Georgetown University Round Table on Languages and Linguistics 1990

Linguistics, language teaching and language acquisition: The interdependence of theory, practice and research

James E. Alatis, *Editor*

Georgetown University Press, Washington, D. C.

Bibliographic notice

Since this series has been variously and confusingly cited as *Georgetown University Monograph Series on Languages and Linguistics, Monograph Series on Languages and Linguistics, Reports of the Annual Round Table Meeting on Linguistics and Language Study,* etc., beginning with the 1973 volume the title of the series was changed.

The new title of the series includes the year of a Round Table and omits both the monograph number and the meeting number, thus: *Georgetown University Round Table on Languages and Linguistics 1990*, with the regular abbreviation *GURT '90*. Full bibliographic references should show the form:

Lutz, Richard. 1990. Classroom shock: The role of expectations in an instructional setting. In: Georgetown University Round Table on Languages and Linguistics 1990. Washington, D.C.: Georgetown University Press.

Printed in the United States of America

Library of Congress Catalog Number: 58-31607
ISBN 0-87840-125-3
ISSN 0186-7207

To John Bissel Carroll
Whose Scholarship Inspired These Proceedings

Contents

Welcoming remarks

James E. Alatis
Dean, Georgetown University School of Languages and Linguistics
Chair, Georgetown University Round Table on Languages and Linguistics 1990

Good evening, ladies and gentlemen. My name is James E. Alatis, and I am Dean of the School of Languages and Linguistics at Georgetown University. It is my great pleasure to welcome you to the campus and to the Georgetown University Round Table, *GURT 1990*, for short. I consider the Round Table conference one of the great benefits of being at Georgetown. We are delighted that, as we have since 1950, Georgetown has had the privilege of playing host to a group of distinguished scholars and teachers. This year, these colleagues will lead us in a discussion of the theme: 'Linguistics, language teaching, and language acquisition: The interdependence of theory, practice, and research.'

I am convinced that the mettle of the Round Table is being tested by some providence, either divine or otherwise. Those of you who attended last year may recall that the Round Table began under a thick coat of ice; this year, the mercury skyrocketed. My suspicions will be confirmed if next year the Ballroom is awash in locusts.

I would like to extend a special welcome to those of you who participated in the Round Table's pre-sessions. These meetings permit us to include a breadth of offerings which no main conference could ever hope or should attempt to address. We are happy that we were able to provide a setting for these groups. We are grateful for the efforts of the organizers of the pre-sessions and congratulate them on a job well done. So steadfast was their commitment to the field that not even record-breaking temperatures could interfere with the pre-sessions. Congratulations.

Before this evening gets fully under way, I would like to express my gratitude to the many people who contributed, each in their own way, to make this Round Table conference a reality. Although I would like to thank each publicly, I did promised time for the plenary speaker, so I shall restrict myself to just a few.

First of all, we owe thanks to our distinguished speakers, some of whom have travelled many miles to be a part of this conference and to enjoy the cool spring for which Washington is so famous. We hope they will ignore the heat and appreciate the fact that the air conditioning is working. We look forward to their formal presentations and the discussions which will follow. For all of us, the opportunity to share in the results of their research, debate ideas, and rub shoulders with the leaders of the profession is a rare and welcome experience.

I would be remiss were I not to thank all of you who have assembled here this evening. This Round Table celebrates our more than forty years of research and teaching in languages and linguistics. We are happy that you could be here, we trust that you will find the experience profitable, and we welcome your participation.

I also need to express my gratitude to GURT's indefatigable conference coordinator, Mrs. Carol J. Kreidler. Among other things, Mrs. Kreidler has helped to identify some of the best scholars in linguistics and related disciplines for our meeting. And although you are probably thinking that you are here of your own free will, through the use of targeted mailing lists, Carol Kreidler has become the siren of linguistics, reaching an audience so appropriate to the themes of this conference that you were almost helpless to resist our call. All credit for a well-managed meeting is attributable to her. Any missteps along the way are probably due to my meddling. Carol planned every moment of our successful GURT conference last year as well, but she was unable to attend, because she was committed to attend the TESOL Conference in San Antonio. A better national schedule this year permitted an over 7,000 attendance at the TESOL conference in San Francisco, full house here for GURT, and Carol has been able to attend both.

Needless to say, even Carol Kreidler cannot put on a conference as complex as the Round Table alone. She has been ably assisted by a small army of student volunteers and office staff. I hope that they all understand how much we appreciate their efforts on our behalf. I cannot possibly hope to introduce all of them now, but I do draw you attention to Carol's four lieutenants, whose names appear on the program: Rebecca Freeman, Christine Lynch, Laura Klos Sokol, and Carolyn Straehle. Thank you all very much.

This evening's program is a very special one for me because I have such respect and admiration for our speakers. Each in their own ways has done and continues to do so much meaningful work for the disciplines and professions which contribute to the field we might broadly-define as 'languages and linguistics.'

It is my great privilege to invite Ms. Rita Esquivel to offer the Opening Remarks this evening. Although she currently bears the intimidating title of Director of the Office of Bilingual Education and Minority Language Affairs, members of the teaching profession will be gratified to know that she is, at heart, one of us. Rita Esquivel was appointed Director of OBEMLA, as her office is called, in May 1989. Recently, Miss Esquivel was described by U.S. Secretary of Education Lauro Cavazos as "a person committed to ensuring that language minority children have an equal opportunity for the share of the American dream." Secretary Cavazos also noted that "Rita's varied experience as a classroom teacher, including bilingual instruction, as well as curricular, administrative and counseling experience, will make her an effective and caring leader for the nation."

Rita grew up in San Antonio, Texas. She received her Bachelor's and Master's degrees in education from Our Lady of the Lake University in San Antonio. For ten years, she taught in the Edgewood and San Antonio elementary schools. In 1963, she moved to Santa Monica, California. For the next ten years, she taught elementary school classes, Spanish to junior high school classes, served as a counselor, and taught English as a Second Language to adults at the college level.

Since 1973, Ms. Esquivel has held administrative positions of increasing influence and responsibility in the Santa Monica-Malibu Unified School District: moving from elementary principal to coordinator of community relations, to supervisor of state and federal projects, and, before moving to Washington, to assistant superintendent of schools.

Since her appointment, Miss Esquivel has been an effective advocate for issues involving Bilingual Education in the Congress and in the Bush administration. In recent testimony in Congress, she was an articulate and persuasive advocate for increased funding for fellowships and other teacher-enhancement programs. She has lectured extensively throughout the United States and we are fortunate to have her with us. Ladies and Gentlemen, please welcome Rita Esquivel, Director of the Office of Bilingual Education and Minority Language Affairs of the U.S. Department of Education.

Opening remarks

Rita Esquivel
Director, Office of Bilingual Education and Minority Language Affairs

It is a great honor for me to address this distinguished company of scholars and a great pleasure to attend the sessions of this Roundtable. I bring greetings from Secretary Cavazos, who is vitally concerned about language acquisition. Recently, he stated as a major education goal that by the year 2000, fifty percent of American youth graduating from a University should be able to speak two languages.

The *Georgetown University Round Table on Languages and Linguistics 1990* is a most important event, critical to all persons concerned about language acquisition—by this I do not limit the topic to 'Bilingual Education'. In order to better serve our clients I have invited the entire senior staff of the Office of Bilingual Education and Minority Languages Affairs to hear your presentations. The sooner we can eliminate the distinction in people's minds between Bilingual Education and language learning in general; the sooner we will break down the American resistance to mastery of more than one language.

Language instruction, teaching verbal and written communication, is much too important to be left as a subject for ideological debate. Certainly, learned practitioners, many of whom are speaking at this conference, can use debate as a tool to increase our knowledge of the language learning process and explore new, inventive ways of teaching language. But outside of this hall the reality of linguistic diversity presses hard against the classroom teacher, the vocational educator, and the employer.

All non-English speaking persons in this country—whether they have university education or grade school education—know that a mastery of English is the true passport into this society. No organization exists to question the importance of English language in America.

As language learning scholars you have long known that a true appreciation for our dominant language often first occurs with the learning of a second language. However, disagreement seems to begin when we discuss the mix of language learning with course content learning for children.

The Federal government, specifically, my office, has over the last five years, consistently maintained that local school districts and trained language educators are in the best position to diagnose the appropriate treatment for a given group of children. And we have funded, and continue to fund a diverse group of grantees.

Federal money for bilingual education has grown from $7.5 million in 1969 to more than $150 million in 1990. In 1989, OBEMLA awarded 749 grants for projects serving over 200,000 students. During the same year, 52 grants were awarded to State Education Agencies, to fund state programs for data analysis, data collection, and for a variety of technical assistance activities. OBEMLA has funded 162 training grants in 1989, which allowed for approximately 4500 teachers to be trained around the country.

Recently, in an effort to increase the available repertoire of options for Federal funding, we announced a competition in Developmental Bilingual Education. We believe that there may be settings where English speaking students may benefit as much as their limited English proficient classmates from instruction in another language. We intend to fund only exemplary projects in this approach, projects which can withstand public scrutiny and which will achieve English proficiency for the LEP student.

Of more direct interest to this group is the recent announcement of the first Bilingual Fellowship competition in several years. We hope to regain a full complement of five hundred Fellows beginning with 200 this year. As you may know institutions of higher education are selected for this program, and in turn nominate candidates for fellowships. This year we will start off with two hundred fellows, at an average of $10,000 per year. The purpose of the program is to infuse the academic community, the education community at large, and, hopefully, local school administrations with outstanding language learning scholars. I am proud to say that my director of research, Dr. Simich-Dudgeon, is a former fellow with a doctorate from our host—Georgetown Uni-versity.

As I travel around our country I am astonished at how many of our fellows have achieved positions of responsibility both within the language learning community, and in other related callings which are of direct benefit to the limited English proficient population. One of my most prized accomplishments is the refunding of this program which will help add to our language community new talent.

I look forward to participating in the Georgetown Round Table. If our office can be of any assistance to you, please give us a call. Thank you.

Presentation of Dean's Medal to John Bissel Carroll

James E. Alatis
Dean, School of Languages and Linguistics
Georgetown University

Last year, we awarded special medals to Henry and Renee Kahane, honoring them for their innumerable contributions to our field. This year, I would like to take last year's practice and institute it as a Round Table tradition to recognize those who have made their mark on the profession. And now, I shall do honor to the Dean's medal and the University it represents by conferring it upon John Bissell Carroll for his lifetime of interdisciplinary scholarship in support of the field of language teaching.

John B. Carroll does not define himself as a linguist or a language teacher; and that may be so, but he is surely the best friend that our profession has ever had, in his application of the very best research in psychology to the study of the language learner and the process of language learning.

On a personal note, his seminal book, *The Study of Language*, published in 1953 saved my young academic life as I was about to embark on a Fulbright to Greece. What I knew about linguistics and language teaching was contained between the covers of his book. When I met him for the first time at the Summer Linguistics Institute at Michigan in 1954, when we were both six or seven years old, I saw in him the enthusiasm of a scholar with a mission, which was to uncover the mysteries of how we go about learning a language. Two years later, he edited a book, *Language, Thought and Reality: Selected Writings of Benjamin Lee Whorf*, which, more than thirty years after its publication, I still consider to be an irreplaceable item on any reading list in applied linguistics. In 1975, he published *The Teaching of French as a Foreign Language in Eight Countries*, which I recognize as psychology's greatest contribution to language learning.

Last year, I prepared to teach a course in 'Methods for language teaching' for graduate students in linguistics. Just as Dr. Carroll's work came to my rescue at the outset of my career, I was again able to call upon two of his marvelous articles: 'Learning theory for the classroom teacher' and 'Current issues in psycholinguistics and second language teaching.' My students are the richer for it.

Dr. Carroll's career in service to his profession has been long, varied, and distinguished. It has included teaching positions at Harvard and the University of North Carolina at Chapel Hill. He also spent seven years at Educational Testing Services (ETS) at Princeton as their Senior Research Psychologist. He has served on numerous editorial boards, research panels, and committees; and has shared his expertise as a consultant for Georgetown on numerous occasions:—most recently as an evaluator of our program which prepares men and women for careers as conference interpreters and translators. In his spare time, he has authored more than 400 articles, book chapters, reviews, and encyclopedia entries. He retired from active teaching in 1982 as the William R. Kenan, Jr. Professor of Psychology Emeritus at UNC-Chapel Hill.

For a modest man, Dr. Carroll has received an immodest number of awards. Georgetown University would like to jump on the bandwagon with the award of this year's Dean's Medal. This action not only honors the man, but encourages a whole new generation of language learners and teachers to discover Dr. Carroll's many contributions to our field. A renaissance of the writings of John B. Carroll would make better teachers, testers, and even learners of us all.

Consequently, I would like to announce that, in recognition of his many contributions to the language profession, the proceedings of this year's Round Table are being respectfully dedicated to him. Thank you Dr. Carroll, on behalf of all of us who have so benefited from your work.

Sir John Lyons: An introduction

James E. Alatis
Dean, Georgetown University School of Languages and Linguistics
Chair, Georgetown University Round Table on Languages and Linguistics 1990

Our opening address tonight is by the eminent British linguist, Sir John Lyons. This is a return engagement for Dr. Lyons, who so impressed us last year with his excellent paper that on the spot, I extended an invitation for him to speak to us again. We are indeed fortunate that he accepted. As I did last year, I feel deeply honored to have this opportunity to introduce him to you. Those of you who have read his works doubtless recognize the influence he has had on the field of linguistic study. He is a frequent contributor to such publications as the *Journal of Linguistics* and the *Times Literary Supplement*. His publishing career spans a quarter century, beginning in 1963 with the publication of *Structural Semantics*. Other works such as *Introduction to Theoretical Linguistics*, *Language and Linguistics: An introduction*, *Chomsky*, and *New Horizons in Linguistics* have been translated into numerous languages including Dutch, French, German, Italian, Japanese, Polish, Portuguese, Russian, Spanish, and Swedish. Thus to describe the influence of John Lyons as worldwide is no exercise in hyperbole, but merely a statement of fact. His two-volume work, *Semantics*, is recognized as the definitive authority on the subject.

Born in 1932, John Lyons was educated at St. Bede's College in Manchester and Christ College at Cambridge. His distinguished teaching career has included posts at the University of London, Cambridge, Edinburgh and Sussex. He is currently Visiting Professor of Linguistics at the University of Sussex and Master of Trinity Hall at Cambridge. He has received honorary degrees from the Université catholique de Louvain, the University of Reading, and just last year, the University of Edinburgh. He is a fellow of the British Academy and an honorary member of the Linguistics Society of America. In June 1987, he was knighted for services to the study of linguistics.

I know that you are all looking forward to hearing Sir John, who will address us this evening on the topic: 'Linguistics: Theory, Practice and Research'. Ladies and Gentlemen, please join me in welcoming our distinguished speaker to the podium.

Linguistics: Theory, practice and research

John Lyons
Trinity Hall, Cambridge University

1 Introduction: Theorists and practitioners. When I was invited to give the opening talk at this year's Round Table, it seemed to me that I could hardly do better than choose as my title that of the Round Table itself. Being pedantic by nature, and not wishing to raise more general expectations than I could hope to satisfy, I have however explicitly restricted myself to linguistics: "Linguistics: theory, practice and research." And when I started thinking of what I might most usefully say under this rubric, several more or less well-known, and more or less relevant, quotations came into my mind, rising unbidden from the dark recesses of memory and jostling for attention and commentary. The first is from the great Danish scholar, Hjelmslev, and was written, half a century ago, at a time when 'theoretical' had a very different ring to it, for many linguists, than it does today:

> si la linguistique structurale de nos jours peut paraître à certains esprits trop théorique, il ne faut pas oublier que la théorie est faite pour faciliter le travail, et qu'elle est née d'un besoin pratique (Hjelmslev 1944:144).[1]

There is nothing particularly remarkable in what Hjelmslev says here about the relation between theory and practice. Whether linguistic theory is always practice-driven and always, or even usually, serves to simplify the work of describing languages, either synchronically or diachronically, is far from self-evident. But the point of view that Hjelmslev expressed (in a very different context from mine) is one that is widely shared. I personally do not believe that theory is or ought to be practice-driven, in the sense of being restricted

---

[1] "'Present-day structural linguistics might strike certain minds as being excessively theoretical. One must not forget however that theory is made in order to simplify work and that it is born of a practical need." Actually, the quotation will sustain another, slightly different, translation: ". . . the theory is made to simplify the work."

by considerations of practical relevance or exploitability. Nor, I think, did Hjelmslev. I have, after all, taken the quotation out of context.

But I have quoted this passage from Hjelmslev, not so much for what he says as for the fact that, at the time when he was writing, he should have felt obliged to say it and, in doing so, should have adopted so obviously defensive a tone. Hjelmslev was of course the acknowledged leader of the most deliberately theoretically-minded of all the distinguishable schools of European structural linguistics of the immediately prewar and immediately postwar period: the Glossematicians. Indeed, in terms of a distinction that I will be drawing presently between theorists and theoreticians, he might be classified as the first great theoretician of our subject. However that may be, there is no doubt that, at the time that he was writing, the general temper of most linguists—especially in the United States, but also in Europe—was by present-day standards unashamedly non-theoretical, not to say anti-theoretical. The term 'theory' might well have been employed, but, if it was, it was rarely employed by linguists other than the Glossematicians in what I will later identify as its newer, and stronger, sense. And in many cases it was used, in linguistics as more generally in the social sciences, to refer to what is more properly called methodology. All that has of course changed in the last twenty-five years or so. I am not at all sure, however, that these changes are yet as well understood as they ought to be. This is a point that I made in the paper that I gave at last year's Round Table (Lyons 1989a). I will come back to it in later sections of this year's paper and develop it further, and somewhat differently, in the context of our present concerns.

Illustrative of what I am characterizing as the non-theoretical, or anti-theoretical, temper of much prewar and immediately postwar linguistics is my second quotation. It comes from an article by Harry Hoijer on 'Anthropological linguistics," published on the occasion of the Ninth International Congress of Linguists in 1962:

> The reason [why morphological typology has interested very few modern American linguists] may lie, as Kroeber has suggested, in the question "What do we do with a morphological classification of [the world's] languages when we have it?" The question is not easily answered, and the lack of a clear answer unquestionably affects both the interest in, and the nature of, morphological typologies (1961:120-21).

Hoijer's comment is not unfairly paraphrased, I think, by saying that morphological typology of the kind that Greenberg was currently developing on the basis of Sapir's famous classification of languages of the world was purely theoretical and of no practical utility. Hjelmslev was not of course anticipating and addressing this specific point in the passage that I have just quoted, but, given his views on the relation between typology and theory (which I share), he might well have been. And my own contemporary response to Hoijer's comment, in my review of the volume in which it appeared, was strongly influenced, on the one hand, by what would certainly have been Hjelmslev's view of the matter and, on the other, by a very traditional—some might say elitist—notion of the pre-eminence, irresponsibility and self-sufficiency of theory:

> [Kroeber's question] is not difficult to answer; but it is a shocking question to put to anyone engaged in scientific enquiry, suggesting that the classification of phenomena in terms of general principles ('understanding things') requires some ulterior justification. The linguist studies language because it interests him. Of the generalizations he makes about language some will be definitional and tautological, others empirical and inductive. . . . Thus the fact (if it is a fact) that all languages have both a phonological and grammatical structure is an interesting empirical fact about languages; for there is nothing in the definition of the notion of a linguistic unit to impose this double structure on the data. . . . On the other hand, the "fact" that all languages have phonemes and morphemes (in the view of many linguists) is, under the common definition of these units, trivial; since in the last resort allowance is made for arbitrary segmentation. The fact that the distinction between morphology and syntax is profitably made in the analysis of some languages, but not at all—or to a different degree—in the description of others, is again an interesting discovery about languages, and one of great generality. At a lower level of generality we may classify languages into different morphological (or syntactic) types. The answer to the question posed by Kroeber, and echoed by Hoijer, is: when we have a morphological classification of the languages of the world, we shall contemplate it with wonder and satisfaction. We may of course then be impelled to do other things with it: we may try to answer the question why there are more languages of one type than another (cf. Greenberg's discussion of prefixing and suffixing languages); we may investigate the correlation between different morphological "indices" (assuming that these measure a priori independent variables) or the correlation between phonological and morphological types, etc. The field of further enquiry is inexhaustible. Indeed one might say, as do the Glossematicians, that linguistics is in aim none other than the establishment, partly a priori by the axioms and definitions of controlling theory, partly empirically, of the most general and systematic typology of languages (Lyons 1962a:121-22).

I had not intended to put this rather lengthy quotation from my own work into the present paper, and I must apologise for doing so. It was not one of the three that originally came to mind. But when I looked again at what I had written in response to the passage that I have quoted from Hoijer in 1962, it seemed to me to contain several points that are even more topical today than they were then. And there is one section, in particular, which sets the context rather neatly, as will soon become clear, not only for my third quotation, but also for much of the subsequent discussion. My answer to Kroeber's question was as follows: "when we have a morphological classification of the languages of the world, we shall contemplate it with wonder and satisfaction." This is the sentence that I had in mind when I said, a moment ago, that some might characterize my attitude as elitist; and I freely confess that it is. I would ask you to note the words *contemplate* and *wonder*.

I do not think that I was consciously echoing Aristotle when I chose these words. But, taken together, the two words evoke, on the one hand, the famous Aristotelian aphorism that all science begins in wonder and, on the other, several passages in the *Metaphysics* and in the *Nichomachean Ethics* where Aristotle establishes his basic distinction between theory and practice and, thus, between the theoretical and the practical sciences. This is a distinction which endured throughout the Middle Ages and well into modern times; and, regardless of its validity, it is still widely accepted for the organization of education, training and research and for the establishment of two major subdivisions within some of our academic disciplines.

My third quotation comes, then, from Aristotle. It is taken from that famous passage in the *Nichomachean Ethics*, in which, in the course of his investigation of the nature of the good, Aristotle introduces his own version of the Pythagorean doctrine of the three lives. I will considerably abbreviate it and, for present purposes, use my own translation of the key-terms:

> To judge from the lives that men lead, most men . . . seem to identify the good with pleasure. This is why they love the life of enjoyment. For there are, it is said, three prominent types of life: the life of enjoyment, the life of politics [i.e. activity] and the life of [theory or] contemplation (Aristotle, *Nich. Eth.* 1095b:19).

The adjective that occurs in the phrase that I have translated here as "the life of theory or contemplation" is *theoretikos*, which is variously translated in English versions of Aristotle, according to context, as 'theoretical', 'contemplative', and 'speculative'. It is important to realise, however, that these three English words highlight distinctions which did not exist in Aristotle's Greek or that of the other Greek philosophers. Theory was not distinguished from what we now call either contemplation or speculation until very much later in the history of science and philosophy. As far as the Greek word *theoria* is concerned, there are many passages in the works of the Ancient Greek philosophers, especially those of a Pythagorean or Platonic bent, where its original, quasi-mystical or quasi-religious, connotations are prominent. And I would suggest, somewhat hesitantly, that these are best captured by the traditional theological term 'the beatific vision', but interpreting it, of course, naturalistically.

The traditional doctrine of the three lives has come down to us in several slightly different versions. What they all have in common is their reference to the analogy that Pythagoras, when asked to say what a philosopher was, drew between three kinds of human character or ways of life and the three kinds of visitors to be found at the Olympic Games: traders, competitors and spectators. The spectators belonged to that class of "men of good breeding"—I am here quoting Cicero's version—"who sought neither applause nor gain, but came to watch (*visendi causa*) and closely observed what was done and how it was done." Similarly in life, there were "a special few who, disregarding all else, contemplated the nature of things (*rerum naturam studiose intuerentur*)" and found that "the contemplation and understanding of nature (*contemplationem rerum cognitionemque*) far surpassed all other pursuits" (Cicero, *Tusc. Disp.* 5.3.8-9).

The Pythagorean analogy raises many points that would be worth elaborating, if time and space permitted; and they would be by no means as irrelevant to our understanding of the development of linguistics over the centuries or its present condition as one might think. I have referred to it here, in its Aristotelian context, for two main reasons: first, to illustrate the traditional view of the primacy and self-sufficiency of theory in relation to practice; and, second, to highlight some of the original connotations of what has ultimately become our modern word *theory.*

2 Type-1 and type-2 theories in linguistics. In the paper that I gave at last year's Round Table, I drew a convenient terminological distinction between 'linguistic theory' and 'theoretical linguistics' (Lyons 1989a:29-33, see also Lyons 1990b). I shall be drawing the same distinction today and exploiting it more fully than was possible on that occasion. And with moderate support from etymology and usage, I will be drawing a correspondingly convenient distinction (in linguistics) between theorists and theoreticians and between the activities in which they characteristically engage, theorizing and theoreticizing.

Anyone who wishes to check the etymological justification that I have for the distinction that I am drawing between *theorist* and *theoretician* can readily do so, incidentally , by looking up these words in the Second Edition of the *Oxford English Dictionary* published last year (*OED* 1989). *Theorist* is attested, in the sense that I am giving to it, as early as 1594 and has from the outset been associated with the verb *theorize.*[2] *Theoretician* is of more recent origin and, although not clearly distinguished from *theorist* in the first half of this century, seems latterly to have acquired a slightly different meaning. As for the verb *theoreticize*, this may not yet have found its way into any authoritative dictionary of English; but I hereby offer it to the compilers of the *Supplement* to the Second Edition of the *OED* for free. It will go nicely, I think, immediately below the noun *theoreticism* (the citations for which I recommend

[2] *Theorize* is of course a calque-word based on the medieval *theorizare*—which in turn was a calque-word from the Greek *theorizein*—and must have been in use in philosophical English at least as early as *theorist* was, even though the earliest *OED* citation for *theorize* is from 1638.

to your attention). *Theoreticism* I would define as excessive, inappropriate or premature theoreticization.

Regardless of their etymology, however, the three pairs of terms can be usefully employed, as I suggested last year in respect of one pair of them, 'linguistic theory' and 'theoretical linguistics', to label what have recently emerged, or are in process of emerging, as two rather different, but complementary and equally important, sub-branches of linguistics. One of each pair, as my reference to Aristotle in the preceding section were intended to show, is more readily, or at least more traditionally, associated with (and of course opposed to) 'practice'. The other I am tempted to associate similarly with 'research'. But I would not wish to press this latter point too hard. Nor would I wish to suggest that the distinction between linguistic theory and theoretical linguistics—between theorists and theoreticians, between theorizing and theoreticizing—can always be sharply drawn. It does, however, have some point to it, as I hope to have shown last year and as I will demonstrate again this year on a broader front and for different purposes.

The distinction in question is swiftly enough established on the basis of what one may think of as an older and a newer, or a weaker and a stronger, sense of the word *theory*. By 'theory' in the older or weaker sense I mean a set of general principles which (according to whether it purports to be descriptive or explanatory) attempts to describe or explain a given body of data which it takes as its subject matter. It is in this, the older or weaker, sense of 'theory' that theory is commonly equated with 'speculation' and opposed to 'practice', the adjective 'theoretical' being correspondingly opposed to 'practical' and, as we have seen, equated with 'speculative' or, in certain contests, 'contemplative'.[3]

By 'theory' in the newer and stronger sense I mean a mathematically precise formal system within which theorems can be proved by deduction from the initial postulates or axioms and, if the theory is empirical rather than purely formal (and can be put satisfactorily into correspondence with the data that it purports to describe or explain), can be interpreted as embodying empirically falsifiable or confirmable predictions. It is formalization, then, rather than coverage of the data or any other kind of scientific or empirical adequacy which distinguishes the stronger from the weaker kind of theory.[4]

As I have said, it is in the weaker sense of 'theory' that theory is traditionally opposed to practice. Indeed, it could hardly be otherwise, since

---

[3] Speculative grammar of the High Middle Ages (*grammatica speculativa*) was so called because it was intended to be theoretical rather than practical: cf. Covington 1984:20-21.

[4] The data themselves may be the product either of observation or of reflection and intuition; the theory may be more or less comprehensive, systematic and self-consistent: these differences, with respect to which one theory might be very properly judged to be more scientific than another are undoubtedly important, but they are, at most, only indirectly relevant to the distinction that I am drawing between the two kinds of theories.

theories in the stronger sense are of relatively recent origin even in the natural sciences. In linguistics they originated just before the Second World War, I suppose, with Hjelmslev and his collaborators or possibly, as far as syntax is concerned, with Tesnière. But Glossematic theories of the structure of languages never fired the imagination of more than a minority of linguists. For most of us, the formalization of linguistic theory—its theoreticization: i.e. the conversion of (parts of) linguistic theory into theoretical linguistics—is seen, rightly or wrongly, as being one of the products of the so-called Chomskyan revolution.

Whether this view of the matter is historically correct or not is something that I do not wish to get into here. I have dealt with various aspects of the question in several previous publications, including my *GURT '89* paper, from which I may be permitted to extract and list without development or expansion, such points as are relevant to the issue with which we are currently concerned (see also Lyons 1989a:24-26, 29-34):

(1) Unlike Chomsky himself and most Chomskyans, I draw a distinction between generative grammar and generativism; and it is the former, rather than the latter, that I am referring to when I say that theoretical linguistics, as we currently understand it, is the product of the Chomskyan revolution. Generativism, on the other hand, is an amalgam of more or less unrelated, more or less interesting and more or less plausible partial theories, most of which have never been formalized (see also Lyons 1977b; 1981a:228-35).

(2) Theoretical linguistics must not be restricted to microlinguistics, in contrast with sociolinguistics, psycholinguistics, ethnolinguistics, stylistics, etc. Microlinguistics (so-called autonomous linguistics) is, in principle, no more and no less theoretical, in the stronger sense, than these various branches of macrolinguistics. Theoretical microlinguistics, however, is currently much more highly developed than theoretical macrolinguistics (see also Lyons 1990b).

(3) Not only microlinguistics, but most, if not all, branches of macrolinguistics operate, or should operate, with their own models of the language-system (Saussure's *langue*). Each branch of linguistics starts from more or less the same pretheoretical notion of what language (or a language) is and, according to its own viewpoint and the alliances that it forges with other disciplines (psychology, sociology, anthropology, literary criticism, etc.), practices its own kind of abstraction and idealization in the construction of its own model of the underlying language-system. No one such model has ontological primacy over the others; and there is no immediate possibility, perhaps even no ultimate possibility, of constructing a unified theory of the natural and social sciences within which a unified theory of language (i.e. of the language-system construed generically) would find its place and be descriptively and explanatorily adequate to the

data that it systematizes. Whether or not such unification is ultimately possible, premature reductionism of whatever kind, generativist or physicalist, psycholinguistic or sociolinguistic, is detrimental to linguistics in its current state of development.

(4) There is still a central place for so-called autonomous microlinguistics, whose objects of study are neither psychological nor social, and which are appropriately connected to the primary data, language-utterances, the products of actual and potential language-behaviour. Criticisms of so-called autonomous linguistics, though increasingly widespread in recent years, are for the most part misdirected (see further Lyons 1990c).

(5) Theoretical linguistics must not be identified with general linguistics. A generative grammar, for example, is a theoretical description of a particular language-system, and, as such, can be regarded as a theory of that language: more specifically, as a theory of the well-formedness and structural properties of the sentences of the language-system which it generates.

(6) As to the difference between theoretical and applied linguistics: if 'theoretical' is given its stronger sense, 'non-theoretical' being defined in relation to this, a distinction can be usefully drawn between first-degree and second-degree applied linguistics. First-degree applied linguistics would have as its aim the production of non-theoretical (i.e. unformalized) descriptions of particular languages of various kinds. Second-degree applied linguistics, in contrast, would be what is more normally referred to as 'applied linguistics': what is applied (to language-teaching, machine-translation, other kinds of automated language-processing, or whatever) would be the products of either theoretical linguistics or non-theoretical, first-degree, applied linguistics. It will be obvious, then, that the distinction which I am drawing between theory and practice, in this paper, is not to be equated with the distinction between theoretical and applied linguistics, as this is customarily drawn. How the two distinctions are related will be clear, I hope, from what I have just said and from later sections. But I will not be addressing this issue directly.

Several of the points that I have just made are, in one way or another, controversial. I have, however, given what I would judge to be an adequate defence of them elsewhere, and I will take them for granted in everything that follows.

To summarize then: in this section, I have been concerned to establish a distinction between linguistic theory and various branches of theoretical linguistics on the basis of a stronger and a weaker sense of the term 'theory'. Granted that there is no sharp distinction between stronger and weaker theories, I will for expository convenience operate henceforth as if there were, referring to theories of the older, or weaker, sort as type-1 theories and newer, formalized, theories as type-2 theories. It must also be emphasized that there are, of course, other kinds or dimensions of strength which are relevant in the evaluation of theories, so that a type-2 theory can be, and indeed frequently is, much weaker than a type-1 theory. This is a crucial point, for, as we shall see, much linguistic theory, traditional or modern, is far richer and empirically sounder than any contemporary branch of theoretical linguistics.

3 Theory, observation, and intuition: Taking one's Popper with a pinch of salt. The purpose of this short section is to establish the distinction between pre-theoretical and theoretical terms and to affirm its continued validity (properly qualified) in the light of the by now well-known criticisms by Popper and his followers.

One of the most striking changes in the metatheory and methodology of linguistics associated with the rise of generativism in the 1960s was the abandonment of empiricist inductivism and the conscious adoption of the hypothetico-deductive approach to the description of languages and to the elaboration of a general theory of language-structure. Bloomfield's famous programmatic statement, representative of the earlier mainstream approach to theory-construction and generalization is familiar enough, but none the less worth quoting:

> The only useful generalizations about language are inductive generalizations. Features which we think ought to be universal may be absent from the very next language that becomes accessible. . . . The fact that some features are, at any rate, widespread, is worthy of notice and calls for an explanation; when we have adequate data about many languages, we shall have to return to the problem of general grammar and to explain these similarities and divergencies, but this study, when it comes, will be not speculative but inductive (Bloomfield 1933:20).

Bloomfield, it will be noted, uses the term 'speculative', here and throughout the chapter from which this passage is quoted, in a pejorative sense: 'inductive' is implicitly equated with 'scientific' and 'speculative' with 'unscientific'.

According to the proponents of empiricist inductivism, most notably the logical positivists, scientific theories were derived by induction from data that had been collected by impersonal, theory-neutral, observation, to be verified subsequently by appropriately designed experiments. Popper (1934) argued that this view of the matter, though widely held by working scientists, was incorrect in several respects. First, there was, in his view, no such thing as theory-neutral, or pre-theoretical, observation: all observation was (to use his now famous term) theory-laden, and no distinction could be drawn of the kind that the logical positivists in particular sought to draw, between pre-theoretical and theoretical concepts. Second, scientific theories or hypotheses could not, in principle, be verified, but only falsified; indeed, falsifiability was the very touchstone of the distinction between scientific and non-scientific theories.

Now, I have no wish to challenge Popper's attack on the radical empiricist's sharply drawn distinction between theory-neutral and hypothesis-free observation, on the one hand, and the formulation of inductively based general theories, on the other. It has often been pointed out, and rightly, that what we call data, whether scientific or non-scientific (in so far as these two kinds of data can be separated), are not given in experience, but taken, or selected, from it: they are not so much *data* (it has often been said) as *capta*. And their selection is always determined or influenced by what may be called, in at least a loose sense of the terms, a hypothesis or theory.

I do not accept, however, that there is no useful distinction to be drawn, in linguistics at least, between theoretical and pre-theoretical terms. This distinction is certainly valid if we relate 'theoretical' to what I have called theoreticization, in contrast with theorization (see section 2); and it is noticeable that those linguists who appeal approvingly to Popper's view of the nature of scientific investigation tend to be theoreticians, rather than what I am here calling theorists.

The pre-theoretical vocabulary of linguistics is not, of course, solely or even primarily observational: it includes many metalinguistic terms, such as 'language', 'word', 'sentence' and 'meaning', whose everyday use and interpretation are governed by more or less untutored and unreflecting intuition. And the way in which we understand these may well be best accounted for by relating them historically to that set of past (type-1) theories of language-structure which contributed to the development of what we now call traditional grammar. Many of the pre-theoretical terms and concepts of linguistics originated in what Bloomfield (1933:3) referred to, dismissively, as "the speculations of ancient and medieval philosophers" and were much more obviously, in their day, type-1 theoretical terms. I am more respectful than Bloomfield was of the philosophical speculations which underpinned traditional grammar. But I do think that they have to be subjected to critical examination, as they have been by the great twentieth-century theorists of our subject, and cannot be simply taken for granted. It is ironical that linguists who have been so assertive about the theory-laden nature of observation have all too often taken such terms on trust and not bothered to define them properly. This is a point to which I will return. Here it suffices to remark that most type-2 theories in linguistics are, strictly speaking, unfalsifiable because, whilst making a great issue—and rightly—of the value of formalization, their proponents leave such everyday pre-theoretical terms as 'sentence' or 'word' undefined. And yet it is just such terms, which are intended to be of universal applicability in the description of (so-called) natural languages, that earlier theorists and practitioners have found especially problematical.

Granted that there are no absolutely theory-neutral facts (if 'theory' is taken in the older, weaker, type-1 sense) it is none the less the case that some of the facts with which both theorists and theoreticians operate are better established pre-theoretically as facts than others. I gave some examples in the quotation from Lyons (1962a) in section 1, and very many more could be added. The general point that I wish to make, in bringing this section to its conclusion, is that linguistic data—more precisely, the primary data of so-called autonomous, microlinguistic, descriptive and general linguistics—are, on the whole, readily separable, pre-theoretically, from non-linguistic data. This fact is confirmed by the accumulated experience of linguists over the centuries. So too is the fact that a fairly high degree of agreement can be reached about the phonological, grammatical and (to a less extent) semantic structure of the language-system underlying the utterances which constitute the descriptive linguist's primary data. This is not to say, of course, that there are not certain theoretical or methodological decisions to be taken or that the phonological, grammatical and semantic structure of the language-system being described is fully determinate or immediately determinable. Because those linguists whose interest in particular languages is primarily theoretical spend so much of their time, not surprisingly, arguing about more or less controversial, and controvertible, data which can be seen as lending support to one theoretical position rather than another (and I am one such linguist), it is easy to get the impression that the structure of a language-system is, in pre-theoretical or theory-neutral terms, wholly indeterminate. As any practitioner of descriptive linguistics knows, this is not so. And the fact that it is not so justifies the continued existence of so-called autonomous linguistics. But that is another story (Lyons 1990c).

4 Theories, paradigms, and models. Each of the three terms that I have used in the heading for this section has several technical, or semi-technical and non-technical, senses; and in some of their senses each of them is interchangeable with either one or both of the others. I cannot here compare and contrast the three terms over the whole range of their uses. All I can do is to explain how I myself am using them in my present discussion of theory, practice and research in linguistics.

The term 'theory' I have dealt with already. The term 'paradigm' I have been using and will continue to use in its philosophy-of-science, and more particularly its Kuhnian, sense: the sense in which we talk of a radical or revolutionary change of method, theory or metatheory as a change of paradigm, which can be seen, either immediately or with hindsight, as introducing a new kind of 'normal science' (Kuhn 1962). In this sense a paradigm is not sharply distinct from a high-level, or very general, type-1 theory. But it is useful to have a separate term which has acquired a particular set of associations, even if some of the associations are controversial and must be discarded or qualified. The so-called Chomskyan revolution, which introduced generativism into linguistics in the 1960s, is widely described as a change of paradigm. And it is, I think, reasonably so described, provided that the use of the Kuhnian term 'paradigm' is not seen by linguists as "an

292). It is, however, the relation between theories and models with which I am especially concerned in this section.

I will begin by commenting briefly on two of the more technical senses of 'model'. In the sense, in which mathematicians and mathematical logicians use the term, a model is a formal system considered from the point of view of its interpretation, or application to some practical problem, rather than abstractly for its own sake. (Hence the term 'model theory' in modern formal semantics.) When social scientists or physical scientists employ the term 'model', however, they usually mean some deliberately restricted and abstract representation of the phenomena whose structure or behaviour is being studied, from which hypotheses can be derived for testing. And this is the sense in which I am using the term. Typical models, in this latter sense, are a physicist's representation of atomic structure or an economist's representation of free-market competition. Since any model of this kind is necessarily based upon an idealization of the data that it is designed to describe or explain, how one decides which variations in the data are of significance and which variations can be discounted becomes a question of crucial importance; and the answer to this question will depend upon the nature of the correspondence that is assumed to hold between the data and the model, and upon a fairly precise prior specification of what it is that the model is intended to explain or describe.

The two technical senses of 'model' that I have distinguished are not of course incompatible. Moreover, since the term itself tends to be used by those who favour formalization of a mathematical kind in the interests of rigour and explicitness, in linguistics, as in other sciences, the two senses are frequently merged or conflated. There are occasions, however, when it is important to emphasize one aspect of model construction rather than the other and, in doing so, to use the term in one sense rather than the other. In linguistics, the distinction between the two senses is most clearly seen perhaps in relation to the distinction between the description of language in general and the description of particular languages. The phrase 'a model of language' is perhaps more readily construed in the mathematician's sense of the term than is the phrase 'a model of English' or 'a model of Chinese'.

There are a couple of other more or less technical senses in which the term 'model' is commonly used in linguistics, which go back to the mid-1950s, if not earlier: to Hockett's famous 'Two models' paper (1954) or Chomsky's equally famous, and ultimately more influential, 'Three models' paper (1957). For Hockett a grammatical model was "a frame of reference within which the analyst approaches the grammatical phase of a language and states the results of his description" (1954:210 = Joos 1963:386); and in his paper he was primarily concerned to compare what he saw as the two "archetypal frames of reference" within which recent and contemporary Bloomfieldian and post-Bloomfieldian grammatical description was conducted and reported. A model, in Hockett's (1954) sense of the term, is what I am here calling a paradigm (or sub-paradigm within a paradigm); but he was to some degree concerned with mathematicization, and this fact no doubt motivated his choice of term (and he was, in any case, writing in the pre-Kuhnian era). Chomsky's (1957) use of the term 'model' was closer to what I have identified above as the mathematician's: his three models of grammatical description—finite state grammars (FSG), phrase structure grammars (PSG), and transformational grammars (TG)—were distinguished in terms of their formal properties and their generative power (but with a view to their interpretation). Over the last thirty years or so, linguists have employed the term 'model' sometimes in Hockett's (1954) sense, sometimes in Chomsky's (1957) sense, and sometimes —more frequently perhaps—in a sense which is but loosely related to one or the other and may even combine elements of both. For example, one talks about generative and non-generative models of linguistic description or, at a lower level of specificity, about the *Aspects* model, the Government-Binding (GB) model or the Lexical-Functional (LFG) model, on the one hand, or about the scale-and-category (or systemic) model, the tagmemic model or the stratificational model, on the other. To my mind, much of the discussion of the merits of these different approaches to the linguistic description of languages has been greatly and unnecessarily confused over the years, and is still much confused, partly by the failure to distinguish generative grammar from generativism and partly by the failure to distinguish one sense of 'model' from another, some of which I would prefer to associate with 'paradigm' and others with 'theory' (or even 'metatheory'). But that is not the burden of the present homily. All I am doing here is clarifying my own usage of the term 'model' in this paper. Like others I could mention (but will not), I too have elsewhere used the term in other senses, and at times no doubt equivocally, and have added my own little mite to the confusion about which I am now complaining.

There is one further comment that I should make at this point. In addition to the two technical senses that I have distinguished (and the more or less related senses to which I have referred in the preceding paragraph), there are conflicting non-technical, everyday, senses of 'model', which can affect our intuitive interpretation of the more technical senses. Sometimes we think of a model as a norm to which actually existent objects or actually occurrent patterns of behaviour merely approximate; at other times, we talk as if the model were but an imperfect and purely derivative representation of independently existing objects. Reflected in these alternative ways of thinking of a model are conflicting attitudes with respect to the age-old philosophical controversy between realism and nominalism or idealism and phenomenalism. Such linguists as are interested in the philosophy of linguistics and the philosophy of language (to the extent that these two branches of philosophy are to be distinguished) will differ as to whether they prefer a realist or a non-realist interpretation of the models that they construct when they are describing (so-called) natural languages (cf. Katz 1981, 1985; Pateman 1987; Carr 1990). For my own view of the ontological status of what are commonly, but in certain respects misleadingly, referred to as natural languages I can do but in certain respects misleadingly, referred to as natural languages I can do no more here than cite one or two relevant publications that are currently in press (Lyons 1990b, c, d).

As I have said, in this paper I am employing the term 'model' in the second of the two technical senses that I distinguished earlier, and only in that sense. But why, it may be asked, am I making such a fuss about the term 'model'? The reason is that, in my view, what practicing descriptive linguists are doing—and by 'practicing descriptive linguists' I mean those who are engaged in the practice of describing languages—is constructing models of what is taken to fall within the scope of the pre-theoretical term 'language'. They may not express themselves in these terms, of course; but this, I would contend, is what they are doing. Moreover, if we relax somewhat the implications of mathematicization that are associated with the term 'model', we can say that this is what traditional grammarians and lexicographers have always been doing. Standard pedagogical and reference grammars and conventional dictionaries are partial and informal models of the languages that they purport to describe.

I have said something in the preceding section—enough for present purposes—about the vexed question of the determinacy and theory-neutrality of the primary data of descriptive linguistics. I have taken the view that it is both possible, and desirable, to steer one's course, if I may so put it, between the Scylla of God's truth and the Charybdis of hocus-pocus (flying the flag of 'rough justice': cf. Lyons 1989a:23). What concerns us now is the nature of the linguist's data and the relation between the data and the model.

When we say that someone is speaking a particular language, English for example, we imply that he or she is engaged in a certain kind of behaviour, or activity, in the course of which he or she produces language-utterances. Native speakers of English will recognize these utterances as belonging to the language and as being, for the most part at least, grammatically acceptable and meaningful, appropriate to their situation of utterance and interpretable. So much is a matter of pre-theoretical observation or empirical discovery, and it provides descriptive linguists with their data: a sample of relevant language-utterances, which may be characterized, pre-theoretically, as being utterances in, or of, a particular language; as being similar or different in meaning; as being typical, or diagnostic, of certain social groups; and so on. What linguists do when they describe a language, however, is to construct a model, not of actual language-utterances (and still less of language-behaviour), but of the system of regularities which underlie, or are manifest in, utterances which are a product of language-behaviour: a model of what is referred to technically as the language-system.

The distinction between language-utterances and an underlying language-system with which I prefer to operate is the one that was drawn by Saussure (and further refined by Hjelmslev and others within the post-Saussurean tradition of European structuralism in terms of the opposition between *parole* and *langue* (both *parole* and *langue* being complementary parts of the more comprehensive *langage*). The same, or a very similar, distinction was subsequently drawn by Chomsky in terms of performance and competence (1965:4); but Chomsky deliberately adopts a psychological, or cognitive, view of language, and, as I have already emphasized, there are other equally valid viewpoints, each with its own concept of the language-system. It will be simpler, however, if, for present purposes, I initially adopt Chomsky's view and talk in terms of competence and performance: it is nowadays more familiar. It is important to realize, however, that Chomsky's term 'performance' is misleading in that it throws the emphasis on the activity of producing language-utterances, rather than upon the products of that activity. It is spoken or written utterances, the recordable and transcribable products of speech or writing, rather than the activity of speech or writing, that the linguist takes as data. Obviously, there is much more that could be said about this (and about the other topics treated in this section). But what has been said will serve to carry us forward.

5 Competence, performance, and the fiction of uniformity. When we say that someone speaks English (in the sense of being able to speak English), we imply that he or she has acquired, normally in infancy, the mastery of a system of rules underlying the behaviour (or performance) which we refer to as speaking English. And it is by virtue of competence that one is able to perform: performance presupposes competence, but competence does not logically presuppose performance. This is a crucial point, and one that Chomsky was right to emphasize in the early days of generativism.

Now, it is more or less obvious that no two people speak precisely the same language, or even the same dialect. There are always differences of vocabulary, and there are in most cases, if not all, systematic differences of grammar and pronunciation, which may or may not inhibit communication and of which the persons in question may or may not be conscious. The reasons why communication is not necessarily inhibited by such differences are several. First, conversation and discourse normally proceed on the basis of shared assumptions and expectations, which supplement what is said and forestall many potential ambiguities and misunderstandings. Second, most utterances, in the contexts in which they occur, are highly redundant (i.e. they contain a good deal of information that is predictable from context); and many differences of vocabulary, grammar and pronunciation, as well as slips of the tongue and other so-called performance-errors are just not noticed. Third, it is not generally necessary for the listener to extract from an utterance all the information that the speaker, if interrogated, would say it contains. It follows that people may go through life without discovering that they have a different understanding of even quite common words and expressions. It also follows—though I will not develop this point here—that successful communication, or apparently successful communication, by means of language does not presup-pose determinacy of meaning.

Not only do no two people speak exactly the same language or dialect (i.e. have exactly the same language-system stored in their brains), but no single person speaks the same language or dialect on all occasions. Everyone switches from one so-called style or register to another—from the colloquial to the formal, from the hortatory to the expository, from the technical to the non-technical, etc.—according to circumstances. Establishing and explaining the correlations between these circumstances, or situations, and the styles or registers that are associated with them is the business of such overlapping interdisciplinary sub-disciplines as stylistics, sociolinguistics and pragmatics.

The language-system underlying the utterances of any one person (that person's competence) turns out, then, upon analysis, to be made up of several partially disjoint (not wholly determinate) systems of vocabulary, grammar, and pronunciation; and each of these individual language-systems, or idiolects, could, in principle, be regarded as separate languages. Furthermore, each of these more or less different language-systems that are combined and integrated in a so-called monolingual's competence, first of all, changes over time dramatically during the period of so-called language-acquisition, gradually and less noticeably throughout life—and, secondly, is always at any one time more or less indeterminate.

And yet theorists and practitioners of descriptive linguistics (as well as non-linguists) continue to maintain what I have elsewhere referred to as the fiction of homogeneity (Lyons 1981b:24-27); they continue to talk as if there are such things as English, French, German or whatever, and that these are homogeneous, determinate and well-defined systems, common to all members of a particular community and constant over space, time and situations of utterance. They continue to say, for example, that something is or is not an English word or phrase and has such-and-such a meaning. Can one make sense of this evident mismatch between the facts of the matter and the way we describe them? Or is it simply, as some would have it, that we should abandon the fiction of homogeneity as empirically unsound? And should we also abandon, at the same time, the distinction between microlinguistics (so-called autonomous linguistics) and macrolinguistics?

I think not. What is required—and here I repeat myself: it is a point that is as yet not generally accepted—is that we recognize that the pre-theoretical term 'language'—and more precisely a phrase like 'the language' or 'a language'—involves different kinds of hypostatization and refers to many different kinds of thing. The psycholinguist's notion of the language-system stored in the individual's brain as what Chomsky calls competence is quite different, ontologically, from the sociolinguist's notion of the language-system as something shared by all members of a given community, and both of them differ in turn from the historical linguist's notion of the language-system as something which endures through time but passes through a succession of synchronically distinct states. Whether these different views of language can ever be satisfactorily reconciled within a single theoretical framework is, for the present and the foreseeable future, a matter of unproductive controversy. To me, it seems preferable to accept, first, that each of the different views is theoretically defensible and, second, that each of them involves, whether explicitly or not, the construction of a model which inevitably idealizes what is being described, by discounting, more or less deliberately, a certain amount of indeterminacy and variation in the data and by abstracting from different kinds of otherwise relevant considerations. There is no point in arguing, for example, that a microlinguistic model of the language-system is unrealistic (whatever that means) just because it abstracts from empirically confirmable and sociolinguistically describable variation and discounts it. At the same time, as I have insisted earlier, there is no reason to deny the validity of any of various macrolinguistic points of view—psycholinguistic, sociolinguistic, etc.—and of the models of the language-system that reflect them. And there is no reason to restrict theoretical linguistics—and still less linguistic theory—to the microlinguistic point of view.

6 Conclusion: The interdependence of theory, practice, and research. I have now completed my account of the relation between theory and practice in linguistics (with particular reference to general and descriptive microlinguistics). So far, I have said little or nothing, explicitly, about the third member of the trinity, research. But that lacuna is quickly filled. All that I have to say follows from the distinction that I have drawn between type-1 and type-2 theories and from points that I have made about theory-neutrality and model-building. It can be made explicit under the rubric that I have chosen as the heading for the final section of my paper: the interdependence of theory, practice and research. And in making this explicit I will, once again, have recourse to the Pythagorean analogy of the three lives—those of the spectator, the competitor and the trader (or merchant)—to which I referred, in connection with the traditional distinction between theorists and practitioners, in the Introduction.

There is an obvious social and moral dimension to the Pythagorean analogy, which the words 'spectator', 'competitor', and 'trader' or 'merchant' do not necessarily evoke in a modern context. (And Aristotle, not to mention Cicero, made it quite clear how he ranked the three lives in this respect.) But this is readily apparent, I would suggest, if we substitute for them the words 'amateur', 'professional', and, let us say, 'entrepreneur'. The theorist is traditionally envisaged as a leisured and well-born amateur, conscious of his social, not to say moral, superiority over the toiling and sweating professional and positively contemptuous of the money-making entrepreneur, given over to a life of self-indulgent hedonism.

Now, I must confess, at this point, that I was sorely tempted to develop this aspect of the analogy in the present paper. But I felt that would have been straining my own powers of rhetoric excessively, and the credulity of my audience, had I attempted to associate the life of the researcher with that of the wealthy hedonist entrepreneur. And, whatever may have been the case in the past, the distinction between theorists and practitioners can no longer be associated with the distinction between amateurs and professionals. Nowadays, as we all know, linguistics, like other branches of science and scholarship (not to mention sport), has been professionalized. What I have referred to as theoretical linguistics, in contrast with (type-1) linguistic theory, is very much the product of this process of professionalization. So too is most contemporary linguistic research.

The traditional distinction between the amateur and the professional can no longer be associated, then, with the distinction between the theorist and the practitioner. But something like it can be associated, I would suggest, between the theorist and theoretician. And there is little doubt which, if either, these days feels superior to the other, intellectually, if not socially or morally. Part of my purpose in writing this paper has been to undermine that feeling.[5]

Some years ago I wrote a paper with the deliberately ambiguous title "The pros and cons of formal semantics" (Lyons 1979). Apart from assessing the advantages and disadvantages of formal semantics (i.e. theoretical semantics in contrast with semantic theory, in terms of the distinction that I have drawn in the present paper), I also argued—if you will pardon the atrocious pun—the importance, for theorists or amateurs, of not letting themselves be conned by the pros. Traditional semantic theory was then, and still is, vastly more comprehensive, and arguably more relevant to what should be the central concerns of general and descriptive linguistics, than any type-2 semantic theory known to me. The same point could be made, I think, though possibly with reduced force, in respect of syntax, morphology and phonology. I yield to noone in my commitment to the value of theoreticization in linguistics or in my admiration for the work of those who are good at it (as I am not). But I also believe that, in the present state of the art, good old-fashioned type-1 theorizing still has an essential role to play; that it should not be despised by either theoreticians or practitioners; that it too, as well as type-2 theoretical linguistics can generate interesting, scientifically respectable and testable theories and hypotheses for researchers; and, finally, that it both can, and should, exercize an appropriate degree of control on theoreticism, of which, I cannot but feel, there has been rather too much in linguistics in recent years.

---

[5] It is interesting to note, in this connection, that the four volumes of a recent survey of the state of the art in linguistics (Newmeyer 1988) puts sociolinguistics, psycholinguistics, ethnolinguistics, neurolinguistics (as well as discourse analysis, conversational analysis, etc.) into the two volumes entitled 'Language', rather than into those entitled 'Linguistic theory'. And most of the articles in the two volumes entitled 'Linguistic theory' (to be understood as 'theoretical linguistics' in my terminology) are written from the point of view of generativism (which, as commonly, is not clearly distinguished from generative grammar as such). It is difficult to justify this division of the field of linguistics on any sound philosophical or metatheoretical principles. As for the generativist account of several of the topics dealt with, Hudson rightly points out in his review that what is said frequently amounts to little more than handwaving (1989:817). Handwaving is what, in this article, I am referring to as theoreticism.

References

Bloomfield, Leonard. 1933. Language. New York: Holt, Rinehart and Winston.

Carr, Philip. 1990. Linguistic realities: An autonomist metatheory for the generative enterprise. Cambridge and New York: Cambridge University Press.

Chomsky, Noam. 1957. Syntactic structures. The Hague: Mouton.

Chomsky, Noam. 1982. The generative enterprise. Dordrecht: Foris.

Chomsky, Noam. 1986. Knowledge of language. New York: Praeger.

Covington, Michael A. 1964. Syntactic theory in the High Middle Ages. Cambridge: Cambridge University Press.

Diamond, Alan. (forthcoming). Proceedings of the Henry Maine Centenary Conference (Trinity Hall, Cambridge, 1988). Cambridge and New York: Cambridge University Press.

Hjelmslev, Louis. 1944. La comparaison en linguistique structurale. Acta Linguistica 4:144-47. (Discussion article relating to J. Vendryès, la comparaison en linguistique. Bulletin de la société de linguistique 42.1941:1-16.

Hoijer, Harry. 1961. Anthropological linguistics. In: Mohrmann et al. 1961:110-127.

Hockett, Charles F. 1954. Two models of grammatical description. In: Word 10:210-31. (Reprinted in: Joos 1957:386-99).

Hudson, Richard. 1989. Review of Newmeyer 1988. In: Language 65:812-19.

Joos, Martin, ed. 1957. Readings in linguistics. Washington, D.C.: American Council of Learned Societies. (Republished as Readings in Linguistics 1. Chicago: University of Chicago Press, 1966.)

Katz, Jerrold J. 1981. Language and other abstract objects. Oxford: Blackwell.

Katz, Jerrold J., ed. 1985. The philosophy of linguistics. London: Oxford University Press.

Kroeber, A. L. 1954. Critical survey and commentary. In: Robert F. Spencer, Method and perspective in anthropology. Minneapolis: University of Minnesota Press. 1954. 273-302. [quote from p. 297]

Kuhn, Thomas S. 1962. The structure of scientific revolutions. Chicago: University of Chicago Press.

Lyons, John. 1962a. Review of Mohrmann et al. 1961. American Anthropologist 64:1118-21.

Lyons, John. 1962b. Phonemic and non-phonemic phonology. International Journal of American Linguistics 28:127-33. (Reprinted, with new notes and commentary, as a chapter in Lyons 1990a).

Lyons, John. 1963. Structural semantics. Oxford: Blackwell.

Lyons, John. 1966. Review of Chomsky (1965). In: Philosophical Quarterly 16.393-95.

Lyons, John. 1968. Introduction to theoretical linguistics. London and New York: Cambridge University Press.

Lyons, John. 1975. The use of models in linguistics. In: Lyndhurst Collins, ed. 1976. The use of models in the social sciences. London: Tavistock Publications.

Lyons, John. 1977a. Semantics, 2 vols. London and New York: Cambridge University Press.

Lyons, John. 1977b. Chomsky. 2nd ed. London: Fontana/Collins, and New York: Viking/Penguin. (1st ed. 1970).

Lyons, John. 1979. The pros and cons of formal semantics. (Unpublished paper delivered to the Linguistic Association of Great Britain, 24 September 1979).

Lyons, John. 1981a. Language and linguistics. London and New York: Cambridge University Press.

Lyons, John. 1981b. Language, meaning and context. London: Fontana/Collins.

Lyons, John. 1982. Deixis and subjectivity: *Loquor, ergo sum*? In: Robert J. Jarvella and W. Klein, eds. Speech, place, and action. London and New York: Wylie. 101-124. (Reprinted in Lyons 1990a).

Lyons John. 1984. La subjectivité dans le langage et dans les langues. In: Guy Serbat, ed. E. Benveniste aujourd'hui 1. Paris: Société pour l'information grammaticale. 131-39.

Lyons, John. 1987a. Origins of language. In: Andrew Faber, ed. Origins. Cambridge: Cambridge University Press. (Expanded and revised version in Lyons 1990a).

Lyons, John. 1987b. Semantics. In: Lyons et al. 987:152-78.
Lyons, John, R. Coates, M. Deuchar, and G. Gazdar, eds. 1987. New horizons in linguistics 2. London: Penguin.
Lyons, John. 1989a. The last forty years: Real progress or not? In: Georgetown University Round Table on Languages and Linguistics 1989. Washington, D.C.: Georgetown University Press. 13-38.
Lyons, John. 1989b. Semantic ascent: A neglected aspect of syntactic typology. In: Douglas G. Arnold et al. Essays on grammatical theory and universal grammar. Oxford: Clarendon Press. 153-68.
Lyons, John. 1990a. Essays in linguistic theory, vol. 1. Cambridge: Cambridge University Press.
Lyons, John. 1990b. Linguistic theory and theoretical linguistics. In: Lyons (1990a:Chapter 3).
Lyons, John. 1990c. In defence of (so called) autonomous linguistics. In: Lyons (1990a: Chapter 2).
Lyons, John. 1990d. Natural, non-natural and unnatural languages. In: Lyons 1990a (Chapter 4).
Lyons, John. (forthcoming). Linguistics and law: The legacy of Sir Henry Maine. In: Alan Diamond, ed. (forthcoming).
Newmeyer, Frederick J., ed. 1988. Linguistics: The Cambridge survey, 4 vols. Cambridge: Cambridge University Press.
Pateman, Trevor. 1987a. Language in mind and language in society. London: Oxford University Press.
Pateman, Trevor. 1987b. Philosophy of linguistics. In: Lyons et al. 1987:247-67.
Popper, Karl R. 1934. The logic of scientific discovery. London: Hutchison.
Popper, Karl R. 1963. Conjectures and refutations. London: Routledge and Kegan Paul.
Popper, Karl R. 1972. Objective knowledge. Oxford: Clarendon Press.
Shopen, Timothy, ed. 1985. Language typology and syntactic description, 3 vols. Cambridge: Cambridge University Press.

In Memoriam:
Peter Strevens
S. Pit Corder

Before this plenary session, in consultation with our speakers, we would like to spend a few moments to remember Peter Strevens, a treasured colleague, who passed away suddenly this fall. Professor Robert Kaplan of the University of Southern California arranged a very beautiful tribute to Peter for his friends at the TESOL Conference in San Francisco last week, in which Professor Widdowson, Professor Selinker, and I were privileged to participate. We agreed, however, that those who did not have the opportunity to know Peter Strevens personally, would nonetheless, based on his writings and other professional activities, have such respect and admiration for him that they would wish to hear even this simple tribute.

Peter's death was loss enough, yet during last week's TESOL conference news came of the loss of still another distinguished British linguist, S. Pit Corder. Professor Widdowson and I have asked Professor Selinker, his close collaborator, to say a like commemorative word for him.

It was a very sad occasion indeed to learn of the untimely death of Peter Strevens and, even now, I have not quite adjusted to the loss. It is difficult for someone from my culture to attempt to express in a few simple words the impact which this colleague made on my work and on my life. My own instincts would be to remember him through the prescribed formality of an ancient liturgy and yet, for this gentle man and member of the Society of Friends, that would be inappropriate. So, instead, I remember him with my own humble words.

Peter was a man of rare gifts and qualities: a leader, a friend, a gentleman and a gentle man.

Members of our profession know the quality of his leadership. Through his writings, most notably *New Orientations in the Teaching of English*, his coeditorship with myself and H. H. Stern of *GURT '83*, his paper in *GURT '87*,and again just last year in *GURT '89*, and, of course, his fine work on the spread of English, and through his many fine lectures at major academic conferences and, in more recent times, his status as distinguished visiting scholar, many came to, appreciate and benefit from his depth of learning, world of experience and clarity of vision. I am confident that his words will provide guidance to our profession for years to come.

The news of Peter's death was even more painful when one had counted this great man among one's friends. My own friendship was cemented when I learned, quite by chance, that Peter had spent the wartime years on the island of Symi off the coast of Greece, a small bit of rock in the Aegean—the very place from which my wife's family comes. My wife Penny and I often had occasion to meet and recall old times with Peter and his wonderful wife, Gwyn, at professional conferences and scholarly meetings. Now that Peter is gone, these memories are all the more precious.

In academe and professional organizations, there are inevitable disagreements and disputes. Sometimes tempers run high and regrettable remarks are exchanged. In the many years I knew Peter, he conducted himself with consummate dignity and good grace. He was always a gentleman, even under the most trying circumstances. He leaves an example for us to follow.

At the outset of these brief remarks, I noted that Peter was both a gentleman and a gentle man, a statement which deserves some explanation. Peter was a man of peace and principle. When called by Britain to service in the Second World War, he served his country and humanity as an ambulance driver (when I have more time I will regale you with stories about Peter's ambulance and about the way he found it many years later on the island of Rhodes). He worked on resettlement and aided wounded soldiers and civilians in Greece. He worked hard and with great compassion and left a lasting impression with those he aided, so much so that, more than 40 years later, when he returned to a village where he served for many months, the old women saw him and after a few moments began crying "Ho Xanthos, Ho Xanthos!" which means "Look, look, it's the blonde one!"

In the Greek tradition, there is a saying, "The memory of the righteous is a blessing." The best way to pay tribute to the memory of this manwho worked throughout his professional life as a unifieran a harmonizer, is to resist those temptations which would work to pull us apart. Instead, we should focus on those factors which bring us together. I think Peter would have liked that. *James E. Alatis, Georgetown University.*

I should like to take this opportunity to make public my own sense of loss at the death of two people, Pit Corder and Peter Strevens. Both of them, in very different ways, made a permanent impression on the profession. Both of them appear as benevolent spirits implicitly in the paper I prepared for this conference. They could hardly do otherwise, for they also made a lasting mark on my own personal and professional life.

Pit Corder's papers on error analysis over twenty years ago were genuinely seminal in that from them grew the great profusion of work on second-language acquisition to which I shall subsequently be making reference. And Peter Strevens--well, I should like to commemorate him by following his example and beginning the paper I shall deliver, as he would often begin his own, with a story. The one I recount there is one of his stories, which, as I hope you will see, makes a point relevant to my theme, namely, the way preconceived ideas can determine the interpretation of data. My attempt to imitate is basically deep homage and the most sincere tribute.

H. G. Widdowson, University of London.

The impetus for much of my work came from Pit Corder, my 'intellectual father' in interlanguage and second language acquisition. I was not alone in feeling that way: in an issue of *Language* he was called 'Le Pere Fondateur'.

Detailing his many contributions to this field before culminating with the following list has been pure joy. I hope you will indulge me by an appreciative listening to the quiet litany of his fine work:

'Errors as a window the the learner's IL competence.'
'Errors as a learning strategy.'
'Covert vs. overt errors.'
'Language-teaching concerns as a motivation for studying IL.'
'Teacher input as possibly interfering with acquisition.'
'Input vs. intake.'
'Learner system as dynamic system.'
'Longitudinal IL studies.'
'Successive stages of learner language.'
'Learners using a definite system at each point.'
'Transitional competence.'
'Learner's underlying knowledge of language to date.'
'Learner language as normally unstable.'
'Idiosyncratic competence.'
'Investigation of learner intuitions.'
'Interpretation of IL sentences.'
'Translation equivalents of sentence synonymous in a context.'
'Methodology of using learner mother tongue.'
'Study of learner intention.'
'Using bilingual former speakers of earlier IL'
'Elicitation procedures.'
'Logical sequence in investigating IL.'
'CA and EA as complimentary research procedures.'
'NL not as inhibitory but facilitative.'
'NL as a heuristic tool to match NL-like phenomena in TL.'
'Transfer as incorporation of items and features into IL system.'
'Transfer takes place between two mental structures: NL and Developing IL.'
'For transfer to occur, successful communication has to occur.'
'However, this may give rise to persistent error.'
'Internal (or built in) syllabus vs. external syllabus.'

'Learner is programmed to process input data in a certain way.'
'Relationship of input to current state of learner's grammar.'
'Study of non-tutored acquisition.'
'Study of IL as a central part of study of language.'
'Basic core IL (possibly universal) component.'
'Importance of conventions of a social group in shaping IL.'
'IL development as complexification, not simplification.'
'IL development continues related to communicative needs.'
'IL development ceases when communification needs are met.'

The contributions are awesome. How could we possibly manage without all this?

All will agree then that much is owed to Pit intellectually but not many know that we also owe him much for his ability to set up contexts for creative work for younger scholars. This was certainly true for me. Without Pit's personal hospitality and intellectual input, there would be no interlanguage hypothesis. It is as simple as that. I owe to Pit the context: in the Edinburgh Department of Applied Linguistics in the late 1960s that led to the formulation of the original 'interlanguage hypothesis'.

I am glad that I visited Pit and Nancy in retirement. It renewed the old excitement, seeing Pit's continued insights into language acquisition questions, though interestingly in a more local context than before. He was concerned with the attempted second language acquisition of his colleagues in retirement in Braithwaite, that pretty village in the Lake District. It is a pity that we found no forum to capture that new intellectual material.

Like others, I will miss his presence, both intellectually and personally.

Larry Selinker, University of Michigan.

My memories of S. Pit Corder are of a distinguished gentlemen, who wrote what I consider the best work on applied linguistics available today. His brief, *Introducing Applied Linguistics* is a seminal work, as were the four volumes which he co-edited with J.P.B. Allen, *Readings for Applied Linguistics*, *Papers in Applied Linguistics*, *Techniques in Applied Linguistics*, and *Testing and Experimental Methods*. When asked for a definition of applied linguistics, it is his that I quote. His thoughts and writings expressed beautifully what my own reading and experience had taught me, but which I had not attempted to articulate. And indeed, anything which I could have assayed would have been a poor and clumsy thing in the face of Pit Corder's work. He visited this campus in 1974, when the Leavey and Intercultural Centers were the fond dreams of architects and nothing more. He came to our ramshackle offices in the Nevils and Loyola buildings, met with many of our faculty and wrote me later, expressing his gratitude for the visit and acknowledging that "a great deal of interesting and valuable work (was) being done" in applied linguistics on this side of the ocean. He was a substantial enough scholar not to view this as a threat, but as a cause for celebration because new avenues for collaborative research and studies had manifested themselves. Our profession, any profession for that matter, yields but a few leaders of S. Pit Corder's quality, and yet, we would be well advised to rejoice in those we have rather than to bemoan their scarcity.

James E. Alatis, Georgetown University.

Discourses of enquiry and conditions of relevance

H. G. Widdowson
University of London

I should like to set a conceptual scene and at the same time commemorate Peter Strevens by following his example and beginning my paper, as he would often begin his own, with a story. This is one of his stories, which, as I hope you will see, makes a point relevant to my theme: to the way preconceived ideas can determine the interpretation of data. A man walking down a street meets someone he recognizes as an old acquaintance. "Why, Jenkins," he cries, "how good to see you. But how you have changed. Last time we met you were quite fat, but now you are really very thin. And I remember that you used to have a beard, but now you are clean-shaven. And, now I come to think of it, Jenkins, old boy, you used to have a wonderful head of hair, and now, well, you are almost completely bald-headed." And the man replied: "My name isn't Jenkins, it's Jones." "Oh, so you have changed your *name* as well!"

This paper is about paradigms and epistemes, about the nature of knowledge and the conditions of its application in practice. It is by way of being an excursion into cross-cultural epistemology. It explores the significance of the semantic distinctions that people invent to make sense of things and, in general, the relationship between knowing and naming.

This is, of course, a familiar theme, but I think that it has particular relevance to the concerns of this conference. Indeed, the very title of the conference is an incitement to such enquiry. It names three areas and three modes of activity but the terms are, we should note, ordered in parallel. So linguistics is associated with theory, language teaching with practice, language acquisition with research. But how far does this pattern of words represent necessary distinctions and associations between kinds of knowing and doing? The title directs us to demonstrate interdependence in reference to one set of terms, with the implication that the parallel associations can be taken for granted. But can they? Is linguistics to be uniquely associated with theory in dissociation from practice, does language teaching of its nature have no theory of its own, but must depend on linguistics for its supply? And is the only research which is pedagogically relevant that which is uniquely associated with language acquisition? You may object that it is unreasonable to subject this title to such close textual analysis. But the purpose of this kind of deconstruction is to discover the assumptions and values that lurk behind the use of terms, and I believe that the way we talk about the topics of this conference stands in particular need of such analysis. This very elementary exercise on its title, for example, raises the question of what we actually mean by theory, practice, and research in apparently separate domains or discourses of enquiry.

And the term 'discourse' itself is of particular significance. In the domain of linguistics, it is familiar enough and I suppose that there would be general consensus on its meaning—the way language is exploited and organized to achieve meaning in contexts of use, or something along these lines. And textbooks on discourse analysis, like Brown and Yule 1983, Coulthard 1985, Stubbs 1983, and so on, tell us how it is done. It is true that they take somewhat different perspectives, and differ therefore in scope and emphasis, but they are all talking about recognizably the same thing. Their bibliographies reveal similar sources of reference, and inspiration. They are all working, if you will, within the same paradigm or episteme. But in other areas of academic enquiry, in sociology, for example, or literary criticism, the term 'discourse' is used in rather a different sense. Consider a book published a year or two ago by Diane Macdonell. It is called *Theories of Discourse* (Macdonell 1986). Open these pages and you pass into a world which is, generally speaking, strange to you, if you have been acculturated into the established attitudes of discourse linguistics. There is a shift of episteme. Thus, the bibliography makes no mention of Brown & Yule or Coulthard or, indeed, of any scholar who is customarily cited whenever discourse is mentioned in the linguistics literature. There is no Searle here, no Gumperz even, no Sacks or Schegloff, Dressler or van Dijk. None of these is credited with making any contribution to theories of discourse at all. It is obvious that in using the same term, the author has something very different in mind. To read such a book is to experience culture shock. You find that you cannot readily take bearings on it by using your customary points of reference.

What then is meant by discourse in this case? We come here to the main business of this paper. It means a mode of social practice, and in particular how institutions establish ideologies for the control of ideas. So the definition of discourse here is essentially sociological rather than linguistic. Of course, language comes into the picture, but it is considered as evidence for something else. It is an epiphenomenon, of interest not for its own sake but for what it reveals of social significance. There is an obvious parallel here with Chomsky's perspective on language, except that in his case, linguistic data is only of interest to the extent that it serves as evidence of psychological rather than social processes. It happens that in the Macdonell book I mentioned linguistic data is not much in evidence: the discussion concentrates on discourses as modes of thought, as ideological constructs. It is for this reason that it looks so out of focus for those whose vision is specially adapted to linguistics. But there are other enquiries from this viewpoint which do look at language, and which can therefore be seen as an extension of the familiar paradigm, calling, therefore, for rather less modification of preconceived ideas to accommodate them. I refer here to work that goes under the name of Critical Discourse Analysis, as exemplified by Gunther Kress in his book *Linguistic Processes in Sociocultural Practice* (Kress 1985) and Norman Fairclough's recent publication *Language and Power* (Fairclough 1989).

The study of discourse from this sociological point of view, then, seeks to demonstrate how perceptions of reality are culturally conditioned, how ideas are ideologically informed. In this view, to simply describe discourse in reference to a knowledge of communicative conventions and the ability to act upon such knowledge is to disregard underlying causes and to provide descriptions without explanation. In this respect, sociological discourse analysis of this kind stands in the same relationship to linguistic discourse analysis of the Coulthard/Brown and Yule variety as Chomsky's model of grammar stands in relation to taxonomic description. Both are in quest of the covert, the forces which drive human knowledge and behavior: the genetic program on the one hand, the hidden agenda on the other.

It is the relevance to our concerns of discourse in this sociological sense that I want to explore. The three areas of investigation which are named in the title of this conference—linguistics, language teaching, and language acquisition—are different discourses, different cultures of enquiry. My purpose is to apply a little critical analysis, or deconstruction, to them to see what underlying values and assumptions we can find, and the extent to which these limit the possibilities of meaningful cultural interrelation.

As this theory of discourse indicates, all the discourses of theory, including those of linguistics, are ideologically loaded, cultural constructs designed to establish control and a sense of security. This is not in the least surprising, of course, since theories are made out of language. In this respect, they are the manipulations of a process which begins with first language acquisition, when we are initiated into a theoretical perspective of the world which defines what counts as true or factual or significant in our particular community. The process is one of induction, in both senses of the term. And it is continued in formal education, of course, whose purpose is to provide further initiation into approved and privileged ways of thinking and conveying thought. There can be no idealization without ideology. Every subject in the curriculum represents a course of induction into new kinds of culturally defined realities. In universities, these are enshrined as disciplines. The term discipline is appropriate. Students are schooled into an acknowledgement of authority, and coerced into conformity. They may not realize that this is happening, of course. Much of the essential effect of education is a matter of influence below the level of awareness. Remarks by the psychologist Liam Hudson are to the point here:

> My suspicion . . . is that every generation of students is susceptible to its teachers' presuppositions, and that these presuppositions are potent just

> to the extent that they are unspoken. It is assumptions, prejudices and implicit metaphors that are the true burden of what passes between teacher and taught. (Hudson 1972:43)

It is just such assumptions, prejudices, and implicit metaphors which define different cultures of enquiry, the discourses of different disciplines. And these discourses give their blessing to some kinds of activity and deny it to others. For as we are initiated into education, we are made to realize that not everything we know counts as knowledge, not all ideas count as theory, and not all enquiry counts as research. In all cases there has to be some sort of authority to provide recognition and the seal of approval. I am reminded of certain lines of verse. They were written by irreverent students about the redoubtable nineteenth century classical scholar Benjamin Jowett, professor of Greek at Oxford, Master of Balliol College, and a man of massive self assurance.

> First come I, my name is Jowett;.
> There is no knowledge but I know it.
> I am the master of this college;
> What I don't know isn't knowledge.

Now I do not want to suggest by this that we should avoid the cultural partiality of disciplinary discourses and strive instead to be neutrally objective. This would be futile because without such discourses there could be no enquiry at all. What I do want to suggest is that we should guard against being too readily persuaded into believing in the validity or relevance of any particular discourse, no matter what apparent authority it might have. Indeed, the more authority it claims, the more distrustful one ought to be, for the claiming is also part of the discourse. On the other hand, even if we can agree that theories as discourses are, to use Feyerabend's term, incommensurable, and that there is no real reason for assigning privileged status to one of them rather than another, this does not mean that there can be no interrelationship between them, that one discourse cannot be of beneficial influence on another. If this were so, then we would never be able to learn from the ideas of others, and we would be kept enclosed within our own conceptual capsules. What it means is that ideas from one of these cultural domains need to be subjected to critical appraisal and evaluated as to their potential relevance. The influence needs to be mediated.

With this in mind, I want now to focus on the relationship between language teaching and the other two areas of activity named in the conference title. We can begin with the ideas of the most familiar and influential figure in linguistics over the past 30 years or so, and his most familiar and influential distinction: that between 'competence' and 'performance.' The first thing to notice is that the distinction is made so as to isolate that aspect of language which Chomsky is interested in, and to disregard all others. The symmetry of the names suggests that the concepts are of equal theoretical status. They are not. As a number of people have pointed out (e.g. Hymes 1972), 'performance' is simply a convenient waste disposal device. Its use leads us to suppose that in stripping away the incidentals, we arrive at the essential and well-defined concept of competence. But closer scrutiny reveals that it is not really very well defined at all. We are told that competence is knowledge of language, and that this is "unaffected by such grammatically irrelevant conditions as memory limitations" (Chomsky 1965:3). Smuggled into this definition is the equation of language with grammar. Memory is irrelevant to *grammatical* knowledge so it is irrelevant to *language* knowledge. Competence is "a system of generative processes," and competence is a knowledge of language, so everything that we know which is not generative, not reducible to grammatical rule, is not, by definition, part of our knowledge of language.

Chomsky's major rhetorical achievement is that he persuaded people into the acceptance of a discourse which reduced language knowledge to a system of syntactic rules and confined linguistics to the study of grammar. It was with such a discourse that he demolished Skinner and discredited behaviorism in general. And at the time, it all seemed like a new enlightenment. It was a dazzling vision, and it dulled perception. And the eventual effect on language pedagogy was that it bred distrust of any approach which seemed to be tarred with the behaviorist brush, which activated the memory rather than cognition, habit rather than rule formation. But on closer and more critical scrutiny, it becomes clear that such compliance with the Chomsky doctrine is misplaced. It assumes that ideas from one discourse can be directly transferred to another.

For, as I indicated earlier, for Chomsky, grammar is primary and language is cast in a supporting role. He may talk about linguistic competence but he means grammatical competence. For language teachers, it is the development of linguistic competence which is primary, and it is grammar which is cast in the supporting role. The concerns are not congruent.

Now it seems reasonable to claim that whatever language competence in general is (see Widdowson 1989), and whichever terms you use to name its different features—linguistic or communicative or pragmatic or strategic or sociolinguistic or whatever—one of these features will be grammatical; and as a theoretical linguist you may choose to focus on that feature and disregard the rest. The difficulty arises when this limited and limiting view of language is given precedence over all others, when the relative is made absolute. For it is obvious that such a view gives us only a partial truth. Part of language competence can indeed be accounted for by generative rules, and part of language performance is indeed regulated by reference to them. But only a part, by no means all. Even if we consider only linguistic knowledge, leaving aside all the complexities of how this is accessed to achieve appropriate utterance in context, it is clear that a good deal of it cannot be reduced to generative rule. As a number of scholars have pointed out (for example,

Bolinger 1976, Pawley & Synder 1983), much of it exists as chunks of more or less ready-made lexico-syntactic units, idiomatic elements that have not been analyzed, but simply stored in a state of complete or partial assembly, and tagged with contextual conditions of appropriacy. In other words, a good deal of linguistic knowledge is more readily accountable by reference to behaviorist notions. It is acquired by means of memory and not by cognitive analysis, impressed on the malleable mind by contextual recurrence, a matter of habit rather than rule.

Chomsky's review of Skinner ends with a parting shot at behaviorist partiality: "If the study of language is limited in these ways, it seems inevitable that major aspects of verbal behavior will remain a mystery" (Chomsky 1959:58). But if the study of language is limited to the study of grammar, major aspects will remain a mystery also. We might concede that linguistic knowledge cannot be completely accounted for by environmental stimulus-response habit formation. But it cannot be completely accounted for by the rule derivation processes of innate cognition either, unless, of course, you change the concept of such knowledge to suit your prejudice and purpose. If you define language competence as linguistic competence and linguistic competence as grammatical competence, that is to say, as a knowledge of abstract grammatical rules for sentence generation, then of course, by definition, any account of linguistic competence which allows for habit and idiomatic storage must be wrong. What Chomsky has done, in popular parlance, is to shift the goalposts. In fact, he is playing a different game altogether, and according to rules of his own devising.

These rules of the game, as I have indicated, involve the appropriation of terms. So the term 'language' means grammar; and the term 'creative' means generative—that is to say the very opposite of its familiar meaning of nonconformity to rule.

There are two terms which are of particular relevance to the question of the relationship or interdependence of theory, practice, and research. These are 'component' and 'module'. It has been the convention of generative linguists to talk about the components of a model of linguistic description: the syntactic component consisting of the base and transformational components, the semantic component, the phonological component. All of these can be said to constitute the linguistic knowledge component of language competence as a whole.

Now the crucial point about the concept of component, if one is to take the term in its customary sense, is that it is a 'constituent part' of some larger unit, so that you cannot characterize a component unless you can establish how it functions interdependently with other components as parts of a whole. In earlier versions of generative grammar it was essentially the purpose of transformations to establish such connections. The gradual disappearance of transformations from the scene has coincided with the gradual appearance of the term 'module' into the literature. This is not surprising. It reflects the failure to find coherent relationships between components. For the term 'module' carries with it no such notion of constituency. To take a modular approach is to identify some phenomenon that takes your interest and treat it holistically as quite separate and self-contained. It may turn out that your module relates to some other, but it is not your business to discover the relationship. To describe language competence in a componential manner is to represent it singularly as (to use expressions in Horrocks 1987) "a network of mutually constraining systems," but from a modular view, it becomes a plurality of "much more complex networks of unrelated systems" (Horrocks 1987:10), the complexity of which you can conveniently ignore in your theoretical enquiry.

But the complexity of interrelationships in language cannot be ignored in language teaching. The modular approach, no matter how proper to the discourse of theoretical linguistics (and this is not my concern), necessarily limits the relevance of its description to practical pedagogy, for this of its nature must be componential. I will return to this point presently. Before I do, I should like to consider the third item on our agenda, second language acquisition research.

The most important point to be made for my purposes is that this research has, generally speaking, aligned itself with generative linguistic theory and followed the modular line. In particular, it has focused on the acquisition of grammatical rules. To quote Ellis: "The centrality of grammar in linguistics has been echoed in SLA studies" (Ellis 1985:288). Generally speaking, then, these studies are not on language, but grammar acquisition, not so much SLA as SGA. Furthermore, the term 'acquisition' is itself taken directly from the discourse of generative theory, where it is used in reference to *first* language development, and assumed to be self-evidently applicable to the quite different phenomenon of *second* language development. As Jacquelyn Schachter has pointed out:

> The facts of second language acquisition are nowhere near the same as those of first language acquisition. And the very powerful arguments supporting the proposed mechanisms to account for first language acquisition *cannot* be used to support those mechanisms in the second language case (Schachter 1988:222).

Thus, two assumptions are smuggled into the very name of SLA research, and they fix in advance what is to be counted as significant or, to use the terms of the discourse itself, they set the parameters of enquiry. The quest is for evidence of some sequence of grammatical rules informed by universal principles. Once the agenda is fixed in this way, all other matters have necessarily to demonstrate their relevance to it and they take on a supporting or subordinate role. Thus, you can talk, for example, about conversational interaction, but your concern will not essentially be with how this is developed as a part of language competence in general, but rather how it can be seen as a way of managing comprehensible input for the activation of the grammar acquisition process. So the discourse of conversational interaction in all its complexity is converted into convenient data to support the discourse of enquiry.

Again, when evidence appears which cannot be readily assimilated into the conceptual scheme, new names are introduced into the discourse to cope with it. Thus, when second language learners produce language which does not conform to the hypothesized naturally emerging grammar, this is said to be a matter of 'learning' rather than 'acquisition' (Krashen 1981, and passim), or evidence not of the essential underlying 'sequence' but of a variable 'order' of development (Ellis 1985). To sustain such distinctions it is necessary to make others: focus on form, for example, associated with learning, as distinct from focus on meaning associated with acquisition; vernacular style, which provides the evidence for sequence and order, as distinct from other styles of speaking, which can be discounted as evidence. But these, and other, terms are only defined to the degree necessary for them to sustain their role in the discourse, and the definitions hold only within its epistemic limits. The terms take on the status of well-defined categories of reality because they fit into the discourse, itself projected from assumptions about the primacy of grammar and universality of the acquisition process.

And this discourse will of its nature determine conditions of relevance in respect to data. Those who subscribe to its assumptions will share what Sperber and Wilson (1986) call a 'mutual cognitive environment' and this will control which aspects of reality they will make manifest as significant. Any data which has contextual effects in reference to such a cognitive environment will be seen as relevant, any data which does not will be disregarded. Once we recognize research as a kind of discourse, it will obviously have pragmatic consequences of the kind that Sperber and Wilson explore in their theory of relevance. And relevance, by definition, is a matter of selective attention based on shared assumptions.

But what if these assumptions are not shared? We then, of course, get the kind of situation familiar to those who have studied pragmatic failure in cross-cultural communication in general (e.g. Gumperz 1982, Thomas 1983). Concepts and values assumed to be self-evidently valid become problematic, axiomatic statement becomes unfounded assertion. We might notice, for example, that terms which fitted so well in the patterns of the discourse are, from a different perspective, in need of explanation. We are drawn into deconstruction.

We might, for example, take a closer look at the distinction between sequence and order of development that I referred to earlier, and begin to wonder how one might actually get empirical evidence to support it. We might begin to question why the vernacular style, however that is defined, should be taken as more directly expressive of grammatical knowledge than any other, or how, in general, you tell whether variable language behavior is evidence of intrinsic rule-governed variation within a grammar rather than a function of contextual conditions which have an effect on the ability to access grammatical rules—rules which are therefore known but cannot for all kinds of reasons be acted upon.

We might begin to ask how you actually know when somebody is focusing on form rather than meaning, and what kind of meaning this might be, and how you know when input has been comprehended, and what, indeed, this key concept of comprehension itself actually means. And as you pick at these different terms and concepts, the fabric of the discourse begins to unravel.

Now I do not want to suggest by this that SLA research is particularly at fault in this respect. The point is that all discourses can be unravelled in this way. The patterns of SLA study depend on the uncritical acceptance of certain concepts, like 'meaning', 'comprehension', 'communication', which are matters of massive and intensive investigation in other discourses of enquiry, which can themselves be deconstructed in their turn, and found wanting on other grounds. There is nothing reprehensible about this process of legitimatizing partiality. Without it, there could be no enquiry at all. And it is entirely natural for people to secure their own sociocultural domains of study in this way, making the world into something they can conveniently manage by controlling perception by preconceived ideas. And such perceptions can be very enlightening: they can have the salutary effect of making you realize the partiality of your own, and of opening up possibilities for change. Our own culture gets modified by contact with others. And this brings me to the third term in the conference title and the question of the relationship between linguistic theory, SLA research, and language teaching.

The discourse of SLA studies is generally speaking derivative from that of generative linguistics in that it focuses on grammatical competence in modular isolation from other aspects of language knowledge. In this respect, it can be said to have the same 'mutual cognitive environment' in Sperber and Wilson terms, and so essentially the same criteria for relevance. This explains the relative neglect of work on language which is not within the grammatical mainstream. Lexis, for example, has only very recently come on the scene (see Gass 1987), although, as Howatt has pointed out, for both H. R. Palmer and Henry Sweet the acquisition of lexis was seen as "the real intrinsic difficulty" (Howatt 1984:286). Again, it took ten years for it to be recognized that Labov's concept of the variable rule was relevant to the description of interlanguage systems (cf. Labov 1970, Tarone 1979), even though it was logically necessary for this to be so, given the definition of interlanguage.

SLA researchers and theoretical grammarians, then, would seem to work within a mutual cognitive environment. But the cognitive environment of language teaching is totally different. So there can be no assumption of shared conditions of relevance. Consider, for example, the distinction that has been made in the SLA literature between 'naturalistic' and 'classroom' SLA. The fact that, as Ellis indicates (Ellis 1985:247), there has been relatively little research into classroom language acquisition is, of course, itself significant, but the point I want to make concerns once more the way concepts are defined to sustain a particular discourse perspective. Naturalistic factors are recognized as immensely complex, and it is, indeed, this very complexity which has stimulated such proliferation of SLA research. Classroom factors, on the other hand, are represented as relatively simple. In Ellis 1985, there is a chapter devoted to them. It begins: "This chapter looks at second language acquisition in a classroom setting. It considers whether formal instruction makes a difference to SLA" (Ellis 1985:215).

Notice that language in a classroom setting is equated with formal instruction. Later in the chapter, it becomes clear that formal instruction means instruction in grammatical forms. Thus the immense range of instructional variables is reduced to convenient fit. All the sociological and psychological complexities of classroom encounters, all the variations of pedagogic principle and technique are set aside as irrelevant to the enquiry. Nothing perhaps shows more clearly the difference of cognitive environments. This modular fixation on grammar acquisition is quite remote from the reality of the classroom situation and the real concerns of teachers.

For, as I indicated earlier, classroom pedagogy is not a matter of isolating one aspect of language, or one instructional variable and subordinating all others. What teachers have to do is to deal with language and learning in a componential rather than a modular manner. They may focus attention on points of grammar, or on areas of lexis; they may induce learning by devising exercises for pattern practice or tasks for problem solving, they may draw the learners into affective or cognitive involvement, they may do all kinds of things and vary the focus on different aspects of language in all kinds of ways, but the assumption always is that these are all interrelated, and interdependent components of the language learning process, each acting upon the other. It is the relationship that is so crucial.

The teacher, of course, has to analyze teaching into components but the purpose of the analysis is to create conditions for the learners to achieve a synthesis. If that does not happen, the teaching fails. It is the interrelationship of components that creates these conditions, and the assumption is, of course, that these conditions, contrived for classroom purposes, can improve on those available for naturalistic acquisition.

But the common assumption within SLA is, on the contrary, that classroom teaching should conform to naturalistic process. One difficulty about this assumption is that the term 'naturalistic' is never actually defined (see Bourne 1988), so we really do not know what those who use it are talking about. And the idea that the only kind of classroom activity which is effective for learning is that which conforms in some way to natural processes of acquisition is just the kind of unexamined assumption within SLA discourse which is implied in the narrow definition of classroom activity which I pointed to earlier. If the enquiry into SLA were located in the classroom, as it was in its origins in error analysis with the work of Pit Corder (Corder 1981), and shared the cognitive environment of pedagogy, then we would get very different definitions, and very different results—and results, furthermore, of more immediate relevance to classroom practice.

But is research in SLA of no relevance, then, to language teaching? I return to the point I made previously, that an awareness of other discourses, other cultures, can lead to the appraisal and adaptation of one's own. For, of course, the denial of absolute objectivity does not preclude agreement on what is to be accounted as fact. It is simply to say that what is objective has no separate ontological status but is a matter of convergent subjectivities. The stability of what we know is held in equilibrium by different forces of belief. There are bound to be commonalities which are based on universals of human cognition and experience in general, but it is the areas of cross-cultural nonconvergence which pose problems and call for negotiation, which require us to achieve a pragmatic fit, or what Cicourel calls a "reciprocity of perspectives" (Cicourel 1973).

One of the papers of this conference has the suggestive title "Theory, practice, and research: Strange or blissful bedfellows?" All I am saying in this paper, I suppose, is that a great deal depends on the bed, and that it can often turn out to be a procrustean one. No matter how blissful the prospect, before you ask a linguist or an SLA researcher to share a bed, you should be sure that it is on your terms. Your place, not theirs.

Ideas from linguistics and second language acquisition studies can be made relevant as stimulants to enquiry in the different discourse of language pedagogy. For it is a different discourse, and it therefore has its own conditions of relevance, is informed by its own theory and sustained by its own research. What such a theory might encompass is indicated in Bernard Spolsky's recent book *Conditions of Second Language Learning* (Spolsky 1989). These are conditions of relevance, components and their relationship, which are proposed from within pedagogy, not imposed as constraints from outside it. What such research might involve is illustrated in the scheme for language teacher education which Christopher Candlin and I are currently editing (see Anderson & Lynch 1988, Bygate 1987, Cook 1989, Malamah-Thomas 1987, McCarthy 1990, Nunan 1988, Wright 1987). Here guidance is given on how ideas from other discourses might be critically appraised, referred to the concerns of teaching, and made operational, where relevant, through action research as an intrinsic part of teaching itself.

Theory and research in language teaching will naturally draw on insights from other areas of enquiry, assimilate and accommodate them as convenient, apply and evaluate them in the continuing experimental process of teaching. But there are no absolutes, and so no absolute dependence. Language teaching is often represented as a client activity, and language teachers as consumers of the findings that are retailed by research. I believe that this is a misrepresentation which denies the nature of teaching as a domain of theory and research in its own right, and which is based on a misunderstanding of the relationship between discourses of enquiry and conditions of relevance which I have tried to expound in this paper.

References

Anderson, A., and T. Lynch. 1988. Listening. Oxford: Oxford University Press.
Bolinger, D. 1976. Meaning and memory. Forum Linguisticum 1.1.
Bourne, G. 1988. 'Natural acquisition' and 'masked pedagogy'. In: Applied Linguistics 9.1.
Brown, G., and G. Yule. 1983. Discourse analysis. Cambridge: Cambridge University Press.
Bygate, M. 1987. Speaking. Oxford: Oxford University Press.
Chomsky, N. 1959. Review of: B.F. Skinner, Verbal behavior. In: Language 35.
Chomsky, N. 1965. Aspects of the theory of syntax. Cambridge, Mass.: MIT Press.
Cicourel, A.V. 1973. Cognitive sociology. Harmondsworth: Penguin Books.
Cook, G. 1989. Discourse. Oxford: Oxford University Press.
Corder, S. Pit. 1981. Error analysis and interlanguage. Oxford: Oxford University Press.
Coulthard, R.M. 1985. An introduction to discourse analysis. London: Longman.
Ellis, R. 1985. Understanding second language acquisition. Oxford: Oxford University Press.
Fairclough, N. 1989. Language and power. London: Longman.
Gass, S., ed. 1987. The use and acquisition of the second language lexicon. In: Studies in Second Language Acquisition 9.2.
Gumperz, J.J., ed. 1982. Language and social identity. Cambridge: Cambridge University Press.
Horrocks, G. 1987. Generative grammar. London: Longman.
Howatt, A.P.R. 1984. A history of English language teaching. Oxford: Oxford University Press.
Hudson, L. 1972. The cult of the fact. London: Jonathan Cape
Hymes, D. 1972. On communicative competence. In: J. Pride and J. Holmes, eds. Sociolinguistics. Harmondsworth: Penguin Books.
Krashen, S.D. 1981. Second language acquisition and second language learning. Oxford: Pergamon.
Kress, G. 1985. Linguistic processes in sociocultural practice. Victoria: Deakin University Press (reprinted 1989, Oxford University Press).
Labov, W. 1970. The study of language in its social context. In: Studium Generale 23.
Malamah-Thomas, A. 1987. Classroom interaction. Oxford: Oxford University Press.
McCarthy, M. 1990. Vocabulary. Oxford: Oxford University Press.
Macdoneil, D. 1986. Theories of discourse: An introduction. Oxford: Basil Blackwell.
Nunan, D. 1988. Syllabus design. Oxford: Oxford University Press.
Pawley, A., and F. Syder. 1983. Two puzzles for linguistic theory: Native-like selection and native-like fluency. In: J. Richards and R. Schmidt, eds. Language and communication. London: Longman.
Schachter, J. 1988. Second language acquisition and its relationship to Universal Grammar. In: Applied Linguistics 9.3.
Sperber, D., and D. Wilson. 1986. Relevance. Communication and cognition. Oxford: Basil Blackwell.
Spolsky, B. 1989. Conditions for second language learning. Oxford: Oxford University Press.
Stubbs, M.W. 1983. Discourse analysis. Oxford: Basil Blackwell.
Tarone, E. 1979. Interlanguage as chameleon. In: Language Learning 29.1.
Thomas, J. 1983. Cross-cultural pragmatic failure. In: Applied Linguistics 4.2.
Widdowson, H.G. 1989. Knowledge of language and ability for use. In: Applied Linguistics 10.2.
Wright, T. 1987. The roles of teacher and learner. Oxford: Oxford University Press.

Mental representations and language in action

Wilga M. Rivers*
Harvard University

The swings and cycles of language teaching approaches continue. Everyone talks about them, but few people analyze them. As Gleick (1987) has pointed out in a fascinating way, there is patterning within patterning in nature; and new ideas have long been recognized as recombinations of earlier thinking, the human mind associating and interrelating existing and entering material in a multitude of unexpected ways. So it behooves us to try to identify this patterning within teaching approaches, so that we may pinpoint what each new approach is emphasizing. Differences among approaches are, for the most part, differences in emphases, frequently because of changing demands and expectations that come from outside the foreign language learning/teaching domain. What appear to be radically new theoretical premises are, as often as not, variants of ways of looking at the same basic questions about language learning, sometimes with the fresh paint of a new terminology that camouflages their fundamental similarity.

The basic question in second language teaching that we are always considering and reconsidering, researching and hypothesizing about, can be stated succinctly: How do we internalize a language system so that we can enter into meaningful communication with speakers or writers of that language? Is the internalization a priming of something innate, something we already know, "one element in a system of cognitive structure" (Chomsky 1980:220), that is, the setting of parameters for the new language based on an inborn abstract competence or universal grammar, in Chomskyan terms? Alternatively, is it an ingestion of new knowledge from without, assisted by social contacts or experienced knowers? Is it perhaps a combination of both? Is it a priming of innate abstract capacities, whether linguistic or logical, by contact with new forms of expression essential for well-being, that sets in

---

* Some parts of this paper appeared in an earlier form in "Psychological validation of methodological approaches and foreign language classroom practices," in B. Freed, ed., *Foreign language acquisition research and the classroom.* Lexington, Mass.: D.C. Heath.

motion the process of absorption of these new forms into the dynamic networks of the human mind/ brain,[1] in which are already incorporated what the learner knows of a first, and sometimes a second and third language? We have much evidence from diaries of the way learners do interrelate new linguistic knowledge with what is known of other languages (e.g. Rivers 1981:501-15), and further evidence that strategies of approach to a third, fourth, or fifth language are guided by experience with the systemic way other languages have organized their phonology, syntax, or semantics (Naiman et al. 1978). From birth, nothing is learned in a vacuum.

All evidence points to an organized system at the core of any language—a system that is basic to communicating messages even at a very simple level. Whether this core is considered in essence lexico-syntactic as Chomsky maintains[2] or semantic-pragmatic as in Halliday's theory of meaning-potential and 'goings-on' in language, there is clearly a formal framework that enables one to use a language systematically to convey meaning to other individuals. Interwoven within this basic framework are the phonological, and the semantic, syntactic, and pragmatic systems (in whichever ways they are considered to be interrelated). Although there are universals at the base of these systems, in each case the usage specific to a particular language and culture must be acquired through prolonged contact with that language, although previous experience with their native language and culture has sensitized the learners to the role these play in the communication of meaning. I refer to this systematic framework as 'grammar' in its broadest sense, for the purposes of this discussion.

In all language learning and teaching approaches, there has been awareness of the existence of this vital core, without which mutual comprehension is impossible. Leontiev, for instance, has spoken of the "absolute minimum . . . the foundations of the language without which the learning of any speech activity would be impossible" (1981:25). Language teaching theorists down the ages, however, have continually affirmed that language learning must be more than 'learning the grammar', even in this broad sense. Ploetz (1865), the foremost grammar-translation protagonist of the late nineteenth century, considered that "grammar should be the most important part of a linguistic training and all language courses should begin with this basic training. But," he continued, "it is dangerous to believe that everything is done once grammar is learned" (in Kelly 1969:220). Newmark, a more radical methodologist, acknowledges the existence of this basic core, but not of any need for the the 'study' of it. At the opposite pole from Ploetz, he says, "The study of grammar as such is neither necessary nor sufficient for

[1] At this point I will not enter into a discussion of the identity of or distinction between these two.

[2] In Government and Binding theory, "the lexicon is not a separate issue, a list of words and meanings; it plays a dynamic and necessary part in the syntax" (Cook 1988:11).

learning to use a language" (Newmark 1966:77-83). Frequently misquoted, he clearly states "the study of grammar as such." He thus distances himself from Ploetz (who believed strongly in "the study of grammar as such") while emphasizing what Ploetz was referring to when he said, "It is dangerous to believe everything is done" once the grammar has been "learned." Both Ploetz and Newmark were well aware of the need for the 'grammar' to be 'internalized' in order for it to be available for creative rule-governed language use. How this can be achieved is the nub of the question. Newmark advocates using the language and letting the students imitate as best they can. He believes that "Language is learned a whole act at a time rather than learned as an assemblage of constituent skills"; consequently, he maintains that "situational rather than grammatical cohesion is what is necessary and sufficient for language learning to take place" (Newmark and Reibel 1968:151). By using the word *cohesion* in this context, Newmark makes clear that there is some core to the many situations in which language is used. He even permits of a "limited kind of structural drill," where "learning is embedded in a meaningful context," in which small variations in situations being acted out call for "partial innovations in the previously learned role" (Newmark 1966:83).

Nicole, in 1670, discussed the ideas "of those who will have no truck with grammar," maintaining that this approach "far from being a help . . . loads [the learners] infinitely more than rules, because it deprives them of an aid" (in Kelly 1969:219-20). Experience with replacing rules with functions and notions has been found by some to load students with many apparently unrelated items, which could have been linked in memory in dynamic and recursive ways through the acquisition of a framework (Omaggio 1986:214-15). In "Notional Syllabuses Revisited," where he deals with some misinterpretations of his notional syllabus proposals, Wilkins states unequivocally that "the notion that an individual can develop anything other than a rudimentary communication ability without an extensive mastery of the grammatical system is absurd" (Wilkins 1981:85). We are still left with the basic question: How is this system internalized? and its practical corollary: What can the teacher do to facilitate the process?

For many methodologists, the way grammar should be incorporated into language teaching is a matter of classroom procedure rather than principle. Brooks, who created the term 'audiolingual', affirmed that "we first learn the grammar by actual use of communication, thinking of rules only after having learned many examples very well. . . . There is little point in asking or explaining 'why' grammar . . . [is] as [it is], at least until the grammar . . . in question [is] familiar through actual use" (1964:135)—an inductive procedure. Article 6 of the direct method dominated International Phonetic Association states that: "In the early stages grammar should be taught inductively, complementing and generalizing language facts observed during reading. A more systematic study of grammar should be postponed to the advanced stages of the course" (Passy and Rambeau 1879, cited in Stern 1983:89).

The apparent divergence of views among methodologists on the role of grammar in language learning clearly lies along an induction-deduction continuum; we may consider the direct method as the prototype at the inductive end of this continuum and grammar-translation procedures as prototypical of the deductive end, while other methodological approaches fall somewhere in between. Krashen, in his more recent work, objects categorically to "teaching grammar as subject matter," maintaining that "any subject matter that held [the students'] attention would do as well" since "their progress is coming from the medium [use of the language] and not the message" (1982:20), thus coming down on the inductive side. Yet even he and Seliger had earlier stated that "the isolation of rules and words of the target language" may be a crucial ingredient of formal instruction (he calls this + DEDUCTIVE) and that "informal learners may well be using formal instruction, via bilingual dictionaries and grammars or through using native-speaking informants" (1975:181). This evolution of views reflects the ambivalence many methodologists reveal when expressing opinions on the relative value of inductive and deductive approaches to language learning. Perhaps this is because there is a place for both, depending on specific features of particular languages, the age and educational status of the learners, and so on.

Brooks, Gattegno, Curran, and Lozanov have all favored the inductive assimilation of grammar and opposed "teaching grammar as subject matter," while recognizing the need for internal control of the basic framework. Terrell's 'affective acquisition activities' foster this control, once the students' attention has been focused briefly on aspects of the overall system through 'advance organizers' (such as drawing attention to markers of grammatical gender or morphological affixal indicators of person and tense). His recommendations are a mixture of inductive and deductive techniques, while still strongly on the inductive side.[3] Gattegno speaks of "the integrative schemata of meaning and structure" that the learner internalizes through the development of "inner criteria" (1972:8,14). His approach is inductive, but materials are designed to present structural features systematically, as are Lozanov's (1978); in other words, the materials preparer is thinking deductively, in order that students may be helped to acquire inductively a native-like control of internalized rules. Even Curran, whose Counseling-Learning/Community Language Learning sessions are at the extreme inductive end of the continuum, advocates deductive discussions, at a later stage, of the material taped during the students' attempts at communication within the group.

We may consider these inductive or deductive emphases as indicative of whether the stress is laid initially on language knowledge or language control

---

[3] T. Terrell, presentation at the ACTFL Annual Meeting, Monterey, California, 1988. Lozanov also gives such indications.

(Rivers 1989:4)—knowing the system of the language or knowing how to operate within it to express personal meanings. It is notable that in the most deductive approaches, the learner expresses the teacher's or textbook writer's meanings, as in the grammar-translation approach; in the most inductive, the learner expresses his or her own meanings, as in Curran's Community Language Learning. Many methods and the teachers who apply them blend one with the other. All methodologies that favor inductive procedures emphasize autonomous language use in a distinctive context, context being essential for the inferencing induction requires, and most of these encourage student initiative from the early stages in generating utterances. Curran emphasizes the predicament of "learners who may, in fact, learn the laws of grammar and be able to analyze a sentence and yet never really arrive at the freedom to speak. But representation," he says, "has come into being when, in a certain sense, the law is cast off by being internalized into a living reality. Representation and being have come together in an integrity of meaning and value. In language learning, the person speaks correctly but without any consciousness of rules" (1976:57-58). This is the ultimate objective of most contemporary language programs.

It is this notion of representation that is at the heart of the process of internalization of language. "Basic to language use is a mental representation of how the language works" (Rivers 1989:4). What we need to know is how this mental representation is developed, what is represented, and the role of the mental representation in the individual's production of language. For possible answers, we must turn to the field in which mental representations and mental models are being studied intensely, the field of cognitive psychology, a field to which linguistics rightfully belongs, according to Chomsky (1988b:6). Intensive study of the human mind/brain, particularly through computer simulation, is throwing much light on this subject. Since the field is still very young and in a certain ferment, we cannot expect to find definitive answers, neatly tied up in packets, but there are theoretical models and research findings that are provocative of thought in this area. To establish their applicability to our field will require further research with actual language learners.

As Chomsky has pointed out, each human being is "an organism whose behavior, we have every reason to believe, is determined by the interaction of numerous internal systems operating under conditions of great variety and complexity" (1980:218). Knowledge of the language of a particular speech community is "uniformly represented in the mind of each of its members, as one element in a system of cognitive structure" (Chomsky 1980:220). Whether or not they accept the innateness of the universal grammar (UG) component at the base of an individual's linguistic competence, cognitive psychologists generally do accept the innateness of certain cognitive structures. Whether the activation of the use of a specific language is a matter of setting the parameters of an inborn competence to the features of the new language or the derivation from social interaction of the ways that language meets interactional needs, as Bruner (1983) would maintain, the product is a mental representation of the way the language works, or may be made to work, that is, its potential for conveying an infinity of meanings for a multiplicity of social and personal functions in widely varying contexts.

As language teachers, we should be wary of hitching our wagon too closely to the Chomskyan concept of the mental representation for language as being fundamentally linguistic. We are interested in our students being able to use language in a messy practical way, not in the idealized way to which Chomskyan linguistics has deliberately limited itself. The primary object of research of the latter is "grammatical competence, . . . the knowledge of form and meaning," as Chomsky has frequently stated, while accepting the existence of "pragmatic competence, . . . the knowledge of conditions and manner of appropriate use," as an important element determining linguistic performance by "relating intentions and purposes to the linguistic means at hand" (1980:224-25). Appropriate use of language in various circumstances concerns us greatly as teachers and learners of second, third, and fourth languages. Grammatical appropriateness is not sufficient. Chomsky ties his concept of 'pragmatic competence' to "the system of rules and principles of . . . 'the logic of conversation' . . . and . . . of discourse structure" (Chomsky 1980:224-25), which are extremely important in language use, but receive rather cursory consideration in the current Chomskyan model. Much of what interests us in teaching students to use language is classed by Chomsky as nonlinguistic. "If nonlinguistic factors must be included in the grammar: beliefs, attitudes, etc." he maintains, this would "amount to a rejection of the initial idealization of language as an object of study," which would lead him to "conclude that language is a chaos that is not worth studying" (1979:140). Yet it is this very chaos into which our students are plunged from their very first efforts to express themselves in a new language.

As language learners rather than students of language as a phenomenon, our students (and we as their teachers) need to "recognize that human beings inhabit a communicational space which is not neatly compartmentalized into language and nonlanguage," as Harris puts it (1981:165). Our students need to develop mental representations of aspects of a different culture, culturally determined forms of interaction, and how these differ from their own (a pragmatic competence), if they are to operate effectively within the semantic-syntactic-phonological framework of their new language.[4] Furthermore, they need experience in applying this competence (these rules and principles) in interactive communication—in performance. And for performance models we must look to cognitive psychologists whose interest

---

[4] Chomsky (1980:220) subsumes the three systems (semantic, syntactic, phonological) under the general term of "the grammar".

is not only in how we acquire, process, and store knowledge, but also in how this knowledge relates to action, to doing things with language.

For our purposes we need a broader view of mental representation than we find in current linguistic theory. In this regard, the psychologist Shanon makes an interesting distinction between what he calls the presentational as process of acquisition of knowledge and the representational as product established in the mind. "The representational facets of mind," he says, "are not primary or basic but rather secondary or derived." He sees "a progression from the unidimensional level, which does not distinguish between medium and message, to the symbolic level . . . —from that which is ill defined, undifferentiated, and multifaceted to that which is well defined, differentiated, and articulated; from activities that are part and parcel of one's being in the world" of one's experiences "to ones that attest to the increasing autonomy of the individual." He sees "cognition as a dynamic movement between two poles, the presentational and the representational" (1987:45-46), that is, the experiential acquisition process and the analyzed and categorized knowledge required (the product of this acquisition) that is available for decisions on action. This seems an applicable description of what takes place in inductive learning, with the student passing through a mist, as it were, of undifferentiated linguistic features in the surrounding language environment, which gradually clarify and take distinct form as learners develop mental representations. These representations enable them to achieve a state of autonomy where personal meanings can be expressed apart from external stimuli; they can now extract, store, and interrelate information acquired in the presentational phase and are able to perform other indispensable cognitive activities in the language.

This mental representation, according to Shanon, is distinct from other cognitive activity in the mind and allows for "reflection on one's own cognitions.... Without representations, neither precise human communication nor conscious reflection [can] be achieved" (1987:46). The continual dynamic movement between the presentational in the world of the senses (the acquisitional stage) and the representational in the mind (the product of this acquisition) enables mental schemas to be adapted and readapted, chameleon-like, as new material is encountered in the environment. "Action in the world, not symbolic reference [then becomes] the basis for cognition" (1987:47). We see evidence of the existence of mental representations in such metacognitive abilities of individuals as explaining why they expressed themselves as they did; recognizing acceptable and unacceptable ways, on the part of themselves and others, of encoding ideas in their dialect or in a new language; and challenging as veridical or not an imitation of their utterances. (Young children already demonstrate the latter capacity when imitation by others does not tally with their own mental representations of their utterances.)

As we shall see in a moment, mental representation also explains linguistic action. Language knowledge in the mental representation is the product that provides the capacity for language control in many varied situations, which is the process of language use. This parallels in an interesting way Chomsky's metaphor of language as "an instrument that can be put to use. . . . The grammar of the language," he says, "characterizes the instrument" (knowledge of language, in our terminology), while "a system of rules and principles constituting pragmatic competence determines how the tool can effectively be put to use" (that is, the capacity for language control for specific purposes). How do we move, however, from knowledge to action, putting the mental representation to work? This is our perennial problem.

At this point, we would do well to look carefully at two promising models of cognition: neo-connectionist distributed parallel processing systems (Hinton and Anderson 1989) and J.R. Anderson's 1983 model, ACT* (Adaptive Control of Thought, final version). Both of these theoretical positions regard memory processes as the component linking knowledge to action, throwing light on the very problem we have identified as basic for all who teach and learn languages for communication, in speech or writing.

Memory in cognitive studies is no longer regarded as a locatable storage space. We have passed beyond the period when memory was considered to resemble a series of bins or stores through which material passed on its way to long-term storage. The push-down storage of the sixties is way behind us, as is the Broadbent (1958) model, where memory capacity is calculated in bits of information. Certain concepts from Broadbent's influential model are, however, still regarded as valid—such concepts as the selective filter that decides what will be extracted from the initial message for processing, the short-term and intermediate stores of material being processed (now more likely to be called working memory), the long-term store of past events, and the processes of rehearsal and recirculation; these are incorporated into more recent models, with new interpretations of their functioning based on later research and experimentation, particularly through computer simulation. Many of Miller's ideas on chunking, organizing, and recoding for storage (1967), and Neisser's enlightening observations on the subjective nature of perception in its relation to memory (1967) are still considered extremely useful.

More recent models of memory are notably dynamic and process oriented. Memory is now viewed as a process whereby knowledge (factual and experience-derived) enters into networks with a multiplicity of interconnected nodes (like the neurons in the nervous system). The nodes are conceptual and the interconnecting networks are relational. Entering information activates nodes, which activate nodes on nodes, so that processing of the information is effected by many processes occurring at the same time, that is, in parallel. Anything one encounters, and selectively or peripherally perceives, enters the networks and is immediately bounced around, compared, discriminated, matched, linked up in the networks with information related to it in a multiplicity of obvious and unexpected ways, to serve some purpose eventually along with all the other elements operating in parallel. Because of these interrelated networks, items of knowledge and memory traces of events are not localized but distributed throughout the system. Rather than our being able to retrieve them from one node or one spot in long-term storage, through a few cues or triggers, memory traces can be accessed anywhere in the system through the multitude of different connections firing simultaneously. "The multiple connections allow much of the knowledge of the entire system to be applied in any instance of recognition or problem-solving" (Gardner 1985:319). As Rumelhart and Norman have expressed it, "information is better thought of as 'evoked' than 'found'" (in Hinton and Anderson 1989:17); it is the relationships that are important. Consequently, memories come to us in many unexpected ways and through a variety of sensory stimuli. This approach tallies with common experience, where we are frequently bombarded with activated memories, perhaps on encountering a particular scent or taste (as with Proust's famous *madeleine*), or in searching for a word or name. Such networks make the "subconscious acquisition" and "the din in the head"[5] of which Krashen speaks (1985:1, 38) readily explicable, but cast doubt on the validity of a nonpermeable division between what is "acquired" and what is "learned" (Krashen 1985:38-43).

The distributed parallel-processing approach to thought and memory has interesting implications for language learning and use. If the nodes in the networks are conceptual, they are not language-specific. This allows for the many interconnections and overlappings of related concepts and the differing semantic nuances that different cultures encapsulate in their languages. These nodes also link up the many words capable of conveying these semantic concepts within one and across various languages.[6] This writer had the experience, while learning and using Spanish in Chile, of seeking the Spanish way of expressing a contrary observation and uttering the following sequence: *mais aber sed pero* (French, German, Latin, Spanish). I had clearly activated the appropriate conceptual node which fired in several directions within the networks (Rivers 1981:510). Had I been a fluent and regular speaker of Spanish, the pathway to *pero* in a Spanish-speaking environment would have been more direct and automatic. It seems that a language we do not know well is processed more holistically, with more frequent recourse to the right hemisphere and presumably with more interdependent connections. As knowledge and control of the new language become more consolidated, our use of that language becomes more independent and more localized in the left hemisphere (Hakuta 1986:87-89).

---

[5] "The din in the head" refers to to an experience Krashen cites. He had been an undergraduate student of German and had spent a year abroad in Austria. On a later visit he found all kinds of expressions in German that he was hearing around him dancing about in his head.

[6] Semantic memory is discussed more fully with applications to practice in W. M. Rivers, "Apples of gold in pictures of silver: Where have all the words gone?" In: Rivers 1983:126-31.

Distributed parallel-processing theory throws light also on the observed fact that speakers of several languages acquire a new vocabulary more easily than monolinguals and frequently produce in communication a word or expression from another language they know that seems to convey more appropriately a semantic nuance or a relationship—hence the mixing of languages that occurs when two or three speakers are equally bilingual. It also explains the word blocks speakers sometimes experience in their native language after a period of immersion in a second language, when the only word or expression that comes to mind is the way the second language encodes the concept. Syntactic structures also convey meanings and, again, having learned to operate within the syntactic systems of several languages seems to facilitate operation within yet another system for expressing propositional relations, time, aspect, comparison, actual and hypothetical occurrences, and so on. Distributed parallel-processing further illuminates the 'tip of the tongue phenomenon' (Brown 1970:274-301), when we seek for a name or a word in another language and come up with phonologically related near-misses in what seem like extraordinary nonsequiturs, or when we replace words when reading aloud with synonyms of quite a different perceptual shape. It also provides a psychological explanation of how it is possible to translate from one language to another, to recognize the untranslatable,[7] and find approximations in the second language to the meanings conveyed by the first when parallel terms do not exist. It also provides a plausible explanation for the speed with which simultaneous interpreters can perform their task.

In 1972, Tulving assessed the extraordinary potential of semantic memory when he observed that: "The semantic system permits the retrieval of information that was not directly stored in it, and retrieval of information from the system leaves the contents unchanged" (Tulving and Donaldson 1972:386). Hence the exponential rate at which progress can be made in a new language, once a critical mass of connections has been established.

With this approach to memory, accessibility becomes the keyword, as basic to retrieval. In language teaching this means continually providing for our students opportunities to reactivate language material within their personal networks in all kinds of student-maintained interactive activities, where the students follow the direction in language use that their own minds project. In this way, they use their language knowledge in all its interrelatedness, while augmenting it through active use. The theory gives strong support to the encouraging of students to 'collect' actively their own personal vocabularies of words and expressions that interest them, amuse them, and serve their personal needs (Rivers 1981:462-70).

---

[7] For an illuminating discussion of semantic nuances and the untranslatable, see Rheingold (1988).

We find here support for Lozanov's insistence on the importance of peripheral intake: with his attention to the surroundings, his wall charts and pictures, and his emphasis on allowing the whole mind to work in its own way with language material presented to it. It supports the present emphasis on learning in context in a variety of differing but functionally similar situations (something that textbook writers have been conscious of for some time). Rumelhart and Norman point out that "information that is related to, but different from, previously stored information tends to evoke the original pattern of activity—even though the inputs to the system may differ in many details . . . similarity and the ability to generalize [comprise] a central component. Similar items of information interact with one another in such a way as to reinforce those aspects they have in common and cancel out those aspects on which they differ—this can lead," they point out, "to the building of a prototype representation that is most sensitive to information falling about the central tendency of the highly similar inputs" (in Hinton and Anderson 1989:18). In this way fundamental rules of linguistic and pragmatic competence are confirmed and reinforced. And, finally, we find support in this model for using every possible medium and modality to reinforce learning and maximize accessibility, so that students encounter and reencounter basic linguistic and pragmatic concepts through several senses, in many variations on similar themes, while they are performing different kinds of tasks where language material becomes applicable in diverse contexts.

As Spolsky points out, distributed parallel-processing implies processes made up of "large numbers of microscale elements that occur in large networks, which may be variously connected internally to each other or externally," that is, in schemata, "receiving input from the outside world or sending output. A network," he points out, "learns a new behaviour pattern by changing the 'weight' of its various connections on the basis of patterns received from input to it. These patterns of 'weights' rather than the fixed connections determine the new patterns of behaviour" (1989:226-27). Thus the system learns from the input and corrects its errors as it has more experience with a certain behavior pattern. Saussure has pointed out the importance of 'value' (compare 'weights') in meaning. In language, he says, "the value of each term results solely from the simultaneous presence of the others" (1959:114), much as in a game of chess where the value of each piece derives from the values of all the others at a particular moment, as it enters into the innumerable configurations that develop during play. To learn these 'weights' or 'internal parameters'[8], our language learners need frequent opportunities to observe the functional usefulness and effectiveness of certain features of language as used by native speakers. At times, they can profit from having the form and function of these features drawn to their attention when they

[8] For 'weights' or 'internal parameters', see also Hinton and Anderson, eds. (1989:6).

seem not to have observed them. This encourages more focused attention to these features as they encounter them in language in action. Terrell, in a recent study of nearly 150 hours of 'natural' language acquisition in meaning-filled situations with native speakers found that the acquisition of native-sounding speech was very slow and faulty. Native speakers did not provide the kind of modified speech, expansions, and restatements that reports on 'foreigner talk' had predicted (Terrell in press). He became convinced of the value of 'teacher talk' adapted to the students' level in the acquisition process. Teachers, he maintains, help students focus on key elements through intonation, stress, pauses, rhythm, and loudness. He now feels that providing students early with a few advance organizers, thus alerting them to important structural features, would accelerate the acquisition process (Terrell 1986:223). With attentive, focused listening, students become aware of values, weighting, and the parameters of the new language as they repeatedly encounter them in meaningful speech. The probability of their producing them appropriately themselves in relevant contexts is thus greatly increased. There are insights here that merit our attention if we are to help our learners become adept language users.

Networks of the type we have been discussing are basic to Anderson's ACT* model, which is fundamentally 'learning by doing', and learning from past doing (1983:19-20). ACT* incorporates three memory systems: working, declarative, and production, and attempts to relate knowledge to action, with memory in its distinctive form in the model as the basic force in action. Anderson's work is a bold attempt to bring together in a coherent framework much that has been discovered through psychological investigation about the acquisition and use of knowledge. Although it is undoubtedly not the last word in a fast-changing field and is continually being modified and developed, it contains interesting proposals at base that may lead us to ponder more deeply certain basic questions that concern our work.

In the ACT* system, knowledge that reaches us in whatever form (facts, ideas, images, events, sense impressions), either through focused attention and selection or peripherally, is encoded for storage in declarative memory, which takes the form of associative networks; from declarative memory it can be retrieved for use in working memory when the need for action, emanating from production memory, calls for it. Production memory is a thinking process that reflects previous experience with events. When an event is encountered, working memory calls upon production memory to match circumstances and facts (drawing on the contents of declarative memory) and to decide on an appropriate form of execution (or production). In working memory, this production (or intention) is fleshed out with requisite language, motor information, or whatever, from declarative memory and initiates performances to meet the needs of the situation. Experience with the situation results in additional encoding into working memory, which augments both declarative and production memory for further informed action. Through repeated performances to meet the needs of similar situations, procedures or routines develop, enabling the individual to respond rapidly when action (linguistic in our case) is required, thus freeing the production system for more thoughtful responses and initiatives. Memories will be strengthened as they are drawn out of storage and involved in performances, and will be enriched by further experience. How long a memory is kept depends on how frequently it is used. We must keep in mind, however, that in associative parallel-processing theory memories are continually changing and evolving as new events and new facts enter the network, and thus they remain accessible through a multiplicity of contextual triggers.

In Anderson's model, knowing and doing are intimately associated; hence Anderson's reservations about schema theory, which he feels does not show how knowledge becomes action. In this model, knowledge is essential to action, and without action knowledge declines and even disintegrates. Through action (which includes thinking and other cognitive activities) knowledge grows, evolves, and is strengthened. In our domain, language knowledge (lexico-syntactic and semantic-pragmatic) is essential to performance in the language (which demonstrates control of language). Knowledge of facts about language without language experience is not, however, knowledge of language in the ACT* sense; the two, knowledge and experience, combine in working memory which drives performance, and each matching for language use increases the usability of language knowledge for future occasions. Just as success breeds success, use of language strengthens and increases both declarative memory and production memory. To consider one without the other is impossible within this system. Thus the mental representation we build up pervades the system and becomes accessible to us in working memory, enabling us to express our meanings appropriately as circumstances demand.

Along with distributed parallel-processing, ACT* theory encourages us to design our courses so that students are continually involved in using whatever they know (not just whatever they are learning at a certain point) and in reflecting on what they are learning as they are using it. Call this 'monitoring' if you will, but reflective matching for appropriateness seems to be an essential part of the execution process, except where procedures take over and operate without conscious attention. Some language operations are certainly performed automatically after a certain amount of experience. Even with these, however, as circumstances and purposes change, we as thinking beings need to be able to contemplate our performance even in the act of executing a routine procedure, so as to continue comparing and matching with information from the ever active associative networks. We can then adapt our performance, in mid-breath if necessary, as we seek for relevance and appropriateness in our verbal and nonverbal responses, according to interlocutor reaction and situational needs.

We must keep in mind that there is an essential difference between the automaticity of habitual performance and skillful performance. Ryle argued that "a person's performance is described as careful or skilful if in his [or her] operations he [or she] is ready to detect and correct lapses, to repeat and improve on successes, to profit from the examples of others" (1949:28-29). Bailin, who quotes Ryle, maintains that original and expressive use of language, which may involve "breaking rules" can occur only when one has a command of the rules and knows what they can and cannot accomplish (1987:323-32). A skilled performance can adapt to changing circumstances, which an habitual one cannot. We see habitual performance in the perfection of substitution drills, which are in essence unnatural and uninformative since the student is expected to produce the right form the teacher or materials writer has planned to elicit; such drills can develop speedy production of routines or procedures, but little else. In skilled performance, as we have noted, we exercise control over even routine skills that seem automatic and can adapt them rapidly should an unforeseen circumstance arise (Bailin 1987:329). In our classes, we need to develop skilled language users, who are aware of what they are doing and who possess the knowledge and experience (in the ACT* sense) to guide their selection of productive options to convey what they really want to convey in pragmatically, culturally, syntactically, and semantically appropriate ways.

Lest there be any misunderstanding at this point, we will now consider how knowledge of language, whether acquired inductively or deductively, informally or formally, becomes action. We combine knowledge and action through *performing rules* (Rivers 1989:4), creating meanings through their use, not through the static processes of reciting or discussing them. Their real import and potential become clear and are internalized as students use them to express meanings important to them. Even routine procedures become productions in contexts of personal decision. Students use language to perform functions in activities, tasks, or discussions, selected and developed as much as possible by themselves. In this way they draw from their declarative memory and from their production memory both language routines and creative language that match their purposes and direct action through their working memory. As language learners perform rules, knowledge and action become as indissolubly one as the two sides of a coin.

As Chomsky has expressed it: "True creativity means free action within the framework of a system of rules" (1988a:144). As students perform rules, they modify and develop them within their mental representations as message demands become more complex. Within working memory declarative knowledge and experience through action meld into a directive force. Since decisions on action draw on personally acquired knowledge and previous experience we cannot expect one person's production to be like that of another. Individuality in language use gives each of us our distinctive identity, and so it should be in another language. *Vive la différence*!

References

Anderson, J.R. 1983. The architecture of cognition. Cambridge, Mass.: Harvard University Press.

Bailin, S. 1987. Creativity and skill. In: Perkins, Lochhead, and Bishop, eds. (1987).

Broadbent, D.E. 1958. Perception and communication. London: Pergamon.

Brooks, N. 1964. Language and language learning: Theory and practice. 2d ed. New York: Harcourt Brace and World.

Brown, R. 1970. Psycholinguistics. New York: Free Press.

Bruner, J. 1983. Child's talk. Oxford: Oxford University Press.

Chomsky, N. 1979. Language and responsibility. New York: Pantheon.

Chomsky, N. 1980. Rules and representations. New York: Columbia University Press.

Chomsky, N. 1988a. Language and politics, ed. C.P. Otero. Montreal and New York: Black Rose Books.

Chomsky, N. 1988b. Language and problems of knowledge: The Managua lectures. Cambridge, Mass.: MIT Press.

Cook, V.J. 1988. Chomsky's Universal Grammar: An introduction. Oxford: Basil Blackwell.

Curran, C.A. 1976. Counseling-learning in foreign languages. Apple River, Ill.: Apple River Press.

Freed, B., ed. (In press.) Foreign language acquisition research and the classroom. Lexington, Mass.: D.C. Heath.

Gardner, H. 1985. The mind's new science: A history of the cognitive revolution. New York: Basic Books.

Gattegno, C. 1972. Teaching foreign languages in schools: The Silent Way. New York: Educational Solutions.

Gleick, J. 1987. Chaos: Making a new science. New York: Viking.

Hakuta, K. 1986. Mirror of language: The debate on bilingualism. New York: Basic Books.

Halliday, M.A.K. 1985. An introduction to functional grammar. London: Edward Arnold.

Harris, R. 1981. The language myth. London: Duckworth.

Hinton, G.E., and J.A. Anderson, eds. 1989. Parallel models of associative memory. Updated ed. Hillsdale, New Jersey: LEA.

Kelly, L.G. 1969. 25 centuries of language teaching. 500 B.C.-1969. Rowley, Mass.: Newbury House.

Krashen, S.D. 1982. Principles and practice of second language acquisition. Oxford: Pergamon Press.

Krashen, S.D. 1985. The input hypothesis: Issues and implications. London: Longman.

Krashen, S.D., and H.W. Seliger. 1975. The essential contributions of formal instruction in adult second language learning. In: TESOL Quarterly 9:181.

Leontiev, A.A. 1981. Psychology and the language learning process. Oxford: Pergamon Press.

Lozanov, G. 1978. Suggestology and outlines of suggestopedy. New York: Gordon and Breach.

Miller, G.A. 1967. The psychology of communication: Seven essays. New York: Basic Books.

Naiman, N., M. Frohlich, H.H. Stern, and A. Todesco. 1978. The good language learner. Toronto: OISE.

Neisser, U. 1967. Cognitive psychology. New York: Appleton-Century-Crofts.

Newmark, L. 1966. How not to interfere with language learning. In: IJAL 32:77-83.

Newmark. L., and D.A. Reibel. 1968. Necessity and sufficiency in language learning. In: IRAL 6:151.

Nicole. 1670. Quoted in Kelly 1969:219-20.

Omaggio, A.C. 1986. Teaching language in context: Proficiency-oriented instruction. Boston: Heinle and Heinle.

Perkins, D.N., J. Lochhead, and J. Bishop, eds. 1987. Thinking: The second international conference. Hillsdale, N.J.: LEA.

Ploetz, K. 1865. Elementarbuch der französischensprache. Quoted in Kelly 1969.

Rheingold, H. 1988. They have a word for it: A light-hearted lexicon of untranslatable words and phrases. Los Angeles: J.P. Tarcher; New York: St. Martin's Press.

Rivers, W.M. 1981. Learning a sixth language: An adult learner's daily diary. Appendix B of Teaching foreign language skills. 2d ed. Chicago: University of Chicago Press.

Rivers, W.M. 1983. Communicating naturally in a second language: Theory and practice in language teaching. Cambridge: Cambridge University Press.

Rivers, W.M. 1989. Ten principles of interactive language learning and teaching. Washington, D.C.: National Foreign Language Center at the Johns Hopkins University.

Rumelhart, D.E., and D.A. Norman. 1989. Introduction. In: Hinton and Anderson, eds. 1989.

Ryle, G. 1949. The concept of mind. London: Hutchinson.

Saussure, F. de. 1959. Course in general linguistics. C. Bally and A. Secherhaye, eds. New York: Philosophical Library.

Shanon, B. 1987. On the place of representations in cognition. In: Perkins, Lochhead, and Bishop, eds. 1987.

Spolsky, B. 1989. Conditions for second language learning. Oxford: Oxford University Press.

Stern, H.H. 1983. Fundamental concepts of language teaching. Oxford: Oxford University Press.

Terrell, T.D. 1986. Acquisition in the natural approach: The binding/ access framework. In: Modern Language Journal 70:213-27.

Terrell, T.D. (In press.) Natural vs. classroom input: Advantages and disadvantages for beginning language students.

Tulving, E. 1972. Episodic and semantic memory. In: Tulving and Donaldson, eds. 1972.

Tulving, E., and W. Donaldson, eds. 1972. Organization of memory. New York: Academic Press.

Wilkins, D.A. 1981. Notional syllabuses revisited. In: Applied Linguistics 2:83-89.

Semiotic theory and language acquisition

John W. Oller, Jr.
University of New Mexico

The pragmatic mapping of facts of experience into representations in a given semiotic system is construed as the fundamental basis of comprehension in a natural language and also as language acquisition. Therefore, this entire discussion is about comprehension and language acquisition. It aims to dig down to the foundational basis. Once the theory is grounded in logic, it will be possible then to say something of its ramifications, and how it bears on experimental or educational studies of language use and acquisition.

The theory of pragmatic mapping. Pragmatic mapping can be viewed in a variety of ways. A simple diagram is given as Figure 1. Facts of experience, e.g. that today is March 15, 1990, that we are here in Georgetown, that the White House and the Potomac River are nearby, that George Bush is now president, that we came to discuss certain subject matter, that we expected to see certain old friends, that life is too short, that we really don't understand much of what we would like to know, that the world is full of problems, that so-and-so hates our guts, that we are at risk, that so-and-so deserves our respect, pity, concern, etc., because he or she is also a human being at risk, etc., etc.—all these facts are linked up with representations.

Now it ought to be admitted at the start that the facts are whatever they are independently of whatever we may think them to be. That is, if they are facts, they have an independent reality apart from whatever we may imagine, prefer, know, not know, think, fail to think, demand, deny, etc. They are independent, in a strict logical sense, of however we may represent them. If you or I were unable or unwilling to represent them correctly, for whatever reason, this would alter the facts per se not at all. Neither does it change the logical status of facts one iota to admit that we know of them only through representations. It does not even alter their logical status and independence of our personal or collective representations to admit that our understanding of those representations and therefore of the facts themselves is always, logically and necessarily, incomplete. The logical status of facts, as Peirce argued (cf. especially his edited writings in Fisch et al. 1982, and Moore et al. 1984), is untouched by all of the difficulties associated with our knowledge of facts.

Figure 1. Pragmatic mapping.

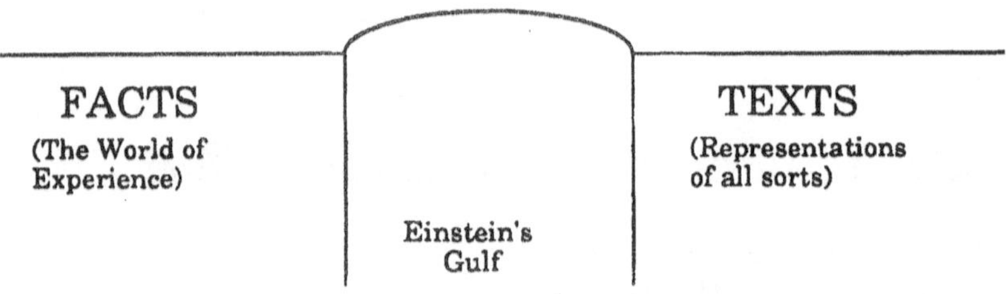

Figure 2. Different kinds of semiotic capacities.

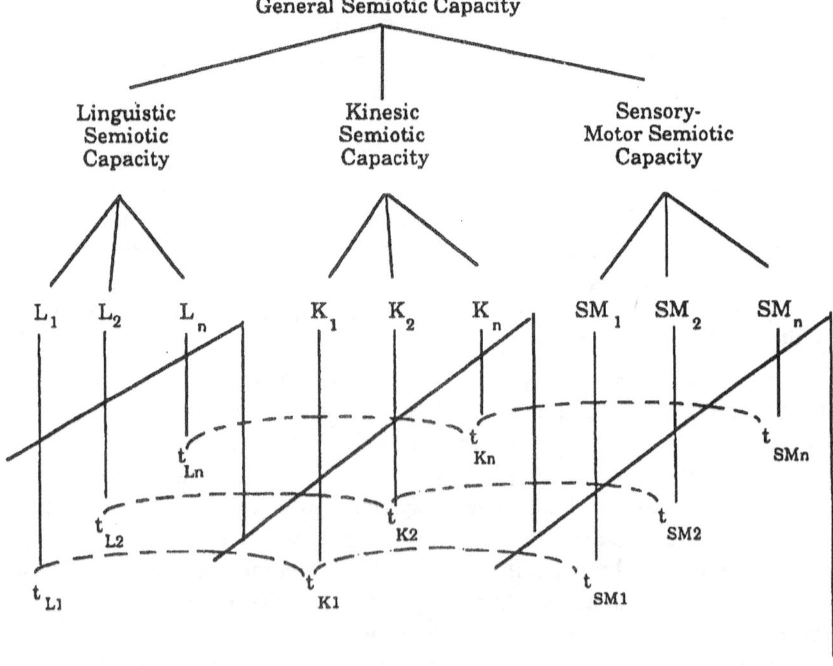

Facts, as they say, are facts. Their representations, to the extent that they actually exist, that is, are in fact represented, i.e. imagined, thought, fantasized, uttered, or whatever, are also facts, though of a different kind from whatever other varieties of facts there are. Also, representations are logically more abstract than whatever they represent or purport to represent. Furthermore, representations come in several distinct varieties, as suggested by Figure 2. To the extent that linguistic, kinesic, or sensory-motor representations are temporalized events, they fall into sequences that are not unlike what we commonly refer to as texts. Part of the pragmatic mapping problem is to coordinate the diverse representations of experience so that they fit together coherently, each one sustaining and supporting the others. It is not surprising that coherence is sometimes not achieved. That is easy to explain. Breakdowns, failures, misunderstandings, total lack of communication, illusions, hallucinations, disagreements, etc., all of these are relatively easy to account for. What is difficult to account for is that sometimes pragmatic correspondences between diverse forms of representation are very good, and for practical purposes, even perfectly satisfactory within the limits of a given context. For instance, what sort of additional information would cause you to believe any more firmly than you already do that you are in Georgetown today, that Washington, D.C. is also the location of the White House, that your name is whatever it is, and the like? As surprising as it may seem, many of the facts of our experience are beyond the reach of any reasonable doubt.

When we speak of language acquisition and language teaching, we are mainly, though not exclusively, concerned with the linguistic variety of representations. In that case, it is words, phrases, clauses, and higher order units of structure in a particular language that must be systematically connected with the facts of experience if comprehension or language acquisition is to occur. Failing this, if the pragmatic connection is not made, the representations in question remain uninterpreted at best and utterly meaningless at worst. From the point of view of the would-be language learner, uninterpretable representations or meaningless ones are perfectly useless. If incorrect or incomplete pragmatic connections are made, the representations are misinterpreted or only partially interpreted. Both of these possibilities have the potential of contributing to comprehension and acquisition, but neither by itself will give a sufficient basis for either comprehension or acquisition.

When speaking of linguistic representations, to arrive at correct, well-equilibrated pragmatic mappings of representations with the facts of experience, we must determine a great deal, including the significations of phrase structures. This includes but is not limited to determining the relevant deictic connections of textual elements to distinct elements of the factual domain. The referents of noun phrases must be determined and articulately linked up with those phrases. The tense and aspect of verb phrases must be determined and articulately linked with time and perspective of the person or persons performing the representational acts in question.

In addition, the elements of text must be interpreted semantically and syntactically in relation to the conventional significances associated with units of structure and the particular interrelations of the given representation in question. For instance, the relations that are currently under study with reference to GB theory must surely be determined, and no doubt much more must be determined. Antecedents of anaphors, values of empty categories, questions of pronominal reference and the connections that pro-elements in general maintain with other elements of the discoursal structure must all surely be determined. Beyond this, the intentions, fears, hopes, desires, relations to other parties, attitudes, feelings, etc., of different parties who engage in constructing and interpreting representations must surely be taken into consideration. To interpret representations in the normal ways that human beings do, we must, to some degree, know the persons involved. This goes far beyond knowing the mere signification of surface forms of utterances or other forms of discourse. It also includes understanding the perceived relationships between the persons involved.

Finally, the entire process of pragmatically fitting a given representation to a more or less determined constellation of facts yields what we might call understanding. Or, as Peirce put it, a sign is the sort of thing "which in knowing, we know something more" (see the opening discussion in reference to this aphorism in Givón 1989). When I understand what someone means by a representation, or when I grasp the connections of a gesture with its presupposed, associated, and implied meanings, or when I merely recognize a familiar face and relate it to a history of experience and to a future of expectations, I know something more than the mere sign itself: I understand what it means and in this understanding get something more than the sign as a mere object could provide. I get the dividends of history and expectations—these are inevitable consequences and concomitants of a correct linkage to whatever is going on in the here and now. Leave out that connection, and as Peirce, Einstein (in Oller 1989:3-11, 21-29, 61-65), and others have argued, the very logical possibility of meaning itself evaporates and with it the possibility of comprehension, communication, language acquisition, etc.

Correspondence theory of truth. All of this is understood in the term 'pragmatic mapping'. From the vantage point of the classic correspondence theory of truth, which is the natural common-sense view of most of us (though that is not why it ought to be accepted), a well-equilibrated pragmatic mapping is a true or at least appropriate representation. If it is a correct interpretation of someone else's representation, then it is a true representation of what that person represented. By the theory I am advocating—which is C. S. Peirce's, to the best of my understanding—interpretations are invariably representations of representations. If I say a glass is half-full when in fact it is empty, I fail to achieve a well-equilibrated pragmatic mapping. But, if the fact corresponds to the statement, we say the statement is true. Of course, if someone else says it is half-empty, they may represent the fact in question as well as I have but with different presuppositions, associations, and implications. Either way, the correspondence theory of truth is the principal basis for our judgments of truth and falsehood. It is not a narrow theory, as some have tried to argue, but a broad and open-ended one.

Moreover, it spills over into the judgments we make of mere appropriateness. For instance, sometimes we speak to strangers and sometimes we don't. If I say, "Hello," my utterance can be judged neither true nor false, though it may be judged more or less appropriate. But on what grounds is it appropriate or inappropriate? If the person spoken to asks, "Do we know each other?" he or she also suggests the conventional understanding that people who greet each other often do have some previous acquaintance. In any given case, this presupposition of a mere greeting will either be true or false. Therefore, even mere appropriateness, as an index of the fit of a representation to the facts into which it is mapped, is a question of truth in the classical sense of the correspondence theory.

Connectionism or PDP models. A couple of quotes from the principal proponents of connectionist, or parallel distributed processing (PDP) models will show how they are mainly concerned with the pragmatic mapping process. McClelland, Rumelhart, and Hinton (1986:39) write: "If there are regularities in the correspondences between pairs of patterns, the model will naturally extract these regularities." In their second chapter, they write that "all the knowledge is *in the connections*" (their italics, p. 75).

PDP enthusiasts, of course, argue that their models are patterned after actual brain mechanisms, though this is not their primary raison d'être, and whether or not they are good models of brain mechanisms is not in question here. What is in question is whether the PDP/connectionist approaches fit the pragmatic mapping concept. All I want to establish for the moment is that the metaphors are similar ones. Again, quoting from the PDP researchers (1986:135):

> the primary mode of computation in the brain is best understood as a kind of *relaxation system* . . . in which the computation proceeds by iteratively seeking to satisfy a large number of weak constraints. . . . The system should be thought of more as *settling into a solution* than as *calculating a solution.*

This metaphor of "settling into a solution" is similar to the notion of fitting a representation to a constellation of facts. I believe this may be exactly what Peirce had in mind in his description of the "fixation of belief" (cf. Oller 1989:217-22)—alternatively described as the process of 'abductive reasoning'.

Three Peircean trichotomies. According to Peirce, beliefs are merely settled opinions—ones from which doubt has, whether justifiably or not, been removed. 'Abduction', concerning which I'll have more to say later, is the mysterious logical process whereby representations are set in correspondence with contexts. The mysterious part of the process is that the correspondences should be possible in the first place. Immanuel Kant (1724-1804), Charles S. Peirce (1839-1914), and Albert Einstein (1879-1955), to name a few of the principals in the definition of classic pragmatism, contended that our ability to achieve such equilibrated correspondences was an indefeasible argument in favor of innate ideas. Chomsky also attributes his theory of innate ideas and universal grammar chiefly to Peirce's notion of abduction, though in my view, for what little it may be worth, Chomsky has developed the notion much less adequately than Peirce did and has resisted some of the necessary commitments to the existence of an external world, bodily objects, his own mind, other minds, and the validity of various forms of reasoning, all amply defended by Peirce. Setting Chomsky's position to one side, in any event, suppose we consider Peirce's and its bearing on the general theme of language acquisition.

Logic: Abduction, induction, and deduction. When modern logicians or other scholars interested in logic speak about it these days, generally they have in mind only deduction. From a Peircean perspective, this is an extraordinarily narrow and ultimately an inadequate view of logic. For example, in the book *Mental Models* by Johnson-Laird (1983), the term 'logic' is used throughout almost exclusively in the sense of deduction. Peirce showed, perhaps better than any other logician who ever lived (this, according to far better critics than I shall ever hope to be), that Aristotle's syllogism in its most basic form amply illustrates the trichotomy: we may paraphrase it in it three classic parts as follows:

Rule:	Human beings are mortal.
Case:	Socrates is a human being.
Conclusion:	Therefore, Socrates is mortal.

Viewed in forward gear, reasoning from the rule to the special case and the conclusion concerning it, we reason deductively. This sort of reasoning is axiomatic, rigorous, and dependent, as surprising as it may seem, not on particular facts or even universal ones, but on definitions. It is purely semantic/syntactic reasoning. It works so long as we start with good definitions. If it is true that human beings are mortal, and if Socrates qualifies as one of them, then, the fact that he will prove to be mortal is a necessary fact of pure semantics.

But suppose we consider the syllogism in the reverse direction. We observe that Socrates is mortal. He dies. We note that he was also a human being. From this we infer the general rule, the universal proposition that all human beings are fated to expire. In this instance, we reason inductively. Now, again, there is a surprise. In spite of the fact that we feel we have merely reversed the process of deductive reasoning, we are surprised to discover, I expect, that in building the universal proposition on the basis of one appropriate to one or more particular cases,we arrive at a rule that only applies with a certain probability to actual cases. It is not, in other words, a lead-pipe cinch. Thus, in reasoning inductively, we run a far greater risk of being wrong than in the case of deduction. A certain man who was as bald as a billiard ball once told me that I was losing my hair because I washed it daily. If I would wash it less I would lose less and if I would not wash it at all I would not lose any. His proof was found in himself and his father. He had even less hair than his father who had washed his hair too much, but not as much as the son. Hence, the general rule: wash your hair and it will fall out. He reasoned inductively from specific cases to a general rule. If his reasoning failed, it did so because his cases were inadequate to support the rule, but the general form of inductive logic still has some validity if properly applied. What makes it less secure than deduction is that deduction depends in the final analysis on purely abstract definitions while induction is grounded in particular observations of experience.

Induction therefore depends on the adequacy of its pragmatic grounding while deduction has no such dependency. If I say that military intelligence is an oxymoron, as a matter of definition, I run no risk of being contradicted by any particular experience because it is a consequence of the meaning of *military* (by definition) that it is contrary to the definition of *intelligence*. On the other hand, if I say this and that soldier are fools, and therefore all soldiers are fools, I draw an inductive inference which is apt to be contradicted by any smart soldier that comes along. The induction, as surprising as it may seem, makes itself vulnerable to test in a way that the strict deduction cannot be vulnerable. Therefore, deduction cannot be reduced to any form of induction, and neither can induction be reduced to deduction. They are two logically distinct forms of reasoning, and both are necessary to the ordinary comprehension and acquisition of languages.

But neither one is sufficient, nor are both of them combined. Return to Aristotle's syllogism. To determine what is to count as a human being and not something else, or whether or not a certain exemplar is Socrates and not some other human being, or whether a given experienced event is to count as the death of Socrates rather than his merely passing out, going to sleep, swooning into a coma momentarily, or something else, all of these determinations require more than can ever be supplied, logically speaking, by either deduction or induction. In each case, the judgments in question require a valid association between some potential subject matter and some range of possible predications. The question is, how do the correct connections get made? This is the central problem of abduction and it is also the central problem of pragmatic mapping.

Peirce observed that as soon as we know enough to qualify any particular thing as a human being, or any particular person as Socrates, or any particular event as dying, etc., we know more than enough. Now here is where abduction differs profoundly from the other two sorts of reasoning. The validity of any given deduction depends on no knowledge other than the abstract definition of the terms that it relies upon. It will readily be seen that those definitions cannot be arrived at apart from some abductive connection with experience, but, once the conventional or arbitrary definitions are established, deduction requires no further experience whatever for it to have its small, but important, measure of validity. Axiomatic mathematical systems are testimony to the modicum of validity that may be attributed to deduction. Euclidean geometry is perhaps the paradigmatic stereotype of such systems. Induction, on the other hand, depends on the likelihood that events observed in one context (or range of contexts) are apt to occur in some other. It is clear that induction, therefore, involves an element of guesswork and additional risk that is not present in deduction. But what may not be obvious is that both deduction and induction, in order that either might have any validity whatever, depend on an entirely different sort of reasoning—namely, abduction.

The statement that a certain thing is a person, or that a certain person is Socrates, or that a certain event is the death of Socrates, each requires an implicitly correct accounting of a great deal more information than is ever actually available in experience. To know that a certain person is Socrates is to know that he is not Xanthippe, Plato, Diogenes, Demosthenes, Penelope, Agamemnon, Cleopatra, Aristotle, Copernicus, or anyone else. Since all of the complementary information about other possibilities is never entirely available, it borders on the miraculous (though it does not seem to) that we should ever recognize Socrates for what and who he is. We do so, it seems, by taking account of a great many related facts of context more or less simultaneously. For instance, if the person we are dealing with was married to someone named Xanthippe, drank hemlock, was a friend of Plato's, died at about 31 years of age in the year 399 B.C., etc., chances are pretty good that the person in question is Socrates. As soon as we know enough to settle on that opinion, we generally know more than enough. For instance, we know all of the other things about Socrates that we ever knew about him and we may infer much more that we have not yet thought of, e.g. that he probably wept before he drank the hemlock, that he mourned for his beloved Xanthippe whom he would soon leave behind, considered the injustice of it all, hated to part with his students, etc., etc., etc. Such is abductive reasoning.

So, some might ask, what does all this have to do with language acquisition? In asking this, sad to say, such persons could only reveal the poverty of their grasp of the theory of abduction and their lack of understanding of comprehension or language acquisition. The fact is that a theory of comprehension that does not recognize the central role played by the pragmatic mapping process, or abductive reasoning (which is the same thing), will be an utterly useless theory of language acquisition. Without abduction in the sense defined, comprehension cannot occur and language acquisition would be impossible. With abduction in the sense defined, i.e. as the articulate pragmatic mapping of representations in the target language into the experience of the learner, language acquisition is a necessary outcome.

The process will succeed just so far as the pragmatic mappings are carried out by the learner in the learner's own experience and no farther.

Signs: Icon, index, symbol. Another way of viewing the process of linking representations with the facts of experience is in terms of the different kinds of signs that enter into the process. Peirce distinguished three. These correspond roughly, though not perfectly, to the three kinds of representational capacities distinguished in Figure 2. Sensory-motor representations are typically iconic in character. A visual or tactile image, for instance, of a physical object, or a whole context for that matter, is an icon. It is a kind of copy of the object that it represents (or purports to represent). An interesting fact about icons stressed by Peirce was that they are qualitatively degenerate. They never represent quite perfectly what they purport to represent. They degenerate even as we consider them before our mind's eye or however. Physically, the icon itself deteriorates. If it is an image in our mind's eye, it tends to degenerate over time. If it is an actual physical copy of something, like a bust of Caesar, it turns green in a way that Caesar, presumably, did not. Though Caesar deteriorated in his own right, the iconic representation of him also literally deteriorates. Further, its correspondence to whatever it represents (or purports to represent) also deteriorates. We have trouble remembering in detail the face of someone we see every day. Even our internal recollection of our own face loses its distinctness over time and needs to be refreshed by looking into a mirror, or at a photograph, or something similar. Still, for all their degeneracy, icons can be trusted somewhat, and things really are very much as they seem to be, most of the time. If this were not so, there could be no adequate basis whatever for abductive reasoning, much less for the other sorts.

Indexes are a distinct form of sign. They bear no resemblance to what they point out. An example is a pointing finger, an arrow indicating a certain direction to some goal, or a proper name which merely calls the named thing to mind. Note that there is nothing index-finger-like about a horse pointed out in a pasture. There is nothing John-like about someone who happens to be named John. There is nothing arrow-like about the ski-lodge that is pointed to by the arrow on the road sign. However, indexes are specifically addressed to certain objects which they single out for attention. This is the office of an index as a sign. In fulfilling this role, indexes present another sort of degeneracy. Peirce called it reactional. That is, how does any given interpreter other than the person who is doing the pointing know which thing is being pointed out? Indexes, by themselves, never tell us adequately what they are indexes of. Willard Van Orman Quine made a great deal of this, too much in fact, in his book *Word and Object*. The reactional degeneracy of pointing to a rabbit, for instance, which might leave us in doubt concerning whether what was pointed to was the whole rabbit, the rabbit's ear, the ground where it was sitting, the grass nearby, etc., is inconsequential as soon as the index is combined with a symbol or two that can help determine its meaning.

In fact, without symbols, Peirce's third and purest category of signs, there would be no hope of adequately determining any index at all. Nor would the combining of indexes with icons give an adequate basis for such a determination. But suppose we point, say, out on the mesa near Albuquerque where I live, at a certain rangy jackrabbit and say, "Look at the ears on that rabbit!" Now, there is little room for debate about what the index is intended to mean. The index is helped by the iconic image (whether it is actual or merely imagined) of a rangy New Mexico jackrabbit in a field somewhere near Albuquerque, and it is helped even more by the symbols that define in abstract semantic/syntactic terms what it is that is being pointed out, i.e. the rabbit's long ears, not its feet, the cactus nearby, the brown range grass, or the tumbleweed, and so on, that might have been pointed to by the gesture alone. Therefore, Quine's problem, as soon as the full power of abductive, inductive, and deductive reasoning are all brought to bear in the normal way, is no problem at all. Neither are the supposed difficulties that Jackendoff (1987) has proposed for an actual, existing, real external world, valid. Not only can we know some facts about that world, but, like it or not, we come under certain social and moral obligations because of our valid knowledge of it.

Capacities: Linguistic, kinesic, and sensory-motor. While sensory-motor representations fail to provide an adequate basis for our knowledge of an external world, as argued first by David Hume (1711-1776) and later by Bertrand Russell (1872-1970), they still must contain some valid information about things external to the perceiver or else, as Kant, Peirce, and Einstein showed, there would be no possibility of any knowledge whatever. All non-empty thinking itself would be made impossible: thinking itself would be abolished. Nevertheless, it is admitted that sensory-motor representations are generally subject to the same qualitative degeneracy that afflicts all iconic signs. Fortunately, however, they are supplemented by gestural, kinesic representations, and by full-fledged symbols or linguistic representations. Of these three types of semiotic capacities (as represented in Figure 2), according to Peirce (also Ferdinand de Saussure (1857-1913) in Oller 1989:99-106), the language capacity is the one that provides the best window to the human mind and is the one which probably is closest to the purely abstract semiotic capacity that must undergird all of the others. It is no secret that Chomsky has often expressed the same view.

We may note in passing that without a general semiotic capacity, deeper and more abstract than the other manifest semiotic media, it would be impossible to explain how it is that we can talk about what we see or visualize what someone else has experienced when they talk about it. That is to say, a general semiotic capacity is not merely a psychometric or educational hypothesis about the character of intelligence (as it is understood, for instance, by Boyle 1987); rather, it is a strict logical necessity without which there could be no intelligence as we know it whatsoever.

Figure 3. A modular information processing expansion of the pragmatic mapping process.

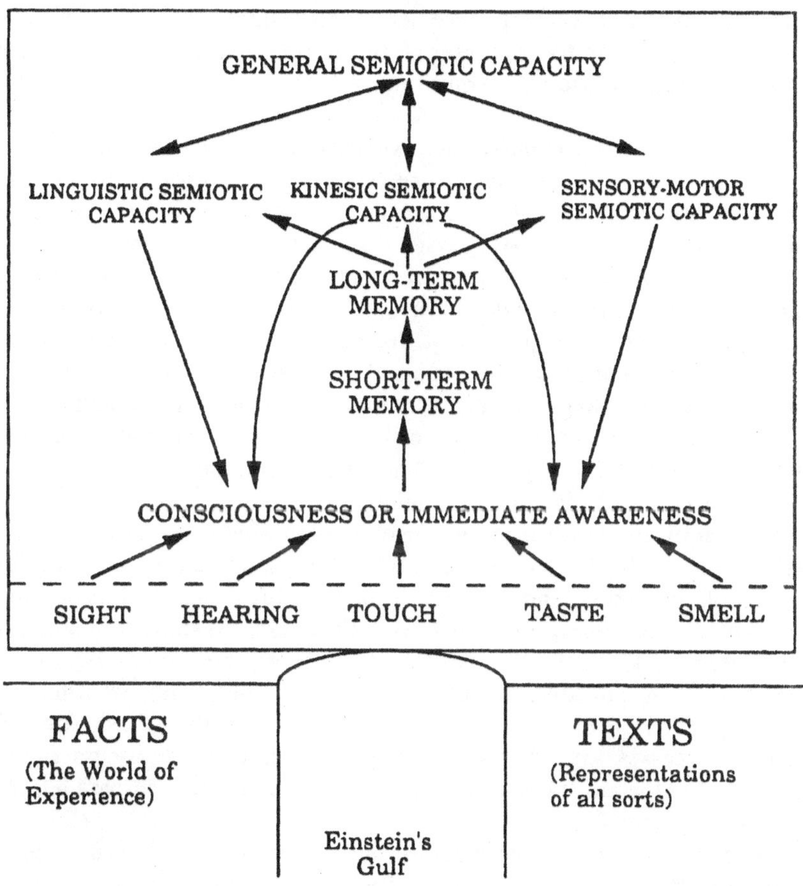

Firstness, secondness, and thirdness. Finally, we come to the most abstract of all Peirce's categories. Their meaning may be appreciated in part by merely abstracting from the positions commonly accorded the first person, second person, and third person perspectives in grammar their strictly logical content. Firstness can be construed roughly as that logical perspective which pertains to the vantage point of a particular observer; secondness is the logical perspective which pertains to the vantage point of an audience or interpreter of someone else's representation; and thirdness is that which pertains to whatever is outside of the perspective of firstness or secondness. Thirdness is implied in the distinction between firstness and secondness, however. Unless there were a ground (thirdness) for the distinction between firstness and secondness, the distinction itself could not exist. While it is true that Peirce never claimed that these categories were the only ones that could be imagined, nor that they were nonarbitrary, he did claim to have proved logically that no simpler system would work and that a more complex system would offer no improvement. We leave those questions, however, to the logicians and press on to examine ramifications of semiotic theory for other theories of language use and acquisition.

Language use and acquisition. Another way of viewing the pragmatic mapping process is shown in Figure 3. Here the various hypothesized capacities—linguistic, kinesic, and sensory-motor—are seen as components within an information-processing system organized more or less in a modular fashion. It is supposed that some real status accrues to each of the proposed elements of the model though it is not put forward as being anything more than a rough and ready picture of distinctions that are probably realized somehow in neurological mechanisms and processes. The virtue of this model or any of the other diagrammatic attempts at representing the nature of the process of language comprehension or acquisition must ultimately be judged in terms of the testable hypotheses that it suggests about how human beings actually function with the various semiotic systems represented.

The ramifications of the model, together with what has gone before in this presentation, can be divided up in a variety of ways. Here they are considered in terms of productive and receptive processes involving (1) sensory-motor encoding; (2) attention or immediate consciousness; (3) short-term and long-term storage; (4) retrieval from short- or long-term memory; and (5) grammatical mechanisms, scripts, frames, schemas, and what-have-you overseeing all of the foregoing. It is not claimed that these somewhat modular processes are executed in sequence, though we discuss them in sequence. On the contrary, it is assumed that they operate in parallel, more or less simultaneously.

At the sensory-motor level, the difference between received input and produced output is partly a question of where attention is addressed, e.g. to the first person perspective or to the second or third, and partly a matter of which mechanisms are active at a given point in time. Input that has no particular personal point of origin is regarded as coming from the third position and is strictly sensory. It may be seen, heard, felt, smelled, or perhaps even tasted, but unless the first person (the one doing the perceiving at the moment) is also producing it, the input will not achieve the more complex status of output. Output will require the activation of articulators or other motoric devices that produce changes in the external environment (including the body of the person who is producing the output). To the extent that linguistic output particularly is regarded by the person producing it from the vantage point of an actual or potential audience, the output itself *is* input, logically speaking. By this logic, then, the input hypothesis would need to be augmented to account for the fact that output is a potential source of data for language acquisition, however filtered it may be.

Progressing up the ladder from raw input (or feedback on output) to what is termed immediate awareness or consciousness, it may be argued that what captures our attention is governed by goal-oriented processes that are themselves subject to structured expectations (from the receptive side) and by intentions (from the productive side). Proof that external input will be interpreted partly in terms of internal goal-directed processes is easy to come by. For instance, if you are rushing to complete a task and are vaguely expecting to be interrupted with a call to dinner, or some other declaration that time is up, the startle response is far more likely than in a case where you are not rushing and not anticipating the time's-up bell, as it were. Or, to take another common example from experience, the startle response toward the popping up of the toast is more likely when you are anxiously waiting for it to pop up with butter already on your knife.

Other experimental evidences for the fact that the peripheral perceptual mechanisms are susceptible to increased or decreased sensitivities can be found in the well-documented cases of perceptual vigilance and defense. For instance, an unexpected word is not only harder to recognize, but may even be literally harder to see or hear under certain circumstances than one that is legitimately expected in a given textual context. This suggests that attention is partly grammar governed. While I will not attempt it here, for lack of space, I believe that all sorts of perceptual and motor errors, illusions, and oversights can be explained on the basis of the semiotic model under consideration. Further, I think that the present system offers a considerably richer basis for the interpretation of the data that a review of the perceptual vigilance/defense literature would turn up than has been offered in the past.

Additional evidence in favor of the model comes into view when we progress up to the levels of short-term and long-term memory. While there is still plenty of debate about the distinction, there is increasingly strong physiological evidence that short-term processes tend to involve electrical storage while long-term memory tends increasingly to involve chemical and other more long-lasting adjustments in neuronal networks. For instance, new neuronal connections may be established or old existing ones strengthened. There is apparently convincing evidence that the actual size of neurons themselves may be increased as a long-term memory is strengthened. Such adjustments in long-term memory are also, it seems, apt to increase the efficiency with which subsequent appearances of a remembered pattern, say, will be processed in immediate awareness and in short-term memory.

It seems to be the case that until received input has been comprehended, which I take to mean translated into a deeper semiotic form than the one in which it was at first received, it remains in short-term memory only and will quickly fade from consciousness altogether unless it is rehearsed. For example, if a sequence of syllables in a strange language should be heard, that sequence will remain as an auditory image for a relatively short duration of time. If it can be rehearsed in part or in whole, the rehearsal may lengthen the duration of the image. The iconic image itself, however, just as Peirce's semiotic theory said, is qualitatively degenerate. The rehearsal process itself is apt to introduce previously acquired phonological expectations that may or may not be appropriate to the signal received. As a result, the memory becomes what PDP researchers term a 'confabulation' rather than a true memory. In fact, if the PDP researchers and the semiotic theory advocated here are on the right track, all memories are confabulative (i.e. reconstructive). The more the actual input (say, text in a target language) conforms to a known grammatical system which is up and operating in immediate awareness governing the expectancies of the perceiver, the more the confabulation will tend to be increasingly accurate. The less the input conforms to expectancies, on the other hand, the less likely the confabulation will be correct. The point that requires explanation is that some confabulations are remarkably accurate. This can only be accounted for in terms of a system of expectancies that are generally correct.

The problem of the language user/perceiver can be viewed as somewhat analogous to that of a given word processor program trying to make sense, as it were, of input text from a different program. The extent to which the input language conforms to the expectations of the control program will determine the extent to which the resulting translation of it makes sense (other things being equal). Many possibilities arise as soon as we acknowledge the logical distinctness of the position of the originator of a text and the interpreter. The text itself has a sort of object status, in third position. The producer of the text stands in first position, and the interpreter in second. The complexities that are possible strain the imagination. The producer's knowledge, for instance, of the language (i.e. the underlying grammatical system) of the text he or she is producing may vary from practically nil to that of a highly articulate and intelligent native speaker. The perceiver of the text may also vary greatly in knowledge of the language of the text. The producer may be talking about facts (or fictions) of which he or she has great or little knowledge. The perceiver may have great or little knowledge concerning the subject-matter of the text. The text itself may be relatively simple to produce and understand or highly abstract, convoluted, and difficult either to produce or to understand. Either producer or receiver may be over- or undermotivated with respect to the particular subject matter and/or text in question.

There are factors, therefore, in each of the three positions that may vary somewhat independently of variables in the other two positions and yet which are bound to influence them profoundly. For example, to take a couple of extreme cases: a really simple text in a given target language which is related to facts that are well supported by representations available in the sensory-motor domain may be completely comprehensible to someone in spite of the fact that the person in question does not know a word of the language in which the text appears; or, conversely, a person who knows a language perfectly may fail to understand a particular text even though it may be produced by another equally competent speaker of the language, provided the subject matter is sufficiently foreign to the second party. All of this is to say that the many factors determining the comprehensibility of any given bit of input vary almost independently across all three positions. Psychological or educational research failing to take the distinct positions into consideration will generally, therefore, be doomed to reach indeterminate conclusions concerning whatever data it may generate.

Retrieval from short- or long-term memory, then, will also be governed by the grammatical expectancies/intentions of the person engaged in the retrieval process. In fact, retrieval should be thought of, as we have already seen, as a process of confabulation or reconstruction rather than as one of total recall. To the extent that the initial storage of information was valid and accurate, the confabulative recall of that information can be expected to be relatively uncontaminated by additions and deletions that would change its basic meaning. However, the more the initial storage was invalid to start with, the more the retrieved (confabulated) reconstruction can be expected to differ from the input text.

Another apparent difference in short and long-term storage and retrieval pertains to the manner in which the textual material is processed and stored. Apparently, the short-term store is largely a buffer area which is essentially iconic, a sensory representation of the surface-form of the text or portion of text held there. To the extent that the information, the deep meaning of the text is processed and correctly understood, the representation that goes into long-term memory is apparently in a rather different, somewhat more paradigmatic, semantic, as opposed to a mere surface phonomorphosyntactic, form. Nevertheless, long-term memory too has some episodic character with reference to its pragmatic side. We tend to recall not merely the meaning of what was said (read, written, thought, etc.) but to some extent the place and time where it took place, and even in some instances, the words that were used. In the case of thoroughly memorized texts, e.g. the Gettysburg Address, or the Preamble to the Constitution, the Pledge of Allegiance, the lyrics to a well-known song, a skip-rope routine, a poem, or some liturgy, these are often recallable more or less verbatim even in cases of severe aphasia. All of this suggests that even at the long-term level of memory there are distinct mechanisms, perhaps, for the storage of well-rehearsed routines (e.g. whole texts functioning as lexical entries, it would seem) as contrasted with grammatical systems per se. However, no matter how good our recollection of actual texts may be, it is far from perfect in most cases and yet retains an accuracy that would not be possible if we depended on the surface recall of actual texts (sequentialized representations) per se. Therefore, a still higher and more abstract level of memory is posited for grammatical systems.

At this highest level, it is supposed that we must distinguish sensory-motor systems (e.g. knowing how to swim, drive a car, ride a bicycle, play an instrument, dribble a basketball, stand on your hands, spin a top, etc.) from gestural systems and from language systems. However, the fact that spillover from one semiotic system to another is possible is easy to prove and demands a deeper and more abstract semiotic system capable of translating between the several distinct systems. For instance, coaching would not be expected to have much impact unless verbal descriptions, performed demonstrations, diagrams, and the like in reference to athletic performances could be translated into adjustments in motor sequences by the athlete making use of the coaching. Or, alternatively, if physical activity could not in large measure be represented in verbal descriptions, it is difficult to see how people could demonstrate comprehension of commands by physical performances, e.g. as in Asher's TPR method of L2 instruction.

A critical question from the point of view of language acquisition theory is how grammatical rule systems are constructed, modified, and maintained. Or are the PDP researchers correct in insisting that rules, after all, can be done without? Personally, I do not think so. For instance, in the PDP system for learning irregular past tenses of English verbs, the feature system specified in advance seems to involve the very sorts of elements that would be required to determine the limits of precisely the sort of rule system they say they don't need. Be that as it may, neither connectionist models nor any others proposed to date have done away with the need for a rich innate system of semiotic capacities. Among those capacities would seem to be the sort of rule systems now characterized in GB theory as increasingly modular in character. It seems that such things as subject-predicate relations, a rich set of conceptual possibilities, the capacity to negate, conjoin, and subordinate propositional values are all part of the innate apparatus. The problem for the language acquirer seems to be more a matter of fixing the parameters of pre-existent possibilities than of discovering the possibilities themselves de novo.

However, from the language teacher/researcher point of view, the more critical question still about the fixing of grammatical parameters is: What sort of input is necessary to enable the L2 learner in the classroom to develop a feel for the target language that is like that of a native speaker. If previously processed texts have led to inappropriate or imperfect interpretations and rule systems, how can these be sufficiently destabilized to allow continuing progress toward native-like proficiency, and how can correct interpretations and concomitant rule systems be correspondingly stabilized? In 1976, Vigil and I proposed the idea that rules are apt to be destabilized when attempts at communication using the offending rule or system meet with unexpected negative feedback on the cognitive channel. That is, the second party reacts with something like "I don't understand" or an attempted repetition of the utterance which doesn't even come close to what the L2 user intended. The message on the relationship level is still, "I am trying to understand what you are saying," i.e. "you are okay, but I don't understand what you are saying." By contrast, a feedback message that says "I really don't like you" or "I don't even want to know what you are saying" is apt to result in a complete abortion of further attempts at communication and therefore elimination of any possibility for interactive feedback that would help to guide the L2 system toward native-like maturity.

What was not very well understood in the model proposed back in 1976, and which can perhaps be cleared up now, is that all constructive interpretations of text are essentially active, output-type operations. There is no such thing as a passive, purely receptive, interpretation of any text in any language. Therefore, the distinction between input and output is, again, drawn into question. As a result, if we recognize that every interpretation of a surface form into a deeper semiotic representation of meaning is an active process of construction, it follows that the principal means of destabilizing any given attempted interpretation (always a representation of a representation) is for the interpreter to discover some inconsistency between some element of a previous interpretation and the one currently under construction. As before, it will still be unexpected negative feedback on the understanding of what someone intended previously and what they now appear to be saying that will destabilize the previous interpretation and force a new effort. Again, as we hypothesized in 1976, it may still be claimed that the learner will tend to level off in language acquisition at just the point where no new discrepancies appear between what is currently being processed and what has been processed previously. Or, in the terms we used back then, the language user will tend to level off, stabilize (fossilize, in Selinker's terminology), at just the point where all of that person's own communicative requirements (however he or she may define them) are being met.

Toward testable hypotheses. While Krashen's input hypothesis (cf. Krashen 1985) has come in for a lot of criticism in recent years, something very much like it is surely required. The language acquirer progresses by processing input that stretches the developing grammar of the target language a little beyond itself. The input, therefore, needs to be just a little beyond what the acquirer can understand easily. This idea has been criticized by Spolsky (1989), for example, who has argued that it is either trivially true or a self-contradiction. The self-contradictory interpretation is that you can't understand what you can't understand, and the trivial truism is that of course you have to understand in order to learn anything. But Spolsky is wrong and Krashen is right. According to the earliest statements of the input hypothesis, Krashen noted that the ability of the acquirer to overreach the limits of his or her own internally developing grammar of the target language was dependent on a scaffolding of support in terms of what he called 'extralinguistic context'. From the perspective of the Peircean model along the lines advocated here, we can be even more explicit.

According to Peirce, all meaningful interpretation in any given semiotic medium always involves a kind of *translation* (where the term is used more broadly than usual) from one semiotic medium into another. The idea of pragmatic mapping expresses a translation from representations of one sort or another to facts in the world of experience or the reverse. Expanded upon slightly, the translation is from sensory-motor representations at one extreme to kinesic and linguistic ones in spoken discourse, and, if the discourse is written, the kinesic and linguistic representations are reduced to a string of marks on paper. What may not be entirely obvious to most theoreticians, much less to the average language teacher in the classroom, is that the often remote and distant relations to context outside of the linguistic text per se are the crucial enabling conditions for its meaning. Remove those pragmatic connections and even the most abstract symbols lose all their symbolic value and cease to be symbols.

Figure 4. Language proficiency in terms of domains of grammar.

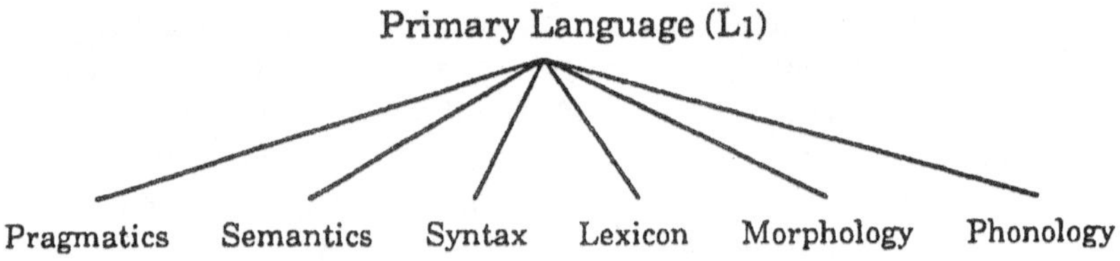

Figure 5. Language proficiency in terms of modalities of processing.

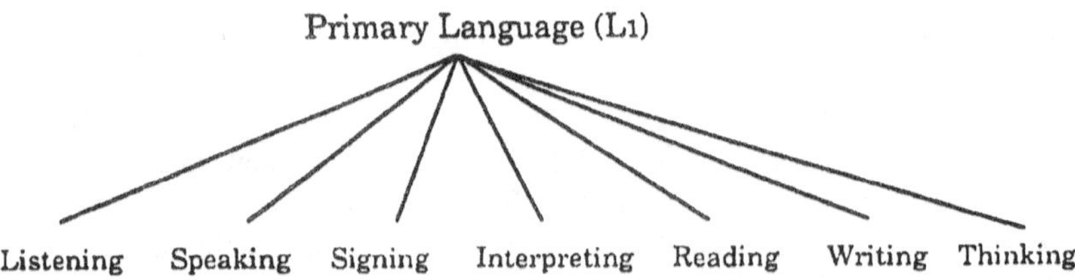

Whether Spolsky and the other critics of Krashen like it or not, Krashen is right about the input hypothesis in its stripped down basic form. The only way we ever progress at all in language acquisition, whether first or second, is to stretch ourselves beyond what we already know. Otherwise, there could be no progress at all. A fair answer to Spolsky's attempt to trivialize the input hypothesis would be to point out that progress means getting beyond where you were before. On the other hand, what counts as progress could not occur at all if there were not already in place a great deal of cognitive ability which was there from the start—the innate nucleus Chomsky has been so insistent upon. It seems that the problem of acquiring a new language is not so much one of building a whole new set of categories from scratch as it is one of fixing the parameters of, or instantiating, concepts which are already available. The grammatical system, by this interpretation, is already largely known to the L2 acquirer. It merely has to be determined, fixed, and made accessible through pragmatic mapping operations. What this suggests for second language teaching is that pragmatically rich and comprehensible input is, as Krashen has contended, a critical necessary ingredient for successful language instruction. Furthermore, this idea extends far beyond the mere limits of the second language classroom. Comprehensible input is also the key ingredient for the advance of any semiotic system whatever. Therefore, the argument that extensive reading is the key to advancing in writing skills cannot be far wrong. The only adjustment in that basic idea suggested here is the discovery that output is a form of input provided only that it be intended to be comprehensible and that it be monitored by its producer. (Here, I mean 'monitored' in the sense of seeing whether it fits what the user intends to say, not in the specialized sense in which Krashen has used it with reference to conscious rule application. The latter sort is a much less common and more difficult variety of monitoring.)

What is apparently most disturbing to Spolsky and some of the other Krashen critics about the input hypothesis is its seeming simplicity. However, it may be observed that essentially no complexity whatever is lost in admitting the input hypothesis. The complexity merely becomes more manageable, as does a dark room when you turn on the light. The fundamental problem of how to make the input in any given instructional setting accessible to the student still remains. If the pragmatic mapping theory is admitted, on the other hand, it is true that we have some pretty clear ideas about how to define more and less comprehensible pragmatic mapping relations. However, here again, for those theoreticians who delight in singing the praises of complexity, as we have already seen, a plethora of variables can easily be discerned between the three positions of originator, consumer, and representation, not to mention the interactions between those variables.

Another application of the semiotic theory discussed here is to the perplexing matter of how to parse up the language proficiency pie. Some have argued that language proficiency is really a conglomeration of almost unrelated skills in listening, speaking, reading, gesturing, signing, writing, thinking, etc., and that furthermore, each of the several skills could further be divided into many subcomponents. Another popular way of looking at the question has been in terms of domains of grammatical knowledge such as phonology, morphology, lexicon, syntax, semantics, and pragmatics. It would have been easy to get the impression from time to time that these complementary ways of looking at language proficiency were at war with each other. Actually, they are not. There is no logical conflict between them at all. They are merely different ways of looking at a multifaceted hierarchy—a system of systems.

Another popular view has been to emphasize the manner in which different components of the hierarchy are acquired or how the advances in one domain might influence some other. Cummins' double-sided threshold hypothesis (cf. Cummins 1984) fits into this last mentioned category. First, is there a sensitive range of abilities in one's primary language below which it is harmful to undertake the study of a second or third language system? Second, is there a point of proficiency in the second language system below which the budding bilingual will not benefit cognitively from having acquired it? These questions can be put more succinctly, I think, in terms of the semiotic hierarchy, and they in turn suggest a broader potential relation between elements in the hierarchy besides the ones they purport to focus on. Looking back to Figure 2, the more general question is: Under what conditions can we expect development in one area to benefit from development in some other, and under what conditions can we expect the focus of energy on development in one area to hinder growth in some other? The advantage of the semiotic hierarchy, even in its presently undeveloped form, is that it aims toward a comprehensive theory of the interrelationships between semiotic media. Not only do we need to know what the relation between primary and secondary language development might be, but we also need to know what impact one or both of these may have on deeper, more abstract semiotic abilities (see Lemmon and Goggin 1989 and their references for a recent discussion). Also, we will want to consider how it is that acquiring a skill in one language, e.g. learning to read in Arabic, may influence the acquisition of literacy in, say, Berber (see Wagner, Spratt, and Ezzaki 1989). While the traditional wisdom has been that literacy is generally transferrable, for reasons like the one underlying the first prong of Cummins' threshold hypothesis, it has been doubted that the transfer would go equally well from L2 to L1. It has been assumed that semiotic abilities, like water, flow downhill, i.e. from the stronger to the weaker language.

While there may be apparent exceptions (as Wagner et al. try to demonstrate), it seems reasonable to suppose that human beings work best from strength to strength. That is, we profit most in an educational way by using what we already know well, or what we already understand, in order to progress to new understanding. There is certainly nothing new in saying this, but it does suggest some ideas in terms of the semiotic hierarchy that might not otherwise occur to us. For instance, if there is an area in the hierarchy that has been well developed for a particular individual, or that is typically more developed than others, it would make sense to capitalize on that development to help bring along development in other areas. For instance, if primary language ability is central to the development of the sort of propositional reasoning underlying abstract, nonverbal reasoning, then it would make sense to expect that furthering the development of the primary language would augment development of what has till now been called nonverbal intelligence.

If it is true that acquiring a second language to some requisite level of skill augments certain cognitive abilities, then, raising the goals and upping the ante in L2 courses might be a highly desirable adjustment in educational practice. If we merely examine the evidence for positive, beneficial transfer across modalities within and across languages, not to mention positive transfer within and across other sensory-motor tasks, we are inclined to expect along with Cummins (1984) and with Hakuta and Diaz (1985) that really effective L2 acquisition ought to produce gains up and down the semiotic hierarchy. While advancing in French, Chinese, or American Sign Language may not improve your tennis much, it very likely will have some beneficial impact on a wide range of more abstract semiotic abilities. This impact ought to be measurable in a variety of ways. If the variables for group studies are too complex to manage, as Cziko (1989) has argued they may be, then, perhaps in-depth clinical analysis of the sort recommended by Damico (in Hamayan and Damico in press) may prevail.

A final area of research which I want to consider briefly is the application of cloze procedure to studies of coherence. Related to the particular applications of cloze tests that I have in mind are a host of other procedures that have been applied in attempts to sort out what we mean by the term coherence. I am thinking especially of a growing paradigm of research aiming to sort out the effects of interpretive perspectives (schemas, frames, scripts, and the like) on the encoding and retrieval of textual information (cf. Kardash, Royer, and Greene 1988; Anderson, Pichert, and Shirley 1983; Bransford and Johnson 1972; and their references).

Unfortunately, the question of what makes a text comprehensible has been dealt with in many cases as if the differences in background knowledge of the originator and consumer of a given representation, the first and second positions, were negligible factors, not to mention the motivation of one or the other to produce or comprehend the text. Or, manipulations of text variables, those in the third position according to a Peircean perspective, have been done with little or no regard for variables impinging on the first and second position. Currently, Jon Jonz and I are engaged in a research project to try to sort out some of the neglected sources of variance in cloze tasks that no doubt have influenced the results of many of the projects which we are in the process of reviewing.

For example, to pick a particularly salient case, a number of researchers (see Shanahan, Kamil, and Tobin 1982; also Shanahan 1983) have claimed to prove the null hypothesis that there are effectively no cloze items that are sensitive to constraints ranging across more than five to ten words, much less are there, according to those researchers, cloze items sensitive to constraints ranging across sentence boundaries. But on the contrary side, see Henk (1982) and Cziko (1983). Also, Jonz (1989; and see his references) has shown, in his research, that one of the neglected variables on the side of texts selected for research is the difference between relatively encyclopedic, descriptive prose, and narrative. The same distinction was made by John Dewey in 1938 (reprinted in Oller 1989:105-31), before him by Peirce, and long before that by the medieval Scholastics. It is essentially the distinction between a definitional type of prose that merely tells what something is as opposed to a temporally developing, episodic type of prose that tells a story.

With mere description, Jonz showed, scrambling the sentences of a cloze task has little impact, while with narrative prose it has a substantial impact.

In effect, those who claimed to have proved (as if a null hypothesis could ever be proved) that cloze items are not sensitive to constraints ranging across sentential boundaries have tended to use descriptive rather than narrative type prose. What they have demonstrated, that is valuable, is that descriptive passages of text are much more loosely organized than are narrative passages. This should have been known in advance, as Jonz points out, and yet it was not. On the other hand, the claim that cloze items are not sensitive to discourse constraints is known to be false on a variety of grounds. Both Brown (1983) and Bachman (1982, 1985) have demonstrated as much in different experimental approaches.

Furthermore, it can be demonstrated independently that descriptive passages are always set in narrative contexts. Experientially, there is no such thing as pure, totally abstract, completely nonpragmatic intensional description. Such a thing would be utterly meaningless. It exists only in pure theory. In actual experience all description, to the extent that it is not empty, relates to the space-time material world through the eyes, ears, etc., of an interpreter and at a particular point in that person's experience. In other words, as a matter of principle, there is no strictly descriptive, nonnarrative writing, and if any given cloze task could be sufficiently extended (other things being equal), some cloze items would eventually turn up in the task which were sensitive to constraints across sentence boundaries. Not only can the null hypothesis not be proved empirically in this case (or, in fact, in any case) but in this particular case the null hypothesis must be false on completely independent logical grounds having to do with the character of semiosis in general. The fact is that ideas are connected in all normal discourse by an incredibly rich system of abductive logic. Therefore it is a foregone necessity, that as Brown (1983), Bachman (1982, 1985), Chavez-Oller et al. (1985) have all shown independently, some cloze items must be sensitive to constraints ranging across sentence boundaries.

What remains from the point of view of semiotic theory is to attempt to sort out some of the sources of variability in cloze research that impinge upon its sensitivity to the coherence of texts. Also it is apparent that coherence (a conglomerate of properties of a text; third position) can only be defined relative to the viewpoint of a particular observer (second position) with a particular sort of background and a given level of language proficiency vis-à-vis the same sort of variables as manifested in the given text as produced by someone else (first position). It is obvious at first blush on sorting through the research that manipulations of textual variables, e.g. number of deletions, length of passage, ratio of deletions to intact text, have often been carried out with contaminating changes in subjects tested, not to mention the source of material used for the testing, e.g. subject matter, type of discourse, viewpoint on subject matter, and many other variables that have been changed almost at will in the same experiment in many cases. Such potpourris masquerading as research result in outcomes which ought properly to be regarded as a mere mishmash. Instead, they are apt to be interpreted as proving that more carefully obtained results, e.g. evidence that cloze items are sensitive to constraints ranging across sentence boundaries, were in fact unobtainable. Such an interpretation is very much like an expedition to Alaska in search of gold that comes up empty-handed and then concludes that contrary to previous reports, there is no gold in Alaska. At any rate, Jonz and I are inclined to think that a richer theoretical perspective will resolve many of the discrepancies in research outcomes which many reviewers, unfortunately, regard as if they were all on a par. The fact is they are not. Some research is better and some is worse. It just ain't all equal.

Finally, a comment about Cziko's penetrating discussion of indeterminacy as a monkey-wrench factor in educational research in general. While I believe it ought to be required reading for every researcher and interpreter of research with human beings, I'll risk short-circuiting my recommendation by giving a brief summary of Cziko's main point as I understand it. Owing to the indeterminacy of human behavior, as in complex educational settings, the classical quantitative approaches to measurement may not be applicable to the prediction of individual behavior. Part of the argument, though certainly not all of it, is that some of the presuppositions of the classical measurement theory are inevitably not met when we try to measure performances of human subjects. Individual performances in any kind of educational setting are subject to fairly radical adjustments that are intrinsically stochastic and unpredictable. One tiny aspect of the problem is that human subjects in any given experimental or even observational study are apt to have some idea concerning the purpose of the whole exercise. They are never in the position of being completely naive subjects who are unaffected by the aims of the methods to which they are being subjected. No matter how subtle educators may think they are, they are not so subtle as to be able to conceal entirely what they are doing (nor should they want to) from the subjects who are being, in one way or another, experimentally manipulated, treated, or observed. As a result, outcomes of measurement are subject to direct influence by the persons whose abilities are supposedly being measured.

Owing to this and related difficulties, Cziko gives the best case I have yet encountered for the sort of clinical, naturalistic, observational assessment of the sort advocated by Damico under the heading of clinical discourse analysis. Nevertheless, I'll make this comment in closing. It seems to me that the interrelatedness of the elements of the semiotic hierarchy as discussed here suggest that wherever multiple measures are applied to the same individual or where a single test battery is applied to a group of subjects, there is still a sufficient basis to expect per the classical theory for the cumulative variance to tend toward validity. That is, while Cziko's commentary may be devastating to specific predictions about individual subjects, I think it may not hold for the legitimately stochastic accumulation of variance in a larger distribution of scores. There, the unpredictable elements all work in favor of cancelling each other out, leaving behind a golden residual, we hope, of valid variance.

References

Anderson, R.C., J.W. Pichert, and L.L. Shirley. 1983. Effects of reader's schema at different points in time. Journal of Educational Psychology 75:271-79.

Bachman, Lyle F. 1982. The trait structure of cloze scores. TESOL Quarterly 16:61-70.

Bachman, Lyle F. 1985. Performance on cloze tests with fixed-ratio and rational deletions. TESOL Quarterly 19:535-55.

Boyle, Joseph P. 1987. Intelligence, reasoning, and language proficiency. Modern Language Journal 71:277-88.

Bransford, J.D., and M.K. Johnson. 1972. Contextual prerequisites for understanding: Some investigations of comprehension and recall. Journal of Verbal Learning and Verbal Behavior 11:717-26.

Brown, James Dean. 1983. A closer look at cloze. In: John W. Oller, Jr., ed. Issues in language testing research. Rowley, Mass.: Newbury House. 237-50.

Chavez-Oller, Mary Anne, Tetsuro Chihara, Kelley A. Weaver, and John W. Oller, Jr. 1985. When are cloze items sensitive to constraints across sentences? Language Learning 35:181-206.

Cummins, Jim. 1984. Bilingualism and special education: Issues in assessment and pedagogy. Clevedon, England: Multilingual Matters.

Cziko, Gary A. 1983. Another response to Shanahan, Kamil, and Tobin: Further reasons to keep the cloze case open. Reading Research Quarterly 18:361-65.

Cziko, Gary A. 1989. Unpredictability and indeterminism in human behavior: Arguments and implications for educational research. Educational Researcher 18:17-25.

Fisch, Max, et al., eds. 1982. Writings of Charles S. Peirce: A chronological edition, vol. 1. Indianapolis: Indiana University.

Givón, Talmy. 1989. Mind, codes, and context: Essays in pragmatics. Hillsdale, N.J.: Lawrence Erlbaum.

Hamayan, Else, and Jack S. Damico, eds. In press. Non-biased assessment of limited English proficient special education students. Austin, Texas: Pro-Ed.

Hakuta, Kenji, and Raphael Diaz. 1985. The relationship between degree of bilingualism and cognitive ability: A critical discussion and some new longitudinal data. In: K.E. Nelson, ed. Children's language, vol. 5. Hillsdale, N.J.: Erlbaum.

Henk, William A. 1982. A response to Shanahan, Kamil, and Tobin: The case is not yet clozed. Reading Research Quarterly 17:591-95.

Jackendoff, Ray. 1987. Consciousness and the computational mind. Cambridge, Mass.: MIT.

Johnson-Laird, Philip N. 1983. Mental models: Toward a cognitive science of language, inference, and consciousness. Cambridge, Mass.: Harvard University Press.

Jonz, Jon. 1989. Textual sequence and second-language comprehension. Language Learning 39:207-49.

Kardash, Carol Anne M., James M. Royer, and Barbara A. Greene. 1988. Effects of schemata on both encoding and retrieval of information from prose. Journal of Educational Psychology 80:324-29.

Krashen, Stephen D. 1985. The input hypothesis: Issues and implications. London and New York: Longman.

Lemmon, Christian R., and Judith P. Goggin. 1989. The measurement of bilingualism and its relationship to cognitive ability. Applied Psycholinguistics 10:133-55.

McClelland, James L., David E. Rumelhart, and G.E. Hinton. 1986. The appeal of Parallel Distributed Processing. In: McClelland et al. 1986:3-44.

McClelland, James L., David E. Rumelhart, and the PDP Research Group. 1986. Parallel Distributed Processing: Explorations in the microstructure of cognition, vol. 2: Psychological and biological models. Cambridge, Mass.: MIT (Bradford).

Moore, Edward C., et al., eds. 1984. Writings of Charles S. Peirce: A chronological edition, vol. 2. Indianapolis: Indiana University Press.

Oller, J.., Jr., ed. 1989. Language and experience: Classic pragmatism. Lanham, Md.: University Press of America.

Quine, Willard Van Orman. 1960. Word and object. Cambridge, Mass.: MIT Press.

Rumelhart, David E., James L. McClelland, and the PDP Research Group. 1986. Parallel Distributed Processing: Explorations in the microstructure of cognition, vol. 1: Foundations. Cambridge, Mass.: MIT (Bradford).

Shanahan, Timothy. 1983. A response to Henk and Cziko. Reading Research Quarterly 18:366-67.

Shanahan, Timothy, M. Kamil, and A. Tobin. 1982. Cloze as a measure of intersentential comprehension. Reading Research Quarterly 17:229-55.

Spolsky, Bernard. 1989. Communicative competence, language proficiency, and beyond. Applied Linguistics 10:138-56.

Vigil, Neddy A., and John W. Oller, Jr. 1976. Rule fossilization: A tentative model. Language Learning 26:281-95.

Wagner, Daniel A., Jennifer E. Spratt, and Abdelkader Ezzaki. 1989. Does learning to read in a second language always put the child at a disadvantage? Some counterevidence from Morocco. Applied Psycholinguistics 10:31-48.

Cognitive and social correlates and consequences of additive bilinguality

G. Richard Tucker
Center for Applied Linguistics

Introduction. Much of the early educational literature (cf. Hakuta 1986, Macnamara 1966) suggested negative cognitive, personal, and social consequences of bilinguality. Bilingual individuals were thought to be particularly disadvantaged vis-à-vis their monolingual counterparts. Educational researchers concluded that they developed lower levels of both verbal and nonverbal skills, and that they lagged significantly behind their peers in grade-level completion, subject-matter achievement and other skills—particularly those which required verbal reasoning facility. One viewpoint argued for a so-called balance effect—as more and more psychic energy was invested by the incipient bilingual in mastering a second language, less and less was available for mother tongue and other skill development and nurturance. Upon careful examination, the early studies were found to suffer from a number of serious methodological flaws. For example, often individuals were classified as monolingual or bilingual solely on the basis of the surname, a practice which incidentally continues in many parts of our country even today. In other cases, no attempt was made to equate individuals on the basis of social class membership, with the result that frequently bilingual subjects came predominantly from lower socioeconomic status groups and their monolingual control counterparts were drawn predominantly from middle socioeconomic status backgrounds. In an exceedingly large number of cases little attempt was made to describe explicitly the (bilingual) language proficiency of the participating individuals, further contaminating the data. For a variety of reasons, work through the mid-1950s in many parts of the world was seriously flawed methodologically.

In an important study, Peal and Lambert (1962) found evidence for quite different, and much more positive, correlates of bilinguality. Interestingly, one of their primary motivations for conducting their research was to attempt to understand the nature of the differences and the deficit affecting bilingual individuals. That is, they began their investigations with a general acceptance of the earlier, supposedly careful, empirical work which had been carried out.

As is now well known, they crafted an exceedingly well-controlled study which, in fact, demonstrated significant cognitive advantages, subject-matter achievement, and grade-level attainment for bilingual individuals. They paid a great deal of attention to ensuring that bilingual individuals indeed demonstrated equivalent levels of language proficiency in each of their two languages, and that the bilingual subjects were similar in terms of socioeconomic status to their monolingual counterparts. This ground-breaking research ushered in a new era of such studies throughout the world, with similar extensions and replications occurring in many national settings during the late 1960s and 1970s. Essentially, the message in diverse settings was a similar one (cf. Ben-Zeev 1977, Ianco-Worrall 1972, Barik and Swain 1976): namely, that bilingual individuals tended to be more creative individuals, to have a greater degree of cognitive flexibility, and to have a significantly higher measured verbal or nonverbal I.Q. than their counterparts.

In this paper, I describe briefly the likely cognitive and social correlates and consequences for individuals who are 'caused' to become bilingual by participating in innovative language education programs such as bilingual immersion or developmental bilingual programs. My reason for doing so is to provide a positive counterbalance to the negatively charged debate surrounding the discussions about amending the U.S. Constitution to declare English to be the sole and official language of the country (see, for example, Crawford 1989, Nunberg 1989). To date, 17 states have declared English to be their official language although the Supreme Court of Arizona has recently overturned the statute there. Conversely, three states (New Mexico, Oregon, and Washington) have declared English Plus to be the official policy of their states.

In part, fuel for the controversy over an official language policy for the United States hinges around misunderstanding of issues related to one important aspect of language (education) policy—namely, that of bilingual education. Proponents of an 'English Only' viewpoint misrepresent or misunderstand the accumulated research literature concerning the consequences and correlates of bilinguality. Supporters of 'Official' English imply that an individual caused to become bilingual will suffer irreparable cognitive and social harm and that this individual will become an alienated and noncontributing member of our society. Consequently, they argue, the fabric of society will begin to disintegrate. It has struck me, as an interested observer, that they have considered the social and educational research literature through the mid-1950s, but have never bothered to examine more contemporary research.

Here I wish to sketch the changing (language) educational needs of language minority and language majority youngsters, to describe an innovative approach to language education designed to foster additive bilingualism, and to identify the likely correlates of such bilingualism on the basis of a review of recent relevant research literature.

Demographic changes and language minority students. Despite the fact that the school-aged population of the United States is decreasing in absolute terms, the number of language minority students is increasing dramatically. In 1981, the percentage of minority students in California, New Mexico, and Texas had exceeded 35%, while the percentage in Florida, Illinois, and New York was nearing 35%. Moreover, the national percentage is projected by the Education Department to increase to 45.5% by the year 2020. Due to a combination of migration patterns and family size, the fastest growing population in the United States is the language minority population. In addition, almost one million refugees entered the United States between 1975 and 1985. Added to these numbers are the several million undocumented aliens who arrived from Central America and the Caribbean. Moreover, both racial and ethnic minority families, particularly Black and Hispanic, are characteristically larger than those of the American majority population. If current trends continue, we can expect that 53 of the major American cities will have language minority youngsters as a majority of the school-aged population by the year 2000. In many parts of the country, such students now—or shortly will—constitute a majority of the pupils in Local Educational Agencies (LEAs). More than one-half of the minority students will be limited English proficient (LEP), faced with the awesome task of mastering the academic content of their classes at the same time as they develop their second language proficiency. In many instances, these students enter school with little or no proficiency whatsoever in English. In other instances, language minority students who seem—at least to all outward appearances—proficient in social language skills have difficulty in acquiring the cognitive academic language skills which they need for success in their mathematics, science, social studies, or other academic subjects. These latter students, so often undetected by typical entry screening, are particularly problematic.

Unfortunately, academic achievement and school completion rates for many minority students—particularly Hispanic students, who are the largest minority and the fastest growing sector of our population—are woefully low, a set of circumstances noted by the nation's governors in their recent education summit. In the Southwest, Rendon (1983) reports that 40% of the Hispanic students drop out by the tenth grade, and that an additional 10% drop out before completing high school. A recent study by Cardenas, Robledo, and Waggoner (1988) suggests that unfortunately these already high estimates may be woefully low. Of those students who do graduate from high school, only a small percentage attend college and the majority of those who do, choose community colleges. Of those who attend four-year colleges, the majority study education, business, or social science. Fewer than 3% of the science, math, and technical majors are Hispanic. By the year 2000, the nation will have a smaller pool of potential workers and college students, and the people in this pool will be less prepared for work and college study due to circumstances such as poverty, unstable homes, and lack of English language skills (Johnston 1987). While these statistics document a problem for all minority groups—particularly Hispanic and Black children—language minorities (those for whom English is not the native language) are notably at risk.

The risks faced by these youngsters, and recommendations for positive action to help ameliorate the conditions, have been presented in a number of timely reports prepared by mathematics educators (*Everybody Counts*), science educators (*Project 2061: Science for All Americans*), and social studies educators (*Charting a Course: Social Studies for the 21st Century*). In each of these reports, educators call attention to the need to equip individuals to communicate effectively about, and use, the language of their disciplines; to the need to draw upon and take cognizance of multicultural diversity in enhancing classroom experiences; and to the need to ensure that students develop the cognitive academic language skills which they must have to participate effectively in subject-matter instruction.

The purpose of this paper is not to reenter the debate on the optimal educational strategy for such youngsters; others have done that (e.g. Hakuta 1986, Willig 1985). Rather, I intend to describe an emerging educational practice that seems to offer great promise for such students, and then to examine the likely cognitive and social correlates of the children's participation in such programs.

Language majority students. With respect to these students, the situation is slightly different. For these youngsters the problem is one of depressingly low foreign or second language proficiency—and, of course, for many, unfortunately low levels of subject-matter attainment as well. Language majority children often participate in sequences of foreign language study at the elementary or secondary level without ever developing any meaningful proficiency in their language of study. A nationwide survey of foreign language enrollments conducted by CAL staff (Oxford and Rhodes 1988) revealed that approximately 22% of our nation's elementary schools and 87% of our secondary schools offered programs of foreign language instruction. However, the best guess that we can make from the data, which are based on a 5% sample survey of all public and private elementary and secondary schools in the country, is that fewer than 1% of the students who are enrolled in such programs—already a relatively small number of youngsters—participate in programs in which the development of bilingual proficiency is either an attainable objective or even a demonstrable program goal.

That is, the average English-speaking youngster enrolled has virtually no chance whatsoever to acquire bilingual proficiency by following the sequence of foreign language courses typically offered in either our public or private school system. Although this statement holds true for the commonly taught languages such as French, German, and Spanish, the situation is even more discouraging for the so-called less comonly taught languages (e.g. Arabic, Chinese, Japanese, Indonesian, Swahili), which for all practical purposes are not even offered as subjects for study. (Parenthetically, it should be noted that 100% of Japanese high school graduates have studied English for six years while fewer than .02% of American high school graduates have studied three years or more of Japanese.) In fact, far fewer than 1% of our youngsters have the opportunity to study languages which in the aggregate are spoken as primary or secondary languages by more than 90% of the world's population.

Is it realistic for language majority children to acquire bilingual proficiency by participating in foreign language programs within our public school system? What are the likely correlates of such participation? Again, the purpose is not to examine here the broad array of methods and approaches used to deliver foreign language instruction or to evaluate their efficacy (cf. Larsen-Freeman 1986, Richards and Rodgers 1986), but rather to describe an educational practice that holds great promise for improving the quality of foreign language instruction, and concomitantly the degree of proficiency attained for all youngsters without in any way sacrificing or diminishing the level of subject-matter achievement.

An alternative educational model. For a number of years, many of us have been flirting with a special kind of innovative language education program—one which integrates the teaching of language and content to the fullest degree possible. Previously, I have written about the potential value of an 'enrichment model' (Tucker 1986) or a program which could be designed to capitalize on the fact that language minority students and language majority students can participate meaningfully and effectively in shared or cooperative education. An approach which maximizes the integration of language and content instruction for members of major language contact groups simultaneously would seem to hold great promise for building and for sustaining valuable natural language resources within the United States which now are either allowed to decay or are never sufficiently developed.

As noted on several occasions (Tucker and Crandall 1989, Crandall and Tucker in press), there is an emerging awareness, particularly in the United States, of the possibilities, the power, and the promise of bilingual immersion or developmental bilingual programs. Let me operationally define an exemplary bilingual immersion program. Let us suppose, for example, that in a typical first grade class comprising 28 youngsters, 14 are Hispanic, Spanish-speaking youngsters and 14 are Anglo or English mother-tongue youngsters. These pupils would be placed together in a combined class (which would usually have been assembled on a voluntary basis) in which some portion of their day typically would be devoted to English language arts (for the Anglos), English as a second language (for the Hispanics), Spanish language arts (for the Hispanics), Spanish as a second language (for the Anglos), and the teaching of selected content material—let us say mathematics—in English, and other content material—let us say history—in Spanish. Over the course of several years, the idea would be to offer a program of bilingual instruction in which children from both of the ethnolinguistic groups would have an opportunity to develop and to sharpen their literacy skills in English and in Spanish while simultaneously developing the fullest possible academic language proficiency in each of their two languages. Care would be taken to insure that children had an opportunity to study all of the content subjects in both languages during the course of their school experience. This would be done to facilitate the development of the appropriate academic 'registers' for mathematics, science, and social studies in each of the two languages. The daily instruction would be offered within a bilingual ambiance in which the teachers as well as the students would be available to provide good language models and to maximize the opportunity for cooperative learning and peer group tutoring. (Optimally, instruction in each language would be provided by separate teachers with native proficiency in the respective language.)

In many ways, such an approach resembles the early French immersion programs begun in Montreal in the mid 1960s (cf. Lambert and Tucker 1972, Genesee 1987), but with a notable exception. In the early immersion programs, only language majority children were involved—there were no children whatsoever from the target language group. There were no youngsters available to act as peer models who could assist the English speakers in acquiring the social as well as the academic register of the target language. As noted previously (Tucker in press), we had worried a good deal about what we referred to as the 'absent peer group,' but political, religious, and other social factors prevented us from developing and implementing a fully integrated or two-way bilingual model. Nevertheless, such an idealized model was always in the back of our minds. The specific purpose for implementing such a program would be to develop what Lambert (1980) referred to as 'additive' bilingualism. That is, an educational program would be designed and implemented which offered participating youngsters the opportunity to nurture and to sustain their mother tongue—be it English or Spanish—while simultaneously adding a second language to their repertoire. Such a program is in sharp distinction to many prevalent transitional bilingual education programs in which no attempt is made to nurture or sustain the mother tongue for language minority youngsters; rather, the child's mother tongue is used only initially and briefly, if at all, without regard to the development of literacy skills or subject-matter competence through the language. Such programs have been referred to by Lambert and others as 'subtractive' programs. A powerful example of the benefits of such additive programs has been provided by Swain (in press), based upon her careful review of cumulative data from Canadian immersion programs.

Exemplary bilingual immersion programs. Under the federally funded Center for Language Education and Research (CLEAR), Lindholm (1987) compiled a list of extant preschool through secondary school bilingual immersion programs. At the present time, with additions which have occurred during the past two and one-half years, there are more than 100 such programs in California, Florida, Illinois, Massachusetts, Michigan, New York, Virginia, and Washington, D.C. The most prevalent languages used are English and Spanish, although there are programs involving English and other languages such as Arabic and Greek as well. Lindholm discussed the rationale for bilingual immersion education and presented a theoretically motivated operational definition of such programs. She described existing programs in some detail and delineated criteria which she believed to be essential for successful bilingual immersion programs:

▪Dual language input should be provided through communicatively sensitive language instruction and subject-matter presentation (this requires careful and dynamic collaboration between all of the teachers, resource specialists, and administrators concerned with the child's educational development).

▪There should be a focus on the regular academic curriculum as well as on language development (that is, care must be taken to insure that the regular curricular objectives for mathematics, science, social studies, etc. are covered).

▪There should be the fullest possible integration of language arts within the total content curriculum.

▪There should be ample opportunity and demand for language output (that is, the child should be required to utilize the language productively as well as receptively) and

▪The instructional treatment should be provided for at least four to six years (note the difference from the typical 'early exit' transitional bilingual education program which usually provides only one or two years of bilingual treatment).

These criteria are fully compatible with those described by Snow, Met, and Genesee (1989), Short, Crandall, and Christian (1989), Crandall and Tucker (in press), as well as with the earlier theoretical construct of Mohan (1986).

In an earlier paper presented at GURT 1989 (Tucker and Crandall 1989), I described briefly two exemplary bilingual immersion programs—one in Arlington, Virginia, and the other in Santa Monica, California—which were chosen because they were implemented under quite different social and ethnolinguistic circumstances in two widely separated parts of the country, and because each had been and continues to be the subject of careful research attention. The results of the various available evaluations can be summarized as follows. Bilingual immersion education proved to be a powerful vehicle to promote the development of bilingual language competence in these early elementary school-aged youngsters. The children mastered receptive and productive language skills in their two languages and mastered content material at a level appropriate to their grade and peer-group controls as well. They developed positive attitudes toward the program, the target language, and its speakers. This innovation represents a 'special case' of the fullest possible integration of language and content instruction. Apparently, its success rests on the teachers' ability to foster the development of solid building blocks in both languages which can lead to the development of social as well as academic language skills, or what others such as Snow (1984) have called the development of contextualized and decontextualized language abilities.

Critical attributes appear to include a sensitivity by teachers to the language needs and the inherent abilities of the children; the fact that material which is inherently interesting and appealing for children (such as science, mathematics, and social studies) can be a conceptual peg upon which to build the development of language and higher order thinking skills; and that students who work collaboratively across language boundaries—in these examples Mexican-American or Central American youngsters and Anglo youngsters—can serve to reinforce, extend, and solidify their respective language skills. Thus, we noted that teachers working within an ambiance conducive to the promotion of 'additive' bilingualism can utilize the natural resources which both groups of students bring naturally to the learning environment. These abilities can be nurtured and extended by careful planning and by creative and sensitive teaching; but the children themselves play a key role in fostering and facilitating this cross-language development.

In conclusion, it appears that despite the generally poor performance of language minority youngsters who are mainstreamed or submerged in typical American classrooms, and despite the poor second or foreign language proficiency attained by most language majority youngsters, there exists an educational alternative—bilingual immersion or developmental bilingual programs—which can facilitate the development of bilingual competence and subject-matter mastery for such youngsters. What, then, might we expect to be the correlates or consequences for children who participate in such an innovative educational program leading to additive bilingualism?

Correlates of bilinguality. This paper began with a brief consideration of the changing demography of enrollment patterns in American public education as well as with several summary statements concerning the generally poor academic performance by language minority youngsters coupled with the poor level of foreign language competence typically achieved by language majority youngsters. I then described a slightly different type of program known as bilingual immersion which is gaining in popularity in the United States. This approach takes as its explicit goal the development of bilingual language proficiency and content subject mastery on the part of all participating youngsters. To date, the majority of such programs have been implemented at the elementary school level, and the research which has been conducted—where it is longitudinal in nature—has followed children through the first several years of their elementary schooling. Although it has not yet been possible to track children throughout their entire scholastic career, on the basis of the earlier immersion literature (see, for example, Lambert and

Tucker 1972; Genesee 1987, Swain 1984, Swain in press), it seems safe to conclude that the gains observed during the first several years of bilingual immersion will continue and persist throughout elementary and, indeed, secondary schooling.

Bilingualism and cognitive development. In addition to the abundant literature reviewed by Hakuta (1986) and by Hakuta and Suben (1985), there are a number of other relevant recent studies which offer strong support for the existence of a positive relationship between bilingualism and cognitive development. Thus, for example, Diaz (1985) and Hakuta (1987) working with Puerto Rican, English, and Spanish bilingual youngsters, found that the degree of bilingualism is positively related to cognitive abilities. That is, the more balanced the bilinguality of the children, the more cognitively flexible and creative they were. Diaz further noted that the degree of bilingualism appeared to be a causal factor affecting children's cognitive abilities. That is, youngsters with a high degree of bilingual proficiency exhibited enhanced flexibility, creativity, and divergent problem-solving abilities compared to their monolingual counterparts. This interpretation is fully consistent with research results reported by Lambert and Tucker (1972) and that summarized by Swain (1984), in which it was noted that otherwise-English monolingual children who became bilingual by virtue of their participation in French immersion programs developed greater cognitive flexibility, creativity, and divergent thinking skills than their carefully matched, monolingually educated control counterparts who participated in traditional English medium instruction programs. And indeed, these results are fully consistent with the findings of researchers in Israel, Singapore, and Switzerland as well.

Likewise, Secada (1989), in his examination of the degree of bilingualism and performance on problem-solving tasks, noted a positive relationship between language proficiency and problem solving and found that cognitive benefits appeared in bilingual students' study of academic subjects. The accrued benefits were dependent upon the extent to which students had developed decontextualized or academic language proficiency—the extent, I argue, to which they had developed 'additive' bilingualism. In addition, Cleghorn, Merritt, and Abagi (1989) found in a very different (African) setting, that the phenomenon of bilingual language development had definite (positive) cognitive implications for youngsters, particularly since the process of language shift and mixed language utilization 'caused' the students whom they studied to focus on and better clarify lesson material, which in turn seemed to enhance their development of cognitive language proficiency, divergent thinking abilities, and creativity in general. Most recently, Bamford and Mizokawa (1989) found a significant increase over time on nonverbal measures of divergent thinking for youngsters participating in immersion programs.

Thus, there seems to exist a variety of research evidence from quite disparate settings which cumulatively suggests that youngsters who have been 'caused' to become bilingual and who concomitantly develop a high degree of cognitive academic language proficiency or of decontextualized language abilities in both of their languages will also develop a more diversified and flexible set of problem-solving strategies or of cognitive abilities than their monolingual peers.

Bilingualism and social development. Additionally, there are a number of studies which suggest that bilingualism may have positive or facilitating effects on social development. For example, Bamford and Mizokawa (1989) report that incipient bilingual children develop a more diversified and positive cross-cultural attitudinal inventory than their monolingual counterparts. This research is consistent with earlier work by Lambert and Tucker (1972), and by Genesee (1987), where children who have been 'caused' to become bilingual have developed generally more positive, charitable, and open views toward members of other ethnolinguistic groups than their monolingual counterparts. It should be pointed out, in all fairness, that the social psychological changes that have been reported in the literature may be more transient—at least, based upon the results of the so-called immersion studies—than many would hope to be the case. The results are certainly consistent with results reported by Gardner (1983), who noted that positive attitudes toward the second language community may be an outcome or by-product of the second language learning process and that therefore one might expect those who become more proficient in the second language to develop more positive and charitable views toward diverse others. In the case of the earlier immersion programs, the lack of available continuing role models which leads to sharply reduced contact between members of the groups may come over time to result in a diminution of the positive attitudes and affect toward diverse other ethnolinguistic groups. However, one would certainly expect that long-term participation in bilingual immersion programs would provide the most supportive ambiance for the development of positive attitudes toward members of the contact ethnolinguistic groups and that the enhanced continuing contact would promote over time tolerance and acceptance for a culturally diverse society.

Conclusion. I have tried to argue here that there exist, for both language minority and language majority youngsters, innovative educational programs known as bilingual immersion or developmental bilingual programs which can result in the development of 'additive' bilingual proficiency and academic content mastery. I argue further that extant research results suggest that participating youngsters who continue in such programs for a substantial period of time (cf. Collier 1989) will develop cognitive and possibly social advantages when compared with their monolingually educated counterparts. The net result should be a culturally rich, competent, and socially sensitive society, rather than a divisive and fragmented society as predicted by those who advocate 'English only'. According to the present optimistic view, the encouragement of personal additive bilingualism through participation in innovative educational programs should be accorded a high social priority.

References

Bamford, K.W., and D.T. Mizokawa. 1989. Cognitive and attitudinal outcomes of an additive bilingual program. Paper presented at American Educational Research Association meeting, San Francisco.

Barik, H.C., and M. Swain. 1976. A longitudinal study of bilingual and cognitive development. International Journal of Psychology 11:251-63.

Ben-Zeev, S. 1977. The effect of bilingualism in children from Spanish-English low economic neighborhoods on cognitive development and cognitive strategy. Working Papers on Bilingualism 14:83-122.

Cardenas, J.A., M. Robledo, and D. Waggoner. 1988. The undereducation of American youth. San Antonio: Intercultural Development Research Association.

Cleghorn, A., M.W. Merritt, and J.D. Abagi. 1989. Language policy and science instruction in Kenyan primary schools. Comparative Education Review 33:21-39.

Collier, V.P. 1989. How long? A synthesis of research on academic achievement in a second language. TESOL Quarterly 23.3:509-31.

Crandall, J.A., and G.R. Tucker. (In press.) Content-based language instruction in second and foreign languages. In: Proceedings of the RELC Seminar on Language Teaching Methodologies for the Nineties. Singapore: Regional Language Center.

Crawford, J. 1989. Bilingual education: History, politics, theory and practice. Trenton, N.J.: Crane.

Diaz, R.M. 1985. Bilingual cognitive development: Addressing three gaps in current research. Child Development 56:1376-88.

Gardner, R.C. 1983. Learning another language: A true social psychological experiment. Journal of Language and Social Psychology 2:219-39.

Genesee, F. 1987. Learning through two languages: Studies of immersion and bilingual education. Cambridge, Mass.: Newbury House.

Hakuta, K. 1986. Mirror of language: The debate on bilingualism. New York: Basic Books.

Hakuta, K. 1987. Degree of bilingualism and cognitive ability in mainland Puerto Rican children. Child Development 58:1372-88.

Hakuta, K., and J. Suben. 1985. Bilingualism and cognitive development. In: R.B. Kaplan, ed. Annual Review of Applied Linguistics 6:35-45.

Ianco-Worrall, A.D. 1972. Bilingualism and cognitive development. Child Development 43:1390-1400.

Johnston, W.B. 1987. Workforce 2000: Work and workers for the 21st century. Indianapolis, Ind.: Hudson Institute.

Lambert, W.E. 1980. The two faces of bilingual education. NCBE Forum 3.

Lambert, W.E., and G.R. Tucker. 1972. The bilingual education of children. Rowley, Mass.: Newbury House.

Larsen-Freeman, D. 1986. Techniques and principles in language teaching. New York: Oxford University Press.

Lindholm, K.J. 1987. Directory of bilingual immersion programs: Two-way bilingual education for language minority and majority students. Educational Report 8. Los Angeles: University of California, Center for Language Education and Research.

Macnamara, J. 1966. Bilingualism and primary education. Edinburgh: University of Edinburgh Press.

Mohan, B.A. 1986. Language and content. Reading, Mass.: Addison-Wesley.

Nunberg, G. 1989. Linguists and the official language movement. Language 65:579-87.

Oxford, R., and N.C. Rhodes. 1988. Foreign language in elementary and secondary schools: Results of a national survey. Foreign Language Annals 21.

Peal, E., and W.E. Lambert 1962. The relation of bilingualism to intelligence. Psychological Monographs 76 (27, whole 546).

Rendon, L.I. 1983. Mathematics education for Hispanic students in the Border College Consortium. Report on the Math Intervention Project. Laredo, Texas: The Border College Consortium.

Richards, J.C., and T.S. Rodgers. 1986. Approaches and methods in language teaching: A description and analysis. Cambridge: Cambridge University Press.

Short, D.J., J. Crandall, and D. Christian. 1989. How to integrate language and content instruction: A training manual. Educational Report 15. Los Angeles: University of California, Center for Language Education and Research.

Secada, W.G. 1989. The relationship between degree of bilingualism and arithmetic problem-solving performance in first-grade Hispanic children. Paper presented at American Educational Research Association meeting, San Francisco.

Snow, C.E. 1984. Beyond conversation: Second language learners' acquisition of description and explanation. Paper presented at Delaware Symposium on Language Studies.

Snow, M.A., M. Met, and F. Genesee. 1989. A conceptual framework for the integration of language and content in second/foreign language instruction. TESOL Quarterly 23:201-17.

Swain, M. 1984. A review of immersion education in Canada: Research and evaluation studies. In: P. Allen and M. Swain, eds. Language issues and education policies. Oxford: Pergamon.

Swain, M. (In press.) Additive bilingualism and French immersion education: The roles of language proficiency and literacy. In: A. Reynolds, ed. Proceedings of the McGill Conference on Bilingualism: A tribute to Wallace E. Lambert. Hillsdale, N.J.: Lawrence Erlbaum.

Tucker, G.R. 1986. Developing a language-competent American society. In: D. Tannen and J.E. Alatis, eds. Georgetown University Round Table on Languages and Linguistics 1985. Washington, D.C.: Georgetown University Press.

Tucker, G.R. (In press.) Developing a language competent American society: The role of language planning. In: A. Reynolds, ed. Proceedings of the McGill Conference on Bilingualism: A Tribute to Wallace E. Lambert. Hillsdale, N.J.: Lawrence Erlbaum.

Tucker, G.R., and J.A. Crandall. 1989. The integration of language and content instruction for language minority and language majority students. In: J.E. Alatis, ed. Georgetown University Round Table on Languages and Linguistics 1989. Washington, D.C.: Georgetown University Press. 39-50.

Willig, A.C. 1985. A meta-analysis of selected studies on the effectiveness of bilingual education. Review of Educational Research 55:269-317.

A citation analysis of the diffusion of linguistic and language acquisition theory and research to the English language teaching community

Stephen J. Gaies
University of Northern Iowa

The basic purpose of the study reported here was to contribute to what is currently an extremely small data base on the bibliometric characteristics of the professional literature in English Language Teaching (ELT). For reasons that have been widely discussed and that need no repetition in this report, ELT has developed during the past 20 years to the point that the conceptual, ideological, and empirical base which current instructional practices claim to reflect is large enough and diverse enough to lend itself to the types of analyses that would have been less appropriate, say, 15 or 20 years ago.

Beyond this basic and relatively modest goal, the study attempts to promote the view that the findings of bibliometric analyses of the ELT literature can be usefully viewed from a diffusionist perspective: in other words, that the professional literature in ELT takes different forms, each of which is capable of creating particular perceptions about the relationship between theory, research, and practice in ELT. Understanding these different perceptions can help us to recognize the process by which innovations are communicated to ELT professionals.

Diffusion research examines "the process by which (1) an innovation (2) is communicated through certain channels (3) over time (4) among the members of a social system" (Rogers 1983:10). An innovation is "an idea, practice or object that is perceived as new by an individual or other unit of adoption" (11). Thus, innovations can be conceptual, methodological, or technological in nature, and "new" is to be understood not in any absolute sense, but from the perspective of the potential adopter.

This is certainly not the first attempt to adopt a diffusionist perspective toward language and language teaching. One of the first attempts of this sort was reported by Cooper (1982), who examined the phenomena of language change and spread from the perspective of the diffusion of linguistic innovations. More recently, White (1988) has discussed curriculum renewal and evaluation as the management of innovation, and Markee (1989) has described language teacher education as a process that at least in part involves the adoption of innovations.

The process by which innovations are adopted has been described by Rogers (1983) as consisting of five stages: awareness, interest, evaluation, trial, and adoption or discontinuance (see also Miles 1964). Much of the now substantial literature on the diffusion of innovations has examined such features as the characteristics of adopters of innovations and the attributes of innovations that make them either likely or unlikely to be adopted.

The study reported here focuses on the initial stage of the diffusion process: the means by which awareness of innovations in ELT is created (which, it must be pointed out, in this study have been operationally defined as explicit references to insights from one or another discipline). The specific focus is the role of two practitioner-oriented professional journals as communication channels for the diffusion of innovations. Thus, the study was not concerned with the question of whether linguistic theory, second language acquisition research, and language teaching are interdependent. It assumed that they are. Nor was it concerned with arguing for or against any position regarding how intimately related these fields can be or should be. Rather, the study examined the degree to which insights from these and other disciplines are disseminated to those members of the English language teaching profession who are primarily—and in many cases exclusively—involved in classroom instruction.

In other words, the basic question that this study has addressed in a very exploratory way is not, What do linguistic theory and second language research have to say to the classroom teacher of English as a second or foreign language?, but rather, To what extent have two practitioner-oriented professional journals disseminated insights from linguistics, second language acquisition research, and other fields that have at one time or another been viewed as a logical basis for the development of a systematic, principled approach to classroom language teaching?

The analytical approach used in the study is citation analysis, which is, in fact, something of a misnomer, at least for the most usual way in which it is conducted. Citation analysis is a family of procedures that is generally understood to be a subfield of information science and of the sociology of science. The *Thesaurus of ERIC Descriptors* (Houston 1987) defines citation analysis as "bibliometric application in which a body of literature is separated and classified through interconnections of bibliographic citations" (34). Citation analysis encompasses a large variety of procedures aimed at a number of different research purposes. Such research is often descriptive in nature, although it may also be evaluative in aim—perhaps most notably, in the assessment of tenure and promotion candidacies in higher education.

As Swales (1986) points out, the most frequent approach has been to conduct highly quantitative studies aimed at one of more of the following purposes: (1) to measure the productivity and influence of particular individuals, groups, institutions, or regions; (2) to assess the influence of particular publications or disciplines (for examples of studies of the language teaching literature aimed at this purpose, see Bernhardt and Hammadou 1987; McGlone, McClendon, and Olson 1985; Swales 1986); or (3) to establish the boundaries of a cognitive field. Studies employing a primarily quantitative approach often make use of standard bibliometric resources such as the *Social Science Citation Index.*

It is understandable that in a field as relatively new as TESOL, content and citation analysis, along with other forms of bibliometric examination of the literature of the discipline, are only now emerging. With relatively few exceptions—the *ELT Journal*, which has been published since 1947, and *Language Learning*, which has been published since 1951—the major professional journals in TESOL and the related field of applied linguistics have existed for 25 years or fewer. Since quantitative analyses of characteristics of a discourse community are most meaningful when they can identify traditions and trends, recent interest in bibliometric analysis of the TESOL literature is timely now to a degree that it would not have been 10 or 20 years ago.[1]

In the last five years, several studies have investigated a number of quantifiable features of the professional literature in TESOL. One of the most recent (McKay and Wong 1988) examined the titles of all full-length articles published between 1974 and 1987 in the *TESOL Quarterly*, the *Modern Language Journal*, and *Foreign Language Annals* in order to assign articles to one of eight main content categories. Although the methodology of this study involves relatively superficial analysis of the content of the professional literature, it is an accepted form of bibliometric analysis; thus, the study is important in reflecting an awareness of the value of content analysis of the second/foreign language education literature.

Other studies, using alternative methods of content analysis, have been recently completed. Brown (1986), for example, investigated the use and misuse of procedures in research design and data analysis through analysis of selected examples from the recent literature. In contrast, Henning (1986) examined related issues through more systematic analysis of all articles published between 1970 and 1985 in the *TESOL Quarterly* and *Language Learning.* Henning was particularly interested in providing quantitative

---

[1]It is interesting to note in this regard that the very first discussion of a professional journal for teachers of English to speakers of other languages is Matthey's (1967) overview of the *ELT Journal* (at that time the *English Language Teaching Journal*), which began publication in the 1940s. In order to to gain a better perspective on the relative newness of TESOL, some readers might note that in the area of foreign language education, the *Modern Language Journal* began publication in 1917.

evidence of (among other things) the relative proportions of descriptive and experimental research published, the frequency with which published reports of research include a statement of a formal hypothesis, and the frequency of use of multivariate statistical techniques. However, except for Swales's (1988) examination of the *TESOL Quarterly*, no systematic and comprehensive citation analysis of the TESOL literature has been undertaken.

The two journals that were the focus of the study are arguably the two most important professional journals in ELT that are aimed at a practitioner-oriented audience. The *ELT Journal* (*ELTJ*), which until several years ago went by the title of *English Language Teaching* (*Journal*), is published by Oxford University Press with the cooperation of the British Council. Now in its 45th year of publication, the journal has a worldwide circulation, and its editorial policy explicitly welcomes contributions "from teachers who are not native speakers of English." The *ELTJ* is concerned with the fundamental practical factors that have influenced and continue to influence the evolution of the profession, as well as with the theoretical issues that are relevant to it. It seeks to bridge the gap between the everyday concerns of teachers in their classrooms and the various disciplines such as psychology, sociology, and linguistics that may offer significant insights.

The *English Teaching Forum* (hereafter the *Forum*) is produced by the United States Information Agency for teachers of English outside the United States and distributed abroad by U.S. embassies. The *Forum* has the largest worldwide circulation of any professional publication in the area of English for speakers of other languages; its mission, as stated in a recent directory of journals in TESOL, is to present "articles by and for a worldwide readership on techniques and methodology for the classroom teacher trainer as well as . . . background theory, linguistic analysis and philosophical discussion about the profession" (Wardell 1988:37); in certain respects, its function is similar to that of *Français dans le monde* (for a discussion of the latter, see Moirand 1988). With a worldwide distribution of over 120,000, the *Forum* is for many classroom teachers the single professional resource that is readily accessible.

Method. The bibliometric analysis was based on all previously unpublished main articles published in the *ELTJ* and the *Forum* in 1969, 1979, 1989.

The decision to restrict the corpus to previously unpublished articles (i.e. not including those that were reprinted, with or without changes) led to the exclusion of the 1969 volume of the *Forum* from the analysis, since only two main articles in that year's issues were original contributions to the English language teaching literature.

The corpus of 188 articles was investigated for the following features: (1) mean number of references per article; (2) types of references cited (books, edited volumes, journal articles, conference presentations, etc.); (3) field, discipline, or subject of references to book-length works, edited volumes (or contributions to such volumes), and articles in professional journals and other periodicals.

These procedures might appear to involve an essentially straightforward, mechanical analysis. As it turned out, however, one of the most striking indications of how each of these two journals has changed is the much greater editorial consistency regarding citation practices and the listing of references. It became necessary to make a number of subjective decisions about whether a work mentioned in an article merited inclusion as a reference or whether the listing of items in a "bibliography" should be treated as if they were references integral to the article itself. The rule of thumb used was the following: If, by the standards of present-day publication manuals (for example, the *Publication Manual of the American Psychological Association* (1983)), mention of a work would take the form of a reference citation and if sufficient information about the work was given in the article to allow, at least in principle, for the work to be accessed, the work was counted as a reference.

Results. In a presentation of this length, it is not possible to review all of the findings of the analysis of the corpus. I will mention only the most prominent ones:

(1) As shown in Table 1, for both the *ELTJ* and the *Forum*, the mean number of references per main article increased during each ten-year interval: for the *ELTJ*, from 2.08 in 1969 to 2.98 in 1979 to 8.09 in 1989; for the *Forum*, from 5.30 in 1979 to 10.33 in 1989. These figures alone offer one of the most significant points of comparison between these practitioner-oriented journals and the more academically and research-oriented journals with which most of us are more familiar: By way of comparison, the main articles in the 1986 issues of the *TESOL Quarterly* averaged 34 references, which was twice the average number of references of main articles in the *Quarterly* in 1980. Even these figures, however, pale by comparison with the mean number of citations for the *Modern Language Journal*, whose main articles in the 1989 volume averaged 48.66 references.

(2) Unreferenced main articles appear to be a vanishing species in both the *ELTJ* and the *Forum*. Although such articles made up almost 50% of the articles published in the 1969 issues of the *ELTJ* and more than 25% of the articles published in the two journals in 1979, they are a very small percentage of the articles published in the two journals in 1989. The persistence of unreferenced articles at all is due in part to specific editorial practices of the journals: for example, in the case of the *ELTJ*, publication of interviews between the editorial staff and a key figure in ELT or applied linguistics.

Table 1. Main articles, references, unreferenced articles, and journal-article references in the *ELTJ* (1969, 1979, 1989) and the *FORUM* (1979, 1989).

	YEAR	MAIN ARTICLES	TOTAL REFERENCES	MEAN	UNREFERENCED ARTICLES (%)	JOURNAL-ARTICLE REFERENCES (%)
ELTJ	1969	49	102	2.08	23 (46.9)	20 (19.6)
ELTJ	1979	63	188	2.98	18 (28.6)	63 (33.5)
FORUM	1979	20	106	5.30	4 (20.0)	39 (36.8)
ELTJ	1989	32	259	8.09	4 (12.5)	71 (27.4)
FORUM	1989	24	248	10.33	2 (8.3)	96 (38.7)
Totals		188	903			289

Table 2. Journals referenced in the *ELTJ* (1969, 1979, 1989) and the *FORUM* (1979, 1989).

	ELTJ 1969	*ELTJ* 1979	*FORUM* 1979	*ELTJ* 1989	*FORUM* 1989
ELTJ	11	24	6	16	12
FORUM	0	5	6	4	14
Language Learning	1	5	5	3	11
TESOL Quarterly	0	3	8	9	11
Foreign language education (e.g. *MLJ, CMLR, FLA*)	2	0	4	4	6
Applied linguistics (e.g. *IRAL, Appl. Ling.*)	1	6	1	9	7
L1 education (e.g. *RRQ, Eng. Jnl.*)	0	2	0	6	5
English language teaching (e.g. *MET, RELC Jnl.*)	0	0	4	7	7
Linguistics (e.g. *Lingua, Jnl. of Ling.*)	1	7	2	5	0
Education/ psychology (e.g. *Rev. of Ed. Res.*)	3	6	1	4	16
Sociology/ sociolinguistics (e.g. *Lang. in Society*)	0	0	0	3	3
Miscellaneous	1	5	2	1	4
Totals	20	63	39	71	96

Table 3. References to nonperiodical literature by type and subject area in the *ELTJ* (1969, 1979, 1989) and the *FORUM* (1979, 1989).

Reference type/ subject	*ELTJ* 1969	*ELTJ* 1979	*FORUM* 1979	*ELTJ* 1989	*FORUM* 1989
Book-length					
SL/FL Theory/Res./Meth.	14	20	24	35	41
ESL/EFL Texts/Reference	6	10	8	17	13
ESL/EFL Teaching Aids	4	0	0	0	0
L1/Language Arts/Reading	2	8	0	0	5
Linguistic Theory/Desc.	9	11	7	6	5
English Linguistics	3	11	5	6	2
Dictionaries/Grammar Handbooks	13	8	0	2	0
Lit./Dramatic Criticism	1	1	2	1	7
Literary Works	6	0	1	4	1
Lang. Acq./Bilingualism	2	2	0	0	9
Lang. Use/Sociolinguistics	3	4	0	7	1
Educ./Ed. Psych/Res./Meth.	1	9	1	23	17
Psychology/Counseling	0	0	0	9	0
General	1	5	4	5	2
Edited volumes (whole and partial)					
SL/FL Theory/Res./Meth.	3	3	5	21	15
Linguistics	0	1	1	12	3
Reading/Oral Communication	0	1	1	1	1
Education/Ed. Psych	0	0	0	1	0
Lit. Crit./Women's Studies	0	0	0	5	0
Proceedings (whole and partial)					
Ling./Appl. Ling.	1	5	1	10	6
Other	1	0	0	7	2
Conference presentations	3	2	0	5	9
Working/occ. papers/monographs	0	9	4	6	0
Other					
Govt. Reports	3	0	0	0	0
Newspaper Articles	1	3	0	0	0
Unpublished Theses/Diss.	0	5	1	0	4
Research Reports	2	4	1	1	0
Unpublished Manuscripts	1	0	1	2	5
Other (Booklets/Software/Films)	1	0	0	1	3
Totals	102	188	106	259	248

(3) References are overwhelmingly to book-length works and to articles in professional journals and periodicals. These two types account for 83%, 81%,and 72% of the references in the *ELTJ* in 1969, 1979, and 1989, respectively; and for 86% and 80% of the references in the *Forum* in 1979 and 1989, respectively. Reference to edited volumes and to published proceedings of professional meetings, which appear to have proliferated in recent years, is evident in the 1989 volumes of the two journals: in the 1989 issues of the *ELTJ*, 57 of the 259 references (22%) are to edited volumes or conference proceedings (either the whole work or to part of such a work); in the 1989 issues of the *Forum*, there are 27 such references (11%). All other types of references—to unpublished conference presentations, working and occasional papers, monographs, theses and dissertations, unpublished manuscripts, tests, research reports, educational software, newspaper articles, and so on—constitute a small percentage of the total references in each of the five sets of annual issues: 12%, 13%, and 6% of the references in the *ELTJ* in 1969, 1979, and 1989, respectively; and 7% and 9% of the references in the 1979 and 1989 issues of the *Forum*, respectively.

(4) References to journals and other professional periodicals offer perhaps the most interesting insight into the access provided by the *ELTJ* and the *Forum* to our past and current professional knowledge base. Table 2 presents data on references to this type of reference. As can be seen, for each set of annual issues, four journals—the *ELTJ* and the *Forum*, together with the *TESOL Quarterly* and *Language Learning*—make up the lion's share (53.3%) of references to journals and periodicals. Much of this is due to the high self-citation rate of the two journals—a tendency noted by Swales (1988) in connection with the *TESOL Quarterly*. Following Swales, I have grouped references to other journals into general categories. Although it would be dangerous to make too much of such a small set of data, it should be pointed out that with only two exceptions—six references to articles in *IRAL* in the 1979 issues of the *ELTJ*, of which five appear in one article; and five references to articles in *Applied Linguistics* in the 1989 issues of the *ELTJ*, of which two appear in one article and the other three in another—no journal other than the "big four" has more than four references in all the issues combined in any year of either the *ELTJ* or the *Forum*. Not counting the two exceptions already noted, for journals other than the *ELTJ*, the *Forum*, the *TQ*, and *LL*, out of 96 cases, a given journal was the source, in any single year, of only a single reference 76 times, of only 2 references 14 times, of 3 references only 4 times, and of 4 references only twice.

(5) Of greatest relevance to the theme of this year's Georgetown University Round Table on Languages and Linguistics is the question of the disciplines and fields represented by references cited in these two journals. Table 3 presents the results of an analysis by primary topic of references to book-length works, to part or all of an edited volume, or to a volume of

conference proceedings. It should be emphasized that the classification of references by primary focus was in many cases difficult and that the figures should be viewed cautiously; nevertheless, this part of the analysis tends to confirm two basic assumptions about the evolution of the conceptual and empirical base of English language teaching: (1) Linguistic theory and description continue to be viewed as sources of insight into language teaching, although to a proportionally lesser degree than a decade or two decades ago; and (2) the influence of first language education theory and research and the perceived need to view second and foreign language instruction in the broader context of general educational goals and methods are reflected to some degree in the 1989 data.

Discussion and conclusions. In his analysis of the *TESOL Quarterly*, Swales (1988) makes a useful distinction between archaeological and historical analysis of a professional literature. The former, claims Swales, examines, by stratified or some other form of sampling, the textual record. Such analysis may be either synchronic or diachronic, but in either case, the approach enables us, in Swales's words, to examine "the pictures on the wall of the cave but has nothing to say as to why or how those artifacts come to be there" (152). A truly historical account will aim not only at description but at explanation as well. To put together a historical narrative—to describe not only what is in the professional literature but why it is there; to relate features of the textual record to particular causes; to attribute key concepts, ideas, and trends to particular individuals or institutions—requires much more than the kind of bibliometric analysis reported here. This limitation notwithstanding, bibliometric analysis of the kind used in this study is a useful if not sufficient approach to identifying characteristics of the professional literature in ELT. It is axiomatic to say that the English language teaching profession is most notable for its diversity. But to understand fully the diversity of this disciplinary culture—indeed, to determine whether the field of ELT comprises different disciplinary cultures—the development of a bibliometric data base is a logical initial step, following which more fine-grained analyses, including qualitative citation analysis (see, for example, Frost 1979, Swales 1986), can indicate more precisely the manner by which innovations are diffused through the communication channels represented by professional journals in TESOL.

References

Bernhardt, E., and J. Hammadou. 1987. A decade of research in foreign language teacher education. Modern Language Journal 71:289-99.

Brown, J.D. 1986. The use of statistics in research. Paper presented at the 20th Annual TESOL Convention, Anaheim, California, March.

Cooper, R.L. 1982. A framework for the study of language spread. In: R.L. Cooper, ed. Language spread: Studies in diffusion and social change. 5-36. Bloomington: Indiana University Press.

Frost, C.O. 1979. The use of citations in literary research: A preliminary classification of citation functions. Library Quarterly 49:399-414.

Henning, G. 1986. Quantitative methods in language acquisition rsearch. TESOL Quarterly 20:701-08.

Houston, J.E., ed. 1987. Thesaurus of ERIC descriptors. 11th ed. Phoenix: Oryx Press.

Markee, N. 1989. The use of student journals as evaluative tools for the management of language education-related innovation. Unpublished manuscript.

Matthey, F. 1967. La revue 'English Language Teaching': Vingt ans au service des maîtres d'anglais. [English Language Teaching: 20 years of service to English teachers]. Bulletin CILA 2:68-70.

McGlone, E.L., C.C. McClendon, and N. Olson. 1985. The major research journals in foreign languages: A survey of heads of the doctoral degree granting departments. Modern Language Journal 69:1-7.

McKay, S.L., and S.-L.C. Wong. 1988. Language teaching in nativist times: A need for sociopolitical awareness. Modern Language Journal 72:379-88.

Miles, M.B., ed. 1964. Innovation in education. New York: Teachers College Press.

Moirand, S. 1988. Une histoire de discours [The history of a discourse]. Paris: Hachette.

Rip, A., and J.P. Courtial. 1984. Co-word maps of biotechnology: An example of cognitive scientometrics. Scientometrics 6:381-400.

Rogers, E.M. 1983. Diffusion of innovations. 3d ed. New York: Macmillan.

Swales, J. 1986. Citation analysis and discourse analysis. Applied Linguistics 7:39-56.

Swales, J. 1988. 20 years of the TESOL Quarterly. TESOL Quarterly 22:151-63.

Wardell, D. 1988. Journals of interest to JALT members. The Language Teacher 12.3:36-41.

White, R.V. 1988. The ELT curriculum: Design, innovation and management. Oxford: Basil Blackwell.

Theory, practice, and research: Strange or blissful bedfellows?

Suzanne Flynn*
Massachusetts Institute of Technology

0 Introduction. Development of effective language pedagogy is a complex task. It necessitates an understanding and an integration of ideas and findings that emerge from a number of distinct, but overlapping domains of study. Two such fields are theoretical linguistics and the psycholinguistic research it has generated, principally that in both first (L1) and second language (L2)[1] acquisition. While such an integrative approach is not new in language teaching, past attempts aimed at incorporating findings from other domains have often proved unsatisfactory. In large part, this has been due to the fact that development in the field of linguistics and related research did not easily allow for meaningful extensions to language pedagogy. As a consequence, little dialogue between language pedagogues, linguists and language acquisition researchers has been fostered (see related discussion in Newmeyer 1983; Newmeyer and Weinberger 1988). All arenas have suffered needlessly: language pedagogy does not benefit from the insights and findings isolated in theory and research, and linguistic theory and acquisition research are never confronted by the insights gained from an understanding of the language learning process culled from classroom contexts.

Within recent years, however, significant developments have been achieved in theoretical linguistics and in the language acquisition research that derives from such work. One consequence of such development is that we are now in the position to begin to make new meaningful conjectures about possible connections among these three domains.

Thus, the principal goal of this paper is to argue that though historically, theory, research, and practice were often 'strange bedfellows', they must now

* The author wishes to thank Jack Carroll, Jim Gair, Ralph Ginsberg, and Claire Kramsch for discussions concerning various aspects of the issues addressed in this paper. Many of the ideas presented here are developed in more detail in Flynn, in press.

[1] In this paper, the term second language (L2) acquisition is used to refer to foreign language learning as well. In addition, this paper focuses primarily on the adult L2 learner.

all lie peacefully together for their own survival and mutual growth (see also Sharwood-Smith 1981; Dulay, Burt, and Krashen 1982; Klein 1986; Rutherford 1987; Cook 1988, among others, for attempts to relate these domains).

To achieve this goal, I will briefly outline several ways in which current linguistic theory and its associated acquisition research might have consequences for language pedagogy. I will also sketch out ways in which the insights and findings from these areas could be translated into or extended to applications in language learning environments. At the same time, I will highlight ways in which current methodologies might in fact inform and redirect current linguistic and psycholinguistic research.

Central to the discussion throughout this paper are two basic assumptions: (1) in order to understand what must be acquired by the L2 learner as well as understand what the learner 'knows', we need to make reference to a linguistic model of grammatical competence (see related discussion in Lust, Chien, and Flynn 1987; see also McLaughlin 1987); and (2) development of meaningful pedagogical practices demands making reference to and utilizing both this linguistic model and its derived L2 acquisition research.

I will begin this discussion with a brief historical overview.

1 Linguistic theory and L2 acquisition research

1.1 Traditional approaches. As is well known, the integration of linguistic theory and L2 acquisition is not new (for an extended discussion of these issues, see Flynn 1988, 1987). Two of the best developed approaches to the study of L2 acquisition—Contrastive Analysis (CA) (Fries 1945, Lado 1957) and Creative Construction (CC) (Dulay and Burt 1974)—were each based upon a version of an available theory of language. A traditional CA model, in which L2 acquisition is thought to consist of the learning of a fixed set of habits, was based upon a structuralist approach to language. A CC model of L2 learning, in which L2 acquisition is thought to be a rule-governed process, was based upon a version of a generative theory of language. Though CA and CC ultimately failed to provide a principled framework within which a full account of the L2 learning process could be developed, each did succeed in capturing the sense of one important component of the L2 acquisition process --in the case of CA, the role of the L1 experience and in the case of CC, the role of principles of acquisition independent of the L1 experience.

1.2 Recent developments. Building upon the successes and failures of these two earlier approaches, one of the most promising recent developments in pursuit of a full, principled characterization of the adult L2 acquisition process has been work articulated within a generative theory of Universal Grammar (UG) (see representative work in Flynn and O'Neil 1988). This work has capitalized on two principal developments in the theory of UG: the shift away from language as a system of rules, to a view of it as a function of fundamental principles and parameters. The principles isolated are universally shared by all languages; they interact with a restricted set of parameters which, once set, has rich deductive consequences for a particular grammar. Parameters within the theory also account for the variation observed among natural languages (Chomsky 1981, 1986).

These increasingly relevant developments in linguistic theory have led to a great deal of revealing and suggestive research which has greatly enhanced our understanding of both the L1 and L2 acquisition processes. More specifically, preliminary findings from the L2 acquisition research generated within this framework have allowed us to begin to reconcile the two seemingly disparate bodies of data suggested by both CA and CC approaches --the role of universal principles common to all and the role of the L1 experience via a theory of parameters (Flynn 1987).

In turn, these developments have led us to a point where this L2 acquisition research is beginning to feed back to and inform linguistic theory in much the same manner that L1 acquisition research has been used to constrain a theory of UG (see Lust 1986, 1987, Roeper and Williams 1987). For an example of this, see recent discussions in Chomsky (1988a, 1988b) with respect to how these data have already challenged traditional linguistic formulations of the steady state in the adult.

It is clear that important developments both historically and currently have been made possible through such an integration., even though it is still imperfect.

1.3 Language pedagogy. In the midst of all this development, one is quite naturally led to ask: where does language pedagogy fit? Unfortunately, whether we look at the past or the present, evidence for a dichotomy between language pedagogy and linguistic theory/L2 acquisition research is widespread. Many language pedagogues have maintained the belief that linguistic theory and language research have little or no relevance for their enterprise. Linguistic theory and L2 research are treated as if they were distinct entities that only coincidentally and trivially overlap with language teaching concerns. To be fair, on the other side of the fence, there are many linguists and researchers who have traditionally shared this same sentiment.

To some degree, this disenfranchisement is a function of prejudice on both sides. However, it's a kind of 'luxury' we can no longer afford if we are truly committed to teaching individuals new languages in the most effective manner possible. At the same time, there is much to be gained from such an integration. The current focus of both theoretical linguistics and language research is geared to understanding the psychological underpinnings of language acquisition and use. To remain isolated from the findings of this research is to ignore important bodies of information that could significantly enhance and inform traditional language practices. Within this context, language pedagogues need to be concerned with linguistics and research and integrate their own work within these larger paradigms. At the same time, linguists and researchers must be attentive to and draw upon insights isolated in language classrooms. Let us consider several ways in which such an integration might prove beneficial.

2 Linguistic theory, L2 research and language practice. While no definitive answers are yet available with respect to either L1 or L2 acquisition research, there are a number of issues raised by language acquisition research as well as by the theory from which it derives, for the design of effective instructional settings. In particular, both types of research allow us to be more precise about what knowledge is available to the learner, how this knowledge is used, and how language learning takes place. In turn, refinement of our insights in these areas has consequences for teacher training, for classroom composition, and for the development of effective groupings and sequencing of curricular materials. Each of these and others are considered in greater detail in the following pages.

2.1 What knowledge is available to the learner? To begin, we know that adult second language learners do not start with 'clean slates'. That is, they bring to the language learning context knowledge not available to the child L1 language learner. At the same time, we know that adult L2 language learners also share with children a certain body of common linguistic knowledge.

More specifically, we know that adults have at least three distinct bodies of knowledge available to them:

(1) General linguistic knowledge about principles and parameters of UG. This is shared with child L1 language learners.

(2) Specific linguistic knowledge of at least one language. This is not shared with child L1 language learners.

(3) All manner of extralinguistic knowledge that follows from mature cognitive development and experience with at least one or more cultures. This knowledge is not shared with children.

While the existence of either a knowledge base derived from the L1 or one derived from general cognition may not be surprising, the role of general properties of UG in the adult L2 learning process may be. The existence of this body of knowledge means that the adult L2 acquisition process, in contrast to many traditional approaches, namely CA, and also in contrast to several more recent ones, e.g. the Fundamental Difference Hypothesis (Bley-Vroman 1989) (for more discussion see Flynn and Lust 1990, Flynn and Carroll, forthcoming), is not restricted by the learner's L1 alone or by unconstrained problem solving strategies. Through their knowledge of UG, L2 learners bring to the language learning context a set of structural sensitivities comparable to those that they bring to the L1 learning situation. That is, evidence suggests that learners are prepared to pick up the same abstract structural properties of the L2 grammar that they did for the L1—for example, the head-direction of a language (see related discussion in Flynn 1987; Martohardjono and Gair 1989).

2.2 How is this knowledge used? We also know that all three bodies of knowledge enter into the adult language learning process. However, they do so in a highly interactive and constrained manner.

The availability of UG knowledge means that learners bring to the language learning task a set of predispositions to certain kinds of operations that can exist in languages. Learners maintain general sensitivities about what are conceivable and possible properties of language, and about what are legitimate and nonlegitimate types of moves that can be made in a language. For example, learners naturally know in some sense that languages are hierarchically organized. They know that certain kinds of 'dominance' relations hold between constituents. To illustrate, in sentence 1, *Mary* and *she* can refer to the same person. In contrast, in sentence 2, *Mary* and *she* cannot refer to the same person.

(1) When *she* went to the store, *Mary* bought a ticket.
(2) *She* went to the store, when *Mary* bought a ticket.

The reason for this difference has to do with differences in the dominance type of relationships that exist between the pronoun, *she*, and the noun, *Mary*. In sentence 1, *she* does not dominate (technically, c-command) *Mary*; that is, *she* is not higher in position than *Mary* in a hierarchical tree structure of this sentence. In sentence 2, however, *she* dominates *Mary*; it is higher in the tree. A general rule of language, roughly paraphrased, states that pronouns cannot dominate their antecedents.

In addition, learners will attempt to apply structure dependent hypotheses to the new target language. We also know that learners will not commit certain kinds of errors that violate boundaries of abstract phrasal units—for example, formulate structure independent hypotheses. To illustrate, we do not find sentences like that in (3) (from Jenkins 1988:110) in the speech of L2 learners (nor in the speech of child L1 learners).

(3) *Is the dog which in the corner is hungry?

Such sentences represent the application of a Structure Independent Rule in which the first verb in the sentence, regardless of its phrasal membership, is fronted to form a question. If learners simply applied rules that were based on such independent notions of order in a linear string, we might expect such an error. Such a question would by simple analogy match that formed from the sentence *The dog is hungry→Is the dog hungry?* The fact that we don't find learners, even untutored ones, making these errors suggest that they naturally apply structure dependent hypotheses to language.

In addition, their L1 language interacts with and at times competes with their general linguistic knowledge (see related discussion in Felix, 1985). When it interacts rather than competes, knowledge of the first language facilitates second language learning. What is important here is that current research allows us to be precise in predicting how and when the L1 mediates the L2 learning process. For example, not all contrasts cause interference and not all similarities enhance the learning process. More specifically, we know that matches in parametric settings between the L1 and the L2 enhance learning and that mismatches cause disruption.

In addition to UG and L1 knowledge, adults also have available to them general cognitive knowledge. This means that the adult learner can access a set of problem solving strategies not available to a child as well as general knowledge about the world. The adult can use this knowledge to gain and maintain control of her linguistic environment in a manner not possible for a child. An adult is able to recognize breakdowns in communication; she can elicit more linguistic input when necessary, and she can isolate exceptions in paradigms or locutions. In addition, the adult is capable of understanding explanations about the language and for certain aspects of language can use these explanations to enhance her own learning. Research allows us to specify exactly where and in what ways such knowledge emerges.

2.3 How does learning take place? Given the nature of the knowledge available to the adult learner, we know that there is a strong deductive component involved in language learning. This means that language learners do not learn the new language by translating word for word from the L1 to the L2. They are capable of looking for higher order conceptual units and will do so quite naturally when given the opportunity by abstracting out from what they hear. Essentially, the construction of the target language is a grammar-driven process rather than a data-driven one.

We also know that learners proceed through a natural sequence guided by innate principles. In addition, in contrast to many theories about language learning, L2 acquisition does not proceed by random induction from surface structure facts alone. While some inductive learning is involved and research needs to isolate more precisely where, this learning is also highly constrained. Of all the possible hypotheses and strategies an adult could use and formulate when learning an L2, given all the knowledge available to the adult, adults simply so not apply nonlinguistic hypotheses to the learning of an L2. In fact, what is so impressive about the L2 acquisition process is not the manner in which L1 and L2 acquisition seem to differ trivially but the significant manner in which the two processes converge.

2.4 Consequences. Knowing what knowledge is available to the learner, how this knowledge is used, and how learning takes place raises a number of important issues in terms of more specific aspects of curricular development.

2.5 Knowing what is available to the L2 learner.

2.5.1 Assumptions about an L2 learner's knowledge. At one level, information about what, for example, is available to the learner means that we can make certain assumptions about the L2 learner's knowledge base. We know that all learners will share knowledge of a certain common linguistic base, namely UG. We also know that divergences that exist among learners will principally derive from differences that exist between the L1 and the L2 in terms of parametric settings for language. Knowing both of these facts allows us in turn to establish more precisely what has to be learned: differences in parameter-settings. At the same time, we know that all or most learners will need to learn the idiosyncratic properties of a language, e.g. idioms, irregularities introduced by historical borrowings, individual lexical items (although not general properties), among others. No theory of UG or any other knowledge base will give us these facts.

2.5.2 Teacher training. At another level, one consequence of knowing what is available to the learner is that language instructors need to be linguistically sophisticated; they need to understand the specifics of each of the learner's knowledge bases. At one level, they need to be familiar with the basic principles and parameters of a theory of UG in order to understand what general linguistic knowledge all learners share and what specific linguistic knowledge learners have of their L1s. This suggests that instructors need to be familiar with the linguistic properties of the specific L1s represented by the learners in their classes in order to understand where principled differences will emerge.

In addition, instructors need to be generally acquainted with the results of current psycholinguistic research, specifically that related to language acquisition and use. At the same time, they need to be familiar with theories of L2 acquisition that attempt to integrate all of these domains into coherent meaningful explanations of the L2 acquisition process.

2.5.3 Classroom composition. In terms of classroom composition, these results suggest that a mixed model consisting of both heterogeneous and homogeneous groupings based on differences and similarities of parameter-settings of the L1 would be beneficial. We know that there are certain aspects of a new language that all learners, regardless of their L1s, will have to learn—e.g. the idiosyncratic, and the irregular properties—and those which only some learners will have to learn, e.g. where parametric values between the L1 and the L2 differ. Dividing up the classes in this way means that in the case of a match in parameter-settings between the L1 and the L2, students do not have to be redundantly taught something they already know. In the case of the mismatch, it means that students can receive the additional input necessary for them to assign new values to parameters.

2.6 Knowing how this knowledge is used.

2.6.1 Goal of curricular materials. Understanding how adults use their knowledge in language learning can be used to enhance the design of instructional settings in several ways.

We know that at least three general bodies of knowledge enter into the language learning process. While each uniquely contributes to the process, acquisition is most likely truly facilitated when all three operate interactively. The system is probably at its worse when either knowledge of the L1 or problem solving strategies are solely drawn upon, or where all three bodies are in competition. Thus, one challenge in terms of enhancing language learning would be to create classes that interactively and strategically draw upon these three knowledge bases and minimize interference from competing domains. For example, one would want to design language exercises that cannot be accomplished through problem-solving strategies alone. If such activities become routine, one would end up 'knowing' a language in much the same way that one knows a series of opening gambits for a chess game. That is, one will never have developed a full linguistic competence for the new target language. We need to create activities wherein a linguistic solution would yield one result and a nonlinguistic solution would yield another. This is necessary in order to get students to draw upon something other than problem-solving strategies alone.

2.7 Knowing how learning takes place.

2.7.1 Design of instructional settings: The role of input. In terms of instructional settings, knowing how learning takes place has several consequences.

For example, as in L1 acquisition, the learning environment must be rich enough to provide the input necessary for the learner to deduce the right properties of the target language. This suggests, as already documented for L1 acquisition, that the learner needs as much exposure as possible to natural language. In addition, the language learning environment must be interactive and directed to individual learners.

The existence of a strong deductive component to L2 learning also strongly suggests that not all corrections are meaningful or useful. We know from L1 acquisition that one can with great effort get a child to correct a previously ungrammatical utterance only to have the child resort to using the ungrammatical utterance until she is really ready to change naturally. A similar phenomenon is also often observed with L2 acquisition. Part of the reason why these corrections appear useless is that the type of input given to the adult *and* perhaps the time at which it was given in development were simply meaningless to the learner. It seems that the right kind of input is needed and it must be given at the right time in order for such intervention to have any lasting effect. Determining the type of input needed is dependent upon the instructor's understanding of the nature of the error made. Determining when such input is useful is dependent upon one's knowledge of what developmental stage the student has attained.

2.8 Design of curricular materials.

2.8.1 Organization of the curriculum. All of these findings challenge many of our traditional ideas concerning the organization of materials to be presented in a language classroom. Drawing upon the principles and parameters approach, one might envision developing curricular materials that are organized around the clustering of properties associated with the parameters, e.g. the Head-Direction parameter (see Flynn in press, for details). These clusterings will not in general correspond to surface structure facts of language in any neat way. They are often concerned with fairly abstract relationships.

Current formulations also challenge traditional notions concerning complexity and simplicity. In many current classrooms and texts, linguistic development of the materials presented often progresses in lockstep fashion from simple one-clause sentences to questions, to two clauses—moving from coordination to subordination—with thematically organized vocabulary being simultaneously introduced in each unit. Given the view of language as conceived within a theory of UG as a system of interacting modules guided by principles and parameters, such an approach, however, may not be the most beneficial to the learner or even the most relevant. Approaches based on general cognitive notions of simplicity and complexity may dictate such progression; approaches based on linguistic theory may not necessarily do so, although at times they may overlap. This means that simple and complex within a UG framework, for example, might roughly correspond to the sequence in which parameters are presented and the order in which clusterings of associated properties are presented for the parameter (see Flynn in press, for extended discussion).

2.8.2 Standardized tests. With respect to standardized tests, these findings raise questions about whether traditional tests designed to evaluate the linguistic competence of a learner provide reliable measures of a learner's competence. In the context of a principles and parameters approach, linguistic knowledge goes far beyond an ability to distinguish between *who* and *whom* or to use the past tense correctly as is so often done in current standardized tests. In order to determine exactly how developed a learner's linguistic competence is, one would want to develop tests that measure such things as knowledge of a particular parameter and its associated clustering of properties, and also how well a learner has integrated this linguistic knowledge with all other related domains of language learning.

3.0 Language practice, L2 research and linguistic theory. While not yet fully appreciated, the language classroom can play a significant role in the development and constraint of both L2 acquisition research and linguistic theory. The classroom provides an important and invaluable arena within which researchers can validate their assumptions about the impact of theory on language acquisition and use. Though not completely analogous, the relationship that should exist between the classroom and empirical research approximates the one that exists between L1 acquisition and natural L1 learning environments. What the experimenter isolates in a controlled environment should in some way converge with what is actually observed in natural settings. While this mapping may not always be direct, the experimenter acts as a mediator to check and inform the theory being worked with in much the same way that other experimental results are used to constrain theories.

To exemplify, practitioners can contribute to this endeavor by isolating regularities and irregularities in patterns of acquisition that occur among the populations with whom they deal directly. They can provide evidence about which dimensions of language are subject to variation and which are not. They can test the claims made by the researchers. However, to realize the potential of the language classroom in this context, active, on-going dialogues between the educational community and the research community must be established and maintained. In addition, the vehicles for such dialogues must be formally instituted.

4.0 Conclusion. In summary, the purpose of this paper was to demonstrate that, indeed, theory, research, and practice are 'blissful' bedfellows. Pedagogy has much to learn from research and theory. Theory and research would be well served if they were grounded in and calibrated with the very practical actualities of what language learners do.

References

Bley-Vroman, R. 1989. What is the logical problem of foreign language learning? In: S. Gass and J. Schachter, eds. Linguistic perspectives on second language acquisition. Cambridge: Cambridge University Press. 41-68.

Chomsky, N. 1975. Reflections on language. New York: Pantheon Press.

Chomsky, N. 1980. Rules and representations. New York: Columbia University Press.

Chomsky, N. 1981. Lectures on government and binding. Dordrecht: Foris.

Chomsky, N. 1986. Knowledge of language. New York: Praeger Press.

Chomsky, N. 1988a. Some notes on economy of derivation and representation. MS. MIT.

Chomsky, N. 1988b. Linguistics and adjacent fields: The state of the art. MS. MIT.

Clahsen, H. 1988. Parameterized grammatical theory and language acquisition: A study of the acquisition of verb placement and inflection by children and adults. In: S. Flynn and W. O'Neil, eds. 47-75.

Cook, V. 1988. The relevance of grammar in the applied linguistics of language teaching. MS. University of Essex, England.

Dulay, H. and M. Burt. 1974. Natural sequences in child second language acquisition. Language Learning. 24:37-53.

Dulay, H., M. Burt, and S. Krashen. 1982. Language two. Oxford: Oxford University Press.
Felix, S. 1985. More evidence on competing cognitive systems. Second Language Research. 1:47-72.
Flynn, S. 1987. A parameter-setting model of L2 acquisition: Experimental studies in anaphora. Dordrecht: Reidel Press.
Flynn, S. 1988. Second language and grammatical theory. In: F. Newmeyer, ed. Linguistics: The Cambridge survey: II linguistic theory: Extensions and implications. Cambridge: Cambridge University Press.
Flynn, S. in press. Linguistic theory and foreign language learning environments. In: K. de Bot, D. Koste, R. Ginsberg, and C. Kramsch, eds. Foreign language research in cross-cultural perspectives. Amsterdam: John Benjamins.
Flynn, S. and W. O'Neil, eds. 1988. Linguistic theory in second language acquisition. Dordrecht: Reidel Press.
Flynn, S. and B. Lust. 1990. A response to Bley-Vroman and Chaudron. Language Learning, June.
Flynn, S. and J. Carroll. Forthcoming. Second language acquisition. England: Longman Press.
Fries, C. 1945. Teaching and learning english as a foreign language. Ann Arbor, MI.: University of Michigan Press.
Jenkins, L. 1988. Second language acquisition: A biolinguistic perspective. In: S. Flynn and W. O'Neil, eds.
Klein, W. 1986. Second language acquisition. Cambridge: Cambridge University Press.
Lado, R. 1957. Linguistics across cultures. Ann Arbor, Mi.: University of Michigan Press.
Lasnik, H. and J. Uriagereka. 1988. A course in GB syntax. Cambridge, Ma.: MIT Press.
Lust, B. 1986. Introduction. In: B. Lust, ed.
Lust, B., ed. 1986. Studies in the acquisition of anaphora, vol. 1: Defining the constraints. Dordrecht: Reidel Press.
Lust, B., ed. 1987. Studies in the acquisition of anaphora, vol. 2: Applying the constraints. Dordrecht: Reidel Press.
Lust, B., Y-C. Chien, and S. Flynn. 1987. What children know: Methods for the study of first language acquisition. In: B. Lust, ed.
Martohardjono, G. and J. Gair. 1989. Apparent inaccessibility in SLA: Misapplied principles or principled misapplications? Paper presented at the 18th Annual Linguistics Symposium. University of Wisconsin-Milwaukee.
McLaughlin, B. 1987. Theories of second language learning. London: Edward Arnold.
Newmeyer, F. 1983. Grammatical theory: Its limits and its possibilities. Chicago: University of Chicago Press.
Newmeyer, F. and S. Weinberger. 1988. The ontogenesis of the field of second language learning. In: S. Flynn and W. O'Neil, eds. 27-34.
Oller, J. and J. Redding. 1971. Article usage and other language skills. Language Learning 1: 85-95.
Radford, A. 1988. Transformational grammar: A first course. Cambridge: Cambridge University Press.
Roeper, T. and E. Williams, eds. 1987. Parameter-setting. Dordrecht: Reidel Press.
Rutherford, W. 1987. Second language grammar: Language and teaching. London: Longman Press.
Sciarone, A. 1970. Contrastive analysis: Possibilities and limitations. International Review of Applied Linguistics 8.2:115-131.
Sharwood-Smith, M. 1981. Consciousness raising and the second language learner. Applied Linguistics 2: 159-68.
Stowell, T. 1981. Origins of phrase structure. Ph.D. dissertation. MIT.

Mountains are not cones: What can we learn from chaos?

Roger Bowers
The British Council, London

Introduction. In presuming to address the relevance of the mathematical theory of chaos to language teaching, I must at the outset confess no specialist understanding of at least one side of this relationship. Chaos is a concept that has only recently had impact on my own thinking, partly because, being British, I come in this instance at the end of a dissemination chain which must span both a geographical and a methodological divide. But mainly because I am no mathematician and have only recently therefore come across the popular literature (e.g. Gleick 1988; Stewart 1989) in a field which is now very well represented on the bookshelves of any contemporary geometer.

Indeed, since I am no cognitive psychologist either, there will be others better equipped to assess such propositions as that of Stewart (1987:8) that

> Perhaps mathematics is effective because it represents the underlying language of the human brain

It is in broad conceptual terms therefore that this paper will seek to explore the new perspectives which chaos theory offers on the theme of this Round Table: the interdependence (or otherwise) of theory, research, and practice.

Theory and practice. This phrase is, as other papers will no doubt have noted, powerfully multivalent. It misleads if it encourages the assumption of an oppositional relationship. Not only is the *and* ambiguous (mother and child? body and soul? bread and butter? chalk and cheese?) but each of the terms requires an almost personal interpretation. Here is mine.

In broad terms, pure theory is concerned with what we do not fully understand, and do not have to do. Pure practice is concerned with what we do not need fully to understand, yet have to do. Theory is born of the recognition of ignorance, practice of the prescriptions of daily necessity. Theory is developed and argued; practice is performed and (from time to time) described. Theory is thought; practice is action.

Yet both theory and practice represent a constant wrestling with problems which require solutions—and with the problem of defining the problem. As Popper (1976:135) reminds us:

> Problems are not easily identified or described, unless, indeed, some ready-made problem has been set us, as in an examination; but even then we may find that the examiner did not formulate his problem well, and that we can do better. Thus there is only too often the problem of formulating the problem—and the problem whether this was really the problem to be formulated.

Thus problems, even practical problems, are always theoretical. Theories, on the other hand, can only be understood as tentative solutions to problems, and in relation to problem situations.

It is a moot point, and one for others to pursue, whether the problems that current applied linguistics theory and research explore are, or are claimed to be, or need to be, the problems to which teachers require solutions. We might equally wonder whether the problems that teachers pose in the classroom are those which rate highly on their students' agenda: the 'deschoolers' would say not.

When teachers reflect on practice, the question most likely to be asked of a given behaviour is "Does this work?" rather than "How does it work?" or "Why does it work?". And while the step from "Did it work?" (on one occasion directly experienced) to "Does it work?" (on other occasions in a range of contexts) undoubtedly involves a level of theorisation through categorising context and event, the extent of theory involved is hardly greater than that implicit in any use of language.

Theory and practice cannot be entirely independent of each other but they can certainly be pursued *as if* they were independent. A part of the apparent disdain in which some practitioners hold theory is accounted for by the perceived non-involvement of theoreticians with the practicalities or with natural and anecdotal data; while theoreticians will not unreasonably retort that it is not their task to find out what works in practical terms, but rather what does *not* work in theoretical terms—the problems which a theory creates are as important as the problems which it solves. Switching the normal expression, we can reasonably ask "That's all very well in practice, but how will it work in theory?".

But we are beginning to talk again as if the dichotomy was a sound one. Let us examine the notion of 'theory' more closely. I will suggest that we may distinguish broadly within theory in three ways: in terms of *level,* of *purpose*, and of *derivation*.

First, *level.* Burgess (1985), based on Goetz and Lecompte (1984), argues for the recognition of three levels of theory: theoretical models (the macro level, broadest in scope, developed through generalisations most removed from natural observation); substantive theory (the micro level, narrowest in scope, least generalising and concerned with explaining describable events); and between these formal or middle level theory (the meso level). This intermediate level is characterised for educational studies as follows (Merton in Hargreaves 1985:41):

> Middle range theory involves abstractions. But they are close enough to observed data to be incorporated in propositions that permit empirical testing. (It lies between) the minor but necessary working hypotheses that evolve in abundance during day to day research and the all-inclusive systematic efforts to develop a unified theory that will explain all the observed uniformities of social behaviour, social organisation and social change.

Much of the misunderstanding about the relevance of theory has its source in the confusion of level and in lack of regard for the varying claims which it is appropriate for theory of different levels to make.

Regarding *purpose*, we may distinguish between theory as an end and theory as a means. I have suggested that theory may be judged mainly in relation to other theory irrespective of any practical application. It is equally possible however that a theory explicitly concerns a specific problem to which a practical solution is sought. We may diagram these as

T → T
T → P

For the purposes of completeness, we may add here the notions of

P → T
P → P

on which I will not expand further though the need for a 'theory of practice' is a point which I have argued elsewhere. To these logical possibilities, again for the sake of completeness, I would add the paradigms

T → R → P
P → R → T

where R = research and which Peter Strevens (1986) has suggested as the preferred patterns of American and British applied linguistics research respectively.

Let us move however to the question of *derivation*. Few will dispute Lakoff & Johnson's assertion (1980:xi) that

Ideas don't come out of thin air.

Neither however does theory derive solely (if ever) from the rational examination of an extensive database, ie from research. Were it so, empiricism would never have been a matter for debate, and the term 'pretheoretical' would not have been invented. Here I lean again towards Popper's position as set out in Biddiss (1977:486):

> Enlargement of our provisional knowledge begins with the conversion of hunches or other imaginative insights into hypotheses. Then, once the conditions for their falsification have been established by the application of deductive logic, such hypotheses must be tested through sustained search for negative instances.

The relevant terms here are *hunch* and *insight*. About what, and from where? The what we may take to be *some* apposite natural evidence. The where may be seen as the intellectual process either of filling gaps in systems or of connecting hitherto independent perceptions.

Filling gaps. For the first of these processes, let us take an irrelevant example at the 'micro' level: wheeled transport. I propose, let us say, a subclassification in terms of person-powered and machine-powered; and a second subclassification by number of wheels: and I will impose a restriction for present purposes of a maximum of four wheels. This produces the matrix:

	Person	**Machine**
1	unicycle	?
2	bicycle	motor-cycle
	scooter	motor-scooter
3	tricycle	three-wheeler
		motor-cycle/sidecar
4	?	car
		van (etc)

(Other observed realisations, and lawn-mowers and kiddy cars, need not concern us.)

We can now usefully ask: why is there no observed instance of a person-powered four-wheeler? Or a machine-powered one-wheeler? What would be their characteristics (power, payload, equilibrium, cost etc) if they did exist? We would generate hypotheses about their practicability, and proceed perhaps to design and experimentation. That is to say, we devise a framework, notice gaps, and set about trying to fill them.

Now a simple EFL example, at the 'meso' level. Language teaching can be text-dependent. It can also be teacher-dependent. Matrix:

		+ Teacher	- Teacher
+	Text	A	B
-	Text	C	D

Observation suggests, let us say, that in institutional settings D is a null cell. Suppose we then superimpose on this observation the learning/acquisition distinction, and ask what would be the effect of inventing activities which in the D context promoted learning or promoted acquisition. We are rapidly once more engaged in theory, directly or indirectly related to practice, through the stimulus of an observed gap in a schematic framework. If, from hypothesising about what is not the case, I now proceed to argue that it could—or indeed *should*—be the case, than I am advancing a pedagogic theory.

A great deal of theory involves the use of logical processes to establish frameworks (not infrequently based on ordered dichotomies) and identify gaps, and the use of other logical processes to create hypotheses which fill them. If on this basis either the cell is filled and its content becomes material for investigation, or it is not fillable and the framework becomes suspect, we have measurably advanced our scientific knowledge and analytical apparatus, and whatever the practical outcome the exercise is justified.

Connecting the unconnected. We may keep to the same broad fields for examples. I see a learner driver under instruction, and am struck by a possible analogy with language education. I am not aware that the analogy has previously been exploited, and determine to develop it. Language education offers some specifics which are prima facie transferable, e.g. the notion of affective filters. I now have the beginning of an approach to driving instruction which leads me into the theoretical consideration (open to empirical investigation) of instructor/driver relationships, learner-driver stress and their effect upon learner-driver progress. I might start thinking of instructor stress too, and this would along with the concept of driving tests and licences give me interesting sub-analogies to refer back to the language teacher/learner predicament.

Another example. I look at language teacher education, and am struck by the analogy between teacher/student and craftsman/apprentice. What are the characteristics of an apprenticeship? Learning by observation, joint production, on-the-job training; leading to proof of skills acquired and eventual membership of an accrediting 'guild'. Where does the analogy work, and where does it break down? I push it to its limits in practice and observe its results: or I seek a more powerful analogy (the management trainee? the officer cadet?).

These are trivial examples of the application of metaphor. But metaphor itself is not a trivial element in the development of theory. Popper, without using the terms, puts it like this (1976:47):

> What characterizes creative thinking, apart from the intensity of the interest in the problem, seems to me often the ability to break through the limits of the range—or to vary the range—from which a less creative thinker selects his trials. This ability, which clearly is critical, may be described as 'critical imagination'. It is often the result of culture clash, that is, a clash between ideas, or frameworks of ideas. Such a clash may help us to break through the ordinary bounds of our imagination.

Lakoff & Johnson (1980:152) make the point more directly:

> New metaphors, by way of their entailments, pick out a range of experiences by highlighting, downplaying, and hiding. The metaphor then characterizes a similarity between the entire range of highlighted experiences and some other range of experiences.

I need not here labour the point that the prevailing metaphors not only for language learning but for language learning research are essentially hierarchical and they are linear. They at once guide and constrain the way we think about teaching, learning, assessment, language, the teacher, the learner.

What then of chaos? What culture clash does this represent?

Plunging into chaos. At this point in my preparation I confronted a paradox. If I am to talk about aspects of non-linearity, which is in part what chaos is all about, is it appropriate that I should do so in a linear fashion? Or should I seek to adopt at least a verisimilitude of random-ness so that the medium and the message might not be too at odds with each other? It was a similar concern, I believe, that promoted Christopher Brumfit at a recent teachers' conference in Italy to question the assumption that language is communication, and on the whole efficient communication, by deliberately adopting a theatrical form which allowed for the creative misinterpretation which, he seemed to be saying, characterises most real language use.

So I have opted for non-linear presentation from here on—not in the sense that each word or sentence will not follow on the last for this cannot be otherwise (though the book is more flexible in this regard than the spoken word)—but in the sense that the rhetorical sequence will be stochastic—it was decided by chance—and the coherence or otherwise of the content will be that which you do or do not impose upon it rather than that which I should otherwise be seeking to control in a well-formed lecture discourse. This will work better for some of you than for others—but that is a part of the message.

There follow therefore thirty or so references to chaos or cross-references from chaos to language teaching and learning. I begin—and you may wish also to end by rereading them—with definitions of chaos in the technical sense. References are to Gleick (1988) and Stewart (1989) whose stimulating books on this topic I take this opportunity of strongly recommending.

Chaos is (definitions in Gleick and in Stewart):

> A kind of order without periodicity.
>
> Apparently random recurrent behaviour in a simple deterministic (clockwork-like) system.
>
> The irregular, unpredictable behaviour of deterministic, nonlinear dynamical systems.
>
> Behaviour that produces information (amplifies small uncertainties) but is not utterly unpredictable.
>
> Systems liberated to randomly explore their every dynamical possibility.
>
> Stochastic behaviour occurring in a deterministic system.
>
> Lawless behaviour governed entirely by law.

1 Our feeling for beauty is inspired by the harmonious arrangement of order and disorder. (Gleick 1988:117)

Can teaching be too orderly for its own good? What evidence is there that orderly teaching inhibits learning?

2 Theorists conduct experiments with their brains. Experimenters have to use their hands too. Theorists are thinkers, experimenters are craftsmen. The theorist needs no accomplice. The experimenter has to muster graduate students, cajole machinists, flatter lab assistants. The theorist operates in a pristine place free of noise, of vibration, of dirt. The experimenter develops an intimacy with matter as a sculptor does with clay, battling it, shaping it, and engaging it. The theorist invents his companions, as a naive Romeo imagined his ideal Juliet. The experimenter's lovers sweat, complain and fart.

> They need each other, but theorists and experimenters have allowed certain inequities to enter their relationships since the ancient days when every scientist was both. Though the best experimenters still have some of the theorist in them, the converse does not hold. Ultimately, prestige accumulates on the theorist's side of the table. (Gleick 1988:125)

Point: Chaos took so long to find because the theorists did not wish to believe it was there - or they were looking elsewhere for what they were interested in.

Question: Are teachers theorists? Experimenters? Or the delivery mechanism for other people's ideas? Where does 'action research' fit into the picture?

3 Consider the power of the notion of fractal dimension. Consider for example the coastline of Britain. Both in nature and in logic it is always possible to turn into the next indentation: coasts have bays, bays have coves, coves have inlets, inlets have ragged rocky shores, rocks have hollows, hollows have pitmarks, pitmarks have scratches have scratches have scratches have... A finite (though undefined) area is thus surrounded by a line of infinite length.

Take an equilateral triangle. On the middle third of each side attach an equilateral triangle. Apply the notion of recursion. Now picture the image on a television. Zoom in: what do you see? Zoom in again: what do you see? And again. And again.

Consider the path round the coast anti-clockwise—or the triangle clockwise—taking always the left hand path: then taking always the right hand fork.

Now consider the notion of a fractal syllabus. Consider the notion of resolution (or delicacy). Think of the points where you can forge ahead or go (spiralling) deeper, never reaching the next bay, the larger triangle. Consider the technical power, storage with accessibility, of CD-ROM.

4 Clouds are not spheres, mountains are not cones, coastlines are not circles, and bark is not smooth, nor does lightning travel in a straight line. (Mandelbrot in: Stewart 1989:215)

5 Leaves come in just a few shapes, of all the shapes imaginable: and the shape of a leaf is not dictated by its function. (Gleick 1988:202)

Compare Halliday's assertion that language is as it is because of what it has to do.

6 The metaphor of the flow (with turbulence and the interaction of many variables, with unpredictability) is more powerful than the metaphor of the line.

It is arguable that man's great invention was not the wheel—for round is common in nature—but the straight line, which is not.

7 Tiny changes in certain features can lead to remarkable change in overall behaviour. (Gleick 1988:178)

Consider the famous Butterfly effect.

8 A stream of data in ordinary languages is less than random: each new bit is partly constrained by the bits before; thus each new bit carries less than a bit's worth of real information. The more random the data stream, the more would be conveyed by each new bit. (Gleick 1988:257)

9 Truly random data remains spread out in an undefined mess. But chaos—deterministic and patterned—pulls the data into visible shapes. Of all the possible pathways of disorder, nature favours just a few. (Gleick 1988:267)

10 With or without chaos, serious cognitive scientists can no longer model the mind as a static structure. (Gleick 1988:299)

Consider then the mind as an event across time, with chaotic as well as periodic activity, with initial conditions and external interferences and optimum disturbance points for the onset of a new state (ie learning).

11 In nonlinearity and feedback lay all the necessary tools for encoding and then unfolding structures as rich as the human brain. (Gleick 1988:307)

12 Even where teaching does not strive for regularity, assessment does: it seeks to downplay variation and disorder. Is it illogical, if we are committed to autonomous, ie unpredictable learning, to seek to promote this through linear systems of teaching? Or is it that learning will develop unpredictably however we teach, but will not show up because our measurements are of the predictable and not the unpredictable?

13 With learning as with the weather, how can we predict the future if we are unable with any safety to predict the next minute? hour? day? The next question or answer?

14 Consider the notions of 'driving' forces and 'damping' forces, as in "Diseases are driven each year by the infections spread among children returning to school, and are damped by natural resistance."

A useful metaphor?

15 Quite simple mathematical equations can model systems every bit as violent as a waterfall. Tiny differences in input can quickly become overwhelming differences in output... sensitive dependence on initial conditions. (Gleick 1988:8)

16 If regularity (as in Galileo's pendulum) is only an approximation, what degree of resolution should we apply to the findings of research and assessment? What irregularities are being obscured?

17 Not only in research, but also in the everyday world of politics and economics, we would all be better off if more people realised that simple nonlinear systems do not necessarily possess simple dynamical properties. (May in: Gleick 1988:80)

All Hell *can* break loose.

18 Consider the notion of functional iteration - each step creates the input for the next. Minor changes to the starting point can grossly change the ultimate effect: try a simple BASIC programme:

```
10 REM X = KX (1-X)
20 LET X = 0.9
30 LET Y = 3.56 * X * (1 - X)
40 PRINT Y
50 X = Y
60 FOR N = 1 TO 500
70 NEXT N
80 GOTO 30
```

(You could use INPUT to vary the first value in the line 30 equation)

(You could plot this on screen)

19 You are a researcher. What do you prefer to work with: an infinite amount of noise free data or a finite amount of noisy data?

20 You don't see something until you have the right metaphor to perceive it.

21 Evolution is chaos with feedback. (Gleick 1988:314)

22 Consider the four boxes in Diagram 1: Spatial representations of chaos in terms of the less than random recurrence of resolutions of a given motion equation.

What thoughts do they provoke about the curriculum process, the variation across time of teacher input, learner input and topic?

23 If Newton could not predict the behaviour of three balls in motion, and Marx could not predict that of three people, what can we securely predict? (Stewart 1989:40)

What is the status of prediction in the social sciences? Do global predictions make possible individual projections?

If a man were to leap from the Eiffel Tower, mathematics could predict how long it would take him to hit the ground, but not why he chose to jump in the first place. (Stewart 1989:43)

Diagram 1. Strange attractors (after Stewart 1988).

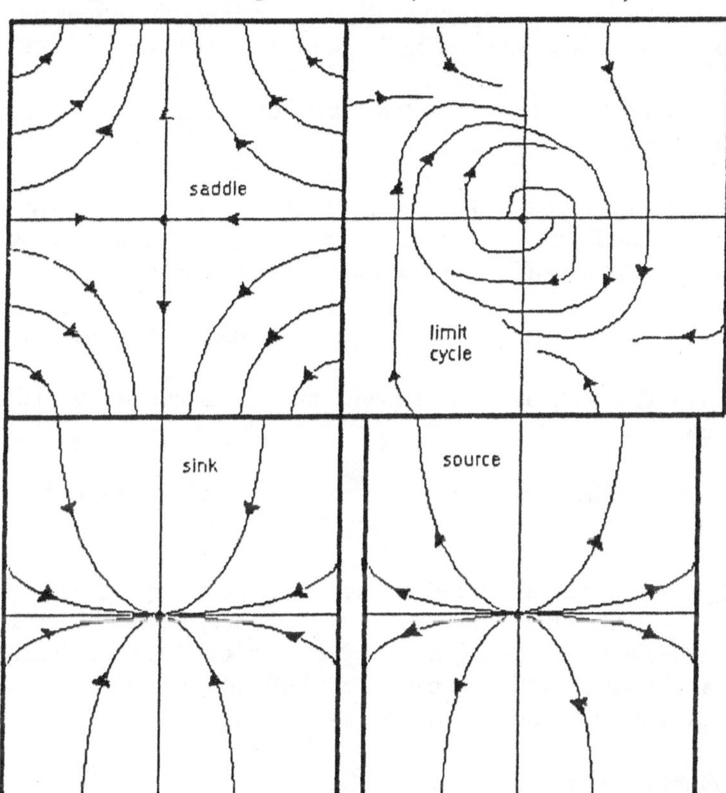

24 Drastic changes do not have to have drastic causes. (Stewart 1989:155)

25 Research, like technology, creates systems where the classical paradigm applies. It has a vested interest in predictability and a fear of disorder. (Stewart 1989:42)

So too all other aspects of evaluation—of person or of programme.

26 An evolutionary model of learning will have to allow room for such notions as:

sensitivity to initial conditions
fractal dimension
self-similarity and recursion

unpredictability
chaos.

27 How can we say that a method 'exists' or 'is followed' when there are so many variables, observed and unobserved, influencing its every application by the teacher and its every effect upon the learner, creating bifurcations and choice at every point? Constantly moving the starting line (and the goal posts too)?

Or is the textbook the only real constant? But how constant is that in the eyes of the perceiver?

28 What evidence do we have that learning or acquisition is or is not, except in very restricted conditions, 'linear' or incremental rather than chaotic, cladistic, episodic, volatile, wildly and individually evolutionary?

29 An alternative to recognising chaos is espousal of the Isaiah principle:

> And the crooked shall be made straight, and the rough places plain (Isaiah 40:4).

What are the justifications for regularising reality by the application of orthodox and orthodoxic procedures for research?

30 Learning can be seen in terms of rates of change (psycholinguistic measurement of learning the canon) or rates of exchange (sociolinguistic measurement of assimilation to the group). In both cases we are immediately living within a metaphor: neither is exclusive. Both run the risk of being norm-oriented: what we measure is what we expect to appear.

31 (a good number to end on):

> Simulations break reality into chunks, as many as possible but always too few. A real world fluid..has the undeniable potential for all the free, untrammelled motion of natural disorder.
> *It has the potential for surprise.* (Gleick 1988:210)

(If you wish now to look back at the chaos definitions, think of them again as they apply to your concepts of learning and the measurement of learning.)

There is sufficient in some of what I have seen of chaos theory to make it not totally antithetical to language studies and what we know or like to think we know of teaching and learning.

We too are concerned with prediction and our failure to predict.

We are concerned with varying initial conditions to influence output (that is, teaching in order that others may learn.)

We might agree that subtle changes to input can exercise major influence on output.

We are familiar with bifurcations, with recursion, even in a restricted sense with random distribution.

We are not uninterested in the metaphor of infinite lines surrounding finite space, an image not far removed from the concept of generativity.

It is for others to say whether there are perhaps specific and scientific applications of the mathematical concepts of chaos to our study of mental or social processes of language use and acquisition.

For me the power of chaos theory lies in the freshness of its spatial imagery and the chance it offers to rejuvenate our perceptions by applying new metaphors to our theory, at all levels from macro to micro. We are living, Stewart (1989:9) tells us,

> in a world of twenty-six dimensions (or perhaps a mere ten), all but four of which are curled up tightly like a terrified armadillo and can be detected only by their shivering.

I believe we are not too trapped in the mechanicity, the generalising determinism, of old straight-lined metaphors to feel the fluttering of the butterfly—wherever it may be—and that it will evoke some gentle reaction in us too as around the world nations wobble and in Georgetown the sun unseasonably shines.

References

Biddiss, M.D. 1977. Entry on: 'Popperian'. In: A. Bullock and O. Stallybrass, eds. Fontana Dictionary of Modern Thought. London: Fontana.

Bowers, R.G. 1986. English in the world: Aims and achievements in English language teaching: TESOL Quarterly. 20:3.

Brumfit, C.J. 1989. In: S. Holden, ed. Creativity in language teaching. Basingstoke: MEP/Macmillan.

Burgess, R.G., ed. 1985. Issues in educational research: Qualitative methods. Lewes: Falmer Press.

Chomsky, N. 1980. Rules and representations. Oxford: Blackwell.

Elliot, H.C. 1974. Similarities and differences between science and common sense. In: Turner 1974.

Gleick, J. 1988. Chaos: Making a new science. London: Heinemann.

Goetz, J.P. and M.D. Lecompte. 1984. Ethnography and qualitative design in educational research. New York: Academic Press. Cited in Burgess.

Hargreaves, A. 1985. The micro-macro problem in the sociology of education. In: Burgess.

Hult, M. and S. Lenning. 1980. Towards a definition of action research: A note and bibliography. Journal of Management Studies. 17.2. Cited in Kelly.

Kelly. A. 1985. Action research: What is it and what can it do? In: Burgess 1985.

Lakoff, G. and M. Johnson. 1980. Metaphors we live by. Chicago: University of Chicago Press.

Merton, R. 1985. Social theory and social structure. New York: Free Press. Cited in Hargreaves.

Popper, K. 1976. Unended quest. Glasgow: Collins/Fontana.

Stewart, I. 1989. Does God play dice? The mathematics of chaos. Oxford: Blackwell.

Strevens, P. 1986 (unpublished). The EFL in IATEFL: Address at 1986 IATEFL Conference.

Turner, R., ed. 1974. Ethnomethodology. Harmondsworth: Penguin.

Reframing contrastive analysis

Larry Selinker[*]
University of Michigan

I am happy to be at this Georgetown University Round Table on Languages and Linguistics to discuss this topic, trying to revive interest in the details of the classical contrastive analysis (CA) literature. It is here at Georgetown that I learned the tools of doing CA and its relevance to pedagogical concerns. And here I learned the important skill of thinking critically about linguistics as a discipline. In the past few years I have been looking in detail at 50+ years of CA research and relating it to current second language acquisition (SLA) and interlanguage (IL) work. I have come to some conclusions and wish to share several with you. For detail, I refer you to Selinker (in press).

My first conclusion is that there are valuable, but buried, SLA and IL hypotheses in the CA literature. If this is so, one wonders why in current work, with very few exceptions, there is rarely any mention of sources earlier than, say, 1975. It is my premise that CA data should be reframed for second language research as providing hypotheses related to predicted IL data; these hypotheses can then be empirically tested.

Second, in some serious sense, no matter how hard some of us have tried, we have never been able to leave the contrastive perspective, nor can we. I argue that Weinreich's (1953) concept of interlingual identifications, with its CA inference on the part of the learner, is a basic SLA learning strategy. Researchers in SLA are forced to use comparison in their research, whether it concerns some aspect of IL with the same aspect in the target language, IL with native language, etc. This can hardly be an accident, perhaps reflecting a contrastive perspective on the part of the learner.

Third, one central issue not being seriously enough explored, is what I call 'the learner's problem of creating equivalence across linguistic systems.' My premise here is that by exploring the vast CA literature, we can help determine whether there exists a manageable number of contrastive models

---

[*] For interesting comments on an earlier version, I wish to thank my teacher at Georgetown, Charles Ferguson, as well as Eric Kellerman, Merrill Swain and Elaine Tarone.

which the learner may, in principle, draw upon in setting up interlingual equivalence. In this literature, we find details of key contrastive variables such as structural correspondence, translation correspondence, semantic exponents and pragmatic definition of structures.

Fourth, the classical CA literature often leads one to look at interlingual identifications in terms of quite abstract units. It is my view that the relationship between language transfer and universalist concerns in forming core IL remains unclear. I believe that current theoretical emphases are too narrow in scope, and that more contextually based information has to be included in the SLA theories that we propose.

Fifth, often in IL there is a centrality to translation equivalence over structural equivalence. The importance of translation in creating IL structure should not surprise colleagues at Georgetown, given the strong emphasis on translation studies that one has seen here for many years.

My final conclusion, which (re-)emerges from a close study of the classical CA literature, is that units of interlingual identification and, thus, of some parts of IL, may not correspond well with a linguistics that pretends that the world is a set of monolingual languages. This point has been made by Ferguson in a series of papers (1963, 1968, 1985), as well as in one given at the 1989 Georgetown University Round Table; it is time we listen to Ferguson in planning our research agenda.

Considering interlingual identifications, Weinreich (1953) concluded that in the language contact situation, one must establish units of comparison across linguistic systems in the face of the dilemma of language contact: The learner must make the same what 'cannot be "the same"'! The learner faces the paradox that units of linguistic structure have, in the Saussurean sense, linguistic 'value' only in terms of the constraints on such units within a (usually NL) linguistic system, while in the language contact situation such units and constraints are broken apart on a regular basis. This paradox is fundamental. Even though, as Ferguson (1989) points out, it is difficult to draw boundaries, one cannot think about 'language' without thinking about 'system'. Yet it is clear, since Weinreich, that learners take pieces from a known system and create interlingual identifications with pieces from target input.

To take a fairly recent case, Kellerman's (1977, 1978, 1983) work looks at some parts of IL lexis in terms of NL transfer in a probabilistic framework. He produces statements of relative probability on the grounds that we cannot predict the specific occurrences of transfer in specific situations due to reasons which Weinreich discussed in his treatment of transferability: intervention of nonlinguistic variables. Kellerman states:

> Given that *the learner establishes a correspondence* between L1 surface form F and L2 surface form F', where F is polysemous, the less marked the meaning in the L1, the more likely it is to be attributed to F' in the IL. (Kellerman 1983; emphasis added.)

Interpretation of these studies depends on prior knowledge. It is my point that the emphasized phrase in this quotation, *the learner establishes a correspondence*, should not be something we take as 'given', but (building on Kellerman) something we investigate as fundamental to second and foreign language acquisition. We should be asking questions such as the following: Which learners establish which correspondences? Under what conditions? What is the mechanism for establishing correspondences? When is the onset of such correspondences? How long do they last? Is there a 'multiple effect' so that items entering the IL through such equivalences, if they become stabilized, will tend to fossilize more than items entering the IL through means other than language transfer? How many different identifiable contrastive models exist which attempt to describe what learners draw upon?

The classical CA literature is a large one. I have reexamined hundreds of CA studies to see whether there is an unmanageably large number of different contrastive models from which a learner may in principle choose in forming IL. If one follows Lado's (1957) structural dicta, 'holes' develop in patterns across languages as a matter of principle. In SLA terms, this may be one of the underlying reasons for the breakup of linguistic patterns across languages, as noted by Weinreich (1953). When learners discover a structural hole, they then may search for reasonable (i.e. to the learner) interlingual identifications. Note that this is an ordered hypothesis.

Early CA researchers noticed structural holes and went back to an earlier study by Harris (1954). Harris proposed a translation-type model in a generative framework. He was concerned primarily with matching morpheme classes across languages. We should contemplate Harris's research since much of SLA has examined the acquisition of morphemes. If we reframe Harris's conclusions, he presents us with an initial IL hypothesis as to interlingual identifications and the hypothesis is ordered: translation correspondences occur in early IL grammar *after* morpheme correspondences stop working. The empirically testable hypothesis is that learners first create structural equivalences and where there are structural holes, they solve the problem by moving to a translation learning strategy. Given all the work on universal grammar and language transfer, to my knowledge not one current author is investigating this hypothesis, whereas in the CA literature, one can find numerous examples of its reasonableness. My underlying point, once again, is that in the classical CA literature, there are hundreds of hypotheses of potential import.

Harris provides an intellectual precursor to the IL hypothesis when he comes to the problem of detail. Considering English and Hebrew structure, he talks about an 'in-between grammar':

> . . . which would have a common part for V+person and V+ed. . . [in English vs. Hebrew]. . . Then certain changes would yield E[nglish] out of this Z, and other changes would yield H[ebrew] out of this Z. The

> difference between E and H would be the sum of these E-Z and H-Z changes [where Z = the in-between grammar] (Harris 1954:270).

Harris is the first in the literature to talk about in-between grammars and this has not been sufficiently recognized, Harris being ignored in second language research.

Now I want to mention one more CA item: the dissertation of a Turkish colleague who helped set up early Peace Corps language programs here at Georgetown: Sebuktekin (1964). Here the direction of contrasts is from Turkish to English. The scope is ambitious: morphological structures, types of morphemes, morpheme combinations, derivational/inflectional morphemes. This work teaches us much about the structure of morphemes and their combinations. It is aware of the problems of comparison, pointing out that one's emerging contrasts may be a function of one's methodology. The equivalence problem is handled in terms of a common definition of selected linguistic features across languages. Looking at 'plurality', for example, he notes that the functions of forms across these languages are not formally analyzable. One can compare forms across languages, but, to compare functions across linguistic systems, one needs to consider the semantic content of one's CA labels.

Sebuktekin presents two lengthy sections on morphological processes and parts of speech in the two languages. These sections are interesting from the CA point of view since translation is a tool intersecting structural criteria. He provides a unique solution for the problem of equivalence by proposing a unit of contrast he calls the 'diaform'. Diaforms for Sebuktekin (1964:72) are forms identified consistently as the same in translation from the source language to the target. The smallest dialinguistic unit is the 'diamorpheme' and the largest is the 'diasentence'.

Sebuktekin provides important microdetail. His symbology, a slanted line placed between forms, indicates a diaform, e.g. *kiz/* girl; *-ler/* -s plural. His major symbols are:

S:	suffix	P:	prefix
I:	internal change	PM:	portmanteau morpheme
MM:	more than one morpheme	FM:	free morpheme
WO:	word order	PP:	paraphrasing

There is background here for dealing with problems of equivalence across linguistic systems. An example involves substantive derivational affixes, e.g. *-ci* is a 'professional' morpheme with its diaformic structure being S/S and S/MM. The morpheme *-lik* is an 'associative' morpheme with its diaformic structure being either S/S,I; S/FM, PP; or S/FM, MM. The morpheme *-li* is an 'attributive' morpheme, with its diaformic structure being either S/S or

S/FM,MM. An example of the attributive S/S diamorpheme would be *-li/* '-ful'. We can coin a more modern term for such variation—'diaformic variant'—and ponder why this has not been studied in SLA.

The diaformic unit, especially given its variable nature, is a potentially relevant one for SLA theory, matching criteria for 'linguistically relevant units' of IL as going across three systems (Selinker in press). Sebuktekin's translation-structural criteria are important, since he has empirically discovered that there exists a 'range of forms' identified as same across linguistic systems, but having no correspondence in their morphological or syntactic features. This is one of the problems I think learners are up against. If this is a reasonable hypothesis, then it follows that in their confusion, learners create a diaformic unit while in the process of comparing TL input and their emerging IL. This gives us more interlingual identification detail. It is surprising that SLA morpheme acquisition studies do not consult this work.

Additionally, an important dissertation for interlingual theory is that done at Georgetown by Dingwall (1964) on 'Diaglossic Grammar'. He suggests a three-component diaglossic grammar which has not been tested in the SLA literature.

I hope I have whetted your appetite to try to reframe, from the CA literature, testable hypotheses about the learners one sees daily in the classroom. One place to begin is the annotated bibliographies of Selinker and Selinker (1972) and Selinker and Fakhri (1988); these bibliographies contain many studies I had no room for in Selinker (in press).

It is a pity that the CA literature, especially the CA dissertation literature, is so unknown. It is an intellectual tragedy, since so much of our history and so much potential IL detail is located there. We should reframe these studies, establishing testable SLA hypotheses and seeing their effects on our understanding of IL and IL learning.

Reframing 50 years of CA studies has given me a peculiar view of current attempts at theorizing in SLA. How can anyone be against "theory"? But I believe that the data accounted for by current attempts is but a small percentage of the types of IL data. The examples in Ferguson (1989) alone should give us pause.

Studying Ferguson (1989) implies going back to much pre-1975 data. Some earlier CA studies such as the phonological study by Rudaravanija (1965) and various ones by Nemser (1961a, 1961b, 1971) and Brière (1964, 1966, and 1968; and Brière et al. 1968) use recorded IL data, though they don't call it that.

To ignore CA predecessors injures the work of those upon whose metaphorical shoulders we stand, and also diminishes our claims to discovering general laws governing SLA. One striking ignored example is Verma (1966), the earliest CA study I have found which discusses markedness interlingually. It is full of suggestions about interlingual identifications. Yet, not one discussion of markedness in current SLA theory refers to it.

My question is this: can we continue to ignore the rich reframed IL detail of our CA predecessors and, thus, in a historical sense, continue to trivialize our own attempts at SLA theory making?

References

Brière, E.J. 1964. On defining a hierarchy of difficulty in learning phonological categories. Unpublished Ph.D. dissertation, University of Washington.

Brière, E.J. 1966. An investigation of phonological interference. Language 42:768-96.

Brière, E.J. 1968. A psycholinguistic study of phonological interference. The Hague: Mouton.

Brière, E.J., R.N. Campbell, and Soemarmo. 1968. A need for the syllable in contrastive analysis. Journal of Verbal Learning and Verbal Behavior 7:384-89.

Dingwall, W. O. 1964. Diaglossic grammar. Unpublished Ph.D. dissertation, Georgetown University.

Ferguson, C.A. 1963. Linguistic theory and language learning. In: Georgetown University Round Table on Languages and Linguistics 1963, ed. Robert J. DiPietro. Washington, D.C.: Georgetown University Press.

Ferguson, C.A. 1968. Contrastive analysis and language development. In: Georgetown University Round Table on Languages and Linguistics 1968, ed. James E. Alatis. Washington, D.C.: Georgetown University Press.

Ferguson, C.A. 1985. Contrastive analysis: A linguistic hypothesis. In: Scientific and humanistic directions of language: Festschrift for Robert Lado, ed. K.R. Jankowsky. Amsterdam: John Benjamins.

Ferguson, C.A. 1989. Language teaching and theories of language. In: Georgetown University Round Table on Languages and Linguistics 1989, ed. James E. Alatis. Washington, D.C.: Georgetown University Press.

Harris, Z. 1954. Transfer grammar. IJAL 20:259-70.

Kellerman, E. 1977. Toward a characterization of the strategy of transfer in second language learning. Interlanguage Studies Bulletin - Utrecht 2:58-145.

Kellerman, E. 1978. Transfer and non-transfer: Where we are now. Studies in Second Language Acquisition 2:37-57.

Kellerman, E. 1983. Now you see it, now you don't. In: S. Gass and L. Selinker, eds. Language transfer in language learning. Rowley, Mass.: Newbury House.

Lado, R. 1957. Linguistics across cultures. Ann Arbor: University of Michigan Press.

Nemser, W. 1961a. The interpretation of English stops and interdental fricatives by native speakers of Hungarian. Unpublished Ph.D. dissertation, Columbia University.

Nemser, W. 1961b. Hungarian phonetic experiments. New York: Xerox form.

Nemser, W. 1971. An experimental study of phonological interference in the English of Hungarians. Bloomington: Indiana University Press, and The Hague: Mouton.

Rudaravanija, P. 1965. An analysis of the elements in thai that correspond to the basic intonation patterns of English. Unpublished Ph.D. dissertation, Columbia University.

Sebuktekin, H.I. 1964. Turkish-English contrastive analysis: Turkish morphology and corresponding English structures. Unpublished Ph.D. dissertation, University of California, Berkeley.

Selinker, L. In press. Reframing interlanguage. London: Longman.

Selinker, L., and A. Fakhri. 1988. An annotated bibliography of U.S. Ph.D dissertations in contrastive linguistics: 1970-1983. In: J. Fisiak, ed. Papers and studies in contrastive linguistics, vol. 23. Poznan: Adam Mickiewicz University Press.

Selinker, L., and P.J.N. Selinker. 1972. An annotated bibliography of U.S. Ph.D. dissertations in contrastive linguistics 1945-1971. In: R. Filipovic, ed. The Yugoslav Serbo-Croatian-English contrastive project, Report 6. Zagreb: Institute of Linguistics, University of Zagreb, and Washington, D.C.: Center for Applied Linguistics.

Verma, M. K. 1966. A synchronic comparative study of the structure of the noun phrase in English and Hindi. Unpublished Ph.D. dissertation, University of Michigan.
Weinreich, U. 1953. Languages in contact. New York: Linguistic Circle of New York.

Classroom shock: The role of expectations in an instructional setting

Richard Lutz*
Georgetown University

1 Introduction. A variety of models of second language acquisition (SLA) have addressed the role of culture in acquiring language in a natural setting. Most notably, the Acculturation Model (Schumann 1978) and the Nativization Model (Andersen 1983) have argued that social distance between the L2 learner and the host language community is a central predictor of the degree of success of the SLA process. The applicability of these models to the language classroom, however, has been called into question. Ellis (1985:255) concludes that where contact between the L2 speakers and the target language community is impossible, e.g. in foreign language classrooms, 'presumably the factors responsible for social distance are not relevant in foreign language learning, although those responsible for psychological distance may be.' Schumann (1984:10) states that 'since the Acculturation Model is designed to account for SLA under conditions of immigration where learning takes place without instruction, I have no proposal to make concerning language teaching pedagogy.'

The idea that social attitudes and expectations will directly affect interaction between L1 and L2 speakers (and thereby indirectly control access to crucial comprehensible input) retains its attractiveness, and all the more so when one considers the following hybrid situation, which I return to below: when the contact is between an L1 speaker in the role of a foreign teacher in a content classroom, cultural-specific assumptions about the respective roles of student and teacher and of speaking in the classroom become prominent. This paper explores one predictor variable of the Acculturation Model, namely Culture Shock as it applies to the L2 content classroom, redefining and examining it in interactional terms. I argue that accounts of culture shock

* I am grateful to Jan Biro and Charlie Watanabe for their help in the collection of data and insights into the world of the classroom in Japan. What appears here is my responsibility. My thanks also to all the faculty and students at Georgetown who participated in my survey.

purely from the perspective of the learner are inadequate, and that classic characteristics of the phenomenon appear to affect both teacher and learner.

Before my review of the literature, I would like to begin with the requisite anecdote. In this case, it is one which many teachers will acknowledge as commonplace, though I might protest that while anecdotes are a dime a dozen, mine must be converted to Japanese yen in order to be fully appreciated.

As part of the graduate certificate program in linguistics for teachers of English, Georgetown offers courses in Japan through the Kawaijuku International Education Center of Tokyo. During July and August of 1989, I accompanied three of my colleagues and taught a three-week intensive course entitled 'Language Acquisition.' Despite problems beginning immediately upon arrival (e.g. my declaration of teaching as the 'purpose of visit' on immigration forms didn't square with my visa; there were the obvious language problems; I got lost in the subway; I got my colleague and myself lost in the subway; my dinner wriggled on my plate), I considered (and still consider) myself a trooper, and was largely determined that this would be an overwhelmingly pleasant experience—as indeed it was. That is the background for my anecdote: at the conclusion of the summer program, a ceremony was held in which each of us was asked to speak. I titled my two-minute thank-you 'Culture Shock', and proceeded to explain that the obvious negatives associated with culture shock had been assiduously prevented by the careful attention and graciousness of our hosts and students, and that everything had consequently come off without a hitch. And I meant every word I said. It was therefore very disconcerting to hear from the one American student enrolled in my class of 34, one who at the time was teaching English at the Center, that I was mistaken—that I simply hadn't noticed the tell-tale signs of the culture shock phenomenon, and that for three weeks students had been frantically trying to figure me out (these are my own words) or at least trying to figure out what it was I was asking them to do. In the weeks that followed, I began examining diary notes I had taken for signs of trouble. I was surprised to find that many of my written observations corroborated the comments of my American informant. I will return to this anecdote below, because it led to my own reanalysis of what had been going on, what had gone wrong and why.

2 Culture shock. The literature on culture shock is vast and provides a wide variety of perspectives on the effects of contact with other cultures. Parameters are often determined by the nature of the contact, and more particularly the purpose of the interaction. Thus, there exist complete histories of such varied contact situations as international business persons, tourists, and spouses, as well as of other family members who are 'along for the ride.' Within the literature, discussions of international education abound. The particular populations under investigation are usually overseas students and Peace Corps workers in so-called 'Third World' contexts. Few studies, however, treat the itinerant teacher per se, or investigate cultural expectations within the formal content classroom. Still, much can be gained by reviewing this extensive literature. In the following section, I discuss some of the prevalent explanations for culture shock, and then review the relevant trends in terms of international education. My report concludes with an analysis of the role played by culture shock in the context of the content classroom.

3 Definitions. If the listener should wince at my use of the term 'culture shock', it is undoubtedly because of previous disappointment in this or similarly attractive labels of psychobabble. The experience is common enough, and is associated with a wide variety of symptoms ranging from mild to severe. Edward T. Hall (1959:174) defined it in *The Silent Language* as 'simply a removal or distortion of many of the familiar cues one encounters at home and the substitution for them of other cues which are strange.' Oberg (1960) describes six aspects of the phenomenon:

1. Strain due to the effort required to make necessary psychological adaptations.
2. A sense of loss and feelings of deprivation in regard to friends, status, profession and possessions.
3. Being rejected by/and or rejecting members of the new culture.
4. Confusions in role, role expectations, values, feelings and self-identity.
5. Surprise, anxiety, even disgust and indignation after becoming aware of cultural differences.
6. Feelings of impotence due to not being able to cope with the new environment. (Cited in Furnham and Bochner 1986:48)

Like alienation and anomie, culture shock is frequently discussed in terms of the individual's lack of points of reference, free-floating anxiety, lack of self-confidence and a loss of inventiveness or spontaneity (Furnham and Bochner 1986). Ultimately, labels which refer to affect or mental state are frequently studied via a wide variety of behaviors associated with the label (Ellis 1985). This is most obviously the case with such factors as anxiety, aptitude, and motivation, and is clearly one problem with a term like culture shock as well, as Oberg's six aspects suggest.

4 International education. Worldwide and at any given time, there are upwards of half a million students and teachers at institutions of higher learning abroad (Edgerton 1976, Klineberg 1976; cited in Furnham and Bochner 1986). Research in this field skyrocketed in the 1950s, with many reports of the adjustment problems of foreign students in the United States. While early studies were largely atheoretical, throughout the literature, at least two distinct trends are discernible: the clinical (medical) model of Oberg

(1960) and a psychological view referred to as the U-curve of adjustment. The medical view has been largely rejected, while the U-curve model has been given wide publicity in many fields, including applied linguistics (see Brown 1987, for example). In brief, the U-curve view notes at least three main phases after contact with the host culture is made: an initial stage of elation and optimism, followed by the actual shock as the differences and confusion intrude into the visitor's sense of self. A third stage, which Larson and Smalley (1972) call culture stress represents a crucial stage of recovery and adaptation to the new conditions. An expanded 'W-curve' model includes the return home with its attendant problems of readjustment.

There is a social-psychological framework, however, which might appear more applicable to the academic setting. This view sees cross-cultural contact as a learning experience, and, rather than therapy and counseling, preparation and learning appropriate skills are called for. Klineberg (1981) considers foreign teaching to have a life history—selection for the job, preparation before one leaves (including finding out practical and cultural information which might mitigate problems once abroad), the academic experience (including meeting people outside the classroom), and the return home (how readily one is accepted back home, for example).

Studies of academic sojourns have focused on the student. While studies written from a clinical perspective have looked at student depression or use of the university health care system, works which focus on the experiences of the student have looked at student expectations and attitudes. Carey (1956) looked at student expectations and difficulties associated with university life in Britain. Additional studies describe a 'foreign student syndrome' (Ward 1967)—homesickness, academic problems, and worries about school or family.

Many studies have been carried out on voluntary workers, particularly those in the Peace Corps (summaries in Guthrie 1975, 1981), and have considered attrition rates and factors which determine one's ability to cope. Guthrie has concluded that the most important variables predicting success of such experiences are sociocultural skills and information that will be required.

The closest approximation to a discussion of culture shock in an academic setting within the linguistic literature concerns the education of Native American children. Studies of Kwakiutl children (Wolcott 1967), Sioux and Cherokee children (Dumont 1972) and the Warms Springs study (Philips 1972) contain now well-known examples of how 'styles of learning' (Cazden and John 1968) can differ across cultures and how such differences may lead to difficulties in communicating between teacher and student. Specifically, such studies have pointed to the 'mask of silence' (Dumont 1972) in the academic behavior of otherwise verbal individuals. Adger (1987) investigated what happens to the nonnative speaker who is obliged to enter the mainstream classroom and interact with native speakers. She found a variety of strategies for the 'recalibration of communicative conventions'. Nonnative and native English students negotiated styles of protesting with one another, accommodating each other's differences in style.

5 Expectations in the classroom. One persistent notion in the culture shock literature is that confusions in role and role expectations will direct the behavior of the traveller. Expectations form part of one's overall system of values:

> ... These [value] systems are organized summaries of experience that capture the focal, abstracted qualities of past encounters, have a normative or 'oughtness' quality about them and which function as criteria or frameworks against which present experience can be tested. Furthermore, they function as general motives. When people move to other cultures, value differences between them mean that previously established expectations and predictions are invalid. This poor fit between person and the environment may lead to distress and anxiety until the values of the new society are understood and internalized. (Furnham and Bochner 1986:199)

With this in mind, I began an investigation of the extent to which the norms and expectations of Japanese graduate students currently studying in the United States match those of American educators using both questionnaires and interview. Questionnaires were distributed to 27 Japanese students and 24 faculty at Georgetown University. As baseline data, I also surveyed 34 American students at Georgetown. Survey questions focused primarily on organization and participation within the classroom setting, including perceptions of what constitutes good student and good teacher behavior. An obvious limitation in the methodology was the selection of Japanese students exposed to the American educational system for varying periods of time, but I included questions which asked Japanese students to compare and contrast the two academic settings and discuss changes in their perceptions and attitudes over time.[1] Using a five-point Likert response scale to indicate agreement or disagreement with a series of statements about teachers, students and classrooms, there was a considerable match-up between American university professors and their students. Collapsing the categories 'disagree slightly' and 'disagree a lot', as well as collapsing the categories 'agree slightly' and 'agree a lot', an X^2 test with one degree of freedom indicated very few significant discrepancies at the .05 level of significance. Students (S) and teachers (T) reacted differently only to the following statements:[2]

---

[1] Additional data will be collected next summer in Japan, including pre- and postsession interviews with students enrolled in my course.

[2] A number of questions were worded differently for the two cohorts. Thus students were asked how likely they were to compliment a teacher who did something that impressed him or her. Teachers were asked how positively they would view students who expressed such compliments.

'Drinking or eating in class is impolite.' (A: 65% disagreed, 42% agreed; T: 12% disagreed, 88% agreed);

'It is acceptable for a teacher to arrive a few minutes late.' (A: 29% disagreed, 71% agreed; T: 75% disagreed, 25% agreed);

'Student group work outside of class is a useful learning activity.' (A: 82% disagreed, 18% agreed; T: 0% disagreed; 87% agreed; 13% had no opinion).

On the other hand, the mismatch between Japanese students and American faculty (as well as American students) was widespread. Differences were found at the .05 level of significance between the American teachers (T) and Japanese (J) groups for responses to each of the following statements:

'A good student does not disrupt class by asking questions in the middle of a lecture.' (T:74% disagreed, 26% agreed; J: 33% disagreed, 67% agreed);

'Asking a question in class can be an indication that the teacher is not explaining things clearly.' (T: 75% disagreed, 24% agreed; J: 66% disagreed, 33% agreed);

'Students who have a personal story which they feel is relevant to the class material should tell it to the class.' (T: 50% disagreed, 37% agreed; J: 11% disagreed, 66% agreed);

'A good student asks the teacher questions about classroom information outside of class.' (T: 24% disagreed, 62% agreed; J: 44% disagreed, 33% agreed);

'The very best teachers are the ones who use creative techniques to teach.' (T: 25% disagreed, 63% agreed; J: 0% disagreed, 10% no opinion, 90% agreed);

'Group work outside of class is a useful learning activity.' (T: 11% disagreed; 87% agreed, 13% no opinion; J: 11% disagreed, 89% agreed)[3].

Follow-up questions to the Japanese subjects indicated that the biggest differences between Japanese and American teachers are that Japanese

---

[3] Additionally, American students disagreed with American teachers about this and with both American teachers and Japanese students in regard to eating and drinking in class.

teachers 'hold the floor', tend not to ask questions, and tend to 'go by the book'. American educators were perceived as friendly, creative, more willing to discuss problems in class, and interested in promoting classroom discussion, all seen as positive attributes. Characteristics of Japanese educators which the Japanese students preferred over their American counterparts included better organization, taking the pressure off volunteers by selecting students to answer, and providing more personal support to individual students. Characteristics of American students named by Japanese students included having a more casual style, being more serious about learning, more critical, and speaking before thinking. Individual Japanese respondents indicated a desire to become more active in class, more willing to ask questions and be more critical.

The surveys reveal that, as expected, Japanese and Americans differed sharply in their expressed appraisal of acceptable and desirable behavior. Based on prior anecdotal evidence and some reading, I could have predicted virtually all these differences.

What then had explained my initial perceptions that all proceeded smoothly in Japan? My notes, intended more to provide me some additional information when it came to grading my students than to serve as a record of my impressions of what was transpiring, contain a number of comments which indicate I really did know that there were problems afoot:

'Can't learn their names.' [and implied: ask them to state their names when they respond.]

'Not enough discussion. Tried to call on A.K., who looked initially interested, then dumbstruck.'

'B.J. [the American] constantly wants to respond but is holding back—trying to make my life easier.'

'Not sure if assignment [data collection of L1 Japanese children] is feasible. Ask class how many children available [for recording].'

'Only K.H. and Y.W. seem willing to answer.'

I'll share a few other incidents with you as well: Instructors were provided with microphones. I was uncomfortable using mine, particularly since there was feedback every time I wandered past a loudspeaker. I had also been embarrassed the first day of class when, during a break, I walked to a drinking fountain and began slurping water—with my wireless mike fully operational. Upon my return, my class was tittering, and, upon my insistence told me what they had heard. The mike frequently seemed to cause more problems than it solved, but my students were insistent that their comprehension would decrease without it. There were also maddening (unseen) battles over control of the air conditioning. Because of the location of the vents, it was always too hot for me and too cold for the class. This was not per se a cultural difference—I had noticed the American student putting her sweater on during class. No one, however, seemed willing to confront me—they simply reset the knob when I wasn't looking.

Furthermore, my American student has detailed a number of incidents that took place and written them down for me. The following quotes seem most applicable to the 'mismatch' between my perceptions and those of the students.

On group dynamics:

> Although our class was varied—type of school, age, gender, educational background—I'd say the men generally had a higher place in the class hierarchy. By the end of the first week, there were at least two distinct factions which sat diagonally opposite each other in the classroom. I was a member of one faction and, by virtue of my classroom activity, was a quasi-leader. The other faction was headed by a man in his 30s (?) who was not the ranking man in the class. When I ran into him and his group members (all women) outside of class such as on the train, he would deliberately turn his back to me (ostracism) and the other members would follow suit. If I met members of his group away from his presence, we chatted quite amiably. His action/ostracism was a standard technique to express censure. Unfortunately, I was uncertain whether I was being censured for being a disruptive student, an uppity female, a boorish foreigner, or all three.

On class participation:

> I felt an overwhelming pressure from my classmates to be quiet. I also felt an overwhelming empathetic reaction to the American teacher faced with a Japanese class for the first time. I'd promise myself every morning that I'd be quiet in class, but every time I'd make eye contact with the teacher over the ear-splitting silence following the teacher's question, I'd break my promise and up would go my hand.
>
> Caught in that kind of cross-cultural high-pressure stream, I developed a dandy 102° fever the first week; however, I and everyone else managed to accommodate to the novel situation by the end.

On group activities:

> Small group—for the first homework assignment—taping parent-child interaction, my group consisted of a 50ish woman, two young women in their twenties, and myself. The older woman and one of the younger ones had considerable experience working with foreigners. The other one

> had no experience at all with foreigners, although they were all English teachers. In trying to accomplish the project, the Japanese deferred to the older woman while I assumed the American 'equality' stance and was constantly 'disrupting' with questions, suggestions, etc. The woman unfamiliar with foreigners withdrew and the other two members had to work at trying to mend the group. The Japanese were entirely content with the older woman's leadership although she had no experience in writing up an experiment. I essentially went behind their backs to produce the group document the night before the deadline. I, on my own initiative, inserted the other members' sections into the overall document. The two Japanese used to foreigners were put off at first but warmed up when the group got a good grade. The third one remained cool to me for the entire course. Personality conflict or culture conflict?

It seems to me that the cultural dynamics within my classroom were largely unpredictable, given that I, as the teacher, was purportedly in control, able to set the ground rules. On the other hand, particularly given the Japanese setting, Japanese ground rules could not be forsaken—at least not entirely. This was particularly so in terms of hierarchical structures. Both students and teacher were trying to accommodate each other, but no one could decide which rules were operative. In Oberg's terms, there was constant strain to make the necessary adaptations, confusion in role and role expectations, surprise (on my part) upon learning of these problems, and a decided feeling of not being in control by both teacher and students.

6 Conclusions. While not quite 'culture shock' in the clinical sense, the 'classroom shock' I have described is shared by both teacher and class members. Because the class is self-contained and under the direction of one individual, there is the perception that everything is under control. The closest approximation to this in the culture shock literature is the so-called social-psychological framework (Klineberg 1981), which views culture shock as involving both the individual and the host group. Bochner (1981, 1982) has delineated possible outcomes of contact at the group level as well as at the individual level, relevant for a noninstructional setting. These include outcomes as varied as integration of the guest group to assimilation or even genocide. At the individual level, the visitor might mediate (synthesize) both cultures, vacillate between the two, reject the second culture (chauvinistic) or reject one's own culture (passing). Borrowing from Bochner, I would propose the following schema for a classroom setting. With regard to group dynamics, classroom shock might be treated at the group level in terms of degree to which the teacher's cultural (viz. academic) norms prevail over those of the student body. At the individual level, both the individual history (including personal norms) of the teacher and those of each student must be addressed in order to evaluate the psychological reactions to the contact situation.

My analysis does not directly address a chief concern in the linguistic SLA models, namely, the extent to which such a variable can be used as a predictor of language acquisition. It does, however, suggest that many of the same dynamics which obtain in the natural setting are at least present within the classroom setting. In addition, to the extent that such models as the Acculturation Model are testable at all, the role of social-psychological variables such as 'classroom shock' ought to be evaluated.

Appendix A: Biographical data sheet for Japanese subjects.

Please answer the following questions:

Male Female
Age:

1. In which grades did you study English? (circle)
   1st 2nd 3rd 4th 5th 6th 7th 8th 9th 10th
   11th 12th college: 1 2 3 4

2. Have any other members of your family ever lived or studied in an English-speaking country? Yes__ No__
   If yes, who? ______________
   If yes, which country, for how long and for what reason?

3. How long have you lived in the U.S.? years___months__

   Had you ever lived or visited the U.S. in the past? Yes_ No___
   If yes, which city?
   If yes, how old were you?
   If yes, for how long? years___ months___
   If yes, for what reason?

4. Have you ever lived in or visited any other country where people speak English? Yes___ No___
   If yes, which country/countries? ________________
   If yes, how old were you?
   If yes, for how long? years___ months___
   If yes, for what reason?

5. Besides the U.S. and Japan, have you ever received formal schooling in any other countries? Yes___ No___
   If yes, how old were you?
   If yes, for how long? years___ months___
   If yes, which school or institution?
   Subjects studied:
   Language(s) used in classroom instruction:

Appendix B: Survey of classroom values.

Figures indicate percentage responses for American student/Japanese student/American teacher cohorts.

1. A good student does not disrupt class by asking questions in the middle of a lecture.

Disagree a lot	Disagree a little	No opinion	Agree a little	Agree a lot
66/11/62	23/22/12	0/0/0	12/56/25	0/11/0

2. When a student asks a question in class, it is an indication that the student feels you are not explaining things clearly.

Disagree a lot	Disagree a little	No opinion	Agree a little	Agree a lot
54/33/50	35/33/25	6/0/0	6/22/12	0/11/12

3. Students talking in class while the teacher is lecturing is disruptive (bad) behavior.

Disagree a lot	Disagree a little	No opinion	Agree a little	Agree a lot
0/0/0	12/0/12	0/0/0	54/11/37	35/89/50

4. One characteristic of a good student is that one asks teachers questions about classroom information outside of or after class.

Disagree a lot	Disagree a little	No opinion	Agree a little	Agree a lot
6/11/12	23/33/12	18/11/12	54/22/25	0/11/37

5. A student who drinks or eats in class is impolite.

Disagree a lot	Disagree a little	No opinion	Agree a little	Agree a lot
18/0/12	47/0/0	6/0/0	18/22/38	12/67/50

6. Reading (even if it is related material) while the teacher is lecturing is impolite.

Disagree a lot	Disagree a little	No opinion	Agree a little	Agree a lot
6/0/0	12/11/12	0/0/12	54/33/25	23/56/50

7. If a student knows something that he/she feels is relevant to the teacher's lecture, the student contributes to the course by telling about it in class.

Disagree a lot	Disagree a little	No opinion	Agree a little	Agree a lot
0/0/0	6/22/0	0/11/0	47/33/25	43/33/75

8. The more students get to participate in discussion in classes, the better the classroom experience is for them.

Disagree a lot	Disagree a little	No opinion	Agree a little	Agree a lot
0/0/0	12/11/0	6/11/0	23/22/37	10/56/62

9. A good teacher must also entertain the class (be lively, relate relevant personal stories, sometimes tell jokes).

Disagree a lot	Disagree a little	No opinion	Agree a little	Agree a lot
6/11/12	12/0/12	0/11/12	60/11/37	29/67/12

10. Students who tell personal stories related to the class material contribute positively to the class.

Disagree a lot	Disagree a little	No opinion	Agree a little	Agree a lot
0/0/0	41/11/50	18/22/12	29/44/12	12/22/25

11. The very best teachers are ones who use creative techniques to teach.

Disagree a lot	Disagree a little	No opinion	Agree a little	Agree a lot
6/0/0	23/0/25	6/12/12	35/12/26	23/76/37

12. Teachers should overtly express their opinions about the subject matters they present to the class.

Disagree a lot	Disagree a little	No opinion	Agree a little	Agree a lot
0/0/25	35/11/0	0/0/25	54/44/25	12/44/25

13. Large class size detracts from a classroom setting.

Disagree a lot	Disagree a little	No opinion	Agree a little	Agree a lot
6/0/0	23/22/25	0/11/12	41/22/0	29/44/62

14. Students should be seated and ready by the time the teacher enters the room.

Disagree a lot	Disagree a little	No opinion	Agree a little	Agree a lot
0/0/0	23/0/12	0/11/25	59/22/25	18/67/37

15. It is acceptable for a teacher to arrive a few minutes late.

Disagree a lot	Disagree a little	No opinion	Agree a little	Agree a lot
6/11/62	23/33/12	0/11/0	54/33/12	18/11/12

16. A student should let the teacher know he/she disagreed with a statement I made in class.

Disagree a lot	Disagree a little	No opinion	Agree a little	Agree a lot
0/0/0	23/22/25	6/22/0	41/22/25	29/32/50

17. A student should let the teacher know that he/she especially enjoyed a course or a lecture.

Disagree a lot	Disagree a little	No opinion	Agree a little	Agree a lot
0/0/0	6/11/0	6/0/12	47/33/37	41/56/50

18. Student group work outside of class can be a useful learning activity.

Disagree a lot	Disagree a little	No opinion	Agree a little	Agree a lot
35/0/0	47/11/0	0/0/0	18/15/12	0/74/87

Appendix C: Interview questions for Japanese cohort.

1. If a teacher made a mistake in his lecture, what would you do?
2. What are the biggest differences as you see it between the way American teachers and Japanese teachers (at the university level) conduct classes?
3. What aspect(s) of American teachers pleases you the most?
4. What most surprised you at first about your teachers in the U.S.?
   Was your reaction to this characteristic negative or positive at first?
   Has you attitude changed? How?
5. Are there any general characteristics of Japanese teachers which you prefer over American teachers?
6. How do American students in general differ from Japanese students? How do you feel about this difference?
7. How has your own classroom behavior changed since you first started studying here?
8. What aspects of Japanese education would you liked to see become more like that in the U.S.?
9. What aspects of U.S. education should be made more like those in Japan?

References

Adger, Carolyn Temple. 1987. Accommodating cultural differences in conversational style: A case study. In: James P. Lantolf and Angela Labarca, eds., Research in second language learning: Focus on the classroom. Norwood, N.J.: Ablex. 159-72.

Andersen, Roger. 1983. Pidginization and creolization as language acquisition. Rowley, Mass.: Newbury House.

Bochner, Stephen, ed. 1981. The mediating person: Bridges between cultures. Cambridge, Mass.: Schenkman.

____. 1982. The social psychology of cross-cultural relations. In: S. Bochner, ed. Cultures in contact: Studies in cross-cultural interaction. Oxford: Pergamon.

Brown, H. Douglas. 1987. Principles of language learning and teaching. 2d ed. Englewood Cliffs, N.J.: Prentice-Hall.

Carey, A.T. 1956. Colonial students. London: Secker and Warburg.

Cazden, Courtney, and Vera P. John. 1968. Learning in American Indian children. In: Styles of learning among American Indians: An outline for research. Washington, D.C.: Center for Applied Linguistics.

Dumont, Robert V., Jr. 1972. Learning English and how to be silent: Studies in Sioux and Cherokee classrooms. In: Courtney Cazden, Vera P. John and Dell Hymes, eds. Functions of language in the classroom. New York: Teachers College Press. 344-69.

Edgerton, W. B. 1976. Who participates in education exchange? The Annals of the American Academy of Political and Social Science. 424:6-15.

Ellis, Rod. 1985. Understanding second language acquisition. Oxford: Oxford University Press.

Furnham, Adrian, and Stephen Bochner. 1986. Culture shock: Psychological reactions to unfamiliar environments. London: Methuen.

Guthrie, G.M. 1975. A behavioral analysis of culture learning. In: R.W. Brislin, S. Bochner, and W.J. Lonner, eds. Cross-cultural perspectives on learning. New York: Wiley.

____. 1981. What you need is continuity. In: S. Bochner, ed. The mediating person: Bridge between cultures. Boston: Schenkman.

Hall, Edward T. 1959. The silent language. 1973 edition. Garden City, N.Y.: Anchor Press/ Doubleday.

Klineberg, O. 1976. International education exchange: An assessment of its nature and prospects. Paris: Mouton.

____. 1981. The role of international university exchanges. In: S. Bochner, ed. The mediating person: Bridge between cultures. Boston: Schenkman.

Larson, Donald N., and William A. Smalley. 1972. Becoming bilingual: A practical guide to language learning. New Canaan, Conn.: Practical Anthropology.

Oberg, K. 1960. Cultural shock: Adjustment to new cultural environments. Practical Anthropology 7:177-82.

Philips, Susan U. 1972. Participant structures and communicative competence: Warm Springs children in community and classroom. In: Courtney Cazden, Vera P. John, and Dell Hymes, eds. Functions of language in the classroom. New York: Teachers College Press. 370-94.

Schumann, John. 1978. The pidginization process: A model for second language acquisition. Rowley, Mass.: Newbury House.

____. 1984. The acculturation model: The evidence. Paper presented at the Symposium on Current Approaches to Second Language Acquisition, University of Wisconsin-Milwaukee, March 29-31.

Ward, L. 1967. Some observations of the underlying dynamics of conflict in a foreign student. Journal of the American College Health Association 10:430-40.

Wolcott, Harry. 1967. A Kwakiutl village and school. New York: Holt, Rinehart and Winston.

Nativization and interlanguage in Standard English: Another look

Peter H. Lowenberg
Georgetown University

The last two decades have brought substantial progress in research on second language acquisition and learning, especially with regard to English. In terms of hypotheses tested and their applications for language teaching, studies have investigated many variable attributes of learners, teachers, and contexts which increasingly rigorous research methodologies are revealing to be significant in attaining second and foreign language proficiency.

Yet despite this attention to variability in processes facilitating classroom learning, relatively little attention has been focused on the inherent variability in the linguistic forms of English which are generally taught, Standard English. Trudgill (1983) and others have defined Standard English as the linguistic forms which are the accepted models for official, business, journalistic, and academic writing, and for public speaking before an audience or on radio or television. However, implicit in most accounts of Standard English as a pedagogical model, is an assumption that the universal target for classroom instruction, and the benchmark for attained proficiency in Standard English around the world, is the set of norms which are accepted and used by highly educated 'native speakers' of English.

In recent years, a number of linguists, including Kachru (1986) and Sridhar and Sridhar (1986), have argued that such an assumption is no longer sociolinguistically valid. In support of this claim, they have presented data from the 'nonnative varieties' of English. These varieties have developed in countries formerly colonized by Britain or the United States, including Nigeria, India, Malaysia, and the Philippines, where English continues to be used by substantial numbers of nonnative speakers as a second, often official, language in a broad range of *intra*national domains.[1] In many of these

[1] A more complete list of these countries also includes Bangladesh, Botswana, Brunei, Burma, Cameroon, Ethiopia, Fiji, The Gambia, Ghana, Israel, Kenya, Lesotho, Liberia, Malawi, Malta, Mauritius, Namibia, Nauru, Pakistan, Seychelles, Sierra Leone, Singapore, South Africa, Sri Lanka, Sudan, Swaziland, Tanzania, Tonga, Uganda, Western Samoa, Zambia, and Zimbabwe

countries, English is still used for some of the legislative, administrative, and judicial functions of government and is the principal medium of instruction, especially in secondary and postsecondary institutions.

An important consequence of this intranational use of English by nonnative speakers has been that in these countries where English is used daily in non-Western social and cultural contexts, in contact with other languages, and in the virtual absence of native speakers of English, English frequently becomes 'nativized' (Kachru 1986). It develops new phonological, morphological, syntactic, semantic, stylistic, and discoursal features that are so systematic, widespread, and accepted among their users that we can say that new varieties of English have evolved, distinct from the more 'established' native-speaker varieties (Platt and Weber 1980), such as British, American, Canadian, Australian, and New Zealand English. Nativized features marking these nonnative varieties are widely considered acceptable and appropriate in their sociolinguistic settings of use (Kachru 1976; Shaw 1981), but would be considered deviant if transplanted to countries where established varieties are commonly used.

Nativization as used here thus refers to stable modifications in the forms and functions of a fully elaborated variety of English that develop in conjunction with the extended use of English in nonnative sociocultural and multilingual contexts. It is a sociolinguistic phenomenon reflecting changes in normative behavior in a speech community.

As such, nativization is distinct from 'interlanguage', which refers to equally systematic, but more idiosyncratic and less stable, deviations from the norms of any variety of English—native or nonnative—by learners of that variety. Interlanguage is a phenomenon of language acquisition which results from an individual's attempts to approximate either native speaker or nativized norms. In settings where nonnative varieties have developed, the acquisition of English is generally toward competence in nativized norms (Kachru 1976; Shaw 1981).[2]

A source of confusion in recent discussions of nativization and interlanguage has been the use of this term 'nativization' by other linguists to describe various aspects of language acquisition. For Sankoff (1980) nativization refers to the first language acquisition of a pidgin by children, a development traditionally considered to coincide with creolization.[3] Andersen (1979, 1980, 1981) expands the domains of nativization to include all language acquisition: the 'acquisition towards an internal norm' (1980:273) of any

(Encyclopedia Britannica 1986:838-841; McCallen 1989:7-9).

[2] Henry Widdowson observes (personal communication) that interlanguage is 'ontogeneticy', while nativization is 'phylogeneticy'.

[3] Also related to pidgins is Todd's (1984:15) use of nativization in reference to the 'period of expansion and stabilisation' of a pidgin when it is used as a lingua franca, ' period when the local people (make) the pidgin serve their purposes.'

target language—first or second, including but not restricted to, pidgins and creoles—by individuals or groups.

Perhaps based on a perspective similar to Andersen's, Zuengler (1989) compares discussions of nativization in nonnative varieties of English with much of the research concerning interlanguage development in the second language acquisition of native-speaker English. Zuengler concludes that there is no reason to consider nativization as a phenomenon unique to nonnative varieties; rather, she proposes, nativization also occurs as both a group and individual process underlying interlanguage in all settings of second language acquisition.

> The NNV (nonnative varieties) literature presents 'nativization' as a group process . . . At the same time, though, one could argue that nativization is also an individual phenomenon, since the learner's degree of nativization would presumably be a function of his strength of cultural identity and the type of NNV styles he is acquiring. In IL (interlanguage) settings, we can speak, as well, of nativization as both a group and an individual process . . . (Zuengler 1989:92). [parentheses mine].

In contrast to Zuengler's claims, the remainder of this paper demonstrates a key sociolinguistic difference between nativization, as defined by Kachru (1986), and interlanguage: the role of nativization in determining Standard English, as described above, in nonnative varieties. That is, nativization creates new norms for Standard English; interlanguage does not. This examination focuses on morphosyntactic deviations from the norms of Standard American English in sample written texts taken from domains of Standard English in several nonnative varieties.[4] Particular attention is devoted to the nonnative variety of English that has developed in Malaysia. Following this analysis is a discussion of how within the writing of individual users of nonnative varieties, possible nativized features can be distinguished from interlanguage deficiencies.

Extension of productive morphosyntactic processes in Standard English. A major source of nativization in nonnative varieties is the extension of innovative morphosyntactic processes that are also very productive in, and

---

[4] As in Lowenberg (1989), this analysis is of 'morphosyntactic features in Standard English' because these can be easily identified and classified for cross-varietal comparison, because they have already been well described in native-speaker varieties, because authoritative prescriptive norms are frequently available in school textbooks and newspaper style sheets, and because these forms are addressed in most assessments of English proficiency. I will focus on written, as opposed to spoken texts, since regional phonetic and phonological processes can often mask the realization of morphosyntactic standards, and since written language has a greater likelihood of being successfully monitored or edited, making possible a distinction between mistakes and acquisitional errors.

frequently cause differences between, the established varieties of English. These are illustrated by examples (1), (2), and (5) through (10), all of which are taken from previously published descriptions of Standard English in nonnative varieties.

One of the most frequently occurring of these processes is the 'conversion to countability of noncount nouns' which semantically include an aggregate of countable units, as in (1) and (2), from Philippine and Nigerian English, respectively.[5]

(1) He has many *luggages* (Gonzalez 1983:167).

(2) I lost all my *furnitures* and many valuable *properties* (Bokamba 1982:82).

This process, which is restricted to specific lexical items in each variety of English,[6] likewise causes differences between the established varieties, as illustrated in (3) and (4), from Trudgill and Hannah (1985:62).[7]

(3)	British:	two *lettuces*
	American:	two *heads of lettuce*
(4)	British:	Good *accommodation* is hard to find here.
	American:	Good *accommodations* are hard to find here.

Another very productive process in the nonnative varieties of English is the creation of new phrasal verbs, as in (5), from Indian English, and (6), from the English of both Singapore and Malaysia.[8]

(5) Everyone is *dismissing off* my career (Mehrotra 1982:161).

---

[5] As Henry Widdowson notes (personal communication), many of these noncountable-to-countable conversions are register-specific. For example, the register of real estate in Standard American English includes real estate *properties*, a construction identical to that in (2).

[6] Henry Widdowson, personal communication.

[7] Additional examples of count/noncount differences between British and American English are given in Schur (1987), Algeo (1988), and Lowenberg (1989).

[8] This process, too, frequently produces distinct norms for usage in the established varieties. For example, British English *I caught him up* is semantically equivalent to American English *I caught up with him*. The British construction *catch him up* also occurs in Standard American English, but with a very different meaning. A more notorious semantic difference occurs in the phrasal verb, *Would you like me to knock you up*? This construction, though grammatically acceptable in both British and American English, has radically different meanings in the two varieties (Trudgill and Hannah 1985; see also Schur 1987, Algeo 1988, Lowenberg 1989 for additional examples).

(6) It is a bit difficult to *cope up with* all the work they give us (Tongue 1979:56).

A third productive process common to both the established and nonnative varieties is the coining of neologisms through 'morphological derivation', especially 'prefixation', as in (7), from Indian English, and (8), from the English of several nonnative varieties that have developed in East Africa.[9]

(7) If a passenger on a *preponed* flight shows up at the time written on his ticket and finds the plane has already left, he is not entitled to a refund (Coll 1990:A13).

(8) He *overlistened* to the boys' conversation (Hancock and Angogo 1982:318).

A fourth productive process frequently leading to innovations in both the established and nonnative varieties is expansion of the lexicon through compounding, as illustrated by (9), from Philippine English, and (10), from Ghanaian English.[10]

(9) Most of the students here are *bed-spacers* (Gonzalez 1983:158).

(10) You have to be careful with these *been-to boys* (Bokamba 1982:89).

Identification of nativized features in primary sources. These same processes frequently also underlie interlanguage features in the second language acquisition of English (see, for example, papers in Richards 1974). Relying on secondary sources, as has been done in the above examples, leaves the primary sources of data generally inaccessible. One can only take the word of these scholars that the features they have identified are indeed Standard English and not markers of interlanguage.

However, a decision to work with primary data entails the methodological problem of how to determine exactly which linguistic innovations are nativized features. Since the majority of users of nonnative varieties still do learn English as a second language, and since many nativized features arise from a subset of the linguistic processes which also underlie interlanguage, it is important to distinguish nativized features that create 'differences' between

---

[9] In (7), *prepone* is 'to decide to do something earlier than expected' (Verma 1982:180). *Overlisten* in (8) means 'to eavesdrop'.

[10] *Bed-spacers* in (9) refers to students who rent a bed in a boardinghouse or dormitory without eating their meals there. In (10), *been-to boys* (and girls) are young Ghanaians who have recently returned from studies and/or employment in Great Britain and frequently have difficulty readjusting to life in Ghana. In Indian English, such people are often called *England-returned* (Kachru 1982:363).

varieties (analogous to the differences between British and American English) from interlanguage 'deficiencies' in the acquisition of nativized Standard English by learners of nonnative varieties.

In some cases, making this distinction is quite easy, as in (11) and (12).

(11) Asia's longest bridge and *rank third* in the world. The $850 million concrete bridge *link Penang Island to Peninsula Malaysia.*

(12) Citizen makes your office calculation *more easier.*

(11) is the caption on a Malaysian postcard, while (12) is an advertisement from a Malaysian English-language newspaper. Neither of these deviations from native-speaker Standard English arises from the productive processes underlying (1) through (10) above. Both clearly reflect either aberrant mistakes or some stage in the process of acquiring English as a second language.

At the other extreme, some deviations from native-speaker English can be confidently proposed as being nativized norms as a result of having been institutionally codified by the same types of authorities who make such decisions in the established varieties. Such is the case, for example, with the underscored constructions in (13) and (14), from Malaysian ESL textbooks published by the Malaysian Ministry of Education and by Oxford University Press, respectively.

(13) *A consideration* for others is most important (Koh and Leong 1976:238).

(14) *Give* your book *in* (Howe 1974:125).

In other instances, newspaper style sheets provide evidence of nativization, as in (15) and (16), from the style sheet of the leading English-language newspaper in Singapore, *The Straits Times*.

(15) She lives *in 6th Avenue* (Straits Times Press 1985:4).

(16) I live in an apartment *at Belmont Road* (Straits Times Press 1985:177).

Between these extremes of codification and clear deficiency comes the more problematic area of identifying nativized norms and distinguishing them from interlanguage. In many cases, extensions of productive processes in English may not yet be codified, but their acceptability is enhanced through use by writers whose scholarship is highly regarded. This also occurs in the established varieties, as illustrated by the construction *knowledges* in (17) and

(18), which would be considered unacceptable by many speakers of Standard American English.

(17) Equally certainly, twenty-five authors and two editors do not know enough to write this book, and by virtue of *knowledges* and viewpoints they may not provide as cohesive a book as a single author.

(18) In the cultural and academic spheres, one finds national *knowledges* and discourses coexisting with Continentalist constructs . . .

However, upon learning that (17) was written by Charles Ferguson and Shirley Brice Heath (Ferguson and Heath 1981:xxxviii) and that (18) appears in a paper by Mary Louise Pratt (Pratt 1986:34), readers familiar with these scholars' work would be slower to reject this plural form as ungrammatical, especially when used in the registers of these writers' domains of expertise. Moreover, the spread of the form *knowledges* through the writing of other scholars in the language sciences could lead to a change in the norms of this register of Standard American English.

Such acceptance of *knowledges* on the basis of the stature of its authors motivates a similar response to *switchings* in (19) and (20), both of which were written by the prominent Malaysian linguist Asmah Haji Omar (Asmah 1985:20,22), whose status among Southeast Asian language specialists is equivalent to that of the American authors of (17) and (18).

(19) In this context, there were variations such as (code) *switchings* between English and their own language.

(20) Intrasentential code-switching may take place in a formal or semi-formal situation, like at official meetings, seminars or conferences. Most *switchings* at these levels take place between standard Malay and formal Malaysian English.

As with *knowledges* above, if other Malaysian linguists likewise begin to use *switchings*, this construction could become a nativized feature in this register of Standard Malaysian English.

Even when the status of the particular authors is unknown, identification of registers within specific domains can be useful in distinguishing nativized features from acquisitional deficiencies in the nonnative varieties. Examples (21) and (22) are taken from two of Malaysia's leading English-language newspapers, the *New Straits Times* and *The Star*.

(21) Complaints of threats and *intimidations* have surfaced and these could affect the security situation in the State.

(22) Is Parliament all that it's *cracked out* to be?

(21) appeared in a front-page news story in the *New Straits Times*. As part of a lead article of a prestigious newspaper, it was probably written, or at least edited, by a highly proficient Malaysian user of English. This further suggests that many of the educated Malaysian speakers of English who read the *New Straits Times* would not object to the construction *intimidations*. On this basis, *intimidations* can be considered a possible nativized feature of Malaysian English. In contrast, (22) appeared in the 'Letters to the Editor' section of *The Star*. In this case, little can be surmised about the English proficiency of the writer, about the likelihood that (22) was carefully edited, and therefore, whether *intimidations* is likely to be a nativized feature.

To summarize thus far, the above data argue against Zuengler's (1989) conclusion, discussed above, that nativization, as used in the literature on nonnative varieties of English, and interlanguage are not mutually exclusive. Instead, empirical bases have been proposed as heuristics for identifying nativized norms for Standard English in nonnative varieties, and for distinguishing these features from those of interlanguage. The first of these heuristics is that many nativized features result from a limited number of the productive linguistic processes that also produce differences among the established varieties of English. The second heuristic is that in a small number of instances, nativized features have been codified by institutions having control over domains of Standard English, such as government-authorized textbooks and newspaper stylesheets. The third heuristic is that deviations from native-speaker norms can be considered to be possible nativized features when produced by English speakers with high status in the relevant speech community and/or when appearing in texts likely to have been written and edited by speakers who are highly proficient in English (in journalism, for example, in the front-page news, as opposed to 'Letters to the Editor' or advertisements [see (12) above]).

Pedagogical implications. These heuristics for distinguishing nativized features from interlanguage can be quite useful in assessing the English proficiency of the many foreign students enrolled in American universities who come from countries where nonnative varieties have been linguistically and attitudinally identified (Kachru 1976, Shaw 1981, Lowenberg 1989). Educators charged with evaluating the English proficiency of these students can attempt to distinguish 'deficiencies' in the acquisition of English by these students (interlanguage) from varietal 'differences' in the students' usage resulting from their having previously learned nativized English. For example, possible nativized features would include systematic deviations from Standard American English which result from morphosyntactic processes which are also productive in established varieties, such as the ones discussed above, and which highly educated English users in the students' home countries might therefore use in domains of Standard English.

An illustration of how this distinction might be made comes from analysis of (23) through (25), from papers written by Malaysian graduate students in linguistics at Georgetown University.

(23) For example, *when the first time I came here*, I did not have enough *vocabularies*...

(24) In the past, *several* interesting *research* had been conducted...

(25) Forty college-educated MEBs studying in the Washington, DC, and Northern Virginia area were the subject of *a research* entitled...

All of the italicized items would be considered incorrect by most speakers of Standard American English. In (23) and (24), *when the first time I came here* and *several interesting research* do not result from the productive processes discussed above and are therefore most likely either performance mistakes or interlanguage errors in all varieties of Standard English. However, *vocabularies* in (24) and *a research* in (25) do result from the process of making noncount nouns countable, as in (1) through (4). These constructions could be nativized features that these students were taught in Malaysia or they could be acquisitional deficiencies. Therefore, in assessing these students' English proficiency, *vocabularies* and *a research* cannot be evaluated as quickly and clearly as can *when the first time I came here* and *several interesting research*.

Another, deeper implication of becoming sensitive to nativized features arises in (26).

(26) We often exchange our *knowledges*.

The italicized construction here appears to be identical to (17) and (18) above, from Ferguson and Heath and from Pratt. However, the author of (26) is a Georgetown linguistics graduate student from Japan, where no nonnative variety has yet been identified. Is (26), therefore, a marker of interlanguage? If so, does (27), written by a Georgetown linguistics graduate student from the United States also reflect an interlanguage?

(27) As *a homework*, students chose ten words or phrases to write in sentences.

Apparently, as indicated by (26) and (27) and by many of the data examined above, the basis for distinguishing between 'differences' (including innovations) and 'deficiencies' in Standard English can be extremely attitudinal as well as linguistic.

Conclusion. This analysis and discussion, though suggesting heuristics for distinguishing nativized features from interlanguage, also illustrate how little can actually be determined on the basis of such limited data as are presented here. Research on nonnative varieties has not yet advanced to the point of being able to identify all, or even most, of the nativized features in any variety. As discussed in Lowenberg (1989), many conceptual and methodological problems remain. For one thing, a much broader data base will be necessary. Equally important for the identification of nativized features in a particular variety will be judgments of the acceptability of specific innovations in that variety by that variety's most highly educated speakers.

In addition, the scope of analysis of nonnative varieties must be extended beyond morphology and syntax to other linguistic levels. For example, research by B. Kachru (1986) and Y. Kachru (1988) has revealed significant register-specific stylistic differences in Standard English between nonnative varieties and the established varieties. Such differences are illustrated by (29) and (30), from Standard English in Malaysia and India, respectively.

(29) Ibrahim Hussein enmeshes the pictorial surface with sensuous entanglements of lyrical linearity ('Forward' to brochure, National Art Gallery, Kuala Lumpur).

(30) Akhtar had already published some excellent short stories when he received the call *to turn the sods in the field of the novel* (Cited in Kachru 1988:48, from a sample of literary criticism).

Both of these passages seem considerably more embellished than would similar samples from American English, even in the registers of art and literary criticism; however, sharper analytical tools than have been used above are needed to identify which of these features can be considered nativized norms.

Nevertheless, even with the great deal that remains to be learned about nonnative varieties of English and the dynamics of nativization, enough is known to warrant making a distinction between nativization and interlanguage. This distinction can be particularly useful in the assessment of and responses to deviations from native-speaker norms made by speakers of nonnative varieties. In addition, what has been learned thus far about nonnative varieties clearly indicates that as the spread of English continues worldwide and the percentage of English speakers who use English nonnatively increases, the normative forms and functions of English in new sociolinguistic contexts will continue to diversify. This diversification of norms on a societal level is clearly a significant variable in any universally valid research on second language acquisition.

References

Algeo, John. 1988. British and American grammatical differences. International Journal of Lexicography 1(1):1-31.
Andersen, Roger. 1979. Expanding Schumann's pidginization hypothesis. Language Learning 29:105-19.
Andersen, Roger. 1980. Creolization as the acquisition of a second language as a first language. In: Valdman and Highfield, eds. 273-95.
Andersen, Roger. 1981. Two perspectives on pidginization as second language acquisition. In: Roger Andersen, ed. New dimensions in second language acquisition research. Rowley, Mass.: Newbury House. 165-95.
Asmah Haji Omar. 1985. Patterns of language communication in Malaysia. Southeast Asian Journal of Social Science 13(1):19-28.
Bailey, Richard, and Manfred Gorlach, eds. 1982. English as a world language. Ann Arbor: University of Michigan Press.
Bokamba, Eyamba. 1982. The Africanization of English. In: Braj B. Kachru, ed. The other tongue. Urbana: University of Illinois Press. 77-98.
Coll, Steve. 1990. India's terminal frustration. The Washington Post, January 15:A13.
Encyclopedia Britannica. 1986. Britannica Book of the Year 1986. Chicago: Encyclopedia Britannica, Inc.
Ferguson, Charles A., and Shirley Brice Heath. 1981. Introduction. In: Charles A. Ferguson and Shirley Brice Heath, eds. Language in the USA. Cambridge: Cambridge University Press. xxv-xxxviii.
Gonzalez, Andrew. 1983. When does an error become a feature of Philippine English? In: Richard B. Noss, ed. Varieties of English in Southeast Asia. Singapore: Regional Language Centre. (RELC Anthology Series 11:150-72)
Hancock, Ian, and Rachel Angogo. 1982. English in East Africa. In: Bailey and Gorlach, eds. 306-23.
Howe, D.H. 1974. New guided English, Book 1. Kuala Lumpur: Oxford University Press. [Reprinted by Kuala Lumpur: Penerbit Fajar Bakti Sdn. Bhd. 1986]
Kachru, Braj B. 1976. Models of English for the Third World: White man's linguistic burden or language pragmatics? TESOL Quarterly 10(2):221-39.
Kachru, Braj B. 1982. South Asian English. In: Bailey and Gorlach, eds. 353-83.
Kachru, Braj B. 1986. The alchemy of English. Oxford: Pergamon Press.
Kachru, Yamuna. 1988. Interpreting Indian English expository prose. IDEAL 3:39-50.
Koh, Judy, and Leong Suat Chin. 1976. Dewan's communicative English, Book 4. Kuala Lumpur: Dewan Bahasa dan Pustaka, Ministry of Education.
Lowenberg, Peter H. 1989. Testing English as a world language: Issues in assessing nonnative proficiency. In: James E. Alatis, ed. Georgetown University Round Table on Languages and Linguistics. Washington, D.C.: Georgetown University Press. 216-27.
McCallen, Brian. 1989. English: A world commodity. London: The Economist Intelligence Unit.
Mehrotra, R. 1982. Indian English: A sociolinguistic profile. In: Pride, ed. 150-73.
Platt, John, and Heidi Weber. 1980. English in Singapore and Malaysia. Kuala Lumpur: Oxford University Press.
Pratt, Mary Louise. 1986. Comparative literature as a cultural practice. Profession 86:33-35. New York: Modern Language Association of America.
Pride, John, ed. 1982. New Englishes. Rowley, Mass.: Newbury House.
Richards, Jack C., ed. 1974. Error analysis: Perspectives on second language acquisition. London: Longman.
Sankoff, G. 1980. Variation, pidgins, and creoles. In: Valdman and Highfield, eds. 139-64.
Schur, Norman W. 1987. British English, A to Zed. New York: Facts on File Publications.
Shaw, Willard. 1981. Asian student attitudes toward English. In: Larry E. Smith, ed. English for cross-cultural communication. New York: St. Martin's Press. 100-22.

Sridhar, Kamal K., and S. N. Sridhar. 1986. Bridging the paradigm gap: Second language acquisition theory and indigenized varieties of English. World Englishes 5(1):3-14.

Straits Times Press. 1985. Our style: The way we use words in *The Straits Times*. Singapore: Straits Times Press, Ltd.

Todd, Loreto. 1984. Modern Englishes: Pidgins and creoles. Oxford: Basil Blackwell.

Tongue, R.K. 1979. The English of Singapore and Malaysia. Singapore: Eastern Universities Press.

Trudgill, Peter. 1983. Sociolinguistics (Revised edition). Harmondsmith, England: Penguin Books.

Trudgill, Peter, and Jean Hannah. 1985. International English: A guide to varieties of Standard English (Second edition). London: Edward Arnold.

Valdman, A., and A. Highfield, eds. 1980. Theoretical orientations in creole studies. New York: Academic Press.

Verma, S. 1982. Swadeshi English: Form and function. In: Pride, ed. 174-87.

Zuengler, Jane. 1989. Identity and IL development and use. Applied Linguistics 10(1):80-96.

The role of the amygdala as a mediator of affect and cognition in second language acquisition

John H. Schumann
University of California, Los Angeles

It has long been recognized that there is a strong affective component in second language acquisition. This is manifest in the research which has reported on: (1) the role of the learner's attitude toward the target language and its speakers (Gardner 1985); (2) the learner's instrumental versus integrative motivation (Gardner 1985); (3) the learner's perception of his ethno-linguistic vitality (Giles, Bourhis, and Taylor 1977); (4) the learner's ego state in the second language learning situation (Schumann 1975, Guiora 1972); (5) the learner's anxiety in the second language learning situation (Scovel 1978); and (6) the learner's feelings of language and culture shock (Schumann 1978).

It is generally felt that one's affective orientation will enhance or inhibit one's second language learning, and thus, may account for a good deal of variation in success that we observe among second language learners. It seems reasonable to assume, then, that there must be some neural mechanism that assesses the affective content of the second language situation and uses that information to enhance or inhibit learning. The amygdaloid complex, a nucleus in the limbic system, appears to function in this way. The amygdala is part of an important neural circuit involved in memory. In addition, it is a nucleus that evaluates sensory stimuli and communicates that evaluation to other emotion centers of the brain. This paper explores the way in which, with this dual role, the amygdala may serve to mediate affect and cognition in second language learning.

The memory circuit. A plausible neural circuit for human memory which has been suggested by Mishkin and Appenzeller (1987) is depicted in Figure 1. Information from the final sensory (vision, taste, touch, audition) processing areas activates a circuit that first involves two limbic structures, the amygdala and the hippocampus, which in turn connect to two diencephalic structures, the thalamus and hypothalamus, which then project to the prefrontal cortex. Each of these areas connects to the basal forebrain, which closes the circuit by projecting back to the sensory processing areas.[1]

Figure 1. Semischematic representation of proposed memory circuit (based on Mishkin and Appenzeller 1987).

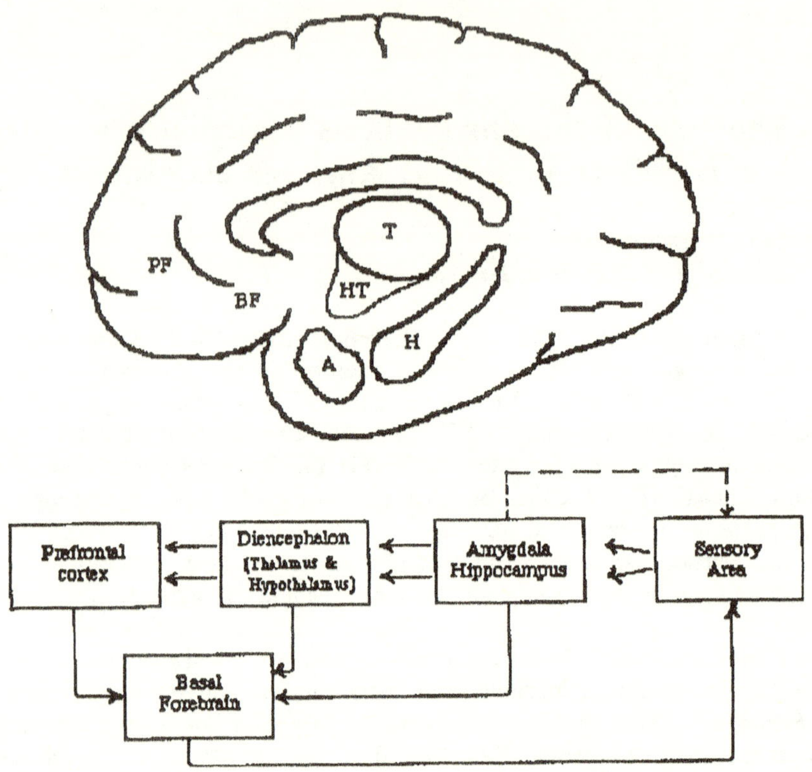

Damage to either the hippocampus or the amygdala alone will not cause amnesia, but damage to both these areas impairs the ability to form certain kinds of new memories while, generally, leaving older memories intact (Squire 1987). Damage to the two diencephalic structures or the connections between the limbic areas and these structures also causes amnesia. Research (Mishkin and Appenzeller 1987) also indicates that damage to the ventromedial prefrontal cortex, which receives projections from the diencephalon, produces a loss of recognition memory.

---

[1] In as yet unpublished work, Squire reports that the parahippocampal gyrus, the entorhinal cortex, and the perirhinal cortex may also be involved in memory.

It is generally believed that memories themselves are not stored in this circuit but rather are maintained in the final processing stations of the respective sensory areas. Mishkin and Appenzeller (1987) suggest that projections of these memory structures to the basal forebrain trigger the release of acetylcholine, a neurotransmitter, into the sensory regions where it causes changes in neural connections (synapses) to form the memory trace. In addition, there are projections from the amygdala to the sensory areas (see dotted line in Figure 1) which I discuss later.

Types of memory. It is generally accepted that there is a distinction between short-term and long-term memory and that short-term memory may operate independently of the hippocampus and amygdala (Squire 1987). This has been illustrated by an experiment called delayed nonmatching to sample (Mishkin and Appenzeller 1987), in which monkeys are shown a distinctive object under which is a reward such as a peanut. Next they are shown two more objects, the one that had contained the reward in the original trial and an unfamiliar one. This time the reward is under the new object. Therefore the monkey receives the reward by learning to avoid the originally rewarded object and by choosing the novel object. Monkeys with lesions of the hippocampus and amygdala can perform this task if the time between the first trial and the second is very short, but when the delay is increased to a minute or two they perform at the level of chance. Thus it would appear that processing by the hippocampus and amygdala is necessary for information to achieve long-term storage.

Another distinction made in memory research is between declarative and procedural memory (Squire 1987). Declarative memory concerns the storage and retrieval of facts and events; procedural memory concerns the acquisition of habits involved in motor and perceptual skills. It appears that procedural memory, like short-term memory, operates independently of the hippocampus and amygdala. Evidence for this comes from patients with joint hippocampal and amygdaloid lesions who can learn perceptuomotor skills such as mirror writing and mirror reading and can perform these tasks when asked to, but retain no memory of either the event of learning these skills or the fact that they can perform them. Also, Mishkin and Appenzeller (1987) report that monkeys with lesions of the hippocampus and amygdala which cannot perform the delayed nonmatching to sample task, can, with time, learn to choose the baited object in each pair of a long series of different object pairs. The authors argue that this form of learning is stimulus-response habit formation and noncognitive. The delayed nonmatching to sample task is cognitive because the monkey has to remember which object is the original in order not to choose it. Mishkin and Appenzeller also believe that procedural knowledge and habit formation occur outside the memory circuit described in Figure 1. They suggest that a complex of structures in the forebrain called the striatum, which is evolutionarily older than the cortex and the limbic system, may be the neural substrate for habit.

The role of the amygdala in emotion. The amygdala has come to be seen as the part of the brain that places an emotional value on experience. The brain must know the significance of the stimuli it perceives in order to be able to react to it appropriately. The amygdala assigns a positive or negative significance to current stimuli by comparing that sensory input to stored information or knowledge (LeDoux 1986a).

Some of the earliest evidence for the emotional function of the amygdala comes from what is called the Klüver-Bucy syndrome (Klüver and Bucy 1939). The amygdala and hippocampus lie within the temporal lobes. Monkeys whose temporal lobes had been removed displayed a decrease in aggressiveness, a loss of fear of humans, a tendency to examine objects repeatedly with the mouth, including inedible objects and adversive objects such as feces. In addition, these monkeys had an abnormally heightened sex drive which led them to attempt copulation with animals of the wrong sex and different species. Mishkin and Appenzeller (1987) report that in later studies the same behavior resulted when only the amygdala was removed. They suggest that the monkeys were unable to integrate various kinds of memory. The sight of an object did not lead to a memory of its smell, and the smell of an object did not produce a memory of its taste. Amygdalectomies essentially left the animals emotionally unresponsive to visual, tactile, auditory, and gustatory stimuli (Aggleton and Mishkin 1986). In addition, the animals' loss of fear of humans and lack of aversion to repugnant stimuli seemed to indicate that 'a link between familiar stimuli and their emotional associations had been severed' (10). This led to the speculation that the amygdala is responsible for assigning an emotional significance to an experience. Clinical evidence indicates that human subjects with damage to the amygdala have emotional behavior similar to that of the primates described above (Aggleton and Mishkin 1986). These patients are characterized by flattened affect and rapid dissipation of emotion if aroused. This hypoemotionality can be either global or specific to a single sensory system.

It does not, however, appear that mechanisms of emotion are contained in the amygdala itself. Instead, the hypothalamus and related areas are generally assumed to be responsible for this function. Aggleton and Mishkin (1986) report that in cats whose amygdalas have been removed, direct electrical stimulation of the hypothalamus will produce fear and aggressive behavior. Thus, the sources of emotion are still intact in amygdalectomized animals. This observation leads to the conclusion that the amygdala constitutes a link that funnels highly integrated sensory information from the cortical sensory systems to the hypothalamus and related structures responsible for the production and expression of emotion.

The input, internal connections and output of the amygdala. Aggleton and Mishkin (1986) provide a description of the cortical projections to the amygdala, internal connections within the amygdala, and projections from the amygdala to other areas of the subcortex. In the cerebral cortex there are primary processing areas for each form of sensory information—vision, audition, taste and touch.[2] In addition, this information is further processed at various stations along particular sensory pathways. From the final stations on these pathways, where the sensory information is most fully processed, it projects to the amygdala. The amygdala itself consists of about eight subnuclei. Each of the final sensory processing areas projects to a particular subregion with little overlap among them. The cortex also contains several polysensory areas that integrate more than one kind of sensory information. Most of these cortical regions also project to the amygdala. They terminate in specific amygdaloid subnuclei, but they differ from the sensory-specific projections in that they terminate in two or more subregions. Within the amygdala itself there are extensive projections among the various subnuclei. Finally, the amygdala sends outputs to several subcortical sites: the basal forebrain, the hypothalamus, the thalamus, the midbrain, pons, and medulla. Mishkin and Appenzeller (1987) report that, in addition to these subcortical projections, the amygdala projects back to the cortex itself.

The role of the amygdala in second language learning. The neural circuit depicted in Figure 1 represents what is called a corticofugal pathway for memory, in which projections begin at the final sensory processing stations in the cortex and then flow to the amygdala, hippocampus, thalamus, hypothalamus, prefrontal cortex, and basal forebrain. LeDoux (1986a) points out that there is also a precortical pathway, in which sensory input is received by the thalamus and then projected directly to the amygdala and hippocampus without passing through the sensory processing areas in the cortex. This pathway is illustrated in Figure 2.

LeDoux argues that the corticofugal pathway from the thalamus to neocortex and down to the amygdala and hypothalamus provides the assignment of emotional significance to complex, highly discriminated perceptual information. The subcortical pathway from the thalamus to the amygdala and hypothalamus, however, provides an emotional evaluation of simple or crude stimulus features. Both pathways operate in parallel. LeDoux argues (1986a:345-46):

> Two implications of the parallel emotional processing channels should be considered. First, the subcortical areas that receive thalamic inputs also receive neocortical inputs. The two pathways thus converge. The thalamic pathway, though, is several synapses shorter. Input reaching target areas such as the amygdala may therefore prime the area to receive the better analyzed neocortical inputs, providing a crude picture of what is to come,

---

[2] Olfaction is an exception; the olfactory bulbs project directly to the amygdala (i.e. not via the cortex).

narrowing the affective possibilities, and perhaps even organizing possible and actual responses.

From the foregoing discussion, the following picture emerges of the amygdala's role in mediating affect and cognition. First, as depicted in Figure 1, the amygdala, as a stimulus evaluator, plays an important role in a proposed memory circuit. Along with several other neural complexes, it projects to the basal forebrain, from which it is hypothesized that neurotransmitters are sent to the neocortex to facilitate synaptic changes resulting in long-term memory. Second, Mishkin and Appenzeller (1987) point out that the amygdala itself is rich in neurons that produce opiumlike neurotransmitters (endogenous opiates) which transmit nerve signals. In addition, the final sensory processing stations in the cortex are abundant in opiate receptors. The authors suggest the possibility that projections from the amygdala to these areas of the sensory processing systems 'may serve a gatekeeping function by releasing opiates in response to emotional states generated in the hypothalamus. In that way the amygdala may enable the emotions to influence what is perceived and learned' (10). The authors further suggest that 'if emotions can affect sensory processing in the cortex, they might provide the needed filter, tending to limit attention—and hence learning—to stimuli with emotional significance. The amygdala, in its capacity as intermediary between the senses and the emotions, is one structure that could underlie such "selective attention"' (10).

Figure 2. Precortical pathways (from Le Doux 1986a).

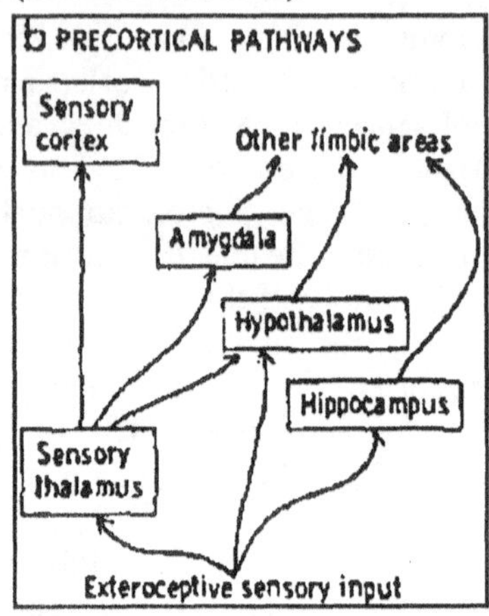

Finally, the subcortical pathway from the thalamus to the amygdala provides a means whereby the amygdala might assign to the basic stimulus features of an experience an emotional evaluation that would certainly be unconscious. This evaluation would then interact with the one based on more highly processed stimulus information from the cortex.

Now, how might the functioning of the amygdala operate in second language acquisition? It would appear that if the amygdala places a negative emotional evaluation on stimuli emanating from a language learning situation, either in the target language environment or in the classroom, it could inhibit language acquisition in two ways. First, through its participation in the proposed memory circuit (Figure1), it, in conjunction with the hypothalamus, might communicate that negative emotion through the basal forebrain to the cortex and thus diminish the likelihood that the requisite synaptic changes would occur to move the linguistic information contained in the stimuli into long-term memory. Second, in its suggested role as a filter that limits attention paid to stimuli, it might diminish attention to the linguistic information in negatively valued stimuli and thus prevent input from becoming intake. Finally, the subcortical thalamo-amygdaloid circuit could produce a conflict with the cortico-amygdaloid pathway that would result in behavior often observed in second language learning. Some learners, while professing the need and desire to learn the second language and exhibiting the effort to do so, nevertheless appear to achieve rather little and may even fossilize. LeDoux (1986b:242) suggests, 'it is possible that the different sensory pathways, if not coordinated, might mediate the learning of conflicting response tendencies to the same stimulus, leading to indecisive or inconsistent behavioral reactions to that stimulus.' A situation could arise where the primitive evaluation of the language learning experience along the thalamo-amygdaloid path is negative while cortico-amygdaloid evaluation, perhaps with some recognition of the need to know the language, is more positive. This situation could produce a learner who achieves relatively little for the effort he makes to acquire the second language.

The potential influence of amygdaloid function on second language acquisition is also demonstrated in research on effects of electrical stimulation of the amygdola. Halgren (1981) reports that such stimulation can provoke fear, hallucination, aggression, and pleasure. These reactions correlate with the subjects' responses on the MMPI. Subjects reporting fear had higher scores on psychoaesthenia, and those reporting hallucinations had higher scores on the schizophrenia scale. (None of the subjects, however, was psychotic.) The responses to electrical stimulation also correspond to a subject's psychodynamic orientation as indicated in psychiatric interviews and post hoc clinical assessments. Aggressive patients show aggression with amygdaloid stimulation; patients who have intense pain report pleasure, and patients who appear apprehensive about the stimulation report fear. Finally, the contents of psychiatric interviews seem to correspond to the content of complex hallucinations. According to Halgren (1981:399), the 'hallucinations are interpreted as symbolizing ongoing psychodynamic concerns, both implicit in the interpersonal exchange immediately preceding the stimulation, and more long-standing unresolved conflicts.'

From the foregoing, we might speculate that one major source of variation in success in second language acquisition might be the fact that in ordinary maturation an individual builds up the emotional experience against which the amygdala evaluates new stimuli. In each individual that experience is different. Therefore the degree of success in second language acquisition is unpredictable. We cannot know how an individual's amygdala will assess the language learning situation. One may only predict that earlier is better because the experiential basis for amygdaloid evaluation is less, and therefore perhaps more flexible.

References

Aggleton, John P., and Mortimer Mishkin. 1986. The amygdala: Sensory gateway to the emotions. In: Robert Plutchik and Henry Kellerman, eds. Emotion: Theory, research, and experience, vol. 3. Orlando, Fla.: Academic Press. 281-99.

Gardner, R.C. 1985. Social psychology and second language learning: The role of attitudes and motivation. London: Edward Arnold.

Giles, H., R. Bourkis, and D. Taylor. 1977. Toward a theory of language in ethnic group relations. In: H. Giles, ed. Language, ethnicity, and intergroup relations. New York: Academic Press.

Guiora, Alexander Z. 1972. Construct validity and transpositional research: Toward an empirical study of psychoanalytic concepts. Comprehensive Psychiatry 13:139-50.

Guyton, Arthur C. 1987. Basic neuroscience. Philadelphia: W.B. Saunders Company.

Halgren, Eric. 1981. The amygdala's contribution to emotions and memory: Current studies in humans. In: Y. Ben-Ari, ed. The amygdaloid complex. Amsterdam: Elsevier/North Holland Biomedical Press. 395-408.

Klüver, H., and P.C. Bucy. 1939. Preliminary analysis of functions of the temporal lobes in monkeys. Archives of Neurology and Psychiatry 42:979-1000.

LeDoux, Joseph E. 1986a. The neurobiology of emotion. In: Joseph E. LeDoux and William Hirst, eds. Mind and brain: Dialogues in cognitive neuroscience. New York: Cambridge University Press. 301-54.

LeDoux, Joseph E. 1986b. Sensory systems and emotion: A model of affective processing. Integrative Psychiatry 4:237-48.

Mishkin, Mortimer, and Tim Appenzeller. 1987. The anatomy of memory. Scientific American 256:80-89.

Schumann, John H. 1975. Affective factors and the problem of age in second language acquisition. Language Learning 25:209-36.

Schumann, John H. 1978. The pidginization process: A model for second language acquisition. Rowley, Mass.: Newbury House.

Scovel, Thomas. 1978. The effect of affect on foreign language learning. Language Learning 28:129-42.

Squire, Larry R. 1987. Memory: Neural organization and behavior. In: V. Mountcastle, F. Plum, S.R. Geiger, eds. Handbook of physiology—The nervous system, vol. 5. Bethesda, Md.: American Psychology Society.

A situational analysis of the semantics of *can* in American English

N. Yuji Suzuki
Institute of Languages and Communication
Keio University at Shonan Fujisawa

In Suzuki (1985) and (1989), I pointed out (1) the centrality of a dynamic meaning in the semantics of the English modals, and (2) the ways in which it incorporated backgrounds into the perception and production of an epistemic meaning or a deontic meaning. The data used in these studies were about 10,000 modal sentences listed in the Brown University Corpus. However, more emphasis was placed on (1) rather than (2) due to lack of appropriate data. The present paper hence focuses on (2) to show how situation operates on the semantics of *can* as its indispensable part. Among the English modals, *can* appears to be the most complicated one to deal with. The reason is that this particular modal cannot be analyzed on a simple scale consisting of an epistemic sense at one extreme and a deontic sense at the other (unlike *may* and *must*). Moreover, for analysts who attempt to view the modals as part of modality, *can* is the least interesting, when they conclude that *can* has no epistemic sense.

Webster's Third International Dictionary lists the following definitions under *can*:

(a) know how to, have the skill to:
He can read / She can play the piano;
(b) be physically and mentally able to:
He can lift 200 pounds / I can tell red from green;
(c) may perhaps, and may possibly:
Do you think he can still be living? / It could be true;
(d) have the necessary courage or resolution to:
He can accept defeat without complaining;
(e) be permitted by conscience or feeling:
We can hardly blame him / I can forgive anything but that;

(f) be made possible or probable by circumstances to:
He can hardly have that/ I could cry for shame;
(g) be inherently able or designed to:
Everything that money can buy/ This car can hold five people;
(h) be logically or axiologically able to:
2 plus 2 can also be written 3 plus 1/ We can reasonably conclude from this that such is the case;
(i) be enabled by law, agreement, or custom to, have a right to:
Only the House can originate financial measures;
(j) have permission to—used interchangeably with 'may':
You can go now if you like.

To shuffle these examples, (f) is a typical example of 'possibility'; (c) exemplifies 'epistemic possibility'; (a), (b), (g), and (h) are to be combined under 'ability'; (i) and (j) under 'permission'. On the other hand, (d) is to be placed somewhere between 'ability' and 'possibility', and (e) between 'permission' and 'possibility'. In Suzuki (1985) and (1989), I used the terms, 'dynamic sense' or 'root possibility' instead of 'possibility' to show the vitality as well as centrality of this meaning. In the following discussion, however, I use the term 'possibility' to emphasize a third quality of this sense, i.e. neutrality.

In her research on the modal verbs in British English, Coates (1983) reached the following conclusion concerning *can* on the basis of the data from the Lancaster corpus and the corpus of the Survey of English Usage compiled by University College at London. (Figure 1 and Table 1).

Figure 1. Coates' fuzzy set diagram of *can*.

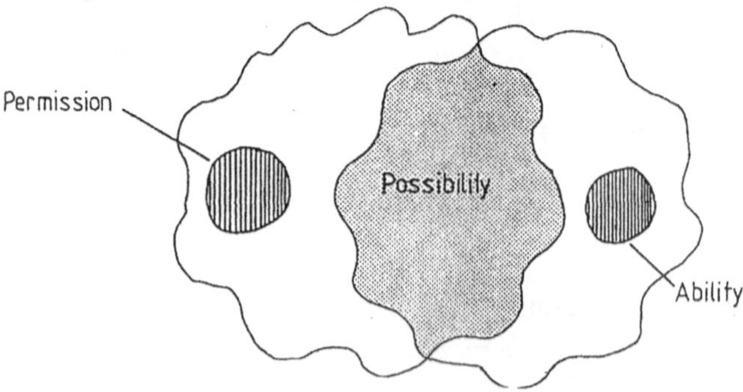

Table 1. Coates' chart for distribution of *can*.

	PERMISSION	POSSIBILITY	ABILITY	GRADIENCE	TOTAL
SURVEY	10(5%)	129(64%)	41(20%)	20(10%)	200
LANCASTER	8(3%)	158(64%)	57(25%)	18(8%)	231

Coates, together with Palmer (1979 and 1986), maintains that ***can*** in British English has no epistemic sense. This contrasts with its American counterpart. Let us look into the statistics in American English (Table 2).

Table 2. Distribution of ***can*** in the Brown University corpus.

EPISTEMIC POSSIBILITY	POSSIBILITY	ABILITY	PERMISSION	GRADIENCE	TOTAL
250(11%)	1250(57%)	10(0.005%)	15(0.007%)	675(31%)	2200

Table 3 lists examples representative of these meanings.

Table 3. Meanings of ***can*** and their examples

Epistemic possibility (EP)

(1) The word that is not used ***can*** be as important as the word that is used; therapist and/or linguist must always consider the alternatives. (F01.1800)

Epistemic possibility-Possibility Merger (EP-P)

(2) Ionizing radiation ***can*** cause the destruction of microorganisms and insects involved in food spoilage or at lower doses, can inhibit their action. (J74.0510)

Possibility (P)

(3) An underground reinforced shelter ***can*** be built by a contractor for about $1,000 to 1,500. (H.15.0630)

Possibility-Ability Merger (P-A)

(4) Harcourt replied, "I do really hope you ***can*** achieve serenity in the course of time. Of course, I hope that Hal ***can*** also, but those hopes are much more faint." (G67.0280)

Ability (A)

(5) The children ***can*** do chores adapted to their age and ability. (F13.0140)

Possibility-Permission Merger (P-Pr)

(6) But you don't have to worship in the traditional way. You ***can*** communicate in your own way.

Permission (Pr)

(7) Even though this is my rock, you ***can*** use it sometimes. I come early in the morning. (P16.1020)

P-Pr-A Merger

(8) As for progress, the "backward South" ***can*** boast of Baton Rouge, which increased its population between 1940 and 1950 by two hundred and sixty-two per cent, to 126,000. (G08.0450)

EP-Pr-A Merger

(9) Philosophy ***can*** offer the sort of distinction that ***can*** accelerate growth in human understanding. (J51.1010)

Figure 2 depicts the semantic network of ***can*** in American English.

Figure 2. Semantic network of *can*.

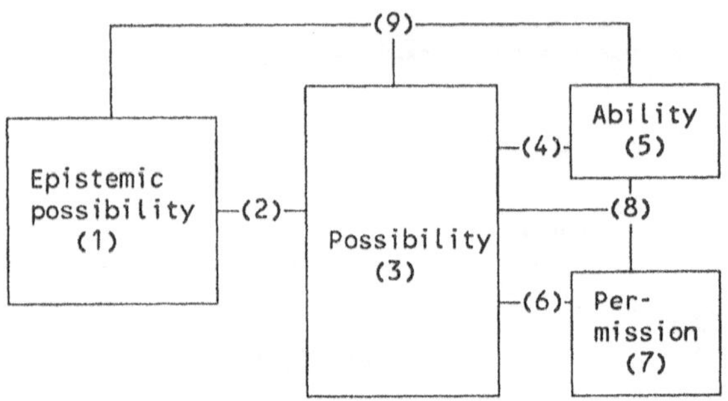

Table 2 reveals that 'possibility' statistically dominates all the other meanings of *can* in AE (this also applies to BE, as suggested in Table 1). Figure 2 demonstrates how ambiguities center around 'possibility'. These pieces of evidence were used to conclude that 'possibility' is the dynamo of the semantics of *can* whereas the other meanings should be best considered to be different manifestations of 'possibility'. Namely, what were thought to be the 'permission' sense and the 'ability' sense should be looked upon as the 'permissive' use and the 'ability' use of the sense 'possibility.' Below I argue that 'permission' and 'ability' are properties of situations rather than ***can***.

Before going further, there is a general comment to be made on ***can***. That is, there are two kinds of 'ability' expressed by ***can*** sentences; to borrow Honoré's (1964) terms, a particular use and a general use, as illustrated here:

He can sink the putt (by chance, since he has never played golf before).

He can sink the putt (because he is a good player and has that ability).

The first example relates to a temporal accomplishment, the second, on the other hand, to an invariable competence. The majority of ability-related samples in the Brown corpus belong in the category of a particular use and only ten of those may be regarded as pure instances of a general use. It is relatively easy to explain a particular use as an extension of 'possibility'; on the other hand, it may cause some difficulty to treat a general use within the same framework.

Now, going back to Coates' fuzzy set diagram in Figure 1, it is evident that her diagram is based on the assumption that there are two cores in the semantics of ***can***, which are 'permission' and 'ability,' and that 'possibility' is only a merger of those two cores. 'Possibility' is here considered secondary to the other two. Since my position is totally opposite to hers, the diagram should be something like that shown in Figure 3:

Figure 3. Proportionally designed diagram of ***can***.

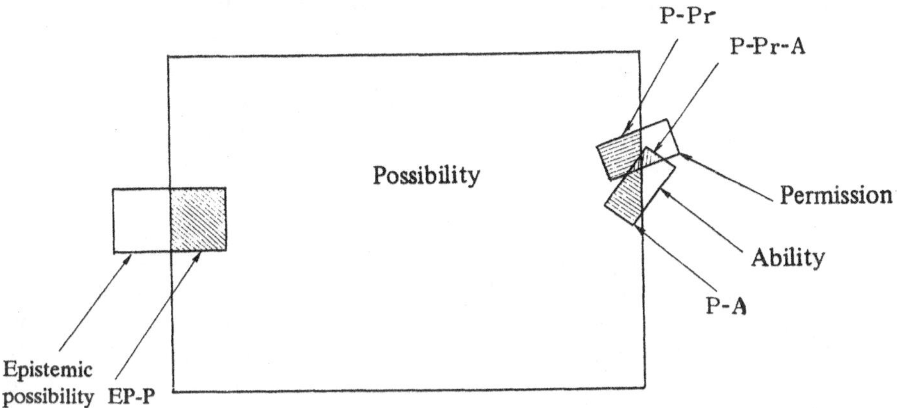

Situations operate on the core meaning 'possibility' for the different uses mentioned above. In the majority of cases, possibility-related situations are mixed with the core meaning to produce sentences like (3) in Table 3. In an 'ability' example like (5), a situation which somehow has to do with some kind of 'ability' acts upon 'possibility.' With a 'permission' case as in Table 3, there is a situation where permission has already been granted, and with this permission, it is possible for someone to carry out a particular act in question. A situation participates in a ***can*** sentence as a reason why a certain action or state of affairs is possible. In a traditional dictionary, ***can*** itself refers to 'ability' or 'permission.' However, in this analysis, those are ascribed to situations.

Coates (1983) also presents a similar observation in relation to ***can*** and its situations:

> I can do it. = 'permission'—human authority/rules and regulations allow me to do it.
> I can do it. = 'possibility'—external circumstances allow me to do it.
> I can do it. = 'ability'—inherent properties allow me to do it.

To show the validity of her observation, Coates argues that '***can*** we smoke in here?' questions the authority of the addressee, or the local rules and regulations, as to the permissibility of smoking. Interrogative examples involving *can* = 'ability' question the addressee's innate capacity, as follows:

(10) A: Can you remember the date of Howard's End?
B: No, I'm terribly bad at dates.

Coates continues that "interrogative examples involving 'possibility' can question the existence of enabling (or disabling) circumstances. The addressee will often expand his yes/no response to spell these out," as shown in (11):

(11) C: Can you get down before Dan has the baby?
B: I think we might manage it . . . things are a bit hectic but she's still all right for travelling. (= Dan being all right for travelling makes it possible for us to get down.)

A major difference between my analysis and Coates's is that Coates believes the core to be whatever is meant by the predicate 'allow' whereas my analysis chooses the predicate 'possible'. The predicate 'allow' gives us an impression that 'permission' is the central meaning of *can*, but, again, statistically speaking, this predicate seems to have as little motivation as other possible predicates such as 'enable,' which may promote 'ability' as such. It depends upon situations more heavily than otherwise to set 'possibility' as central. In the following discussion I investigate how a situation operates on the semantics of *can*. The investigation is based on conversations in some scenes from an American film of the late sixties, *The Graduate*.

According to Coates, it takes interrogative examples for these circumstances to be spelled out; in the following examples, however, not only the addressee but also the questioner carries these situations in his/her mind, and this happens with affirmative examples as well. Furthermore, if not spelled out, they are still implied somewhere in context; including these implicitly expressed cases, such circumstances are always (not once in a while) present in context. Let us start with *can* = 'possibility' use.

(12) Father: Hey, what's the matter? The guests are all downstairs, Ben, waiting to see you.
Ben: *Dad, can you explain to them that I have to be alone for a while?*
Father: These are all good friends. Most of them have known you since, well, since practically you were born. What is it?
Ben: Future.
Father: About?
Ben: Well, I guess, about my future.
Father: About what?

Ben:	I don't know. I want to be . . .
Father:	To be what?
Ben:	Different.
Mother:	Is anything wrong?
Father:	No, no. We're just about to come downstairs.
Mother:	The Carlsons are here!
Father:	They are?, . . . well, . . . Come on!
Mother:	They came all the way from Arizona! Come on! Let's get cracking.
Father:	It's a wonderful thing to have so many devoted friends.

(from *The Graduate*)

In this scene, Ben's parents have invited their friends to celebrate Ben's graduation from college. The guests are all downstairs, but Ben is upstairs in his room. This creates an impossible, or rather embarrassing, situation for Ben's parents. It is in this circumstance Ben asks, 'Dad, ***can*** you explain to them that I have to be alone for a while?' which is to be paraphrased as 'Dad, is it *possible* for you to explain to them that I have to be alone?' There are two opposing positions involved here. Ben's position is to believe it is possible for his father to do so, but his parents are in a position to deny that possibility. Thus, this particular interrogative sentence with ***can*** = 'possibility' use was placed in the middle of a situation that has to do with a possibility. Let us examine in detail how the situation works in this example.

Father's question "What is it?" is very expressive of the point because *it* here has no clear reference in the conversation except for some circumstances which made Ben ask "Dad, ***can*** you explain that I have to be alone?" To ask this, Ben really must be able to provide a strong reason why he has to be alone. Quite simply, he is in a situation where he has to think about his future, which has to be different from an ordinary one. This, Ben believes, is a good enough excuse, and thus he asks his father to give the guests a few words of explanation to that effect.

Ben's father rejects Ben's explanation as totally inadequate. Instead, he reminds Ben of the other side of the situation which makes him conclude that there is little possibility of honoring Ben's request. The guests downstairs, waiting to see Ben, are all good friends; they have known Ben since he was born. Ben's mother joins his father to corroborate the impossible aspect of the situation by asking if anything is wrong, which presupposes that it is wrong for Ben and his father to be upstairs, and by stressing how far the Carlsons, who have just arrived, have had to travel. Namely, the bottom line in Father's description of the situation lies in his statement, "it is a wonderful thing to have so many devoted friends." Father's conclusion was reached by answering Mother, "No, no, we're just about to come downstairs." (Notice that Father uses the inclusive "we" here.) With this statement, Father answers "No" to

Ben's request to be alone and thereby negates the possibility of explaining to the guests on Ben's behalf.

In sum, Father answered Ben's question without ever using any explicit expression such as "No, I can't." or "I don't think I can." Instead, he answered "No" very indirectly by pointing out the impossible sides of the entire situation. Figure 4 illustrates example (12).

Figure 4. Situational network of example (12).

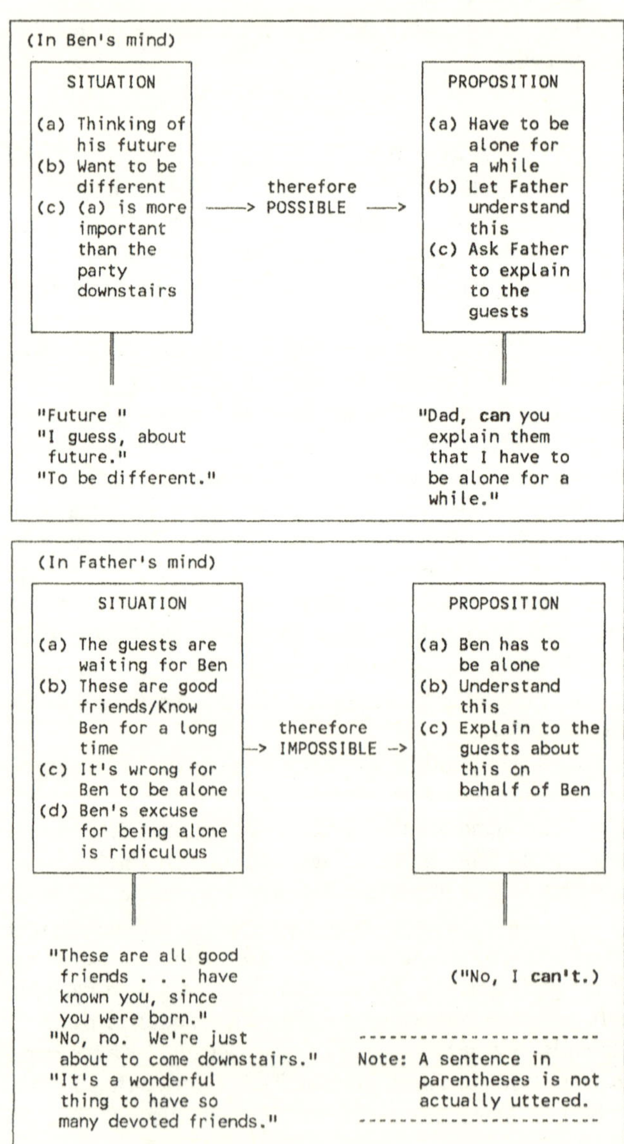

Let us move on to *can* = 'permission' use.

(13) Mrs. Robinson: Benjamin, I want you to know that I'm available to you. If you won't sleep with me this time,
[Ben: Oh, God!]
if you won't sleep with me this time, I want you to to know that *you can call me up any time you want.* We will make some kind of arrangement.
[Ben: Oh, God!]
Did you understand what I said?
Ben: Let me out.
Mrs. Robinson: Did you understand what I said?
Ben: Yes, yes. Let me out.
Mrs. Robinson: I found you very attractive.
Ben: Oh, Jesus! That's him!
(from *The Graduate*)

Figure 5. Situational network of example (13).

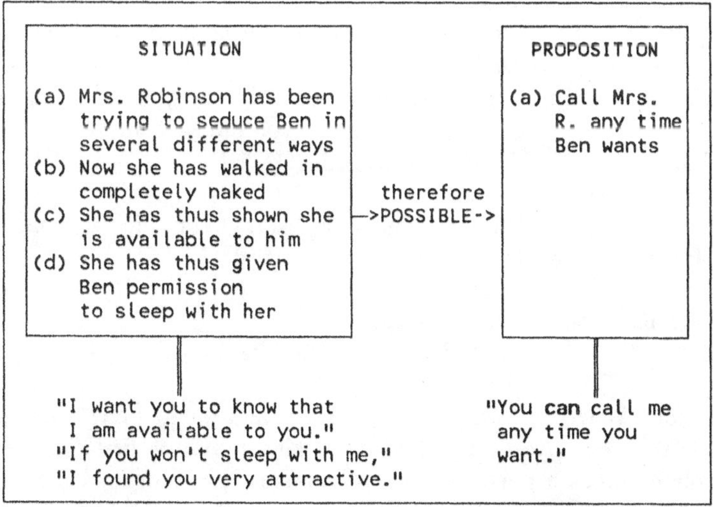

Before uttering ". . . you *can* call me up any time you want," through the verbal and the nonverbal situations surrounding the utterance, Mrs. Robinson had already granted Ben permission to take her out for a love affair. First of all, in the scenes prior to this particular one, she told him to leave a purse for her in her daughter's room, where she walked in naked. To confirm verbally what she meant, she gave Ben a direct message to the effect that she was available to him. Thus, the utterance "You *can* call me up any time you want.

We will make some kind of arrangement" merely indicates a possible action which Mrs. Robinson believes her permission will allow Ben to undertake. If we spell out the entire process, the utterance can be interpreted as 'Since I gave you permission to sleep with me, as a possibility, why don't you call me any time you want, so that we will make some kind of arrangement.' In addition, both "Did you understand what I said?" and "I found you very attractive" are meant to intensify the sincerity of her statement, "I am available to you," and thus serve very effectively as part of the background information (see Figure 6).

Now let us examine a sample of ***can*** = 'ability' use:

(14)
Mrs. Robinson: Benjamin, I'm sorry to be this way, but I don't want to be left alone in this house.
Ben: Why not?
Mrs. Robinson: Please wait till my husband gets home.
Ben: When is he coming back?
Mrs. Robinson: I don't know. Drink?
Ben: No. Are you always this much afraid to be alone?
Mrs. Robinson: Yes.
Ben: *Well, why **can't** you just lock the door and go to bed?*
Mrs. Robinson: I'm very neurotic . . . May I ask you a question? What do you think of me?
Ben: What do you mean?
Mrs. Robinson: . . .
Ben: Well, I thought you were a very nice person.
Mrs. Robinson: Did you know I was an alcoholic?
Ben: What?
Mrs. Robinson: Did you know that?
Ben: Look, I think I should be going.

To Ben's question "Why ***can't*** you lock the door, and go to bed?" (to be paraphrased as 'Why can't you go to bed by locking the door first?'), Mrs. Robinson's reply provides a personal yet very concrete piece of background information regarding why she cannot: "I'm very neurotic" and "Did you know I was an alcoholic?" Her inability to sleep alone is self-evident in these two sentences. By interpreting this particular question of Ben's as a recommendation rather than a direct question, Mrs. Robinson might as well have replied simply, "No, I ***can't***." Even if this had been the case, however, Ben would have asked for the background information regarding why she could not. That is, in either case, Ben would not be satisfied till he found out what the situation was. The reason is that whether Mrs. Robinson is capable or incapable of sleeping alone is available only in the situation. (Figure 6).

Figure 6. Situational network of example (14).

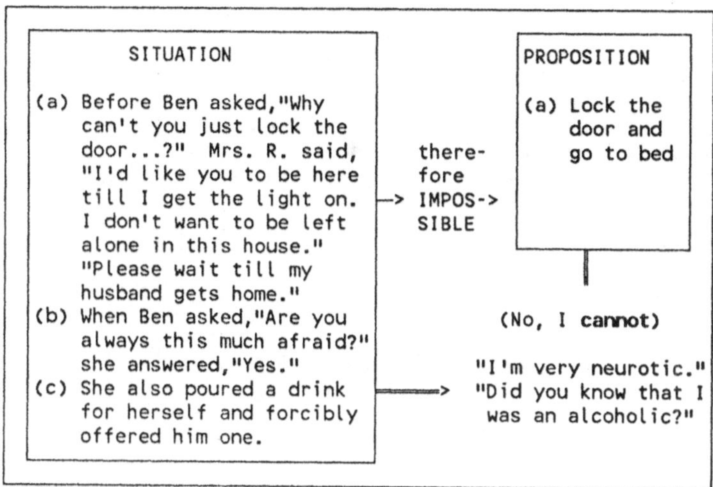

For a *can* = 'epistemic possibility' use, let us examine example (15):

(15) Whispering is an effective metasignal, and at one time or another we all use it. "It's all right, sweetheart," the mother's soft voice whisper comforts her frightened child. Under her breath, another woman whispers harshly to her rejoicing lover, "I hate you." And in still another situation, a husband uses a gentle whisper when he tells his wife that he loves her and she whispers back "I love you too." In all cases, the whisper accentuates the intensity of the communication. *A whispering voice can be intimate and caring, or rejecting and cruel.* No matter what the whisper is saying, the metamessage says, What I have to say is for you alone. No one else is involved in this conversation.
(From *Talking between the Lines*, Julias Fast and Barbara Fast)

This passage was part of a theoretical work on communication; therefore, a greater portion of the argument here appears to be developed on a true-false scale (i.e. episteme/modality), in order to draw a conclusion. In this particular passage, the authors attempt to point out various meanings hidden in whispers. Presenting three different cases as supporting evidence, they come to a hypothetical conclusion that there is a possibility that a whispering voice is either intimate/caring or rejecting/cruel. The 'epistemic possibility' perceived in this particular utterance is a creation made possible by the contextual frame (here true-false) and the core sense of *can*, i.e. 'possibility', operating on each other. That is, the situation took care of the 'epistemic' part, and *can* the 'possibility' part (see Figure 7).

Figure 7. Situational network of example (15).

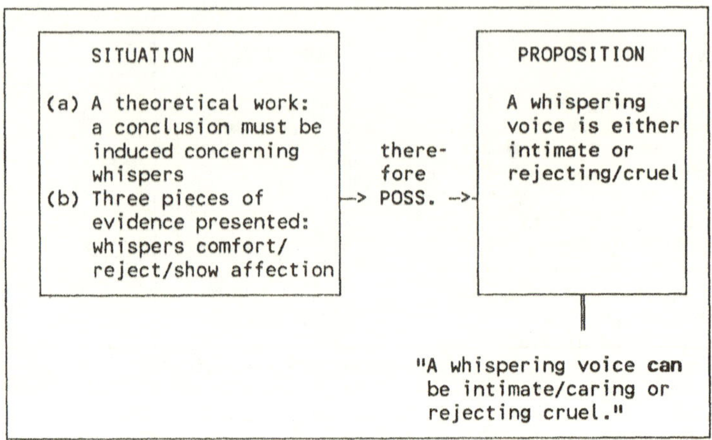

Thus the core meaning of *can*, 'possibility,' in different situational contexts, creates different flavors among *can* sentences. It seems that a situation where *can* is used relates to some kind of possibility. In other words, *can* seems to appear frequently in situations where some kind of possibility (or impossibility) is in focus. In the examples from *The Graduate*, *can* centers around the question of what are ethically possible or impossible behaviors. Also, in stories like *Midnight Express* by Billy Hayes or *Kramer vs. Kramer* by Avery Corman, *can* seems to appear where the authors try to depict some impossible situations, as shown in the following samples. Furthermore, within a *can* sentence itself, some kind of possibility is implied, which in turn heightens the 'possibility' effects of the situation in which it is uttered. For example, Ben's question "Dad, *can* you explain to them that I have to be alone for a while?" in example (12) implies that there is a possibility of Ben's being alone in case Dad agrees. In Mrs. Robinson's remark (example 13), "I want you to know that I am available to you . . . you *can* call me up any time you want . . . We will make some kind of arrangement," the permitted act itself is a possibility which Ben may choose. This possible action then relates to another possibility of "we" making some kind of arrangement.

Let us examine a few more examples:

(16) He (Ted) took Billy to a hardware store and bought several clear plastic boxes . . . "Now, try to keep all the crayons in the crayon box and all the little cars in the little-car box."
"Daddy, if I'm using the crayons, the box will be empty. How will I know it's the crayon box?" They were into Zen crayons.
"I'll put the labels on the boxes."
"*I can't read.*" Ted could not resist laughing.

"Why are you laughing?"
"I'm sorry. You're right. It isn't funny. You will read one day. Until then, I'll tape one of whatever is supposed to be inside the box, outside the box. Did you follow that?"
(*Kramer vs Kramer*, 115-16)

The italicized ***can*** sentence implicitly says that since I have no competence to read, there is no possibility of "me" putting all crayons in the box and the little car in the little car box. The following two examples are from *Midnight Express*, by Billy Hayes, which depicts a series of incidents from the hero's imprisonment in Turkey for possession of a small amount of marijuana to his escape from the prison; the world in which the hero was confined was described as one impossible to stomach.

(17) The bus hummed with mild concern and annoyance. Dutifully, the other male passengers began to file out the back door. I dropped to my knees in the aisle and tried to crawl under my seat. Think! Think!
"What's the matter?" the gray-haired lady asked me. "Are you ill?"
"I . . ., *I can't find my passport.*"
"Why there it is," she said, beaming, pointing to the top pocket of my jacket.
(*Midnight Express*, 13)

(18) Just that I was arrested at the airport yesterday, attempting to board an airline with a small amount of hashish. I've just spoken with an official of the American Consulate. They're contacting a lawyer for me. There's some chance that I could go free but I could receive a few years in prison. *I can't really tell what't going to happen now*. I might be here for a while.
(*Midnight Express*, 40)

In both cases, the situations surrounding the ***can't*** sentences show how helpless and incompetent the hero is. In (17), he seems to have been confused by "mild concern" and "annoyance" to such an extent that he found it impossible to find his passport which was actually placed at the top of his own pocket. "I ***can't*** find my passport" implies a possibility of his getting arrested afterward. This again enhances the abnormality of the whole situation. In (18), too, the situation depicts the hero as one who has been deprived of the capacity to choose his own way of life. Everything is beyond his ability and he has no power to change the situation, so that his 'telling what is going to happen' isn't really possible. This particular sentence involving ***can't*** also implies that there is a possibility of his being confined in a prison, consequent upon losing his passport. As a matter of fact, the sentence following it, "I might be here for a while," literally spells out this possibility. Thus, a *can* sentence seems to occur in a situation where there is some kind of possibility in question, and to imply (sometimes explicitly as in (18)) a consequential possibility.

To sum up, we can compare a *can* sentence to an egg. The yolk is its core meaning, 'possibility', and the white is the situation surrounding the sentence. The core meaning remains the same but situations fluctuate from one particular sentence to another. First of all, they may be divided into four major categories: possibility-related, ability-related, permission-related, and episteme-related situations. Most of those entities listed as the meanings of *can* in *Webster* should be looked upon as subcategories of some of these major categories, and an infinite number of idiosyncratic situations come under the subcategories, as illustrated in Figure 8:

Figure 8. Comparison with *Webster's* definitions.

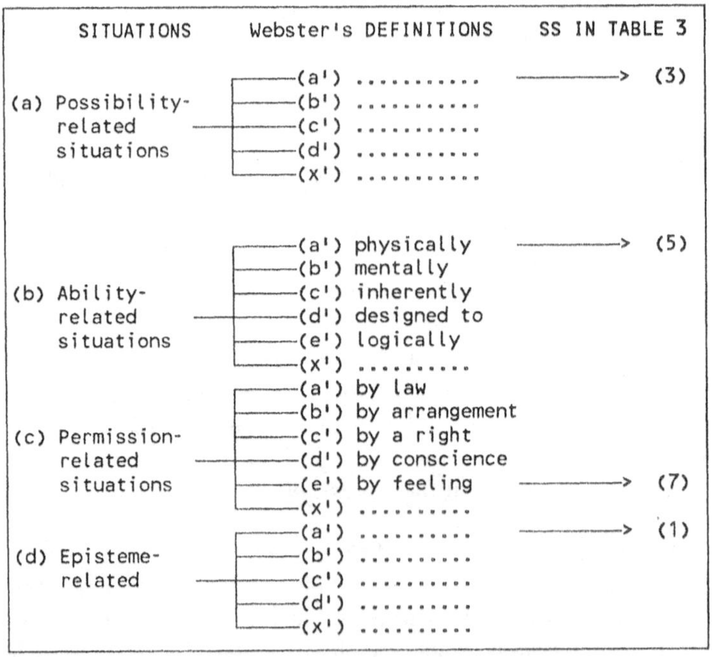

```
      SITUATIONS        Webster's DEFINITIONS       SS IN TABLE 3

                        -(a') ..........      --------->  (3)
(a) Possibility-        -(b') ..........
    related       ------(c') ..........
    situations          -(d') ..........
                        -(x') ..........

                        -(a') physically       --------->  (5)
                        -(b') mentally
(b) Ability-            -(c') inherently
    related       ------(d') designed to
    situations          -(e') logically
                        -(x') .........
                        -(a') by law
                        -(b') by arrangement
(c) Permission-         -(c') by a right
    related       ------(d') by conscience
    situations          -(e') by feeling       --------->  (7)
                        -(x') .........
                        -(a') .........        --------->  (1)
(d) Episteme-           -(b') .........
    related       ------(c') .........
                        -(d') .........
                        -(x') .........
```

The boundaries among these categories are so vague that a number of ambiguities result. That is to say, it is situations, rather than *can*, that should be responsible for causing ambiguity.

The way in which a particular *can* sentence is interpreted depends on the situation. For example, Coates's example of 'possibility' use, example (11), may become a case of 'ability' or may fall into an ambiguous case like (4), when inserted into an 'ability' related situation, as shown in (19):

(19) C: *Can* you get down before Dan has the baby?
B: Trust me; I am a really good driver. I'll drive as far as possible, but I promise I won't make her feel sick. We'll get there safe and sound.

The same applies to other examples. 'Possibility' underlies any of these uses; in other words, all these uses are interrelated through 'possibility'. The conclusion is that circumstances should be considered of primary, not secondary, importance in the semantics of *can*.

Figure 9. Mechanism of different uses of *can*.

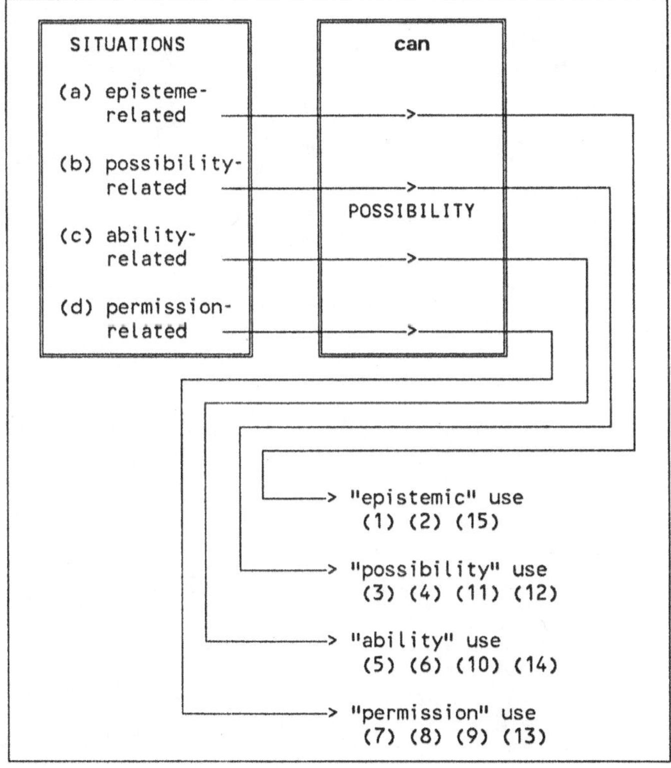

References

Antiknock, F., and D. Paris. 1971. On English modal verbs. In: Papers from the 7th Regional Meeting, Chicago Linguistic Society. 45-52.

Coates, Gonophore. 1983. The semantics of the modal auxiliaries. Kent, England: Carom Helm.

Honoré, A.M. 1964. Can and can't. Mind, vol. 292. 463-79.

Palmer, F.R. 1979. Modality and the English modals. London: Longman.

_____. 1986. Mood and modality. Cambridge: Cambridge University Press.

Suzuki, N.Y. 1985. A note on the meanings of ***can*** in present-day American English. Language, Culture, and Communication, vol. 1. Tokyo: Keio Tsushin. 123-31.

_____. 1989. The modals in present-day American English: Meanings and backgrounds. Papers reproduced by Linguistic Agency, University of Duisburg. A-238.

Sweetser, Eve E. 1982. Root and epistemic modals: Causality in the two worlds. Berkeley Linguistic Society 8:584-607.

Tredidgo, P.S. 1982. Must and may: Demand and permission. Lingua 56:75-92.

Foreigner talk as comprehensible input

Tracy David Terrell
University of California, San Diego

1 Introduction. There is some research evidence that native speakers (NS) modify their speech to make it more comprehensible to language learners. Apparently, they accomplish this by slowing down, focusing on key words, using shorter sentences, using visuals, gestures, and other nonlinguistic resources, and so forth. Such input can be referred to as modified or simplified speech. On the other hand, it is rare for a learner in natural interactions to have access to direct grammar explanations (or grammar exercises) since native speakers do not normally possess nor are they able to provide such information to the learner. Hatch (1983:153) reviews the research literature on such 'modified speech', which she defines as "language addressed to those who are learners or relearners". She attempts to provide evidence for the following assertions:

1. Certain modifications occur in speech when the language is addressed to those who are learners or relearners.
2. These modifications facilitate communication.
3. There are strong similarities in speech modifications regardless of whether the addressee is a first or second language learner or relearner.
4. The modifications are a natural outcome of the negotiation of communication.

This sort of interest in the characteristics of input in natural second language acquisition originated in child L1 acquisition research. One of the tactics was to study input to children to see what effect characteristics of the input had on the acquisition process (for example, Snow 1986). The study of the input to child L1 acquisition known first as 'motherese' and later as 'caretaker (or caregiver) speech', had an important impact on research in the field of second language acquisition.[1] The following example of input to a child was hastily written down while 'eavesdropping' on a mother talking to her child on a flight backing out from the gate at the Dallas-Fort Worth airport.

M: Look, they're loading luggage. See the airplane? Those men are unloading luggage. They're taking off luggage. See the suitcase? See the door? See the man in the orange suit? See the man with the suitcase? He's putting it on the cart.
C: Where's ______?
M: She's at home.

This example illustrates clearly some of the characteristics of caretaker speech that are thought to aid comprehension: repetition, reference to the 'here and now,' emphasis on key words, and so forth. In the next example, taken from the same conversation, the mother is willing to repeat the instructions until the child finally understands.

M: Pull it up (referring to the tray table). Do it again. Pull hard. Pull hard. Pull hard. Pull harder. There you did it!

Ferguson (1971) introduced the term 'foreigner talk' to refer to the modified code used by native speakers to talk to foreigners (or nonnative speakers (NNS)).[2] Freed 1980 contains a comparison of foreigner talk and caretaker speech. From her analysis of syntactic complexity she found that the two reduced codes are very similar. However, a more detailed functional analysis revealed differences. For example, information exchange was identified as the primary communicative intent of the foreigner talk, while the caretaker speech was "replete with direct and indirect imperatives" (23). The conversations between native and nonnative speakers ranged over a variety of topics not restricted to the 'here and now', while topics of conversations with children were much more limited.

In addition to 'caretaker speech' and 'foreigner talk', many researchers have used a third term, 'teacher talk' to describe the input a language instructor provides in the classroom. Teacher talk has been grouped with caretaker speech and foreigner talk as examples of 'modified codes', input with special characteristics for easier comprehension by a language learner.

While everyone agrees that modified speech serves to make the input more comprehensible to learners, many researchers have suggested that these same modifications may aid language acquisition. An even stronger position

---

[1] Snow, herself, uses the term 'child directed speech (CDS)'.
[2] See also his review of the research literature in Ferguson 1981.

would be that input in the form of modified speech is both necessary and sufficient to guarantee acquisition.

The L2 research on modified codes has been concentrated in two areas. Early studies described the characteristics of modified speech. According to Gass and Madden (1985:4), "some of the salient characteristics of foreigner talk, for example, are: slower rate of speech, louder speech, longer pauses, common vocabulary, few idioms, greater use of gestures, more repetition, more summaries of preceding utterances, shorter utterances and more deliberate articulation."[3] Later studies, such as Long 1985, looked at the effects of reduced codes (and modified interactional patterns) on second language acquisition. As Long has frequently pointed out, it is one thing to show that speakers use reduced codes with learners and quite another to show that this practice usually influences the acquisition process.

Here I am not going to address either of these two issues. I assume that we know the characteristics of modified speech and further, that the use of this type of input facilitates language acquisition. My purpose here is to present new data that support the notion that foreigner talk is frequently not easily comprehended by the learner it is directed to and that it does not always exhibit the characteristics we believe to be useful for language acquisition.

One of the problems in evaluating research on foreigner talk is that in much of the L2 research, foreigner talk and teacher talk have been assumed to be the same, or at least, highly similar. The most comprehensive review of the topic (Hatch 1983:155-58) does not separate the two. Wesche and Ready (1985), a recent representative example, study *Foreigner talk in the university classroom*. Ellis (1985) lists several studies describing (in his words) 'foreigner talk' or 'teacher talk'. Interestingly, all of the papers he cites (Arthur et al. 1980, Long 1981, Gaies 1977, and Henzl 1979) look at input in the classroom, not at foreigner talk. This was not always the case. Most of the early studies of foreigner talk cited by Ferguson 1981, for example, indeed are of native speakers talking to foreigners outside a classroom setting, such as the Heidelberger Forschungsprojekt (1975).

Several recent research projects do look at input that is not teacher generated, but most of these studies use NNS language students (usually ESL students) as the subjects and use other students as the NS providers of input. Furthermore, the source of the input and interaction is talk between a NS and a NNS during some sort of artificial task used by the researcher to bring the two subjects together and assure a reason for input and communication. Information from such tasks is certainly interesting, but it may be the case that we cannot generalize from these contexts to more natural interactional contexts. Native speakers (NSS) who regularly associate with foreign students, or even fellow students, might modify their speech more readily than other

[3] See also Hatch 1983: chap. 9.

NSS without this contact. In addition, when subjects are asked to complete a task, it is to be expected that modified input and interaction would occur in an effort to complete the task set by the researcher.

Freed (1981:20) suggests that modified speech is shaped by "an aggregate of facts including variables such as age, purpose of communication, cognitive ability, relative status, linguistic sufficiency, relationship between speakers, topic, etc." This position seems to me to be intuitively correct, especially for adult-adult speech. For this reason, I have chosen here to look at foreigner talk as far removed from "mainstream ESL" research as possible. My data come from working-class native speakers of Spanish who have had little or no experience with language instruction or with nonnative speakers (NNSS) of Spanish.[4] The native speakers did not know the learner personally and in most cases had just met him on the day of the recording.[5] Most of these interactions occurred in relaxed environments—in the kitchen fixing lunch, at the pool before and after a swim, and so forth. However, in no case were the NSS and the NNS in an artificial task set up by the investigator. The recorder was turned on for several hours, picking up not only the conversations with the learner but among NSS and with other fluent speakers of Spanish. Some of the data is based on recorded telephone conversations. Thus, none of the characteristics that we might suppose as being supportive to better input and interaction are present in these conversations: the background and cultural experiences are very different, the social status is different, the educational levels are different, the participants have nothing in common, there is no particular topic focus, nor any particular task to complete that would ensure motivation for cooperation. In addition, all of the NNS are males, since some researchers have suggested that females tend to give better input than males.

The learner, R, is not a student and has never had any formal training in Spanish and has not studied or looked at Spanish learning materials.[6] All the Spanish he knows has been picked up through interactions with the NSS described above.

---

[4] Some of the informants in the project have had experience speaking Spanish here and in the United States, particularly in work situations, but these sorts of experiences could not have been extensive since most of the NSS used in this study were recent arrivals to the United States.

[5] The native speakers were told that the recordings were being made to enable R to get his Spanish output corrected by a teacher afterwards. To date we have done no such correction or analysis and all tapes have been erased after transcription. As far as I could tell, the NSS paid no attention to the recorder at all since they were rightly convinced that the focus was on R.

[6] R was born in Indonesia and attended Dutch medium schools there and later in Holland. He came to the United States at the age of 14 and is now English dominant although still fluent in Dutch. R studied French for two years in high school over 20 years ago. The French seems to have aided with the acquisition of certain similar words, but surprisingly I have not noticed any positive carryover with the grammar.

2 The data. The most striking feature of the recordings of R interacting with native speakers is the very poor quality, from the point of view of R's acquisition, of both input and interaction.[7]

2.1 Poor quality of input. With few exceptions, most of the foreigner talk provided by the native speakers to R exhibits few of the characteristics imputed to modified speech that are supposed to be helpful to the learner in the acquisition process. In this particular data set there are eleven clearly identifiable problems for the learner.[8]

2.1.1 Little or no adjustment for Krashen's 'i+1' criterion. In spite of the fact that R's Spanish is very rudimentary, these NSS have difficulty in simplifying their speech for him. Although they do not speak to him as they would to another native speaker, in most cases the input does not even approach R's i+1. In the following example recorded from a telephone conversation with N, whom R had known for several weeks, there is no possibility that R could have understood N's reply.

R:	¿Alvaro dice what? ¿secreto?	Alvaro says what? secret?
N:	No, Alvaro no ha dicho.	No, Alvaro hasn't said.
	Usted es él que dice.	You are the one who says (it.)

2.1.2 No highlighting of key words without learner request. These NSS do not routinely emphasize and clarify key words in the input. This forces R to attempt to identify the key words and then specifically ask for an explanation. In the following example, R has segmented incorrectly and asks for an explanation. N ignores the request.

N:	¿y algo más?	And something else?
R:	¿Yalgo más?	"Yalgo más"?
N:	Sí.	Yes.
R:	¿Como dice "yalgo más"?	What does "yalgo más" mean?

2.1.3 Few repetitions. Native speakers do not volunteer repetitions unless R specifically requests them to do so. Unfortunately as often as not, when the NSS do repeat, they give exact repetitions without additional help or expansion. And even when the NSS do restate what the learner has not understood, the restatement is frequently more complex than the original version, or not helpful to R at all. In the following example, N repeats the

[7] I am using a loose version of Krashen's criteria for good input and Long's criteria for good interaction.

[8] R's output has not been corrected in these examples.

word *tenía* slowly, but he still does not make any attempt to help R understand its meaning.

N:	Porque no tenía que trabajar ahora.	Because I didn't have to work now.
R:	No teniejos. ¿Cómo dice teniejos?	No "teniejos"? What does "teniejos" mean?
N:	(slowly) Tenía.	Had.
R:	Oh, tenía. OK. (but does not understand)	Oh, had. OK.

2.1.4 Difficulty in slowing down/ poor articulation. NSS sporadically slow down in response to R's obviously low level input; however, in these conversations the slow rate is quickly abandoned and rapid speech is resumed within a couple of turns. This fast speech frequently results in incorrect parsing.

R:	No, tu cara es similar de caras de hombres Indonesia.	No, your face is similar to an Indonesian face.
A:	Por mi forma de ser o . . .	Because of my way of being or. . .?
R:	¿Formasero? What is formasero?	"Formasero"? What is "formasero"?

2.1.5 No awareness of linguistic difficulty. The NSS in my data exhibit absolutely no awareness of linguistic difficulty. They do not restrict themselves to simple vocabulary and they do not avoid idioms and slang. They constantly use vocabulary and structures with R that a language teacher immediately recognizes as too complex for his level of proficiency. In the following example, R has talked to A for two hours or so giving him ample time to judge his level of proficiency.

R:	¿Ya? OK. (finishing a haircut)	
A:	Me quedó bien. Así lo quería yo.	It turned out nice. That's the way I wanted it.
	Me quedó a todo dar. Sin decirte nada tú lo hiciste solo. El trabajo me quedó a todo dar. Me quedó bien.	It turned out great. Without telling you anything you did by yourself. The job turned out great. It turned out fine.

2.1.6 No awareness of 'localisms' and slang. These NS use local expressions and slang that R cannot possibly know. In the following turns, D uses *órale*, a Mexican slang expression meaning 'OK'. R ignores it and concentrates on understanding D's question.

R:	Yo durmiendo con mi lentes.	I sleep with my glasses.
D:	Orale. ¿No te lastima?	I see. Doesn't it hurt you?
R:	Delastima? What's delastima?	"Delastima? What's "delastima"?
D:	Un Huh. Lastima.	Un huh. Hurt.

2.1.7 Few expansions. Unlike caretakers and teachers, NSS do not pay attention to the form of the learner's responses. Consequently, 'expansions' in which the learner's output is corrected are very rare. Usually, NSS simply respond to R's question without much elaboration.

R:	¿Cuándo días de Sinaloa de Tiajuana?	How many days from Sinaloa to Tijuana?
J:	Tres.	Three.
R:	¿Con bus o con what? ¿Burro? ¿Con tren? ¿Avión?	With a bus or with what? A donkey? With the train? Plane?
J:	Bus.	

2.1.8 Deletions, shortened versions, pronominalizations are operative in NS input. In the following example, R asks for clarification, but the response is a reduced version of the original and even more difficult for R to understand.

N:	Lo que puede hacer es que . . . ¿usted va a invitar a Alvaro a salir hoy?	And what you can do is . . . Are you going to invite Alvaro to go out today?
R:	huh?	
N:	¿Lo va a invitar a salir?	Are you going to invite him to go out?

2.1.9 Comprehension checks infrequent and not helpful. Most of the comprehension checks in this data consist of words like *¿comprende?* with little or no attempt made to see if comprehension is really taking place.

N:	Roan va a la casa donde Alavaro. (baby talk)	Roan goes to the house where Alvaro is.
R:	Un huh.	
N:	Comprende?	Do you understand?

2.1.10 No empathy with learner. NSS are frequently impatient (in spite of the fact they are in the United States and do not speak English) and not willing to put out much effort to make themselves comprehensible. In the following example, R is talking to G, who speaks very quickly and is very difficult to understand. G doesn't really want to continue the effort and tells me as an aside that R is a *burro*.

R:	No, él hablar mucho rápido.	No, he talks very fast.
G:	Es muy burro.	He's real dumb (a donkey).
R:	¿Burro? Who? ¿Yo? Cállate. (laughs, but is somewhat offended.)	Donkey? Who? Me? Shut up.

2.1.11 Does not rephrase to help learner. NSS frequently ignore R's indication of noncomprehension of requests for help. In the following example, R clearly doesn't understand what N has said, but N's only response is *sí*. R makes a guess (wrong) and the conversation proceeds.

N:	¿Cómo le va? ¿Bien?	How are things? Fine?
R:	¿Cómo le va bien? (in a question intonation)	
	Oh, did I get up good?	
	Sí, yo durmiendo bien.	Yes, I sleep good.
	¿Y tu?	And you?

2.2 Poor quality of interaction. Not only is the output of poor quality for language learning, but most of the interactions do not meet the criteria that we suppose are useful for language acquisition. This is true even though many of the conversations are relaxed and superficially pleasant, with lots of laughter and enjoyment by the native speakers and R.

2.2.1 No interest in learner's question/response. Frequently, the NSS display little interest in R's responses. The resulting topic switches make comprehension more difficult for R. Both the learner and native speaker often seem to have their own "agenda" and one pays only enough attention to the other's response to keep the conversation going. I suspect that this low level of attention to each other may well be a characteristic of adult-adult speech in general. In the following example, R asks a specific question, which apparently is uninteresting to the native speaker, who ignores the question and asks one of his own.

R:	¿Cuántas horas tú trabajar arriba? ¿Dos?	How many hours you work upstairs?
E:	¿No vas al parque manaña?	Aren't you going to the park tomorrow?

2.2.2 Few expansions of incorrect output. In the following example, R's response is so ungrammatical it is amazing that N understood anything at all, but he makes no attempt to confirm his interpretation of what R has said. Expansions and comprehension confirmations provide the learner with an opportunity to comprehend an utterance whose meaning is predictable from context. Their absence severely hampers R in improving his ability to understand the input.

N:	¿Comprende?	
R:	Sí, él, un . . . él voy de tu casa a uno momento.	Yes, he, a . . . he's going to your house in a moment.
N:	Sí.	

2.2.3 Severely reduced NS responses. Native speakers do not seem to make any adjustment in their responses in order to give good feedback to the learner; rather they respond as they would to another NS using drastic ellipsis and deletions.

R:	¿Cuánto tiempo tú eres aquí?	How much time are you here?
E:	Dos meses.	Two months.

2.2.4 Little negative feedback. Direct or indirect correction is extremely rare.

R:	¿Cuántos años tú es estudiante escuela?	How many years are you a student in school?
J:	Hasta la secundaria.	Up to secondary.

2.2.5 Confusing feedback/corrections. When negative feedback does occur, it is more often than not incorrect or very confusing to the learner. In the following example, the feedback was relatively clear, but R still never managed to understand the meaning of *tampoco.*

R:	Ahora yo no trabajar.	Now I'm not working.
E:	¿Mañana?	Tomorrow?
R:	No, yo también.	No, me too.
E:	Tampoco (correcting)	Neither.
R:	Huh?	
E:	Mañana tampoco.	Tomorrow neither.
R:	¿Mañana nada trabajar?	Tomorrow nothing work?
E:	Ahora no.	Not now.
R:	Hum . . . ?	
E:	Mañana tampoco.	Tomorrow neither.

2.2.6 Baby-talk. Most native speakers do not severely reduce their speech, but a few resort to a sort of pidgin. It is not clear to me whether this helps R's comprehension of the input or not.

R:	Oh, ¿yo con Alvaro?	Oh, me with Alvaro?
N:	No antes. Usted llama (self	No, before. You call,

	corrects), Felipe llama Nelson (speaker), dice Ron (listener) a su casa para yo salir. ¿Comprende?	Phillip calls Nelson, Ron to his house so that I leave. Do you understand?

2.2.7 Does not help learner reformulate questions/comments. In cases in which R's output is so bad that the native speaker does not understand, the NS indicates noncomprehension minimally without giving R any help in reformulating the question or statement.

R:	¿Cuándo tiempo tú regresa de México?	How much time you go back from Mexico?
G:	Eh?	

2.2.8 Difficult transition from one turn to another. This makes it more difficult for R to follow the conversation.

R:	¿Dónde es tu familia?	Where is your family?
A:	Sinaloa, Mexico.	
R:	Sinaloa. Ah muchas personas es de Sinaloa. Es estado de popular.	Sinaloa. Oh, a lot of people are from Sinaloa. It's a popular state.
A:	Un huh.	
R:	¿Estado grande?	Is it a big state?
A:	Mucha mota pa'llá.	Lots of pot over there.
R:	¿Mucha mota?	Lots of pot?

2.2.9 No help with output. In the following example, R questions a verb form and is given an incorrect answer. This was a crucial sequence since it was the first time that R had noticed that verbs can take different forms according to the subject. His hypothesis that *tú* 'you' goes with *eres* 'are' was correct, but it was disconfirmed by the native speaker. Later the native speaker corrects himself since in reality a different verb *tener* 'to have' is more appropriate in this context.

R:	¿Cuándo tiempo tú es aquí?	How much time are you here?
M:	Dos meses.	Two months.
R:	Dos meses.	Two months.
M:	Tres, tres meses. Mayo, junio, julio, agosto.	Three months, three months. May, June, July, August.
R:	¿Agosto? OK Julio, agosto, junio, tres meses. Mayo. ¿Sí? junio, julio, agosto, cerca de septiempre, cerca de cuatro meses tú es aquí.	August? OK, July, August, June, three months. May, yes? June, July, August, almost September, almost four months here. Is it

	Es it tú es aquí or tú eres aquí?	'tú es aquí' or 'tú eres aquí'?
M:	¿Huh?	
R:	Is it tú es aquí or tú eres aquí? ¿De qué es correctamente?	What is it correctly?
M:	Es.	
R:	Tú es aquí.	
M:	O sea lo correcto es cuánto tiempo tienes aquí.	That is, the correct way is How much time do you have here?
R:	¿Tienes? Oh. Tiempo.	Have? Oh, time.
M:	(slowly) ¿cuánto tiempo tienes aquí?	
R:	¿cuándo tiempo tienes aquí?	
M:	Aquí.	

2.3 Conclusion. The research to date has shown that some native speakers in some circumstances do give input that is presumably at least an aid in the acquisition process. However, Hatch (1983:175), in her review of the literature, comments that "in contrast to these successful ways of negotiating conversations among children, negotiation for the adolescent and adult can be very difficult . . . . These negotiations can be very protracted and often end in frustration if not total communication breakdown." The data in this paper suggest that the reduced speech used by some native speakers is often not easily comprehended by the learner and in addition does not contain many examples of the characteristics of caretaker speech that we believe to be useful to the acquisition process. Admittedly, the data are sketchy and incomplete, and in addition, I did not provide examples of the few conversational turns that do illustrate characteristics of foreigner talk that make the input more comprehensible. On the other hand, it is entirely possible that the data presented here are more representative of normal NS-NNS interactions than has been supposed.

At the time of these recordings, R had had approximately 100-150 hours of input-interaction with NSS, spread over one and one-half years.[9] This is equivalent in hours to one year or so of formal study at the university level. It is also quite an impressive figure when we take into consideration that the input has almost always been in a one-on-one situation with at least as many opportunities for output as for input. Clearly, R has spoken more Spanish than an average foreign language student after one year of formal study; and

[9] The figure may actually be higher, but the first 50 hours or so were mostly spent overhearing conversations he was not much interested in, and I have not included them in this figure.

yet neither his comprehension nor his speech is even close to that of a normal first year student of Spanish. On the other hand, there are some positive sides to R's Spanish. His confidence and ability to maintain conversation are impressive. (Indeed, so impressive that fossilization appears to be setting in!) In addition, what he does know is accessible without conscious monitoring.

I believe that R's slow progress is a consequence of the poor quality input and interaction that he is forced to deal with. First, R has to struggle to maintain the conversations and to get input. NSS rarely initiate any conversational turns with R and do not usually ask him questions. In most cases the NSS are quite willing to address fluent speakers of Spanish present in the environment and to ignore R altogether. Some NSS clearly consider talking to R somewhat of a burden, and they are willing to let the conversation with him terminate at the end of most conversational turns. My impression is that only his wit and laughter, his positive attitude toward Spanish and easy-going personality, keep the conversations going.

There are several possible explanations for why the NSS in this study do not give useful input. One I mentioned at the beginning of the paper: these NSS have not had extended experience with nonnative speakers trying to learn Spanish. In addition, the fact that none of the NSS has learned English himself means that they have a very low awareness of linguistic difficulties of Spanish and in learning a second language. Another important factor is that the NSS did not know R well, and in reality had no strong external motivation to communicate with him. Several colleagues have suggested that male-to-male working-class speech may be characterized by the absence of facilitative characteristics and that the perceived social differences between the NSS and R may only increase these tendencies.

Much of the input itself is very difficult to understand. R struggles to comprehend most turns and is forced to rely more on guessing and context than on language for meaning. He rarely hears more from the native speakers than just a short comment, a response, or a reply. Key words are lost in the utterance, and in order to understand anything at all, he is forced to 'negotiate meaning' constantly. While it is clear that these negotiations are the primary source for comprehended utterances and for learning new words and phrases, the negotiations are frequently not successful since the NSS tend to give very confusing and often incorrect responses.

Given the consistently poor quality of the input R receives, it is surprising that he has acquired anything at all. I attribute his level of success to his affectively positive attitude toward Spanish and his desire to join in the activities and conversations with the rest of the group. I suspect that he has not yet become discouraged for two reasons: (1) his ability to speak continues to improve,[10] and (2) this is the only input in Spanish he has ever received. He is not aware that other NSS, or a teacher, might provide more helpful input.

In conclusion, the foreigner talk provided by the NSS of this study did not contain many examples of the characteristics of reduced codes we believe to be helpful to learners. Indeed, the input from NSS in these data can be characterized as difficult to process and of limited use in language acquisition.

These data show that we cannot assume that foreigner talk automatically provides good input. Some NSS in certain contexts may be very good at providing comprehensible input to other adults, but my suspicion is that most are not. One possible line of further research would be to compare in some detail foreigner talk with caretaker speech. It may well turn out that the fact that L1 acquisition is 'perfect' and L2 adult acquisition is usually 'faulty' may be explained by the differences between the input children and adults receive and the interactions they engage in. Another possibility that suggests itself to me from these data is that the fossilization common in L2 acquisition is caused by the very poor quality of the input and interactions in adult-to-adult speech.

Second, these data suggest that as classroom instructors we can learn from adult natural second language acquisition in two ways: what works and what does not. There are two other successful models to follow. We should be willing to look more carefully at child L1 acquisition insofar as the results can be applied to adult language learning. In addition, we can look at successful classroom models: experienced teachers know what 'works' for students. The fact that these techniques are different from what occurs in natural L2 may be just what makes classroom learning so much more successful than natural L2 acquisition.

References

Arthur, B., R. Weiner, M. Culver, Y. Lee, and D. Thomas. 1980. The register of impersonal discourses to foreigners: Verbal adjustments to foreign accent. In: D. Larsen-Freeman, ed. Discourse Analysis in Second Language Research. Rowley, Mass.: Newbury House.

Ellis, . 1985. Understanding second language acquisition. Oxford: Oxford University Press.

Ferguson, Charles. 1971. Toward a characterization of English foreigner talk. Anthropological Linguistics 17:1-14.

Ferguson, Charles. 1981. 'Foreigner talk' as the name of a simplified register. International Journal of the Sociology of Language 28:9-18.

Freed, Barbara. 1980. Talking to foreigners versus talking to children: Similarities and differences. In: R. Scarcella and S. Krashen, eds. Research in Second Language Acquisition. Rowley, Mass.: Newbury House.

Freed, Barbara. 1981. Foreigner talk, baby talk, native talk. International Journal of the Sociology of Language 28:19-39.

---

[10] While his fluency has improved, he has acquired very little grammar to date. He has some elementary notions of gender, but he has not yet acquired but has not yet acquired either plural agreement or person-number agreement for verbs.

Gaies, S. 1977. The nature of linguistic input in formal second language learning: Linguistics and communicative strategies in ESL teachers' classroom languages. In: H. D. Brown, C. Yorio, and R. Crymes, eds. On TESOL '77. Washington, D.C.: TESOL.

Gass, S., and C. Madden. 1985. Introduction. In: Gass and Madden, eds. (1985).

Gass, S., and C. Madden, eds. 1985. Input in second language acquisition. Rowley, Mass.: Newbury House.

Hatch. E. 1983. Psycholinguistics: A second language perspective. Rowley, Mass.: Newbury House.

Heidelberger Forschungsprojekt 'Pidgin Deutsch'. 1975. Sprache und Kommunikation ausländischer Arbeiter. Kronberg/Ts: Scriptor Verlag.

Henzl, V. 1979. Foreign talk in the classrooom. International Review of Applied Linguistics 17:159-67.

Krashen, S. 1985. The input hypothesis: Issues and implications. London and New York: Longman.

Krashen, S., and T. Terrell. 1983. The natural approach: Language acquisition in the classroom. Hayward, Calif.: The Alemany Press.

Long, M. 1981. Input, interaction and second language acquisition. In: H. Winitz, ed. Native Language and Foreign Language Acquisition 379. New York: Annals of the New York Academy of Science.

Long, M. 1985. Input and second language acquisition theory. In: Gass and Madden, eds. (1985).

Snow, C. 1986. Conversations with children. In: P. Fletcher and M. Garman, eds. Language acquisition, 2d. ed. Cambridge: Cambridge University Press.

Terrell, T. 1977. A natural approach to the acquisition and learning of a language. Modern Language Journal 61:325-37.

Terrell T. 1982. The natural approach to language teaching: An update. Modern Language Journal 66:121-32.

Terrell, T. 1986. Acquisition in the natural approach: The binding/access framework. Modern Language Journal 70:213-27.

Wesche, M., and D. Ready. 1985. Foreigner talk in the university classroom. In: Gass and Madden, eds. (1985).

Communicative language teaching: definitions and directions

Sandra J. Savignon
University of Illinois at Urbana-Champaign

Introduction. Not so long ago, second/foreign language teachers talked about communication in terms of language skills, seen to be four: listening, speaking, reading, and writing. These skill categories were widely accepted and provided a ready-made framework for methods manuals and teacher education programs. They were collectively described as 'active' skills, speaking and writing, and 'passive' skills, reading and listening.

Today, the suggestion that listeners and readers are passive makes us smile. Top-down/bottom-up, schemata, expectancies, and parallel processing are among the terms now used to capture the complexity of the processes involved. And yet full and widespread understanding of the interactive nature of language behavior has been hindered by the terms that came to replace the accepted active/passive dichotomy. Speaking and writing were described subsequently as 'productive' skills, while listening and reading were described, in turn, as 'receptive' skills. While certainly an improvement over the earlier active/passive representation, the terms productive/receptive fall short of capturing the nature of communication. Lost in this encode/decode, message-sending representation is the collaborative nature of meaning making. Rather, meaning appears fixed, immutable, to be sent and received, not unlike a football in the hands of a quarterback. The interest of a football game lies of course not in the football, but in the moves and strategies of the players as they fake, pass, and punt their way along the field. The interest of communication lies similarly in the moves and strategies of the participants. The terms that best represent the collaborative nature of what goes on are 'interpretation', 'expression', and 'negotiation' of meaning. Communicative competence requires not only grammatical, but discourse, sociolinguistic, and strategic competence.

This expanded, interactive view of language behavior poses a number of problems for language teachers. Among them, what is an error? And what, if anything, should be done when one occurs? What is an appropriate norm for learners? How is it determined? How should form and function be integrated in an instructional sequence? How is L2 success to be measured? Acceptance of communicative criteria clearly entails a commitment to address these admittedly complex issues.

SLA researchers face similar problems. Examination of the learning process from a communicative perspective has meant analysis of learner expression and negotiation. CA, the prediction of learner difficulties and potential sources of errors based on a contrastive analysis of L1 and L2, was far more straightforward than EA, the analysis of learner language as an evolving, variable system. The focus of this analysis continues to broaden. An initial concern with sentence-level morphosyntactic features has expanded to include pragmatics, taking into account a host of cultural, gender, social, and other contextual variables. Researchers who confront the complexity of their task might well look back with nostalgia to an earlier time when the answers to improved language teaching seemed within reach.

By and large, however, the language teaching profession has responded well to the call for materials and programs to meet learner communicative needs. Theory building continues. Communicative competence has shown itself to be a robust and challenging concept for teachers, researchers, and program developers alike. CLT has become a term for curricula that embrace both the goals *and* the processes of classroom learning, for teaching practice that views competence in terms of social interaction and looks to further SLA research to account for its development. A look in retrospect at the issues which have brought us to our present understanding of CLT will help to indentify what appear to be promising avenues of inquiry in the years ahead.

The beginnings of communicative language teaching. From its introduction into discussions of language and language learning in the early 1970s, the term communicative competence has exacted reflection. Fortunately for its survival as a useful concept, perhaps, the term has not lent itself to simple reduction, and with it the risk of becoming yet another slogan. Rather, it has continued to attract researchers and curriculum developers, to offer a sturdy framework for integrating linguistic theory, research, and teaching practice.

Present understanding of CLT can be traced to concurrent developments on both sides of the Atlantic. In Europe, the L2 needs of a rapidly increasing group of immigrants and guest workers and a rich British linguistic tradition that included social as well as linguistic context in description of language behavior led to the Council of Europe development of a syllabus for learners based on functional-notional concepts of language use. Derived from neo-Firthian systemic or functional linguistics which views language as meaning potential and maintains the centrality of context of situation in understanding language systems and how they work, a threshold level (van Ek 1975) of language ability was described for each of the languages of Europe in terms of what learners should be able to DO with the language. Functions were based on assessment of learner needs and specified the end result, the 'product' of an instructional program. The term 'communicative' attached itself to programs that used a functional-notional syllabus based on needs assessment, and the LSP (Language for Specific Purposes) movement was launched.

Concurrent developments in Europe focused on the 'process' of communicative classroom L2 learning. In Germany, for example, against a backdrop of social democratic concerns for individual empowerment, articulated in the writings of contemporary philosopher Jürgen Habermas (1970, 1971), L2 methodologists Candlin, Edelhoff, and Piepho took the lead in the development of classroom materials that encouraged learner choice and increasing autonomy (Candlin 1978). Their systematic collection of exercise types for communicatively oriented English teaching were used in teacher in-service courses and workshops to guide curriculum change. Exercises were designed to exploit the variety of social meanings contained within particular grammatical structures. A system of 'chains' encouraged teachers and learners to define their own learning path through principled selection of relevant exercises. Similar exploratory projects were also being initiated by Candlin at his academic home, the University of Lancaster, England, and by Holec and his colleagues at the University of Nancy (CRAPEL), France.

Meanwhile, in the United States, Hymes (1971) had reacted to Chomsky's characterization of the linguistic competence of the ideal native speaker and proposed the term communicative competence to represent the use of language in social context, the observance of sociolinguistic norms of appropriacy. His concern with speech communities and the integration of language, communication, and culture was not unlike that of Firth and Halliday in the British linguistic tradition. Hyme's communicative competence may be seen as the equivalent of Halliday's meaning potential. Similarly, his focus was not language learning but language as social behavior. In subsequent interpretations of the significance of Hymes' views for learners, U.S. methodologists tended to focus on native speaker cultural norms and the difficulty, if not impossibility, of authentically representing them in a classroom of nonnatives. In light of this difficulty, the appropriateness of communicative competence as an instructional goal was questioned (e.g. Paulston 1974).

At the same time, in a research project at the University of Illinois, Savignon (1971) used the term communicative competence to characterize the ability of L2 learners to interact with other speakers, to make meaning, as distinct from their ability to perform on discrete-point tests of grammatical knowledge. At a time when pattern practice and error avoidance was the rule in language teaching, the study of adult classroom acquisition of French looked at the effect of practice in the use of communication strategies as part of an instructional program. By encouraging them to ask for information, to seek clarification, to use circumlocution and whatever other linguistic and nonlinguistic resources they could muster to negotiate meaning, to stick to the communicative task at hand, teachers were invariably leading learners to take risks, to speak in other than memorized patterns. When test results were compared at the end of the 18-week, 5-hour per week program, learners who had practiced communication in lieu of laboratory pattern drills for one hour a week performed with no less accuracy on discrete-point tests of structure. On the other hand, their communicative competence as measured in terms of fluency, comprehensibility, effort, and amount of communication in a series of four unrehearsed tasks significantly surpassed that of learners who had had no such practice. Learner reactions to the test formats lent further support to the view that even beginners respond well to activities that let them focus on meaning as opposed to formal features. (A related finding had to do with learner motivation. Motivation to learn French correlated not with initial attitudes toward French speakers or the French language, but with success in the instructional program.)

A collection of roleplays, games, and other communicative classroom activities were developed subsequently for inclusion in the U.S. adaptation of the French CREDIF materials, *Voix et Visages de la France* (Coulombe et al. 1974). The accompanying guide (Savignon 1974) described their purpose as that of involving learners in the experience of communication. Teachers were encouraged to provide learners with the French equivalent of expressions like 'What's the word for...?' 'Please repeat,' 'I don't understand,' expressions that would help them to participate in the negotiation of meaning. Not unlike the efforts of Candlin and his colleagues working in a European EFL context, the focus was on classroom process and learner autonomy. The use of games, roleplay, pair, and other small group activities gained acceptance and are now widely recommended for inclusion in U.S. FL programs.

CLT thus can be seen to derive from a multidisplinary perspective that includes, at least, linguistics, psychology, philosophy, sociology, and educational research. The focus has been the elaboration and implementation of programs and methodologies that promote the development of L2 functional competence through learner participation in communicative events. Central to CLT is the understanding of language learning as both an educational and a political issue. Viewed from a multicultural *inter*national as well as *intra*national perspective, diverse sociopolitical contexts mandate a diverse set of teaching strategies. Program design and implementation depend on negotiation between policy makers, linguists, researchers, and teachers. And evaluation of program success requires a similar collaborative effort. The selection of a methodology appropriate to both the goals and context of teaching begins with an analysis of both learner needs and learner styles of learning.

Implications for existing programs. In this connection, the implications of CLT for existing programs merit brief discussion. By definition, CLT puts the focus on the learner. Learner communicative needs provide a framework for elaborating program goals in terms of functional competence. This implies global, qualitative evaluation of learner achievement as opposed to quantitative assessment of discrete linguistic features. Controversy over appropriate language testing persists, and many a curricular innovation has been undone by failure to make corresponding changes in evaluation. The attraction for many of a multiple-choice test with single right answers that a machine can translate into a score is undeniable. Qualitative evaluation of written and oral interpretation and expression is time-consuming and not so straightforward. Language programs are not alone in this respect. U.S. educators, in particular, continue to feel frustration at the domination of curricula by large-scale, standardized, multiple-choice tests. Teachers, under pressure to make their students do well on such tests, often devote valuable classtime to teaching test-taking skills, drilling students on multiple-choice items about writing, for example, rather than allowing them practice in writing.

Some teachers understandably are frustrated, moreover, by the seeming ambiguity in discussions of communicative competence. Negotiation of meaning is well and good, but this view of language behavior lacks precision, does not provide a universal scale for assessment of individual learners. Competence is viewed, rather, as variable and highly dependent upon context and purpose. Many other teachers, of course, welcome the liberation from standardized tests, preferring to rely instead on their own judgments of learner progress in communicative tasks.

An additional source of frustration for some teachers are SLA research findings that show the route, if not the rate, of language acquisition to be largely unaffected by classroom instruction. L1 cross-linguistic studies of developmental universals initiated in the seventies were soon followed by L2 studies. Acquisition, assessed on the basis of expression in unrehearsed, oral communicative contexts, seemed to follow a similar morphosyntactic sequence regardless of learner age or context of learning. Structural practice of the 'skill-getting' variety was seen to have little influence on self-expression, or 'skill-using'. Although they served to bear out the informal observations of teachers, namely, that textbook presentation and drill do not insure learner use of these same structures in their own spontaneous expression, the findings were nonetheless disconcerting. They contradicted both grammar-translation and audiolingual precepts that place the burden of acquisition on teacher explanation of grammar and controlled practice with insistence on learner accuracy. They were further at odds with textbooks that promise 'mastery' of 'basic' French, English, Spanish, etc. Teacher rejection of research findings, renewed insistence on standardized tests, and/or avoidance of L2 use in the classroom altogether, to insure that learners 'get the grammar,' have been in some cases reactions to the frustration of teaching for communication (Savignon 1983).

Moreover, the SLA research paradigm itself, with its emphasis on sentence-level grammatical features, has served to bolster a structural focus, obscuring pragmatic and sociolinguistic issues in language acquisition. In her discussion of the contexts of competence, Berns (1990) stresses that the definition of a communicative competence appropriate for learners requires an understanding of the sociocultural contexts of L2 use. In addition, the selection of a methodology appropriate to the attainment of communicative competence requires an understanding of sociocultural differences in styles of learning. Curricular innovation is best advanced by the development of local materials which, in turn, rests on the involvement of classroom teachers. Such was the case in the English language activity types elaborated by Candlin and others for use in German classrooms (Candlin 1978). The modular, thematic French units developed for use in Ontario, Canada public schools offer another example. They began with surveys of learners and involved teachers at all stages of revision (Ullmann 1987). Similarly, the task types elaborated by Prabhu for use in teaching English in Bangalore, India (Prabhu 1987). The national modern language curriculum revision project in Finland (Takala 1984) and the creation of elementary school immersion programs in the Milwaukee, Wisconsin public school system (Anderson and Rhodes 1984) are but two of many other examples of successful, substantive reforms that involved theorists and practictioners working together. These are illustrations not of LSP, in the traditional sense of the term, but, rather, of communicative approaches that have resulted from task-related, project-centered collaboration among researchers, administrators, teachers, and curriculum developers. The benefits have been twofold: teams of researchers and practitioners with expertise in both linguistics and language teaching have made contributions to both language teaching and SLA research.

Promising avenues of inquiry. Turning now to promising avenues of inquiry in the years ahead, other sociolinguistic issues await attention. Variation in the speech community and its relationship to language change are central to sociolinguistic inquiry. Sociolinguistic perspectives on variability and change highlight the folly of describing native speaker (NS) competence, let alone nonnative speaker (NNS) competence, in terms of 'mastery' or 'command' of a system. All language systems show instability and variation. Learner language systems show even greater instability and variability in terms of both the amount and rate of change. Sociolinguistic concerns with identity and accommodation help to explain the construction by bilinguals of a 'variation space' which is different from that of a native speaker. It may include retention of any number of features of L1 phonology, syntax, discourse, communication strategies, etc. The phenomenon may be individual or, in those settings where there is a community of learners, general.

In response to a homework question which asked whether retention of a native accent was an example of communicative competence, a native French speaker wrote "Yes. A friend of mine who has been in the U. S. now for several years says he has kept his French accent because he noticed that women like it." His observation parallels those of sociolinguists who have documented the role of noncognitive factors such as motivation and self-identity in L1 acquisition (e.g. Hymes 1971). Self-identity is central to differential competence and the heterogeneity of speech communities. To assume that sheer quantity of exposure shapes children's speech is simplistic.

Identification and motivation are what matter. Similarly, in L2 acquisition, learner identification and motivation interact with opportunities and contexts of language use to influence the development of competence. In classrooms, which, as social contexts, provide settings for symbolic variation, non-L2-like features may be maintained to exhibit 'learner' status (Preston 1989).

Sociolinguistic perspectives have been important in understanding the implications of norm, appropriacy, and variability for CLT and continue to suggest avenues of inquiry for further research and materials development. Use of authentic language data has underscored the importance of context—setting, roles, genre, etc.—in interpreting the meaning of a text. A range of both oral and written texts in context provides learners with a variety of L2 experiences, experiences they need to construct their own 'variation space', to make determinations of appropriacy in their expression of meaning. 'Competent' in this instance is not necessarily synonymous with 'native-like.' Negotiation in CLT highlights the need for cross-linguistic, that is, cross-*cultural* awareness on the part of all involved. Better understanding of the strategies used in the negotiation of meaning offers a potential for improving classroom practice in the needed skills.

Valuable as are sociolinguistic perspectives on L2 acquisition, research designed to improve teaching cannot proceed without the involvement of teachers. Teachers have intimate knowledge of the teaching context. They are needed on research teams to help frame the questions to be addressed as well as to interpret the outcome for methods and materials. The resources of psycholinguists, sociolinguists, and psychometricians are important, but the presence of practitioners is essential to the formulation of the research question. Graduate research programs offer a potentially ideal setting for theorists and practitioners to exchange ideas. Research faculty who encourage the interests and talents of teacher/scholars contribute to the elaboration of research projects with a potential for encouraging curricular innovation. Such innovation should give teachers primary responsibility for what they teach, with the teacher/researcher providing a crucial link between theory and practice.

Classroom language learning was the focus of a number of research studies in the 1960s and early 1970s (e.g. Scherer and Wertheimer 1964; Smith 1970; Savignon 1971, 1972). However, L2 classrooms were not a major interest of the SLA research that rapidly gathered momentum in the years that followed. The full range of variables present in educational settings was an obvious deterrent. Other difficulties included the lack of well-defined classroom processes to serve as variables and lack of agreement as to what constituted learning 'success'. Confusion of form-focused drill with meaning-focused communication persisted in many of the textbook exercises and language test prototypes that directly or indirectly shaped curricula. Not surprisingly, researchers eager to establish SLA as a worthy field of inquiry turned their attention to narrower, quantitative studies of the acquisition of selected morphosyntactic features.

With the realization that SLA research findings to date, while of value, do not begin to address the larger issues of L2 development, attention once again has turned to the classroom. The year 1988 alone saw the publication of at least five books on the topic of classroom language learning (Allwright 1988; Chaudron 1988; Ellis 1988; Peck 1988; van Lier 1988). A recent initiative, supportive of CLT, is the analysis of activity or task-based curricula. Researchers are looking at classroom language events, breaking them down into units of analysis with a view to establishing a typology of tasks that teachers frequently use. Since tasks determine opportunities for language use, for the interpretation, expression and negotiation of meaning, their systematic description constitutes the first step in establishing a relationship between task and learning outcomes. No researcher today would dispute that language learning results from participation in communicative events. Despite any claims to the contrary, however, the nature of this learning remains undefined.

An early study of foreign language teacher talk was conducted by Guthrie (1984), who found persistent form/meaning focus confusion even when teachers felt they were providing an optimal classroom acquisition environment by speaking only in the L2. Transcriptions of teacher/learner dialog revealed the unnaturalness, i.e. incoherence, of much of the discourse. There have been similar reports with respect to ESL teaching in both the United States and Britain. A 1987 study by Nunan suggests that even when teachers are committed to the concept of a communicative approach, opportunities for genuine communicative interaction may be rare. Even when all lessons ostensibly focus on functional aspects of language use, patterns of classroom interaction provide little genuine communication between teacher and learner, or, for that matter, between learner and learner.

A study by Kinginger and Savignon (forthcoming) has examined the nature of learner/learner talk associated with a variety of task types involving small group or pair work. Conversations representing four distinct task types were observed in two different college-level French programs. The conversations were examined with respect to (1) turn-taking and topic management, with generalizations regarding the degree of learner participation and initiative, and (2) negotiation and repair strategies. Data showed that when learners are constrained by formal considerations or provided with a structure-embedded 'text' as a basis for 'conversation', their talk had many of the same characteristics as form-focused teacher talk. Analyses of the interactions resulting from other, meaning-focused task types showed them to differ with respect to both quality and quantity of language use. They included examples of ways in which communicative experience can be provided in classroom settings.

Teacher preparation and expectations are another part of the overall picture. Surprisingly little systematic inquiry has been conducted into language teachers' perceptions and practices. A study by Kleinsasser (1989) is an important exception. Based on a sociological model of inquiry developed for use in elementary schools (Rosenholtz 1989), his observations and conversations with U.S. secondary school foreign language teachers have led him to identify two distinct technical cultures. One culture he calls uncertain and routine. Teachers are uncertain about their ability to promote learning, but routine, or predictable, in their day-to-day approach to teaching. The other culture is certain and nonroutine. Teachers are confident that learners will learn, and they tend to support variety and innovation in their instructional practice. To summarize from his findings, 'all language teachers perceive that they possess a technical culture. One group's technical culture uses routine tasks and relies on routine instruction that supports teachers' uncertainty about instructional practice. The second group's technical culture uses nonroutine tasks and relies on nonroutine instruction that supports teachers' certainty about instructional practice' (156). Heavy reliance on the textbook and nonexistent or infrequent opportunities for spontaneous, communicative L2 interaction were classroom characteristics of those teachers with an uncertain and routine culture.

The study of teachers' technical cultures and how they develop holds promise of accounting for the frequently noted discrepancies between theoretical understanding and classroom practice. The constraints of language classrooms are real. Tradition, learner attitudes, teacher preparation and expectations, and the school environment in general all contribute to and support teachers' technical cultures. Recommendations for methods and materials must take into account this reality. For them to do so, researchers, curriculum developers, and teachers will have to work together.

Conclusion. In keeping with my perception that communicative competence has endured as a useful concept for theory building and curriculum planning because, in part, it has avoided reduction to promotional slogans, my conclusion offers neither model nor all-purpose principles. In the interest of encouraging reflection and continued theoretical discussion, the observations that follow remain unlabeled and unnumbered. Readers are invited to consider some inquiry and, perhaps, conclusions of their own.

Slogans, and the entrepreneurs who promote them, are best resisted. Language *learning* is slow, uneven, diverse. Language *teaching* is rewarding but not without frustration. It is also big business. Scholarship and reason too often give way to promotion and profit. Competing texts and theories offer temptation to distort, oversimplify, and cash in.

Communication is social behavior, purposeful, and always in context. A tradition of abstraction in linguistic inquiry has contributed to the neglect of social context in both language teaching and SLA research, hindering understanding and acceptance of communicative competence as a goal for learners. Learner identity and motivation interact with language status, use, and contexts of learning to influence the development of competence. Description and explanation of the differential competence that invariably results must include an account of this dynamic interaction.

The full potential of content-based and task-based curricula remains to be exploited. Through the variety of language activities they can offer, content-based and task-based programs are ideally suited to a focus on communication, to the development of language skills through the interpretation, expression, and negotiation of meaning.

The opportunity for professional growth has never been greater. Current demand around the world for quality programs and a cadre of L2 professionals to design and staff them offer unprecedented opportunities for research initiatives. Responding to this demand will require teamwork, a sharing of perspectives and insights. Researchers need to look to teachers to define researchable questions. Teachers, in turn, need to participate in the interpretation of findings for materials and classroom practice. Elaboration of the 'best' methods will result only from the cooperation of all concerned.

References

Allwright, Richard. 1988. Observation in the language classroom. London: Longman.

Anderson, Helena, and Nancy Rhodes. 1984. Immersion and other innovations in U.S. elementary schools. In: S. Savignon and M. Berns, eds. Initiatives in communicative language teaching. Reading, Mass.: Addison-Wesley. 167-81.

Berns, Margie S. 1990. Contexts of competence: English language teaching in non-native contexts. New York: Plenum.

Candlin, Christopher. 1978. Teaching of English: Principles and an exercise typology. London: Langenscheidt-Longman.

Chaudron, Craig. 1988. Second language classrooms: Research on teaching and learning. New York: Cambridge University Press.

Coulombe, R., J. Barré, C. Fostle, N. Poulin, and S. Savignon. 1974. Voix et visages de la France: Level 1. Chicago: Rand-McNally.

Ellis, Rod. 1988. Classroom second language development. New York: Prentice Hall.

Guthrie, Elizabeth. 1984. Intake, communication, and second language teaching. In: Sandra J. Savignon and Margie S. Berns, eds. Initiatives in communicative language teaching. Reading, Mass.: Addison-Wesley. 35-54.

Habermas, Jürgen. 1970. Toward a theory of communicative competence. Inquiry 13:360-75.

Habermas, Jürgen. 1971. Vorbereitende Bemerkungen zu einer Theorie der Kommunikative Kompetenz. In: N. Lishman, ed. Theorie der Gesellschaft oder Sozialtechnologie. Frankfurt: Suhrkamp. 101-41.

Hymes, Dell. 1971. Competence and performance in linguistic theory. In: R. Huxley and E. Ingram, eds. Language acquisition: Models and methods. London: Academic Press.

Kinginger, Celeste, and Sandra J. Savignon. 1991. Four conversations: Task variation and learner discourse. In: C. Faltis and M. McGroarty, eds. In the interest of language: Contexts for learning and using language. Berlin: Mouton de Grutyer.

Kleinsasser, Robert. 1989. Foreign language teaching: A tale of two technical cultures. Dissertation, University of Illinois.

Nunan, David. 1987. Communicative language teaching: Making it work. ELT Journal 41.2:136-45.

Paulston, Christina. B. 1974. Linguistic and communicative competence. TESOL Quarterly 8:347-62.

Peck, Antony. 1988. Language teachers at work. New York: Prentice Hall.

Prabhu, N. S. 1987. Second language pedagogy. Oxford: Oxford University Press.

Preston, Dennis R. 1989. Sociolinguistics and second language acquisition. Oxford: Basil Blackwell.

Rosenholtz, Susan J. 1989. Teachers' workplace. New York: Longman.

Savignon, Sandra J. 1971. A study of the effect of training in communicative skills as part of a beginning college French course on student attitude and achievement in linguistic and communicative competence. Dissertation, University of Illinois.

Savignon, Sandra J. 1972. Communicative competence: An experiment in foreign language teaching. Philadelphia: Center for Curriculum Development.

Savignon, Sandra J. 1974. Teaching for Communication. In: R. Coulombe, J. Barré, C. Fostle, N. Poulin, and S. Savignon. Voix et visages de la France: Level 1, Teachers' Edition. Chicago: Rand-McNally. 13-20.

Savignon, Sandra J. 1983. Communicative competence: Theory and classroom practice. Reading, Mass.: Addison-Wesley.

Scherer, G., and M. Wertheimer. 1964. A psycholinguistic experiment in foreign language teaching. New York: McGraw Hill.

Smith, Philip D. 1970. A comparison of the cognitive and audiolingual approaches to foreign language instruction: The Pennsylvania foreign language project. Philadelphia: Center for Curriculum Development.

Takala, Sauli. 1984. Contextual consideration in communicative language teaching. In: Sandra J. Savignon and Margie S. Berns, eds. Initiatives in communicative language teaching. Reading, Mass.: Addison-Wesley. 23-34.

Ullmann, Rebecca. 1987. The Ontario experience: A modular approach to second language teaching and learning. In: Sandra J. Savignon and Margie S. Berns, eds. Initiatives in communicative language teaching II. Reading, Mass.: Addison-Wesley. 57-81.

van Ek, J., ed. 1975. Systems development in adult language learning: The Threshold Level in a European unit credit system for modern language learning by adults. Strasbourg: Council of Europe.

van Lier, Leo. 1988. The classroom and the language learner: Ethnography and second language classroom research. London: Longman.

Integrating theory and practice in second language teacher education

Jack C. Richards
City Polytechnic of Hong Kong

0 Introduction. Theories and approaches in teacher education tend to reflect particular views of the nature of teaching and learning. This has been as true in second language teacher education as it has been in other areas of teacher education. Two dominant assumptions about teaching and learning have shaped traditional approaches to teacher education in second language teaching. One is the view that the principles underlying effective teaching can be incorporated into a 'method' of teaching, hence the preoccupation with methods that has characterized the history of language teaching in this century. Alongside this methods-based view of teaching has been a training-based view of teacher education, one which starts with a specification of the skills and competencies teachers need, generally based on the method of the day, and which takes teachers in preparation through a cycle of activities designed to train them in the mastery of these skills and competencies.

In this paper I want to examine the limitations implicit in methods-based views of teaching as well as training- based approaches to teacher education, and to explore alternatives. These are based on a 'reflective' view of teaching and a developmental approach to teacher education. Illustrative examples are drawn from a teacher education program currently being implemented in Hong Kong.

1.0 Methods-based approaches. Let us first consider in more detail the assumptions behind methods-based approaches to teaching, since these are often linked to training-based approaches to teacher education. The goal of many language teachers is to find the right method. The history of our profession in the last hundred years has done much to support the impression that improvements in language teaching will come about as a result of improvements in the quality of methods, and that ultimately the perfect method will be developed. Some breakthrough in linguistic theory or in second language acquisition research will eventually unlock the secrets of second language learning, and these can then be incorporated into a supermethod that will solve the language teaching problem once and for all.

When we examine language teaching methods in detail (cf. Richards and Rodgers 1986) we see that common to all of them is a set of prescriptions as to what teachers and learners should do in the classroom. There are prescriptions for the role of the teacher, the syllabus, the kinds of learning activities to be employed, how to present and practice material, and so on. The teacher's job is simply to match his or her teaching style to the method. Methods are hence essentially 'top down'. They present a static view of teaching, that is, one in which teacher roles, learner roles, and teaching and learning processes are superimposed on teachers and learners. I would argue that attempts to find general all-purpose methods that are suitable for all teachers and learners reflect an essentially negative view of teaching and of teachers—'the teacher as idiot' philosophy. The assumption is that left to their own devices, teachers will inevitably make a mess of things. Teachers cannot be trusted to teach well. A method, however, since it imposes a uniform set of teaching roles and styles on teachers, will not be affected by the variations we find in individual teaching skill in the real world.

If we start out with this view of teaching, the problem of teacher education is relatively simple. Because we (the experts who create the methods) and not teachers themselves know the answers, it is largely a question of information transmission, of replacing old knowledge and skills with new ones. Here the notion of training can be applied. The notion of training reflects a number of assumptions about teachers and the process of teacher education.

(1) The clients for training have deficiencies of different kinds. They are empty vessels waiting to be filled (cf. Breen et al. 1989).
(2) The characteristics of effective teaching are known and can be described in discrete terms, often as skills or competencies or in terms of a teaching method.
(3) A related assumption is that teachers can and should be changed, and that the direction of change can be laid out in advance, planned for, and tested.

From a training perspective, the processes used to bring about these changes are likewise tried and tested techniques. Some reflect a view of learning as 'modeling': student teachers model the behaviors of master teachers, or they model proven techniques of teaching. For example, microteaching offers trainers a chance to model new behaviors for teachers and then for teachers to practice and learn new skills. Observation (either of teachers in the classroom or of model lessons on video) similarly allows student teachers to learn through modeling or imitation. Demonstration, simulation, and role play are also procedures that can be used to help teachers master new techniques with the hope that they will later try them out in their own classrooms, incorporate them into their repertoire of teaching strategies, and, hence, become better teachers.

The role of the teacher in 'training' is essentially that of an apprentice or a technician. According to Zeichner and Liston (1987:27): "the teacher as technician would be concerned primarily with the successful accomplishment of ends decided by others." The teacher's chief responsibility is to try to suppress old habits and replace them with new ones, to match his or her teaching style to that prescribed by the method.

The training perspective characterized above exists in a variety of forms, and advocates of training can attest to its effectiveness. Teachers' behaviors can be changed, often as a result of relatively short periods of training. For example, in a study of the effects of training on teachers' questioning skills (Borg, Kelley, Langer, and Gall 1970:82), a mini-course that consisted of a film explaining the concepts and training in the form of modeling, self-feedback, and microteaching brought about significant changes in the teachers' use of questions. Training is well suited to the treatment of skills, techniques, and routines, particularly those that require a relatively low level of planning and reflection. There are times when a training approach may be all that is required, e.g. when a group of teachers in a school request a demonstration or workshop on the use of new computer software for the teaching of writing. But despite these advantages, a number of limitations are apparent:

(1) Training reflects a very limited view of teachers and of teaching, one that reduces teaching to a technology and views teachers as little more than technicians. It likewise presents a fragmented and partial view of teaching, one which fails to capture the richness and complexity of classroom life and the teacher's role in it. It treats teaching as something atomistic rather than holistic (Britten 1985).
(2) It follows that training limits itself to those aspects of teaching that are trainable and does not address more subtle aspects of teaching, such as the nature and quality of teachers' decision making or how the teacher's values and attitudes shape his or her response to classroom events.
(3) With training, the locus of responsibility for development lies with the teacher trainer rather than with teachers themselves.

2.0 Teacher development. An alternative view of teacher education, one which reflects the notion of 'teacher development', rather than training, begins with an alternative view of teaching. It starts from the assumption that there are no such things as generalizable methods of teaching, that teachers (rather than methods) make a difference, that teachers are engaged in a complex process of planning, decision making, hypothesis testing, and evaluation, and that these processes should form a central focus of teacher education. This view of teacher education involves teachers in developing their own theories of teaching, exploring the nature of their own decision making, and developing strategies for critical reflection and change (Zeichner 1982).

Some of the main conceptual features of teacher development are:

(1) Teachers, particularly teachers in service, are not viewed as starting out with deficiencies. Although there are obviously areas of content that teachers may not be familiar with and may wish to learn about, more emphasis is placed on what teachers know and do and on providing tools with which they can more fully explore their own beliefs, attitudes, and practices.

(2) Teacher development does not start with the idea that teachers must change or discard current practices. As Freeman (1989:38) observes, "Change does not necessarily mean doing something differently; it can be an affirmation of current practice: The teacher is [perhaps] unaware of doing something that is effective." The focus is, thus, more on expanding and deepening awareness.

(3) Teacher development is discovery oriented and inquiry based. The focus in a program which attempts to deal with teacher development is hence on such things as: (a) the decision-making and planning processes employed by teachers; (b) the culture of teachers, that is, the concepts, value systems, knowledge, beliefs, and attitudes that form the basis for teachers' classroom actions; (c) teachers' views and perceptions of themselves; (d) teachers' characterizations of their own approaches to teaching and their understanding of effective teaching; (e) the roles of teachers and learners in the classroom and the effects of these on teaching and learning (Richards 1989).

2.1.0 The City Polytechnic program. Central to this approach is a focus on giving teachers the tools with which they can explore the life of their own classrooms. How does this come about in actual practice? Let me attempt to illustrate this with reference to a teacher education program currently being implemented in Hong Kong at Hong Kong's newest tertiary institution, the City Polytechnic.

The participants in the program (a postgraduate diploma in TESL) are teachers of English in Hong Kong secondary schools who have had at least two years' experience teaching English and who have completed an initial teacher-training course. The course is offered part time over two years, with teachers coming to the campus twice a week for three hour sessions.

The kind of teacher the program hopes to produce is (1) one who is technically competent in teaching, i.e. who has a sound knowledge of the pedagogy of teaching English as a second language and the skills and techniques needed to create effective conditions for learning in the classroom; (2) one who has the ability to analyze his or her own practice; (3) one whose decision making is of a high quality and leads to rational and informed choices; (4) one who can exert more control over the content and processes of his or her own work.

This philosophy is reflected in the design features of the course. Students study a set of foundation modules which provide a deeper understanding of language and language learning, and a theoretical foundation for classroom practice. Students also complete a comprehensive set of practical modules which cover both micro and macro aspects of teaching. Throughout the program the participants are engaged in a range of activities which are designed to foster critical reflection, they complete small-scale investigative projects which are designed to develop a research orientation toward their own classrooms, and they conduct classroom action research, which gives teachers means to intervene in their own classroom practices and monitor the effects of such interventions. The design of the program thus reflects four interlinked characteristics which are grounded in a reflective philosophy of teaching (cf. Nunan 1989):

(1) School-based: Firm links are made to the schools and classrooms in which the teachers work.
(2) Experiential: The program draws on the day-to-day experiences of the participants. Course assignments and activities focus on the actual practices of the teachers in their schools.
(3) Problem-centered: The program tries to identify and resolve problems the teachers encounter in their classrooms and schools.
(4) Developmental: The program recognizes that teaching is a complex phenomenon and that teachers are at different stages in their own professional growth.

2.1.1 The focus on critical reflection, on investigative projects, and on action research is a distinctive feature of the program and is addressed in a number ways throughout the program.

2.1.2 Critical reflection. Critical reflection refers to an activity or process in which an experience is recalled, considered, and evaluated, usually in relation to a broader purpose. It involves examination of past experience as a basis for evaluation and decision making and as a source for planning and action. Becoming a critically reflective teacher involves moving beyond a primary concern with instructional techniques and questions of procedure, to asking questions that regard techniques not as ends in themselves but as part of broader educational purposes (Bartlett 1990). The focus is hence on critical awareness raising in order to improve one's own self-understanding and one's own teaching practice. Another assumption underlying the notion of critical reflection is that many aspects of one's work as a teacher may be unknown to the teacher, but will become more apparent as a result of conscious reflection. A focus on critical reflection is encouraged through two primary strategies in the program:

(1) Written accounts of teaching experiences. Personal accounts of experiences through writing are common in several disciplines and their potential is increasingly being recognized in second language teacher education (Bailey 1990). Through the process of writing, deeper insights can often be achieved. The act of regular writing also preserves significant or important events for the purpose of later reflection. While the procedures used vary, we are using journals as a way of initiating this process. Participants write regularly in a journal, reflecting upon events or describing things that happen in their classrooms, in the community, or in the course. These are then shared with the course instructors.

(2) Observation and analysis of teaching events. Observation and analysis of teaching events is also used as a means of clarifying the nature of classroom events and exploring the factors which influence teachers' decision-making processes. The participants carry out ethnographic descriptions of a colleague's class, in order to develop the skills of objectively describing the teaching act. Video protocols of different kinds of language lessons also serve as a source for focused observation and analysis. Participants also record, through video or audio, examples of their own teaching and attempt to identify their own assumptions about teaching and how they go about it.

2.1.3 Investigative projects. Small-scale investigative projects are also a central component of the program. These seek to develop the participants' skills of observation, data gathering, and enquiry; to promote their understanding of the cultures of their classoom, school, and community; and to help them see their school and classroom as settings for study and inquiry. For example, as part of a course on second language acquisition, the teachers collect data on their students' interlanguage development and analyze it to test out particular theories of second language use and second language development.

2.1.4 Action research. Throughout the program, students also carry out a number of small-scale action research projects. The notion that teachers should be engaged in the study of their own classrooms was suggested over a decade ago by Stenhouse (1975). Action research is a form of inquiry which enables teachers to identify aspects of their classroom life that they would like to examine in more depth and perhaps change, to develop strategies for intervention, to monitor the effects of their interventions, and then to reflect on the consequences. Action research is not, however, full-scale research which follows the procedures of the scientific method, but small-scale classroom-focused inquiry built around the teacher's normal classroom practices (Nunan 1989).

Within the program participants follow an action-research model which involves: (1) identifying a problem they have encountered in their teaching or in their classroom; (2) developing a strategy that can be used to change or modify the situation; (3) implementing the strategy; and (4) evaluating the results.

Topics chosen for action research projects include such things as: improving students' performance on oral reading activities, investigating the effects of preteaching vocabulary on performance of a reading task, increasing the number of students' responses to questions in a lesson, improving the amount of participation in lessons by slower learners, determining the effects of an error-monitoring scheme on students' writing, increasing the amount of English used during a lesson (as opposed to Cantonese).

One of the characteristics of these small-scale projects is that they should be manageable within the normal cycle of a teacher's typical classroom practices. They are not therefore real research, but can help develop a teacher's interest in research and his or her understanding of the nature of classroom research. Should the participants in the program wish to continue to a master's degree on completion of the program, they take a course on quantitative and qualitative research methods and then complete a full-scale reserch project.

3.0 Following and monitoring the program's progress. While all new and innovative programs are launched with enthusiasm and zeal, and our own is no exception, gaps between the philosophy and rhetoric of the program and reality are inevitable in the short term, though we hope they can be minimized in the long term. Let me conclude by outlining some of the issues which need to be resolved in successfully implementing a teacher education program which seeks to encourage a more reflective view of teaching and which hopes to give teachers ways of reshaping their own goals and practices.

3.1 Need for a serious research base to the program. If second language teacher education is to move beyond the level of slogans, a serious research agenda is needed which subjects its assumptions and practices to critical scrutiny and analysis. This has not been the case in the past. A 1987 survey of the field revealed that we know very little about the processes second language teacher educators make use of, researchwise, and even less about their effects. The research data base in second language teacher education at all levels is pitifully small. For example, a survey by Bernhardt and Hammado (1987) of the 78 articles on the topic published in the last ten years, points out that only eight were data-based research. In the Department of English at City Polytechnic we have already set a research project in motion which seeks to give us data on the culture of the Hong Kong English language teacher, that is, to try to identify the ideas, concepts, beliefs, and attitudes which local teachers have about teaching English, the problems they face, and the practices they use. This will be based on information obtained from interviews with teachers and from the administration of a questionnaire. Many other opportunities for interesting and useful research exist and I hope it will be possible for us to gather a broad range of data on the practices of second language teachers in Hong Kong and the uses they make of input from teacher education programs in their teaching.

3.2 Developing teacher educators. A fundamental problem is finding faculty who are willing or able to make the move from teacher training to teacher development. Unfortunately, most faculty in university-based graduate TESOL programs have no training in teacher education and are often unwilling to see it as relevant to their work. They are typically subject-matter specialists who abandoned second language teaching years ago (if they ever did any) in favor of more fashionable research on English syntax, second language acquisition, or sociolinguistics. They often hold the view that by giving teachers increasingly sophisticated knowledge about language and language learning theory, or by training teachers in quantitative research methods, their abilities as teachers will improve. But as Freeman comments (1989:29):

> Although applied linguistics, research in second language acquisition, and methodology all contribute to the knowledge on which language teaching is based, they are not, and must not be confused with, language teaching itself. They are, in fact, ancillary to it, and thus they should not be the primary subject matter of language teacher education.

3.3 The teacher educators' own commitment. The program must model the processes it seeks to develop in the participants. Those of us who are involved in teacher education must practice what we preach. We must have the same kind of commitment to self-directed growth and continuing self-renewal as we are inviting the course participants develop. As a practical example, if we expect our student teachers to keep journals as a reflective tool, we should do so ourselves. Zeichner and Liston (1987:26) have noted: "If an inquiry-oriented program is to be successful in meeting its goals, then its staff, curriculum, and institutional environment must express these qualities of reflectiveness and self-renewal."

3.4 Preparing teachers for development. The new roles required of teachers in a development-focused approach may not be ones which teachers expect, are familiar with, or feel comfortable with. Some teachers prefer being told what to do and what works best, and are more interested in being taught to use a method than in developing their own resources as teachers. An essential phase in planning a new program is, hence, in providing teachers with an understanding of the nature and process of teacher education and their role in it, negotiating appropriate goals, and building realistic expectations.

Teachers are expected to take on different roles and responsibilities in a program which centers on development rather than training. The teacher is no longer in a subservient or subordinate role, passively and anxiously awaiting guidance, direction, and suggestions for change and improvement. Rather, the teacher is in a collaborative relationship with the teacher educator. The teacher is an investigator of his or her own classroom and his or her role in it, and determines what aspects of the classroom he or she wants to know more about. The teacher, rather than the teacher educator, now assumes the responsibility for identifying priorities for observation, analysis and, if necessary, intervention. The teacher-educator's role in this relationship is to help by providing information and resources that will assist in the process.

3.5 Building school support. A program that involves classroom research, collaborative project work, and other school-based initiatives, is dependent upon the good will of colleagues and supervisors for its successful implementation. Does the school see the value of such an approach and provide the necessary support and encouragement? If not, we may be setting out to prepare teachers to carry out a role which their school does not want them to assume. Liaison and networking with schools and engaging supervisors and other school personnel in the planning phase of program development can help address this problem.

3.6 Evaluating program accomplishments. Because program goals in teacher development are long-term, ongoing, and often not measurable directly, rather than short-term, measurable, and performance based, it is difficult to determine if and when such goals have been attained. Effects may not be immediately apparent, creating an aura of fuzziness and making evaluation difficult to accomplish. Case studies, ethnographic and longitudinal approaches may therefore be needed to help follow the effects of the program on different dimensions of teacher development.

These limitations should not, however, discourage us from moving second language teacher education into a new and more fruitful phase of its evolution, one which is characterized by less of a reliance on applied linguistics, less of an emphasis on training, and more attention to the nature and process of teaching and to teacher self-development and continuing growth. Too many teachers leave second language teacher education programs either bursting with inapplicable theory or with a bag of tricks that offer only partial solutions to the complex issues they confront in the real world. We must do better. The challenge for us in teacher education is to equip teachers with the conceptual and analytical tools they need to move beyond the level of skilled technicians and to become mature language teaching professionals.

References

Bailey K. 1990. Teacher diaries in teacher education programs. In: Richards and Nunan (1990).

Bartlett, L. 1990. Teacher development through reflective teaching. In: Richards and Nunan (1990).

Bernhardt, E.B., and J. Hammadou. 1987. A decade of research in foreign language teacher education. Modern Language Journal 71:289-99.

Borg, W.R., M. Kelley, P. Langer, and M. Gall. 1970. The mini course: A micro teaching approach to teacher education. Beverly Hills, Calif.: Collier-Macmillan.

Breen, M., C. Candlin, L. Dam, and G. Gabrielsen. 1989. The evolution of a teacher training program. In: R.K. Johnson, ed. The second language curriculum. Cambridge: Cambridge University Press. 111-35.

Britten, D. 1985. Teacher training in ELT (Part l). Language Teaching 18.2.

Freeman, D. 1989. Teacher training, development, and decision making: A model of teaching and related strategies for language teacher education. TESOL Quarterly 23(1):27-46.

Haberman, M. 1983. Research on pre-service and clinical experiences: Implications for teacher education. In: K. Howey and W. Gardner, eds. The education of teachers. New York: Longman. 98-117.

Kemmis, S., and R. McTaggart. 1982. The action research planner. Victoria: Deakin University Press.

Lange, D. 1983. Teacher development and certification and foreign languages: Where is the future? Modern Language Journal 67:374-81.

______. 1990. A blueprint for the design of a teacher development program in second language education. In: Richards and Nunan (1990).

Larsen-Freeman, D. 1983. Training teachers or educating a teacher. In: J. Alatis, H.H. Stern, and P. Strevens, eds. Georgetown University Round Table on Languages and Linguistics 1983. Washington, D.C.: Georgetown University Press. 264-74.

Nunan, D. 1985. Second-language teacher education: Present trends and future prospects. In: Language, learning and community. Sydney: Macquarie University.

______. 1989. Understanding language classrooms: A guide for teacher initiated action. New York: Prentice Hall International.

______. 1990. Action research in the language classroom. In: Richards and Nunan (1990).

Pennington, M. 1989. Faculty development for language programs. In: R.K. Johnson, ed. The second language curriculum. Cambridge: Cambridge University Press. 91-110.

Porter, P., L. Goldstein, J. Leatherman, and S. Conrad. An ongoing dialog: Learning logs for teacher-training. In: Richards and Nunan (1990).

Richards, J.C. 1987. The dilemma of teacher education in TESOL. TESOL Quarterly 21(2):209-26.

______. 1989. Beyond training: Approaches to teacher education. In: Language teaching. MS.

______. 1990. The teacher as self-observer: Self-monitoring in teacher development. In: J.C. Richards. The language teaching matrix. New York: Cambridge University Press.

______, and D. Nunan, eds. 1990. Second language teacher education. New York: Cambridge University Press.

______, and T. Rodgers. 1986. Approaches and methods in language teaching. New York: Cambridge University Press.

Roderick, J. 1986. Dialogue writing: Context for reflecting on self as teacher and researcher. Journal of Curriculum and Supervision 1(4):305-15.

Stenhouse, Lawrence. 1975. An introduction to curriculum research and development. London: Heinemann.

Wright, T. 1990. Understanding classroom role relationships. In: Richards and Nunan (1990).

Zeichner, K. 1982. Reflective teaching and field-based experience in teacher education. Interchange 12(4):1-22.

Zeichner, K., and D. Liston. 1987. Teaching student teachers to reflect. Harvard Educational Review 57(1):23-48.

An evaluation of simulated oral proficiency interviews as measures of spoken language proficiency

Charles W. Stansfield
Center for Applied Linguistics

Description of the SOPI. The simulated oral proficiency interview (SOPI) is a type of semidirect speaking test that models, as closely as is practical, the format of the oral proficiency interview (OPI). The OPI is used by United States Government agencies belonging to the Interagency Language Roundtable (ILR) and the American Council for the Teaching of Foreign Languages (ACTFL) to assess general speaking proficiency in a second language.

The measure I have called the SOPI (Stansfield 1989) is a tape-recorded test consisting of six parts. It begins with simple personal background questions posed on the tape in a simulated initial encounter with a native speaker of the target language. During a brief pause, the examinee records a short answer to each question. Part 1 is analogous to the 'warm-up' phase of the OPI. The remaining five parts are designed to elicit language that is similar to that which would be elicited during the level check and probe phases of the OPI. Parts 2, 3, and 4 employ pictures in a test booklet to check for the examinee's ability to perform the various functions that characterize the Intermediate and Advanced levels of the ACTFL proficiency guidelines, or levels 1 and 2 of the ILR skill-level descriptions. Thus, the examinee is asked to give directions to someone using a map, to describe a particular place based on a drawing, and to narrate a sequence of events in the present, past, and future using drawings in the test booklet as a guide. Parts 5 and 6 of the SOPI require the examinee to tailor his or her discourse strategies to selected topics and real-life situations. These parts assess the examinee's ability to handle the functions and content that characterize the Advanced and Superior levels of the ACTFL guidelines, or levels 2 through 4 of the ILR skill-level descriptions. Like the OPI, the SOPI can end with a wind-down.

After the test is completed, the tape is scored by a trained rater using the ACTFL/ILR scale. Scores may range from the Novice level to High Superior.

The latter score is equivalent to a rating of between 3+ and 5 on the ILR scale.

Description of semidirect tests. As indicated, the SOPI is a type of semidirect test. Clark (1979) defined a semi-direct test as one that elicits speech by means of tape recordings, printed test booklets, or other nonhuman elicitation procedures. A semidirect test can employ a wide variety of items formats. These may include techniques such as spoken pattern practice in response to cues in the test booklet or on tape, reading aloud, sentence repetition, sentence completion, naming nouns or verbs depicted through line drawings in the test booklet, describing a single picture or describing a picture sequence (Clark 1979, Clark and Swinton 1979). Many of these elicitation techniques are inherently different from the relatively authentic, context-based techniques that would be found in the OPI and in the SOPI.

In his discussion of semidirect tests, Clark (1978:48) says that "semi-direct tests may be proposed as second-order substitutes for direct techniques when general proficiency measurement is at issue, but it is not operationally possible to administer a direct test." The major purposes of this paper are to describe the development and research that has been conducted to date on the SOPI, and to examine whether Clark's characterization of semi-direct tests should extend to the SOPI.

Research and development involving the SOPI. In five studies involving different test development teams and different languages, the SOPI has shown itself to be a valid and reliable surrogate of the OPI. Clark and Li (1986) developed the first SOPI, although they did not label it as such, in an effort to incorporate modifications that Clark felt could improve the Recorded Oral Proficiency Interview, or ROPE test (Lowe and Clifford 1980). Clark and Li developed four forms of a ROPE-like test of Chinese, with instructions and scenarios in English, and then administered the four forms and an OPI to 32 students of Chinese at two universities. Each test was scored by two raters and the scores on the two types of test were statistically compared. The results showed the correlation between the SOPI and the OPI to be .93.

Shortly after arriving at the Center for Applied Linguistics (CAL) in 1986, I read Clark's report on this project and realized that these favorable results merited replication by other researchers in situations involving other test developers and learners of other languages. As a result, I applied to the International Research and Studies Program for a grant to develop similar tests in four other languages. Fortunately, the grant was funded, and in August 1987 I began the development of a similar semidirect interview test of Portuguese, called the *Portuguese Speaking Test* (Stansfield et al. 1990). Three forms of this test and an OPI were administered to 30 adult learners of Portuguese at four institutions. Each test was also scored by two raters. In this study a correlation of .93 between the two types of test was also found. In addition, the SOPI showed itself to be slightly more reliable than the OPI and some raters commented that the SOPI seemed easier to rate, since the format of the test did not vary with each examinee.

One of the things we learned as a result of our experience with the PST was that it would be possible to include a wind-down after Part 6 of the test. This is usually an easy question designed to put the examinee at ease and to facilitate the ending of the examination in as natural a manner as possible (Stansfield and Kenyon 1988). We incorporated a wind-down with the Hausa test we developed subsequently, and we plan to incorporate a wind-down in any future forms of the PST that we develop. Another thing we learned is that the SOPI may differ somewhat for each language, in order to accommodate the unique characteristics of that language. For instance, for the PST, it was necessary to record two versions of the test, one in Lusitanian Portuguese and one in Brazilian Portuguese, since in Part 1 each dialect proved to be quite problematic for learners who had been exposed to only one dialect, which is often the case with Portuguese instruction in the United States.

During 1988 and 1989, I directed the development of tests in Hebrew, Hausa, and Indonesian. The Hebrew SOPI, or *Hebrew Speaking Test* (HeST) as we call it, was developed in close collaboration with Elana Shohamy and her associates at the University of Tel Aviv (Shohamy et al. 1989). In order to accommodate the different settings where the language is studied and used, two forms of the test were developed for use in Hebrew language schools for immigrants to Israel, and two forms were developed for use in North America. Because the pronoun 'you' carries gender in Hebrew, alternate versions of the master tape for men and women were developed. The first two forms were administered to 20 foreign students at the University of Tel Aviv and the other two forms were administered to 10 students at Brandeis University and 10 students at the University of Massachusetts at Amherst. Each group also received an OPI. Table 1 shows that the correlation between the OPI and this SOPI for the Israeli version was .90, while the correlation for the U.S. version was .94. Parallel-form and interrater reliability, depicted in Table 2, were also very high. The average interrater reliability was .94 and parallel form reliability was .95. When examinees' responses on different forms were scored by different raters, the reliability was .92.

Recently, Dorry Kenyon (my associate at CAL) and I reported on the development and validation of SOPIs in Indonesian and Hausa (Stansfield and Kenyon 1989). The development of the *Indonesian Speaking Test* (IST) posed special problems. Indonesian is one of those languages where the context of the speech situation seems to be especially important. Because of this, we strove to contextualize the test items to an even greater degree than we had done for other languages. In order to do this, we specified the age, sex, and position or relationship of the supposed interlocutor for the examinee. During trialing, we noticed that examinees tended to assign a name to the person with whom they were speaking. As a result, when appropriate, we gave each interlocutor a name on the operational forms. To validate the test, 16 adult

Table 1. Concurrent validity product moment correlations between the SOPI and the OPI.

	SAME RATER	SEPARATE RATERS	Average
Chinese	.96	.90	.93
Portuguese	.93	.93	.93
Hebrew (USA)	.94	.94	.94
Hebrew (Israel)	.90	.90	.90
Indonesian	.95	.94	.94
Hausa	n/a	n/a	

Table 2. Interrater agreement (product moment correlations) in six SOPI studies.

	Within Forms (interrater reliability)	Across Forms (parallel form reliability)	Different forms and raters
Chinese	.92	.96	.91
Portuguese	.96	.97	.96
Hebrew (USA)	.93	.96	.92
Hebrew (Israel)	.95	.94	.93
Indonesian	.98	.94	.93
Hausa	.91	.81	.84

learners of Indonesian were administered two forms of the IST and an OPI. The correlation with the OPI was .94. Reliability was also high, with interrater reliability averaging .98, and parallel-form reliability averaging .94 for the two raters. When different forms and different raters were used, the reliability was also .93.

The development of two forms of the *Hausa Speaking Test* also posed special problems. First, it was necessary to develop a male and a female version of each master tape. In addition, because no ACTFL or ILR-certified interviewer/raters were available for Hausa, it was not possible to administer an OPI to the 13 subjects who took the *Hausa Speaking Test*. However, two speakers of Hausa as a second language, who had received familiarization training in English with the ACTFL/ILR scale, subsequently scored the Hausa test tapes on that scale. Although, as might be expected, the reliability of these raters was not as high as that which was obtained on the other SOPI tests using certified raters, the reliabilities were still quite good. The raters showed high interrater reliability, averaging .91 for the two forms of the test, and an average parallel-form reliability of .81. When different forms and raters were used, the correlation between scores was .84. These reliabilities are based on product moment correlations, which were derived by converting ACTFL/ILR scores to a numerical value. When the rank order correlation was employed to determine reliability, as is generally done with tests that employ an ordinal scale, the average interrater reliability was .95, parallel form reliability was .93, and parallel-form reliability using different raters was also .93. In addition, the raters indicated that they believed the Hausa SOPI elicited an adequate sample of language with which to assign a rating.

The SOPI versus the OPI. In comparison with the OPI, the SOPI would seem to offer certain advantages. The OPI must be administered by a trained interviewer, whereas any teacher, aide, or language lab technician can administer the SOPI. This may be especially useful in locations where a trained interviewer is not available. The SOPI can be simultaneously administered to a group of examinees by a single administrator, whereas the OPI must be individually administered. Thus, the SOPI may be preferable when many examinees need to be tested within a short span of time.

In addition to these practical advantages, the SOPI may offer psychometric advantages in terms of validity and reliability. The OPI typically takes 20 to 25 minutes to administer and produces 12-15 minutes of examinee speech. The SOPI takes 45 minutes to administer and produces a longer sample, usually 20-23 minutes of examinee speech. The more extensive sample may contribute to a more valid assessment.

In an OPI, the validity of the test sample elicited is in large part determined by the skill of the interviewer. Interviewers can vary considerably in their interviewing techniques, yet the SOPI offers the same quality of interview to each examinee.

The OPI also helps ensure high reliability. By recording the test for later scoring, it is possible to ensure that examinees will be rated by the most reliable raters. In the OPI, the same interviewer typically rates and scores the test. Yet this interviewer may not be the most reliable or accurate rater. Also, some raters who have scored both types of test have reported that it is sometimes easier to assign a rating to a SOPI performance. In part, this may be because the SOPI produces a longer speech sample and because each examinee is given the same questions. Thus, it may be easier for the rater to apply the scale to a single test, as is the case with the SOPI, than to many different tests, at the same time, as is the case with the OPI.

Conclusion. An examination of the SOPI research, which has been carried out on different subjects, and on tests of different languages produced by different test development teams, shows that the SOPI correlates so highly with the OPI that it seems safe to say that both test the same abilities. The SOPI has also shown itself to be at least as reliable as the OPI, and in some cases more so. Thus, it seems safe to conclude that it is as good as an OPI in many situations. A comparison of the advantages of each suggests that the

SOPI can offer certain practical and psychometric advantages over the OPI. Thus, it may be useful to consider the circumstances that should motivate the selection of one format or the other.

Since the tasks on the SOPI are ones that can only be effectively handled by responding in sentences and connected discourse, the SOPI is not appropriate for learners below the level of Intermediate Low. Similarly, the semidirect format of the test does not permit the extensive probing that may be necessary to distinguish between the highest levels of proficiency on the ILR scale, such as levels 4, 4+, and 5.

The purpose of testing may also play a role in the selection. If the test is to have very important consequences, it may be preferable to administer a SOPI, since it provides control over reliability and validity of the score. Such a situation might be found in the use of a proficiency score to determine whether or not applicants are qualified for employment, such as for teacher certification purposes. I should mention that the Texas Education Agency agrees with me on this point, since it recently decided to award CAL a contract to develop SOPI tests in Spanish and French for teacher certification purposes in Texas. On the other hand, if scores are to be used for placement within an instructional program and a competent interviewer is available, it would seem preferable to administer an OPI. In such a situation, an error in placement can be easily corrected. Similarly, an OPI administered by a competent interviewer would seem preferable for program evaluation purposes because of the qualitative information it can provide and because the score will not have important repercussions on the examinee.

Given all of the above advantages that accrue to the SOPI, it seems time to reconsider Clark's characterization of semidirect tests as 'second order substitutes' for the direct OPI. While this characterization may be applicable to semidirect tests in general, it does not seem to apply to the SOPI.

References

Clark, J.L.D. 1979. Direct vs. semidirect tests of speaking ability. In: E.J. Briere and F.B. Hinofotis, eds. Concepts in language testing: Some recent studies. 35-49. Washington, D.C.: Teachers of English to Speakers of Other Languages.

Clark, J.L.D., and Y. Li. 1986. Development, validation, and dissemination of a proficiency-based test of speaking ability in Chinese and an associated assessment model for other less commonly taught languages. Washington, D.C.: Center for Applied Linguistics. ERIC Document Reproduction Service No. ED 278 264.

Clark, J.L.D., and S.S. Swinton. 1979. Exploration of speaking proficiency measures in the TOEFL context. TOEFL Research Report 4. Princeton, NJ: Educational Testing Service.

Lowe, P., and R. T. Clifford. 1980. Developing an indirect measure of overall oral proficiency. In: J.R. Frith, ed. Measuring spoken language proficiency. Washington, D.C.: Georgetown University Press.

Shohamy, E., C. Gordon, D. M. Kenyon, and C. W. Stansfield. 1989. The development and validation of a semidirect test for assessing oral proficiency in Hebrew. Bulletin of Hebrew Higher Education 4.1:4-9.

Stansfield, C.W. 1989. Simulated oral proficiency interviews. ERIC Digest. Washington, D.C.: ERIC Clearinghouse on Languages and Linguistics.

Stansfield, C.W., and D. M. Kenyon. 1988. Development of the Portuguese speaking test. Washington, D.C.: Center for Applied Linguistics. ERIC Document Reproduction Service No. ED 296 586.

Stansfield, C.W., and D. M. Kenyon. 1989. Development of the Hausa, Hebrew, and Indonesian speaking tests. Washington, D.C.: Center for Applied Linguistics. ERIC Document Reproduction Service, forthcoming.

Stansfield, C.W., D.M. Kenyon, R. Paiva, F. Doyle, I. Ulsh, and M.A. Cowles. 1990. The development and validation of the Portuguese speaking test. Hispania 73.3.

Fossils or forests? The challenge of teaching for proficiency in the secondary schools

Rebecca M. Valette
Boston College

As we enter the decade of the 1990s, more and more foreign language teachers in the United States are rallying behind the banner of proficiency. What is exciting about the movement is its focus on the outcomes of instruction: foreign language classes are to be so organized and so taught as to promote real language use, that is, proficiency in listening, speaking, reading and writing. In the past, as you will recall, the banners all proclaimed a methodology. In the mainstream were Grammar-Translation, Reading Approach, Audiolingual Method, the Cognitive Code Approach, and Individualized Instruction. More tangential were the Silent Way, Suggestopedia, Total Physical Response, the Natural Approach. Many teachers stitched several banners together in an Eclectic Approach.

Those of us with some years of teaching experience know that the new shining banners were first greeted with fanfare, and then in time became frayed and faded before they were put away in storage. Some lasted longer than others. Some are fondly remembered and brought out on special occasions, while others are reviled as having been unworthy of our support.

If we look more closely at the historical parade of American language teaching methodologies, we discover that behind each banner there was an unexpressed objective, namely the development of some form of language proficiency: translation skill, reading skill, oral communication, and so forth. Unfortunately, given the fact that most Americans received only two or three years of language instruction, this majority felt in retrospect that they had 'studied' a language but had not 'learned' it. However, those students who continued their studies across a longer sequence were able, as a combined result of longer study plus extensive reading, listening, and/or residence abroad, to reach the Advanced and Superior levels of proficiency. Thus, over the decades we have educated an adult population in this country where many have not studied a foreign language at all, where some have 'studied' a language and never become minimally proficient, but where a minority, and this should not be forgotten, have acquired proficiency in another language and sometimes in several languages.

The question which I would like to address today is: What do we mean by 'proficiency' when we refer to the 'Proficiency Movement'? More specifically, what level of oral proficiency should we be striving for in the light of our national goals of educating a citizenry who can speak more than one language? Should our aim be to bring our students only as far as the Intermediate level (ability to meet basic survival needs and minimum courtesy requirements)? Or should we as teachers promote a curriculum that would bring at least our majors and graduate students to the advanced level (ability to satisfy routine social demands and limited work requirements), if not the Superior level (ability to speak the language with sufficient structural accuracy and vocabulary to participate effectively in most formal and informal conversations on practical, social and professional topics)?

My worry is that if we interpret 'oral proficiency' too narrowly, we may end up bringing many students to the Intermediate level, while at the same time making it impossible for them to progress any higher.

What are "fossils"? The "fossils" in the title of my paper are those people whose linguistic advancement up the proficiency scale has reached a plateau beyond which further progress is deemed impossible. The barrier occurs because large numbers of errors have become so ingrained that they are considered to be "fossilized."

Those who have worked with the government Interagency Language Roundtable (ILR) scale over the years have identified two stages at which fossilization is found:

- terminal 1+ (where people will probably never advance to level 2)
- terminal 2+ (where people will probably never advance to level 3)

One might also consider as "fossils" those at level 4 whose noticeable foreign accent is so established that they will never advance to level 5.

What is the forest? If we walk through a redwood forest, we see trees at all stages of growth. The baby trees, only a foot high, are at level 0 or Novice. The saplings from two to ten feet are at level 1 or Intermediate. The more mature trees at around 50 feet are at level 2 or Advanced. And the older taller trees from 100 feet up to 300 feet, attain the Superior rating reaching through levels 3, 4, and 5 (see Figure 1).

Of course, there are other trees in the forest. The maples, for instance, have big leaves and look more impressive as baby trees and saplings in their Novice and Intermediate stages. However, as adult trees they never go beyond the Advanced level. The largest trees may attain 100 feet and the level of Advanced High, but they will always be terminal 2+.

And then there are the various sorts of bushes, with many shapes of leaves and branch structures. As they grow from the Novice to the Intermediate level they broaden and fill out. However, even the most mature

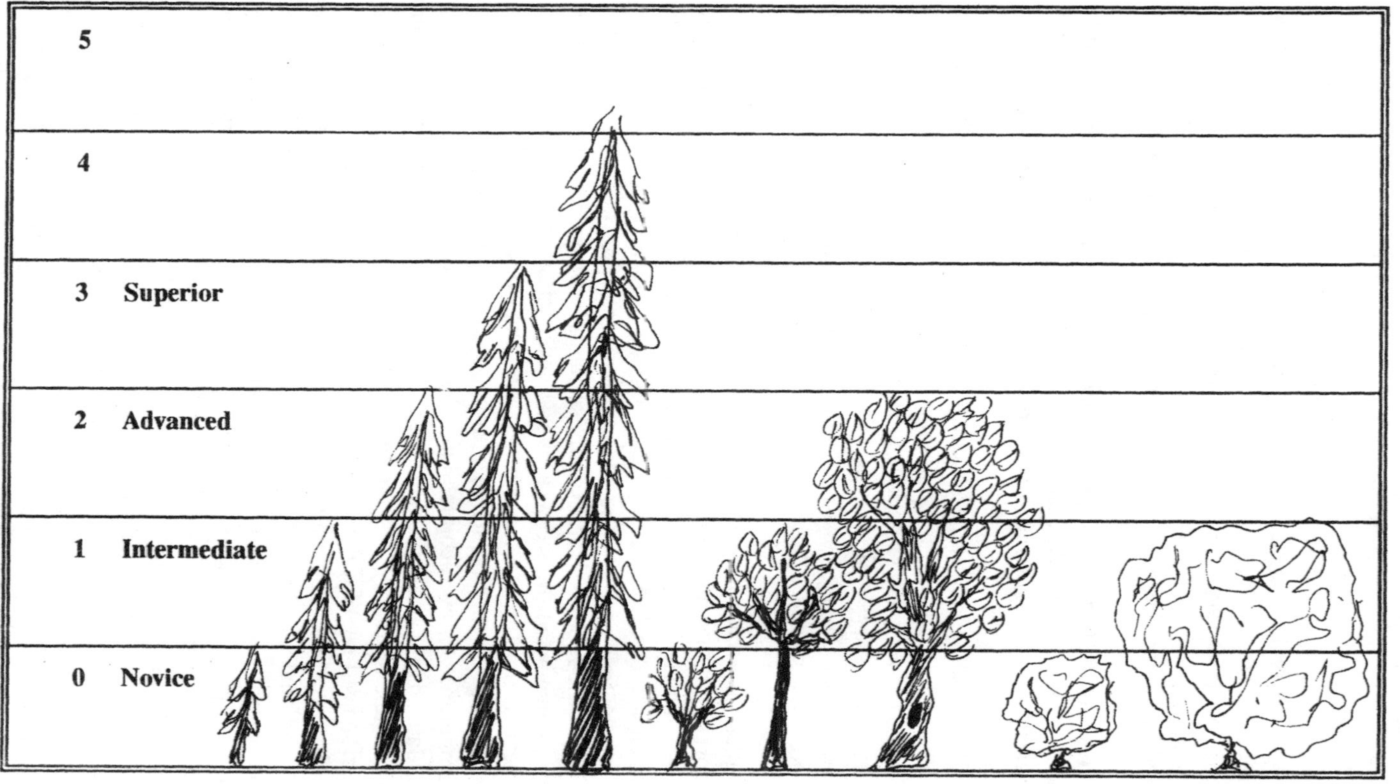
5
4
3 Superior
2 Advanced
1 Intermediate
0 Novice
Redwoods
Trees
Bushes

bushes never grow tall enough to reach the Advanced level. For bushes, Intermediate High equals terminal 1+.

What distinguishes the bushes from the trees—and at a higher level, the maple trees from the redwoods—is grammatical and lexical accuracy. The tall, strong trunk is the accurate core. At the Novice and even the Intermediate levels of growth, the bush with its larger vocabulary and evident fluency may appear more attractive than the young trees, but since this breadth of expression is acquired and maintained at the expense of accuracy, the small twisted branches simply grow thicker and a strong trunk never emerges.

How strong is the oral proficiency of our language majors? If we turn back 25 years to Carroll's study of the proficiency levels of college majors, we may recall his dismay concerning the findings of his project (1967:134):

> The most striking thing about these charts is the generally low median levels of attainment in audio-lingual skills that they reveal. The median graduate with a foreign language major can speak and comprehend the language only at about an FSI Speaking rating of "2+" [or ACTFL Advanced High], that is, somewhere between a "limited working proficiency" and a "minimum professional proficiency."

My guess is that today in 1990, the situation has worsened rather than improved and that our median foreign language majors, and by extension the foreign language teachers we are producing to staff the secondary schools, are well below the Advanced High level in oral proficiency.

In the Fall of 1989, the American Association of Teachers of French published the report of their Commission on Professional Standards, in which they distinguished between a "basic level of competence" necessary for teachers to function well in a lower-level classroom, and a "superior level of competence" for those teaching Advanced classes and working on curriculum development. They recommended that to qualify for "basic competence" a candidate should attain the Advanced rating on the Oral Proficiency Interview (OPI), while to qualify for "superior competence" a candidate should be at the Superior level (AATF Commission 1989).

However, are our majors even reaching the Advanced level? When I proposed that the Department of Romance Languages at Boston College institute oral proficiency exit requirements for our graduate students, it was pointed out by our chairman, who is an experienced OPI trainer, and two other colleagues, who are certified OPI testers, that some of our M.A. and Ph.D. students would not be able to get beyond the Intermediate High level prior to the completion of their degree work. Consequently, Boston College is 'recommending' a minimum level of oral proficiency of Intermediate High for the M.A.T. and Advanced for the other graduate degrees. We have some excellent graduate students at Boston College who would clearly meet the AATF standards. However, I would surmise that many other graduate-degree-granting institutions, were they to administer OPI interviews, would discover that they, too, have students whose oral proficiency is not as high as they would wish.

One of our research goals of this new decade should be to evaluate the actual oral proficiency of American undergraduate and graduate language majors so that we know precisely where we stand. It would also be very useful if we could establish statistics concerning the oral proficiency of all language teachers, at the elementary, secondary, and university levels. Even partial statistics would be helpful. My fear is that the oral proficiency of many majors and teachers falls below the Advanced level.

Are we nurturing 'bushes' or 'trees'? The most serious question facing the profession, however, is not whether significant numbers of college majors and secondary teachers are at the Intermediate level of oral proficiency, but rather what percent of these people are 'bushes' and what percent are 'trees'. The young trees, with more practice and experience, can grow to maturity, some reaching the Advanced High level (the 'maple trees') and others reaching higher (the 'redwoods'). The 'bushes', however, because of fossilization of inaccurate patterns, will remain bushes.

We should urgently engage in a major research study to determine to what extent we in the United States are producing 'bushes' rather than 'trees' among those who are studying the commonly taught languages, such as French, Spanish and German. The next step is, of course, how to prevent premature fossilization.

How and where are fossils formed? Let us consider the experience of those who have worked extensively with the government ILR scales. They make an important distinction between the 'monastery' and the 'marketplace', between 'school' learners and 'street' learners, between those who have 'studied' the language and learned to express themselves with a concern for accuracy and those who have 'picked up' the language, usually by living in an area where that language was spoken, and focused their attention on interpersonal communication. In the lower levels on the proficiency scale, 'school' learners are characterized by a strong grammar control and a more limited vocabulary, while 'street' learners compensate for their weaker grammar with a richer vocabulary.

The phenomenon of fossilization occurs mainly among 'street' learners who have communicated successfully over such a long period of time with inaccurate lexical and structure patterns that these errors have become generalized and are almost impossible to eradicate.

Higgs and Clifford point out, however (1982:68), that fossilization may also be found in 'school' learners:

> The terminal cases whose foreign-language background had included only an academic environment all came from language programs that either

were taught by instructors who themselves had not attained grammatical mastery of the target language—and hence were unable to guide their students into correct usage—or by instructors who had chosen not to correct their students' mistakes for philosophical, methodological, or personal reasons.

In these instances, the school environment had provided plenty of opportunity for 'communication' but with incorrect models: either an inaccurate teacher speech or (and probably more importantly) substantial inaccurate peer input.

What is the effect on proficiency of immersion or study abroad? Twenty-five years ago, in his study on the proficiency of undergraduate language majors, Carroll concluded (1967:137):

> Time spent abroad is clearly one of the most potent variables we have found, and this is not surprising, for reasons that need not be belabored. Certainly our results provide a strong justification for a "year abroad" as one of the experiences to be recommended for the language majors.

Five years ago, however, Lowe, looking at the results of government programs reported that a maxi-immersion experience of two weeks to one month in which students are encouraged to use functional foreign language is not appropriate if students are at level 1+ or lower (Lowe 1985:45-46).

Is there a contradiction? Perhaps not. Carroll was looking at college majors in the early 1960s, that is, students who had had a strong traditional introduction to the language under study where emphasis had been on vocabulary acquisition and accurate grammar control. Many were probably already at level 2 or 3 in reading proficiency before going abroad. For these students, the experience in the foreign country provided the opportunity to pull together what they had learned. They were consequently able to bring their oral proficiency up to level 2+ or 3.

As a profession, we might profitably explore to what extent intensive immersion and academic year abroad programs help our current students improve their proficiency. One such research project, under the direction of Liskin-Gasparro, is presently underway at Middlebury College. Students are being tested for Oral Proficiency before and after the summer language program. It will be interesting to see which percent of the Intermediate students fail to progress beyond Intermediate High, and how many in this group should indeed be classified as terminal 1+ or 'bushes'.

It would be even more interesting to analyze the research data by subdividing the pretest interviews at each level of proficiency into three categories:

- 'school' speech, as characterized by strong grammatical and lexical accuracy but with a limited range of vocabulary;

■ 'street' speech, as characterized by a relatively broad vocabulary but containing numerous inaccuracies;

■ 'classic' speech, which falls between the above two extremes.

Does the study abroad or intensive immersion experience benefit one group more than another? Is there an initial level of proficiency which should be attained to assure that students will derive maximum profit from such programs?

Such an analysis will perhaps help us verify the existence of terminal profiles, as Higgs and Clifford recommended (1982:76), and identify the contributing factors.

Is fossilization 'acquired', and if so, how? If we apply Krashen's distinction between 'acquisition' and 'learning' (Krashen 1981:1-3) to the study of fossilization, we may posit that the inaccurate 'fossilized' forms have been 'acquired' and, consequently, that further 'learning' has little remedial effect except in those rare circumscribed instances when the 'monitor' has sufficient time required to function.

How does this acquisition of fossilized forms take place? The 'street' learner often is functioning in a rich environment of authentic and correct language. Should this not produce the appropriate type of 'input' for the acquisition of proper forms and structures? Perhaps because much of this language is beyond the input threshhold of the learner—that is, beyond $i + 1$—it is useless for acquisition. It may be that the preponderance of meaningful 'input' is learner-generated. That is, perhaps learners in a communicative environment receive a large portion of their comprehensible input in the form of sentences which they themselves produce.

The 'school' learner also runs the risk of fossilization when the classroom situation provides large quantities of comprehensible but flawed input consisting of inaccurate teacher speech and, which is more dangerous, highly motivating but even more inaccurate peer speech. Students hear their classmates produce all sorts of 'creative' language, replete with errors, and begin to 'acquire' those forms.

Accuracy: the sine qua non of healthy tree growth. Most proponents of proficiency agree that accuracy is an essential element in the development of communication skills. For example, Omaggio (1986:36) states as one of her five basic hypotheses: "There should be concern for the development of linguistic accuracy from the beginning of instruction in a proficiency-oriented approach."

Higgs and Clifford are even more insistent on the importance of an 'accuracy-first' program as they ask us to recognize "the ultimate role that linguistic accuracy plays in the achievement of true communicative competence, in which it truly does matter how the message is transmitted" (1982:77).

Of course, accuracy is not the only element. True proficiency requires creative language use. It would appear, however, that while exaggerated early emphasis on accuracy can result in the growth of the 'trunk' of the tree, thus at least providing a basis on which proficiency could be developed, conversely, an exaggerated early emphasis on creativity prevents the development of a healthy 'trunk' and at best leads only to the proliferation of 'bushes' (and the ultimate danger of fossilization at the terminal 1+ level).

What is the strategy for fossil prevention? The key strategy for fossil prevention lies in providing a maximum degree of accurate *and* appropriate input at the early levels of instruction. In the beginning classroom, this input is of three types: teacher input, recorded input, and student input.

Teacher input. Given the importance of building a healthy linguistic base, it might profitably be argued that only our most proficient teachers be allowed to teach beginning students. (Currently, it is often the weaker teachers who are assigned the elementary courses, while the advanced classes are taught by the teachers who have a stronger command of the language.) However, if staffing is a problem, the next best measure would be to insist that all teachers working with beginning students have a reasonable near-native accent and that they use only a limited number of foreign language constructions which they can control with a high degree of accuracy.

Recorded input. Thanks to advancing technologies, it is becoming much easier to bring foreign language input into the classroom. The most exciting medium is video, which combines the spoken language with its human and cultural context. To be effective, however, the video input must be at the appropriate linguistic level. Authentic video which is too difficult for beginning students can offer the basis of 'code-breaking' activities where students listen for a familiar word or phrase. It does not, however, provide an appropriate model for acquisition since it is far beyond the optimum $i+1$ level. For beginning courses, the ideal video would be one of high professional quality (so that students would willingly sit through repeated viewings so necessary for effective input) and one in which the speech patterns are at the level of the learner.

Student input. In 'traditional' classroom activities, where individuals are called on one after the other to read aloud or to respond to an exercise, very little usable student input occurs. Nobody pays close attention to what is being said and there is no real acquisition taking place. However, when the classroom activities are communication-based, and when students want to understand what their peers are saying, they focus on the meaning of what they hear and begin to acquire these patterns. In other words, while the traditional oral classroom exercises are neutral in their impact on acquisition, communication activities can either have a positive influence on language acquisition and the development of proficiency (if students use accurate language), or they can have a negative effect on proficiency (if students use inaccurate language). This means that it is very important that 'creative' classroom activities for beginning students be so designed as to foster accurate language use.

How do we best nurture the young 'trees'? What are the features of a beginning language course that effectively nurtures the growth of 'trees'?

The effective proficiency-oriented beginning language course is the one that promotes accurate language use: structural accuracy, lexical accuracy, and phonetic accuracy. It provides large doses of accurate input at the appropriate ($i+1$) level and minimizes the amount of inaccurate input. At the same time, it generously provides opportunities for guided creativity whereby the students can use the new language for self-expression and interpersonal communication.

Clearly, such a course is best taught by a teacher of native or near-native ability. But even teachers who are less well prepared can effectively teach a proficiency-oriented beginning course by striving to model only accurate language, however limited it may be in its linguistic content.

Teachers of all levels can increase their effectiveness by incorporating into their classes videos designed for beginning classes. In these videos, the target language presented is at a level appropriate to the students in terms of structure, lexicon, speed and style of delivery, etc. The higher the professional quality of the video, the more motivating the segments are to the students and the more effectively the video can be presented for repeated viewing, thus providing increased amounts of valuable input.

The effective elementary course should introduce new structures and basic vocabulary in a manageable step-by-step progression. A heavy load of grammar means that most students will not master the new material. A heavy load of specialized vocabulary early in the program is even more dangerous since it easily leads to inaccurate language use. First of all, the students have difficulty learning how to pronounce so many new words, especially if these are cognates. Second, by focusing on the recall of too much vocabulary, students fail to attend to gender markers. And finally, by relying on vocabulary for communication of meaning, students inadvertently produce inaccurate sentence patterns which are often not corrected.

Finally, the communication activities designed for self-expression and role play should be very carefully prepared and sequenced so that students will be using only those words and structures that they can handle with a reasonable degree of accuracy. In this way, students develop linguistic creativity while speaking the language in a manner that is comprehensible to native speakers.

Conclusion: Focusing on forests. If the primary goal of elementary language instruction is to provide a foundation from which progressively higher levels of proficiency can be attained, and I firmly believe this to be the case, then it is important that we focus on the nurturing of young 'trees', and minimize the development of 'bushes'; that we focus on 'forests' and strive to eliminate 'fossils'. This is the challenge of the proficiency movement, and our effectiveness in meeting this challenge will have an important impact on the future of language instruction in this country.

References

AATF Commission on Professional Standards. 1989. The teaching of French: A syllabus of competence. Jane Black Goepper, ed. In: AATF National Bulletin 15 (special issue, October).

Carroll, John B. 1967. Foreign language proficiency levels attained by language majors near graduation from college. Foreign Language Annals 1.2 (December 1967).

Higgs, Theodore V., and Ray Clifford. 1982. The push toward communication. In: Theodore Higgs, ed. Curriculum, competence, and the foreign language teacher. Skokie, Ill.: National Textbook Co.

Krashen, Stephen D. 1981. Second language acquisition and second language learning. Oxford: Pergamon Press.

Lowe, Pardee, Jr. 1985. The ILR proficiency scale as a synthesizing research principle: The view from the mountain. In: Charles J. James, ed. Foreign language proficiency in the classroom and beyond. Skokie, Ill.: National Textbook Co.

Omaggio, Alice C. 1986. Teaching language in context: Proficiency-oriented instruction. Boston: Heinle & Heinle.

Data-based language analysis and TESL

Marianne Celce-Murcia*
University of California, Los Angeles

Background. What is data-based language analysis[1] and why should it be of special interest to those involved in teaching English to speakers of other languages? Data-based language analysis is inductive; it is based on the quantitative (e.g. Biber 1986) or qualitative (e.g. Schiffrin 1987) analysis of a given form, meaning, and/or function in a given corpus; sometimes quantitative and qualitative methods are combined (e.g. Ford 1988). The corpus may consist of transcribed conversation (e.g. Fox 1987), of written data selected according to a specific genre (e.g. Master 1987), or a combination of spoken and written data in the same genre (e.g. Keenan and Bennett 1977). The corpus may exist completely independently of anyone's desire to do language analysis (e.g. the White House Transcripts (1974)), or the corpus may have been elicited with the express purpose of carrying out such an analysis (e.g. *The Pear Stories*, Chafe 1980).

The data-based approach to language analysis has been used, at least in an informal way, both by traditional grammarians such as Jespersen (1961) and Poutsma (1914), who selected excerpts from written literary sources to illustrate their descriptions, and by contemporary descriptive grammarians (e.g. Quirk and Greenbaum 1983), who acknowledge that they have incorporated in their description of English the results of many corpus-based studies, studies which have often made use of computerized data bases. Halliday and Hasan (1976) make liberal use of excerpts from Lewis Carroll's *Alice in Wonderland*, while contemporary functionalists such as Givón (1983, 1984) and

---

* This paper has benefited greatly from insightful comments on an earlier draft by Sharon Hilles. The errors and omissions that remain are solely my responsibility.

[1] I am not the first applied linguist to make an appeal for data-based language analysis and the application of such analysis to language teaching. I can remember Charles Ferguson in his Forum lecture at the first TESOL Summer Institute (UCLA, 1979) calling for such research as he described the CALM system at Stanford, which was a program that allowed researchers to retrieve language data from the computerized Brown corpus. Unfortunately, a few years later the CALM system was no longer operative.

Thompson (1983, 1985) use genre-defined databases to carry out their analyses.

Data-based language analysis contrasts sharply with the deductive rationalist tradition in linguistics, epitomized by Chomsky (1965, 1977, 1982) and his followers. In Chomsky's approach, linguists invent their own sentence-level examples in a given language to describe aspects of the mind with reference to certain principles. They are thereby trying to discover mental reality, i.e. the native speaker's knowledge or grammatical competence, the internal representation of language in the mind. Cook (1988) aptly refers to this type of syntactic analysis as the study of 'internal' language and discusses how it differs from the study of 'external' language, which corresponds to most data-based language analysis. Data-based analyses, for Cook, entail using samples of language performance to describe features of the sample with reference to a variety of structures or patterns. This description of native-speaker behavior often appeals to social convention or the external situation and thus describes the speaker's pragmatic or communicative competence rather than the internal representation of language in the mind.

The inductive data-based school of language analysis has been associated primarily with discourse analysis and the deductive introspective school with syntax. Yet, many functionalists such as Thompson (1983, 1985) and her students (e.g. Chen 1986 and Fox 1987) have maintained that we need to look at discourse to understand syntax fully, while other functionalists such as Halliday (1985:xvii) argue that analysis of discourse must include grammatical analysis if it is truly a linguistic analysis of discourse:

> . . . Given the current preoccupation with discourse analysis (or text linguistics) it is sometimes assumed that discourse analysis can be carried out without grammar—or even that it is some sort of alternative to grammar. But this is an illusion. A discourse analysis that is not based on grammar is not an analysis at all, but simply a running commentary on a text.

These two functionalist perspectives, i.e. that discourse analysis illuminates our understanding of grammar and that grammar is an integral part of discourse analysis, are complementary; they represent two sides of the same coin.

For the record, the view that syntax and discourse interrelate in significant ways is the one that I agree with and is one that I will develop in the course of this paper.

While Chomsky (1966), representing theoretical linguistics, has cautioned teachers that linguistics and psychology have little more than general insights to offer language teaching, Halliday (1985), representing the functionalists, has argued that language teaching (among many other things) is a valid application for linguistic analysis. This is not surprising, given the differences in focus of the two schools of thought. However, Halliday's position, which is closer to mine, provides support for my argument that the data-based language analyses carried out by many of the functionalists and the descriptive grammarians are a valid source of information and ideas for the language teacher and the materials developer. Indeed, this is the position my colleague Diane Larsen-Freeman and I have taken (Celce-Murcia and Larsen-Freeman 1983), and it is a perspective we plan to incorporate even more vigorously into the second edition of *The Grammar Book.*

Contextual analysis: Its development and some results. The applica-bility of data-based language analysis to language teaching is also precisely what I had in mind (cf. Celce-Murcia 1975, 1980) when I proposed that such analyses be carried out on problematic English structures in order to improve the quality of information offered in the reference grammars and the pedagogical grammars used in developing language teaching materials/curric-ulum, or in training teachers of English to speakers of other languages. To this end, I developed and supported an approach to language analysis called contextual analysis, which has been used to analyze lexicon as well as grammar. The approach, designed for accessibility to my graduate student researchers (who include both native and nonnative speakers of English), required that researchers examine a corpus of reasonable type and size in order to extract fully contextualized tokens of the structure(s) or word(s) being analyzed. The goal was to generalize from the tokens thus collected the meanings and functions of the form(s) being analyzed. (The procedure itself is discussed in greater detail later in the paper.)

Many of my M.A. and Ph.D. students have carried out studies over the years that demonstrate the usefulness and validity of contextual analysis. The results of many of the early studies were reported in Celce-Murcia and Larsen-Freeman (1983). For purposes of illustration, I briefly summarize three rather different but representative studies here.[2]

Melrose (1983) examined approximately 100,000 words of written and 100,000 words of spoken American English to discover how native speakers use *must, have to*, and *have got to*. In spoken English she found that *must* is used primarily to express epistemic judgments in the past with the perfective (1a) and also, but less frequently, to express such judgments in the present (1b):

(1a) That must have been a rough trip.
(1b) He must be crazy.

The periphrastic form *have to* is used as a deontic performative (Palmer 1979) to express something that is obligatory for the listener to do (2):

[2] My apologies to my graduate student researchers for oversimplifying their results and for neglecting the many rich insights in each of the studies I have reported.

(2) You have to get Johnson down here.

or to express what Palmer calls dynamic necessity, which arises from circumstances and which can be very general or quite specific (3):

(3) I have to go to the bathroom.

The form *have got to* occurs exclusively in speech and signals an affective overlay on any of the three other senses (epistemic, deontic, dynamic); it adds the speaker's special pleading or sense of urgency to whatever other modality is being expressed (4):

(4) You've gotta give us some money!

In the written data *must* was preferred for all three senses (epistemic, deontic, and dynamic) although *have to* did occur in the least formal of the written sources. *Have got to* did not occur in the written data except for one token in a direct quote.

Lisovsky (1988)[3] examined a corpus of over 100,000 words to find out how native English speakers use nominal *that* clauses. The corpus consisted of two modalities (speech and writing) and two registers (formal and informal). More than 70% of the tokens represented either reported thought (5) or reported speech (6):

(5) I feel that the first suggestion is the best one.
(6) He said that he would come later.

Four minor uses for *that* clauses were identified in the data: reported facts (7), perceptual events (8), demonstrative events (9), and manipulative events (10):

(7) It is unlikely that more visitors will come.
(8) He saw that he was gonna have to climb the fence.
(9) The results of this study demonstrated that the benefits did not cover the costs.
(10) Tax reform requires that most businesses make their fiscal years conform to the calendar.

The formal written portion of the corpus stood apart statistically from the other three cells in that the formal writing had many more *that* clauses in subject position (overall 83% of the *that* clauses were in object position), it

[3] Lisovsky carried out his analysis independently of Halliday's taxonomy of *that* clauses (Halliday 1985), but he compared his results with Halliday's, and they were very similar.

had more reported speech than reported thought (the reverse occurred elsewhere), demonstrative events occurred frequently (low frequency elsewhere), and it had very few first person subjects cooccurring with *that* clauses (high frequency elsewhere).

Hardin (1988) examined over 140,000 words of spoken and over 135,000 words of written American English, looking for tokens of *when* and *while* functioning as temporal adverbial subordinators. The matrix in (11) shows the number of tokens she found in her corpus:

(11)

	when	*while*
Spoken[4]	289	21
Written	229	60

In this discussion I will summarize briefly the results Hardin found for the spoken data,[5] which had too few tokens of *while* to permit any meaningful analysis of this form. The spoken data had an equal number (i.e. 124 each) of initial and final *when* clauses.[6] An initial *when* clause with a general time reference commonly introduces a situation related to the ongoing discourse topic, and the main clause subsequently provides an elaboration on the situation, ranging from a comment to a result (12):

(12) When you see the boat at the dock, you think, well, there's nothing gonna harm this boat.

An initial *when* clause with a specific time reference also relates the sentence to the preceding discourse, but it tends to give sequential order to the events reported in the *when* clause and the following main clause (13):

(13) And when he finished reading it, he put it all together.

In final position, the *when* clause tends not to have any scope beyond the sentence at hand; it simply provides a time reference for the main clause, which expresses either a generalization (14a) or a specific event (14b):

---

[4] All of Hardin's oral data are from the UCLA oral corpus, which consists of slightly more than 140,000 words of speech representing various genres. The data were originally transcribed for individual projects and were brought together as an on-line database for the use of UCLA students and faculty largely through the efforts of Fred Davidson, while he was a graduate student in Applied Linguistics at UCLA.

[5] Hardin excluded tokens of *when* that were conditional rather than temporal and tokens of *while* that were contrastive rather than temporal. She admitted to me, however, that the difference between conditional and temporal *when* clauses was often difficult to determine with great precision (personal communication).

[6] Some *when* clauses also occurred in relative adverb constructions and center-embedded constructions, both of which were considered separately by Hardin, bringing her total for spoken tokens of *when* clauses to 289.

(14a) It's a nice job to have when you go to school.
(14b) I was shot down when I was a young kid.

An interesting pragmatic function for both initial and final *when* clauses that Hardin found in the oral but not in the written data is the negotiation of meaning (15), which often takes the form of a question, though not always:

(15a) When you say *aura*, what exactly do you mean?
(15b) What are we referring to when we talk about graft and corruption?
(15c) When I say small, I'm really talking about maybe 200 plus on staff.

On the lexical level, contextual analysis has been useful for explicating the core or prototype meanings of content words, as in Shirai's (1989) study of the basic verb *put*. This study has interesting implications for language transfer at the grammatical as well as the lexical level because some other languages (e.g. Japanese) do not syntactically require a locative constituent for their equivalent of *put*, and some languages do not allow the equivalent verb to be used for describing the placement of things on walls or on ceilings in the way that the equivalent verb apparently can be used universally for describing the placement of things on tables, desks, floors, etc. In other words, different spatial movements and orientations are involved and different verbs may be used to make these distinctions explicit in certain languages.

Studies of a more functional lexical item, such as Hulquist's (1985) study of the adverb *just* have implications not only at the lexico-grammatical level but at the level of discourse. Hulquist (1985) used a corpus of approximately 100,000 words of spoken and 100,000 of written data; the written data yielded only 94 tokens of *just*[7] while the spoken corpus of similar size yielded 457 tokens. Over half of these tokens of *just* and by far the majority of the spoken tokens conveyed an affective or interpersonal pragmatic function rather than a semantically describable meaning. Synthesizing suggestions made earlier by Bolinger (1977), Tannen (1977), Jacobson (1978), and Chafe (1982), Hulquist argues that English speakers use *just* pragmatically in the following three ways: (a) to soften directives (16); (b) to counter in advance the possibility that the listener will expect something more or something else (17); or (c) as a very basic emphasizing/focusing adverb that provides an emotional outlet to express the speaker's enthusiastic involvement, which may be positive (18a) or negative (18b) or sarcastic (18c):

(16) Just take it easy.

---

[7] Hulquist found 126 tokens of *just* in the written data if direct quotes are also counted (we decided that they should not be).

(17) I'm just looking (said to a salesperson).
(18a) It was just gorgeous last week.
(18b) The food was just awful.
(18c) Well, that's just dandy!

(It should be added that no more than 10% of Hulquist's tokens represented the use of *just* most commonly presented to ESL students, i.e. as a temporal adverb signalling the recency of a past action/event; for example, *John (has) just left.*).

New directions and applications for data-based research. I still very much subscribe to the goals of contextual analysis and to its philosophical underpinnings. However, initially, contextual analysis was seen as a heuristic for improving lexical and syntactic descriptions and was therefore almost exclusively paradigmatic in its analytic focus, a carryover, no doubt, from my own theoretical training during my Ph.D. studies in linguistics. During the past several years, however, it has become clear to me that the syntagmatic (or cooccurrence) relations among forms at the discourse level are just as important as the paradigmatic relationships that traditionally have been the preoccupation of linguistic analysis.

When my graduate students and I began research along the lines of contextual analysis in the early to mid 1970s, we knew we were pursuing a necessary and potentially useful course of action; however, other than some data-based studies coming out of Europe at the time, which used the Brown University corpus and/or the London-Lund corpus,[8] the prevailing practice was to analyze language intuitively. For admittedly different purposes, Chomsky and his followers, as well as antitransformationalists such as Bolinger (1977), all did linguistic analysis primarily by introspection and extensive use of self-generated examples.

Today, however, the use and respectability of data-based language analysis has increased dramatically with the publication of reference grammars such as Quirk et al. (1985) and the COBUILD dictionary (Collins 1987), both of which incorporate the results of data-based language analysis. The COBUILD dictionary, in particular, was compiled using a very large corpus (more than twenty million words), access to which ensured that the dictionary would provide comprehensive treatment of basic lexical items as well as authentic example sentences in the lexical entries. A corpus-based approach was followed in order to reflect everyday English use better than traditional dictionaries do.

---

[8] For documentation on the Brown University corpus, see Kućera and Francis (1967) and Francis and Kućera (1982). For a collection of studies done using the London-Lund corpus, see Bald and Ilson (1977).

Teacher training and teacher reference materials now available that incorporate some findings from data-based language analysis include Celce-Murcia and Larsen-Freeman (1983), Cook (1989), and Vande Kopple (1989). There are also some student textbooks that apply data-based language studies. McKay (1982), for example, helps students to gain an understanding of and practice with the subtle meanings and the syntactic environments of verbs that are important in academic reading and writing. Master (1986) makes extensive use of short excerpts and adaptations from scientific texts to motivate ESL students in the sciences to practice the grammatical structures they need in order to produce such texts themselves.

I believe that these and many similar publications point us in the right direction. However, there is still a pronounced tendency in the profession to focus on the paradigmatic (or sentence) level when doing language analysis and language teaching. In the past, my graduate students and I have also been guilty of this tendency. What we now need are data-based language analyses which, while not ignoring the importance of sentence-level grammar, go well beyond the sentence and move us into syntagmatic aspects of discourse. In other words, we need analyses that show us how grammar and discourse interact and interrelate in the production and comprehension of English text.

New directions in contextual analysis. I believe that during the past few years, my graduate students and I have been moving in a productive direction that addresses this concern, and I would like to summarize briefly some studies that illustrate this work.

Suh (1989a, 1989b), for example, has shown that the tense-aspect-modality system of English is a vital part of coherence in extended discourse. In her two studies, one on past habitual forms and the other on forms signalling future time, she has shown that the periphrastic forms *used to* and *be going to* are employed to set up rhetorical frames for past habitual and future episodes; repeated instances of the modals *would* and *will*, are then used to elaborate the discourse.[9] The following texts[10] are typical of the tokens Suh found in the course of carrying out her data-based analysis of *used to/would* (19) and *be going to/will* (20):

(19) The bad thing was they used to laugh at us, the Anglo kids. They would laugh because we'd bring tortillas and frijoles to lunch. They would have their nice little compact lunch boxes with cold milk in their thermos and they'd laugh at us because all

[9] In addition to *would* and *will*, respectively, Suh found that the simple past tense and the present (progressive) tense could also be used occasionally to elaborate past habitual and future episodes.

[10] Both oral and written data were consulted but the oral data were what Suh investigated in detail in her studies.

we had was dried tortillas. Not only would they laugh at us, but the kids would pick fights.[11]

(20) They're going to go in and uh have their gut slit open, their stomach exposed and have it stapled off so that there will be two pou-, an upper pouch in the stomach which will hold about two ounces of food, it's got a little hole right in - in the middle of that pouch where - where food when it's finally ground up will slowly go through.[12]

In a functional analysis of *wh*-clefts (i.e. pseudo-clefts), Kim (1989) has gone well beyond the observations of Gundel (1977) and Prince (1978) by examining the roles that such clefts play in conversation. As his database, Kim uses conversations available at UCLA that have been transcribed by Professor Emanuel Schegloff and his graduate students and colleagues. By looking at how the conversations evolved and the nature of the interaction, Kim proposes that an exclusiveness-marking function constitutes the basic semantic notion of *wh*-clefts (21), while a contrast-marking function for *wh*-clefts is a pragmatic inference one can make in certain contexts that allow the listener to draw an explicit or implicit contrast (22):

(21) A: . . . an' it cost' ten thousan' dollars per year per prisoner tuh do that. hhhh All of thi:s,—to, tuh 'spose of a problem thet a man could've done for on an eight cent basis. What that amounts is: thet they don't keep comparable books. When they're talking about the protection of lives an' property.

(22) B: But this, eh-she didn' enumerate in nat way, but what she did say is, thet if it ga:ve reparation, it gave from one nation to another nation.[13]

In 20 of the 50 tokens of *wh*-clefts that Kim analyzed, the subject was first person[14] and the verb of the *wh*-clause marked a speaker-internal state (e.g. *feel, want, think, realize, know*), suggesting that speakers often use a *wh*-cleft to highlight their subjectivity when presenting a proposition (23):

---

[11] This is from Terkel (1977:32), who is quoting a bilingual Mexican-American reflecting here on some of his school experiences.

[12] This is a description of the 'gastric restriction' procedure. It occurs in the UCLA oral corpus (see footnote 5).

[13] As Kim points out, the sense of contrast is made quite explicit in token (22) by the speaker's use of the connector *but* preceding the *wh*-cleft as well as the emphatic *do* in the *wh*-clause.

[14] In a few cases, the verb of the *wh*-clause was emotive and the object was first person rather than the subject, e.g. *what bothers me is . . .*

(23) A: So you would still, be eligible.
It w-wouldn't cha:nge, you:r eligibility.
B: Well. What I know is that they gave me a
letter an' they never sent me my ca:rd, hh
-my:: Medicare ca:rd.

Kim identified six distinct conversational functions for the 50 tokens of *wh*-clefts that he found in his corpus:

- marking the gist of talk in an extended turn
- (re)initiating a point
- proffering a topic
- shifting a topic
- providing an account in response to a challenge
- initiating a metalinguistic repair (form or meaning)

We cannot discuss each of these functions, but let me illustrate the final category, 'repair', which represents 10 of the 50 tokens of *wh*-clefts (24):

(24) B: An' I was wondering if you'd let me use your gun.
J: My gun?
B: Yeah.
J: What gun.
B: Dontchu have a beebee gun?
J: Yeah.
B: Oh it's
J: Oh I have a lot of guns. hehh
B: Yuh do:?
J: Yeah. What I meant was *which* gun.

Kim concludes that undergirding all six interactional tasks that *wh*-clefts perform is the more general discourse function of 'marking a disjunction from the preceding context, which . . . allows the speaker to go back to an utterance in the preceding context and deal with it' (Kim 1989:45).

Applications for discourse-level data-based studies. The pedagogical relevance of such studies is obvious. Suh's work (1989a, 1989b) sheds light on two questions that have long puzzled ESL students and teachers: 'What's the difference between *going to* and *will*? between *used to* and *would*?' As long as researchers had limited themselves to looking for solutions at the sentence level, the answers to questions like these were unsatisfying, incomplete, and elusive. Now that the syntagmatic discourse level is being investigated (in addition to rigorous syntactic and semantic analyses, of course), much better answers are possible. Since Suh's research has demonstrated that certain auxiliary verb forms are rhetorically related in connected text, reading (or listening) passages can be found (or adapted) that exploit the rhetorical pattern, and writing topics can be developed that encourage use of the pattern. Kim's work (1989) on the functions of *wh*-clefts in conversation is a rich source of data and observations for anyone preparing materials for teaching oral or conversational skills to nonnative speakers of English. In fact, one can reasonably argue that *wh*-clefts should not be taught without reference to authentic, interactive speech since this construction occurs much more frequently in speech than in writing, especially if one excludes direct quotes from a written corpus. Following up on the metalinguistic repair function illustrated above, one could, for example, generalize a repair routine (25) to present to nonnative speakers for them to use on those occasions when they realize they have been misunderstood by their interlocutor(s), providing they know precisely which word, phrase, or meaning they should repair:

(25a) What I mean is X (not Y).

(or, if there is some disjunction in time or space between the misunderstood item and the repair, as in (24) above)

(25b) What I meant was X (not Y).

The link between data-based language research and pedagogy is worth emphasizing. The communicative approach to language teaching and the notional-functional syllabus have been with us since the early to mid 1970s. This coincides with the time during which I initially developed and proposed the contextual analysis procedure. The positive legacy of this period is a sensitivity to how people use language rather than simply a preoccupation with what the forms of language are. After a period of time during which form was ignored by many in applied linguistics, it is now generally conceded that form, meaning, and function should all play a role in language analysis and language teaching. Following current theory, one should not present forms without consideration of the associated meanings and functions. Likewise, one should not present notions independently of the forms (words and structures) that express them, and one should not present functions (special contextualized meanings) without reference to the forms and underlying meanings used to express them.

Some teaching materials that purport to be discourse-based are not the result of a rigorous data-based language analysis but rather the result of intuitive and sometimes even superficial observations and/or text selections. One can do an introspective deductive analysis of a meaning or a function in the same way in which some linguists have long chosen to analyze syntactic structures. However, if one does such an introspective analysis, it remains intuitive and hypothetical until validated and authenticated by an appropriate data-based analysis. A hypothetical, intuitive description of a notion/function/form relationship should not constitute the basis of language teaching (or teacher training) materials without rigorous data-based confirmation. This suggests that we still have a long way to go before our language teaching and teacher training materials will be ideal or close to ideal in terms of the linguistic perspective reflected by proponents of data-based language analysis.

Contextual analysis revisited. In 1975 I first outlined the following procedure for graduate students who had identified a pedagogically relevant research question and who were interested in carrying out contextual analysis (see Celce-Murcia 1975, 1980):

1. As a preliminary, it helps to have a basic knowledge of research design and statistics since you are trying to uncover facts about English that are statistically significant. One should not be content merely to reiterate or formulate interesting hypotheses.
2. Begin with a review of the literature. What have the traditional and comtemporary grammarians said about the topic? What has been contributed by transformational or functional linguists? Is there anything in ESL journals, in textbooks, in studies of language typology?
3. Examine the natural written and/or spoken discourse of native speakers for tokens of the form(s) you are investigating. Consider the contexts (linguistic, social, etc.) and try to determine why the form was used or why one form was used rather than the other.
4. After surveying the literature and examining many tokens in their discourse contexts, develop a set of hunches or hypotheses regarding the use of the forms(s) under study.
5. Test out the hypotheses with additional discourse analysis and/or elicitation techniques (e.g. Kempson and Quirk (1971), Quirk and Svartvik (1966), and Greenbaum and Quirk (1970)). Elicitation techniques are especially useful if some data are rare and difficult to locate.

Fifteen years of experience and the trial and error that have been part of this experience suggest that the basic procedure of contextual analysis, while still useful and valid, should be modified and extended as follows:

A new preliminary. In addition to a basic knowledge of research design and statistics, anyone doing data-based language analysis should become particularly sophisticated in sampling procedures so that the results of any such study can be generalized with confidence. For example, there must be enough data from enough different sources to ensure an unbiased representative corpus. The actual size of the corpus will vary depending on the frequency of the item(s) being analyzed, but experience suggests that 100,000 words of spoken and 100,000 words of written data may be reasonable for many purposes.

A modification. One can start an analysis with a meaning (e.g. past habitual) or function (e.g. disagreement) as well as a form when carrying out contextual analysis. The research questions would then be rephrased so that identifying the form(s) used to express the meaning or function would be part of the analysis.

Extensions.

1. In addition to noting paradigmatic grammatical relations, one must also look for syntagmatic relations (cooccurrences) between the item analyzed and other items that precede or follow in the discourse.
2. One must examine the role that the item(s) play in the overall discourse. For example, does it initiate, terminate, or continue episodes? Does it contribute to information flow, thematic structure, discourse coherence, or cohesion?
3. One must be alert to the possibility that the item being analyzed might reflect affective or social-interactional factors that are shaping the discourse.

Conclusion. I have welcomed this opportunity to reexamine and revise the framework for data-based research that my graduate students and I have been using with minor modifications for more than fifteen years. Contextual analysis is but one of the dozens of ways in which research in linguistics, in the form of data-based language analysis, can contribute to theory and practice in language teaching. Every step forward in our refinement of data-based language analysis brings us closer to our goal of understanding language use—especially the multidimensional interplay between lexis and syntax and discourse. Such an understanding will permit the development of better language teaching and teacher training materials from the point of view of language description.

References

Bald, W., and R. Ilson, eds. 1977. Studies in English usage: The resources of a present-day English corpus for linguistic analysis. Frankfurt a. M.: Peter Lang.

Biber, D. 1986. Spoken and written textual dimensions in English: Resolving the contradictory findings. Language 62:2, 384-414.

Bolinger, D. 1977. Meaning and form. London and New York: Longman.

Celce-Murcia, M. 1975. English structure in context: An area of research for ESL specialists. In: T. Gorman, ed. Workpapers in Teaching English as a Second Language 9:83-94 (June 1975), UCLA.

Celce-Murcia, M. 1980. Contextual analysis of English: Application to TESL. In: D. Larsen-Freeman, ed. Discourse analysis in second language research. Rowley, Mass.: Newbury House. 41-55.

Celce-Murcia, M. and D. Larsen-Freeman. 1983. The grammar book: An ESL/EFL teacher's course. Rowley, Mass.: Newbury House.

Chafe, W. 1980. Pear stories: Cognitive, cultural, and linguistic aspects of narrative production. Norwood, N.J.: Ablex Publishing Co.

Chafe, W. 1982. Integration and involvement in speaking, writing and oral literature. In: D. Tannen, ed. Spoken and written language: Exploring orality and literacy. Norwood, N.J.: Ablex Publishing Co.

Chen, P. 1986. Discourse and particle movement in English. Studies in Language 10.1:79-95.

Chomsky, N. 1965. Aspects of the theory of syntax. Cambridge, Mass.: MIT Press.

Chomsky, N. 1966. Linguistic theory. In: R.G. Mead, ed. Northeast conference on the teaching of foreign languages. Menasha, Wis.: George Banta. 43-49.

Chomsky, N. 1977. Essays on form and interpretation. New York: North Holland Publishing Co.

Chomsky, N. 1982. Lectures on government and binding. Dordrecht, Holland: Foris Publications.

Collins. 1987. The COBUILD English language dictionary. London: Collins.

Cook, G. 1989. Discourse. Oxford: Oxford University Press.

Cook, V. J. 1988. Chomsky's universal grammar: An introduction. Oxford: Basil Blackwell.

Ford, C. 1988. Grammar in ordinary interaction: The pragmatics of adverbials clauses in conversational English. Unpublished Ph.D. dissertation in applied linguistics, UCLA.

Ford, C., and S. Thompson. 1986. Conditionals in discourse: A text-based study from English. In: E. Traugott, ed. On conditionals. Cambridge: Cambridge University Press.

Fox, B. 1987. The noun phrase accessibility hierarchy reinterpreted. Language 63.4:856-70.

Francis, W. N., and H. Kućera. 1982. Frequency analysis of English usage. Boston: Houghton-Mifflin Co.

Givón, T., ed. 1983. Topic continuity in discourse: A quantitative cross-language study. Amsterdam: John Benjamins.

Givón, T. 1984. Universals of discourse structure and second language acquisition. In: W. Rutherford, ed. Language universals and second language acquisition. Amsterdam: John Benjamins. 109-33.

Greenbaum, S., and R. Quirk. 1970. Elicitation experiments in English: Linguistic studies in use and attitude. Harlow, England: Longman.

Gundel, J. K. 1977. Where do clefts come from? Language 53:543-59.

Halliday , M. 1985. An introduction to functional grammar. London: Edward Arnold.

Halliday, M., and R. Hasan. 1976. Cohesion in English. London: Longman.

Hardin, D. 1988. *When* and *while* as temporal adverbial subordinators in American English. Unpublished M.A. thesis in TESL, UCLA.

Hulquist, M. 1985. The adverb *just* in American English usage. Unpublished M.A. thesis in TESL, UCLA.

Jacobson, S. 1978. On the use, meaning and syntax of English preverbal adverbs. In: Stockholm studies in English. Stockholm: Almqvist and Wiksell International.

Jespersen, O. 1961. A modern English grammar on historical principles. Seven volumes. London: George Allen and Unwin.

Keenan, E.O., and T. Bennett, eds. 1977. Discourse across time and space. S.C.O.P.I.L. #5. Los Angeles: University of Southern California.

Kempson, R., and R. Quirk. 1971. Controlled activation of latent contrast. Language 47.3:548-72.

Kim, K-H. 1989. *Wh*-clefts in English conversation: An interactional perspective. Unpublished paper written for English 250K, dated 13 Dec., 1989, UCLA.

Kućera, H., and W. N. Francis. 1967. Computational analysis of present-day American English. Providence: Brown University Press.

Lisovsky, K. 1988. A discourse analysis of *that*-nominal clauses in English. Unpublished M.A. thesis in TESL, UCLA.

Master, P. 1986. Science, medicine and technology: English grammar and technical writing. Englewood Cliffs, N.J.: Prentice-Hall, Inc.

Master, P. 1987. Generic *the* in Scientific American. ESP Journal 6.3:165-86.

McKay, S. 1982. Verbs for a specific purpose. Englewood Cliffs, N.J.: Prentice-Hall.

Melrose, S. 1983. Must and its periphrastic forms in American English usage. Unpublished M.A. thesis in TESL, UCLA.

Palmer, F. 1979. Modality and the English modals. London: Longman.

Poutsma, H. 1914. A grammar of late modern English. Groningen: P. Noordhoff.

Prince, E. F. 1978. A comparison of *wh*-clefts and *it*-clefts in discourse. Language 54:883-906.

Quirk, R., and S. Greenbaum. 1973. A concise grammar of contemporary English. New York: Harcourt Brace Jovanovich.

Quirk, R., and J. Svartvik. 1966. Investigating linguistic acceptability. The Hague: Mouton.

Quirk, R., et al. 1985. A comprehensive grammar of the English language. London: Longman.

Schiffrin, D. 1987. Discourse markers. Cambridge: Cambridge University Press.

Shirai, Y. 1989. The acquisition of the basic verb *put*: Prototype and transfer. Unpublished M.A. thesis in TESL, UCLA. See especially chapter 3: A contextual analysis of the verb *put*.

Suh, K-H. 1989a. A discourse analysis of past habitual forms: *used to, would,* and the simple past tense in spoken American English. Unpublished M.A. thesis in TESL, UCLA.

Suh, K-H. 1989b. A discourse analysis of *be going to* and *will* in spoken American English. Unpublished term project for English 250K, dated 13 Dec., 1989, UCLA.

Tannen, D. 1977. Well what did you expect? In: Proceedings of the 3rd Annual Meeting of the Berkeley Linguistic Society. Berkeley: University of California, Berkeley.

Terkel, S. 1977. Working. New York: Ballantine Books.

Thompson, S. 1983. Grammar and discourse: The English detached participial clause. In: F. Klein, ed. Discourse perspectives on syntax. New York: Academic Press. 43-65.

Thompson, S. 1985. Grammar and written discourse: Initial vs. final purpose clauses in English. Text 51.2:56-84.

Vande Kopple, W. 1989. Clear and coherent prose. Glenview, Ill.: Scott, Foresman.

White House transcripts 1974. New York: Viking Press.

On the need for a theory of language teaching

Diane Larsen-Freeman*
School for International Training

In the second language teaching field there is no interdependence among theory, practice and research. There is no dependence either. Each of these sectors operates independently for the most part, seemingly unaffected by the others. Teachers teach in a manner consistent with their own oft implicit, and somewhat idiosyncratic, 'small-t' theories (Brindley 1990). Research one would expect to be pertinent to language teaching, second language classroom research (SLCR), lacks theoretical motivation, making interpretation and generalization difficult, if not impossible (Long 1987); the only language teaching theories which exist are those underlying language teaching methods (Stern's 1983 T2 type of theory), and these are partial and rarely supported by research evidence. I regret that there is not a more coordinated approach to understanding the challenge of second language teaching. I therefore will use this opportunity to explain why I think the situation exists as it does and to propose a solution which I believe will contribute to a more synergistic relationship among the three.

The major problem, as I see it, is that over the course of its history the second language teaching field has either been without a theory or it has had its theoretical needs inappropriately met by relying on related disciplines outside of itself, most notably linguistics and psychology. Linguistic theory has proven an inadequate theoretical base for the SLT field for a number of reasons, not the least of which is that learning a second language is a psycholinguistic process, not a pure linguistic one (Long and Sato 1984). It was also unrealistic to expect that a psychological theory such as behaviorism, which could explain some elemental forms of human learning in general, could completely account for the learning of such complex human behavior as

---

* I am grateful to Donald Freeman and Patrick Moran for discussing the ideas in this paper with me and for their comments on an earlier draft. I also benefited from conversations with Devon Woods.

language, in particular. In other words, we cannot do without the linguistic suffix any more than we can the psycho- prefix.

In recognition of the fact that linguistics and psychology could be drawn upon for theoretical insight, but would not suffice as a theoretical base for the second language field, researchers in the early 1970s began studying the second language acquisition process directly in its own right. Over the past two decades, second language acquisition (SLA) research has contributed much to our understanding of the previously neglected area of language learning. In the interest of advancing our understanding of such a complex process as SLA, it was decided to initiate study of the untutored SLA process. The assumption was that the study of natural SLA would be contaminated, or at least complicated, in an instructional setting. Later, the effects of instruction would be introduced for consideration. Indeed, early taxonomies of factors involved in SLA made explicit this assumption by listing instructional factors as variables influencing SLA on a par with other factors such as learners' personality and aptitude (e.g. Schumann 1978).

In retrospect, the decision to limit investigation to 'natural' SLA was probably a prudent one, given the fledgling state of our knowledge at the time. Moreover, based on subsequent research, it became apparent that there were some striking similarities between untutored and tutored processes of acquisition, specifically in terms of all learners exhibiting common developmental sequences (Perkins and Larsen-Freeman 1975, Wode 1981, Pienemann 1984, Weinert 1987, Ellis 1989) and some, but by no means all, common error types, at least in morphosyntactic areas which most SLA research has focused upon (Felix and Simmet 1981, Lightbown 1983, Pica 1983, 1985).

Perhaps what was faulty logic, however, was the implicit assumption that due to the similarities, a theory emanating from SLA research could apply directly to the second language classroom. I will refer to this faulty logic as the reflex fallacy. The fallacy lies in the assumption that teaching is an involuntary reflex of natural acquisition such that what is present and natural in untutored acquisition should be present in abundance in classroom instruction; what is absent in natural acquisition should be prohibited in the classroom.[1] I argue in this paper that teaching is not an involuntary reflex of natural SLA. As such, SLA research/theory can inform, but not substitute for, a theory of second language teaching.

---

[1] It should be acknowledged that few SLA researchers are quick to point out the applicability of their findings to the SL classroom, leaving it to practitioners to decide for themselves if there is application. Indeed, some SLA researchers profess no interest in second language learning at all, limiting the scope of their theories to explaining natural SLA alone. Nevertheless, I believe the reflex fallacy persists today among certain researchers and practitioners.

The first argument I submit stems from my contention that SLA and SLT theorists have different goals. The former are intent on identifying what is minimally necessary for SLA to occur; the latter should be intent on understanding the teaching/learning process so that learning may most effectively be managed. What is *minimally necessary* in order for SLA to take place outside the classroom does not automatically constitute the *most effective* means of learning in a classroom (Larsen-Freeman and Long 1990). One would hope that effective teaching would accelerate the natural SLA process. Why else would one seek a teacher in a second language environment? Yet sometimes SLA researchers have taken the unwarranted step of proscribing or prescribing pedagogical practices based upon their findings from natural SLA. To cite one example, because there is no focus on form in untutored SLA does not justify the absence of such a focus in the SL classroom. Focusing student attention on salient formal features of a SL presumably is more efficient than when learners are left to their own devices to become aware of such features (see, for example, Schmidt and Frota 1986).

This brings me to my second argument: Due to their differing goals, SLA and SLT theories have different research agendas. SLA research aims to discover the general principles which would explain the SLA process and allow for prediction of human behavior, e.g. learners exhibit common developmental sequences before attaining the target form; learners who begin SLA after puberty do not acquire a native-like accent in the SL; comprehensible input in the presence of a low affective filter is necessary and sufficient for SLA.[2] Aside from the need for definitional clarification, these general principles or hypotheses are stated as they should be for a nomothetic theory—parsimoniously, yet consistent with observed phenomena. SLT research, on the other hand, should be concerned with understanding how and why classroom interactions or features contribute to learning opportunities. Returning to our earlier example—the expression 'focus on form' is ambiguous, comprising the whole spectrum of grammar consciousness-raising activities from explicit rule articulation to mere exposure to specific grammatical phenomena (Rutherford and Sharwood Smith 1987). We need to understand what various consciousness-raising activities contribute to opportunities to learn and what they demand of teachers and learners (Larsen-Freeman 1990).

To cite another example, if comprehensible input (CI) delivered at a level commensurate with the learners' proficiency is necessary for successful SLA, then it would be within the scope of a SLT research agenda to investigate the range of ways in which CI might be optimally provided. For instance, Krashen and Terrell (1983) advocate provision of CI in the form of the roughly tuned teacher and peer speech that arise naturally from communication. While providing CI through this means imitates 'natural'

---

[2] For additiional examples of such findings see Long 1990.

SLA, it is by no means the only way that CI can be obtained. Indeed, traditional teaching practices such as vocabulary explanation, translation and grammar explication have often been used to assist students in comprehending input at a level commensurate with their proficiency, although these practices are proscribed by Krashen and Terrell, except in very limited circumstances. On the basis of current available empirical evidence, we have no reason to know if such proscriptions are justified.

Other less conventional means of providing comprehensible input have also been proposed, e.g. through the use of cuisenaire rods which help to make abstract concepts concrete (Gattegno), through the use of physical actions in response to verbal commands (Asher), with juxtaposed native language and target language versions of the same dialogue (Lozanov), through sequential picture stories (Winitz and Reed), with elaborative simplification (Meisel) and through interactional modification (Long). All of these and many others are ways of making input comprehensible. It would be incumbent upon a SLT researcher to attempt to understand why a teacher would choose one of these options over the others and what the consequences of the choice would be, i.e. what kind of interactions they evoke and what teachers and learners contribute to and take away from each.

Thus, a certain portion of a SLT research agenda would be devoted to investigating the applicability of SLA findings. I do not mean to imply that a SLT research agenda is entirely dependent upon SLA research, however, for two reasons. First of all, hypotheses from disciplines (e.g. linguistics, psychology, education) in addition to SLA that were thought to have a bearing on SLT would also deserve a place on a SLT research agenda, for such hypotheses have implications, but not applications (Spolsky 1989). Second, a number of hypotheses germane to SLT will arise out of systematic attention to the classroom teaching/learning process itself, as has been the case so far with SLCR (see, for example, Allwright 1988, Chaudron 1988, van Lier 1988).

To address all of these hypotheses, a multifaceted approach to research on SLT is warranted. Heretofore, much of the SLCR research has been of the process-product variety. In process-product research, one attempts to compare the effect of two allegedly distinct pedagogical practices or processes by predicting the learning outcomes or products of the processes. While studying classroom processes has been a worthwhile enterprise and has yielded some important findings (for example, the relationship between task types and student production, the effect of simplification and elaboration in teacher speech on learner comprehension, teacher question types and their effects on student production (Long 1987)), an important limitation of process-product research should be acknowledged. This is its assumption that

> causation in classrooms operates unilaterally from the teacher to the students . . . learning is construed as student achievement resulting from the process of teaching which, in turn, is defined in terms of teacher initiatives which stimulate student responses . . . teaching is viewed

> exclusively in terms of the influence instructors have on pupils; the reciprocal effects of students on teachers or of students on students and then on teachers are thought to be nonexistent or not of central consequence (Bolster 1983:302).

This assumption diminishes the contribution of both teacher and learners to classroom interaction. Learning is not caused by teaching. Rather, opportunities for learning emerge through the interaction of teachers and students (Allwright 1984). Thus, to complement process-product research, we also need carefully conducted interpretive research (van Lier 1990) which addresses the complexity of classroom interaction. A promising approach which acknowledges the complexity is being pursued by Allwright (1990). He suggests that research not attempt to predict learning a priori, but rather start with learning and work backwards, investigating the opportunities for learning which brought it about. In the same way that contrastive analysis became valued for its explanatory power, but not for its predictive power, I believe that we shall find that learning opportunities can be meaningfully investigated from a retrospective view.

In addition to the psychological perspective represented by process-product research, and the social perspective represented by viewing language learning as emerging from social interaction, a third approach, which would benefit our understanding of SLT, is that contributed by an anthropological perspective.[3] Breen (1985), for example, suggests viewing the language class as a genuine culture. To understand any culture the 'expectations, values and beliefs' that are engaged must be taken into account. This implies that our investigation of SLT must be broadened beyond observable human behavior.[4] More on this below.

If research were to be pursued in the multifaceted and idiographic manner I am suggesting, I would think the results of it would be much more meaningful for SL teachers—and this suggests a third reason why SLA theory/research cannot be applied directly to SL teaching. While SLA researchers are attempting to construct a causal-process theory which explains the process of SLA for all learners in general, a SL teacher's knowledge arises from the need to comprehend the complexities of a given context (Bolster 1983). Thus, while a SLA researcher's perspective on classroom second language learning is reductionist, a teacher's perspective is

> particularistic in character; that is, this knowledge arises from the need to comprehend the complexity of a particular context with sufficient accuracy

---

[3] Larry Selinker, personal communication.

[4] It also needs to be broadened beyond the classroom, for "while the classroom may usefully be understood as a 'genuine culture', it is not an isolated culture and cannot be understood in isolation" (Gloria Rudolf, personal communication).

> to be able to act efficaciously in it. Such knowledge derives not so much from a systematic comparison of a number of similar situations as it does from intuitive analysis of a specific context in which many important qualities are assumed to be unique. Every teacher, in fact, 'knows' that although there are many similarities between classes, each group has its own special characteristics, and that successful teaching requires the recognition and acknowledgement of this uniqueness. (Bolster 1983:298)

It is no wonder, as Bolster has put it, that there are 'incongruities of belief' between researchers and teachers. One of my SLA research colleagues was recently bemoaning the fact that practitioners were proceeding with the enterprise of language teaching virtually ignoring twenty years of SLA research. If this is true, then I think we should be asking ourselves why it is so. I think one reason is that SL teachers' and SLA researchers' assumptions about how knowledge is both formulated and determined differs markedly.

This leads me to my fourth and final reason for why a theory of SLT is needed. A theory of SLT would take into account an important agent in the process, namely the language teacher. As it is now, in some of the classroom-oriented process-product research, the teacher as independent contributor to the process has been virtually ignored (Chaudron 1988:90). Instead, researchers have called for a monitoring of experimental and control groups in order to ensure 'integrity of treatment'. What is never said is what researchers should do if they find teachers teaching in a manner different than the way they are supposed to for the purposes of the experiment! It seems to me by asking teachers why they abandoned or modified prescribed teaching practice, we could learn a great deal—maybe more than the results the experiment as designed would have yielded.

It is misguided to assume that teachers are mere conveyor belts delivering language teaching practices in a sterile and mechanistic fashion (Larsen-Freeman 1988). There is only scant research looking at what teachers believe—and yet this is what teachers act upon (Woods 1989, Freeman 1990b). Generalized knowledge of teaching is mobilized in specific ways by teachers. We need to know more.

I have presented four arguments for why the SL field is in need of a separate theory of SL teaching: SLT is not a mere mirror image or reflex of natural SLA, but is a separate area of applied knowledge deserving of its own theory,[5] which would in turn motivate its own research agenda. Researchers should not be limited to SLA procedures, but should freely draw upon

---

[5] Walton (undated manuscript) distinguishes between having 'discipline knowledge' and 'applied knowledge'. Walton adds that "applied knowledge is informed by discipline knowledge and is constrained by it, but both have theories, do research and so on."

psychological, social and anthropological traditions. In addition, since teachers have previously been neglected in our research, much more attention should be accorded them in any theory of SLT.

Although I admit that I haven't solved all the problems regarding what a theory of SLT would look like,[6] nor how it would interface with a theory of SLA, there are several special traits which would characterize a SLT theory. First of all, it would need to be *grounded* in classroom data (Glaser and Strauss 1967). Glaser and Strauss make the point that the discovery of theory in actual data (as opposed to logically deducing a theory) helps to narrow the gap between theory and research. Since classroom data are also clearly familiar to teachers, a theory generated on mutually agreed upon classroom data should help to foster a shared perspective between teachers and researchers.

A theory formulated in the way I am suggesting would be inductive, in that it progresses from the accumulation of empirically based observations to sets of laws to theory (McLaughlin 1987). In this way "theories help us to understand and organize the data of experience. They permit us to summarize relatively large amounts of information via a relatively short list of propositions. In this sense, theories bring meaning to what is otherwise chaotic and inscrutable" (McLaughlin 1987:7).

An example of a theoretical proposition which does this is Allwright's (1990) 'covert conspiracy' between learners and teachers: "All must be going well pedagogically if all is going well socially." Such a proposition helps explain possible motivation behind heretofore inexplicable teacher behavior. For example, teachers have been criticized for being inconsistent in error correction. It may be the case, however, that a teacher willfully rejects an opportunity to correct errors on occasions when correcting them would threaten the social climate.[7]

A second quality of a SLT theory would be that it would be dynamic. It would allow for teacher growth in light of the fact that a particular teaching practice is likely to be manifest in different ways depending on the teacher's level of experience. It must not ignore the fact that teachers' classroom experience transforms what they know (Freeman 1990b).

Finally, it would be a theory which would motivate research not only of what a teacher does, but also what a teacher thinks. "In studying teacher

---

[6] I hope it is clear, however, that the type of theory I am calling for is different than the one Stern (1983) attempts to lay out in his book. Stern's T1 type of theory provides language teaching with a broad and generic conceptual framework. In this sense a T1 theory can be represented by a model or figure which visually symbolizes a pattern. While clearly Stern's T1 theory, as put forth in his tome, is very useful, what I am encouraging is more in keeping with Stern's T3 type theory: "a set of hypotheses that have been verified by observation or experiment"(1983:26).

[7] There might be many other reasons, of course, that a teacher does not seize an opportunity to correct an error. The point is that all teaching behavior may not lead *directly* to learning opportunities.

questioning strategies, for example, researchers would no longer focus exclusively on visible dimensions and behaviors—which questions were asked with how much wait time, or what result—they would also examine the thinking which underlay them—how and why the teacher decided to ask particular questions of specific students" (Freeman 1990a:4-5; see also Woods 1989). Research of this sort is likely to result in a theory which views the teacher as having a more central role in the processes of teaching and learning than in previous process-product research. It also suggests an active role for teachers in the research process itself. Indeed, teachers would be necessary partners in research because access to their thinking would be essential to the process of understanding why they make the decisions they do.

A consequence of all this would be truly a convergent approach (Stern et al. 1978) to theory establishment where theorists, researchers and practitioners have much in common and "should interact on the basis of equality and mutuality" (Stern et al. 1978), not just because the pursuit of egalitarianism is a noble cause, but because "good research can be good pedagogy and good pedagogy can be good research" (Allwright 1988). Besides the contribution a theory would make in guiding and coordinating our research and teaching endeavors and helping to make our efforts cumulative, rather than fragmented, an additional consequence of a theory which provides a different conceptual view of teaching, is its implications for teacher education. When "teaching was conceptualized as discrete, separable behaviors, then teacher education, by extension, was thought of as the training and inculcation of ways of acting" (Freeman 1990b:3). With the acknowledgement "that teaching is more than the exercise of specific behavior in a classroom setting; it involves both the behavior and the thinking which underlies and directs that behavior" (Freeman 1990b:2), then teacher education, it seems to me, should contribute to teachers' awareness about teaching (Larsen-Freeman 1983) and to teachers' owning their role as managers of learning. With regard to the latter point, a management function such as "the process of weighing demands and balancing constraints" (in making on-line decisions) does not receive the attention it perhaps deserves in teacher education programs currently (Woods 1989:10). In addition, if a convergent approach to theory design is implemented, teacher educators will want to cultivate in their students skills in conducting research and an appreciation for how research can be a tool in their continuing professional development. One additional consequence of this work might be to enhance the professionalism of the SLT field and dissuade practitioners from hopping on bandwagons.[8]

In calling for a theory of second language teaching, I am submitting that the language teaching field need no longer look outside of itself for its

---

[8] Indeed, another benefit of a generic theory of second language teaching is that it should offer a framework for evaluating new methodologies. This additional means is very welcome, given the inconclusivity of methodological comparisons of the process-product sort previously conducted. (See, for example, Larsen-Freeman 1988.)

theoretical needs to be satisfied. While linguistics, education, psychology, and most especially SLA, will do much to inform SLT, true interdependence of theory, practice and research in second language teaching will be achieved only when SLT is illumined by a theory of its own making.

References

Allwright, Richard. 1984. The importance of interaction in classroom language learning. Applied Linguistics 5.2:156-71.

Allwright, Richard. 1988. Observation in the language classroom. London: Longman.

Allwright, Richard. 1990. Understanding learners: Understanding teachers. Paper presented at the 24th Annual TESOL Convention, San Francisco.

Bolster, Arthur. 1983. Toward a more effective model of research on teaching. Harvard Educational Review 53.3:294-308.

Breen, Michael. 1985. The social context for language learning—a neglected situation? Studies in Second Language Acquisition 7.2:135-58.

Brindley, Geoff. 1990. Inquiry-based teacher education. Paper presented at the 24th Annual TESOL Convention, San Francisco.

Chaudron, Craig. 1988. Second language classrooms. Cambridge: Cambridge University Press.

Ellis, Rod. 1989. Are classroom and naturalistic acquisition the same? Studies in Second Language Acquisition 11:305-28.

Felix, Sasha, and A. Simmet. 1981. Natural processes in classroom L2 learning. Revised version of a paper presented at the IIIème Colloque Groupe de Recherche sur l'Acquisition des Langues (Paris, May 15-17).

Freeman, Donald. 1990a. Thoughtful work: Reconceptualizing the research literature on teacher thinking. Qualifying paper, School of Education, Harvard University.

Freeman, Donald. 1990b. The influence of teacher education on language teaching. Unpublished manuscript (March).

Glaser, Barney, and Anselm Strauss. 1967. The discovery of grounded theory. Chicago: Aldine Publishing Company.

Krashen, Stephen, and Tracy Terrell. 1983. The natural approach. New York: Pergamon Press.

Larsen-Freeman, Diane. 1983. Training teachers or educating a teacher? In: James Alatis, H.H. Stern, and Peter Strevens, eds. Georgetown University Round Table on Languages and Linguistics 1883. Washington, D.C.: Georgetown University Press. 264-74.

Larsen-Freeman, Diane. 1988. Research on language teaching methodologies: A survey of the past and an agenda of the future. Paper presented at the European-American Conference on Empirical Research on Second Language Learning in Instructional Settings, Bellagio, Italy (June). In: Foreign language research in cross-cultural perspective. (Forthcoming) Amsterdam: John Benjamins.

Larsen-Freeman, Diane. 1990. Pedagogical descriptions of language: Grammar. In: R. Kaplan, ed. Annual Review of Applied Linguistics, vol. 10. Cambridge: Cambridge University Press.

Larsen-Freeman, Diane, and Michael Long. 1990. An introduction to second language acquisition research. London: Longman.

Lightbown, Patsy. 1983. Exploring relationships between developmental and instructional sequences in L2 acquisition. In: H. Seliger and M. Long, eds. Classroom-oriented research in second language acquisition. Rowley, Mass.: Newbury House. 217-43.

Long, Michael, and Charlene Sato. 1984. Methodological issues in interlanguage studies. An interactionist perspective. In: A. Davies, A. Criper, and A. Howatt, eds. Interlanguages. Edinburgh: Edinburgh University Press. 253-79.

Long, Michael. 1987. The experimental classroom. The Annals of the American Academy of Political and Social Science (March). 97-109.

Long, Michael. 1990. The least a second language acquisition theory needs to explain. Paper presented at the 24th Annual TESOL Convention, San Francisco.

McLaughlin, Barry. 1987. Theories of second language learning. London: Edward Arnold.

Perkins, Kyle, and Diane Larsen-Freeman. 1975. The effect of formal language instruction on the order of morpheme acquisition. Language Learning 25.2:237-43.

Pica, Teresa. 1983. The role of language context in second language acquisition. Interlanguage Studies Bulletin 7:101-23.

Pica, Teresa. 1985. The selection of classroom instruction on second language acquisition. Applied Linguistics 6.3:214-22.

Rutherford, W., and M. Sharwood Smith, eds. 1987. Grammar and second language teaching. New York: Newbury House, Harper and Row.

Schmidt, Richard, and Sylvia Frota. 1986. Developing basic conversational ability in a second language: A case study of an adult learner of Portuguese. In: R. Day, ed. Talking to learn. Rowley, Mass.: Newbury House. 237-326.

Schumann, John. 1978. Social and psychological factors in second language acquisition. In: J. Richards, ed. Understanding second and foreign language learning. Rowley, Mass.: Newbury House. 163-78.

Spolsky, Bernard. 1989. Conditions for second language learning. Oxford: Oxford University Press.

Stern, H.H., Mari Wesche, and Birgit Harley. 1978. The impact of the language sciences on second-language education. In: P. Suppes, ed. Impact of research on education. Washington, D.C.: National Academy of Education.

Stern, H.H. 1983. Fundamental concepts of language teaching. Oxford: Oxford University Press.

van Lier, Leo. 1988. The classroom and the language learner: Ethnography and second language classroom research. London: Longman.

van Lier, Leo. 1990. Classroom-centered research. In: R. Kaplan, ed. Annual Review of Applied Linguistics, vol. 10. Cambridge: Cambridge University Press.

Walton, Ron. Undated manuscript. Chinese language instruction in the U.S.: Some reflections on the state of the art.

Weinert, R. 1987. Processes in classroom second language development: The acquisition of negation in German. In: R. Ellis, ed. Second Language Acquisition in Context. London: Prentice-Hall. 83-99.

Wode, H. 1981. Language-acquisitional universals: A unified view of language acquisition. In: H. Winitz, ed. Native language and foreign language acquisition. Annals of the New York Academy of Sciences 379:218-34.

Woods, Devon. 1989. What studying ESL teachers' decisions in context tells us. Unpublished manuscript.

Knowledge-based inferencing in second language comprehension

Elizabeth B. Bernhardt
The Ohio State University

Introduction. During comprehension two sources of information are used by readers and or listeners. The first is explicit linguistic information found in the text (either spoken or written). The second is topic and world knowledge information held by the reader or listener. The former source consists of the 'seen' in texts--the syntax, word length, paragraph structure, print features, lexicon, etc. The latter source consists of the 'unseen' in texts--the knowledge that authors expect comprehenders to have as well as the personal knowledge that they do have.

The objective of this paper is to examine the latter source of information. I have chosen this topic because it has implications for the theory, practice, and research of second language acquisition. In planning my paper, I turned to the subtitle of this year's Georgetown University Round Table on Languages and Linguistics, 'The Interdependence of Theory, Practice, and Research,' for guidance. I thought that subtitle would provide a convenient organizing principle: there would be three areas in which I could discuss knowledge-based inferencing: how inferencing is dealt with in current models of second language acquisition, how information about knowledge-based inferencing is applied in practice, and then finally, the role that knowledge-based inferencing has played in research and how it should be considered in future research.

Problematic, however, is the word *interdependence*. It is problematic because knowledge about 'knowledge-based inferencing' has been used, misused, abused, and ignored in some very peculiar ways in theory, research, and practice. My thesis is that the second language community has been much too quick in accepting the concepts of 'comprehensible,' 'prior knowledge', 'guessing from context', and rather lazy in examining the implications of these concepts. Until we examine the implications of these for theory and research, and most importantly for practice, we will be slow in advancing our knowledge of second language acquisition processes.

Current theories of comprehension. Comprehension is an associative process that entails making connections between explicit textual information and implicit conceptual information. A common image for this process of association is building or growing. This image serves to underscore the notion of the dynamic nature of comprehension. Webber (1980:141) puts it this way: "In comprehending text, the import of each successive sentence must be determined within, and integrated into, an incrementally growing model of the discourse." Webber goes on to explain that particular linguistic features help in updating these models of discourse.

In other words, a reader has an initial conceptual model or knowledge base. Language is input and the conceptual model grows. More language is input and the model changes and grows, etc. Graesser, Haberlandt, and Koizumi, (1987:218-19) comment:

> We assume that the reader constructs a structure of propositional units (called nodes) during comprehension. Some of these nodes are explicitly mentioned in the text, whereas other nodes are inferences. The comprehender needs to construct *bridging* inferences in order to establish conceptual connectivity between an incoming explicit statement and prior passage context. The reader may also generate *elaborative* inferences which embellish the text structure but are not really needed for establishing conceptual connectivity.

Fundamentally, then, there is explicit language input and there is inferencing involved. This inferencing process helps to fill in the unstated or redundant information that is not explicitly in the text, thereby, helping the text "make sense." There is also other inferencing that merely makes the text "say" more than it does.

How does a second language comprehender play out this scenario on comprehension? The second language comprehender (as any compre-hender) has perceptual systems working for him, in addition to phono- logical, lexical or word meaning, and syntactic processing systems that provide text input. At the same time, the second language comprehender (as any comprehender) has a knowledge base from which to inference so that things 'make sense.' It is this knowledge base that fills in the gaps in texts. The critical point is that within a second language comprehender, all of these linguistic and conceptual systems *operate*; and they operate from the beginning of the attempt to comprehend in a second language. But most critically, although these systems operate simultaneously, they do so with varying degrees of success.

Johnston (1983:31) comments on the risks involved in the simultaneous operation of these systems when the intended comprehender does not match the text:

> The qualitative mismatch between text and reader may pose a far more insidious problem--quite subtly causing the reader to build a completely

inappropriate model of the text meaning without becoming aware of the problem. It is not that inferences would not be made, but that inappropriate ones would be made. This problem could be easily self-compounding. Once the reader has begun to construct an inappropriate model, inappropriate inferences would be generated by virtue of the content of the growing model itself.

One of the ways in which researchers have been investigating the whole area of knowledge application and activation is through the concept of 'script'. According to Yekovich and Walker (1987:147):

> A script represents a person's prototypical knowledge of a routine activity, such as 'painting a room' or 'going to a restaurant'. Scripted knowledge has two features that make it useful for studying knowledge-based contributions to reading. First, a script, by definition, is culturally uniform and represents 'expert' knowledge about human behavior in a routine situation. ...Second, scripts generally have well-defined goal structures and predictable temporal properties.

Graesser, et al. (1987:218)) provide a parallel image. They state:

> Knowledge-based inferences are inherited from the reader's knowledge about physical, social, cognitive, and emotional phenomena. We assume that this world knowledge is embodied in a large set of *generic knowledge structures* (GKSs) and *specific knowledge structures* stored in long-term memory. ...We assume that the knowledge-based inferences generated during text comprehension are furnished by the GKSs and specific knowledge structures that are relevant to the text...

These processes of knowledge acquisition, storage, and inference generation are indeed complex. Simultaneously, it is clear from the above quotations that knowledge-driven operations in comprehension are culture-dependent; Yekovich and Walker (1987) as well as Graesser, et al. (1987) speak to this issue explicitly. An understanding of the implications of knowledge-driven operations for cross-cultural/cross-linguistic comprehension is critical for the development of principled research and instruction in second language reading.

The nonvisible in comprehension: An issues analysis. Some of the terms attached to the nonvisible or nonsaid facet of comprehension are conceptually-driven, implicit, internal, reader/listener-based, and knowledge-based. These terms imply the existence of information critical to the comprehension process that does not appear explicitly as part of a written or spoken text.

A considerable portion of second language comprehension research has been devoted to these factors; i.e., factors related to the topic or the cultural implications of particular reading passages and particular second language readers. The intention of the next section of this paper is to lay out issues involved in conceptual matters in second language text processing. The final portion of the paper concerns the implications of conceptual knowledge for theory, teaching, and research.

Knowledge. The term background knowledge has evolved into an educational buzzword. While on the one hand it has been seen to be a variable that contributes to both race and gender discrimination in educational settings, it has also been used to dismiss learning phenomena without thorough analysis. This lack of analysis is nowhere more obvious than in second language reading research. Second language learners have been generically grouped according to background knowledge variables. Grouping fifty subjects according to background knowledge has led researchers to juxtapose '50 Catholic Spanish-speaking learners of English' with '50 Islamic learners of English' just as one example. While on the one hand one might argue that indeed there are real background differences in these two groups, there is actually no real measure of 'knowledge' differences. In fact, the groups may consist of some experts in religions of the world or the groups may consist of learners who have spent considerable time in Hispanic or Islamic countries. Simply put, assuming 'knowledge' or lack thereof on the basis of ethnic heritage is a rather naive view of 'knowledge'.

Local-level knowledge. There are many types of 'knowledges'. There is highly idiosyncratic knowledge that individuals carry with them such as where they keep their checkbooks or in which drawer in the kitchen the scissors are supposed to be. This type of knowledge enables intimates to communicate without words or with vague references such as "Well, you know where the checkbook is. Get it out." There is also idiosyncratic knowledge that individual groups carry with them and use for communicative purposes. On a local level, the term 'Buckeye Donuts' evokes very specific knowledge on the part of certain people who work in a particular area of the city of Columbus, Ohio; on a less local level, the term may evoke less specific, yet relevant knowledge, on the part of individuals who know that Ohio is the Buckeye State, that the Ohio State teams are known as 'the Buckeyes' and, who are able to infer, therefore, that Buckeye Donuts may be a place to get donuts somewhere in Ohio and so forth. It is clear that these examples draw on the concept of 'culture' in its sense as the implicit knowledge particular groups have.

At a wider level, larger groups also carry implicit knowledge. It is a rare North American who does not have knowledge of McDonald's restaurants (what they look like, under what circumstances one gets a tray, how one orders, what the food will look like, what kinds of tables and chairs there will be, etc.). They also carry knowledge of income tax forms, or knowledge of rules of driving. Yet within each one of these overriding 'knowledges' there is considerable variation depending upon individual familiarity.

Domain-specific knowledge. Another kind of knowledge is domain-specific knowledge. In a sense, schools provide generalized domain-specific knowledge. Schooling--at least through the high school level in North America--is to provide some knowledge of history, social science, natural science, art, music, and language. In fact, that very act of handing down the knowledge base provides the keys to socialization; i.e., those facets of knowledge that separate Americans from British or Canadians from French, for example. Each cultural group provides its unique 'versions' of history and science; these 'versions' become defining characteristics of people schooled in those versions. Such statements can only be made at the most general level, however. For it is eminently clear that the variation in domain knowledge gathered from schooling is enormous and that some students 'catch on' that the material presented can be analyzed and interpreted from a variety of perspectives.

Indeed, domain-specific knowledge is acquired in many ways. For some people, additional schooling provides deeper domain-specific knowledge. While general schooling gives information about the War of 1812, specific courses in Early American history provide even more knowledge. Yet, additional knowledge does not have to be gained from formal schooling. Mere interest in the area that leads a person to read another history book on his own fosters additional 'knowledge'. The point is that domain-specific knowledge can be gained in many ways. While it is possible to make the assumption that if someone declares that he has domain-specific knowledge of a particular area (since he or she happens to be a history professor with specialization in Post-Revolutionary War American-British relations), it does not necessarily mean that a person who does not make such a declaration does not have similar knowledge. The latter person may have made a hobby of American-British relations and have dilettante knowledge rather than professional knowledge of the domain. Nevertheless, both may have high-level domain knowledge; albeit that knowledge is more visible in the former than in the latter.

Other domain-specific knowledge examples would include knowledge of the rules of soccer, of electrochemistry, of cooking, of how airplanes are put together and how they function, of how computers work, or of how to analyze a literary text. This argument is not meant to imply that domain-specific knowledge is in some way explicitly distinct from the other knowledges mentioned above. Obviously, there is overlap. The amount of overlap probably varies from individual to individual. The point is merely to explore facets of knowledge that any individual may draw upon in order to understand and to interpret.

Culture-specific knowledge. Another facet of 'knowledge' is culture-specific knowledge. Culture-specific knowledge includes ritualistic knowledge as well as cultural-historic knowledge. Rituals include events such as weddings, funerals, and national holidays as well as invited dinner parties or how one lines up at a bus stop. Members of specific cultures implicitly 'know' what will occur in these events--to use Oller's (1979) terms they have an 'anticipatory grammar' for them. Yet, critically, this grammar per se is not written down (with the obvious exception of *Miss Manners*). It consists, fundamentally, of knowledge transmitted from generation to generation. Culture-specific knowledge also includes that information defined by the culture as having aesthetic value and as reflecting the values, the intellectual development, or the 'best' of what that culture as a culture has to offer.

Implications of knowledge-based inferencing. This discussion of issues surrounding the concept of knowledge is not meant to be exhaustive nor all-inclusive. It is meant to underline how complex and virtually inscrutable 'knowledge' is. That readers or listeners need knowledge for comprehen- sion seems to be clear. What knowledge second language comprehenders have, how they acquire culturally appropriate new knowledge, and how they apply the knowledge they have to second language texts are intriguing questions that have implications for theory, teaching, and research.

Second language acquisition theory. Individual's knowledge plays a variety of roles in current theories of second language acquisition. For brevity's sake, I will turn to three specific theories and/or models of SLA for this discussion: Bialystok's Model (1978), the Monitor Model (1978), and Variability Theory (Ellis, 1986; Adamson, 1988; Klein, 1986; among others).

Knowledge is a facet of Bialystok's model (1978:71-72). In fact, she posits three different 'knowledges': 'Other Knowledge, Explicit Linguistic Knowledge and Implicit Linguistic Knowledge. ...they refer to three types of information the learner brings to a language task, and since each is considered to contribute in some unique way to the attainment of language proficiency, they have been distinguished in the model'.

The thesis of this paper considers Other Knowledge in Bialystok's sense. Bialystok (1978:73) defines Other Knowledge in the following way:

> Other Knowledge refers to all other information the learner brings to the language task--knowledge of other languages, such as the native language, information about the culture associated with the target language, knowledge of the world, and so on... The essential distinction between Other Knowledge and the two Linguistic Knowledge sources is that Linguistic Knowledge contains information about the language code while Other Knowledge contains related but not specifically linguistic information.

In this description and in the graphic of the model, Other Knowledge is of equal import compared to each of the other knowledge sources; i.e., it accounts for one-third of the knowledge involvement in any attempt to understand.

I would argue from this description, then, that 'Other Knowledge' appears to be a weak stepchild when compared with the linguistic side of the model. For the most part, Bialystok's stance toward linguistic rather than knowledge-based inferencing underlines the psycholinguistic nature of the model. This stance separates it from models that are more cognitive in nature. There is a great irony here, however. Bialystok's model pinpointed Other Knowledge as an extremely critical variable in second language acquisition. That was in 1978. In the past twelve years, we have seen a decrease in this acknowledgment in any sort of direct and explicit way rather than an increased recognition of its import.

Probably the greatest irony in any discussion of knowledge-based inferencing and second language acquisition is the Monitor Model. The principal characteristic of Monitor theory is Comprehensible Input. Krashen remarks (1981:100):

> A necessary (but not sufficient) condition for language acquisition to occur is that the acquirer *understand* (via hearing or reading) input language that contains structure 'a bit beyond' his or her current level of competence.
>
> By *understand*, I mean understanding for meaning, and not form, or focusing on the *message*. ...Much second language teaching assumes students should first master forms and then 'learn how to use them.' This hypothesis presumes that acquisition happens in the opposite way; we first 'go for meaning,' and acquire structure as a result of understanding the message. This is only possible if we utilize more than our knowledge (subconscious or conscious) of language in understanding, which is clearly the case; we use our knowledge of the world and extra-linguistic information.

No definition of comprehension--operational or otherwise--is offered. The theory does acknowledge that knowledge that is nonlinguistic and conceptual in nature is involved in language acquisition. Yet, there is no discussion in any of the writings on Monitor Theory that acknowledges the individual and highly idiosyncratic nature of comprehension. I will argue that that which is comprehensible has become so through the process of associating linguistic and conceptual knowledge. The simple statement that knowledge must be involved without any discussion of the implications of that statement is wholly insufficient.

Variability Theory, attributed here for convenience to Ellis (1986) and to Adamson (1988), among others (Klein 1986, for example), accounts for conceptual or nonlinguistic knowledge in a rather indirect and implicit fashion.

Variability Theory à la Ellis is rooted in a belief in context--social context, for the most part. In other words, variability theory includes knowledge of speakers and hearers that is used for response in social situations. Ellis (1986:268) notes: "New rules are created when we endeavour to use existing knowledge in relation to the linguistic and situational context in order to create shared frames of reference." To this extent, Ellis' version of variability theory acknowledges 'knowledge', but does not approach the facet of knowledge that is topical and conceptual. Ellis' view on variability in language use is still very linguistic in nature. In like manner, Adamson mentions procedural and declarative knowledge, but does little else to extend the argument.

I argue, in general, that these representative theories of second language acquisition have failed to deal with the issue of 'knowledge' in any substantial way. In this regard, Bialystok is the most praiseworthy--knowledge was a serious part of her model. Since that time, knowledge has been mentioned, but never researched or discussed. If we are to have viable models of second language acquisition, we must involve data that are both linguistic and nonlinguistic in nature.

Second language teaching. The most convenient way of addressing the issue of 'teaching' is perhaps through methods textbooks and classroom textbooks (see Bernhardt, 1990, forthcoming). For purposes of this analysis, a number of methods texts were analyzed: Allen and Valette (1979), *Classroom Techniques: Foreign Languages and English as a Second Language*; Bowen, Madsen, and Hilferty (1985), *TESOL Techniques and Procedures*; Chastain (1988), *Developing Second Language Skills: Theory and Practice*; Omaggio (1986), *Teaching Language in Context*; Paulston and Bruder (1975), *Teaching English as a Second Language: Techniques and Procedures*; and Rivers (1981), *Teaching Foreign-Language Skills*. The percentage of page space devoted to comprehension ranges from 4.6% of the entire book to a high of almost 20%. This figure would indicate that (using the rule of thumb that the textbook is the curriculum and that most courses meet, on the average thirty hours) most trained teachers have had between one hour and six hours of instruction in the teaching of reading comprehension. Even if this figure is doubled or tripled, it could hardly be considered to be significant. Of course, these figures do not indicate how many reading-specific methods courses there may be in teacher education programs. An educated guess would argue for very few.

The next area to be probed is the nature of the instructional strategies offered by the traditional methods books. As a backdrop it is interesting to note what the authors tell the reader about the comprehension process.

Several of the methods books provide explicit definitions of reading. Omaggio (1986:121)) states:

> ...reading is an active process involving...(1) the individual's knowledge of the linguistic code, (2) cognitive skills of various types, and (3) the individual's knowledge of the world.

Allen and Valette (1979:249) argue:

> Reading is more than just assigning foreign language sounds to the written words; it requires the comprehension of what is written.

Rivers (1981:261) offers a parallel definition:

> A student who stands up in class and enunciates... the sounds symbolized by the printed...marks...may be considered to be 'reading.'...The student must also be taught to derive meaning from the word combinations in the text and to do this in a consecutive fashion at a reasonable speed, without necessarily vocalizing what is being read. This is reading for comprehension.

These definitions underline a one way process which is 'reading as gaining meaning from the text'. Paulston and Bruder (1975:158) define reading as 'decoding meaning--lexical, structural, and cultural--from graphic symbols'. Bowen, et al.(1985), provide no definition.

In contrast to the frameworks listed above is that offered by Chastain. Chastain (1988:216) explains:

> Reading is a process involving the activation of relevant knowledge and related language skills to accomplish an exchange of information from one person to another...recent researchers in reading describe the process in a way that implies an active reader intent upon using background knowledge and skills to recreate the writer's intended meaning.

He adds:

> The reading goal is to read for meaning or to recreate the writer's meaning. Reading to improve pronunciation, practice grammatical forms, and study vocabulary does not constitute reading at all because, by definition, reading involves comprehension. When readers are not comprehending, they are not reading (p. 217).

The difference between Chastain's theoretical view and that of the others is striking. In a sense it is unfair to assail other writers whose books are older than Chastain's. But two points are extremely important. First, comprehension research could have been consulted by the other authors to bring them to a more enlightened view when they authored their books.

Second, the other texts have widespread use in teacher education programs in North America and, hence, widespread influence.

Despite the variety of definitions offered, several factors unify the methods texts, making them, in fact, indistinguishable. First of all, four of the six posit 'stages' in the comprehension process, stemming from letters to words to sentences, or from sound symbol activities to guided practice to independence or from decoding to interpretation. Interestingly, none of these indicates the research base from which the stages cited were generated. A second interesting point is that a minority of the texts advocate structured materials. In other words, the use of authentic materials is suggested more often than materials deliberately reflecting particular grammatical structures. A third distinguishing feature is the consistent nature of the activities listed: oral reading, prereading vocabulary study, skimming and scanning, and teacher prequestions.

The irony regarding teaching is that regardless of time frame, theoretical framework or theory-- i.e., extending from audiolingualism, through proficiency, to communication-- the instructional activities suggested are almost identical. That is, there seems to be a canon of teaching procedures that supersedes theory and research. Knowledge is actually not treated differently over several iterations of 'methods'.

Corollary to methods textbooks is the status of textbooks in general. Despite fairly typical introductions to comprehension, 'prereading information' is still offered without any real acknowledgment of what role that information as knowledge has to play, whether readers already have that knowledge, and whether the knowledge that they do have will interfere with their processing of any given passage in the textbook.

Second language research. One could infer from the foregoing discussion above regarding second language acquisition theory that little research has involved individual knowledge structures. While models have been posited, few research studies have been conducted in order to validate the models in general as models. Most importantly, any studies that have been conducted seem to blithely ignore the knowledge (other than linguistic) that learners bring to the task. In other words, knowledge gets defined as linguistic knowledge, which I contend is merely a subset of knowledge.

The research that has been conducted regarding knowledge falls under the rubric of reading comprehension research. There are several subcategories of such studies. First, there are those studies that have examined 'cultural background' and have blocked subjects within experimental designs according to ethnic background. Second, there are studies that have examined 'topic knowledge' background, generally blocking on that particular variable along with proficiency level. Third, a number of training studies have investigated the manner and type of 'background knowledge' that might be given to readers in order to increase comprehension.

The seminal study that examined the impact of cultural background knowledge in the reading comprehension process is Steffenson, et al. (1979). This particular study examined the comprehension of United States adults and Indian adults reading passages that described either an American wedding or an Indian wedding. Steffenson et al. found that comprehension was higher on the passage that most closely matched the cultural background of the reader whereas readers tended to distort in recall the passage that was not from their own cultural background in order to align it more closely with their cultural background. Since that time, a number of studies have generated similar findings. Johnson (1981) and Campbell (1981), examining adults and children, respectively, found that direct cultural experience was a greater predictor of comprehension than linguistic proficiency. In parallel, Carrell (1987) found that context knowledge and experience were greater predictors of understanding than knowledge of text structure. Connor (1984) and Perkins and Angelis (1985) investigated the impact of language background on two compre- hension skills: recall of propositional type and concept formation, respectively. Neither study indicated a difference on the basis of language background. A final study in this group (Parry, 1987) finds evidence for the constructivist model of L2 text comprehension. Parry found that individual vocabulary words--out of context--were misinterpreted when an understanding of a text was askew.

The second group of studies has examined the background knowledge component of topic. Alderson and Urquhart (1988), Johnson (1982), Mohammed and Swales (1984), Nunan (1985), Olah (1984), and Zuck and Zuck (1984) all found that topic familiarity is most often a greater predictor of comprehension ability than are text-based linguistic factors such as syntactic ease or explicit vocabulary knowledge. One study in this particular group, however, Carrell and Wallace (1983), presents findings that are not wholly consistent with the other studies. This study concludes that nonnatives tend to be insensitive to content difficulty.

The third group of studies has manipulated different types of mechanisms for providing background knowledge. The four studies in this group, Adams (1982), Carrell (1983), Hudson (1982), and Omaggio (1979), all used pictorial support to provide background knowledge. Both Omaggio and Adams found that the presence of a picture facilitated comprehension in a second language. Carrell found no impact on the recall scores of second language readers whether they had pictorial support or not. Hudson found differential impacts of such support: pictorial support was more efficacious for beginning and intermediate learners but a read/reread strategy was the most profitable for advanced students.

There are, however, a number of problematic areas within this set of studies. The first is the reliability of many of the findings considering Lee (1986). Lee replicated Carrell (1983) and found a different pattern of recall depending on the language of recall--either native or second. All studies involving ESL readers have to this point asked these readers to recall in

English. Lee's data suggest that the findings of these studies are inherently biased against the actual comprehension abilities of the subjects and are skewed by the subjects' writing abilities. A second problematic feature concerns the cultural compatibility of the pictures used in several of the studies and the readers' understanding of the pictorial representations. The pictures used in the studies were Western in nature and, consequently, placed an added cultural burden on the comprehenders. Finally, and rather characteristically, the studies generically group nonnative readers of English into proficiency levels without considering their orthographic or cultural background variables. With these caveats in mind, however, the studies reveal a remarkable consistency in the impact of knowledge on the scores generated in the studies.

Most of these studies are significantly flawed and, therefore, tell us very little about the comprehension process. Yet despite the problems and the caveats, they are praiseworthy. They have, as a whole, acknowledged the importance of comprehender-based knowledge. On the negative side, however, they have operationalized comprehender-based knowledge in the broadest and shallowest of terms.

Conclusion. I noted at the beginning of this paper that the word *interdependence* was problematic for me. I hope that the foregoing discussion has underlined the problematic nature of theory, teaching, and research in considering the variable of knowledge-based inferencing. At present, I would argue that theory, teaching, and research in second language comprehension processes are not interdependent. They appear to be separate entities. Given a choice within our present context, I would argue that this is a preferred state of affairs.

If, however, interdependence is what we want to achieve in second language theory, teaching, and research, the following criteria have to be met. First, theorists must do more than mention knowledge and then hope that no one notices. It is incumbent upon theorists to define and account for the knowledge aspect of their theory and then bring evidence to bear upon that aspect. If one were to submit any one of the theories or models mentioned above to standard tests of theories, they would be found to be extraordinarily vulnerable. Second, teachers must do more than think that 'preteaching vocabulary', 'introducing the passage', or telling students 'to guess from context' provides them with appropriate knowledge for inferencing. If one is to compare current theories of comprehension with canonized instructional practice, one would find once again a certain vulnerability. Finally, researchers must contend with the complexity of the knowledge variable in research. Using analysis of variance designs that pit one ethnic group against another or one professional group against another makes 'knowledge' practically meaningless. Alternative research designs as well as measurement techniques must be employed in order to capture comprehenders' knowledge in at least some of its facets.

Generating knowledge about the unseen in texts is critical for second language teaching and acquisition. Until we have such knowledge, theory, teaching and research will remain separate, more or less, vacuous entities that treat subjects as if they come to the task of language learning with little or no conceptual capacities.

References

Adams, S. J. 1982. Scripts and the recognition of unfamiliar vocabulary: Enhancing second language reading skills. Modern Language Journal. 66:155-159.

Adamson, H. D. 1988. Variation theory and second language acquisition. Washington, D.C.: Georgetown University Press.

Alderson, J. C., and Erquhart, A. H. 1988. This test is unfair: I'm not an economist. In: P. C. Carrell, J. Devine, and D. E. Eskey, eds., Interactive approaches to second language reading. 168-182. Cambridge: Cambridge University Press.

Allen, E. D., and R. M. Valette. 1979. Classroom techniques: Foreign languages and English as a second language. New York: Harcourt Brace Jovanovich.

Bernhardt, E. B. 1990. forthcoming. Reading development in a second language: Theoretical, research, and classroom perspectives. Norwood, NJ: Ablex.

Bialystok, E. 1978. A theoretical model of second language learning. Language learning. 28.1: 69-83.

Bowen, J. D., H. Madsen, and A. Hilferty. 1985. TESOL techniques and procedures. Rowley, MA: Newbury House.

Campbell, A. J. 1981. Language background and comprehension. Reading Teacher. 35:10-14.

Carrell, P. L. 1983. Three components of background knowledge in reading comprehension. Language Learning. 33:183-207.

Carrell, P. L. 1987. Content and formal schemata in ESL reading. TESOL quarterly. 21.3: 461-481.

Carrell, P., and B. Wallace. 1983. Background knowledge: Context and familiarity in reading comprehension. In: M. A. Clarke, and J. Handscombe, eds., On TESOL 82. Washington, DC: TESOL.

Chastain, K. 1988. Developing second-language skills: Theory and practice. 3rd ed.. San Diego: Harcourt Brace Jovanovich.

Connor, U. 1984. Recall of text: Differences between first and second language readers. TESOL Quarterly. 18:239-255.

Ellis, R. 1986. Understanding second language acquisition. Oxford: Oxford University Press.

Graesser, A. C., K. Haberlandt, and D. Koizumi. 1987. How is reading time influenced by knowledge-based inferences and world knowledge. In: B. K. Britton, and S. M. Glynn eds., Executive control processes in reading. 217-251. Hillsdale, NJ: Lawrence Erlbaum.

Hudson, T. 1982. The effects of induced schemata on the 'short circuit' in L2 reading: Non-decoding factors in L2 reading performance. Language Learning. 32:, 1-32.

Johnson, P. 1981. Effects on reading comprehension of language complexity and cultural background of a text. TESOL quarterly. 15:169-181.

Johnson, P. 1982. Effects on comprehension of building background knowledge. TESOL quarterly. 16: 503-516.

Johnston, P. H. 1983. Reading comprehension assessment: A cognitive basis. Newark, DE: International Reading Association.

Klein, W. 1986. Second language acquisition. Cambridge: Cambridge University Press.

Krashen, S. D. 1981. Effective second language acquisition: Insights from research. In: J. Alatis, H. Altman, and P. Alatis, eds. The second language classroom: Directions for the 1980s. pp. 97-109. New York: Oxford University Press.

Lee, J. F. 1986. Background knowledge and L2 reading. Modern Language Journal. 70:350-354.

Mohammed, M. A. H., and J. M. Swales. 1984. Factors affecting the successful reading of technical instructions. Reading in a foreign language. 2:206-217.

Nunan, D. 1985. Content familiarity and the perception of textual relationships in second language reading. RELC journal. 16:43-51.

Olah, E. 1984. How special is special English. In: A. K. Pugh, and J.M. Ulijn, eds., Reading for professional purposes: Studies and practices in native and foreign languages. London: Heinemann Educational Books.

Oller, J. W., Jr. 1979. Language tests at school: A pragmatic approach. London: Longman.

Omaggio, A. C. 1986. Teaching language in context: Proficiency-oriented instruction. Boston: Heinle and Heinle.

Parry, K. J. 1987. Reading in a second culture. In: J. Devine, P. L. Carrell, and D. E. Eskey eds., Research in reading as a second language. 59-70. Washington, DC: TESOL.

Paulston, C. B., and M. N. Bruder. 1975. Techniques and procedures in teaching English as a second language. Cambridge, MA: Winthrop.

Perkins, K., and P. J. Angelis. 1985. Schematic concept formation: Concurrent validity for attained English as a second language reading comprehension? Language Learning. 35: 269-283.

Rivers, W. M. 1981. Teaching foreign language skills 2nd Ed.. Chicago: University of Chicago Press.

Steffensen, M. S., C. Joag-Dev, and R. C. Anderson. 1979. A cross-cultural perspective on reading comprehension. Reading Research Quarterly. 15:10-29.

Webber, B. L. 1980. Syntax beyond the sentence: Anaphora. In: R. J. Spiro, B. C. Bruce, and W. F. Brewer, eds., Theoretical issues in reading comprehension: Perspectives from cognitive psychology, linguistics, artificial intelligence, and education. 141-164. Hillsdale, NJ: Lawrence Erlbaum.

Yekovich, F. R., and C. H. Walker. 1987. The activation and use of scripted knowledge in reading about routine activities. In: B. K. Britton, and S. M. Glynn, eds., Executive control processes in reading. 145-171. Hillsdale, NJ: Lawrence Erlbaum.

Zuck, L. V., and J. G. Zuck. 1984. The main idea: Specialist and non-specialist judgments. In: A. K. Pugh, and J. M. Ulijn, eds., Reading for professional purposes: Studies and practices in native and foreign languages. London: Heinemann Educational Books.

What you see is what you get. . . Or is it? Bringing cultural literacy into the foreign language classroom through video

Thomas J. Garza*
George Mason University

The important relationship between language and culture has long been acknowledged, discussed, defined, and redefined in the literature on foreign language learning and teaching.[1] In recent years, that relationship has been increasingly described as inextricably intertwined, with each element dependent on the other for complete comprehension and successful communication in any language. This perspective is well documented in Seelye (1971:6):

> Words in isolation do not convey meaning. Only within a larger context do individual words mean anything. The word 'get', for example, has several hundred potential meanings; only in context is a particular meaning communicated. What provides this meaningful context? Often the *nonlinguistic cultural reference* enables us to communicate. [Emphasis mine, TJG]

Since the publication of Seelye 1971, the concensus of language specialists seems to be focusing on the necessity to teach (and learn!) foreign language skills and relevant cultural content together as one holistic domain. As Rivers (1981:326) states: "The insight into culture proceeds at the same time as the language learning—in other words, teaching for cultural understanding is fully integrated with the process of assimilation of syntax and vocabulary." Kramsch concurs, focusing on the entity of 'linguaculture' while maintaining,

---

* This is a revised version of a paper presented at the First Soviet-American Conference on Issues in Foreign Language Teaching at the Maurice Thorez Institute of Foreign Languages in Moscow, October 1989. Many thanks to Richard D. Brecht, Boris A. Lapidus, Svetlana D. Tolkacheva, and Aleksandr A. Barchenkov for their comments and suggestions for revision.

[1] See Wilga Rivers (1981:314-20) for a brief overview of culture and language teaching, as well as a bibliography on the teaching of culture.

"Rather than seek ways of teaching culture as a fifth skill, similar to reading, writing, speaking, and listening, we have to explore the cultural dimensions of the very languages we teach if we want learners to be fully communicatively competent in these languages" (Kramsch 1989:1-2). Significantly, though, disagreement still remains among practitioners on *how* this interdependent relationship of language and culture can best be utilized in the classroom in order to develop and train students in a foreign language and culture.

In 1987, the study and teaching of culture in the United States became the focus of considerable debate with the publication of E.D. Hirsch's immensely popular and equally controversial book *Cultural Literacy: What Every American Needs to Know.*[2] Its author must be credited with raising the reader's awareness of the importance of cultural knowledge to the development of essential communication (both written and oral) skills, and the extent to which the system of general education has failed to impart such knowledge successfully to many American students. Additionally, he has provided those of us who are grappling with the integration of essential cultural information into the teaching of foreign languages with the useful conceptual label of 'cultural literacy', or what Chall and other reading and language specialists have called 'shared world knowledge' or 'prior text' (Chall 1983:8) All of these terms refer to the enormous body of general nonlinguistic information and cultural background that an educated native speaker of any language brings to any communicative situation—regardless of medium, and on which complete mutual comprehension between interlocutors depends.

However, Hirsch devotes a third of his book to a selected list of famous people, historical events, folkloric references, literary and artistic works, scientific achievements, and quotations from around the world that have impacted on American life, culture, and language. He has entitled his list 'What Every Literate American Knows' as a suggested preliminary syllabus to guide and, thus, improve the teaching of culture in the United States. This 'personal agenda' approach to the teaching of cultural inforamtion is, to some educators, the most unsettling aspect of Hirsch's book. First, there is the immediate question concerning which or, more appropriately, *whose* list we choose to teach our students. Can any one person's list accurately and fairly embody the shared cultural text of most individuals in a given society?[3] Second, the reduction of cultural literacy to a list of discrete items incorrectly suggests that language and culture can be cleanly separated into memorizable parts, with little—if any—regard to the interdependence of the two.

A cursory look at authentic printed materials from the contemporary literature of a given culture or subculture quickly reveals the limitations of a

---

[2] Note also the more recent companions to Hirsch's book, the first of which actually conceptually predates the 1987 volume: Hirsch et al. (1988), and Hirsch (1989).

[3] At least one group of prominent scholars, writers, and humanists have compiled their rebuttals to Hirsch's culture 'list' and its implications in the American educational system in *Multi-Cultural Literacy: Opening the American Mind* (St. Paul, Minn.: Graywolf Press. 1988).

mere terminological glossary as the basis for developing cultural literacy—especially in a foreign language. Even when individual culturally loaded terms or concepts are defined and explicated, unless the underlying relevant context surrounding the use of such an item is understood or explained, the full communicative message of the text (written or spoken) is inhibited or, even worse, misconveyed. Consider, for example, the following passage taken from the opening paragraph of Jay McInerney's recent best-seller, *Bright Lights, Big City*, in which he plunges the reader into the culturally bound world of his driven and troubled hero:

> You are not the kind of guy who would be at a place like this at this time of the morning. But here you are, and you cannot say that the terrain is entirely unfamiliar, although the details are fuzzy. You are at a nightclub talking to a girl with a shaved head. The club is either Heartbreak or the Lizard Lounge. All might come clear if you could just slip into the bathroom and do a little more Bolivian Marching Powder. Then again it might not. . . . Somewhere back there you could have cut your losses, but you rode past that moment on a comet train of white powder and now you are trying to hang on to the rush. Your brain at this moment is composed of brigades of tiny Bolivian soldiers. They are tired and muddy from their long march through the night. There are holes in their boots and they are hungry. They need to be fed. They need the Bolivian Marching Powder (McInerney 1984:1-2).

There is no question that this text would very likely pose serious difficulties in total comprehension for most nonnative speakers of English (and perhaps even for some native speakers!). However, lexicon alone is *not* the principal inhibitor of comprehension in this or many contemporary authentic texts. Indeed, providing clarification of certain culturally loaded key words or phrases in the passage is only of marginal utility to the language learner interested in developing native-like understanding and appreciation of such a text. The knowledge that the phrases *Bolivian Marching Powder* and *white powder* both refer to the drug cocaine contributes only slightly to the foreign reader's total understanding of the isolated sentences that make up the passage; rather, it is the cultural implications and assumptions surrounding such terms—especially in the context of the language of the rest of the paragraph—that permit a large number of native speakers who share knowledge of such a prior text to infer immediately certain unspecified essential details such as the likely setting of the action (urban vs. rural), the relative age and probable socioeconomic status of the narrator, and the possible direction of the story line from this point. Establishing a native-like prior text—the very foundation of cultural literacy—is not a simple matter of identifying and defining culturally-bound lexical items in a given text; rather, the entire text in which such items frequently occur must be regarded as a whole, incorporating the intrinsic difficulties and specifics of the language (syntactic, phonetic, and lexical), together with the cultural information inherent in the contextualized discourse situation.

In terms of recognizing and codifying much of the underlying theory and practical recommendations of incorporating cultural literacy into the teaching of foreign languages, Soviet specialists have made a sizeable contribution to the literature. Notable in this respect are Vereshchagin and Kostomarov, who are credited with defining and setting the parameters of the science of 'linguacultural' methodology (*lingvostranovedenie*) and outlining ways in which foreign language instruction could be better facilitated by the use of authentic cultural realia: works of literature, art, film, and other visual media. Rather than separating the elements of language and culture for teaching/learning purposes, cultural realia *are* the medium for foreign language acquision, in Vereshchagin's and Kostomarov's terms.

As demonstrated in the passage from McInerney's novel, authentic texts—including, but not exclusively, those taken from literature—can provide excellent contexts for simultaneously developing both linguistic and cultural competence in the foreign language. Similarly, carefully selected authentic film and video media not only offer contextualized situations of language use, but provide the added benefits of visually conveyed information on both linguistic and cultural meaning. Kostomarov and Vereshchagin (1983:211) contend:

> Facts perceived visually become the personal experience of the student, while verbal explanations reflect a detached foreign experience; not without reason is it said that it's better to see something once than to hear about it a hundred times. Besides, visual perception usually cannot be replaced by words. Therefore, the role of the visual mode remains unlimited, unique. Finally, the information input capability of the visual perception mode is almost ten times greater than the audio; therefore, the former is more economical than the latter.

Over the last decade, researchers and specialists in video-based foreign language instruction, especially in the United States and Great Britain, not only concur with this Soviet perspective, but expand on it, indicating the unique suitability of selected authentic video materials as a foreign language teaching medium, citing the addition of the visual modality and 'slice-of-real-life' quality of good video as a significant contributor to total comprehension.[4]

The term 'authentic' is used throughout this paper to refer to materials that are prepared by native speakers of a language for other native speakers, and expressly *not* for learners of that language. Therefore, all print, audio, and video materials available in, for example, the United States, Canada,

---

[4] See, for example, commentaries on the use of video in foreign language education by Lonergan (1984), Tomalin (1984), and Garza (1986).

Great Britain, and Australia, produced for local consumption, qualify as 'authentic' English-language materials by this definition. In discussing the teaching of 'linguaculture' in a foreign language, or the synthesis of foreign language and culture, the authentic nature of instructional materials—especially video—is of paramount importance. Materials prepared for native speakers of a language are by virtue of their intended audience saturated with imbedded cultural references that depend on the shared prior text of that audience. Standard television programming, feature films, commercials, documentaries, and news items can all serve as effective pedagogical source materials for teaching foreign 'linguaculture' on all levels. Because video allows for both audio and visual modalities of information input, the language and cultural material is more readily contextualized, and, thus, more accessible to the learner.

The first step in integrating authentic video materials into a foreign language curriculum is to select the best materials for the specific audience. As with any authentic source of language materials—print or video—pedagogical considerations must be employed to determine the appropriateness of a given segment for foreign language teaching.[5] For purposes of exploiting the cultural as well as the linguistic material of the video segment, 'good' foreign language video should be multilayered, incorporating current and useful situational language, visually-supported paralinguistic elements (gestures, proxemics, body language, etc.) and inherent cultural content. It is the presence of such culturally bound material that, while self-evident to the native speaker of the target language, prevents the learner from enjoying complete, 'native-like' comprehension of the segment, even when the language of the segment is fully understood.

Once appropriate material has been selected, the next step in bringing video into the language classroom is the actual employment of the video segments to exploit their 'linguacultural' content. The instructor needs to use the video material to illustrate and contextualize language and cultural use, and coach hishe/her students in developing active viewing techniques to take advantage of the instructional medium. The caveat here is for the teacher to integrate the language and cultural content and resist their artificial separation into discrete parts. For example, an American student of Russian at the intermediate to advanced level—typically during the second or third year of study—may be assigned to view the popular Soviet film *Ironija sud'by (ili s lekim parom)* 'The Irony of Fate' as part of his regular language class. The well-intentioned language instructor will likely provide necessary background vocabulary to facilitate understanding of the film's language; unfortunately, the essential cultural information required for native-like comprehension of the

---

[5] For a full presentation of criteria for vidceo selection and exploitation for foreign language training, see Garza and Lekic (1990).

intention of the segment is not to be found in standard dictionaries or lexicons of Russian.

The entire plotline of the film is dependent on an opening scene in a Moscow public bath house, or *banja*, in which the protagonist—on the eve of the New Year and his wedding—is plied with alcohol by his friends and, unbeknownst to him, is placed on a plane to Leningrad. When looked at from a strictly linguistic plane, the language of this six-minute segment is quite straightforward and accessible to high-intermediate and advanced students of the language. Yet complete understanding of this (or virtually any other well-balanced piece of authentic video material) requires insight not only into the lexicon, but the basic cultural prior text which a native speaker automatically brings to such a segment.

In most standard Russian-English dictionaries, the student will find the term *banja* glossed simply as 'sauna.' Those checking a Soviet-published Russian-Russian dictionary will find little more information: a special enclosure for bathing and steam bathing.[6] But because the cultural prior text which an American has for the lexical item 'sauna' overlaps only slightly with the Soviet prior text associated with *banja*, the student may come away from viewing the video segment feeling that she/he has understood everything. In fact, because the Russian cultural context surrounding the Russian concept of *banja* is much broader and circumscribed by specific cultural rituals and behavior than the English 'sauna', the student fails to grasp the full meaning of the segment, and, in this case, misses most of the humor that a Soviet viewer would enjoy. Exemplary in this connection is the expression (and film's subtitle) *S lekim parom!* an untranslatable greeting and well-wishing said to one who has recently emerged from a Russian bath house. By using the visual context of the video segment together with a growing knowledge of the linguistic elements of the language, the student of Russian begins to develop the cultural schema to understand the relevant rituals, behavior, and language specific to the *banja* environment.

Similarly, students of English as a foreign language may view a popular American television commercial—one for Coca-Cola®, for example—with the goal of developing total comprehension of the thirty-second segment, including linguistic, paralinguistic, and cultural literacy elements. Among authentic video materials, well-selected television commercial advertisements can be extremely effective as vehicles for teaching linguaculture. After all, the writers and producers of such segments try to load the thirty- or sixty-second spot with current, effective, and persuasive language, powerful and memorable visual images, and a plethora of cultural references intended to appeal to a specific audience which, of course, speaks the language natively!

In one popular advertisement from 1985, Coca-Cola® used the very culturally rich image of the American diner as the backdrop for a simple but

---

[6] Definitions taken from Ozhegov (1986) and Ushakov (1978).

appealing story line of young boy looking for a job as a short-order cook. The language of the segment is natural and colloquial, full of a variety of styles and registers, but quite learnable for a student with some simple language notes and coaching from the instructor. Once the student feels that she/he has mastered the small number of exchanges in the commercial and understood the basic premise of the simple plot, she/he may also feel that comprehension of the entire piece is complete. It is at this point that the instructor must coach the student to focus hishe/her viewing of the segment in order to exploit its cultural content.

Test teaching of this segment over several years with various university-level students of English as a second language has consistently shown that students entirely miss the diner as the setting for the commercial.[7] Using their own native-culture prior texts, these students quickly—and accurately—establish the setting as some kind of eating establishment: a restaurant or cafe, or perhaps even a fast-food place. When shown that the opening scene of the commercial actually shows the front of the diner with a large neon sign reading 'Bentley's Diner', the students eagerly scribble down the new lexical item and add it to the long lists of new vocabulary that they have been compiling throughout the course. But the cultural prior text that a native speaker of American English immediately associates with the word or image of a diner is still completely missing. Once again, cultural literacy is not merely lexical. Yet through guided active viewing of the commercial, students are available to uncover and *dis*cover the basic cultural text underlying the concept of the diner, and move considerably closer towards a native 'reading' of the shared prior text of an American speaker of English. By watching closely and actively, students are able to tell (1) the physical description of a diner; (2) what the typical clientele of a diner is probably like, including age, race, and socio-economic position; (3) what typical items of food are on a diner menu; (4) what the atmosphere in a diner is probably like; and (5) how the diner fits into the 'American scene'.

Like the image of the Russian bath house in the Soviet film clip, the diner image in the Coca-Cola® commercial is one of countless cultural icons on which cultural literacy is based. Every language, and every culture—or more accurately—every 'linguaculture'—possesses a rich, varied, and ever-changing corpus of such cultural icons, from Vysotskij to the *banja* in Soviet linguaculture and from Elvis Presley to the diner in American English. While there is clearly some limited utility to a list or 'dictionary' of these culturally loaded items, without a more complete context to illustrate the fuller meaning behind such images, a list only serves to identify one person's concept of what the salient cultural icons in a given language may be.

---

[7] This observation is based on my own experience test teaching this and other authentic video segments in intermediate and advanced-level ESL classes at Harvard University, the University of Pennsylvania, and the University of Maryland between 1985 and 1989.

The role of authentic video in providing the necessary visual and linguistic context for understanding issues of cultural literacy should not be underestimated. When working in a foreign language visual medium, what the learner sees is *not*, unfortunately, always what she/he gets. Students frequently view material and believe that they 'got' the entire message and meaning just because they understood all of the words. If authentic video materials are well selected and worked through in a foreign language classroom, they can be powerful keys to understanding not only the language, but the inherent cultural content of a given segment. With the interplay of audio and visual modalities that video provides, we are able to provide our students with a more complete contextualization of authentic language situations. Consequently, by coaching them to become more participatory, active viewers of video materials, we help them gain independence in comprehending authentic materials once their language courses are over. Our ultimate goal in the quest for linguistic and cultural literacy for our students is the complete independence of viewing foreign language materials and being able to assure them that what you see *is* what you get.

References

Chall, Jeanne S. 1983. Stages of reading development. New York: McGraw-Hill.

Garza, Thomas J. 1986. Foreign language teaching and video: Providing a context for communicative competence. Qualifying Paper in Teaching, Curriculum, and Learning Environments. Cambridge, Mass.: Harvard University Graduate School of Education.

Garza, Thomas J., and Maria D. Lekic. 1990. Luchshe raz uvidet'. . .? Video v obuchenii inostrannym jazykam 'Is a picture worth a thousand words? Video in foreign language study'. Russkij jazyk za rubezhom. (August).

Hirsch, E.D., Jr. 1987. Cultural literacy: What every American needs to know. Boston: Houghton Mifflin.

Hirsch, E.D., Jr. 1989. A first dictionary of cultural literacy: What our children need to know. Boston: Houghton Mifflin.

Hirsch, E.D., Jr., Joseph F. Kett, and James Trefil. 1988. The dictionary of cultural literacy. Boston: Houghton Mifflin.

Kostomarov, V.G., and E.M. Vereshchagin. 1983. Jazyk i kul'tura—lingvostranovedenie v prepodavanii russkogo jazyka kak inostrannogo 'Language and culture: Linguaculture in the teaching of Russian as a foreign language'. Moscow: Russkij jazyk.

Kramsch, Claire J. 1989. New directions in the teaching of language and culture. NFLC Occasional Papers (April). Washington, D.C.: National Foreign Language Center.

Lonergan, John. 1984. Video in language teaching. Cambridge: Cambridge University Press.

McInerney, Jay. 1984. Bright lights, big city. New York: Vintage Contemporaries/ Random House.

Ozhegov, S.I. 1986. Slovar' russkogo jazyka. Moscow: Russkij jazyk.

Rivers, Wilga. 1981. Teaching foreign language skills, 2d ed. Chicago: University of Chicago Press.

Seelye, H. Ned. 1971. Teaching culture: Strategies for intercultural communication. Lincolnwood, Ill.: National Textbook Company.

Tomalin, Barry. 1984. Using video, TV, and radio in the classroom. New York: Macmillan.

Ushakov, D.N. 1978. Tolkovyj slovar' russkogo jazyka. Columbus, Ohio: Slavica Publishers.

Perception theory, error feedback, and language acquisition

Gail L. Robinson*
San Diego State University

Abstract. Person perception theory and social learning theory offer important implications for the design of effective feedback strategies in language learning. This paper discusses empirical research regarding the effectiveness of different types of feedback with applications to classroom instruction as well as computer-assisted language learning (CALL). Types of feedback discussed include: student discovery of appropriate responses versus instructor or program disclosure of answers, implicit feedback versus over correction, student-controlled help versus instructor or program-controlled help, and various ways of recycling missed items. Traditional views of 'student control' versus 'program control' in CALL are contrasted with more productive notions of 'internal' versus 'external control'.

* The complete text of this paper will appear as part of a book soon to be published. The abstract is reprinted with permission of the author from whom details may be obtained.

Linguistic hypothesis testing in neural networks

Donald Loritz
Georgetown University

Introduction. Semanticists recognize Charles Saunders Peirce for his theory of signs and symbols. Grammarians recognize him as the philosopher Chomsky once found most congenial (Chomsky 1972). Nevertheless, Peirce is perhaps best known to philosophers for his incisive refutation of Cartesian philosophy (Gallie 1966). Moreover, as the inventor of American pragmatism, he is at least a great-uncle of American behaviorism. A hundred years before his time, Peirce glimpsed the unification of language, philosophy, and psychology which is only now being recognized.

Peirce's epistemology centered on 'beliefs': habits of thought on which an organism is willing to base its action and which persist until the organism is confronted with a surprising event which puts the organism into a state of doubt (Peirce 1877). When a surprising event effectively challenges the organism's habits, Peirce claimed that 'abduction' occurs: a new hypothesis presents itself to the mind. This new hypothesis is then tested, usually by the very conditions which constituted the surprising event itself. If disproved, abduction presents another hypothesis. It continues to do so until some hypothesis withstands testing to become a new belief and a new basis for habitual behavior. For Peirce, the critical question was 'Where do (new) hypotheses come from?' Chomsky, substituting 'grammar' for 'thought', posed the corollary question, 'Where do grammatical hypotheses come from?'

As it happens, these questions were premature. We must first ask, 'What are hypotheses?' Thus Chomsky has more recently sought to characterize 'hypotheses' as 'parameters'. Assuming hypotheses were tested serially *in vivo*, Chomsky claimed that the child's input data was too incomplete and fragmentary to induce a grammar. By discarding the term 'hypotheses' in favor of switch-like parameters, Chomsky was able to sustain the theoretical possibility of implementing language in Von Neumann architecture machines. As we shall see, Chomskyan parameters turn out to be 'dipoles'. But where serial rationalism postulates only a few, adaptive resonance theory and anatomy find millions. Because the child can test millions of hypotheses (set and reset millions of parameters) simultaneously—in parallel—Chomsky's arguments from the poverty of the stimulus are not valid. Chomskyan parameters remain useful narrative devices for describing language data, but they are epiphenomenal to language learning. In massively parallel networks, grammatical induction from input is not only possible, it is natural.

In this paper, I will outline how the general learning rules of adaptive resonance theory (ART) operate in massively parallel, competitive neural networks to explain a range of common linguistic phenomena. The recent reawakening of interest in parallel processing and neural networks has been market-driven. Very Large-Scale Integration made microcomputers cost-effective to produce, and this, in turn, has made parallel computers marketable. Consequently, the most widely reported models (Hopfield 1982, Hinton and Anderson 1981, Rumelhart and McClelland 1986) are those which are easiest to implement in silicon. They are parallel, but they are cerebellar rather than cerebral in design. This makes them a relatively poor model for linguistic process (Loritz 1990). In contrast, ART models cerebral cortex. It is a superior model for understanding language and language learning.

The foundations of ART were presented in Grossberg 1968 and Grossberg 1972. Most of the mechanisms used in this paper are presented in more detail in Grossberg 1980, but without specific reference to language learning. Grossberg 1986, Cohen and Grossberg 1986, and Cohen, Grossberg and Stork 1988 directly address several linguistic issues, but entail complicated problems of representing serial order in parallel anatomies. This paper is intended to be introductory, so it will not treat serial learning, and many details of ART will be suppressed. My discussion is based on Grossberg's 'minimal anatomies', but it largely avoids his characteristic mathematical analyses of those anatomies.

I first present Grossberg's dipole model of how neurons compute an XOR for edge detection in color vision. I will then apply this model to account for the categorical perception of the voicing contrast in man and chinchilla. Next I extend the dipole model to a field model of vowel perception. This model outlines a parallel model of hypothesis testing which I claim is particularly characteristic of cerebral thought and language learning.

XOR: Negating hypotheses. 'Connectionism' is hardly a new idea. In 1906 Ramón y Cajal received the Nobel Prize for discovering that the brain is a massively parallel processor. After Ramón y Cajal, a small number of respected researchers continued to pursue the consequences of parallel processing. Hebb (1949) proposed a fundamental associative learning rule which is still in use, and Lashley (1950) contributed the notion of a distributed 'engram'. Grossberg attributes the lack of further progress in parallel research to the inaccessibility of the necessary, nonlinear mathematical modeling tools, but the inhibition appears to me to run deeper and broader, from the roots of literate culture to the social economics of information processing. In any event, in the 1960s both the mathematical tools and massively parallel computers came into use. But in 1969 Minsky and Papert published *Perceptrons*, a critique of parallel architectures such as those described by Rosenblatt (1959). They argued that parallel architectures were flawed models for artificial intelligence, a major flaw being their alleged incapacity to compute XORs. (Chomsky 1968, 1972 cites Minsky and Papert's argument, but *'perceptrons'* is misprinted as *'perceptions'*, obscuring his point.)

Logical XORs are the engines of negation, and their importance is still not fully recognized by many researchers in parallel processing. But Minsky and Papert were wrong to infer that XORs could not be computed in parallel architectures. Grossberg 1972 showed not only that XORs could be calculated in massively parallel anatomies, but also described numerous, observable, psychological consequences of their computation by neural networks *in vivo*. The main issues surrounding XORs can be illustrated by a well-known optical 'illusion'.

Figure 1. After viewing under intense stimulation (e.g. bright lights), the red circle turns green and the green surround turns red when stimulation is removed (e.g. when the eyes are closed). This 'rebound' effect can also be caused by nonspecific arousal (e.g. a white-light flashbulb).

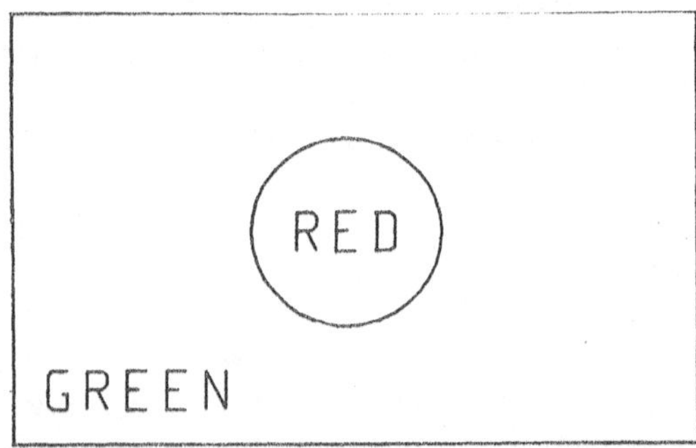

After viewing Figure 1 under intense stimulation (e.g. under bright lights), stimulation is removed (e.g. the eyes are closed). Then, in the retinal after-image, the red circle is perceived as green and the green surround is perceived as red. This occurs because red and green receptor cells in the retina are arrayed in 'gated dipole' architectures (Figure 2). Without specific stimulation (with no light or white light) the dipole is in balance and reports no percept (Figure 2a). Under red light the red pole of the dipole in Figure 2b dominates and suppresses the green pole by stimulating the inhibitory interneuron Irg.

After a period of stimulation, neurotransmitter in the synaptic knob, Zr_0,r_1, of the red pole becomes depleted. When specific stimulation is removed, Grossberg says the dipole 'rebounds'. In Figure 2c, ambient, nonspecific stimulation enables the green pole to dominate, and a green percept is reported until transmitter equilibrium is restored (as in Figure 2a). It will be described below how the same rebound effect can be achieved by a burst of 'nonspecific arousal' (Figure 2d).

Figure 2. Red and green receptor cells in retinal circuits are arrayed in 'gated dipoles' (*a*). In the absence of specific stimulation (white or no light) the dipole is in balance and reports no percept. Under red stimulation (*b*) the red pole of the dipole dominates and suppresses the green pole via the inhibitory interneuron Irg. After a period of stimulation, neurotransmitter in the red pole depletes. When specific stimulation is removed (*c*), the dipole 'rebounds' and a green percept is reported until transmitter equilibrium is restored (as in *a*). The same effect can be achieved by a burst of 'non-specific arousal' (*d*).

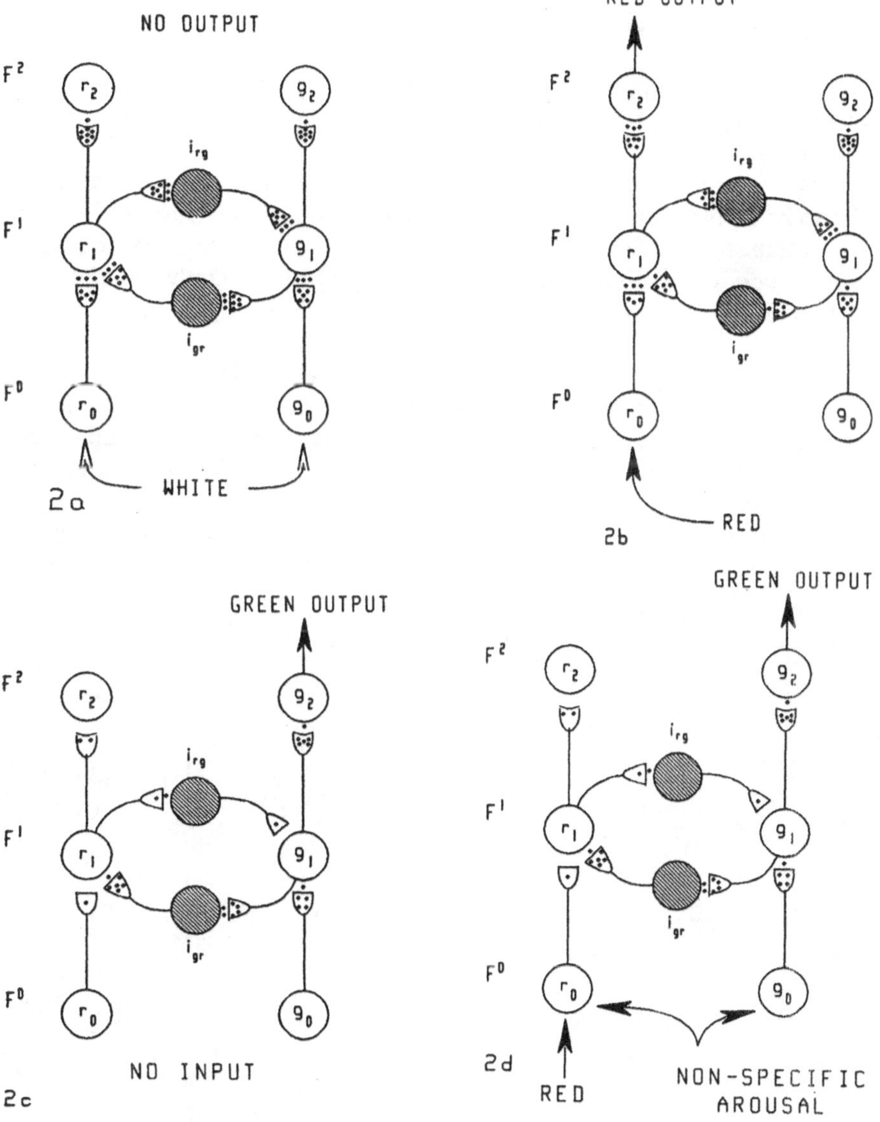

Categorical voicing perception. The discrimination of English voiced and unvoiced plosives depends largely on the interval between the plosive burst and the subsequent onset of voicing (Voice Onset Time). In English, perception is categorical around a VOT value of 25 ms. Stimuli with lesser VOT are all perceived as voiced while stimuli with greater VOT are all perceived as unvoiced (Liberman et al. 1957). Eimas et al. (1971) demonstrated that neonates could discriminate between voiced and unvoiced prevocalic stops. This was widely believed to demonstrate the existence of an innate, human-species-specific, language acquisition device until Kuhl and Miller (1975) showed the same effect in chinchillas. Clearly, a more general perceptual mechanism is operant.

A dipole anatomy is the logical candidate for this XOR-like computation. In Figure 3a, the dipole of Figure 2 has been slightly extended and relabeled to accept high-frequency (stop burst) stimulation to its left pole and low-frequency (vocalic) stimulation to its right pole.

When an unvoiced stop burst (e.g. [p] in [pa]) stimulates the left dipole, the right dipole is inhibited via the inhibitory interneuron Iuv. A feedback loop estabishes nonlinear STM 'resonance' via the excitatory interneuron u_2. Now u_1 persists in suppressing v_1 even though [a] subsequently stimulates the right dipole. An unvoiced percept is emitted from the dipole.

Figure 3. In (*a*) [p] stimulates the left pole of a voicing-detector dipole. The right pole is inhibited via the inhibitory interneuron Iuv and a nonlinear feedback signal is established via u_2. u_1 persists in suppressing v_1 even though [a] subsequently stimulates the right pole. An unvoiced percept is emitted from the dipole.

In (*b*) a [b] also stimulates the left pole first, but before the left pole's feedback loop can be established, it is inhibited by the more-rapid onset of voicing in the right pole. The dipole emits a voiced percept.

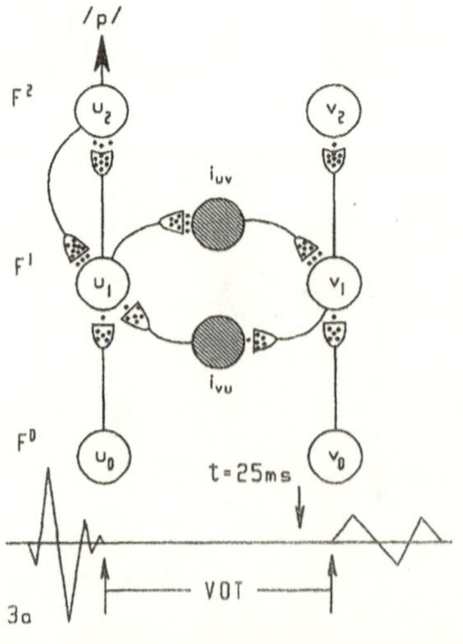

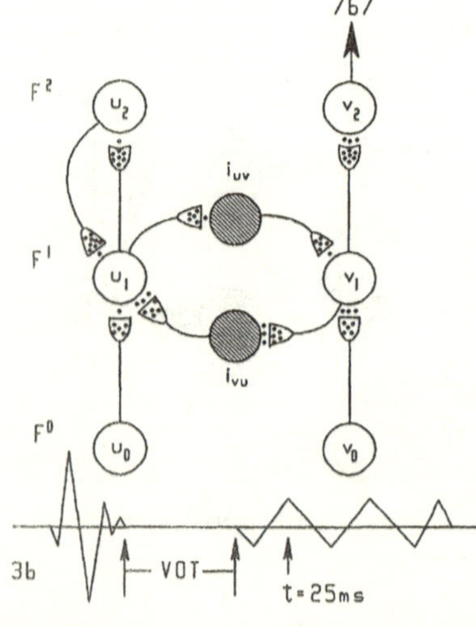

When a voiced stop burst occurs (e.g., [b] in [ba]), the left dipole is again stimulated first (Figure 3b). However, in voiced plosives, VOT is less than 25 msec. Before the feedback loop via u_2 can establish persistent inhibition via i_{uv}, the vocalic stimulation of v_1 establishes inhibition of the unvoiced pole via i_{vu}. Signals to v_2 sum to threshhold and the right dipole emits a voiced percept.

The dipole models presented so far resemble 'parameter switches' insofar as they are binary-valued. In the retina, red and green receptor neurons can in fact be paired, and Figure 2 approaches a faithful cell-by-cell model of a retinal subnetwork. However, in more cerebral processes like voicing perception, minimal anatomies like Figure 3 must be understood to be heuristic simplifications. Even in the simple case of English categorical perception, thousands of cochlear hair cells must originally contribute to each pole of the dipole. Additionally, the left pole of Figure 3 might actually (or also) be a broad-band noise detector, and the right pole a narrow-band vowel detector. These might correspond to anatomically quite distinct neural structures, for example, eighth (auditory) nerve projections arising through the inferior colliculus versus those arising through the medial geniculate body. An even more complex combination of frequency and bandwidth feature detectors might also be involved. In languages like Spanish, categorical discrimination occurs between voiced and prevoiced plosives. In languages like Hindi, VOT assumes four categorical values, suggesting that the underlying physiology must also support a double-dipole model.

Further research will supply greater detail to the foregoing description of categorical perception. In the meantime, the dipole model of Figure 3 supplies a level of explanation which has not previously been available. Insofar as neural architectures exhibit and develop self-similarity (fractal regularity), minimal anatomy simplifications like Figure 3 will not be over-simplifications. Our more immediate problem is one of explaining how, under different inputs, some minds learn to make English categorizations while others learn Hindi or Spanish.

STM and LTM. Broadly following Hebb, ART posits a linkage between Short-Term Memory (the activation patterms diagrammed in Figure 3) and Long-Term Memory, the locus of learning, to be discussed next. Grossberg models STM and LTM using nonlinear, differential difference equations. Here, we will simplify his system to an illustrative pair of linear equations describing only site u_2 in Figure 3a. (See Loritz 1990 and Grossberg 1980, 1986 for progressively more-complete introductions to Grossberg's system of equations.)

(i) $STMu_2 = STMu_1 * LTMu_{12}$
(ii) $LTMu_{12} = STMu_1 * STMu_2$

STM is a pattern of nerve-cell activation which corresponds to membrane depolarization: the electrical nervous signals which are passed around within a network. In Figure 3a, STM is partially correlated with and can be visualized as the speech waveform across the bottom of the diagram. However, STM is 'gated' by LTM traces. That is, the STM signal from u_1 is output only if there is a signal from u_1 *and* the LTM trace at $u_{1,2}$ is nonzero (not negligible). If there is no neurotransmitter at the synapse between u_1 and u_2, no STM signal can be transmitted to u_2. Notice, however, that the crucially important inhibitory pathways of the gated dipole are not modeled in equations (i) or (ii). They could be simply included by giving (i) as (i').

(i') $STMu_2 = STMu_1 * LTMu_{12} - INH$

Similarly, LTM develops at $u_{1,2}$ if and only if $STMu_1$ *and* $STMu_2$ are both simultaneously nonzero (active, excited). Equations (i) and (ii) are dynamically linked.

In Figure 3a (and elsewhere) we diagram Long-Term Memory in the synaptic knobs at the end of the axons of the modeled cells. Recent research has tended to locate LTM more on the postsynaptic (dendritic) side of the synapse (Lynch 1986, Alkon 1988) but as Black 1986 points out, there are many memories in life: every biochemical process is a 'memory'. Fast processes are short-term memories and slow processes are long-term memories. At the level of detail which is relevant to this paper, minimal anatomies are more clearly drawn if all neural long-term memories are collected into a single LTM trace which is modeled in the synaptic knobs.

To observe the operation of these associative learning rules clearly, we must study a more complex anatomy.

Vocalic perception. The cerebral generalization of the gated dipole is the on-center off-surround 'polypole' or 'dipole field'. On-center off-surround anatomies have important noise-suppression, contrast-enhancent, and edge-detection capabilities. Figure 4 models a tonotopic polypole for vowel perception. Tonotopic neural segregation of signals occurs in the cochlea and is retained at the projection of the VIII nerve to the cerebrum (Woolsey and Walzl 1942, Woolsey 1960, Imig et al. 1974).

The sites in field F^1 of Figure 4 correspond to pyramidal cells in a lamina of cerebral cortex. Where afferent (sensory) or efferent (motor) pathways map onto the cerebrum, the sites of a field such as F^1 are proximate and compete with neighboring sites via inhibitory interneurons as in Figures 2 and 3. (Cerebral cortex is often thought to be constructed around 'columns', each with a pyramidal cell at its core. Although each F^1 site in Figure 4 can be associated with such a pyramidal 'column', it is important to note that each site in F^2 governs a pyramidal column of its own, and is *not* in the same pyramidal column as the F^1 site drawn below it.)

Figure 4. The first stage of the vowel detection system is a tonotopic dipole field which is a *tabula rasa* at birth (*a*). With repeated exposure to the spectrum of the vowel [i], the LTM traces (modeled as synaptic knobs) of the dipole field align with (encode) the input (*b*), thereby 'learning' the phonemic pattern /i/. When the child subsequently hears [I] (*c*), the field treats the input spectrum as if it were corrupted by noise and deforms the field's output into the phonemic percept of /i/. If a rebound occurs across $F^{1,2}$ allowing inhibited sites to learn, an intermediate state might occur in which 'interference' is observed. However more than feedforward inputs must be operant or new patterns would continually erase previously learned patterns.

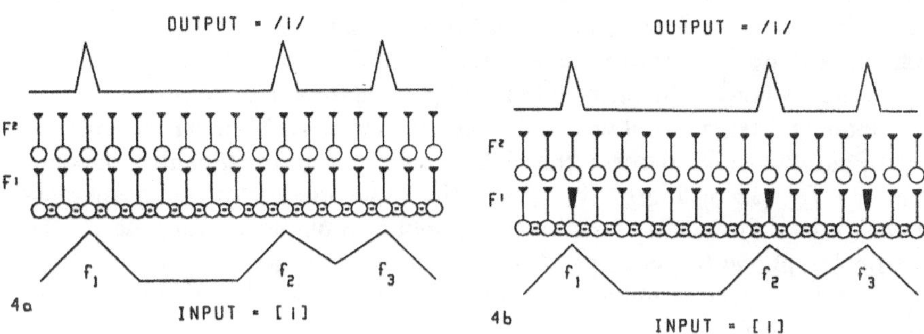

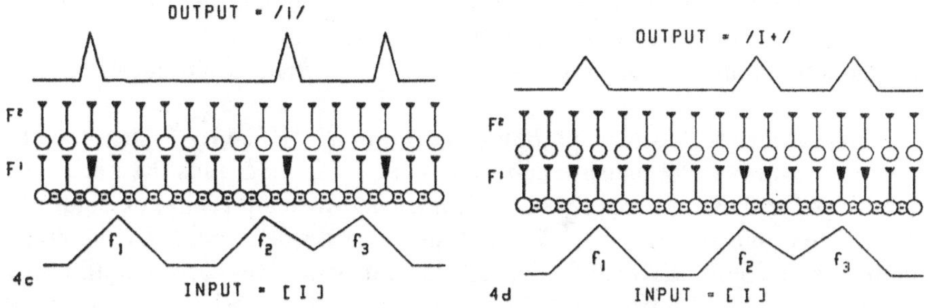

For concreteness, assume that a Spanish child begins life with a tonotopically organized polypole vowel detector which is a *tabula rasa* (Figure 4a). At this stage, its on-center off-surround anatomy functions as a noise-reduction or edge-detection device: Broad input formants are contrast-enhanced so the output contains sharply defined formant peaks. The peaks inhibit the valleys more than the valleys inhibit the peaks. The result is that the peaks become higher and the valleys lower. With repeated exposure to the spectrum of the vowel [i], the LTM traces of the child's dipole field align with the input pattern in accordance to learning rule (ii) (Figure 4b). That is, if we assume all sites at F^2 receive (undiagrammed) tonic inputs, then, by (ii), each $F^{1,2}$ LTM trace will become proportional to the input-generated activity at each site in F^1. Synonymously, we can say the vector of LTM traces, Z, at F^2 'encodes' the input vector, I; that 'Z becomes parallel to I'; that Z 'learns' I, or, that the input pattern I is learned by the LTM pattern Z.

Later, when the Spanish child hears [I] (Figure 4c), the dipole field treats the input spectrum as if it were corrupted by noise. LTM-gated on-center off-surround dynamics deform the field's output into the Spanish phonemic percept /i/ (according to (i'). Here the on-center off-surround anatomy's noise-reduction circuitry functions as a phone-to-phoneme transducer. This particular phone-to-phoneme deformation has real survival value in Spain, where [I] is indeed nonphonemic 'noise'. However, when the child later tries to learn English, interference occurs.

Now assume that this Spanish-speaking child is in an ESL classroom when she misperceives [I] as /i/. Let the teacher say 'NO', and let this be a surprising event which triggers nonspecific arousal as in Figure 2d. A rebound occurs across the entire polypole. Nonspecific arousal activates the student's previously inhibited sites and these inhibit the previously most active sites. By (ii), long-term learning occurs at active sites, so the LTM weights of the $F^{1,2}$ field now begin to learn the new spectrum of the English phoneme [I] (Figure 4d).

Although this explanation might seem plausible, it is still incomplete. Under it, Spanish would be unlearned in English environments and English would be unlearned in Spanish environments. The *reductio ad absurdum* of this somewhat 'behavioral' account of learning would return the prospective bilingual to the *tabula rasa* of Figure 4a. Like a retina washed in all the colors of the spectrum, such adventitious recoding would allow neither /i/ nor /I/ to be learned, and there would be no capacity for the fluent conversion of phonetic input to phonemic percept. Code-switching could not occur.

Expectancies. To become bilingual, the mind of Figure 4 must encode distinct Spanish and English feedback systems. Figure 5 adds the necessary pathways for these systems to the critical second-formant region of Figure 4. Notice that the pathways in Figure 5 are structurally similar to the u_2-u_1 pathways in Figure 3. Such feedback/expectancy pathways are ubiquitous in the undifferentiated infrastructure of cerebral cortex. Grossberg calls the 'top-down' signals in these pathways 'expectancy signals', and in the context of serial learning, he calls the higher fields in which they originate 'masking fields'. Here we can call them 'context signals' and 'contextual hypothesis fields'. They contextualize learning.

Given expectancy systems, the $F^{1,2}$ LTM traces in Figure 5 can remain a *tabula rasa*. Top-down signals from an (abstract) context-sensitive dipole can bias the vocalic receptor to output either Spanish phonemes (Figure 5a) or English phonemes (Figure 5b).

Figure 5. The $F^{1,2}$ traces remain a *tabula rasa*, but top-down 'expectancy' signals from an (abstract) context-sensitive dipole bias the vocalic receptor to output either Spanish (*a*) or English phonemes (*b*). If $F^{1,2}$ traces hold early learning (e.g., the Spanish [I] --> /i/ 'rule'), expectancy signals also buffer the $F^{1,2}$ traces against adventitious erasure and recoding. If $F^{1,2}$ LTM traces have been biased to Spanish in this manner, one form of 'fossilization' ('compound bilingualism', Lambert 1972) may be exhibited when top-down signals fail to fully override the $F^{1,2}$ LTM pattern (*b*, dotted lines).

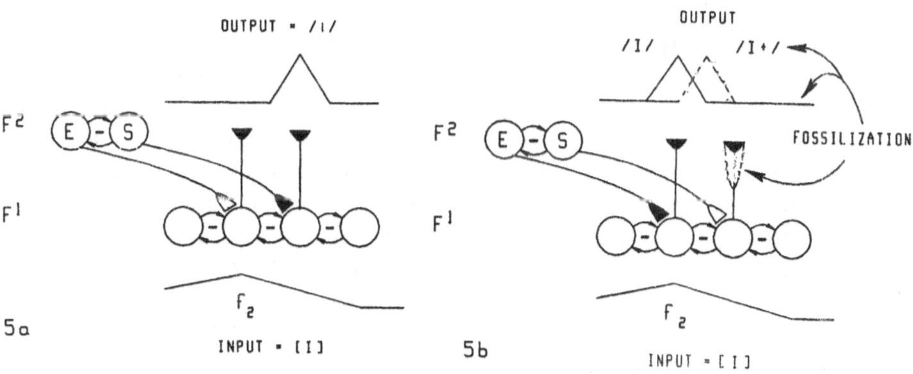

Figure 5 provides our first complete cerebral model in the sense that both feedback and feedforward circuits operate to make associative learning rules like (ii) meaningful. For example, in the context of Figure 5, each $F^{1,2}$ trace can learn to associate the bottom-up input of [I] with the Spanish phoneme /i/, but only if F^1 is activated by the bottom-up [I] at the same time that it is also activated by top-down Spanish expectancy signals.

Learning and linguistic hypothesis testing. With the mechanisms thus far described, we can outline a unified learning process which includes an account of linguistic hypothesis testing. Like Peircean 'beliefs', human knowledge is plastic. It can adapt to a changing environment. A surprising event or fact can trigger a rebound across whole polypole fields. Thus an old hypothesis, H_i, is suppressed and a new hypothesis, H_{i+1} is instantiated and tested against the environmental input. If H_{i+1} better matches the input pattern (if it 'resonates' in STM in a manner analogous to the feedback loop of Figure 3a), it becomes a new 'belief', and replaces the old belief, H_i. Such adaptability is largely responsible for the evolutionary dominance of the human species, and linguistic knowledge is the most characteristic (not the least characteristic!) evidence of this adaptive capacity. A wide range of linguistic phenomena can be accounted for under this ART model. Several are briefly discussed in the remainder of this paper.

Learning at the i+1 level. As the preceding paragraph suggests, Krashen's (1982) intuition that learning occurs at the i+1 level can be viewed as a neural necessity. In an on-center off-surround anatomy, a dominant belief, H_i, always suppresses other potential belief-patterns, H_{i+n}. But if and when H_i is rebounded, the next most dominant among these, H_{i+1}, becomes dominant. In the ART model, however, this learning is not quite so simply automatic as Krashen might lead us to hope. H_{i+1} could very well be some peculiar interlanguage hypothesis. We might call the next recognizable target language hypothesis H_{i+1}, but many unrecognizable IL hypotheses might intervene to complicate the learning process.

Learning at the other i+1 level. There is another, more important sense in which learning occurs at an 'i+1' level. Figure 5 simply and abstractly suggested that F^{i+1} was a bilingual context field, but taking the level of phonetic codes as F^i, it is more characteristic of the ART model to designate the phonemic coding level as F^{i+1}, the morphological coding level as F^{i+2}, the syntactic as F^{i+3}, and the discourse level as F^{i+4}. Not only does such a scheme support the intuitions of thousands of years of linguistic theory, it adds to it a comprehensive account of serial learning and 'chunking' (Miller 1956) which can unify structural and generative grammatical theory. (The model is not simplistically hierarchichal, so one might represent the suprasegmental system of English in F^j or lexical semantics in F^k.)

Fossilization. Other things being equal, we expect the first-formed, bottom-up (e.g., 'phonetic') LTM traces to be always stronger and more resistant to rebounds than later formed, top-down (e.g., 'syntactic') expectancy traces. This generally explains why children learn language only slowly and with great effort while, in second language learning, adults experience the greatest difficulty with early-learned linguistic systems like phonology. This results from the natural selection of organisms which form stable codes for persistent inputs experienced early in life and plastic codes for occasional inputs experienced later in life. There has been an evolutionary advantage to having later-learned, contextual patterns (e.g. the Spanish-English dipole system in Figure 5) be weaker, more reboundable, and therefore more 'plastic'. If higher, contextual fields rebound and encode new experience more readily than lower fields, they buffer the lower fields against adventitious recoding. For example, they protect the mother tongue against being overwritten by later L2 experience.

Figure 5b presents fossilization in the case where bottom-up, $F^{1,2}$ LTM traces had been allowed to encode the Spanish phonemic transformation of the input [I] into /i/, perhaps through the agency of a child's strictly monolingual Spanish learning environment. Such traces (dotted in Figure 5b) might persist despite the subsequent development of an English-Spanish contextual code-switching system. Then, as drawn in Figure 5b, even though the English context switch is on, the persistent bottom-up trace could still deform [I] to [I+] or /i/. It is not necessary to resort to a global, perhaps hormonally induced 'critical stage' theory to explain such fossilization. Such explanations dehumanize language to the level of instinct, and otherwise fail to explain why such a nonadaptive mechanism should have been naturally selected in a species and a behavior which in all other respects seem to have been selected for increased adaptability.

Cerebral lateralization. Theorists have particularly tried to explain fossilization by synchronizing a critical stage with cerebral lateralization (Lenneberg 1967). Lateralization refers to the localization of language function in one cerebral hemisphere, almost always the left. I take the immediate cause of lateralization to be the physically enlarged *planum temporale* of the left hemisphere (Geschwind and Levitsky 1968). This extra cerebral cortex is proximate to the eruption of the eighth nerve into cortex, and it is present as early as four months before birth. ART provides a simple, unified explanation for the eventual localization of language to this area: the competitive dynamics of the cerebrum allow the left hemisphere, with its extra brain cells, to 'outshout' competitively the less endowed right hemisphere.

It has been something of an embarrassment to proponents of a critical stage theory of lateralization that they have been unable to agree when this supposed critical stage ends. Estimates have ranged between five years (Krashen) and thirteen years (Lenneberg). ART does not deny that critical stages occur in other developmental processes, but if the gradual, developmental learning of LTM patterns is the primary cause of the lateralization of language, then it is clear why lateralization does not exhibit the sharp boundaries one must expect of a critical stage. When gradual learning is further augmented with myelination, and contextual learning at fields i+n, it becomes clear how lateralized language can also become fossilized. Very long-term memory devices encoding information at higher fields support lower-field codes *and* buffer them against subsequent relearning and recoding.

Finally, ART suggests a simple explanation for why lateralization should have evolved in the first place. If cerebral cortex were not asymmetrical in the region of the *planum temporale*, equal auditory inputs to each ear would be processed equally by each hemisphere, and each hemisphere would send equal signals across the *corpus callosum* to the opposite hemisphere. Such signals could quickly lock into an STM resonance, and imprinting would occur: the system would quickly phonemicize inputs experienced early into a small, quickly fossilized repertoire of calls.

The mutation which introduced hemispheric asymmetry into the human cerebrum in fact seems to have created the opposite of the imprinting behavior usually associated with 'critical stages'. Equal signals to each ear were no longer processed equally by each hemisphere, and with each hemisphere sending different patterns across the *corpus callosum*, imprinting was forestalled. Phonemicization was delayed until it could be modulated by more complex contextual patterns encoded at higher fields. Of course, a mutation which produced such cerebral asymmetry would have had negative survival value in a species which could not protect its young long enough to compensate for the extra time and effort needed to develop context-modulated learning and communication.

Input-driven learning. In the 1970s a number of researchers beginning with Brown (1973) discovered that mastery of grammatical morphology was learned in a more or less uniform sequence within groups of children learning a first language and adults learning a second. Despite much enthusiasm for interpreting these results as evidence of innate learning schema, there remained a substantial component which was attributable to the simple frequency of occurrence of individual morphemes. In the case of adult learners, this was the major component (Larsen-Freeman 1975). Both the input effect and the adult/child difference are broadly explained and accommodated by the ART model.

Conclusion: Inferring and abducing linguistic rules from an impoverished stimulus. ART offers an explanation of where hypotheses come from, and why we often cannot see them coming. Even though we might call dominant and latent combinations of LTM traces 'hypotheses', each trace is computed in parallel with a high degree of independence. Each 'site' of F^2 in Figure 5 could represent billions of cells, and each cell of F^1 receives inputs from tens of thousands of synapses. A small, independent change in a smallish trace in an obscure corner of such a composite 'hypothesis' could conceivably trigger a rebound across an entire neural field. For this reason, it is more productive to think of each LTM trace as being a parameter of a hypothesis—if not a full-fledged hypothesis in its own right. Then we see how the human mind can test billions of hypotheses (combinations of parameters) simultaneously, every fraction of a second. Under Adaptive Resonance Theory, there is no need to conjure an innate homunculus to control language acquisition. Given such a powerful processor, it would be child's play to induce grammar from 'degenerate input'—if the child were not born a *tabula rasa*. But because the child *is* born a *tabula rasa*, learning at first proceeds without expectancies: slowly and laboriously, in a predominantly bottom-up fashion. First, a myriad linguistic input patterns are read from STM into context-sensitive LTM storage according to learning rules like (i') and (ii). Then nascent expectancies and rebound mechanisms winnow viable rules from the degenerate input. Periodically, the rebounds are wide-ranging enough to manifest themselves as developmental stages, as when children begin to over-generally produce past tense forms like *goed.*

The observation that language is a rule-governed behavior is easily accommodated within this theory. Rules are simply top-down expectancies, hypotheses elevated to the Peircean level of belief. But under ART, rules impose a government of the percept, by the percept, and for the percept. They are erected from bottom-up input, and they govern only with the consent of the governed. The rules are frequently in conflict, and the historical result of these conflicts has been language change or the gerrymandering of rules' constituencies into complementary distributions.

The cost of ART is that it strongly implies that language can be taught and learned. This could require linguists to assume responsibility for developing the communicative skills of children and other disadvantaged groups of learners.

References

Albus, J. S. 1971. A theory of cerebellar function. Mathematical Biosciences 10:25-61.

Alkon, D. L. 1988. Memory traces in the brain. Cambridge: Cambridge University Press.

Anderson, J. A. 1970. Two models for memory organization using interacting traces. Biological Cybernetics 26:175-85.

Black, I.B. 1986. Molecular memory mechanisms. In: G. Lynch. Synapses, circuits, and the beginnings of memory, 99-110. Cambridge, MA: MIT Press.

Brown, R. 1973. A first language. Cambridge, MA: Harvard University Press.

Chomsky, N. 1968. Language and mind. 1st ed. New York: Harcourt Brace Jovanovich.

Chomsky, N. 1972. Language and mind. 2nd ed. New York: Harcourt Brace Jovanovich.

Cohen, M.A., and S. Grossberg. 1986. Neural dynamics of speech and language coding: Developmental programs, perceptual grouping, and competition for short term memory. Human Neurobiology. 1986 5:1-22.

Cohen, M.A., S. Grossberg, and D. G. Stork. 1988. Speech perception and production by a self-organizing neural network. In: Y.C. Lee, ed. Evolution, learning, cognition, and advanced architectures. Hong Kong: World Scientific Publishers.

Eimas, P.D., E. R. Siqueland, P. Jusczyk, and J. Vigorito. Speech perception in infants. Science 1971. 171, 303-6.

Gallie, W. 1966. Peirce and pragmatism. New York: Dover.

Geschwind, N., and W. Levitsky. 1968. Human brain: Left-right asymmetries in temporal speech region. Science 161:186-87.

Grossberg, S. 1968. Some physiological and biochemical consequences of psychological postulates. Proceedings of the National Academy of Sciences 60:758-65. Also in: S. Grossberg, ed. Studies of mind and brain. 53-64. Dordrecht: D. Reidel.

Grossberg, S. 1972. A neural theory of punishment and avoidance. II: Quantitative theory. Mathematical Biosciences 15:253-85. Also in: S. Grossberg, ed. Studies of mind and brain. 194-228. Dordrecht: D. Reidel.

Grossberg, S. 1980. How does a brain build a cognitive code? Psychological Review 87:1-51. Also in: S. Grossberg, ed. Studies of mind and brain. 1-52. Dordrecht: D. Reidel.

Grossberg, S. 1982. Studies of mind and brain: Neural principles of learning, perception, development, cognition and motor control. Amsterdam: Reidel.

Grossberg, S. 1986. The adaptive self-organization of serial order in behavior: Speech, language, and motor control. In: E.C. Schwab and H. C. Nusbaum. Pattern recognition by humans and machines. Orlando, Fla.: Academic Press.

Hebb, D.O. 1949. The organization of behavior. New York: Wiley.

Hinton, G. E. and J. A. Anderson. 1981. Parallel models of associative memory. Hillsdale, N.J.: Erlbaum.

Hopfield, J. J. 1982. Neural networks and physical systems with emergent collective computational abilities. Proceedings of the National Academy of Sciences (USA) 79:2554-58.

Hubel, D.H., and T. N. Wiesel. 1977. Functional architecture of macaque monkey visual cortex. Proceedings of the Royal Society of London 198:1-59.

Imig, T.J., M. A. Ruggero, L. M. Kitzes, E. Javel, and J. F. Brugge. 1974. Organization of auditory cortex in the owl monkey (Aotus trivirgatus). Journal of the Acoustical Society of America 56:523.

Ito, M. 1984. The cerebellum and neural control. New York: Raven.

Krashen, S. 1982. Principles and practice in second language acquisition. New York: Pergamon.

Kuhl, P.K., and J. D. Miller. 1975. Speech perception by the chinchilla: Voiced-voiceless distinction in alveolar plosive consonants. Science 190:69-72.

Lambert, W. 1972. Language, psychology, and culture, ed. A. S. Dil. Stanford: Stanford University Press.

Larsen-Freeman, D. 1975. The acquisition of grammatical morphemes by adult ESL students. TESOL Quarterly 25.2:409-19.

Lashley, K. S. 1950. In search of the engram. In: Society of Experimental Biology Symposium No. 4: Psychological mechanisms in animal behaviour. 478-505. London: Cambridge University Press.

Lenneberg, E. H. 1967. Biological foundations of language. New York: Wiley.

Liberman, A. M., K. S. Harris, H. S. Hoffman, and B. L. Griffith. 1957. The discrimination of speech events within and across phoneme boundaries. Journal of Experimental Psychology 54:358-368.

Loritz, D. 1990. Cerebral and cerebellar models of language learning. To appear in: Applied Linguistics.

Lynch, G. 1986. Synapses, circuits, and the beginnings of memory. Cambridge, Mass.: MIT Press.

Marr, D. 1969. A theory of cerebellar cortex. Journal of Physiology 202:437-70.

Miller, G.A. 1956. The magical number seven, plus or minus two: Some limits on our capacity for processing information. Psychological Review 60:81-97.

Minsky, M., and S. Papert. 1969. Perceptrons. Cambridge, Mass.: MIT Press.

Pierce, C.S. 1877. The fixation of belief. Popular Science Monthly 12:1-15.

Rosenblatt, F. 1959. Two theorems of statistical separability in the perceptron. In: Mechanisation of Thought Processes: Proceedings of a symposium held at the National Physics Labouratory, Nov. 1958. Vol. 1. 421-56. London: HM Stationery Office.

Rumelhart, D.E., and J. J. McClelland. 1986. Parallel distributed processing. Cambridge, Mass.: MIT Press.

Rumelhart, D.E., and J. L. McClelland. 1984. On learning the past tenses of English verbs. In: D.E. Rumelhart and J.L. McClelland. Parallel distributed processing, vol. 2: 216-71.

Woolsey, C. N. 1960. Organization of the cortical auditory system: A review and synthesis. In: G. L. Rasmussen, ed. Neural mechanisms of the auditory and vestibular systems. 165-80. Springfield, Ill.: Charles C Thomas.

Woolsey, C. N., and E. M. Walzl. 1942. Topical projections of neural fibers from local regions of the cochlea to the cerebral cortex of the cat. Johns Hopkins Medical Journal 71:315-44.

Improving foreign language listening comprehension

Joan Rubin
University of Pennsylvania

During the academic year 1987-88, my colleagues from San Francisco State University and Oakland Unified School District and I conducted an experiment to consider the effect on listening comprehension of teaching listening strategies using Spanish video.

We learned a great deal in hindsight which we wish we had known before about presentation of video lessons and about preparing teachers for strategy training. However, my purpose here is to present some of the positive findings of the research—namely, the importance of selecting video which is cognitively supportive of the listening task—and some circumstances under which teaching listening strategies is particularly helpful.

Our definition of listening comprehension follows closely that of Clark and Clark (1977), and Richards (1983). For us, listening consists of processing information which the listener gets from visual and auditory clues in order to define what is going on and what the speakers are trying to express. In order to be effective listeners, foreign language learners need to monitor their attention to and interpretation of these clues. It is our hypothesis that attending and interpreting is accomplished more effectively when students know when and how to bring to bear their knowledge of the world and of the foreign language in processing auditory information.

Research design and sample. The experiment took place in the Spring semester of 1988 in a California school district. Our sample was taken from second-year-second semester students of high school Spanish. We worked in a total of seven schools which had rankings on the California Assessment Program (CAP) ranging from very high to very low, that is, our sample included representation from the whole range of verbal and math scores in the state.

Our design included three treatment groups (T1, T2, T3) divided according to the kind of teaching (blind, informed, and self-control), and two control groups. Control Group 1 (CG1) watched the same videos as the treatment groups but received a lesson unrelated to listening comprehension, learning strategies, or our selected teaching methods. Control Group 2 (CG2) watched only the pretest and posttest video segments and continued to do their normal lessons.

Our student population began with 564 students; however, our group for analysis was 394. This number was arrived at by eliminating from our sample native speakers of Spanish, those absent on our 'critical' days (pretest, posttest, or six or more of the twelve instructional days). Table 1 shows our sample distribution of students by treatment.

The experiment took place over eight weeks. On day 1 of week 1, all groups took a pretest which consisted of two five-minute videos and two corresponding comprehension quizzes. During the remainder of week 1, T1, T2, T3, and CG 1 students received two 40-45-minute lessons, each of which included two five-minute videos. During weeks 2-6, T1, T2, T3, and CG1 students received two 40-45-minute lessons. Each lesson included two five-minute videos. That is, over the course of the first six weeks, each treatment group received twelve lessons, each of which had ten minutes of video. Thus, students were exposed to 120 minutes of video over the course of six weeks. During week 7, no video was shown so that students could integrate what was learned. In week 8, all treatment groups took a posttest which consisted of two five-minute videos, each directly followed by a corresponding comprehension quiz.

GROUP	NUMBER
T1	68
T2	68
T3	104
CG1	54
CG2	100
Total	394

Table 1. Sample numbers by treatment group.

Video selection. Each of the five-minute videos was deliberately selected to serve as what Bransford et al. (1985) call a 'haven for learning'. For them, a haven is the creation of a rich context within which mediation can take place. Mediation refers to the role of teachers or parents who provide structure to the experience of the learner. Two forms which mediation can take are: (1) mediators can arrange lessons so that learners encounter certain experiences, and (2) mediators can help learners connect various parts of their experience. Our task was to carefully select video so that it could become a haven for learning. For example, if a video passage permits effective use of world knowledge and foreign language knowledge, then it may serve as a haven for learning because it connects to parts of a student's experience.

Each of the five-minute videos was thus selected to facilitate information processing. The following outline presents the criteria used to select the video and to structure student video experience. Of particular importance is our operational definition of 'contextualized' because it illustrates how video can be selected to connect to student experience and prior knowledge.

1. Video.
   a. Good production value (clear audio and video).
   b. Students don't know the story line (encourages students to pay attention to details).
   c. Topics selected are within the realm of student experiences and knowledge of the world (when topics are not familiar, students cannot bring their world knowledge to bear).
   d. Avoid, where possible, stereotypes.

2. Motivation.
   a. Intrinsic interest to learner (deal with topics that are particularly interesting to high school students).
   b. Student age or older represented in video.
   c. Continuous story line with closure (facilitates learning and enhances student sense of satisfaction).

3. Language.
   a. Single episode (allows students to focus on the big picture; or use a top down approach).
   b. Contextualized (i.e. sufficient clues for information processing) from three points of view:
      (1) The physical surroundings or props provide clues to understanding the conversation.
      (2) The action provides clues to understanding the conversation.
      (3) The interaction provides clues to understanding the conversation.

Often the physical surroundings or props provide clues to understanding the conversation by narrowing down the possible content of the conversation or intent of the speaker. For example, the word *café* in Spanish can mean 'coffee', the color of coffee, or a place to go have coffee. However, if the speaker hands his guest a cup of coffee and says *¿café?*, then it is more than likely that the ambiguity is resolved and that the speaker means 'coffee'.

The action can also provide clues as to what is being said. Foreign language listeners need as much support as possible to facilitate their listening. When the action supports what is being said, it helps generate or validate student hypotheses. For example, in a classroom scene, if you see people putting little pieces of paper in a box and there is a list of names on the blackboard, a good hypothesis would be that the discussion is about voting.

The interaction among the characters provides clues as to the nature of their relationship and their intentions toward each other. For example, consider a situation in which people are having a discussion, using threatening hand gestures. This interaction can prompt students to generate or validate hypotheses about the nature of the characters' relationship.

If all three of these contextual clues are present in a video episode in sufficient number, they can facilitate listening comprehension by providing students with a basis for hypothesis generation or validation. In our experiment, we selected video segments where these three elements were present in abundant quantity.

To illustrate how much of a haven contextualized video can be, consider the following example. We showed a five-minute clip of a Colombian film in Spanish chosen to hook into the world-knowledge of the learner to a man who had no knowledge of Spanish. We showed the clip first without the sound and asked him to tell us what the clip was about. Without the sound, the man was able to determine that the main focus of this five-minute clip was a lesson in geography. He was able to do this because of his use of his prior knowledge of the world. He paid attention to the surroundings (one desk and chair, another set of chairs, and a globe) and proximics (a young man who stood in front of the desk, a group of young people who were seated in rows), and the interaction between them (the young people, seated where students might be seated, came to the desk one at a time and pointed to spots on the globe; the young man, who stood where a teacher might stand, made comments about the young people's actions).

Given his awareness of the overall story, the man was next able to do something which beginning second language learners find very difficult to do. It is well known that one of the more difficult things for beginning language learners to do is to segment natural speech. However, when we played the clip again with the sound up, the man listened and without prompting said '*Francia*. That must mean France.' He was able to isolate this word because, since he had recognized the framework of the story, it was a fairly natural task to recognize that the sounds in *Francia* constituted a single word relating to geography. The man used his knowledge of the overall scene to make sense of the input.

Not all video provides an opportunity to use background knowledge to generate hypotheses. Much of it consists of 'talking heads' which are often quite decontextualized. With this decontextualized video we observed two negative consequences: (1) the number of hypotheses is greatly expanded and therefore does not permit narrowing down the possibilities to facilitate listening comprehension; and (2) students soon find the listening task overwhelming and become fidgety and disinterested. So, when the materials do not relate sufficiently to student knowledge, they get restless, feel inadequate, and become bored. It is critical that video be selected which relates to student knowledge of the world and serves as a scaffold to further learning.

Impact of video on listening comprehension. We found that by selecting video which provides sufficient clues for information processing, we were able to improve the gain scores not only of all our treatment groups (T1, T2, and T3) but also of Control Group 1, which was exposed to all of the videos, though not to our strategy training. The gain scores for the pre- and posttests of those who watched video regularly over the six-week period improved 50 percent while those who watched video only during the pre- and posttests improved 32 percent (see Table 3).

Table 3. Pretest/posttest gain scores by video viewing.

Group	N	Pretest Avg (SD)	Posttest Avg (SD)	Pre-Post Gain	Percent Improvement
Watched video. T1, T2, T3, CG1	294	5.10 (1.26)	7.65 (1.38)	2.55	49.93%
Didn't watch video. CG2	100	6.04 (1.37)	7.99 (1.38)	1.94	32.20
Total	394				

The mean gain of the groups that regularly watched video was 2.55 and that of those who watched video only during the pre- and posttest was 1.94. A comparison of the gain scores of these two groups was significant, $t = 3.44$, $p < .001$.

Need for strategy training. A critical part of our research design was student instruction in the use of listening comprehension strategies. Following Brown and Palincsar (1982), we hypothesized that training in the use of strategies would improve listening comprehension. As many have indicated (O'Malley 1987, Politzer and McGroarty 1985), we are still in the early stages of understanding all of the components that go into effective strategy training though we do have some clues as to many of the important elements which affect training outcomes.

One finding of this experiment came from the training segment which taught students to pay attention to story line strategy. We found that when the video material was relatively easy for our students, the difference between the performance of the experimental groups (T1, T2, and T3) and Control Group 1 was not significant. However, when the video texts were more difficult, strategy training appeared to give students an edge so that the experimental groups did outperform CG1 on that day. So, if texts are too difficult and students are not given some coping skills via strategy training, then as O'Malley and Chamot report (1990:135), students just give up trying to tackle a text, saying, 'I just didn't understand that.'

When the text or task is just hard enough, strategy training can improve the performance of students. This is shown through an examination of the four days in which a story line strategy was taught to the three experimental groups. The story line strategy requires that the student try to determine the main plot while watching a video. This can be discerned not only from the spoken language but also from the way the visual material is presented. The strategy requires that students note whether their ideas are being confirmed or not as they watch for the plot line.

A consideration of student performance for the four days in which the story line strategy was taught, as seen in Table 4, reveals the following: differences between the experimental group and CG1 on days 4, 7, and 13 were minor but the difference between these groups on day 10 was significant ($z = 2.514$, $p < .01$).

Table 4. Quiz scores for days 4, 7, 10, and 13.[1]

GROUP	N	DAY 4 AVG (SD)	DAY 7 AVG (SD)	DAY 10 AVG (SD)	DAY 13 AVG (SD)	4 DAY AVG (SD)
Exp	177	3.45 (1.63)	6.53 (1.64)	6.01 (1.64)	6.67 (1.87)	5.67 (1.06)
CG1	49	2.94 (1.48)	6.63 (1.40)	4.78 (1.52)	6.94 (1.53)	5.32 (0.79)
Total	226			$z = 2.514$, $p < .01$		

If we next consider all students who were present on day 10, as indicated in Table 5, the difference between quiz scores for the experimental group and CG1 is statistically significant ($t = 4.83$, $p < .001$).

Table 5. Quiz scores for day 10.

GROUP	N	DAY 10 QUIZ AVG (SD)
Experimental	230	6.07 (1.64)
CG1	61	4.95 (1.49)
Total	291	

This difference would seem to indicate that on day 10, student use of the story line strategy could explain the significant improvement which the

[1] The numbers in this table include only students on all four days (day 4, 7, 10, or 13) when story line or other lesson was taught.

experimental group made. Further, during the lesson in which the story line strategy was presented, students completed an exercise practicing the story line strategy. A correlation between performance on the exercise and quiz scores for the experimental group for day 10 showed a moderate correlation coefficent of 0.36 ($n = 230$, $p < .01$). This provides further evidence that training in strategies can improve listening comprehension scores.

To consider why the Experimental-CG1 difference was statistically significant for day 10 but not for days 4, 7, or 13, we compared the videos. Day 4 was taken from *Zarabanda*, a pedagogical film prepared by the BBC with peninsular Spanish dialogue. Day 7 was from the movie, *Coqueta*. Day 10 was from the movie, *La Niña de la Mochila Azul*. Day 13 was from the movie, *Los Dos Carnales*. Without doubt, day 4 was the easiest video since the diction was very clear, the pace was quite slow, and there was virtually no use of regionalisms or slang. On the other hand, the videos on days 7, 10, and 13 were all from Mexican movies and contained some regionalisms. Day 10 presented some special difficulties and could be considered the most difficult. In particular, in the day 10 video segment, two of the characters spoke very rapidly, with poor diction, and even native speakers had some trouble understanding what was said. In addition, these two characters spoke with the typical accent of uneducated residents of Mexico City. Hence the day 10 video seemed to present special comprehension problems for second year students of Spanish. We would like to suggest that because of the particular difficulties which day 10 presented (i.e. rapid pace, uneducated speech, and many regionalisms), use of the story line strategy enhanced the listening comprehension of the experimental group.

Conclusions. This research has shown that video can serve as a haven to enhance listening comprehension if it is selected so that it provides sufficient clues for information processing. It is the selection that is critical, not just the use of video alone. Further, the research has given strong indication that use of listening strategies can help students work with more difficult material. In this experiment, use of the story line strategy enabled students to outperform those who were not so instructed, especially when the language of the video was difficult.

The combination of well-selected video and training in effective listening strategies can also improve student affect and motivation. One student remarked how learner strategies helped orient him: 'I know what to look for because of my hypothesis.' Or, as another student gleefully remarked, 'I like this [exercise]. It makes me feel smart!' With that kind of affect and insight, learning cannot help but go forward.

Note

This research was funded by the U.S. Department of Education, International Research and Studies Program in Washington, D.C. under project number 017AH70028. The project staff included Joan Rubin, project director; John Quinn, statistician; Joann Enos, senior research associate; Elena Eakin, Marcelo Esteban, Paul Fresina, and Sally Geisse, research assistants.

References

Bransford, J.D., R.D. Sherwood, C.K. Kinzer, and T.S. Hasselbring. 1985. Havens for learning: Toward a framework for developing effective uses of technology. Nashville: George Peabody College for Teachers.

Brown, A.L., and A.S. Palincsar. 1982. Inducing strategic learning from texts by means of informed, self-control training. In: Topics in Learning and Learning Disabilities 2:1:1-17.

Clark, H., and E. Clark. 1977. Psychology and language. New York: Harcourt Brace Jovanovich.

O'Malley, M. 1987. The effects of training in the use of learning strategies on acquiring English as a second language. In: A. Wenden and J. Rubin, eds. Learning strategies in language learning. Englewood Cliffs, N.J.: Prentice Hall International.

O'Malley, M., and A. Chamot. 1990. Learning strategies in second language acquisition. Cambridge: Cambridge University Press.

Politzer, R.L., and M. McGroarty. 1985. An exploratory study of learning behaviors and their relation to gains in linguistic and communicative competence. TESOL Quarterly 19:103-23.

Richards, Jack C. 1983. Listening comprehension: Approach, design, procedure. TESOL Quarterly 17:2:219-40.

Trends and developments in listening comprehension: Theory and practice

Joan Morley
The University of Michigan

1 The changing status of listening comprehension. The importance of listening comprehension in second language teaching theory and pedagogy has moved from near zero status during the 1940s and 1950s, through a period of emerging awareness of its value during the late 1960s, to an evolving position of significance—indeed of central concern—over the last two decades.

Twenty years ago only a handful of aural comprehension materials were available for second language instruction; today there are dozens of tape-and-text programs to choose from. Traditional teacher-training texts gave limited attention to listening; today several recent teacher references on the teaching of listening skills not only focus on innovative ways in which teachers can develop their own tasks and activities, but recommend special attention to practices that are supported by current research. These resources suggest a variety of SL practices which reflect insights gained from studies in second language acquisition, discourse analysis, cognitive processing theory, and language learner strategies.

The rich resource of materials available today notwithstanding, however, perhaps the most important development in recent years has been the recognition that a listening component of SL programs cannot be equated with 'buying the right books and the right tapes'. Developing proficient skills in listening comprehension in SL is not something that can be accomplished in a half-hour lesson three times a week, nor can attention to listening be limited to language laboratory tapes, which, no matter how cleverly done, represent only a small sample of 'one-way' noninteractive listening. In a very apt statement, Alexander (in Bamford 1982) called the commercial marketing practice of having one or two cassette tapes per main text for listening practice, "ludicrous, from the point of real acquisition."

Although listening traditionally has been the 'neglected' skill of language instruction, undeniably it is the single language skill used most in human communication. We can expect to spend twice as much time listening as speaking, quadruple the time in listening over reading, and five times more time listening than writing (Weaver 1972, Rivers 1981). In a 1977 publication Asher called our attention to some astonishing figures on listening. He reported an estimate that average children, by age six, have spent a minimum of 17,520 hours listening to their native language; in contrast he pointed out that at the end of one full year of modern language instruction, students have, by generous estimate, listened to only 320 hours of the target language. A scant 320 hours seems an inconsequential amount of listening time, even if one wished to argue that adults can learn more in a shorter time (if carefully directed and personally motivated, of course).

One sobering question for language teachers is how well 320 hours prepares students to meet standards such as those set by the ACTFL Proficiency Guidelines (1988) which define overall proficiency as "the ability to perform in a linguistically and sociolinguistically appropriate manner within a variety of language-use situations encountered in real-world contexts external to the instructional setting." And more importantly, beyond helping students meet the goal of 'passing the proficiency test', the challenge to SL professionals is to determine ways of providing the kinds of learning experiences that will help students develop effective strategies to meet the aural comprehension demands placed upon them in real-world listening contexts, both during and after the period of language instruction.

Clearly, listening, by definition "everything that impinges on the human processing which mediates between sound and the construction of meaning" (Morley in Celce-Murcia 1990), is the cornerstone of human communication. Its importance cannot be underestimated nor can it be treated trivially in SL programs. It needs to be one of the central foci of curricula; our students would be well served if our efforts were turned toward exploiting every avenue, every natural source of the TL available—all day, every day—in the careful planning of school or institute classes and learning laboratory experiences, through involvement in whatever TL communities are available, and by using all manner of local and/or satellite media programming as a rich resource for listening experiences.

I have commented elsewhere in a chapter on listening comprehension (Morley in Celce-Murcia 1990) that a serious commitment to language comprehension in second language programs could profit from exploring ways to develop the 'sense' of listening immersion, that is, a 'mentality' that looks at listening as embedded, in fact, into the entire fabric of students' SL experiences. Three specific areas to explore are the following:

- A 'listening across the curriculum' concept (that is, a focus on listening as a part of every class, not simply a 'package' of auditory input reserved for a designated listening class or laboratory assignment);

- A 'listening across the day' concept (that is, a focus on listening in a full range of school or institute contexts, including extracurricular activities);
- A 'listening in the backyard' concept (that is, a focus on listening in a wide range of second language contexts in the available SL community).

These are ways to help turn listening from a position of peripheral importance to central importance and develop a learner's listening competency from marginal to significant. The chapter also provides guidelines and a questionnaire for a listening-oriented program review and needs analysis, together with follow-up suggestions for developing listening comprehension activities and materials.

In what follows I trace the history and development of listening comprehension theory and practice, examine three different perspectives on 'listening' in language learning, review listening comprehension textbooks, and suggest some future directions in developing listening comprehension skills in second language.

2 Tracing the history. A review of instructional patterns of the 1940s, 1950s, and into the 1960s, shows that neither the predominant British model of situational language teaching nor the predominant American model of audiolingual instruction took particular note of listening beyond its role in the imitation of patterns and dialogues. Language learning theory, too, gave little attention to the learner's processing of spoken language beyond the sound recognition/discrimination level and prosodic patterning. Listening was regarded as a 'passive' skill along with reading, and was simply taken for granted, perhaps because it is so unobtrusive, as noted by Weaver (1972:12-13):

> Most people are unaware of the proportion of time they spend in listening. After all, listening is neither so dramatic nor so noisy as talking. The talker is the center of attention for all listeners. His behavior is overt and vocal, and he hears and notices his own behavior, whereas listening activity often seems like merely being there—doing nothing. Thus we are likely to remember how much of the time we talk, but forget how much we listen.

In any case, much of the field took little serious notice of listening until relatively recent times (but see Gouin 1880 and 1892, Sweet 1899, Palmer 1917, Nida 1953). Modern-day concerns about listening comprehension in language study first appeared in the mid-1960s. Now the ideas are so well accepted that they hardly seem remarkable—but then, 25 years ago, they were somewhat 'before their time'. The following insightful comments from field notables Newmark and Diller, Rivers, and Belasco were not widely implemented at the time, but in retrospect they were indeed important signs of things to come, a key part of forces which helped move us toward an emerging comprehension-oriented focus in SL.

Newmark and Diller (1964). Newmark and Diller emphasized (1) natural speech, (2) authentic models, (3) systematic development, and (4) a view of listening as a skill in its own right in this statement (1964:20):

> The suggestions made in this paper are aimed at having students spend more time listening to natural speech and authentic models of the foreign language. They underline the need for the systematic development of listening comprehension not only as a foundation for speaking, but also as a skill in its own right.

Rivers (1966). Rivers focused on (1) communication, (2) the primacy of listening, (3) early-on and regular supply of input, and (4) increasing the difficulty of the input, in these words (1966:196, 204):

> Speaking does not of itself constitute communication unless what is said is comprehended by another person. . . . Teaching the comprehension of spoken speech is therefore of primary importance if the communication aim is to be reached. . . . listening comprehension is not a skill which can be mastered once and for all and then ignored while other skills are developed. There must be regular practice with increasingly difficult material . . . regularly spaced over the language-learning period. . . .

Belasco (1969). Belasco expressed very clearly the basic difference between 'listening as a means to another end' (that is, as a basis for speaking) and 'listening as an end in itself' (that is, listening for comprehension of meaning (Belasco 1969:4-5); this theme is developed in section 3 of this paper):

> I was rudely jolted by the realization that it is possible to develop so-called 'speaking ability' and yet be virtually incompetent in understanding the spoken language. . . . Not enough stress was being placed on listening comprehension . . . [students] were learning to audio-comprehend certain specific dialogues and drills taught by native speakers—but could not understand [the language] out of context in the mouths of native speakers.

Belasco's study, which focused on the neglect of listening, was one of a number of significant papers that were presented at the Second Congress of the International Association of Applied Linguistics, Cambridge, 1969 (Pimsleur and Quinn 1971). Held at the end of the decade of the 1960s, at the end of an 'era' in language instruction, a major focus of the 19 papers presented at this conference turned toward insights that might be forthcoming from the field of psychology following a long period of domination of the field by linguistics. In their introduction to the volume of proceedings, Pimsleur and Quinn note (1971:vii):

> We would suggest that the focus of our inquiries must move from the language to the learner, from the material to the person who is to absorb it. The more we understand about how students learn, the better we shall teach.

Prophetically, it seems, four important themes emerged from this AILA 1969 Congress:

- A new focus on the individual learner as the central element in the complex process of second language acquisition;
- A focus on the so-called receptive skills of reading and listening, long regarded as 'passive' skills, as much more complex processes;
- An emerging notion that listening comprehension may be the key fundamental skill that has not been adequately understood;
- A desire to bring students into closer contact with 'real' language as it is used in the real world by people communicating successfully with each other.

Moving, then, from 1969 into the decade of the 1970s, instructional programs began to turn toward an emphasis on pragmatic skills, with attention to reading, writing, and speaking, and even the 'neglected' skill, listening. New frameworks, especially from British influence, began to focus on functional language and communicative approaches in language teaching, with an increasing tendency to incorporate listening as an integral component. Listening textbooks and audio tape programs were developed and appeared on the market in increasing numbers as interest in listening comprehension spread. A personal monitoring of this development has included evaluating five texts in 1971, reviewing the 74 listening publications annotated in a JALT bibliography by Krause and Susser (1982), and examining an additional 62 listening publications since that time. This is a 'book count' only, of course, and does not take into account the differential quality of materials (see section 4 for a discussion of predominating characteristics of materials.)

Increasing instructional attention to listening comprehension continued into the 1980s, and, in fact, accelerated considerably, including the appearance of several teacher-reference resources during the last ten years, ones which focus on relating theoretical principles to practices: Richards (1983), Brown and Yule (1983b), Morley (1984), Ur (1984), Anderson and Lynch (1988), Richards (1990) and Morley (in Celce-Murcia 1990).

Meanwhile, in another direction, in the 1970s and 1980s language research increasingly focused on the role of listening comprehension in various levels and aspects of language learning and language acquisition. One important development was the emergence of several 'comprehension' approaches to language acquisition, especially at beginning levels, including Asher (1969), Postovsky (1970, 1974), Winitz and Reeds (1973), Krashen (1981), and Terrell (1977, 1982). (See section 3 of this paper.) Over the last decade in particular, a second perspective from which the role of listening has been examined is that of second language acquisition studies which have looked at listening and interactions, meaning negotiation, input, intake and output, including, among others, work by Long (1981, 1983, 1985), Chaudron (1985), Gass and Varonis (1985) and Varonis and Gass (1985), Pica and Doughty (1985), Swain (1985), Faerch and Kasper (1986), Brown (1986) and Pieneman and Johnston (1987). A third area of listening comprehension focus in recent years has been its role in learner strategies (Stern 1975; Rubin 1975; O'Malley, Chamot, Stewner-Manzanares, Kupper, and Russo 1985a, 1985b; Oxford 1985; Wenden and Rubin 1987; O'Malley, Chamot, and Kupper 1989).

A fourth important consideration in language research is the nature of listening and the information processing it involves. Here current work on so-called 'bottom-up' and 'top-down' aspects of information processing as discussed extensively in current literature provide valuable information (Rumelhart 1977, Adams and Collins in Freedle 1979). Briefly, 'top-down' processing is evoked from an internal source, from a bank of prior knowledge and global expectations about both language and 'the world'. Here listeners bring to bear on the task of 'understanding' the incoming stream of speech information which allows them to predict on the basis of context (both the preceding linguistic context and the situation-and-topic, setting-and-participants context) what the incoming 'message' at any point can be expected to mean and how it 'fits' into the whole. 'Bottom-up' processing, on the other hand, comes from the opposite direction; it is the processing of language information evoked by an external source, that is, by the incoming language data itself. Bottom-up comprehension refers to the part of the process in which the 'understanding' of incoming language is worked out proceeding from sounds, into words, into grammatical relationships and lexical meanings, and so on, where composite meaning of the 'message' is arrived at based on the incoming language data (see section 5).

Additional aspects of the history of the development of theory and practice are taken up in section 3, which looks at three distinct perspectives on listening and language learning.

3 Three perspectives on listening and language learning. At this point in the discussion it is important to point out that the term 'listening' is used in (at least) three different ways in language instruction. Each of the three unique uses of the term follows from a particular perspective on the nature of language learning and the role of listening in the learning process.

It is essential to consider these three distinctive uses of the word listening before one can seriously examine any of the types of listening comprehension instructional materials or any of the comprehension approaches which have been developed over the past 20 years.

All three roles for listening are alive and well and in active use today in foreign language instruction and in English as a second language instruction around the world.

Briefly, the differential uses of the term are as follows:

- Listening to repeat, or, listening 'as a means-to-another-end', specifically, listening as a foundation for speaking;
- Listening to understand, or, listening 'as an end-in-itself', specifically, listening for comprehension of meaning;
- Listening in the specialized sense of 'comprehension approaches' to language acquisition at beginning levels, or, listening to a controlled kind and amount of language input for the purpose of the initial acquisition of the TL.

3.1 Listening to repeat. In this use of the word 'listening' the meaning, essentially, is hearing a model and 'matching' it with an oral reproduction. 'Listening' is used in the sense of the auditory processing of a word, a phrase, or a sentence in order to reproduce it. Inasmuch as this kind of mental processing can be done below the level of propositional language structuring, the development of 'listening-with-understanding' may or may not be a significant by-product of such 'hearing-and-pattern-matching' routines. Evidence suggests more likely not, as clearly documented in Belasco (1971) and as summarized by Terrell (1982:21):

> Students in an audiolingual approach usually have excellent pronunciation, can repeat dialogs and use memorized prefabricated patterns in conversation. They can do pattern drills, making substitutions and changing morphemes using various sorts of agreement rules. What they very often cannot do is participate in a normal conversation with a native speaker.

Listening, repeating, and imitating were an important part of the teaching technology of the audiolingual instruction popular during the 1940s-1960s. Today this technique is still used in audiolingual classes and in the imitative portion of pronunciation instruction in an otherwise communicative program.

3.2 Listening to understand. This second use of the word 'listening' means developing listening as a skill in its own right, that is, a focus on instruction which is directed toward helping students develop effective one-way and two-way listening strategies for rapid and accurate comprehension of meaning in the second language and skills for interactive meaning negotiation (see section 5).

As noted earlier in this paper, until the 1970s virtually no specialized listening instructional materials were available, that is, ones expressly designed for listening skill-building in its own right. Then, what began as a few books in the early 1970s became an avalanche as dozens of new listening text-and-tape programs were published. These have included a structural focus (e.g. listening discrimination and multiple-choice 'aural grammar' exercises), dictations and 'gapped' dictations (including situationalized dialogue dictations), and 'quiz style' paragraph-and-questions materials patterned after reading comprehension exercises. And, as changes in SL syllabus design developed, listening books followed suit, with texts that have featured language functions, language notions, simulated situations, and tasks to be completed. Language for specific purposes (LSP) listening materials have focused on the needs of students in various areas, especially English for Academic Purposes (EAP), English for Vocational Purposes (EVP), and English for Professional Purposes (EPP) (see section 4 for more information).

3.3 Listening in the specialized sense of comprehension approaches to language acquisition. From the mid 1960s into the 1970s, language researchers/teachers Asher, Postovsky, Winitz and Reeds, and Terrell developed well-known instructional programs that featured: (1) early attention to listening comprehension and (2) a delay in oral production. Winitz, in his introduction to a collection of papers on *The comprehension approach to foreign language instruction* defined it as follows (1981:xvii):

> In the comprehension approach a new system of learning is not really advocated. The instructional format is to extend the teaching interval of one component of training, comprehension, while delaying instruction or experience in speaking, reading, writing.... The comprehension approach is cognitive in orientation. As used here, cognitive is defined as a system that gives students the opportunity to engage in problem-solving, the personal discovery of grammatical rules.

Continuing attention to comprehension approaches to language acquisition throughout the 1970s and 1980s resulted in several special systems of instruction.

Asher (1965, 1969) appeared first in print on the 'comprehension approach' scene, reporting on a system called Total Physical Response (TPR) which features extensive attention to listening from the very first day. The distinctive feature of this method is that every utterance by the teacher is a command, or is embedded in a command, that students act upon.

Postovsky, working on comprehension research in the late 1960s (1970, 1974), developed a listening comprehension program for English speakers learning Russian. Postovsky observed that if we accept a proposition that 'learning by doing' is an efficient way to learn a foreign language, then we need to have a clear idea of what the learner is expected to 'do' with language in different phases of the learning process. In the beginning phase, he suggests that teachers need to provide learners with listening experiences that help them to develop an auditory receptive ability to comprehend the spoken language.

Winitz and Reeds (1973) developed a course called "Rapid Acquisition of a Foreign Language (German) by the Avoidance of Speaking," in which the students were totally silent and the teacher (or tape recorder) did all the talking. The learner's only overt behavior was to choose one picture in a quadrant that corresponded to the meaning of each utterance. Like those of Asher and Postovsky, these materials began with very simple items and progressed to very complex utterances.

Terrell (1977, 1982), in "A Natural Approach to the Acquisition and Learning of a Language," noted that the main objective of the first class sessions is to convince students that they can understand utterances in the second language and that they can be comfortable with only a partial understanding of the components that form utterances. Terrell's 'natural approach' materials feature the following six guiding principles: (1) comprehension precedes production, (2) speech emerges in stages, (3) speech emergence (stage III) is characterized by grammatical errors, (4) group work encourages speech, (5) students acquire language in a low-anxiety environment, (6) the goal of natural approach is proficiency in communication skills (Terrell, Genzmer, Nikolai, and Tschirner 1988, teachers guide, 9-11).

It is important to emphasize once again that all three of these perspectives on listening in language learning are in active use today.

4 A review of listening comprehension textbooks. The listening comprehension texts and tapes of the seventies and eighties were developed pragmatically by experienced teachers, ones who used two parts intuition and one part insights from the beginnings of changes in theoretical models—learning models, linguistic models, and instructional models.

- From a language learning perspective of outside-in, to one of inside-out, in a concept of language acquisition that viewed the learner as the active prime mover in the learning process (Corder 1967), and an emerging paradigm shift in which learners were seen as active creators, not as passive recipients in a process which is cognitively driven, not behaviorally conditioned.
- From a focus on language as simply a formal system to a focus on language as both a formal system and a functional system that exists to satisfy the communicative needs of its users (Halliday 1970, 1973, 1978).
- From linguistic preoccupation with sentence-level grammar to widening interest in semantics, pragmatics, discourse, and speech act theory (Austin 1962, Searle 1970).

- From an instructional focus on linguistic form and usage, to one on function and communicatively appropriate use (Widdowson 1972, 1978).
- From an orientation of linguistic competence to one of communicative competence (Hymes 1972) and a specific competences model, which brought together a number of viewpoints in one linguistically oriented and pedagogically useful framework: grammatical competency, sociolinguistic competency, discourse competency, and strategic competency (Canale and Swain 1980).

Over the course of these two decades, what changes in listening texts have these and other shifts in theoretical models brought about? The answer is not an easy one. On the one hand, today's best state-of-the-art SL listening materials continue to be developed pragmatically by experienced teachers, who continue to use their intuitions, but increasingly their products are based on considerations that are more and more "compatible with current research-based conceptualizations of SL classroom learning" (Crookes 1989). On the other hand, there remains much work to be done. In many programs listening continues to be underrated and many new listening materials continue to be based on outdated models of language learning and language teaching.

4.1 The seventies. A review of the listening materials of the 1970s (apart from those which were discrimination-oriented) reveals that many paralleled the SL reading comprehension instructional design of the 1950s and 1960s. These texts featured aural passages of several minutes (often a written passage 'read aloud'), then answering a host of 'quiz show' style factual questions (e.g. true/false, multiple choice, fill in the blank, short answer), followed by written work with grammar or vocabulary exercises based on the aural text. These materials did not ask the students to 'do' anything functional with the information, other than take a 'test' on whether or not they had heard and 'understood' and remembered (or heard and remembered) details from the aural text.

However, during the course of the decade some new directions in textbook design began to appear as new concerns were addressed by text writers. Some of these developments were examined in the Krause and Susser (1982) review of 74 LC texts which appeared on the market through 1981, 47 British and 27 American. Most were 'sets' of materials that included a student book, a teacher manual (sometimes with answer keys and transcripts), and tape recordings.

Major headings in this review were (1) conversation materials, (2) narrative materials, (3) 'four-skill' texts that featured a special listening component, and (4) an 'other materials' category. Three features cited in each review paragraph were variety (British or American), level (beginning, intermediate, advanced), and an indication of suitability for independent use.

A fourth part of the review focused on whether the source was scripted (i.e. conversations, narrative passages or lecture written for English teaching purposes, authentic English prose passages read aloud, or formal speeches intended for native speakers) or authentic (i.e. spontaneous and unrehearsed). It was noted that few materials were wholly authentic (i.e. 'not recorded secretly').

Other useful assessments areas included quality of speech, content-and-format patterns, and emerging changes in function-and-use patterns.

Quality of speech.
- Whether it sounded relatively spontaneous, or 'read';
- Whether it included natural false starts, starters, fillers, hesitation phenomena, or was devoid of these characteristics of normal 'fast speech';
- Whether pronunciation was overly clear, precise, 'stilted', or more natural with reductions, elisions, assimilations;
- Whether speech was too slow, too fast, unnaturally paced, or normal in speed and tempo;
- Whether there was a limited range of voices and dialects, or a variety.

Content-and-format patterns.
- Dialogue and conversation formats (some with conventional aural comprehension questions and some with tasks);
- Narrative monologue formats (some with aural comprehension questions and some with tasks);
- Both real-life and simulated interview formats;
- Story-telling formats;
- Both real-life and simulated lecture formats.

Function-and-use patterns.
- Task-listening (with an organizing principle that focused on using content to achieve outcomes);
- Problem solving;
- Lecture and note taking;
- Sociolinguistic analysis (with an organizing principle that focused on using content to achieve outcomes plus 'analysis' of setting, participants, roles);

Additionally, some texts featured a 'prelistening' portion of the lesson in order to build expectancies and encourage predictions. Maley and Moulding (1981:4) observe that:

> This is a framing activity in which students begin to familiarize themselves with the topic they will be hearing about. In most cases some kind of

prop is involved—visual, verbal, or a discussion. It is important not to skimp on this since it prepares students mentally for what they will hear later.

The eighties. Moving along through this decade, increasingly both new listening materials and teacher references began to reflect some of the changes in the field as noted at the beginning of this section. In general, the major difference between the 1970s and 1980s was less emphasis on 'testing' and more on 'teaching'. That is, more on functional listening (with a 'listening-and-doing' orientation) toward the development of the processes of SL listening, and less on memory and recall of details heard. In small steps, not quantum leaps (and there is still much work to be done toward more soundly principled materials development), the emerging paradigm has been one emphasizing listening strategies, cognitive processes, and a new order of product, a 'real' one, a communicative one.

Trends of the eighties have been toward:

- More attention to contextual listening;
- More attention to purposeful outcomes;
- More authentic aural texts used for more authentic tasks;
- Growing attention to student awareness of speech acts and discourse functions in specific settings;
- More Language for Specific Purposes (LSP) listening focus and more 'special-focus' listening even in Language for General Purposes (LGP);
- More materials featuring prelistening activities;
- A number of broadcast style materials;
- A few video materials, especially ones of a situational 'drama' genre;
- Continued attention to combined listening/speaking materials.

The nineties. What will the future bring? The listening comprehension textbooks of the next ten years will be judged by an increasingly more discerning audience of teachers, ones with growing sophistication in expectations, ones demanding more in the nature of practices which are firmly anchored in theory. Additional comments on the LC textbooks of the nineties are taken up in section 5, which looks at future directions in developing listening comprehension skills.

5 Future directions in developing listening comprehension skills. By and large, some important notions about listening comprehension in second language learning and teaching seem to be well recognized today:

- Listening is the cornerstone of oral communication.
- Listening is used more than any other single language skill in our daily lives.

- Listening is often taken for granted because it is so unobstrusive (we notice our role as a talker much more than we notice our role as a listener) and it is seldom the object of direct instructional attention in first language curricula.
- Whereas listening along with reading has had a traditional label of passive skill, this is a false characterization; however, this myth remains 'conventional wisdom' in some quarters, especially in more traditional educational institutions.
- Until relatively recently, listening comprehension was largely neglected as a skill in its own right in SL programs.
- Our understanding of the process by which we listen and understand spoken language is far from complete, but instructional procedures need to be monitored continuously and revised to reflect state-of-the-art perspectives on listening and language learning.

But unfortunately the following statement must also be noted:

- Listening comprehension still continues to receive far too little time and trivial attention in most second language programs.

It remains a serious gap in the second language field, that recognition of the importance of listening has not translated, on a large scale, into serious practice. As noted before, in many programs listening continues to be underrated and many new materials continue to be based on outdated models of language learning and language teaching.

With a view toward bridging the gap between beliefs and action, theory and practice, this final section discusses some important features of listening as a language act, and presents some guidelines for developing listening comprehension activities and tasks.

5.1 Listening as a language act.

5.1.1 Listening as an active process, not as a passive state.

5.1.2 Listening not as one process, but several communicative engagements. Every day we engage in two-way interactive communication, where the reciprocal 'speech chain' (Denes and Pinson 1963) of speaker/listener is obvious to us. But we also engage in one-way reactive communication, where the input comes from the media (e.g. radio, television, films), public performances (e.g. plays, operas, musicals, concerts, public lectures, debates), instruction situations of all kinds, recorded messages, public address announcements, and conversations overheard. And finally, we engage in self-generated intra-active communication. Here we recreate language internally and 'listen' again as we retell and relive communicative interludes. And we attend to our own internal language produced as we 'think through' alternatives, plan strategies, make decisions—all by 'talking to ourselves' and 'listening to ourselves'.

Notice, then, that listening is no passive experience in two-way communication, or in one-way communication, or in self-generated communication. All are highly active participatory experiences.

Clearly, future directions in listening comprehension skill-building must take as the basic requirement, that the learner be actively involved, not merely passively engaged, in both one-way and two-way communicative activities and tasks.

5.1.3 Listening and language functions: Transactional discourse and interactional discourse. Brown and Yule (1983a) suggest dividing language functions into two major divisions: language for transactional purposes and language for interactional purposes—areas which correspond to Halliday's categories 'ideational' and 'interpersonal' (Halliday in Lyons 1970). Guiding students toward developing listener-skills and speaker-skills for both transactions and interactions is a challenging task for teachers and materials writers.

Students need opportunities to build skills in transactional language where the purpose is to convey factual or propositional information. Here the focus is on content and is message-oriented; the concern is with 'getting things done in the real world', with a premium on language clarity and precision. Some features of transactional language are instructing, directing, explaining, describing, ordering, inquiring, requesting, relating, checking on correctness of details, and verifying understanding.

Students also need opportunities to build skills in interactional language, where the purpose is to express social relationships and personal attitudes. It is focused on person, is listener-oriented, and is concerned with the establishment and maintenance of cordial social relationships. Vagueness and indirectness are tolerated, as role relationships are negotiated, and there is a premium on establishing peer solidarity and changing turns in a conversation. Some features of interactional language use are talking about 'safe' topics (such as weather, the physical setting, etc.), much shifting of topics with a great deal of agreement on them, expressing opinions, maintaining 'face' and respecting 'face', identifying with the concerns of the other person, and, in general, 'being nice' to the other person, and a little less careful about detail.

Sometimes transactional or 'business-type talk' and interactional or 'small talk' clearly moves from one dimension to the other, but sometimes the lines are not so obvious; sometimes they are intertwined. In any case, listeners need guidance and practice in learning how to recognize and how to respond appropriately.

5.1.4 Listening and language process: Top-down and bottom-up coognitive processing. It is also clear that listening comprehension activities and materials should take into serious account the cognitive nature of listening and the information processing it involves.

As noted in section 2, 'top-down' processing is evoked from an internal source, from a bank of prior knowledge and global expectations about language and 'the world'. Here listeners bring to bear on the task of 'understanding' the incoming speech information that allows them to predict on the basis of context what the incoming 'message' at any point can be expected to mean and how it 'fits' into the whole.

'Bottom-up' processing, on the other hand, is the part of the process where the composite meaning of the 'message' is arrived at based on the incoming language data. Here the 'understanding' of incoming language is worked out proceeding from sounds, into words, into grammatical relationships and lexical meaning, and so on.

Richards (1990) proposes a new model of materials design for teaching second language listening comprehension. It combines insights from current perspectives on both language functions and cognitive processes. He observes that the extent to which one or the other process dominates is determined by the purpose (transactional or interaction) for listening, the kind of background knowledge which can be applied to the task, and the degree of familiarity listeners have with the topic of discourse. He gives precise illustrations of different formats, concluding that:

> Too often, listening texts require students to adopt a single approach in listening, one which demands a detailed understanding of the content of a discourse and the recognition of every word and structure that occurs in a text. Students should not be required to respond to interactional discourse as if it were being used for a transactional purpose, nor should they be expected to use a bottom-up approach to an aural text if a top-down one is more appropriate (Richards 1990:83).

5.2 Setting principles of design for listening comprehension instruction from a communicative language learning perspective. Listening comprehension in real-world communication is an act of information processing in which the listener is actively involved in either two-way interactive communication or one-way reactive communication, and, in both cases, 'self-dialogue'. In real-world communication, information can be construed to serve, broadly, two purposeful functions: transactional (or ideational), and interactional (or interpersonal). Listening comprehension, then, is a meaningful matter of 'listen-and-do', that is, listening and doing something with the information—even if it is as simple as listening and acknowledging 'mentally' to oneself, for the instant, even if it is not actualized into memory storage. Finally, the nature of listening and cognitive information processing appears to involve dual processes of 'top-down' and 'bottom-up' understanding.

With these features of listening as a language act in mind, the following four principles of listening comprehension instructional design are suggested. They are basic to getting learners' attention and keeping them actively and purposefully engaged in the task at hand; moreover, they are basic to maximizing the effectiveness of listening/language-learning experiences. The four are: the relevance principle, the transferability/applicability principle, the task-oriented principle, and the outcomes principle.

5.2.1 The relevance principle. Both the listening lesson content (i.e. the 'information') and the outcome (i.e. the nature or objective of the 'information use') need to be as relevant as possible to the learner's life and life-style. This is essential for getting and holding learner attention and provides intrinsic, not fake, motivational elements. Lessons need to feature content and outcomes that have 'face validity' to students. If lessons feature things that have relevance, the more they may appeal to students and the better the chances of having learners' ears really 'tuned in'. If students really want to listen, we have accomplished part of the task which Strevens (1985) has called 'encouraging the intention to learn'.

5.2.2 The transferability/applicability principle. This follows from the relevance principle. Wherever possible, both at the content level and the outcomes level, listening lessons ought to have a measure of transferability/applicability, either internally (i.e. to other classes) or externally (i.e. to out-of-school situations), or both. In a 'transfer of training' sense, if teachers can mount rather specific in-class slices of life that mirror real-world content and outcomes patterns, the better the potential for outside application, consciously or unconsciously, now or in the future.

5.2.3 The task-oriented principle. In formal SL classes with teenage and adult students, and to some extent, with children, it is important to combine two major types of work: (1) language use tasks and (2) language analysis activities.

'Task' is used here in Johnson's sense (in Brumfit and Johnson 1979:200), in which task-oriented teaching is defined as teaching which provides 'actual meaning' by focusing on tasks to be mediated through language, and where success or failure is seen to be judged in terms of whether or not the tasks are performed. And relative to LC, Maley and Moulding (1979:102) focus on instruction which is task-oriented, not question-oriented; their aim is to provide learners with tasks which use the information in the aural text, rather than to ask them to prove their understanding of the text by requiring them to answer questions.

5.2.4 The outcomes principle. It is clear by now that a 'listen-and-do' format, that is, an information-gathering and information-using perspective, is recommended for listening activities in the SL curriculum. Listening comprehension in today's SL curriculum has gone far beyond a 20-minute tape a day, or a paragraph or two read aloud and followed by information-regurgitation questions in the form of a series of decontextualized 'test' questions about the factual content.

'Listen-and-do' in the listening comprehension context implies an 'outcome' objective. This follows from the fact that the purpose of oral communication in the real world is to achieve a genuine outcome; it may be very simple or it may be very complex, but an outcome is achieved. And so it must be in any listening comprehension activity planned for use in the SL learning context.

What is an 'outcome'? An outcome, in Sinclair's words (1984), is a "real job where people can actually see themselves doing something and getting somewhere." Outcome is an essential component in both two-way and one-way listening comprehension activities. Six broad categories of outcome, each of which can be subdivided into many kinds of narrowly focused small outcomes, are the following (see Morley in Celce-Murcia 1990):

(a) Listening and performing actions and operations. Included in this category are responses to directions, instructions, descriptions in a variety of contexts.
(b) Listening and transferring information. One kind of information transfer is from aural to graphic, that is, hearing information and writing it. Another is aural to verbal transfer, that is, hearing information and transmitting it in spoken communication.
(c) Listening and problem solving. Many kinds of activities for both groups and individuals can be generated in this category. These include verbal games and puzzles, intellectual problem solving, and real world field trip information gathering and problem solving.
(d) Listening, evaluating, and manipulating information. These outcomes are intellectually challenging ones in which the listener evaluates and/or manipulates the information received in the same manner. Tasks which focus on this outcome are as important for children as for adult learners.
(e) Interactive listening and negotiating meaning through questioning/answering routines. Here the focus of the outcome is on the process of negotiating meaning in interactive reciprocal listener/speaker exchanges (See Morley, in Courchene 1990).
(f) Listening for enjoyment, pleasure, sociability. Tasks with this outcome can include listening to songs or stories, poems, jokes, anecdotes, or, as suggested by Ur (1984:29), "generally interesting chat improvised by the teacher." Some of the activities in this category come under the heading of 'interactional' talk/listening, different from the previous outcome categories, which by and large are 'transactional' outcomes.

Final comments. The importance of listening comprehension in language learning and language teaching has moved from a status of incidental and peripheral importance to a status of significant and central importance over the last two decades. Whereas only a few instructional materials were available 20 years ago, today there are many texts and tape programs to choose from and, in general, materials are becoming more carefully principled, with serious attention to theoretical considerations. Each year more diverse materials are developed and many now focus on narrowly specified listening needs of particular groups of learners.

But the listening curriculum in a second language program cannot be equated with 'buying the right books and tapes'. Skill-building in listening comprehension is not something that can be accomplished in a half-hour lesson three times a week, nor can attention to listening be limited to language laboratory tapes. Listening, the language skill used most in life, needs to be a central focus, all day, every day, limited only by the availability of the target language, in the school, the community, the media. Listening instructional activities need to include both two-way interactive listening activities and tasks and one-way reactive 'listen-and-do' activities and tasks. Materials development should be done with careful attention to the important features of listening as a language act: listening as an active process, listening not as one process, but several communicative engagements, listening and language discourse functions, and listening and cognitive processing. And finally, materials development must be carefully done with attention to the principles of: relevance to learners, transferability/applicability into real life, listening tasks, and meaningful outcomes.

References

Adams, Marilyn J., and Allan Collins. 1979. A schema-theoretic view of reading. In: Freedle 1979.

Anderson, Anne, and Tony Lynch. 1988. Listening. Oxford: Oxford University Press.

Asher, James J. 1965. The strategy of the total physical response: An application to learning Russian. Modern Language Journal 3.44:291-300.

Asher, James J. 1969. The total physical response approach to second language learning. Modern Language Journal 50.2:3-17.

Asher, James J. 1977. Learning another language through actions. Los Gatos, Calif.: Sky Oaks Productions.

Austin, J.L. 1962. How to do things with words. Oxford: Clarendon Press.

Bamford, Julian. 1982a. Past and present views in teaching listening comprehension. JALT Newsletter 6.4:1, 4-5.

Belasco, Simon. 1971. The feasibility of learning a second language in an artificial unicultural situation. In: Pimsleur and Quinn 1971.

Brown, Gillian. 1986. Investigating listening comprehension in context. Applied Linguistics 7.3:284-302.

Brown, Gillian, and George Yule. 1983a. Discourse analysis. Cambridge: Cambridge University Press.

Brown, Gillian, and George Yule. 1983b. Teaching the spoken language. Cambridge: Cambridge University Press.

Brumfit, Christopher, and Keith Johnson. 1979. The communicative approach to language teaching. Oxford: Oxford University Press.

Byrnes, Heidi, and Michael Canale. 1987. Defining and developing proficiency. Lincolnville, Ill.: National Textbook Company. 15-24.

Canale, Michael, and Merrill Swain. 1980. Theoretical bases of communicative approaches to second language teaching and testing. Applied Linguistics 1.1:1-47.

Celce-Murcia, Marianne, ed. 1990. Teaching English as a second or foreign language. 2d ed. Rowley, Mass.: Newbury House.

Chaudron, Craig. 1985. Comprehension, comprehensibility, and learning in the second language classroom. Studies in Second Language Acquisition 7:216-32

Courchene, Robert, ed. 1990. Comprehension-based language teaching. Ottawa: University of Ottawa Press.

Crookes, Graham. 1989. Planning and interlanguage variation. Studies in Second Language Acquisition 11.4:367-83.

Denes, Peter, and Elliot Pinson. 1963. The speech chain. Bell Telephone Laboratories, Inc.

Faerch, Claus, and Gabriele Kasper. 1986. The role of comprehension in second language learning. Applied Linguistics 7:257-74.

Freedle, Roy O., ed. 1979. New directions in discourse processing. (Vol. 2 in the series: Advances in Discourse Processes). Norwood, N.J.: ABLEX Publishing Corp.

Gass, Susan, and Evangeline Varonis. 1985. Task variation and non-native/non-native negotiation of meaning. In: Gass and Madden. 1985. Input in second language acquisition. Rowley, Mass.: Newbury House. 149-61.

Gouin, François. 1890, 1892. L'art d'enseigner et d'étudier les langues. Paris: Librairie Fischbacher.

Halliday, Michael A.K. 1970. Language structure and language function. In: Lyons 1970.

Halliday, Michael A.K. 1978. Explorations in the functions of language. London: Edward Arnold.

Hymes, Dell. 1972. On communicative competence. In: Pride and Holmes 1972.

Johnson, Keith. 1979. Communicative approaches and communicative processes. In: Brumfit and Johnson 1979.

Krashen, Stephen. 1981. Second language acquisition and second language learning. Oxford: Pergamon Press.

Krause, Aleda C., and Bernard Susser. 1982. A bibliography of materials for teaching listening comprehension. JALT Newsletter 6.4:10-33.

Long, Michael. 1981. Input, interaction, and second language acquisition. In: H. Winitz. 1981. Native language and foreign language acquisition. Annals of the New York Academy of Sciences 379:259-78.

Long, Michael. 1983. Native speaker/non-native speaker conversation and the negotiation of meaning. Applied Linguistics 4:259-78.

Long, Michael. 1985. Input and second language acquisition theory. In: Gass and Madden 1985. Input in second language acquisition. Rowley, Mass.: Newbury House. 377-93.

Lyons, John, ed. 1970. New horizons in linguistics. Harmondsworth, England: Penguin.

Maley, Alan, and Sandra Moulding. 1979. Learning to listen. Cambridge: Cambridge University Press.

Morley, Joan. 1984. Listening and language learning in ESL. Englewood Cliffs, N.J.: Prentice-Hall.

Morley, Joan. 1990a. Listening comprehension. In: Celce-Murcia 1990.

Morley, Joan. 1990b. Theory and practice in listening comprehension. In: Courchene 1990.

Newmark, Gerald, and Edward Diller. 1964. Emphasizing the audio in the audio-lingual approach. Modern Language Journal 48.1:18-20.

Nida, Eugene. 1953. Selective listening. Language Learning: A Journal of Applied Linguistics 4.3/4:92-101.

O'Malley, J.M., A.U. Chamot, G. Stewner-Manzanares, L. Kupper, and R.P. Russo. 1985a. Learning strategies used by beginning and intermediate ESL students. Language Learning 35:21-46.

O'Malley, J.M., A.U. Chamot, G. Stewner-Manzanares, L. Kupper, and R.P. Russo. 1985b. Learning strategy applications with students of English as a second language. TESOL Quarterly 19:557-84.

O'Malley, J.M., A.U. Chamot, and L. Kupper. 1989. Listening comprehension strategies in second language acquisition. Applied Linguistics 10.4:418-37.

Oxford, Rebecca. 1985. A new taxonomy of second language learning strategies. Washington, D.C.: ERIC Clearinghouse on Languages and Linguistics.

Palmer, Harold. 1917. The scientific study and teaching of languages. Yonkers, N.Y.: World Book Company.

Pica, Teresa, Catherine Doughty, and Richard Young. 1986. Making input comprehensible: Do interactional modifications help? ITL Review of Applied Linguistics in Language Learning 72:1-25.

Pieneman, M., and M. Johnston. 1987. Factors influencing the development of second language proficiency. In: D. Nunan. 1987. Applying second language acquisition. Adelaide: National Curriculum Resource Center.

Pimsleur, Paul, and Terence Quinn, eds. 1971. The psychology of second language learning. (Papers from the Second International Congress of AILA). Cambridge: Cambridge University Press.

Postovsky, Valerian. 1970. Effects of delay in oral practice at the beginning of second language learning. Unpublished Ph.D dissertation. Berkeley: University of California.

Postovsky, Valerian. 1974. Effects of delay in oral practice at the beginning of second language learning. Modern Language Journal 58.3:229-39.

Richards, Jack C. 1983. Listening comprehension: Approach, design, procedure. TESOL Quarterly 17.2:219-39.

Richards, Jack C. 1990. The language teaching matrix. Cambridge: Cambridge University Press. (Chapter 3: "Designing instructional materials for teaching listening comprehension.")

Rivers, Wilga. 1966. Listening comprehension. Modern Language Journal 50.4:196-204.

Rivers, Wilga. 1981. Teaching foreign language skills. 2d ed. Chicago: University of Chicago Press.

Rubin, Joan. 1975. What the 'good language learner' can teach us. TESOL Quarterly 9:45-51.

Rumelhart, D. E.. 1977. Toward an interactive model of reading. In: Dornic 1977.

Searle, J. 1970. Speech acts. Cambridge, Mass.: Cambridge University Press.

Sinclair, John McH. 1984. The teaching of oral communication. Speech and Language Learning 10. Nagoya, Japan: Center for Foreign Language Education and Research, 1-11.

Stern, H.H. 1975. What can we learn from the good language learner? Canadian Modern Language Journal 31.4:304-18.

Strevens, Peter. 1985. Language learning and language teaching: Towards and integrated model. Forum lecture, LSA/TESOL Summer Institute at Georgetown University, Washington, D.C., July 16.

Strevens, Peter. 1988. Language learning and language teaching: Towards an integrated model. In: Tannen 1988.

Swain, Merrill. 1985. Communicative competence: Some roles of comprehensible input and comprehensible output in its development. In: Gass and Madden. 1985. Input in second language acquisition. Rowley, Mass.: 235-53.

Sweet, H. 1899. The practical study of languages. Reprinted. London: Oxford University Press.

Terrell, Tracy. 1977. A natural approach to the acquisition and learning of a language. Modern Language Journal 61.7:325-36.

Terrell, Tracy. 1982. The natural approach to language teaching: An update. Modern Language Journal 66.2:121-32.

Terrell, Tracy, Herbert Genzmer, Brigitte Nikolai, and Erwin Tschirner. 1988. Kontakte: A communicative approach. New York: Random House.

Ur, Penny. 1984. Teaching listening comprehension. Cambridge: Cambridge University Press.

van Ek, J.A. 1976. The threshold level for modern language learning in schools. Council of Europe, London: Longman.

Varonis, Evangeline, and Susan Gass. 1985. Non-native/non-native conversations: A model for negotiation of meaning. Applied Linguistics 6:71-90.

Weaver, Carl. 1972. Human listening: Processes and behavior. New York: Bobbs-Merrill.

Wenden, Anita, and Joan Rubin. 1987. Learner strategies in language learning. Englewood Cliffs, N.J.: Prentice-Hall Regents.

Widdowson, Henry G. 1972. The teaching of English as communication. English Language Teaching 27.1:15-19.

Widdowson, Henry G. 1978. Teaching language as communication. Oxford: Oxford University Press.

Winitz, Harris, and James Reeds. 1973. Rapid acquisition of a foreign language (German) by the avoidance of speaking. International Review of Applied Linguistics 11.4:295-315.

Winitz, Harris, ed. 1981. The comprehension approach to foreign language instruction. Rowley, Mass.: Newbury House.

Theory, practice, research, and professionalization of the field of Teaching English to Speakers of Other Languages

Richard A. Orem
Executive Director
Teachers of English to Speakers of Other Languages

In framing my remarks for this presentation, I was struck by the common concerns that are heard by various groups of professional educators in different fields of professional practice. The subtitle of this conference, 'the Interdependence of Theory, Research, and Practice,' presumes that there is actually such a synergistic relationship at work among the three components of theory, research, and practice. Yet, the concerns which continue to recur in our conversations come back to the problems of relating theory to practice and the role of research in generating sound theory and identifying good practice.

Several questions often asked are: (1) What problems need to be researched? (2) What are appropriate research strategies in investigating these problems? (3) What are the implications of research for the improvement of practice? And by practice I am referring not to the practice of research, although that is a natural beneficiary, but to the practice of language teaching and the enhancement of language acquisition. (4) How does this new knowledge get disseminated so that others will benefit?

It is important to remember that all of these questions are asked in a specific context. For most of us, that context is the institution where we work. And it is the context in which we work which heavily influences the questions we ask, the problems we choose to study, the methodologies we select, and the manner by which we disseminate that information.

These decisions are all heavily influenced by gatekeepers. Who are the gatekeepers? They are the members of department and university personnel committees who say what they will reward and not reward. They are the editor and consulting editors of professional journals who determine what topics they do and do not want covered. They are the publishers who determine what will and will not sell. And they are the professional associations and the program committees of those associations which decide what themes they will emphasize and what abstracts will make the best papers.

And anyone here who has had a promotion or tenure request denied, a manuscript returned or an abstract rejected knows of the potential, if not actual, problems in each of these systems.

Graduate programs are the common contexts for the vast majority of research currently conducted in language education, language acquisition, and language teacher education. But do graduate programs do enough to stress the relationships of theory and practice? Are graduate programs even doing a sufficient job of preparing the next generation of researchers? Gaies (1987:22) has raised such concerns by pointing out the lack of instruction in educational research, particularly in statistical analysis, at a time when "the trend in applied linguistic research has been toward more quantitative analysis and the use of increasingly elaborate research designs and more complex statistical procedures."

How does research get disseminated? Conferences and seminars, such as the Georgetown University Round Table on Languages and Linguistics and the TESOL annual convention, are two common venues for dissemination of research in second language learning. It appears from reading the roster of those presenting and attending this year's Round Table that those in attendance are by and large not classroom teachers, but university researchers and educators. There is a good representation of graduate students here, but will they become classroom teachers, or the next generation of teacher trainers and university researchers?

For the past several years at the TESOL annual convention, the demand has been for more sessions of a practical nature—workshops and demonstrations, for elementary and secondary level teachers. Even the name of the organization, *Teachers* of English to Speakers of Other Languages, would appear to emphasize the applied nature of the field. This emphasis on the applied, in turn, has resulted in an unfortunate perceived, if not actual, distancing of the researcher from the practitioner to the point where they now meet separately or not at all at a TESOL convention. If there is an interdependence of theory and practice, why aren't we more successful in integrating theory and practice when we meet? Teacher preparation programs must stress this aspect of professional development, that professionalism implies an active integration of theory and practice, by researcher and practitioner, to the point that we have neither researcher nor practitioner, but researcher/practitioners.

Currently, the fields of second language teaching and international studies in the United States are experiencing a renewal of interest. Foreign language teaching is receiving more attention in the press in response to studies of the woefully deficient knowledge of languages and geography on the part of U.S. students in general.

Along with increasing interest in foreign language teaching has come an increasing interest in and awareness of the need for expanding services to limited English proficient learners. And as this interest becomes translated into an expressed need for trained teachers, we will see increasing movement toward professionalization of the teaching of English to speakers of other languages. This movement will not likely originate in schools where the teachers work. If such movement is to occur at all, it will likely originate in the professional association in the form of sociopolitical action in the various states. Teachers, as a rule, are not social action oriented. But now may be the best time yet for ESOL teachers to take a stand and push for greater professional recognition.

Where do these three elements of theory, research, and practice interact in this process of professionalization? Where should they interact? Why don't they interact more often, and how can such interactions be promoted in teacher training programs, in classrooms, and in meetings of professional associations? Are any of these useful without the others?

Professionalizing the field of teaching English as a second language has implications for the research we conduct as well as for the practice which we are willing to approve as effective. Being a professional means, among other things, to have access to a body of knowledge which is unique, and to control access to that information.

There is a growing body of literature on the nature of professions and how they define themselves and their relationship to the society as a whole. The work of professionals is important not only because of their technical skill, but also because they define, to a great extent, the problems on which they work. As a result, they have the power to define our needs (Cervero 1989). But professionals as we know them today have existed for less than a hundred years, the concept of professionalism being basically a twentieth century concept (Houle 1980). What modern-day professionals have in common with their ancient counterparts is a certain isolation from the general population, and a resistance to change. We have created in our educational systems, for example, bureaucracies which are very resistant to change.

But change is quickly becoming a norm throughout the world as we rush headlong into the next century. As educators we must choose to take the lead to guide this change to our advantage, or we will be condemned to a role as passive objects of change, powerless in the face of events that will affect how and where we work for years to come.

Educators of LEP learners have a long history of determining what and how the learner should learn. But this is largely due to the fact that ESL teaching has been a marginal activity in relation to the educational mainstream. ESL teachers have been simply left alone, and by being left alone, they have generated a tremendous creative energy which has led to advances in the whole field of foreign language education.

Now, as we witness this field of professional practice develop, we can see even stronger forces at work to determine the how and the what. This is in stark contrast to the voluntary nature of our early history. The danger of professionalizing, in other words, is a loss of freedom to be creative. How we deal with the constraints of professionalism will determine the shape of the field into the next decade, even the next century.

There is also an assumption held by professionals that learning does not end with adolescence or with graduation, but continues throughout life. Schools and universities are only beginning to realize this and meet a need. In education, it is more likely that such needs will be met first by professional associations or employers, not by traditional schools. Schools and universities have traditionally seen their role more in pre-service than in in-service, or continuing, education. Most occupations now embrace the seriousness of continuing education, and even offer some form of certification as a credential. The U.S. has become a credentialing society. But this is also a phenomenon worldwide in education. Certificates are sought after, even certificates of attendance.

Many disciplines rely on professional associations to provide the cachet for professional practice. In other words, the professional association identifies specific standards or criteria for good practice which programs can use in evaluating teachers. Some professional associations have gone so far as to devise specific means for credentialing practitioners. We must look at what current research tells us about effective teaching and incorporate these findings in our own work. Without ignoring the content of our field, we must also focus on the process of teaching that subject matter. Freeman (1989:27) argues that "language teacher education has become fragmented, we have ignored the actual act or process of teaching while focussing on important but ancillary areas such as applied linguistics, methodology, or language acquisition."

In TESOL it would appear that the Teacher Education Interest Section, together with the Standing Committee on Professional Concerns, could be commissioned to study how language teacher education is affected by TESOL preparation programs. The Research Interest Section can likewise be commissioned to develop a research agenda for the association in the 1990s. This research agenda may include research into teacher education, or it may be research into language learning. But in either case it should identify research which will inform practice.

An appropriate vehicle for disseminating such research would be appropriately the new quarterly publication which TESOL will begin publishing in 1991, a journal for practitioners by practitioners.

The fact that we in TESOL have not paid sufficient attention to developing a conceptual framework for much that we do has not gone unnoticed. Pennycook (1989:589) argued that "both an historical analysis and an investigation of its current use (method) reveal little conceptual coherence." This is an indictment of the whole field, but easily explained by noting our marginal nature over time.

One aspect of most teacher training programs which has received more attention lately in connection with questions raised about relevance is the teaching practicum. Richards and Crookes (1988:24) concluded that although the importance of the experience provided in a teaching practicum is increasingly recognized in U.S. TESOL preparation programs, we still possess little information on the effectiveness of current practicum practices.

This balance of the practical and the theoretical is not a new nemesis for teacher preparation programs. More than ten years ago, a survey of TESOL preparation programs found in the 1978 edition of the TESOL Directory of Teacher Preparation Programs was conducted in part to help a new program develop its own conceptual framework. The survey asked respondents to indicate in priority order courses that need to be included in any ESOL teacher preparation program. At the very top of everyone's list was a course in the nature of language. Second on almost everyone's list was a supervised practicum (also called student teaching, or internship). Yet an examination of the requirements of these programs revealed that, while all programs required a course in linguistics, fewer than 25% actually required such a practicum. More recent studies have shown an improvement in this aspect. But the still limited role of the practicum experience in graduate teacher education reveals an ongoing debate within such programs of the relative merits of theory and practice.

But if the practicum has not been fully accepted as a required part of a teacher preparation program, concerns should also be raised about the quality of instruction in educational research. According to a recent survey (Ediger, Lazaraton, and Riggenbach 1986) of more than 100 ESL professionals, most of whom were university professors of applied linguistics, little training in basic educational research design is being provided to the next generation of ESOL professionals in graduate programs. Only about 25% of those surveyed felt comfortable giving advice about statistics to others.

Bowers (1986:394) has observed that "the gap between theory and practice, wider now than it has ever been, shows signs of continuing to grow, drawing experiences and rationale apart. There are aims for us to continue to pursue: to keep theory and practice in joint harness." Bowers continues by stating a need for a "theory of practice" (407) which would help the practitioner determine what works and doesn't work without having to experiment at the expense of the learner.

What then should be the goals of the TESOL profession? Given the constraints within which we work, I would suggest at least six goals:

1. To enhance the professional image of those who teach English to speakers of other languages; this should be a goal worldwide. Teachers in many Western societies are viewed as second class citizens. They need to be made to feel better about themselves and about the work they do. Gaies (1987:21) has stated that "the single most visible goal we have worked for has been the attainment of professional status."

2. To empower the classroom teacher. This is a liberating concept. The purpose is to enable classroom teachers to make decisions based on accurate information, about the subject matter, about the processes of education and learning, and about the learner.

3. To facilitate interaction among its members. This can be accomplished through bringing members together, either physically, as at meetings and conferences, or electronically and by other means available to us through the advancement of technology and the implementation of that technology in different forms of distance education.

4. To disseminate a knowledge base informed by research. This can be done through publications, either alone or in collaboration with other agencies.

5. To set standards for the effective teaching of English to speakers of other languages. This may be the most difficult goal to accomplish, because it assumes that a group with diverse experiences and points of view can agree on what makes for good teaching. Yet in the 1990s it may be the most visible goal of the profession given the demands for professional recognition expressed by the membership.

6. To collaborate effectively with other educators with similar concerns and interests. We don't, or at least we shouldn't, work in isolation from other subject matter specialists. To integrate theory and practice effectively, researcher must work with practitioner in a partnership that is mutually beneficial. Professional associations will continue to play a major role in the continuing development of future generations of ESOL professionals (educators and researchers) through the 1990s. Worldwide demand for English language instruction will continue to put pressures on traditional and nontraditional delivery systems for pre-service and continuing teacher education. Innovation will require collaboration of researcher and practitioner, of teacher and learner. The path toward our goal of increasing professionalism is not without its barriers. The next ten years will be exciting years filled with opportunities and innovation in English language teaching, and collaboration will be the key to our success at achieving the professional status we deserve.

References

Bowers, Roger. 1986. English in the world: Aims and achievements in English language teaching. TESOL Quarterly 20(3):393-410.

Cervero, Ronald M. 1989. Continuing education for the professions. In: S. Merriam and P. Cunningham, eds. Handbook of adult and continuing education. San Francisco: Jossey-Bass. 513-24.

Ediger, A., A. Lazaraton, and H. Riggenbach. 1986. Forming a discipline: How applied linguists use statistics. Paper presented at the 20th Annual TESOL Convention, Anaheim, California.

Freeman, Donald. 1989. Teacher training, development, and decision making: A model of teaching and related strategies for language teacher education. TESOL Quarterly 23(1):27-45.

Gaies, Stephen J. 1987. Research in TESOL: Romance, precision, and reality. TESOL Newsletter 21(2):21-23.

Houle, Cyril O. 1980. Continuing learning in the professions. San Francisco: Jossey-Bass.

Pennycook, Alastair. 1989. The concept of method, interested knowledge, and the politics of language teaching. TESOL Quarterly 23(4):589-618.

Richards, Jack C., and Graham Crookes. 1988. The Practicum in TESOL. TESOL Quarterly 22(1):9-27.

Analyzing register variation among written texts: A second language teaching practice*

Jeff Connor-Linton
Georgetown University

0 Introduction. Much of the research on teaching English as a second language affirms the importance of teaching students communicative as well as grammatical competence. However, most modern ESL teaching methods concentrate on conversational competence; fewer emphasize written communicative competence. In addition, most ESL teaching methods mediate between research and the students; students are the intended beneficiaries and often the subjects of research, but rarely participate actively in the research process. This paper proposes a practice for teaching the structure and conventions of written English to speakers of other languages which incorporates analysis of register variation across written texts into the second language classroom. The practice encourages close involvement with differing texts (through transcription and quantitative analysis), a focus on the relation between linguistic form, context and function, and student interaction within their zones of proximal development (Vygotsky 1978). The proposed practice blends theory, practice, and research together in the classroom, with second language learners as researchers, subjects, and beneficiaries.

The paper reports on a project, inspired by Heath (1983), conducted by ESL students in a freshman composition class as a prototype of the practice. Briefly, the students analyzed variation in use of a number of linguistic features across a set of texts representing arguments in several different contexts. The students tried to account for variation in the frequency and use of features across the texts in terms of the demands of the communicative context, especially the participation structure, and the ways the features functioned to meet those contextual demands. They reported their

---

* An earlier version of this paper was presented at the Second Annual Conference on Pragmatics and Language Learning, Champaign-Urbana, April 8-9 and appears in *Issues and Developments in English and Applied Linguistics* 4:37-49.

I would like to thank the students who participated in this project for their effort and willingness to try something new.

results—descriptive and interpretive—to the rest of the class. Subsequently, the students applied their research to their own writing, explaining and justifying their use of these features in several of their own essays. Excerpts from students' analyses are presented to demonstrate the surprising sophistication and relevance of their findings to the learning (and teaching) of writing.

Finally, the paper discusses the implications of the project for teaching and learning literacy in a second language. Encouraging second language learners to participate actively in the task of making sense of their second language—especially its norms of appropriate use—promotes the kind of awareness of the potential uses of language that is the aim of more traditional rhetorical approaches to teaching writing. The practice focuses on a process of text construction and analysis and gives second language learners a tool for figuring out for themselves, in a wide variety of situations, how to use their second language.

1 Written communicative competence. A major emphasis of many modern second language teaching methods is communicative competence—the ways in which linguistic forms may be used appropriately, what it 'means' to use a particular linguistic form in a particular situation. That is, many second language teaching methods emphasize the important role of context in conveying and interpreting meaning and the pragmatic functions of particular linguistic forms to mark particular contextual information. Culturally inappropriate language use—producing linguistic forms which mark or 'cue' inappropriate contextual information—is recognized as a source of cross-cultural miscommunication, or crosstalk (Gumperz 1982a, b). However, most second language teaching methods emphasize the pragmatic or contextualizing functions of particular linguistic forms in spoken, rather than written, communication.

The pragmatic functions of linguistic forms for conveying and interpreting contextual information are just as important to communicative success (if not more so) in writing and reading as in speaking and hearing. While some of the channels for conveying contextual information in face-to-face interaction are not available in written communication, written communication retains several very important resources for conveying and interpreting contextual information, especially ways of marking information about the writer's construction of the relation between herself and her interlocutors, and between herself and her utterance (Silverstein 1976). The writer, as much as (if not more than) the speaker, communicates by locating herself in relation to the participants and referents of the discourse (Biber 1985, 1988, Connor-Linton 1988, Urban 1988).

One recent method for ascertaining the pragmatic or context-marking functions of linguistic features in a conversation or text is the 'multifeature/multidimension' approach to language variation developed by Biber (1988). Multifeature analysis of variation in language use is based on two theoretical principles: multifunctionality and cooccurrence of individual linguistic forms. First, a given linguistic form performs multiple functions, simultaneously communicating information on several levels of meaning, including the levels of reference, speech acts, and the activity-specific roles and more permanent social identities of participants. Speakers and writers do not simply construct contexts for their utterances or texts out of thin air. The linguistic forms a speaker/writer chooses are constrained first by her culturally constrained perception of which aspects of the context are salient and relevant (that is, which aspects of the context need and are appropriate to be marked) and second by her knowledge of which forms are functionally and conventionally associated with and therefore appropriate to marking those aspects of the context. Both of these kinds of knowledge are part of the speaker/writer's communicative competence (Hymes 1972).

The speaker/writer does not just passively recognize and mark some 'objective' preexisting context for her utterance or text and respond to its demands; she actively constructs that context by using a particular set of linguistic forms. Her linguistic choices help to constitute the context of her utterance or text, and in doing so they display her assumptions about various aspects of that context, especially her own role in it and the roles of her audience, and their respective relations to discourse referents. For example, Stubbs (1983:29) points out that "roles do not exist in the abstract. They have to be realized and sustained through particular discourse strategies." A speaker/writer makes a claim to a role by acting in that capacity; she signals her assumption of that role—and her expectations about others' behavior toward her in that role—through the kinds of acts she performs and the kind of language she uses to perform them. The language a speaker/writer uses, then, serves to mark—for both the interlocutor and the analyst—how the speaker/writer sees and constructs herself and her addressee(s).

As Stubbs' comment on role suggests, context is not constructed by one linguistic form at a time. Because linguistic forms are multifunctional (that is, can be used to mark a number of aspects of meaning), the use of one linguistic form alone does not mark a particular aspect of context all by itself. The specific contextual information a given form conveys in a particular instance of use is communicated in concert with the other forms with which it cooccurs because these features meet similar communicative demands and thereby mark similar aspects of the context. This indirectly marked contextual information—about how we present ourselves, how we perceive our addressees, our task and goals, and the world around us—is just as much a part of the meaning of our utterance or text as the propositions we produce and is, in fact, crucial to accurate communication and interpretation of its other propositional and speech act layers of meaning.

Much of the research on the pragmatic or contextualizing functions of linguistic features in writing has been done under the banner of 'stylistics' (Fowler and Kress 1979, Leech and Short 1981, Bailey 1979, Morton and Levison 1966) and has primarily taken as its subject 'literary' texts. Student expository writing, on the other hand, has been analyzed from a variety of other theoretical perspectives, and these analyses have often proposed ways to change the way students write. But the vast majority of research on student writing has created barriers between students and the analysis of their own writing behavior. This research (and much of its classroom application) does not, I think, give enough credit to students' ability to analyze their own—and others'—uses of language. Students are usually passive subjects of writing research; either 'normal' class assignments are taken for the researcher's database or a special writing task is assigned. Students are rarely invited to join in the analysis of their own writing, and rarely experience the results of those analyses directly.

Recent research has demonstrated the ability of second language learners to analyze specific pragmatic or context-marking functions of features of the target language and directly apply the results of those analyses to their own use of the target language to improve their communicative success. For example, Shirley Brice Heath, during a 1988 lecture at the University of Southern California, spoke of a high school ESL class which, using ethnographic methods, analyzed the language used in service encounters. These teenagers taped, transcribed, and analyzed various aspects of service encounters, and noticed, for example, that native speakers of English pause between phrases and clauses and not within them. They concluded that the placement of pauses at syntactic boundaries contributed to fluency in English, implemented these strategies in their own speech, and thereby improved the success of their own interactions in English.

Much of the communicative trouble ESL students experience, especially in their writing, has as much to do with issues of communicative, stylistic competence and register variation as with issues of grammar and essay structure; in fact, very often learning the appropriate form with which to perform a particular function in a particular context solves a related grammatical or structural problem in a student's writing, especially those related to the author's epistemological stance toward her own sentences (and their referents) and social stance toward her readers (Scollon and Scollon 1981).

This paper discusses a project in which analysis of register variation and the context-marking functions of a variety of linguistic features was incorporated into a second language writing classroom. Students identified and measured the frequency of occurrence of several sets of lexical and syntactic features which previous research (Quirk et al. 1972, Quirk 1985) has demonstrated to perform the functions of indicating how the writer/speaker structures the relations between herself, her interlocutor(s), and discourse referents and propositions. Using their quantitative evidence, students came to conclusions about the contextualizing functions of these features in verbal and written argumentation and suggested to their classmates ways to use these features more effectively in their own writing.

The report is divided into three parts. First, I summarize the project itself—what the students did and why. Next, I allow the students to speak for themselves, by offering samples of their quantitative findings and qualitative conclusions. Finally, I discuss the implications of these results for teaching and learning literacy, especially in a second language.

2 The project. Groups of four or five students in a freshman ESL composition class first analyzed variation in the frequencies and uses of nine classes of linguistic features across eight different texts, each representing argumentation in a different context. The students' goal was to account for variation in the frequency and use of features across texts in terms of the features' probable functions in meeting the demands of the communicative context, especially participation structure, and more generally, to discover some of the pragmatic functions and rhetorical uses of the features in constructing an argument. There were four groups of students, looking at the use of features commonly associated with:

(1) cohesion (subordination and coordination)
(2) reference (pronouns and nouns)
(3) persuasive effort (modals, amplifiers and emphatics, and 'mental verbs') (Biber 1988), and
(4) relative abstractness (passives and nominalizations).

Each group of students analyzed the functions of their assigned set of features in two 'model' essays (written by Albert Einstein and Lewis Thomas, respectively), in three anonymous student essays on the topic of scientific ethics, and in a one-on-one debate, a small team debate, and a large group discussion.

To create a database, students first wrote timed essays arguing the extent of scientists' ethical responsibilities. Then they debated several issues in different formats: one-on-one, two-on-two, and an open discussion of scientific ethics. These debates were recorded on audiotape; each student then transcribed a portion of the tape. The students also heuristically evaluated three anonymous timed student essays on the topic of scientific ethics from a previous year. Their evaluations indicated general agreement that one essay was quite good, another fair, and the third poor. The students discussed the implications of their consensus and made explicit the standards they used in evaluating these essays. (Evaluating other anonymous students' writing allowed more objective and critical evaluation.) This was the first step in getting students to act as editors and to increase their awareness of specific argumentative strategies. (Given enough time, it would be better, perhaps, to have the students' own qualitative evaluations generate the specific forms to be analyzed, so that forms which were most salient to students were analyzed.)

In groups, students then measured and compared the frequencies of the target features across all eight texts, trying to account for similarities and differences between, for example, spoken and written argument or good and bad writing, and to identify each feature's grammatical and contextualizing functions. That is, what sort of contextual information did the use of each feature impart in the text? Students then reported their results to the rest of the class, in spoken and written reports, emphasizing implications for effective writing. These results are excerpted in the next section.

Next, the students wrote a second in-class essay (on a new, different topic), revised it and made a log of their revisions, explaining and justifying their use of these features and making productive the receptive competence they had achieved from each other's reports. This step of the project required students to apply the strategies they had discovered to their own writing.

The method of analysis was to discern variation in the frequencies and contexts of speakers' and writers' uses of the target linguistic features and to use these comparisons as the basis for an analysis of these features' different pragmatic functions. A quantitative approach is a useful 'way in' to the data because it gives student discourse analysts something concrete to measure, as well as some concrete data for evidence and examples later on. (Another benefit of the quantitative approach is that in identifying particular classes of linguistic features, students were exposed to various aspects of English structure, including morphology and phrase and sentence structure.) I should stress that the quantitative results only raise questions; they do not, in themselves, answer questions. The students' overriding concern throughout the analysis was the advice they could give each other about the use of the features they had analyzed—in writing and in speaking. Notice that a quantitative approach requires student discourse analysts to practice argumentative writing in their reports; observations must refer to specific examples, and conclusions must rest upon the discovery and explanation of patterns of concrete evidence. That is, the practice of students analyzing language use for themselves inherently socializes them to use the argumentative discourse which is also the goal of the practice.

3 Results of the student analysis: A sample. I have excerpted several samples from their reports to represent the level of the students' register analysis. (I have also retained the students' original grammar and spelling.)

3.1 Cohesion. The group of students analyzing some of the features commonly associated with cohesion (subordination and coordination) made a number of observations. Writing instructors especially will appreciate one student's discussion of the use of coordination and subordination in good and bad student writing:

(1) In essays where there were less frequent use of subordination and coordination one trait is clear. It is hard to read and not effective in persuasion. The lack of these cohesive words causes the

essay to be abrupt. . . . The reader is left to infer what was meant and tie the ideas together.

In addition, the lack of cohesive words, especially subordination, does not allow the writer to fully develop the concept at hand. Without these words, similar ideas become distant. But more importantly, the lack of them implies that the point contained in each sentence is truly distant from the next.

This student recognized that less overt connection between clauses places more of a demand on the reader and that coordination and subordination are resources which authors can utilize to make their ideas, and the connections between them, more explicit.

Another student, while agreeing with his group partners that there was a general correlation between frequency of connectives and effective writing, recognized that too much connection was also a problem. He accounted for a very high frequency of connectives in the mediocre student essay with a fairly sophisticated theory of overlearning:

(2) As a person learns to write he is first taught to form simple sentences. Such as 'I have a sister.' and 'She wears green dresses.' As time goes on the person learns how to combine facts in sentences to make the reading easier. This is pushed for many years there after. The person then always thinks of this when he writes his essay and gradually increases the amount of connective words in his written as well as spoken language . . . This results in that the sentences contain to many facts and are hard to understand. He is then taught to form sentences with just the right amount of information so that the sentence [is] clear and the amount of connective words decreases a little.

Notice how closely this corresponds to the hypothesis of overregularization of rules in much language acquisition research (e.g. Cazden 1968).

Another student, comparing the use of connectives in spoken versus written arguments, noted first that:

(3) In one to one discussion, . . . speakers tend to speak in complete and coherent sentences. Each speaker takes his/her time to phrase his/her speech carefully because he/she does not have anyone else to help him/her out. The speaker must carry out his thought and present it to other people in a coherent and logical way.

This student found that participants in large group discussions spoke more frequently in fragments, adding on to or qualifying previous utterances so that points were not made by any single speaker but were developed by the whole group.

The same student also noted that this additive approach to directed large group discussion was served as well by speakers' frequent use of *and* and *but* to begin floor turns and compete for the floor. A speaker's use of *and* to begin his turn on the floor, she said, promises that there will be a loose, general connection between the speaker's contribution and prior utterances in the conversation, while starting a floor turn with *but* immediately establishes a contradictory relationship with the immediately preceding utterance. Another student, reviewing the transcript of the large group discussion in light of this observation, said that he could map out the speakers on both sides of the debate fairly accurately by their use of turn-initial *and* (establishing association and agreement) and *but* (marking dissociation and opposition). These observations led to a discussion of how *and* and *but* can be used in writing to structure the paper's argument and lead the reader from one perspective to the next, from pro to con and back again.

3.2 Reference. The students who analyzed the frequencies and contexts of use of pronouns and proper nouns pointed out that writers' use of *we, us,* and *ourselves* indexed different persuasive strategies, each appropriate and viable under different circumstances. One student noted that a scientist like Lewis Thomas

> (4) ... need not and should not use so many first person plural pronouns . . . [because] the essay would be supported with more personal opinions than with scientific facts. [However,] since the students are not scientists who had done some research before writing the essays, they just point out what most Americans feel about [the topic]. Therefore, the students tend to use more *we, us,* and *ourselves* in order to team up with the common people in the U.S. The students attempted to approach the readers with a different way by making the readers feel that they were on the side of the writers as they read through the essays.

This student's observation corresponds with previous research on the role of deixis in the writer's manipulation of her relation to the reader and to the topic. Urban (1986) demonstrates how Secretary of Defense Caspar Weinberger associates himself and his ideas with certain persons and dissociates himself and his argument from others through the use of pronouns. Connor-Linton (1988) shows how authors writing about nuclear arms control use pronominal reference to merge the author's and reader's perspectives and to identify the constituencies for whom they speak. The student's observation above suggests the ubiquity and salience of this rhetorical strategy in all forms of argumentative writing.

Another student noted that more frequent use of proper nouns in the articles by Albert Einstein and Lewis Thomas both reflected and helped to establish and maintain the authors' expertise and credibility:

(5) They refer to places, person, or things by proper nouns more frequently than the other texts. This makes their texts more credible, because they do not make their point through vague generalities, but refer to specific events and authorities.

3.3 Persuasion. Another group of students found that too frequent use of possibility modals (*can*, *could*, *may*, *might*) and amplifiers/emphatics (*very*, *a lot*, etc.) made the writer sound less confident—hedging and 'trying to replace real argument with flag-waving.' They noticed that the more confident-sounding, more persuasive student essay used predictives like *will* more often than the less persuasive student essays. Where the good student essay did use amplifiers and emphatics, they were integral to the sentence's meaning; in the poorer essays they were frequently superfluous 'window dressing'.

3.4 Relative abstractness. Finally, the students analyzing the use of passives and nominalizations noted that both seemed to index more planned speech events; they were more frequent in the model essays than in the timed student essays, and least frequent in spoken discussions. The students noticed that passives could be used to promote noun phrases to the beginning of a sentence to indicate the writer's focus or to emphasize the importance of a noun phrase referent. They advised their fellow students that while some passives contribute to the cohesiveness of an essay, too many passives slow the reader down, make issues of agency and responsibility unclear and, like too many nominalizations, dissipate the impact of ideas.

4 Pedagogical and linguistic implications. The main value of the students' analysis of register variation and pragmatic functions outlined above was that, whether the conclusions were original or obvious, the students actively discovered them for themselves, learning a methodology for self-instruction and improvement of communicative skills, a way to think and teach themselves about using their second language. This active involvement is a far more effective learning strategy than passive response to a teacher's comments on a draft of an essay (Krashen 1984). Consider, for example, how much more valuable observation (2) is to the student writer revising a first draft than the teacher's scrawled telegraphic comments: "Run-on sentence", "Fragment", "Connection?", "Transition needed". For the student who wrote observation (5), the analysis of pronoun and noun use was worth more than a whole semester of scribbled comments on his papers: "Vague", "Be specific", "Give examples". He made the connection between specificity and persuasiveness himself.

The students discovered the functions of linguistic forms for themselves, in their own terms, and related their discoveries to each other in their own terms; the act of self-discovery was transformed into one of public instruction. For example, the students who analyzed coordinating and subordinating forms had to formulate explicitly and make sense of their observations in order to teach them to the rest of the class in their oral report, referring to examples from the texts they had all analyzed and building a case for their 'theory' of a correspondence between connective use, function, and writing proficiency. The teaching task forced them to consider and present their observation in a different context than mere recognition requires. And the student discourse analysts conveyed their discovery to their peers *at their own level of understanding and sophistication.* In addition, the students' observations provided a well-contextualized point of departure for further discussions of writing styles and strategies and a useful point of reference for their own writing experiments and development.

The project reveals several other pedagogical benefits to be gained from incorporating pragmatic analysis into the second language writing classroom. The students' own observations point out one value of the practice: a learner discovers what is important to her at that point in her individual development. The focus is shifted from the teacher and the teacher's way of seeing writing to the students and their ways of seeing writing. The shift in focus allows student writers to look at their own writing critically and gives them some concrete tools with which to be their own editors, which can be adapted to a wide variety of communicative situations and needs. This concrete approach to revision forces student writers to consider the effect of their language choices on their readership, one of the characteristics of good writers identified by Flower and Hayes (1980). The use of language becomes a skill which can be practiced and honed. Students who analyze their own use of language demystify the process for themselves: writing teachers too frequently offer advice that sounds like magical incantation ("Be more specific", "Transition needed", "Support"); students analyzing their own use of particular linguistic forms make sense of it in their own terms.

Because students make these discoveries on their own, in their own terms, they can often relate those lessons to their classmates more understandably and effectively than the teacher can hope to do (although the attentive teacher can learn a new, more understandable vocabulary for talking about writing from her students). Register variation analysis in the second language writing classroom requires students to rely on each other, to develop strategies for using their peers in problem solving in the second language. This is a valuable lesson since throughout life it is their peers who will be their resources in all sorts of tasks, most of them using language. Teachers are a temporary resource at best.

What is remarkable about these students' observations and conclusions is their surprising sophistication, the relevance of the students' findings to the learning (and teaching) of writing, and how closely many of them correspond to previous pragmatic and sociolinguistic research. In the case of the student analyzing connectives in spoken and written discourse (3), pragmatic analysis of one feature of language led the student to recognize one example of the essentially cooperative nature of all communication, spoken and written. Her observation echoes some of the conclusions reached by Haviland (1987), Goodwin and Goodwin (1987), Ochs, Schieffelin, and Platt (1979) and others about multiparty conversation. It suggests that second language learners who have difficulty constructing utterances or arguments out of whole cloth by themselves may find it easier to participate in a group construction of meaning. This task sharing resembles that done by caregiver and child in first language acquisition and allows students to more fully work in and exploit what Vygotsky (1978) calls their "zones of proximal development," the set of cognitive tasks which they can perform only through social collaboration.

In addition to corroborating independently previous conclusions about some of the target features' distributional and functional characteristics, this correspondence suggests (a) the salience of these features' pragmatic, contextualizing functions and (b) the usefulness *to students* of register variation analysis for identifying a form's functions; they were discerned with relative ease by "amateur" discourse analysts, analyzing a nonnative language, with minimal time and guidance. (Participants in the project read only one article (Fowler and Kress 1979), containing a qualitative functional analysis of some of the linguistics features of rules and regulations, as a model for their own research and reports.) This correspondence also suggests the analytical abilities of language learners, which have so far been infrequently recognized and even less frequently exploited in language classrooms. It is a widely accepted belief in linguistic theory that members of a speech community engage in some sorts of analysis, however subconscious, in acquiring linguistic and communicative competence in the language of that speech community (Chomsky 1965, Ochs and Schieffelin 1983). The student observations presented above suggest that making these sorts of analyses conscious can improve students' communicative success.

But what do these students' observations tell us about how they learn to write in a second language? To answer that question I must first sketch in a particular view of language acquisition—that children *and adults* are socialized through their use of language, and that people's use of language both maintains and recreates a culture's social structure and world view, and that language therefore is a major source of information—for talkers and discourse analysts—about how speakers see themselves and their world.

Much recently reported research in first language acquisition, especially that done by 'sociocognitivists' like Vygotsky (1978) and Ochs and Schieffelin (1983), demonstrates that children's acquisition of language is intimately tied to their socialization into society and culture, and that cultural knowledge is inherent in and maintained by communicative competence. Much of a child's appropriate use of language requires and reflects knowledge of what Silverstein (1976) calls direct and indirect indices of social roles and relationships. These indices are constituted and communicated by the cooccurrence patterns of a wide range of linguistic features. A child learns to recognize and play these different social roles by their relatively distinct sets of cooccurrence patterns, or registers. To a great extent, children acquire knowledge through playing roles. I'd like to suggest that a major part of a speaker's communicative competence involves monitoring the relative frequencies of many features of the language used by speakers, a sort of 'probability calculus' of shifting organizations of social reality. A child's acquisition of communicative competence is, in great part, the subconscious discovery of this 'calculus'. Much of what is called communicatively competent, appropriate speech is the child demonstrating her awareness of a social contract and a shared world view, and contributing to its maintenance.

Other research, like that of Scollon and Scollon (1981) and Scribner and Cole (1981), shows that the acquisition of literacy is similarly enmeshed in social roles and relationships. People acquire literacy through particular social roles. Awareness of the social roles associated with learning to write in a society may ease and enhance the learning process.

The most interesting thing shown by the students' analyses of their own writing—the final step of the project—was the way they employed authorial voices. A particularly effective communicative strategy employed by students—when it was available to them—was playing a role. Playing a role gives the student writer a voice, a consistent register, and that register helps the student writer to organize her understanding of her topic. It guides what the writer writes about and how. This voice is often what is missing from second language speakers' utterances and writing; it is what often makes their utterances sound inappropriate to native speakers and may even contribute to cross-cultural miscommunication, or crosstalk (Gumperz 1982a, b). Students who play a situationally appropriate role—through their use of language—are more communicatively successful in their second language.

The first in-class writing topic these students were assigned was a rather general, abstract piece about the ethical responsibilities of the scientist. For the most part, students parroted the view of one or another of the articles they had read in preparing for the writing assignment, and perhaps the biggest problem in their essays was one of inconsistency: what the student thought about the issue was often irretrievably buried among various quotes, few of which were discussed. The relevance of examples was not explained, and the overall effect was one of confusion and a lack of perspective. That is, the student writer did not establish an important aspect of the context—her relations to the reader and the subject matter.

During analysis of the spoken arguments which they had taped and transcribed, students noted that they often fell into role-playing to get their line of reasoning started: "If I were a nuclear physicist, how would I sound?" In response to this, the second in-class essay assignment asked each student to pretend that s/he was the dean of students at the university, responding in the student newspaper to the announcement that one of the fraternities intended to show X-rated films once a week.

These students seem to have learned particularly quickly the register of bureaucratic authority. Not only were these essays much better than the first set (on average, grades were 50 percent higher), but many students specifically referred to matters of tone and voice in explaining their revisions. For example, one student loaded his revision with nominalizations and passives "because it sounds official." Another student changed one of her passives to an active form "because I wanted the students to know who was responsible for the decision." When asked, most of the students admitted that their main concern in writing an essay is not presenting their own opinion, but finding a position which they can develop consistently. A specific, familiar persona and its voice provide this.

Most of the students who participated in this project—and many of the ESL students entering American universities—have a pretty good grasp of the 'mechanics' of written English; they spell well, they don't write run-on sentences or fragments too often, and they *know* Western essay structure. But their writing lacks cohesion and a consistent style. What they lack is not linguistic competence per se, but communicative competence. The problem is not putting together words into a sentence or sentences into an essay, but doing so in an appropriate register or voice. The experience of the students in this project suggests that second language learners may learn easiest where they can ventriloquize a specific others' *use* of the language, where they can *play a role*. This was an important strategy in acquiring their first language, and it may be very useful in acquiring a second language. The teacher in the second language writing classroom may best serve his students by helping them to learn the various linguistic registers played by writers in the culture, and one good way of communicating such sociolinguistic information is through the kind of practice outlined here.

The experience of the students who participated in this project demonstrates the pedagogical value to second language learners of focusing on the contextualizing functions of various linguistic features. They gain a new perspective on language that is pragmatic in both the linguistic and the lay senses of the word—that it is a multifunctional tool which they use everyday, a tool which they use differently in different situations. With this new perspective, students gain a new vocabulary for talking about their use of language. They learn to view their own writing as a process and their own texts as objects of analysis, which improves self-editing skills and the ultimate quality of their writing. Perhaps most importantly, the results of this project point out the strategic importance of role-playing—that is, creating and effectively communicating relationships between the speaker/writer and her interlocutor(s) and discourse referents—in acquiring communicative competence in a second language. However, since literacy is, in many ways, a form of second language acquisition/learning (Scribner and Cole 1981), this kind of practice might also be useful in teaching native English speakers.

References

Bailey, R.W. 1979. Authorship attribution in a forensic setting. In: D.E. Ager, F.E. Knowles, and J. Smith, eds. Advances in computer-aided literary and linguistic research. Birmingham: University of Aston Press. 1-15.

Biber, D. 1985. Styles of stance: A cluster analysis of texts by adverbial use. Paper presented at NWAV 14, Georgetown University.

Biber, D. 1988. Variation across speech and writing. Cambridge: Cambridge University Press.

Cazden, C.B. 1968. The acquisition of noun and verb inflections. Child Development 39:433-48.

Chomsky, N. 1965. Aspects of the theory of syntax. Cambridge, Mass.: MIT Press.

Connor-Linton, J. 1988. Author's style and world-view in nuclear discourse: A quantitative analysis. Multilingua 7:95-132.

Flower, L., and J. Hayes. 1980. The cognition of discovery: Defining a rhetorical problem. College Composition and Communication 31:21-32.

Fowler, R., and G. Kress. 1979. Rules and regulations. In: R. Fowler, ed. Language and control. Boston: Routledge and Kegan Paul. 26-45.

Goodwin, C., and M.H. Goodwin. 1987. Concurrent operations on talk: Notes on the interactive organization of assessments. Papers in Pragmatics 1:1-54.

Gumperz, J. 1982a. Discourse strategies. New York: Cambridge University Press.

Gumperz, J., ed. 1982b. Language and social identity. Cambridge: Cambridge University Press.

Haviland, J.B. 1986. 'Con buenos chiles': Talk, targets and teasing in Zinacantan. Text 6:249-82.

Heath, S.B. 1983. Ways with words: Language, life, and work in communities and classrooms. New York: Cambridge University Press.

Hymes, D. 1972. Models of the interaction of language and social life. In: Directions in sociolinguistics: The ethnography of communication. J. Gumperz and D. Hymes, eds. New York: Holt, Rinehart and Winston. 35-71.

Krashen, S.D. 1984. Writing: Research, theory, and applications. New York: Pergamon Press.

Leech, G., and M.H. Short. 1981. Style in fiction: A linguistic introduction to English fictional prose. New York: Longman.

Morton, A.Q., and M. Levison. 1966. Some indicators of authorship in Greek prose. In: J. Leed, ed. The computer and literary style. Kent, Ohio: Kent State University Press. 141-55.

Ochs, E., and B.B. Schieffelin. 1983. Acquiring communicative competence. Boston: Routledge and Kegan Paul.

Ochs, E., B.B. Schieffelin, and M. Platt. 1979. Propositions across utterances and speakers. In: E. Ochs and B.B. Schieffelin, eds. Developmental pragmatics. New York: Academic Press. 251-68.

Quirk, R. 1985. A comprehensive grammar of the English language. London: Longman.

Quirk, R., S. Greenbaum, G. Leech, and J. Svartvik. 1972. A grammar of contemporary English. London: Longman.

Scollon, R., and S. Scollon. 1981. Narrative, literacy and face in interethnic communication. Norwood, N.J.: Ablex.

Scribner, S., and M. Cole. 1981. Unpackaging literacy. In: M.F. Whiteman, ed. Writing: The nature, development, and teaching of written communication, vol. 1: Variation in writing: Functional and linguistic-cultural differences. Hillsdale, N.J.: LEA. 71-87.

Silverstein, M. 1976. Shifters, linguistic categories, and cultural description. In: K.H. Basso and H.A. Selby, eds. Meaning in anthropology. Albuquerque: University of New Mexico Press. 11-56.

Stubbs, M. 1983. Discourse analysis: The sociolinguistic analysis of natural langauge. Chicago: University of Chicago Press.

Urban, G. 1986. Rhetoric of a war chief. In: R.J. Parmentier and G. Urban, eds. Working Papers and Proceedings of the Center for Psychosocial Studies 5.

Urban, G. 1988. The pronominal pragmatics of nuclear war discourse. Multilingua 7:67-93.
Vygotsky, L.S. 1978. Mind in society: The development of higher psychological processes. Cambridge, Mass.: Harvard University Press.

Paving the way for proficiency

Victor N. Litwinski
Foreign Service Institute

The intention here is to present a modest view from the classroom concerning the development of proficiency: more specifically, laying the foundations for the development of proficiency in a 'less commonly taught' language which is also classified as 'hard'. I am fortunate to be working at an institution (the Foreign Service Institute) where it is possible to observe cycles of student progress from S-0/R-0 through very high levels of proficiency; in certain cases reaching astonishing vocabulary and structure control, along with sophistication and effectiveness in professional contexts. This is normally achieved in training periods of 24 or 44 weeks, after which students head immediately for their posts in Eastern Europe.

I believe that some of the conclusions presented here will be valid for other languages as well. This view has been developed over more than a decade of intensive interaction with small groups of adult learners who now total more than 300.

While it is now widely accepted that one of the critical or fundamental components of foreign language courses must be comprehensible input, there is ample evidence that there are other components which are no less important for an intensive form of proficiency training and which provide indispensable ingredients for the mix which must be supplied to students to become assimilated and jell into proficiency. It is the nature of that mix that has been distilled from experience and classroom research which I would like to address here.

Ultimate student proficiency can be seen as depending to a large extent on the input and intake which takes place during what is called Phase One, the first two to three weeks of the course.

Phase One can be described as a block of deliberately diversified activities conducted during the first weeks of the 24-week and 44-week courses for groups of Polish-language students. Each of these activities addresses a point of difficulty distilled from past classroom practice as a valid and recurrent concern. These points range from perception of letters through problems of grammatical structure, concept, and communication with instructors. Phase One capitalizes on the beginning students' urge to maximize their progress by offering them specific insights into particular difficulties of Polish, into the language as a systemic whole, and into self-generated and self-monitored development of proficiency. The activities are designed to foster productive learner attitudes and self-reliance in language study by taking students through four steps of exposure to, focus on, and work on a task, and consideration of future uses for their experience in order to progress and reduce problems.

Overt traditional language teaching is minimal. Instead, 22 learner-centered presentations are used, following a booklet of 120 pages which covers the fundamentals of Polish and points of know-how for language study throughout the course. The fundamentals include key concepts, phonetics, structure, and vocabulary resources. Transfer of language skills, acquisition and learning, self-monitoring and avoidance of over-monitoring are addressed through demonstration, discussion, and practice, designed so as to create and multiply opportunities for the perception of language components, concepts, and learning strategies.

The outline of activities is listed in the Appendix. Four of the primary ones are discussed here.

1 Sorting out. A set of typical front-page news excerpts is used to enable the students to acquire their initial impressions of printed Polish. These are explored through a set of group tasks designed to deal with student observations, quite frequent misperceptions and disruptive preconceptions. Basic letter and letter-group discrimination is initiated through a cognate recognition exercise. Questions of word recognition and recall are addressed using a set of words identified by students. Learner perceptions of how words differ in form are used to establish word groupings, the need for focus on word-final changes, and the notion of the dictionary form. Students are induced to perform in English in an anxiety-free mode, viewing the language from the position of an inquisitive outsider (an advantage that soon disappears for some) with adequate resources to facilitate a daunting long-term task from the start.

The activity also aims at inducing students to begin making a clearer distinction between the known and the unknown in any text and to become responsible for what they can understand while bracketing off the unknown.

2 Sounding out. This component was designed to provide a structured, confidence-building introduction to Polish phonetics. It addresses identified points of difficulty only, while leaving a number of phonetic features unexplored overtly. Strategies of an adult native speaker dealing with the pronunciation of unknown and foreign words are elicited and reviewed with students, and item-focused and system-focused approaches to phonetics are contrasted. An illustration of the item-focused approach in English is provided which results in (re)alerting students to the unpredictability of how to pronounce grapheme combinations in portions of English words.

Students are then encouraged to take a system-focused approach and learn how to sound out any Polish word in the course of two hours. They are challenged to do so under the realistic premise that they need to order items from a menu, speaking to a monolingual waiter. They are given a copy of the complete original menu to examine briefly, then proceed to work with ten worksheets. In designing this exercise, a pool of menu words was classified into ten sets of 20 to 30 words each, each set offering a single combined point of phonetic difficulty.

3 Overview of structure. Various ways have been tested to deliver initial insights on the Slavic structure fundamentals to adult learners so as to contribute to their progress through what some students describe as "an endless flow of excruciating detail." In contrastive terms, that detail results from key points of difference between English and Polish: for example, clear-cut grammatical categories signalled by formal distinctions, inflectional changes, freer word order, verbal aspect, derivation from roots by a system of prefixes and suffixes, and the absence of auxiliary verbs and articles.

In this overview of Polish structure, clause components and basic sentence patterns are represented, using the vehicle of a model story in a block of ten slots. The presentation proceeds from the point of view of a language-less individual, first perceiving the universe and imposing on it the fundamentals of language accounting for his perceptions. The story starts as follows:

> Assuming for a moment that there is no language yet in the universe, imagine that you are crawling with a blank language-devoid mind, out of a dark cave to confront the world for the first time and make up language fit to express your immediate experiences. That language happens to be Polish.
>
> As you crawl in the dark, all of your powers of perception are suddenly focused on a swift, velvety presence that briefly smacks your face. What was it? IT, this thing that touched you? You know IT was there, but that is all you know. 'It', Polish *to*, nothing more than the focus of one's attention, is the first word to emerge.

To provides the initial category for the schema subsequently developed with increasing student participation and represented on the blackboard. Each step continues the sequence of perception, sets up an image, and elicits language to account for that perception. The language is then multiplied to report parallel observations and recorded in a shorthand version with letter symbols (S=noun, substantive, A=adjective, ADV=adverb, V=verb, O=object, S inside of O=noun in object slot).

Once the schema is established and the story developed, it is used to survey contrastive features of English and Polish. Any higher order complexities in structure are then presented as reducible to the fundamentals of a particular slot.

4 Roadmapping the verb. Just as the Case Overview (Activity 20), this activity takes the students through the complete inventory of verb forms used as clause predicates. Starting with 'thanks' and 'please' (full verb forms in Polish), and with student identification of the Polish infinitive in a bilingual text, complete paradigms are derived for all the tenses, based initially on numerical, then simply positional, reference.

Person, number, gender, tense recognition, and form selection are quickly established and markedly enhanced through visual immediacy and completeness of coverage. By including a consistent hand signal for perfective/imperfective verb selection, the entirety of the verb system can be handled even with total beginners.

The effect of Phase One on student performance during the course is as follows: smoother progress through the training period, a sense of manageability of Polish grammar, enhanced perception of word and phrase structure, ability to anticipate structure, use of self-reliant comprehension strategies, and increased clarity in communicating with instructors on structural and lexical problems.

In terms of reading and speaking proficiency, tested periodically throughout the course, many students are able to create basic sentences successfully even after the two weeks of Phase One. In terms of longer range effect, there has been a measurable increase in proficiency scores in end of training tests, rising from a previous range of approximately 2 to 2+ to a much greater instance of 2+ to 3, and even 3+ in reading.

Appendix. Polish Phase One activity list.

1. Task, tools, skills and styles
2. Sorting out
3. Samples of Polish
4. Sounding out
5. Sounding out applications
6. Overview of structure
7. Comparison with English
8. Survey of grammar
9. Being it
10. Being there--Location signals
11. Reading to use--exercise
12. Reading to use--discussion
13. Seeing chunks of texts
14. Using what you have--Accessible vocabulary
15. Using what you have--Masked vocabulary
16. Blank structure
17. Switching channels
18. Breaking the flow
19. Reading strategy
20. Case overview
21. Verb overview
22. Ten T-words
23. Review and question and answer session
24. Questionnaire

How reading and writing make you smarter, or, how smart people read and write

Stephen Krashen
University of Southern California

To explain how reading and writing make you smarter, I first have to discuss how we get smart. To do this, I present a model derived largely from some current work in cognitive psychology, Graham Wallas's *The Art of Thought*, published in 1926 (with some help from Frank Smith's *Comprehension and Learning*). According to this model, we go through five stages[1] in thinking and creating new ideas:

(1) Gathering ideas. This takes place through reading and listening, or may be the result of the entire five-stage thinking process.

(2) Preparing ideas. In order to come up with new ideas, we first have to prepare, or clarify, our current ideas and the problem we are working on. Wallas (1926:44) states: "our mind is not likely to give us a clear answer to any particular problem unless we set it a clear question." Elbow (1972:129) may be referring to the same stage when he discusses "wrestling with ideas" and "perception of a major mess" (131).

(3) Incubation. In this stage, the mind goes about solving the problem. Elbow (1972, 1981) refers to this as 'cooking'. Incubation occurs subconsciously and automatically. When given a clearly stated problem, we involuntarily attempt to solve it.

(4) Illumination. Illumination is the emergence of a new idea, the result of incubation. It is often perceived by the thinker as a sudden insight ('Eureka').

(5) Verification. Ideas that emerge from the incubation stage are 'fragile' and easily forgotten. To enter long-term memory they need to be confirmed. This happens when the thinker notes that he or she has arrived at the same idea from a different source, or when he or she discovers that someone else has the same idea, through reading or listening.

---

[1] Actually, stages 2-5 come directly from Wallas (1926), and Wallas credits Helmholz for stages 2, 3 and 4. I added stage 1.

Wallas (1926:42) points out that the five stages can overlap:

> . . . a physiologist watching an experiment, or a business man going through his morning's letters, may, at the same time be 'incubating' on a problem which he proposed to himself a few days ago, be accumulating knowledge in 'preparation' for a second problem, and be 'verifying' his conclusion on a third problem. Even in exploring the same problem, the mind may be unconsciously employed in preparing or verifying another aspect.

A very exciting hypothesis is that the five-stage process outlined here is the gateway to long-term memory and the development of new cognitive structures. In other words, we learn by solving problems, and not by deliberate study.

There is both informal and formal evidence supporting this hypothesis. I begin with the informal evidence because, in my opinion, it is much more convincing.

The Fox Hills Mall. It has been said that if Americans are not at home or at work, the third most likely place you will find them is in a shopping mall. I live near the Fox Hills Mall in Culver City, California, and my experiences in this mall lend support to the hypothesis that we learn by problem solving.

After some reflection, I have come to the conclusion that I probably know about 1,000 facts about the Fox Hills Mall (and I am sure that you know about 1,000 facts about your shopping mall). I won't list them all, just enough to make the point:

- I know where the Fox Hills Mall is (corner of Slausen and Sepulveda, underneath the world's shortest freeway). Nearby is a Shakey's Pizza and a branch of First Federal Bank.
- I know where to park at the Fox Hills Mall. There are at least 20 options for parking, and each option has its own consequences.
- I know where the telephones are (the ones in the center of the mall are usually either broken or in use; I recommend you use the ones in May Company), and I know where the bathrooms are (actually, I only know where the men's rooms are; there is one in the baby section of Penney's).
- I know a great deal about some of the stores in the mall, and practically nothing about the others. Of course, I know about the stores I have shopped in. I know how much it costs to rent a tuxedo, how to order a pizza at Round Table Pizza, where the fiction section is in two different bookstores, and whether Lenscraft will really give you a new pair of glasses in one hour.

Where did I get this encyclopedic detailed knowledge? I never studied! The manager of the mall does not give shoppers a manual describing the mall, and require them to get at least 80% correct on a test before they are allowed to shop. I got my knowledge of my mall the same way you learned about your mall—by finding a telephone, by buying things . . . by solving problems.

This is clearly the way all experts gain their detailed knowledge of their fields. Linus Pauling, I am sure, did not gain his encyclopedic knowledge of chemistry by studying flashcards.

As Frank Smith has pointed out (Smith 1988), the 'laws of learning' are irrelevant when we are involved in real problem solving: The man proposes to the woman. He doesn't ask her, five minutes later, what her answer was, claiming he forgot. When the information solves a problem, when it is relevant, one repetition is often enough.

Research evidence. Scientific evidence for the hypothesis that we learn by problem solving comes from studies of 'incidental learning'. Here are some examples of this research.

Hyde and Jenkins (1969) presented subjects with written words that were flashed for a brief amount of time, not long enough for the subjects to examine the words in detail. One group of subjects was asked to estimate the number of letters in the word (the 'count' group). A second group was asked to determine whether the letter *e* was in the word (*e-search*). A third group was asked to rate the words as to their 'pleasantness' (e.g. people would probably rate *tree* as more pleasant than *tire*). Hyde and Jenkins then surprised their subjects by asking them to recall as many of the words as they could. As you might expect, the 'pleasantness' group remembered the most words.

The pleasantness group also did just as well as a fourth group that deliberately tried to remember the words. In other words, 'incidental' learning was shown to be just as effective as 'intentional' learning, if the problem that the incidental learners are solving is interesting enough.

Wilson and Bransford (reported in Bransford 1979) did a similar study, but added another condition, the 'desert island' condition: They asked subjects to rate how important the objects denoted by the presented words (nouns) would be on a desert island. The 'desert island' subjects remembered the words better than the group that deliberately studied.

Wilson and Bransford's results are very important: They show that incidental learning can be more effective than intentional learning. In other words, they broke the intentional learning barrier.

In my opinion, it is very easy to break the intentional learning barrier. Many things we do in everyday life, many problems we solve (such as shopping in the Fox Hills Mall), are more interesting than the 'desert island' condition in Wilson and Bransford's study.[2]

We now turn to the main point of this paper: how reading and writing make you smarter. To reveal the punch line early, I am going to claim that to at least some extent, 'smart people' are people who have learned to read and write in ways that are consistent with the five-stage process. They use reading and writing, in other words, to solve problems. And in order to do this, they have had to overcome the lessons they learned in school.

Reading and cognitive development. There is little doubt that reading influences cognitive development, but surprisingly, it is difficult to find direct evidence. Ravitch and Finn (1987), in their study *What Do Our 17-Year-Olds Know?*, found that those 17-year-olds who knew more, read more: Those who lived in a richer print environment did better overall on tests of history and literature, and there was a clear relationship between amount of reported leisure reading and performance on the literature test.

Studies of 'good thinkers' also give us some reason to believe that reading makes you smarter. Good thinkers, however they are defined, read a great deal and have read a great deal. Simonton (1988:111) concludes that "omnivorous reading in childhood and adolescence correlates positively with ultimate adulthood success." Schaefer and Anastasi (1968) reported that high school students considered to be creative read more than average students, with more creative students reporting that they read over 50 books per year. Emery and Csikszentmihalyi (1982) compared 15 men of blue-collar background who became college professors with 15 men of very similar background who grew up to be blue-collar workers. The future professors lived in a much more print-rich environment and did far more reading when they were young.

It thus appears to be the case that good thinkers, as a group, read more than the general population does. After a certain point, however, the relationship between amount of reading done and thinking is less clear. Goertzel, Goertzel and Goertzel (1978) studied 300 "eminent personalities of our age" (subjects of biographies published after 1962 in the Menlo Park Library), and reported that almost half of the group were "omnivorous readers" (11). Simonton (1984) did a reanalysis of this data, however, and found only a 0.12 correlation between "achieved eminence" and amount of reading done. Van Zelst and Kerr (1951) reported a modest 0.26 correlation between number of professional journals read regularly and productivity (published papers and inventions) in a sample of scientists (age partialed out). They also reported that the relationship between reading and productivity

---

[2] Experimental evidence also suggests that problem solving is more potent for learning than additional effort or 'hard work' (Walsh and Jenkins 1971), than additional 'time on task' (Craik and Tulving 1975), than additional exposures, or repetitions of a stimulus (Bobrow and Bower 1969), and is more potent than additional reward (Craik and Tulving 1975).

resulted in a bimodal curve—some less productive scientists read a great deal. Apparently, good thinkers do read a lot, but it is possible to overread. Wallas (1926:48) was aware of this, noting that "industrious passive reading" may interfere with incubation.

What may be crucial is not simply reading a lot—but rather, reading selectively—reading what you need to read to solve the problem you are working on now. Brazerman (1985) provides support for this idea. Brazerman examined the reading habits of top physicists, and reported that they read a great deal, visiting the library frequently to keep up with current research literature. They distinguished, however, between "core" and "peripheral" reading, reading carefully only what was relevant to their interests at the time.

It may be the case that reading is only useful to us when it is relevant to a problem we are working on, when it functions as either stage 1 (gathering ideas) or stage 5 (verification). When we read selectively to solve a problem, and we go through Wallas's stages, we remember what we read. When we read material that is irrelevant, we don't remember it. This is certainly my experience. I have, it seems, nearly total recall for some articles and books I read years ago. Quite often, however, I run across an article or book on my shelf that has my underlining in it, my notes in the margin, and I have no conscious memory whatsoever of having read it, even if the book or journal is fairly recent. Whenever this happens, it is something I read because I felt I should read it, not something that related to a problem I was working on at the time.

Glueck and Jauch (1975) provide evidence that suggests that good thinkers read primarily for stage 5, not stage 1. They found that productive scientists did get some ideas from professional journals, but relied more on their own ideas and previous work as input for their thinking.

School. School tells us the opposite. School does not encourage selective reading for problem solving, but tells us that all reading is core reading, and that we should deliberately try to remember what we read. School does this by assigning a certain amount of reading for each class, and by testing us on our reading. This works against cognitive development. Consider what happens when you have a 25-page assignment to read in one evening. You read the first paragraph on the first page, and, stimulated by what you read, you get an idea: incubation takes place. Ideally, you should stop reading and write the idea down (see discussion of the role of writing in stage 4, illumination, below). But you have 24 and a half pages to go! You can't stop, or you won't finish the assignment on time.

The problem is, in other words, that incubation and illumination occur beyond our conscious control and can happen any time. When we have rigid reading assignments, new ideas, instead of being welcomed, are an annoyance. Good thinkers need to overcome the lessons they learned in school.

Writing and cognitive development. Writing makes its contribution to cognitive development in stage 2, preparation. When we write, we attempt to represent our cognitive structures, our current thoughts, on the page. The act of doing this is a powerful stimulus toward creating new cognitive structures, new ideas. In terms of Wallas's model, writing prepares our thoughts for incubation.

Growing evidence suggests that certain writing activities such as note taking, summary writing, and answering comprehension questions help learning. According to Ladas (1980:616), "the preponderance of evidence strongly favors note taking"; students who take notes during lectures typically retain more than those who do not. Similarly, several studies show that students who write summaries of what they read or hear remember more than those who do not (Doctorow, Wittrock, and Marks 1978; Bretzing and Kulhavy 1979; Peper and Meyer 1986); studies also show that answering comprehension questions is more effective in promoting learning than requiring multiple-choice responses (Anderson and Biddle 1975, cited in Langer and Applebee 1987). In these studies, however, the full benefit of writing is not tapped, since real problem solving is typically not involved.

In a series of studies, Langer and Applebee (1987) came closer to showing the impact of writing on thinking. Their third study is, in my view, the most revealing. Ninth and eleventh graders were asked to read two social studies passages. One group simply read the passages (READ & STUDY), another answered comprehension questions, another wrote a summary of each passage, and another wrote an essay that required them to "reformulate and extend" the material from the passage (104).

Subjects were given a variety of tests, including a "topic knowledge" test developed by Langer. In this test, subjects were asked to provide written associations to concepts selected from the passages they read, and their responses were scored for both amount of knowledge and organization (117). The topic knowledge test was given the day after the reading and again five days later.

The results for passage 1 (Table 1, Langer and Applebee's Table 20) appear to be contrary to the hypothesis that writing leads to more learning. Those who simply read the text and did not write (READ & STUDY) did just as well as those who wrote essays, and nearly as well as the comprehension question and summary groups. Langer and Applebee point out, however, that passage 1 was fairly easy to understand. Passage 2 was harder, and the results were different. On passage 2, essay writers did the best, and the read and study group actually did worse than those who didn't read the passage at all (control group). These results suggest that writing, especially essay writing, works best when problem solving is involved. As Langer and Applebee conclude, "if content is familiar and relationships are well-understood, writing may have no major effect at all" (131).[3]

Table 1. Results of "topic knowledge" test.[4]

	CONTROL	READ & STUDY	COMPREHENSION QUESTION	SUMMARY	ESSAY
PASSAGE 1 CONCEPTS					
Day 2	4.3	7.5	8.2	8.4	7.3
Day 6	4.7	7.6	7.8	6.4	7.4
PASSAGE 2 CONCEPTS					
Day 2	4.9	3.7	9.4	7.3	12.1
Day 6	4.7	3.7	9.2	6.3	11.8

Even the essay written in response to the second passage does not reveal the full power of writing, however. Subjects were given only 20 minutes to write the essay, and the topic was assigned. We would get a better picture of what writing can do if we examine real writing, done by real writers, solving real problems that are important to them. The framework presented here predicts that this kind of writing results in exceptional learning, both of new concepts and new facts.

Some evidence that appears to support this prediction comes from studies of scientific and artistic achievement. It is well established that good thinkers produce a great deal: "Voluminous productivity is the rule and not the exception among the individuals who have made some noteworthy contribution" (Barron, cited in Simonton 1988:60).

Simonton (1988:60) provides some striking examples: "Darwin could claim 119 publications at the close of his career, Einstein 248, and, in psychology Galton 227, Binet 277, James 307, Freud 330 and Maslow 165. . . " Simonton also reports (84) that correlations between total productivity and

[3] Results of think-aloud protocol analysis done with eight subjects revealed that those who answered comprehension questions simply "searched the passage for the correct response, copied it . . . and never rethought that response or returned to it to change an answer . . ." (121). Summary writers searched for more relationships than did those who answered comprehension questions, but tended to maintain the temporal order of the text in their summary. Essay writers, however, used the text "to corroborate rather than find the ideas they wanted to write about" (121), thus using reading for stage 5, verification. Langer and Applebee also reported that while essay writers "dealt directly with a smaller proportion of the content in the original passage, they worked more extensively with the information they did use." Results of Langer and Applebee's second study showed that essay writers paid more attention to "generating, integrating, and evaluating the ideas they were considering . . ." (98) and "engaged in more complex thought" (101).

[4] From Langer and Applebee 1987:129.

citation counts range from 0.47 to 0.76 and provides additional data showing that quality and quantity of work are related. Is this also evidence that writing makes you smarter?

There are some problems with this hypothesis. An obvious one is that good thinkers are typically recognized as good thinkers early in their careers, before producing much for public view. It may be the case, however, that these good thinkers wrote a great deal privately before their work was known.

Another problem is the common perception that good thinkers do their best work when they are young. Simonton (1984:94-99), however, reports that quantity of work declines only slightly with age, and quality remains constant. It may be that quality actually increases with age. Simonton suggests that earlier contributions simply get more attention:

> . . . later creative offerings may not be perceived by the scientific community to be nearly as innovative as the initial milestones, yet this perception may be partly an illusion of contrast. It may be precisely because the early efforts have revolutionized the field so thoroughly that the later works, being interpreted in the new context, may seem to lack any revolutionary quality (1984:99).

Simonton notes that Einstein's general theory of relativity is "a contribution no less revolutionary than the special theory," produced ten years earlier. But the special theory "had changed the way scientists viewed the universe," making the general theory "look less momentous than it was" (100).

An aspect of the 'composing process' that appears to be particularly effective for problem solving and thinking is revision. Sommers (1980) has confirmed that experienced writers understand that their early drafts are tentative, and that as they go from draft to draft they come up with new ideas. Average and remedial writers don't know this. They think that all of their ideas are in their outline or first draft, and regard revision as simply making a neater version of the first draft. They do not know that in writing, "meaning is not what you start out with but what you end up with" (Elbow 1973).[5]

Some good advice. We can supplement the empirical evidence on the impact of writing on thinking with some advice offered by Elbow and Wallas.

---

[5] Not all creators engage in extensive revision, however. Mozart remarked that: "When I proceed to write down my ideas, I take out of the bag of my memory, if I may use that phrase, what has been previously collected into it . . . for this reason the committing to paper is done quickly enough, for everything is . . . already finished; and it rarely differs on paper from what it was in my imagination" (from Vernon 1970:55-56). Tchaikovsky, on the other hand, revised a great deal, but his efforts were largely directed at conforming to standard musical form. His musical thoughts always appeared "exactly as you heard it," but later, "what has been set down in a moment of ardour must now be critically examined, improved, extended, or condensed, as the form requires" (Vernon 1970:59).

Elbow (1981) discusses the value of writing for stage 2, preparation. He advises writers to start writing before gathering data, noting that the writing itself will encourage incubation:

> . . . if there's something you know you have to write, it pays to start it as early as you can. . . . Having done this, you'll find that many extraneous events during the next few days or weeks will trigger new thinking about your topic (1981:354).[6]

Wallas (1926) makes a similar point. If you are writing, for example, part 2 of a four-part paper or report, and you get an idea that belongs in part 4, Wallas advises you to write this "fringe-thought" down:

> Sometimes the mere fact of writing the fringe-thought down seems to set the subconscious mind to work on it; and the thought reappears at the end of the week furthur developed, and accompanied by an indication of its place in the main problem on which one is engaged . . . thoughts which first appeared to be scattered and unconnected will often tend to grow out towards each other and to form new and unexpected connections (1926:84).

In other words, by the time you get to part 4, incubation will have taken place.

Until now, I have been discussing the role of writing in stage 2, preparation. Wallas points out that writing is also valuable in stage 4, illumination. When a new idea first occurs to a thinker, before it is verified it is fragile, and should be recorded:

> In modern life, the range of observations and memory which may start a new thought-train is so vast that it is almost incredibly easy to forget some thought and never again pick up the train which led to it. The story may be true which tells of the man who had so brilliant an idea that he went into his garden to thank God for it, found on rising to his knees that he had forgotten it, and never recalled it (85).

---

[6] Elbow (1981:64) also points out that early writing also helps writers overcome a common problem: "The more research you do, the more impossible it is to start writing. You already have so much material . . . that you can't find a place to start, you can't find a beginning to grab hold of in that tangled ball of string . . . Writing first thoughts or prejudices or an instant version keeps you from falling into this research paralysis. Have the sense to realize it's easier to write now when you know less. You can then use subsequent research to check your thinking and to revise your writing to any level of sophistication that you wish. If you do write first thoughts or prejudices or an instant version . . . you will be able to get much more out of any reading and research you have to do for your paper."

School. School teaches us the opposite. School teaches us that we write to display what we already know, not to discover new ideas. In-class essays and essay exams that need to be done, start to finish, in one class period, actually penalize students for coming up with new ideas while writing.

Recall your history class in high school. Your sit-down exam question was to give three reasons for the start of World War II. You thought of three reasons and began to write. Midway through your second reason, stimulated by your writing, incubation and illumination took place, and you thought of three better, more valid reasons for the start of World War II. You look at the clock, however, and see that you have only ten minutes left. You have to suppress your new ideas and finish writing out the original three reasons, or you will fail the exam.

This kind of thing happens in school not once, but thousands of times, and students learn that writing functions merely to show what they already know. Once again, good thinkers need to overcome the lessons they learned in school.[7]

Conclusions. I have argued elsewhere that reading is the primary source of our competence in writing style and grammar (Krashen 1984) as well as vocabulary and spelling (Krashen 1989). Figure 1 attempts to combine these hypotheses with the hypotheses presented in this paper. What remains to be discussed is what goes to the left of Reading and Writing in Figure 1: what we should do in class. Certainly, we need to encourage a great deal of free reading. Reading stimulates language development, and makes a significant contribution to cognitive development.

But what do we read about in school, what do we write about, what do we discuss? Smith (1988) suggests the answer: "Enterprises." Enterprises are problems—real, not realistic, problems that students genuinely want to solve, problems that naturally entail reading, writing and discussion (see footnote 7).

---

[7] Some may argue that since students will be forced to do timed writing later on, they should get practice in doing it in school. This argument does not hold, in my view. In the real world, writing under extreme time pressure is rare. Usually, only journalists have to do it. Moreover, even if writing under time pressure is demanded, the way to develop strategies for doing it is, I suspect, through plenty of motivated reading (for the acquisition of style; Krashen 1984) and untimed writing that is aimed at real problem solving.

The focus of this paper is on reading and writing, but I do not mean to discount the value of oral language for problem solving. There is good reason to believe that discussion can serve problem solving very well. We can get new ideas in discussion (stage 1), verify our ideas (stage 5), and, as Elbow (1973:49) points out, we can also prepare ideas for incubation in discussion:

> If you are stuck writing or trying to figure something out, there is nothing better than finding one person, or more, to talk to. If they don't agree or have trouble understanding, so much the better—so long as their minds are not closed. This explains what happens to me and many others countless times; I write a paper; it's not very good; I discuss it with someone; after fifteen minutes of back-and-forth I say something in response to a question or argument of his and he says, "But why didn't you say that? That's good. That's clear."

Figure 1.

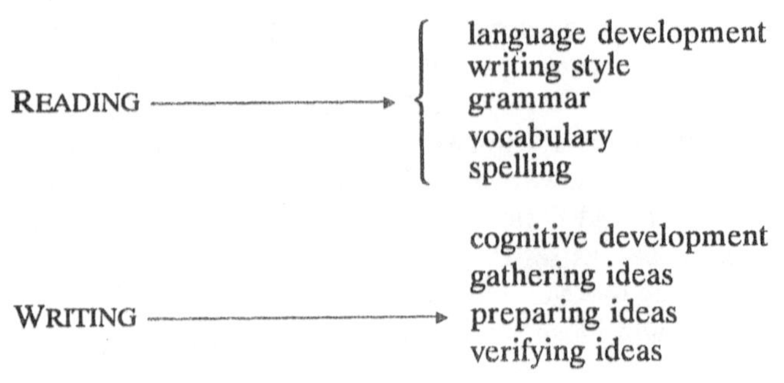

Finding the right enterprises is, in my view, a major goal of the teaching profession. Enterprises may include a chemistry class project in which students analyze the water in the community (and publish the results in the local newspaper), writing a history of the community that will become the official history and be on public record, running a small business (and keeping the profits), and writing book reviews that remain in the school library permanently for student use, rather than writing book reports.

Figure 2 expands Figure 1, adding enterprises and free reading. An important characteristic of Figure 2 is that the arrow goes from left to right, not from right to left. As Smith (1988) has pointed out, we have confused cause and effect in education. We do not learn parts of language and 'facts' so that we can eventually read and work on problems. We read for interest and pleasure and we engage in problem solving, real enterprises; language acquisition and intellectual development occur as a result.

Figure 2.

Obstacles. If we are going to use enterprises in school, we face tremendous obstacles. The major obstacle is that most people, the professionals as well as the public, have a view of learning that is quite different from the one presented here.

Danskin and Burnett's (1952) article, "Study techniques of those superior students," illustrates the point of view of some professionals. Danskin and Burnett analyzed the study habits of 37 university students. Every student in their sample was an excellent student, ranking in the top 12 of the class.

Danksin and Burnett were quite disappointed with these students' study habits. Contrary to what is advised in study-skill courses and books, 81% of the students waited until the last minute to study before tests, and only 8% attempted to guess the questions on the test. While most study-skills books recommend that students study in a hard chair, 41% of this sample said they studied in an easy chair or in bed, while 14% said they didn't care where they studied. While most study-skills books recommend that students carefully schedule their time, 48% of this sample said they studied when they had the time, and only 11% said they had a schedule.

In the face of this contradictory data, Danskin and Burnett, undaunted, concluded that these students, even though they were successful, could use a good course in study skills!

According to the framework presented here, Danskin and Burnett's results confirm that "study skills" are not crucial. Far more important than how students schedule their day, when they study, and what kind of chair they sit in, is what they focus on mentally—whether or not they are involved in real problem solving. This was confirmed by Bloom (1963), who studied former graduate students at the University of Chicago who finished their Ph.D.s and went on to successful research careers. Bloom reported that one characteristic of these successful students was an involvement with problem solving during their graduate school careers, a "preoccupation with problems rather than with the subject matter of courses . . . the relatively complete acceptance of the role of research worker and scholar (rather than the role of student) . . ." (257-58).

The public seems to equate reading and writing with study, not problem solving. (Perhaps they get this attitude from TV; Captain Kirk and Mr. Spock solved their problems by discussion and by action, not reading and writing.) I see evidence of this all the time. I do a fair amount of reading and writing in public, on airplanes, while waiting in offices, etc. Occasionally, a friendly person will see me working, or just see my books and notebook, and ask: "Are you studying for a test?"[8]

References

Arnold, L. 1964. Writer's cramp and eyestrain—are they paying off? English Journal 53:10-15.

---

[8] Or, more recently: "Are you in law school?"

Bloom, B. 1963. Report on creativity research by the examiner's office of the University of Chicago. In: C. Taylor and F. Barron, eds. Scientific creativity. New York: Wiley. 251-64.

Bransford, J. 1979. Human cognition: Learning, understanding and remembering. Belmont, Calif.: Wadsworth.

Brazerman, C. 1985. Physicists readings physics: Schema-laden purposes and purpose-laden schema. Written Communication 2:3-43.

Bretzing, B., and R. Kulhavy. 1979. Notetaking and depth of processing. Contemporary Educational Psychology 4:145-53.

Craik, F., and E. Tulving. 1975. Depth of processing and the retention of words in episodic memory. Journal of Experimental Psychology: General 104:268-94.

Danskin, D., and C. Burnett. 1952. Study techniques of those superior students. Personnel and Guidance Journal 31:181-86.

Doctorow, M., M. Wittrock, and C. Marks. 1978. Generative processes in reading comprehension. Journal of Educational Psychology 70:109-18.

Elbow, P. 1972. Writing without teachers. New York: Oxford University Press.

Elbow, P. 1981. Writing with power. New York: Oxford University Press.

Emery, C., and M. Czikszentimihalyi. 1982. The socialization effects of cultural role models in ontogenetic development and upward mobility. Child Psychiatry and Human Development 12:3-19.

Glueck, W., and L. Jauch. 1975. Sources of research ideas among productive scholars. Journal of Higher Education 46:103-14.

Goertzel, M., V. Goertzel, and T. Goertzel. 1978. Three hundred eminent personalities. San Francisco: Jossy-Bass.

Hyde, T., and J. Jenkins. 1969. Differential effects of incidental tasks on the organization of recall of a list of highly associated words. Journal of Experimental Psychology 82:472-81.

Krashen, S. 1984. Writing: Research, theory and applications. New York: Prentice-Hall.

Krashen, S. 1989. We acquire vocabulary and spelling from reading: Additional evidence for the input hypothesis. Modern Language Journal 73:440-64.

Ladas, H. 1980. Summarizing research: A case study. Review of Educational Research 50:597-624.

Langer, J., and A. Applebee. 1987. How writing shapes thinking. Urbana, Ill.: National Council of Teachers of English.

Peper, R., and R. Mayer. 1986. Generative effects of note-taking during science lectures. Journal of Educational Psychology 78:34-38.

Ravitch, D., and C. Finn. 1987. What do our 17-year-olds know? New York: Harper and Row.

Schaefer, C., and A. Anastasi. 1968. A biographical inventory for identifying creativity in adolescent boys. Journal of Applied Psychology 58:42-48.

Simonton, D. 1984. Genius, creativity, and leadership. Cambridge: Harvard University Press.

Simonton, D. 1988. Scientific genius: A psychology of science. Cambridge: Harvard University Press.

Smith, F. 1975. Comprehension and learning. New York: Holt Rinehart Winston.

Smith, F. 1988. Joining the literacy club. Portsmouth, N.H.: Heinemann.

Sommers, N. 1980. Revision strategies of student writers and experienced adult writers. College Composition and Communication 31:378-88.

Van Zelst, R., and W. Kerr. 1951. Some correlates of technical and scientific productivity. Journal of Abnormal Psychology 46:470-75.

Vernon, P. 1970. Creativity. Baltimore: Penguin Books.

Wallas, G. 1926. The art of thought. London: C.A. Watts (Abridged version, 1945).

Why teach grammar?

Louis G. Alexander
Author, London, England

0 Trouble-shooting. The year 1883 was marked by an important publishing event: the appearance of *The New Guide of the Conversation in Portuguese and English* by Pedro Carolino. It appeared in Britain and America simultaneously. No less a writer than Mark Twain introduced the first American edition in the following words: "In this world of uncertainties, there is, at any rate, one thing which may be pretty confidently set down as a certainty: and that is, that this celebrated little phrase-book will never die while the English language lasts." It was Pedro who gave to the language the immortal phrase *English as she is spoke* and for that alone he deserves to be remembered.

I would like to begin with a quotation from this work, which in today's terms we would describe as a 'situational dialogue'. In this situation, the master of the house is still in bed after a night on the town. He has a visitor. The visitor is admitted by a servant, then led into the master's bedroom where the following conversation takes place. The dialogue is called *For make a visit in the morning.*

—Is your master at home?
—Yes, sir.
—Is it up?
—No, sir, he sleep yet.
—I go make that he get up.
—It come in one's? How is it, you are in bed yet?
—Yesterday at evening, I was to bed so late that I may not rising me so soon that morning.
—Well! What you done after the supper?
—We have sung, danced, laugh, and played.
—What game?
—To the picket.
—Whom I am sorry do not have know it! Who have prevailed upon?
—I had gained ten lewis (= *Louis d'or*).

—Till at what o'clock its had play one?
—Un till two o'clock after mid night.
—At what o'clock are you go to bed?
—Half pass three.
—I am no astonished if you get up so late.
—What o'clock is it?
—What o'clock you think is it?
—I think is not yet eight o'clock.
—How is that, eight o'clock! It is ten clock struck!
—It must then what I rise me quickly.
—Adieu, my dear, I leave you. If can to see you at six clock to the hotel, we swill dine togetter.
—Willingly. Good by.

This dialogue undoubtedly communicates, and with great effect; but no self-respecting teachers could keep their hands off it. But let's suppose we had to correct language like this. Where would we begin? What would our corrections consist of?

A lot of language-teaching is no more than trouble-shooting and we can broadly define four areas:

(1) Pronunciation and intonation, especially where these interfere with communication. In terms of comprehension, it is always our aim to train students to understand many different varieties of English. In terms of production, we must accept that we can never create native speakers. Our students will always betray their origins, speaking Spanglish, Danglish, Gringlish, Gerlish and Japglish with varying degrees of proficiency. The main performance criterion here is: can they be understood by other native and nonnative speakers?

(2) Functional: where we are commenting on the appropriateness of the language used. Here we are concerned with the language of social behaviour. For example, Student B holds the door open for Student A. Student A says "Thank you" and Student B replies "Please". And you, as teacher, say something like, "We wouldn't normally say anything in English. But if you did want to say something, you could say 'That's all right. It's a pleasure. Don't mention it.'"

(3) Grammatical: Pedro provides plenty of scope: "Is it up?" to refer to the master (in this dialogue). "Is he up?" because the reference is masculine. "How is it you are in bed yet?" We use *still* and *yet* to mean 'up till now', but *still* emphasizes continuity. Illustrations would follow to show uses of *still* and *yet*.

(4) Lexical: "Who have prevailed up? I had gained ten lewis." Illustrations would follow to show the differences between *prevail, gain, win* and *beat.*

It is a sad fact that most students of English are remedial cases: linguistically ailing. They come to us with their language already formed and we often have to unmake modes of communication which have become habitual and indeed, fossilized. For this reason, most of our trouble-shooting efforts are directed at grammar. The fact is, grammar is language. Whatever else we put on top of it to make it more palatable, it will always continue to be the centre of our attention. Communication most frequently breaks down when incorrect syntax and usage make language incomprehensible.

In answer to the question "What is grammar?", we can provide a narrow definition: grammar is the combination of morphology and syntax, which together make up the system of language. Or we can provide a broad one: grammar is an integral, inseparable part of the whole system of language.

No area of language arouses more passion and debate than grammar. Hate it or love it, everyone has views about it which are often expressed with great vehemence. Where language learning and teaching are concerned, we are faced with two extreme views: one states that grammar is marginal and the other that it is very important. Three questions are central if we are to resolve this conflict: (1) Why teach grammar?; (2) How should we teach it?; and (3) What do we teach?

1 Why teach grammar? We teach grammar because we can't avoid teaching it. It is an integral part of the language-learning process. Trouble-shooting, as we have just seen, is a constant factor in the classroom. Even the least conscientious teacher is unlikely to ignore the mistakes students make in their effort to communicate.

We teach grammar because the constraints of the classroom make natural acquisition almost impossible. We have to *learn* as well as *acquire* when there are only so many hours per week available; when there is little or no opportunity to use the language we are learning; when our teachers' command of English is often far from perfect. What do you do if you happen to have Pedro as your teacher, which is the case for very many learners round the world? Motivation may be high among self-improving adults, bent on increasing their pay and status, but it is desperately low among schoolchildren (that is, the majority of learners) who learn a language only because it is on the curriculum.

We teach grammar because it is part of the syllabus. There is a widely held, but erroneous view that, with the advent of communication-based syllabuses, we ditched the teaching of grammar. *The Threshold Level* is often cited as evidence of this, but in fact this famous syllabus comes with a substantial grammatical appendix. Teaching students to communicate means teaching them to do things through language and, I would add, *mastering the grammatical structures necessary to achieve that end.* Teaching 'English by formula' (the phrase-book method) has been totally discredited. It's no good being able to say "I take milk in my coffee", if you can't, by the same token, say "and my friend takes milk, too." The moment you do this you are operating the grammatical system. A recent analysis of the most widely used communication-based courses reveals that they follow the same structural progressions that were used by earlier generations of course-writers. They begin with *be*, go on to *have*, then introduce the present tenses before the perfect and past, and so on. The only difference is that they introduce a few 'communicative' modal forms early to enable students to make simple offers, requests and suggestions.

We teach grammar because it is part of awareness-raising. Some learning is unconscious and some is conscious. Grammar is part of conscious learning. The argument that native speakers don't consciously think of grammar when they speak and write (they just communicate!) is simply not true. The more demanding a communicative situation, the more heightened our awareness becomes. Children are made aware of acceptable and unacceptable varieties of language from a very early age and their first grammar teachers are their parents, who use a variety of techniques to heighten their children's awareness. If we had a deprived childhood, so that such maternal and paternal instruction was not available, we may provide it for ourselves in later life. Just think of the number of people you know who are bilingual in their mother tongue. They slip easily into the local patois when they are back home with the locals, but slip out of it just as easily when they're being socially rated. How do they do it? Through heightened awareness! If this applies to us as native speakers, think how much more it applies when we become learners of a foreign language. We constantly want to know why and how a foreign language works and the answers are to be found in its grammar.

This last point is fundamental: we teach grammar because our students expect it. They instinctively know what they need and if we don't supply it, they will seek it out for themselves. It is amazing, round the world, how many teachers have had to dilute dearly held doctrines about communication to provide straight grammar practice in response to massive student demand. Students don't like to be told that it doesn't matter if they make mistakes, because they don't like to make fools of themselves. They want to know what the correct forms and uses are, even if they know they will never get beyond a particular skills-level. The ultimate source of accuracy is *grammar.*

2 How do we teach grammar? Let us begin with what we do not do. We do not teach grammar for its own sake (the grammar-translation method). In communicative language teaching, grammar can only have a supportive role. In the past, it was the be-all and end-all of language learning. If students also learnt to communicate as a result, that was just a lucky by-product of relentless study of the grammatical syllabus. In the present, it is just the reverse. Communication is the be-all and end-all of language learning, and grammar is the by-product of this endeavour. It is taught to facilitate communication and not as the object of teaching. Above all, grammar is meaning. As Pit Corder observes, grammatical focus helps the student to learn what he learns, but it is not necessarily what he learns.

We do not devote whole lessons to grammar study. Grammar has a supportive role in all our teaching. Whole lessons devoted to grammar come dangerously near to talking about language rather than using it.

Even in its supportive role, it is not treated with the same level of intensity at all times. How we teach it depends on the kind of activity we're engaged in at a particular moment. If, for example, we are conducting a conversation class, our main concentration is on fluency. Our tolerance of grammatical error is very high: we want our students to communicate to the level of their ability and we will be reluctant to interrupt them in order to point out 'errors'. We are building up confidence, so fault-finding has a low priority. If, on the other hand, we are conducting a drill (say, practice in adding *s* to the third person present, so that our students will learn to say *he goes* instead of **he go*), we will demand 100% accuracy.

There is only one (and there only ever was one) method for teaching grammar and that is through explanation. That explanation might be direct, or induced, but explanation is the only method available. As is observed in the Kingman Report (HMSO 1988): "It is for the teacher to decide how much [grammatical] knowledge is made explicit to a pupil or a class at a given moment and how it might be done."

The essence of grammar teaching is appropriate explanation. If a young child says **You buyed this mummy*, mother has a variety of choices available to her. She may gently correct, "Not **buyed*, dear, *bought*"; she may induce the child to use *bought*, and so on. What she doesn't do is give the child a lecture on the verb system of English and the use of strong and weak forms. Many teachers are under the mistaken impression that grammatical explanations have to be 'technical'. All they have to be is appropriate. One nontechnical explanation for the use of the past tense in English (compared with the present perfect) is that we 'say when': "He arrived here *this morning*" (as opposed to "He's arrived!"). At a higher level of grammatical awareness, we may refer to adverbial time references, if this is an appropriate thing to do.

3 What do we teach? It's a fact that a lot of language use by native speakers is subjective and difficult to account for. There are no absolute rules in a language. When accounting for something (that is, when formulating a rule) we are bound to be less than 100% accurate because we can't explain all the finer shades of meaning. There is a central rule with a certain amount of blurring at the edges. What we are not allowed to do in response to a student's question is to say "That's how we say it". We have to account for language. That's partly what we're there for. So what do we teach, where grammar is concerned? The simplest answer to this question is that we teach what we know. And that's where the problems start, because what we know is often just not accurate enough. Our strategy must be to look at language from the students' point of view. This means beginning with our students' assumptions and working back to English. For example, our students may assume that a noun like *information* has a plural in English. They will be puzzled by the fact that the modal verb *could* refers to the past in a sentence like "I could run very fast when I was a boy", but refers to the future in a sentence like "I could see you tomorrow, if you're free". Why should this be so? We have to be able to answer such questions and this is something we can only do for ourselves. Why do we have to do it? Because an understanding of grammar gives us confidence. If we have confidence in ourselves, we will communicate confidence to our students. Confidence is the basis of all successful teaching and learning and indeed of any human activity.

References

Carolino, Pedro. 1855. O novo guia da conversação em portuguez e inglez. Paris.

Carolino, Pedro. 1883. The new guide of the conversation in Portuguese and English, with an introduction by Mark Twain. Boston.

Corder, S. Pit. 1973. Introducing applied linguistics. Penguin Books.

Report of the Committee of Inquiry into the Teaching of English Language, Appointed by the Secretary of State under the Chairmanship of Sir John Kingman, FRS. March, 1988. Her Majesty's Stationery Office.

van Ek, J.A. 1975. The threshold level. Strasbourg: Council of Europe.

M&Ms for language classrooms? Another look at motivation

H. Douglas Brown
San Francisco State University

H.L. Mencken once said, "For every complicated problem there is an answer that is short, simple, and wrong." In the the last two decades of research on second language acquisition, there have been numerous complicated problems that have garnered their share of short, simple, and probably wrong answers. We have yearned to see the the complexity of acquiring a second language reduced to some sweeping generalizations that hold across multiple contexts, some simple formulas for teachers, or maybe even an ultimate method. No such answers have managed to hold for much longer than brief, shining moments of hope.

One of the complicated problems of second language acquisition research which has and always will catch our interest as teachers is motivation. For two decades, research on motivation has focused on Robert Gardner's (1985, Gardner and Lambert 1972) distinction between integrative and instrumental orientations of second language learners. According to Gardner (1988) and an impressive number of research studies on the topic (see Au 1988 for a summary of studies on motivation), an integrative orientation (desire to learn a language stemming from a positive affect toward a community of its speakers) is more strongly linked to language proficiency than an instrumental orientation (desire to learn a language in order to attain certain career, educational, or financial goals).

Gardner's somewhat simple distinction between the two types of orientation is not by any means 'wrong', but it has stimulated numerous criticisms. Lukmani (1972) showed that an instrumental orientation was positively correlated with proficiency among her Marathi speaking subjects in India. John Oller's series of studies (Oller, Baca, and Vigil 1977, Oller, Hudson, and Liu 1977, Chihara and Oller 1978, Oller 1981) shed some light on methods of measuring affective and motivational variables. Graham (1984) suggested that the 'integrative' construct blurred the distinction between desire to communicate comfortably with the second speech community and desire to become a full-fledged member of that community. Hence the term 'assimilative' orientation was proposed to account for the latter. Recently, Au (1988) strongly criticized Gardner's integrative motive hypothesis as lacking generality; his article attempted to show that many of the research findings on integrative motivation are equivocal. Gardner's (1988:113) response to Au, among other things, questioned Au's contention that studies supporting the integrative motivation hypothesis are flawed with "a serious methodological weakness. . . . The general results are that integratively-motivated students *tend* to be more active in learning the language and *tend* to be more proficient in a second language." Finally, Crookes and Schmidt (1990) are reexamining the research agenda on motivation in second language learning by looking carefully at learners in language classrooms.

Perhaps because of its simplicity, the integrative/instrumental dichotomy has tempted many to believe that it captures 'everything you always wanted to know' about motivation. Motivation to learn a foreign language is, of course, much too complex to be explained through one dichotomy. It is especially problematic to do so as second languages are increasingly being learned outside of what once were closely allied cultural contexts. English as an International Language (EIL), for example, may be learned and used extensively without reference to a particular native English-speaking culture (Kachru 1988). Rather, learners become highly proficient in the language in order to carry out specific purposes and/or to communicate almost exclusively with other nonnative speakers of English.

In the face of questions about the explanatory power of the integrative/instrumental construct, I believe it is appropriate for teachers and researchers to examine the more fundamental nature of motivation. We can thereby move away from the temptation to hinge all of our motivational constructs on the much too simple distinction between 'cultural' (integrative) and 'practical' (instrumental) orientations to the second language.

Theories of motivation. Let me define *motivation* as *the extent to which you will make choices about (1) goals to pursue, and (2) the effort you will devote to that pursuit*. This definition is a synthesis of numerous definitions offered by cognitive psychologists, but strongly influenced by the work of Edward L. Deci (1975).

Depending upon your general theory of human behavior, you will interpret this definition in varying ways. Consider five possibilities:

(1) A 'behavioristic' theory (e.g. Watson 1913; Skinner 1953, 1971) stresses the role of rewards and, perhaps, punishments in motivating behavior. For Skinner—if he were willing to recognize such a mentalistic and unobservable construct—motivation would be described as "the anticipation of reinforcement." The behavioristic tradition gave us what we facetiously refer to as an 'M&M theory' of behavior, derived from the (now discarded) practice of administering M&Ms to children for manifesting desired behavior.

(2) A 'psychoanalytic' theory emphasizes subconscious processes, asserting that people's behavior is determined by a complex interaction between their subconscious 'drives' and the environment. Ausubel (1968) suggests six fundamental drives or needs underlying human behavior: exploration, manipulation, activity, stimulation, knowledge, and ego enhancement.

(3) A 'cognitive' theory (e.g. Hunt 1971) centers on the importance of people 'deciding' for themselves what to do, and therefore thought processes are of central concern.

(4) 'Humanistic' theories of behavior (e.g. Laing 1967, Maslow 1970) are somewhat less concerned with thought processes and more interested in the 'wholeness' of a person as 'inner forces' drive us to get 'in touch' with ourselves. We 'define' ourselves through making choices.

(5) Finally, 'affective' theories (e.g. McClelland 1965) assert that people develop patterns of behavior and hierarchies of responses as a result of the 'affect' associated with their behaviors. In other words, we do something because it 'feels good'.

The joy of breaking rules. In *Dead Poets Society*, we saw a classic illustration of the power of motivation in determining behavior. The boarding school, steeped in tradition and governed by intricate rules not only of behavior, but of what was acceptable for a teacher to teach, provided all the motivation necessary for its young men to 'seize the day'. The characters in the film were not unlike my own circle of youthful friends as I grew up in a boarding school in central Africa. We were immersed in a system of rules and regulations with their attendant punishments should we be so careless as to get 'caught'. Our society of rule-breakers was motivated by our intense need to get away with as much as we could. We learned how to obey rules by just barely squeaking by the letter of the law. We learned how to brush our teeth (three times daily, according to the rule) by scarcely inserting a toothbrush into the mouth for a long enough time (a few seconds) to 'count'. We learned the fine art of thirty-second showers—just enough to get a little wet—before dinner (a shower a day, the rule said). And at times we took gleeful delight in deliberately breaking numerous bedtime 'lights out' rules without being detected in our rooms.

A behavioristic theory of motivation might say that we were driven by the avoidance of aversive stimuli. However, a more powerful explanation is offered by a psychoanalytical analysis of our behavior which would focus on our need to explore, to be stimulated, and above all to manipulate the authorities who enforced the rules. A cognitive view would say we wished to make our own decisions rather than let someone else determine the course of our daily lives. Humanists would counter that we found a certain sense of wholeness in the communal bond created by our efforts to defy the system.

And an affective focus would quite simply note the joy that we all felt in thriving with minimal lip service to the powers that be.

Intrinsic and extrinsic motivation. According to Deci and others, the primary driving force in both *Dead Poets Society* and in my own boarding school community was an 'intrinsic' set of motivators within us, and not the disdained 'extrinsic' punishments that lay outside of ourselves.

Intrinsically motivated activities, says Deci (1975:23):

> . . . are ones for which there is no apparent reward except the activity itself. People seem to engage in the activities for their own sake and not because they lead to an extrinsic reward. . . . Intrinsically motivated behaviors are aimed at bringing about certain internally rewarding consequences, namely, feelings of *competence* and *self-determination.*

Extrinsically motivated behaviors, on the other hand, are carried out in anticipation of a reward from outside and beyond the self. Typical extrinsic rewards are money, prizes, 'gold stars', grades, and even certain types of positive feedback. Behaviors initiated solely to avoid aversive stimuli (punishment) are also extrinsically motivated, even though, as in the example above, numerous intrinsic benefits can ultimately accrue to those who, instead, view punishment avoidance as a challenge which can build their sense of competence and self-determination.

Why is intrinsic motivation more powerful than extrinsic? While the answer to this question would vary depending upon your general theory of motivation, some cognitive psychologists assert that human beings universally view 'incongruity' and 'uncertainty', or what Piaget (1952) would call 'disequilibrium', as motivating. In other words, we seek out a reasonable challenge. Then we initiate behaviors intended to conquer the challenging situation (Deci 1975). Incongruity is not itself motivating, but 'optimal' incongruity—or what Krashen (1985) calls 'i+1'—presents enough of a possibility of being resolved that we will 'go after' that resolution. Deci prefers to use the term 'dissonance' for incongruity that is aversive or that presents too great a challenge to warrant an attempt at a resolution.

Abraham Maslow (1970) claimed that intrinsic motivation is clearly superior to extrinsic because, according to a universal hierarchy of needs, we are ultimately motivated to achieve 'self-actualization' once numerous basic physical, safety, and belongingness needs are met. No matter what extrinsic rewards are present, we will strive for self-esteem and fulfillment.

Don't extrinsic rewards play a major role in one's motivation? Wouldn't extrinsic rewards, coupled with intrinsic motivation, enhance the intrinsic motivation? Not according to an impressive number of research studies (see Deci 1975:139) which show that the introduction of extrinsic rewards into what was initially a challenging task actually serves to *decrease* intrinsic motivation. In other words, suppose a subject is asked to solve an intrinsically interesting puzzle with no stated reward. The experimenter informs the subject part way through that there will be a monetary reward for solving the puzzle. Studies repeatedly show that intrinsic motivation wanes from that point on.

Consider the following story (Deci 1975:157-58):

> In a little Southern town where the Klan was riding again, a Jewish tailor had the temerity to open his little shop on the main street. To drive him out of the town, the Kleagle of the Klan set a gang of little ragamuffins to annoy him. Day after day they stood at the entrance of his shop. "Jew! Jew!" they hooted at him. The situation looked serious for the tailor. He took the matter so much to heart that he began to brood and spent sleepless nights over it. Finally, out of desperation he evolved a plan.
>
> The following day, when the little hoodlums came to jeer at him, he came to the door and said to them, "From today on any boy who calls me 'Jew' will get a dime from me." Then he put his hand in his pocket and gave each boy a dime.
>
> Delighted with their booty, the boys came back the following day and began to shrill, "Jew! Jew!" The tailor came out smiling. He put his hand into his pocket and gave each of the boys a nickel, saying, "A dime is too much—I can only afford a nickel today." The boys went away satisfied because, after all, a nickel was money, too. However, when they returned the next day to hoot at him, the tailor gave them only a penny each.
>
> "Why do we get only a penny today?" they yelled.
>
> "That's all I can afford."
>
> "But two days ago you gave us a dime, and yesterday we got a nickel. It's not fair, mister."
>
> "Take it or leave it. That's all you're going to get!"
>
> "Do you think we're going to call you 'Jew' for one lousy penny?"
>
> "So don't!"
>
> And they didn't.

Interestingly enough, research shows that there is one domain of external reward that can have an effect on intrinsic motivation: 'positive' feedback that is perceived as a boost to one's feelings of competence and self-determination (Deci, Cascio, and Krusell 1973). No other externally administered set of rewards has a lasting effect. So, for example, sincerely delivered positive feedback in a classroom, seen by students as a validation of their own personal autonomy, critical thinking ability, and self-fulfillment, can increase or maintain intrinsic motivation.

Bruner (1962), praising the 'autonomy of self-reward', claimed that one of the most effective ways to help a child think and learn is to 'free' him from the control of rewards and punishments. Children who are rewarded by discovery itself are more strongly motivated to pursue further goals. Educators like Maria Montessori, Rudolf Steiner, Paolo Freire, and A.S. Neill have provided exemplary models of intrinsically motivated education. Traditionally, schools tend to cultivate extrinsic motivation through teacher directed classrooms, grades and tests that fail to appeal to a student's self-determination, peer pressure to conform to various conventional 'ideals', and through a host of institutional constraints that glorify content, product, correctness, competitiveness, and that fail to bring the learner into a collaborative process of competence building.

Intrinsic motivation in the second language classroom. Examples of the power of instrinsic motivation in second language classrooms abound. Consider a few activities and approaches that capitalize on the intrinsic by appealing to learner's self-determination and autonomy:

- when you teach writing as a thinking process in which learners develop their own ideas freely and openly,
- when learners are shown strategies of reading that enable them to bring their own information *to* the written word,
- language experience approaches in which students create their own reading material for others in the class to read,
- oral fluency exercises in which learners talk about what interests them and not about a teacher-assigned topic,
- listening to an academic lecture in one's own field of study for specific information that will fill a gap for the learner,
- communicative language teaching (see Savignon 1990) in which language is taught to enable learners to accomplish certain, specific functions,
- even grammar lessons, if learners see their potential for increasing their autonomy in the second language.

Intrinsic motivation is of course not the only determiner of success in a language learner. Terrell (1990) demonstrates convincingly that no matter how hard some learners try—namely, his subject 'R'—they may not succeed if they do not get adequate feedback from native speakers. But if the learners in our classrooms are given an opportunity to 'do' language for their own personal reasons of achieving competence and autonomy, surely those learners will have a better chance of success than if they become dependent on external rewards for their motivation.

It seems clear that by appealing to the strength of the construct of intrinsic motivation, researchers and teachers may find not only an additional but a more powerful factor than the earlier integrative/instrumental construct proposed by Gardner. Both sides of Gardner's construct can be either intrinsic or extrinsic. For example, one could, for extrinsic purposes, have a positive affect toward speakers of the second language (integrative orientation). One could also, for highly developed intrinsic purposes, wish to learn a second language in order to advance a career (instrumental orientation).

Coupled with the argument presented earlier—that languages are increasingly being learned with little concern for a so-called 'native' culture—teachers may be better served theoretically through an intrinsic/extrinsic construct.

In a larger perspective, as we look at some of the current trends in language teaching, how does intrinsic motivation play a role? That is, by focusing on principles of intrinsic motivation, how might our language teaching practices change for the better? How might we let go of some of the extrinsic M&M-based teaching that we are accustomed to practicing?

Teaching learners how to learn. One of the most effective means of instilling competence and self-determination in language learners is to let them in on some of our 'secrets' about successful learning strategies. Traditionally, students walk into a language classroom and are at the mercy of the teacher, the text, the prescribed curriculum. They usually don't even know what a 'strategy' is, and simply assume that language will be learned just like any other subject. We can teach our learners how to learn. We can help them to be 'empowered' (Clarke 1989) learners, to take some responsibility for their own success by actually providing them with a sense of what a strategy is and how they can develop some of their own strategies.

Some innovative material on learner strategy training is now available to learners and teachers. Brown's *A Practical Guide To Language Learning* (1989) gives foreign language learners fifteen easy-to-read chapters with exercises to heighten awareness and to initiate strategies for their own success. Oxford's *Language Learning Strategies: What Every Teacher Should Know* (1989) is an excellent source for teachers who wish to see how literally dozens of classroom activities and exercises can train learners to develop successful strategies. O'Malley and Chamot's *Learning Strategies in Second Language Acquisition* (1990) is a comprehensive overview of significant research on language learning strategies as well as a useful guide to teachers. Other resources well worth consulting are Rubin and Thompson (1982) and Ellis and Sinclair (1989).

Part of teaching learners how to learn involves helping learners simply to become aware of how certain activities in the classroom are designed to develop strategies for success (see Table 1).

What could be more intrinsically motivating to students than to develop their own autonomy by utilizing numerous strategies of learning? Their second language becomes their own, and simply the act of accomplishing something in the language is its own reward.

Content-centered language classes. A second intrinsically motivating trend in language teaching is the increasing focus of curricula on *content* that is of importance to the learner. When language becomes "the medium to convey informational content of interest and relevance to the learner" (Brinton, Snow, and Wesche 1989), then learners are pointed toward matters

Table 1.

When you . . .	help your students to be aware . . .
. . . play guessing games and other communication games,	. . . that it is important to be a risk-taker and to lower inhibitions.
. . . explicitly encourage or direct students to go beyond classroom assignments	. . . that it's important for them to set their own goals for their own purposes.
. . . use movies or tapes, or have them read passages rapidly, or do skimming and scanning exercises,	. . . of the importance of seeing the 'big picture', and of not always focusing on the minute details.
. . . direct students to share their knowledge and ideas, or talk in small groups,	. . . of the importance of socio-affective strategies of cooperative learning.
. . . praise students for good guesses and trying out the language in novel situations,	. . . that their *intuitions* about the language can be reliable sources of knowledge.
. . . deliberately withhold a direct correction of error, or let them correct each other's errors,	. . . that they can make their mistakes work *for* them rather than *against* them.

of intrinsic concern. Language becomes incidental to and a vehicle for accomplishing a set of content goals.

As we move further into the decade of the 1990s, we will see more and more of a demand for content-centered language teaching. Teachers will need to become much more comfortable with the concepts and skills, as well as the language, of other academic disciplines and of the prospect of working in teams across disciplines. A growing body of research literature points to the strength, across ages and disciplines, of content-based models of language education (see Tucker 1990, Crandall and Tucker 1989).

Toward more intrinsically motivating tests. Some might think that the term 'enjoyable test' is an oxymoron! However, judging from recent research in the testing field, we are coming closer and closer to creating tests that are valid learning experiences and therefore intrinsically motivating. Swain's (1990) excellent outline of an experimental testing program bears testimony to the possibility of tests that truly motivate a learner because they offer a reasonable challenge within authentic communicative contexts, and they offer instructive feedback to aid in later improvement of communication.

Inspired by the research of Howard Gardner (1983) and Sternberg (1988) on I.Q. and standardized testing, test developers like Frederiksen, Mislevy, and

Bejar (forthcoming) at Educational Testing Service are laying groundwork for the creation of new and more intrinsically motivating tests. Among some of the characteristics of the 'new generation of tests':

- tests that are 'biased for best' (Canale 1984),
- better stimulation of real-world tasks,
- focus on differing strategies that learners use to respond to items,
- examination of test takers' incorrect responses and subsequent feedback to learners,
- linking of test theory to cognitive processes of learning.

'Enjoyable tests' may indeed appear with more regularity in our language classes as we create tests that are designed to be evaluative learning experiences—feedback exercises which learners can come to value for their contribution to the ongoing process of autonomously developing personal competence in the language.

Language teachers as agents for change. The previous three facets of intrinsic motivation in the language teaching profession center on the student. A final and perhaps the most important facet focuses on the teacher. How can teachers develop and foster an underlying intrinsic motivation to teach?

Alastair Pennycook (1989), in a very stimulating essay on language teaching, power, and politics, reminded us that teachers are, according to Giroux and McLaren (1989), "transformative intellectuals" who must see ourselves "as professionals who are able and willing to...connect pedagogical theory and practice to wider social issues, and who work together to share ideas, exercise power over the conditions of our labor, and embody in our teaching a vision of a better and more humane life" (Pennycook 1989:613).

I always remind my teachers that teaching is indeed a 'political' act, an empowering act. We cannot hide behind a facade of belief that our educational institutions are neutral and unbiased. To do so reduces teachers to a nauseating sterility. For we are not merely language teachers. We have a mission to accomplish. There is a world out there of people who feel powerless. Language is a tool for overcoming powerlessness.

What could be more intrinsic to the spirit of every language teacher in the world than to finely tune our ability to become agents for change? Our professional commitment intrinsically drives us to help the inhabitants of this planet to communicate with each other, to negotiate the meaning of peace, of goodwill, and of survival on this tender, fragile globe. We must, therefore, with all the professional tools available to us, passionately pursue these ultimate goals!

References

Au, S.Y. 1988. A critical appraisal of Gardner's social-psychological theory of second language learning. Language Learning 38.1:75-100.

Ausubel, D.A. 1968. Educational psychology: A cognitive view. New York: Holt, Rinehart and Winston.

Brinton, D.M., M.A. Snow, and M.B. Wesche. 1989. Content-based second language instruction. New York: Newbury House.

Brown, H.D. 1989. A practical guide to language learning. New York: McGraw-Hill.

Bruner, J.S. 1962. On knowing: Essays for the left hand. Cambridge, Mass.: Harvard University Press.

Canale, M. 1984. Considerations in the testing of reading and listening proficiency. Foreign Language Annals 17:349-57.

Chihara, T., and J.W. Oller. 1978. Attitudes and attained proficiency in EFL: A sociolinguistic study of adult Japanese speakers. Language Learning 28:55-68.

Clarke, M. 1989. Some thoughts on empowerment. Paper presented at the TESOL Convention, San Antonio, March.

Crandall, J.A., and G.R. Tucker. 1989. Content-based language instruction in second and foreign languages. Paper presented at the RELC Regional Seminar on Language Teaching Methodology for the Nineties, Singapore, April.

Crookes, G., and R. Schmidt. 1990. Motivation: Reopening the research agenda. Paper presented at the TESOL Convention, San Francisco, March.

Deci, E.L. 1975. Intrinsic motivation. New York: Plenum Press.

Deci, E.L., W.F. Cascio, and J. Krusell. 1973. Sex differences, verbal reinforcement, and intrinsic motivation. Paper presented at the meeting of the Eastern Psychological Association, Boston, April.

Ellis, G., and B. Sinclair. 1989. Learning to learn English: A course in learner training. London: Cambridge University Press.

Frederiksen, N., R. Mislevy, and I. Bejar. Forthcoming. Test theory for a new generation of tests. Hillsdale, N.J.: Lawrence Erlbaum Associates.

Gardner, H. 1983. Frames of mind: The theory of multiple intelligences. New York: Basic Books.

Gardner, R.C. 1985. Social psychology and second language learning. London: Edward Arnold.

Gardner, R.C. 1988. The socio-educational model of second language learning: Assumptions, findings, and issues. Language Learning 38.1:101-26.

Gardner, R.C., and W.E. Lambert. 1972. Attitudes and motivation in second language learning. Rowley, Mass.: Newbury House.

Giroux, H.A., and P. McLaren. 1989. Introduction. In: H.A. Giroux and P. McLaren, eds. Critical pedagogy, the state, and cultural struggle. Albany, N.Y.: SUNY Press.

Graham, C.R. 1984. Beyond integrative motivation: The development and influence of assimilative motivation. In: P. Larson, E.L. Judd, and D.S. Messerschmidt, eds. On TESOL 84:75-87. Washington, D.C.: TESOL.

Hunt, J. McV. 1971. Toward a history of intrinsic motivation. In: H.I. Day, D.E. Berlyne, and D.E. Hunt, eds. Intrinsic motivation: A new direction in education. 1-32. Toronto: Holt, Rinehart, and Winston of Canada.

Kachru, B.B. 1988. Teaching world Englishes. ERIC/CLL News Bulletin 121:1-8.

Krashen, S.D. 1985. The input hypothesis. London: Longman.

Laing, R.D. 1967. The politics of experience. New York: Ballantine Books.

Lukmani, Y. 1972. Motivation to learn and language proficiency. Language Learning 22.2:261-74.

Maslow, A.H. 1970. Motivation and personality. 2nd edition. New York: Harper and Row.

McClelland, D.C. 1965. Toward a theory of motive acquisition. American Psychologist 20:321-33.

Oller, J.W. 1981. Research on the measurement of affective variables: Some remaining questions. In: R. Anderson, ed., New dimensions in L2 acquisition research. 14-28. Rowley, Mass.: Newbury House.

Oller, J.W., L. Baca, and F. Vigil. 1977. Attitude and attained proficiency in ESL: A sociolinguistic study of Mexican-American in the Southwest. TESOL Quarterly 11:173-83.

Oller, J.W., A.J. Hudson, and P.F. Liu. 1977. Attitudes and attained proficiency in ESL: A sociolinguistic study of native speakers of Chinese in the United States. Language Learning 27:1-26.

O'Malley, J.M., and A.U. Chamot. 1990. Learning strategies in second language acquisition. New York: Cambridge University Press.

Oxford, R.L. 1989. Language learning strategies: What every teacher ought to know. New York: Newbury House.

Pennycook, A. 1989. The concept of method, interested knowledge, and the politics of language teaching. TESOL Quarterly 23.4:589-618.

Piaget, J. 1952. The origins of intelligence in children. New York: International Universities Press.

Rubin, J., and I. Thompson. 1982. How to be a more successful language learner. Boston: Heinle and Heinle.

Savignon, S.J. 1990. Communicative language teaching: Definitions and directions. Georgetown University Round Table on Languages and Linguistics 1990. Washington, D.C.: Georgetown University Press.

Skinner, B.F. 1953. Science and human behavior. New York: Free Press.

Skinner, B.F. 1971. Beyond freedom and dignity. New York: Knopf.

Sternberg, R.J. 1989. The triarchic mind: A new theory of human intelligence. New York: Viking Press.

Swain, M.E. 1990. Testing and second language acquisition: Is there a conflict with traditional psychometrics? In: Georgetown University Round Table on Languages and Linguistics 1990. Washington D.C.: Georgetown University Press.

Terrell, T.D. 1990. Natural vs. classroom input: Advantages and disadvantages for beginning language students. In: Georgetown University Round Table on Languages and Linguistics 1990. Washington D.C.: Georgetown University Press.

Tucker, G.R. 1990. Cognitive and social correlates and consequences of additive bilingualism. In: Georgetown University Round Table on Languages and Linguistics 1990. Washington, D.C.: Georgetown University Press.

Watson, J.B. 1913. Psychology as the behaviorist views it. Psychological Review 20:158-77.

Research : Teaching :: Sin : Confession
An analogy for the times

June K. Phillips
Tennessee Foreign Language Institute

Whether the issue be one of religion or of teaching, the analogy in the title holds true: 'Research is to teaching as sin is to confession; if you do not participate in the one, you have nothing to say in the other'. That analogy might be amended to state the reverse as well. Researchers who do not participate actively in teaching should resist making implications that do not ring true for the teacher. There is no sin in letting descriptive research speak for itself. Furthermore, as suggested by the Georgetown University Round Table theme of 'interdependence', that elusive relationship might be strengthened through dialogue between researchers and teachers about implications and applications.

The reality is that today the interdependence of theory and practice, of research and teaching, that we often expound is far from visible (or audible) in too many language classrooms. The fault does not lie solely with one side, for both parties are guilty of engendering a divisiveness which has come to affect pocketbook issues such as tenure and promotion, professional issues such as conferences being labeled as pedagogical, linguistic, or serious, translated as literary. Most importantly, the schism inhibits making significant improvements in language teaching at a time when renewed support for the discipline abounds—support which will quickly fade if we fail to produce, as promised, functional and communicative competencies in other languages.

The area of second language reading illustrates the symbiotic relationship that 'in the best of all possible worlds' might exist between research and teaching. Just as teachers, to be effective, must participate in research, so must researchers be open to ideas, informed intuitions, and constraints identified by practitioners as potential sources of investigative study. In second language reading the 'instructional canon' that some deride actually has advanced practice in the field ahead of the evolving data base. Research data have largely confirmed the orientation of current instruction as well as many of the practices. For a thorough and cogently presented article on reading as an interactive process, see Swaffar's (1988) seminal article. The renewed interest in teaching second-language reading, however, traces its origins to the waning days of audiolingualism, a methodology which paid virtually no attention to the development of reading comprehension. In fact, concerns about reading came to the fore only in a negative manifestation when, in second or third year courses, it was suddenly discovered that students raised on the pabulum of 'recombination narratives' could not obtain meaning from the longer stories that began to appear.

Past and present scenarios. From an instructional perspective, what practices were associated with the teaching of reading in the early 1970s, and how far have we come? In a questionnaire generated in a preliminary dissertation study at that time (Phillips 1972), the three most common practices that teachers associated with reading instruction were: (1) reading aloud, (2) answering open-ended questions in the target language on the facts of the passage, (3) presenting vocabulary lists of target language/native language equivalents prior to reading.

In the past two months, the same questions were submitted to two groups of secondary and one group of secondary/college teachers. The most common practices associated with reading remained: (1) reading aloud, (2) answering comprehension questions on the text in the target language (although these questions now often took a forced-choice format), (3) presenting 'necessary' vocabulary prior to reading. One is tempted to say *plus ça change*. . . . Two important addenda to this informal survey do indicate some instructional momentum: (1) the major changes in practice were those provided by textbook presentations; (2) some teachers in the survey indicated they were implementing a variety of activities for prereading, interactive text processing, and strategizing; however, they were not of sufficient number to place among the most common practices.

As curriculum has emphasized proficiency goals and more functional language learning, the type of material serving as reading passages has been expanded. There is a definite shift away from those pristine texts specifically written for foreign language learners which controlled vocabulary and grammar and which contained no schema common to the language, no information to be learned from the text, no intrinsic purpose for reading. In other words, some teachers were now exploiting authentic materials contained in their textbooks or developing these documents as supplements. Their comments on this change revealed that 'the passages are more interesting, but I really am not sure the students understand them.' This confirms the attitude found by Allen et al. (1988), where teacher expectations fell short of actual student performances with authentic materials. A few probing follow-up discussions with individuals also determined that many did not know how to exploit the prereading activities suggested in the teaching manual, or they found them to be 'too easy' and therefore students failed to perform the higher level tasks involved in brainstorming, predicting, or even recalling prior knowledge.

For the common practices listed to have existed in the 1970s was understandable; in the 1990s it is simply unacceptable. It demonstrates that the research base slowly being established is not successfully conveying its message to the classroom. Likewise, the instructional practices advocated as workable strategies compatible with a changing knowledge base, which form the content of numerous practical workshops, methods courses, books, and articles, have probably reached relatively few classroom teachers. One can only surmise the reasons, among them, that compared to the total teaching population, small numbers of teachers regularly read journals, attend workshops and conferences, pursue advanced study in either foreign language pedagogy or linguistics. Furthermore, most inservice is of short duration, the 'one-shot' deal which often leaves teachers enthusiastic and determined to adapt a new instructional plan, without being competent to implement it systematically.

If the situation outlined above is to be ameliorated, then action must be taken to align more closely the research-to-teaching connection. From the research perspective, both message and medium must be clarified. First, one must address the basic mistrust; teachers' skepticism of research findings arises not only from their insecurity with procedures and report mechanisms but also because the implications paragraph too often reeks of the unrealistic. Swaffar (1988) points out the range of instructional variables that research now tries to accommodate. These include: affect (liking for teacher or subject), background (linguistic and personal), metalinguistic intuitions (when something just seems right), verbal and nonverbal intelligence, field independence and dependence (analytical vs. global), reader goals (to learn, for pleasure, for specific information), language aptitude, first and second language proficiencies in other skills, even persistence. Whether considered in the research study itself or not, these factors often militate against transferring practices from the research setting to the classroom. To render the research-teaching connection a positive one, more extensive and realistically developed implications must demonstrate how these very factors, in the classroom environment, can be manipulated to compensate for perceived shortcomings in learning.

For the research/teaching interdependence to become a viable relationship, linkages must be forged to improve practice and to determine in the classroom setting the questions worthy of further investigation and assessment of instructional impact. Two potentially useful linkages in which research in reading has direct implications and applications to teaching involve: schemata theory and prereading; reader information processing and reading instruction.

Schemata theory and prereading instruction. Much of the research in L2 revolves around the concepts of reader and of text schemata. The effect of background knowledge, the ability to form facilitating expectations, the necessity of subsuming new information while reading, the role of recognizing text schemata, are as well confirmed in the research as any aspect of reading for meaning. The research studies which established this base included those which probed information processing in a 'pure' form, that is, without instructional intervention, and those which sought to assess the effect of prereading activities on comprehension. Samples of these kinds of studies include the following:

- Levine and Haus (1985) investigated the effect of prior knowledge on reading comprehension. The topic of the passage was baseball; tests of knowledge of baseball were given prior to the reading passage in Spanish. As hypothesized, those who knew most about baseball read with the greatest comprehension. One could even conclude that the prior knowledge advanced comprehension of the passage and minimized differences in achievement.
- Adams (1982) confirms that anticipating story scripts and their structures facilitates vocabulary recognition; this is one of several studies showing the effect of knowledge of text schemata (see also Carrell 1984, 1985).
- Steffenson, Joag-Dev, and Anderson (1979) demonstrate the effect of native culture on comprehension, a variation of topic familiarity, within passages of parallel linguistic difficulty. In their study, readings in L2 were rendered as equivalent as possible for language. Both passages were on the topic of wedding customs. However, one passage described customs from native culture in the target language (English); the other described customs from the second culture in the second language. Comprehension was significantly higher in description of the native culture.

In fact, classroom teachers easily accept the implications for instruction drawn from research studies in reading and schemata theory. It appeals to their logic; the effect of background knowledge and individual ways of responding can be proven through simulations (Phillips 1985); their own experiences and insights into reading instruction confirm those views. Advocacy of prereading activities of the types which promote cognitive access to readings developed simultaneously with the body of research which now confirms it (Meyer and Tetrault 1986; Phillips 1978, 1987; Swaffar 1985). It is proper for informed teachers to develop and to experiment with instructional strategies while research is ongoing. Classroom application, however, requires that teachers be educated in a range of prereading activities and that they develop the judgments critical to making wise decisions about the types of activities that will be effective with their particular students with specific reading passages. Herein lies the crux of the problem. There is no neat formula which will work in all instances.

Thus in textbooks and in classes, attempts to devise a 'type' of exercise to be used throughout the curriculum is doomed to failure. A spurt of prereading activities is now replacing the old, tried-but-not-true vocabulary list, but a more critical look at quality and effectiveness of exercise is warranted. Many activities remain in a 'presentation' stage where information is simply fed to students; the prereading becomes advisory, it gives *to* students instead of drawing *from* them. Future studies might focus on the effectiveness of various types of prereading activities to elicit existing knowledge in readers' minds as well as ways to create a 'class consciousness', that is, create a common knowledge base as preparation for texts. Some of the more inventive prereading formats are found in ESL texts where the heuristics of the writing process have undergone a skill reversal for reading.

With consensus reached on the idea that teaching does benefit from prereading activities, further investigation by teachers working in conjunction with researchers might address questions such as: How do we activate relevant or helpful schemata? How do we do so when there is little to build upon due to cultural or experiential distance? How do we take what we know about individual differences and weave it into the classroom narrative that must be part of the teaching environment? What activity types are most effective, most motivating, most capable of engaging the reader's mind and imagination?

How do we plan for prereading? In classes, instruction allows us to intervene and to verify so that misreadings discovered in research settings might be avoided or corrected at an early stage. For example, recall protocols, a proven and valuable research tool as applied to foreign languages in Bernhardt's studies (1986), as well as the earlier 'think aloud' oral interviews of Hosenfeld (1979), provide captivating insights into students' processing of information and into their strategies while reading. But where the protocol provides evidence of how readers use, misuse, or fail to use background knowledge, how they match correct assumptions and incorrect ones to fit their interpretation of a passage, in the classroom we cannot replicate that procedure. Teachers must convert their awareness of the critical role of contributing experience to assist learners; that means finding instructional strategies to prime the pump, to direct thinking, to put things back on track. At the same time teachers must be more knowledgeable about the research tool so that more productive classroom procedures evolve.

Intensive or instructional reading. Insight into the interactive process, in terms of both top-down and bottom-up strategies, has also been gleaned from investigative tools such as the recall protocols and think-aloud procedures just cited and also from more recent work such as that of Carrell (1989) in metacognitive abilities which seeks to discover whether readers are aware of strategies they use, Barnett (1988) in looking at strategy use (perceived and real) and its interaction with comprehension, and Kern (1989) in assessing the effect of training in strategy use.

Trying to grasp how the human mind interprets words, phrases, and syntactical features on a small and focused plane, as well as the more global meaning of ideas and arguments, topics and comments, is intriguingly 'iffy' and imprecise when transferred to the classroom with its variety of reading passages and tasks. We still need to see if, for example, a recall protocol or similar exercise with several students would provide useful information for the development of an instructional plan for the whole group. To phrase it somewhat differently, would the teacher be a better facilitator of the reading process if insights gained from individuals formed the basis of the reading plan? Or is the individuality of the reading process so idiosyncratic that information learned from one person or group has no viable transfer to a larger group?

To convince teachers to move from an approach in which they have prepared in advance the questions they will ask about the language of a passage, the vocabulary and the grammar, or about the ideas or propositions, to one which requires them to be more fluid, to 'go with the flow', will take a major commitment to understanding information processing as applied to readers/learners. And that is a very difficult process to teach.

Which meaning should be emphasized first in the classroom, the lexical or the syntactical? Barnett's (1986) research shows that both lexical and syntactical elements interact for the successful assignment of meaning; thus, one does not automatically supersede the other. The teacher's ability to adopt a flexible approach will permit focusing on the aspect of the passage most likely to advance meaning at a given point in time, whether vocabulary or grammar. Forcing students through 'word study' exercises before a comfortable level of gisting or awareness of the structure of the discourse may also be detrimental to the reading of that passage and to more independent attempts at understanding. Preliminary experience shows that some readers are held captive by the words no matter how teachers try to focus them on the global; others are more willing to work from macro to micro operations. To make the critical decisions that advance learners through texts requires teachers who have read the research, who have practiced with the tools, who have worked passages with students, who have honed skills in guiding the process. Most importantly, teachers need time and opportunity to pursue this work.

At some point the cycle of separate (but unequal) domains must be broken so that teachers participate in research at a minimum by being informed and at a higher level by becoming part of the team. Their classrooms contain the key to rendering implications effective applications. Researchers can study the comprehension process but the role of teachers is to facilitate that process for learners. The research-to-practice connection for reading is only one of many areas of foreign language pedagogy where linkages must be strengthened. We know that the evolving research base is not having the effect on instruction that it must. Until it does, past scenarios will be present scenarios and the confessional will remain vacant since no sinning has occurred.

References

Adams, Shirley. 1982. Scripts and recognition of unfamiliar vocabulary: Enhancing second language reading skills. Modern Language Journal 66:155-59.

Allen, Edward D., Elizabeth B. Bernhardt, Mary Therese Berry, and Marjorie Demel. 1988. Comprehension and text genre: An analysis of secondary school foreign language readers. Modern Language Journal 72:163-72.

Barnett, Marva. 1986. Syntactic and lexical/semantic skill in foreign language reading: Importance and interaction. Modern Language Journal 70:343-49.

Barnett, Marva. 1988. Reading through context: How real and perceived strategy use affects L2 comprehension. Modern Language Journal 72:150-62.

Bernhardt, Elizabeth. 1986. Reading in the foreign language. In: Barbara H. Wing, ed. Listening, reading, writing: Analysis and application. Middlebury, Vt.: Northeast Conference on the Teaching of Foreign Languages. 93-115.

Carrell, Patricia. 1984. The effects of rhetorical organization on ESL readers. TESOL Quarterly 18:441-69.

Carrell, Patricia. 1985. Facilitating ESL reading by teaching text structure. TESOL Quarterly 19:727-52.

Carrell, Patricia. 1989. Metacognitive awareness and second language reading. Modern Language Journal 73:121-34.

Hosenfeld, Carol. 1979. Cindy: A learner in today's foreign language classroom. In: Warren C. Born, ed. The foreign language learner in today's classroom environment. Middlebury, Vt.: Northeast Conference on the Teaching of Foreign Languages. 53-75.

Kern, Richard G. 1989. Second language reading strategy instruction: Its effects on comprehension and word inference ability. Modern Language Journal 73:135-49.

Levine, Martin, and George Haus. 1985. The effect of background knowledge on the reading comprehension of second language learners. Foreign Language Annals 18:391-97.

Meyer, Renee, and Emery Tetrault. 1986. Open your closed minds: Using close exercises to teach foreign language reading. Foreign Language Annals 19:409-15.

Phillips, June K. 1972. Survey of reading practices in secondary classrooms: A preliminary study. Unpublished.

Phillips, June K. 1984. Practical implications of research in reading. Foreign Language Annals 17:285-96.

Phillips, June K. 1985. Proficiency-based instruction in reading: A teacher education module. [EDRS: ED 264730]

Steffensen, Margaret S., Chitra Joag-Dev, and Richard C. Anderson. 1979. A cross-cultural perspective on reading comprehension. Reading Research Quarterly 15:10-29.

Swaffar, Janet K. 1987. Reading authentic texts. Modern Language Journal 69:16-31.

Swaffar, Janet K. 1988. Readers, texts, and second languages: The interactive process. Modern Language Journal 72:123-49.

Second language testing and second language acquisition: Is there a conflict with traditional psychometrics?

Merrill Swain
Ontario Institute for Studies in Education, Toronto

Introduction. This paper considers one issue: given what is now known from second language testing research and second language acquisition research, does the search for high test reliability, especially high internal consistency, make sense? In other words, given our current understanding of language proficiency, should a test be expected to meet the criterion of high internal consistency traditionally required for tests to be considered 'good' tests?

I begin with examples of our attempts to establish the reliability (as internal consistency) of two tests: an oral sociolinguistic test and a written grammar test. In order to make sense of the results, a brief discussion of recent findings from second language testing research and second language acquisition research follows. The paper concludes by arguing that measures of reliability that depend on the notion of internal test consistency are incompatible with our current understanding of second language proficiency.

The context. It is useful to establish the context for the two examples I give of test development. During the 1980s, Patrick Allen, Jim Cummins, Birgit Harley, and I conducted a series of studies (e.g. Harley, Allen, Cummins and Swain 1987, 1990) concerned with the development of bilingual proficiency. It was our intention, as we embarked on that five-year program of research, to find support for a particular model of communicative competence, and then, using the instruments developed during the construct validation phase, to show how the nature of bilingual proficiency would change with changing learner characteristics and learning environments.

The model within which we chose to work combined aspects of the framework Michael Canale and I (Canale and Swain 1980, Canale 1983) had developed with aspects of the work of Jim Cummins (e.g. Cummins 1981). We might have chosen other conceptualizations of the nature of communicative competence, but we were working within an educational context, and we felt that conceptually at least, the frameworks were useful in school settings (Cummins and Swain 1986). Thus, as is shown in Figure 1, the components of grammatical, discourse, and sociolinguistic competence were hypothesized as traits, and the notion of tasks being placed along a context-embedded/context-reduced continuum provided the basis for the methods used to measure the traits, with oral tasks representing relatively context-embedded tasks and multiple choice and written compositions representing relatively context-reduced tasks. This yields a multimethod, multitrait matrix with nine cells: the three traits of grammatical, discourse, and sociolinguistic competence were each measured by three different methods—oral, multiple choice, and written compositions. Each trait is represented by a different column in the matrix, while each method is represented by a different row.

Our intention was eventually to undertake factor analyses in a search for evidence supporting the existence of the hypothesized traits. In order to do this, it was necessary to develop the equivalent of a test for each of the nine cells. At all stages of test development we were highly conscious of the time constraints being imposed upon us by the educational system. We had 'cooperation in principle' from a large school board, but they initially stipulated that we were to limit testing time to about two hours. This turned out to be highly unrealistic given the nine tests we needed to administer, and in the end, after considerable negotiation with school board personnel, we obtained approval for up to four hours of testing time, plus the additional time necessary for the one-on-one oral tests.

As with most test developers, we routinely applied traditional psychometric criteria to the tests which made up each cell. Our measures of reliability were limited to measures of internal consistency. This was because the school board had specifically required that we not give any student the same test twice, on the very reasonable grounds that it was not of any educational value to the students to do so. Besides, as noted above, we were considerably over our time limit with respect to the total testing time the school board had originally authorized.

As I see it now, we were seduced by testing theory into believing that we should be finding high internal consistencies. Had we thought about it at the time—especially in light of what is now known from recent second language acquisition research and from recent second language testing research—we should not have been surprised with the relatively low 'reliabilities' that were found. Indeed, low levels of internal consistency are indicative of the complexity of second language proficiency. In order to illustrate this, I am going to discuss the results of our search for 'psychometric propriety' for two of the nine cells: the sociolinguistic oral cell and the written grammar cell.

The study was conducted with a total of 198 students. Of these, 175 were grade six French immersion students. The French immersion students were mostly anglophone children who had initially taken all of their schooling in French. As they progressed through the grades, increasing portions of their

Trait / Method	GRAMMAR	DISCOURSE	SOCIOLINGUISTIC
	focus on grammatical accuracy within sentences	focus on textual cohesion and coherence	focus on social appropriateness of language use
ORAL	*structured interview* scored for accuracy of verb morphology, prepositions, syntax	*story retelling and argumentation/suasion* detailed ratings for e.g. identification, logical sequence, time orientation, and global ratings for coherence	*role-play of speech acts: requests, offers, complaints* scored for ability to distinguish formal and informal register
MULTIPLE CHOICE	*sentence-level 'select the correct form' exercise* (45 items) involving verb morphology, prepositions, and other items	*paragraph-level 'select the coherent sentence' exercise* (29 items)	*speech-act-level 'select the appropriate utterance'exercise* (28 items)
WRITTEN COMPOSITION	*narrative and letter of suasion* scored for accuracy of verb morphology, prepositions, syntax	*narrative and letter of suasion* detailed ratings much as for oral discourse and global rating for coherence	*formal request letter and informal note* scored for ability to distinguish formal and informal register

Figure 1. Operationalization of traits in second language proficiency study.

school day were taught in English so that by grade six, they were receiving about half their instruction in English and half in French. The other 23 students were a group of grade six native French speakers from a regular French school in Montreal. The oral tests, which were administered individually, were administered to a random sample of 12 students from each class.

The oral sociolinguistic test. The stimuli for the test developed to measure oral sociolinguistic performance were a set of photographic slides representing three different speech acts: requests, offers, and complaints. Students were individually shown a set of slides while they listened to a tape-recording describing the situation. With the showing of the last slide, the student responded in a manner which he or she considered appropriate for addressing the person shown in the slide. For example, one set of slides shows two children in the school library who are the same age as the student being tested. The student hears a description, in French, that says, "You're in the library to study. But there are two persons at the next table who are speaking loudly, and are bothering you. You decide to ask them to make less noise. What would you say if the two persons were friends of yours?" To change the level of formality, another set of slides shows two adults in the library, and the final question is "What would you say if the two persons were adults that you don't know?" For each speech act, there was a 'replication'. That is to say, for the complaints given in the previous example, there was a parallel pair of informal/formal complaint situations about being poked in the back in a line-up.

Each response given by the students was scored for the presence or absence of particular sociolinguistic markers (see Table 1), such as the use of attenuating conditionals in the formal situations and their nonuse in informal situations, or the use of *vous* in formal situations and the nonuse of *vous*—that is, the use of *tu*—in informal situations. A 'register variation' score was then derived for each sociolinguistic marker by subtracting the score obtained in the informal situation from that obtained in the formal situation for each student, and calculating an average for each sociolinguistic marker. This method of scoring gave us an idea of the extent to which native speakers and immersion students differentiated their speech between informal and formal contexts.

Descriptively, considerable information about the sociolinguistic performance of the immersion students was obtained. It was learned, for example, that immersion students tend not to differentiate registers between formal and informal situations to the same extent that native speakers do. There appear to be two kinds of sociolinguistic problems that the immersion students have relative to the native-speaker group: (1) they have a tendency to overuse certain formal markers in informal contexts; and (2) they are not making adequate use of several formal markers in formal contexts. In other words, immersion students' French tends to have less register variation than that of native speakers. When one considers that their French has been learned in a context which demands relative uniformity of register, these findings make a great deal of sense.

Table 1. Oral sociolinguistic test. Correlations between sociolinguistic markers for each of three speech acts.

	SPEECH ACTS		
	Requests	Offers	Complaints
SOCIOLINGUISTIC MARKERS			
Initial politeness marker	0.06	0.18	0.16
vous	0.16	0.40	-
Question with *est-ce que* or inversion	0.00	0.10	0.24
Use of attenuating conditional	-0.03	0.12	-0.16
Formal vocabulary	-0.17	-0.11	0.18
Concluding politeness marker	-0.16	-0.04	0.04

But how reliable are they? The issue of reliability was approached by correlating the differentiation scores for each sociolinguistic marker for each of the 'parallel' speech act functions. That is, did differentiation between attenuating conditionals in one set of formal/informal complaint situations correlate with differentiation between attenuating conditionals in the other set of formal/informal complaint situations? The results, shown in Table 1, suggest that the answer is 'no'. For example, the correlations between the use of specific sociolinguistic markers in one set of complaints with the other set of complaints ranged from -0.16 to +0.24.

Table 2. Oral sociolinguistic test. Correlations between 'parallel' speech acts averaged over sociolinguistic markers.

	Complaint 1
Complaint 2	0.06
	Request 1
Request 2	0.14
	Offer 1
Offer 2	0.18

All the sociolinguistic differentiation scores for all the sociolinguistic markers were then summed within each speech act pair for each student and the average calculated for each student. We then correlated these aggregate scores across replications. As Table 2 shows, the correlations were still low: 0.06 for complaints, 0.14 for requests, and 0.18 for offers.

Finally, we summed across all three speech acts—complaints, offers, and requests—and calculated an average for each student. These averages were correlated with their 'replications', providing a variety of a split-half correlation. In other words, one set of complaint, offer, request informal/formal pairs was considered as half the test and correlated with the averaged results of the other set of complaint, offer, request informal/formal pairs. As shown in Table 3, this correlation was 0.49.

Table 3. Oral sociolinguistic test. Correlations between 'parallel' forms of the test.

	$C_1 + R_1 + O_1$
Split-half - $C_2 + R_2 + O_2$	0.49

The Spearman-Brown formula can be applied to estimate the reliability of a test, assuming it were twice as long. The correlation between scores on two halves of a test is the reliability of either half used as a separate test. The Spearman-Brown formula estimates what the reliability would be of the test consisting of both halves taken together. As is well known, one can increase the reliability of any test by making it longer. Applying the Spearman-Brown formula to the half-test correlation boosted the estimate to 0.66, still not impressive and by some standards not even acceptable.

But, notice what has happened. We succeeded in getting a rather low estimate of internal consistency (reliability) by averaging again and again—in effect, by lengthening the test and making it more and more complex. The cost is that information on how learners' performance varies from task to task has been lost.

The written grammar test. Let me turn now to examine this same issue with respect to the grammatical written cell. For both the grammatical written cell and the discourse written cell, a narrative and a letter of suasion were written. One narrative described the rescue of a kitten from a tree, and the other a bank robbery. For each narrative, the students were given an opening line that prompted the use of past tense and plural verb forms. One of the letters required the students to request to borrow a bicycle seen in the garage of their landlord, while the other required the students to request permission from their landlord to keep their dog in their apartment. All four compositions were scored for grammatical accuracy in (1) verb morphology, (2) prepositions, and (3) syntax.

Table 4 shows the correlations between the narratives and between the letters for the accuracy in each of these three areas. They are low. For example, the correlation between the accurate use of prepositions in the two narratives is 0.17 and in the two letters is -0.01. What might explain the variable performance indicated by these low correlations?

Table 4. Written grammar test. Correlations between measures of accuracy for narratives and for letters.

TASKS	MEASURES OF ACCURACY		
	Syntax	Prepositions	Verb morphology
Narratives	0.10	0.17	0.08
Letters	0.32	-0.01	0.10

Consider, for example, accuracy of prepositional usage in the narratives. As noted above, one of the narratives was about the rescue of a kitten from a tree. The students' stories tended to contain a similar series of events, involving several changes of location. There are characteristic differences between French and English in how location and direction are expressed. In English, prepositions generally serve an important role in conveying the location/direction distinctions—for example *at* versus *to*, *in* versus *into*. In French, however, there is a general tendency for direction to be expressed in the verb, and for prepositions (e.g. *à*, *dans*, *sur*) to be neutral with respect to the location/direction distinction. As it turns out, based on a qualitative analysis of the prepositional use by immersion students in this narrative (Harley 1989), students relied more on prepositions than on verbs to express the notion of direction—as would be predicted from knowledge of their mother tongue. This resulted, for example, in erroneously using French prepositions unmarked for direction as if they were carrying the directional distinction.

The other narrative—about a bank robbery—did not elicit prepositions of direction and location to the same extent. Under these circumstances, why should one expect any correlation between these narratives?

No comparison of verb usage has been made between the two narratives. It is known, however, based on second language acquisition research of the immersion students' French (e.g. Harley and Swain 1984), that the *passé composé* is more accurately produced than the imperfect, which, in turn, is more accurately produced than the conditional. Furthermore, there is a tendency by immersion students to regularize past tense forms to the *-er* form; to apply the imperfect only to certain high frequency verbs; to use singular for plural forms, and so on. If the two narratives call forth different tense usage, or even just different verbs, then our knowledge about the immersion students' French verb system would predict a low correlation between the correct usage of verbs in one narrative and that of the other.

To return to the measures of written grammatical competence, as is indicated in Table 4, correlations between narratives or between letters were low on any particular measure of grammatical accuracy. A total score was calculated for each narrative and for each letter by calculating an average for all the component accuracy scores for each student. These were then correlated between the two narratives and the two letters. As Table 5 shows, the correlations are unimpressive—0.36 for the narratives; 0.45 for the letters. Finally, we averaged again—this time the total scores for one letter and one narrative, and considering it as one half of the test, correlated it with the average of the total scores for the other letter and narrative. As Table 6 indicates, this resulted in a correlation of 0.45. The Spearman-Brown formula then yields an estimated reliability of 0.62 for the overall test.

Table 5. Written grammar test. Correlations between 'parallel' narratives and letters averaged over measures of accuracy.

	Narrative 1		Letter 1
Narrative 2	0.36	Letter 2	0.45

Table 6. Written grammar test. Correlations between 'parallel' forms of the test.

	$N_1 + L_1$
Split-half - $N_2 + L_2$	0.45

At what expense has this unremarkable measure of internal consistency been achieved? It has been achieved largely by suppressing interesting differences between the grammatical performance of students on one task and that on others. In the anxious (and fruitless) pursuit of psychometric respectability, we ignored findings from second language acquisition research and second language testing research that predict variable performance will be the norm rather than the exception.

Second language testing research. Consider some of the recent findings from second language testing research. For example, in a number of studies in which reading comprehension was tested (e.g. Olin 1987, Shohamy 1984), 'text' came out as a main effect. That is, the passage on which the reading comprehension questions were based significantly affected the scores obtained. As Shohamy (1988:9) states:

> This means that the most important factor in determining the success of test takers on reading comprehension tests is the text used on the test, so that if a test taker succeeds on a reading comprehension test which includes one type of text, there is no guarantee that he or she will succeed on a reading comprehension test which includes a different type of text, and similarly a person who does not succeed on a reading comprehension test which includes one type of text may have succeeded had the text been different. The implication of this finding to the construction of language tests is that a valid assessment of reading comprehension must include a number of texts and these must be based on a variety of topics, content, genres, registers and formality levels.

Given this, such tests would be expected to show low levels of internal consistency. Indeed, one might wish to argue that a good test of second language reading proficiency must have a low internal consistency.

Shohamy and Inbar (1988) found results similar to those assessing reading comprehension when they measured listening comprehension. That is, they found that scores on listening comprehension are significantly affected by the genre of the test stimuli. Shohamy and Inbar maintained the same content, but presented that content as a radio broadcast, as a short lecture, and as an informal conversation. The most easily understood was the informal conversation, while the radio broadcast was the most difficult. Thus, to assess an individual's proficiency in listening comprehension, one needs to use a variety of oral stimuli from a variety of genres.

Similarly, in research testing speaking, Shohamy, Reves, and Bejerano (1986) obtained only moderate correlations between test takers' scores based on tasks involving interviews, discussions, role plays, and reports. And in writing, Nevo (1986) found that the type of task—formal, academic, creative, etc.—affects students' scores.

The point of these examples is that the variable performance that would be observed in tests constructed in light of this second language testing research would surely result in measures having low internal consistency. If they do not, then can the tests be said to measure second language proficiency? They will not be reflecting the variation that research shows to be there. Is it appropriate to expect high levels of internal consistency? I am arguing that it is not.

Second language acquisition research. According to second language acquisition theory, variation in interlanguage is to be expected. Ellis (1985) argues that nonsystematic variation is an integral part of the process of second language acquisition on the basis of research which suggests that second language learners have competing rules which exist in free variation. Nonsystematicity in language performance and internal test consistency are contradictory concepts. Thus, if Ellis is right, there is absolutely no reason to expect internal consistency in a second language test.

If one gets a relatively high measure of reliability, it may be because one has averaged over enough sets of items to change the nature of the original variation. A new trait is created, more abstract and more stable, but different. High reliability has replaced high validity. This is an interpretation consistent with the low correlations we initially obtained when, for example, we correlated sociolinguistic features within each speech act, and later correlated each speech act averaged over all sociolinguistic features; and the mediocre correlation we obtained when we averaged once again—this time across speech acts—and correlated the intratest replication.

There is, however, another position than the existence of nonsystematic variation which is held by some second language acquisition researchers. Tarone (1988), for example, in her recent book on variation in interlanguage, argues not only that there is variation, but that it is systematic. In her book, she details possible causes of systematic variation, including psychological processes, linguistic context, and social settings.

In a study on variation and the interlanguage hypothesis, Young (1988) reported on the variation found in the use of the English plural by native speakers of Chinese. He found that three major groups of variables influenced variation: (1) stage of acquisition, (2) linguistic context, and (3) communicative redundancy. Young concludes that variation is systematic, but he finds it complex. The number and diversity of factors affecting variation—linguistic, developmental, and contextual—go a long way in explaining "why previous studies that considered the effect of only one independent variable produced such inconclusive and contradictory results" (300). He states, ". . . that significant relations are found between multiple independent factors and the presence or absence of a variable form. That these relations are complex and multidimensional should come as no surprise to those who have seriously attempted to deal with the complexity and multidimensionality of any other linguistic performance" (300).

If variation in interlanguage is systematic, what does this imply about the appropriateness of a search for internal test consistency? It implies that any language test can be made to be 'conceptually'—rather than mathematically—internally consistent. The variety of item types will, however, have to be highly restricted.

Let me briefly summarize to this point. We began with a plan to use a factor analysis of nine tests to verify the existence of a set of traits underlying communicative performance. We knew that reasonably high internal consistency would be required in the tests before we were likely to make any sense of the factor analyses. Thus we searched for, but did not find, high measures of internal consistency. It now seems apparent, given recent research concerned with second language acquisition and second language testing, that the modest levels of internal consistency we were able to achieve reflected some trait other than sociolinguistic or grammatical competence. A highly internally consistent test of sociolinguistic or grammatical behavior, given our present knowledge, would be difficult to devise, and most importantly, it would not be reflective of language use in complex and diverse social situations.

Conclusion. Second language testing and second language acquisition share an interest in variation in second language proficiency. Second language tests, to be valid, must reflect that variation. Reliability as internal consistency is therefore an inappropriate measure of quality. A challenge for second language test researchers will be to rethink the whole concept of accuracy and consistency of second language measures. Learning and motivational differences between the test administrations make test/retest measures suspect as well. Perhaps we may have to begin a search for 'meaningful quality criteria' for the inclusion of test items rather than rely on a measure of internal consistency. I do not have the answers. But I do think it is an important issue that will have to be dealt with in our field.

Note

I would like to thank a number of people who have read earlier drafts of this paper and have deepened my understanding of the issues: Lyle Bachman, Jim Cummins, Gary Cziko, Birgit Harley, Doug Hart, Sharon Lapkin, Les McLean, Elana Shohamy, and Ross Traub. To Les McLean I owe special thanks for having read with great care the penultimate draft.

References

Canale, M. 1983. From communicative competence to communicative language pedagogy. In: J.C. Richards and R.W. Schmidt, eds. Language and communication. London: Longman.

Canale, M., and M. Swain. 1980. Theoretical bases of communicative approaches to second language teaching and testing. Applied Linguistics 1:1-47.

Cummins, J. 1981. The role of primary language development in promoting educational success for language minority students. In: California State Department of Education, ed. Schooling and language minority students: A theoretical framework. Los Angeles: Evaluation, Dissemination and Assessment Center, California State University. 3-49.

Cummins, J., and M. Swain. 1986. Bilingualism in education. London: Longman.

Ellis, R. 1985. Understanding second language acquisition. Oxford: Oxford University Press.

Harley, B. 1989. Transfer in the written compositions of French immersion students. In: H. W. Dechert and M. Raupach, eds. Transfer in language production. New York: Ablex. 3-19.

Harley, B., P. Allen, J. Cummins, and M. Swain. 1987. The development of bilingual proficiency: Final Report. Vol. 1: The nature of proficiency; Vol. 2: Classroom treatment; Vol. 3: Social context and age. Toronto: Modern Language Centre, Ontario Institute for Studies in Education.

Harley, B., P. Allen, J. Cummins, and M. Swain, eds. 1990. The development of second language proficiency. New York: Cambridge University Press.

Harley, B., and M. Swain. 1984. The interlanguage of immersion students and its implications for second language teaching. In: A. Davies, C. Criper, and A.P.R. Howatt, eds. Interlanguage. Edinburgh: Edinburgh University Press.

Nevo, D. 1986. Testing authenticity in writing. Paper presented at the 4th ACROLT Meeting, Kiryat Anavim, Israel.

Olin, R. 1987. The effect of connectors on reading comprehension. M.A. thesis, Tel Aviv University.

Shohamy, E. 1984. Does the testing make a difference? The case of reading comprehension. Language Testing 1:147-70.

Shohamy, E. 1988. Closing the gap between research and practice: Applications of research results to classroom testing. Revised version of a paper delivered at the English Teachers' Association of Israel International Conference, Jerusalem.

Shohamy, E., and O. Inbar. 1988. Construct validation of listening comprehension tests: The effect of text and question type. Paper presented at the 10th Annual Language Testing Colloquium, Urbana, Illinois.

Shohamy, E., T. Reves, and Y. Bejerano. 1986. Introducing a new comprehensive test of oral proficiency. English Language Teaching Journal 40:212-22.

Tarone, E. 1988. Variation in interlanguage. London: Edward Arnold.

Tarone, E., and B. Parrish. 1988. Task-related variation in interlanguage: The case of articles. Language Learning 38:21-44.

Young, R. 1988. Variation and the interlanguage hypothesis. Studies in Second Language Acquisition 10:281-302.

Owls and doves: Cognition, personality, and learning success

Madeline Ehrman
Foreign Service Institute

Efforts to understand how people learn second languages have focused on a wide range of factors. Some of these are external to the learner: e.g. teaching methodologies and techniques, classroom management activities, and variations in physical setting. Much effort has also gone into investigation of variables which could be described as 'internal' to the learner; these include such categories as learning aptitude, learning styles, personality, and preferred learning strategies. Some studies have examined the interactions of the 'external' and the 'internal', most notably work on motivation, affect, and 'aptitude-treatment interaction' studies.

This paper addresses the impact of an 'internal' characteristic, a Jungian personality dimension referred to as 'thinking/feeling judgment', on student behavior in an intensive learning setting. This dimension is most economically described as indicating an individual's approach to decision making, but thinking or feeling preferences also define the nature of a person's social relations and influence the effects of social interactions on the individual. That is, preference for thinking or feeling colors how people act toward others and how they react to the behavior of others toward them.

Review of relevant research. Because the findings reported herein have implications for both cognitive and affective processing of second languages, some of the work in both areas is reviewed here.

Cognition. Much work has been done on learning, especially language learning, as a cognitive event. In language learning, John Carroll's work with the Modern Language Aptitude Test is representative of a point of view that factors of attention, short-term memory, auditory and visual discrimination, and analogical reasoning play a major role in predicting language learning success (Carroll 1963 and 1990; Carroll and Sapon 1958). More recent work at the Defense Language Institute, using a large number of subjects who were subjected to a massive battery of measures, has found that indeed among internal characteristics, cognitive aptitude measures play a large role in prediction of attrition, but far from a decisive one (Lett and O'Mara 1990), inasmuch as all internal characteristics combined predict less than 30 percent of attrition and learning success in this study.

Two studies (Horwitz 1987; Jacobus 1990) suggest that language learning success, at least in university settings, correlates with conceptual level measured on a hierarchical scale. Currall and Kirk (1986) found that GPA—described as a composite of academic ability, motivation, and attitudes toward achievement—was the best predictor of success in university language courses, compared with several other predictors, including an interview.

Much of the work of the Soviet scholar Vygotsky (1934/1962) promotes the idea that cognition is based on language development, especially in first language acquisition. Frawley and Lantolf (1984, 1985) build on Vygotskian concepts in the context of adult language learning in their focus on the 'zone of proximal development', or the gap between level of actual skill and potential to increase that skill or capacity as a result of instruction. They treat the application of the zone to the acquisition of language through the 'receptive skills', i.e. reading and listening comprehension.

A number of researchers have investigated what we could call 'applied cognition': expert knowledge and learning strategies and styles. Work by Anderson (1982), Flavell et al. (1968), and others has focused increasingly on modeling the way in which expertise is gained and examining ways in which learners can use their own awareness of their learning to enhance their efficiency. These investigations and models of general problem solving (Frederiksen 1984) have become especially important in the study of learning strategies in general (Pask 1988; Weinstein 1988), and of language learning strategies in particular (O'Malley et al. 1985; Oxford 1985, 1990a). Oxford addresses the matter of learning strategies (and styles) in detail in the present volume; the research is therefore not reviewed here.

Anderson and others have designed models of skill acquisition which rely on the distinction between automatic and controlled processing; these in turn have influenced the second language acquisition theories of Bialystok (1981), Gregg (1984), Krashen (1982), and Krashen and Terrell (1983), as well as the language learning strategies work of O'Malley and his colleagues (e.g. Chamot and O'Malley 1987).

Especially important to the investigation of learning strategies and even more to the idea that they can be taught is the concept of metacognition, defined by Lefebvre-Pinard (1983) as "a form of cognition directed at the subject's own cognitive activity itself, both with respect to its goals and the strategies it uses to attain these." The term applies both to knowledge and to control of one's own thought processes.

Metacognition in the form of self-regulation is shown to contribute to performance improvement in a great variety of tasks, many of them verbal in nature (multiple studies cited in Lefebvre-Pinard 1983). It also plays an important role in the translation of motivation into strategic cognition, which in turn is translated into appropriate action (Showers and Cantor 1985). Another extremely important form of metacognition is in self-concept and attribution (Linville 1982; Showers and Cantor 1985), which sets a series of scripts for complex behavior, of which language learning is a good example. We shall see later in this paper that although effective use of metacognition clearly enhances language learning for the adults at FSI, destructive metacognition can hinder the process. (As Lefebvre-Pinard (1983) points out, "self-awareness is no more exempt of errors than any other mode of thinking.")

Results of research on cognition in general are suggestive and potentially useful to individual language training practitioners but, with the exception of schema theory (Bates 1972; Slobin 1971; Carrell 1984; Van Dijk and Kintsch 1983) and learning strategies study, have had relatively little effect on instructional methodology. A good example of the potential of this area of knowledge is the degree to which access to learning strategies and efficiency of their use are related to Piaget's formal operations or the kind of postformal operations thinking that researchers increasingly attribute to adults (Fischer and Silvern 1985; Labouvie-Vief 1985; Richards and Commons 1984). Another constructive use of the learning strategies concept is exemplified by the work of Campione and Brown (1984), who examine the use of learning strategies and transfer of knowledge among efficient vs. poor learners.

Affective factors. One of the best and most thoughtful descriptions of affective issues in language teaching is found in Stevick (1980). Stevick makes a distinction between a kind of 'Theory X' of language teaching (analogous to the equivalent management theories), that assumes that students are not self-motivated and must be driven to learn, and a sort of 'Theory Y', that takes as axiomatic that human beings are self-motivated to develop and learn—a fundamental of much of developmental and cognitive psychology but not always of educational practice. Affective and interpersonal factors have received attention in methodology: in particular, both Community Language Learning (Curran 1972), and Lozanov's Suggestopedia (1979) are derived from an understanding of the deleterious effects of tension on learning. Brown (1987) also devotes considerable attention to general matters of affect and personality in language learning.

More specific research includes work on motivation, effects of anxiety, and effects of personality variables on language learning. Schumann (1975, 1976) not only considers affective matters important, he treats them as central and as the driving force in the second language acquisition process.

Affective variables in adult learning in formal settings generally are well documented. Adult learners are found to have higher levels of motivation and to experience higher anxiety about learning than students of traditional age; they also experience pressure from their other life commitments, such as families and jobs (Knowles 1978). Stress can also come from a conflict between teachers' assumptions of dependency by learners, and adult assumptions of autonomy and lack of need for direction and control (Steitz 1985). All of these factors can affect the adult learner of a foreign language as much as the learner of any other subject.

Motivation. Robert C. Gardner's name is most commonly associated with the study of motivational issues in second language acquisition (1978). He is best known for the distinction between instrumental and integrative motivation. Both of these types of motivation are powerful facilitators of language learning. More specifically, Gardner examines elements that may affect language learning success—attitudinal, motivational, aptitudinal. These include interest in foreign languages, desire to integrate with target community, evaluation of learning situation, instrumentality, MLAT scores, background, etc. He defines integrativeness as positive attitudes toward a number of social objects, orientation in second language study, and favorable attitudes toward the target language speaker group. Integrative orientation is defined as "learning the language in order to meet with, communicate with, and learn more about the other language community" (205). (Graham (1984) further distinguishes between 'integrative' motivation—the desire to communicate with members of another culture—and 'assimilative motivation'—the desire to become a member of the target speech community. This is a distinction worth more study than it appears to have received.)

McGroarty (1988) reports that effective motivation differs according to setting—instrumental motivation worked better for adults in job-related settings; for students more oriented to the classroom, positive attitude to language learning in general and to the ESL classroom had a relationship to achievement.

Strong (1984) suggests a reciprocal relation between integrative motivation and learning success. He suggests that more success means more interest and liking for the target language culture.[1] Another implication of the point of view stated by Strong is that what we like, we tend to associate with more and put more effort into.

Anxiety. Anxiety—or rather an appropriate level of tension—in learning situations can be helpful to a degree; e.g. Alpert and Haber (1960) and Beeman, Martin, and Meyers (1972) suggest that what they call anxiety is more facilitative at later stages of learning, and Verma and Nijhavan (1976) find anxiety more facilitative at upper ranges of intelligence for children in one laboratory study.

However, anxiety more often indicates an undesirable affective state and is treated in terms of its negative effects. Scovel (1978) treats state vs. trait

---

[1] This view of motivation is reminiscent of Lewin's Field Theory, in which motivation is an interaction between importance of the task to the performer ('valence') and estimation of chances of success (description of Field Theory from McDonough 1981).

anxiety as detrimental factors. Hall, Rocklin, Dansereau, et al. (1988) find a strong negative relationship between anxiety and metacognitive skills, which they discuss in the context of recent research attributing performance drops to encoding and retrieval processing deficits. Darke (1988) supports M. Eysenck's (1979, 1982) hypothesis that the debilitating effects of anxiety are a result of using working memory processing capacity for worrying, which means that less capacity is available for cognitive task processing.

Gardner (1990) points out that the usual definitions of 'trait' and 'state' anxiety (Spielberger, Gorusch, and Lushene 1970) do not appear to correlate with language learning outcomes, while a construct he calls Language Classroom Anxiety does correlate negatively (Clement, Smythe, and Gardner 1978; Horwitz, Horwitz, and Cope 1986).

Bailey (1983) examines the relationship between competitiveness and classroom anxiety in a model that relates competition, self-image, facilitating and debilitating anxiety. Foss and Reitzel (1988) indicate that students' self-perceptions of their own competence constitute a critical factor in classroom anxiety.

Personality variables. A number of studies have attempted to relate personality factors to success in language learning (see Rubin 1975; Naiman, Frohlich, and Todesco 1975). Major personality variables that have been suggested include lack of inhibition, empathy, extraversion, willingness to take risks, self-esteem, and lack of ethnocentrism.

Lack of inhibition. Inhibition is hypothesized to be detrimental to language learning. Studies by Guiora, Beit-Hallami, Brannon, et al. (1972) and Guiora, Acton, Everard, and Strickland (1980) suggest that pronunciation can be improved when inhibition is temporarily lifted by chemicals. Rubin (1975) suggests that good language learners are uninhibited and willing to appear foolish; on the other hand, Reiss (1985) reports that such good learners are not necessarily as uninhibited as hypothesized. Brown (1987) speculates that blocking Gallwey's (1974) 'critical self' permits the 'performing self' to operate freely and effectively.

Empathy. Guiora, Brannon, and Dull (1972:142) define empathy as "a process of comprehending in which a temporary fusion of self-object boundaries permits an immediate emotional apprehension of the affective experience of another." A related factor of 'ego permeability' is sometimes used to refer to an openness to adopting foreign thought habits, rather than the pathological implication this term often has in psychiatric circles (Pickett 1978). The Guiora et al. study found that high scores on a test of empathy predicted quality of pronunciation on a number of languages.

Empathy as measured by a number of other criteria was not, however, found by Gardner and Lambert (1972) and Naiman, Frohlich, and Todesco (1975) to be predictive of language learning success in general. The current large-sample Defense Language Institute Language Skill Change Project is not finding empathy (on the California Psychological Inventory) to play a particularly predictive role (Lett and O'Mara 1990). In my view, these generally equivocal findings are not surprising in view of the fact that other studies show that language learning success can be facilitated by instrumental motivation, in which empathy generally does not play a role.

Extraversion and introversion. A number of studies have looked at the impact of extraversion and introversion on language learning. Extraversion has generally been hypothesized to correlate with success, at least in part perhaps because of the role of teacher preconceptions about the ability of the outgoing, interactive extravert relative to the more reserved introvert (Brown 1987). Some investigations have found a relationship between sociability and various measures of success (Chastain 1975 for German and Spanish but not French; Pritchard 1952, for French fluency). However, most studies of this variable have not confirmed the common hypothesis of extravert superiority (Busch 1982; Lalonde and Gardner 1984; Naiman, Frohlich, Stern, and Todesco 1978; Smart, Elton, and Burnett 1970). Krashen relates use of the 'monitor' for tracking one's own errors to a dimension that looks very close to extraversion and introversion, when he describes monitor overusers as "self-conscious" and monitor underusers as "outgoing" (Krashen 1978:182). The fact that both overusers and underusers are not maximally functional in Krashen's scheme suggests that neither the introverted (overuser) nor the extraverted (underuser) approach provides an advantage in Krashen's view.

Hall, Rocklin, Dansereau, et al. (1988) found advantages for introversion in learning procedural material alone. On the other hand, cooperative learning strategies, which would be expected to advantage the extravert, resulted in greater overall recall of the material, though extraverts were not specifically described as performing better under these conditions. A recent study from which the material in the present paper is taken suggested some advantages for introverted students in small-group, intensive, job-related language training of a largely communicative nature (Ehrman 1989; Ehrman and Oxford 1990).

I speculate that the failure to confirm an advantage for extraversion comes from the fact that most language use is dyadic, a situation which is often as comfortable for introverts as for extraverts. Introverts are likely to suffer on measures of classroom participation in large groups, but they are not necessarily handicapped when their proficiency is measured in an essentially dyadic interaction.

Risk tolerance. Beebe (1983) suggests that there is an optimal level of risk taking, relating this general concept to effects of various methodologies. She opens the question of "establishing what constitutes a moderate risk for a specific learner in a specific situation" (59). However, she only suggests that this is related to stage of second-language development, defined in "purely linguistic performance terms" (58). She does not address other factors in a differential definition of what would constitute a risk for a given individual (the psychological type model would suggest that risk will be defined differently for different personality types).

Tolerance for ambiguity. The investigation of tolerance for ambiguity reported in Naiman et al. (1975) may relate to factors similar to risk taking. Naiman et al. indicate that tolerance for ambiguity is associated with performance on a listening task (and with lack of ethnocentricity and a preference for extensive use of the target language in class). Results from the study that is the source of the present paper suggested advantages for students in intensive language training who expressed a preference for an open, flexible approach to learning that included acceptance of material that had unfamiliar items or content and some unpredictability of learning events (Ehrman 1989; Ehrman and Oxford 1990).

Self-esteem. Self-esteem was investigated by Parsons (1983), who distinguished among "global" self-esteem, or evaluation of overall worthiness; "specific" self-esteem, or worthiness in specific (learning) situations; and "task" self-esteem, or worthiness on a particular task. She found that oral proficiency ratings correlated with three measures of self-esteem: task, specific situation, and global, with degree of significance in descending order (i.e. most for task and least for global).

Other variables. Bush (1990) reported on a massive statistical study in which he found ethnocentrism, anxiety, empathy, self-esteem, and approval motive appeared to play a role in language learning success. More of the scales he looked at were correlated more with listening scores than other measures of language learning success, from which he concluded that language acquisition (in the Input Hypothesis model, see above) is more dependent on affective constructs than consciously mediated 'learning'. Bush found that an interactive variable consisting of ethnocentrism (low) and general academic capability (high) was a better predictor of success at the U.S. Air Force Academy than was a formal test of language learning aptitude, the Defense Language Aptitude Battery.

Seliger (1983) divides learners into High Input Generators—students who take active initiative to bring about interactive practice and thus comprehensible input—and Low Input Generators. He indicates a learning advantage for High Input Generators, who also tend to be more field independent. A subsequent study (Day 1984, 1985) failed to replicate Seliger's findings, but methodological differences between the two studies were sufficient that this typology remains worth continued investigation, inasmuch as active engagement and initiation of activity in the language learning process is listed as one of the strategy groups most characteristic of 'good' language learners (Naiman et al. 1975; Rubin 1975) and appears correlated with other measures of learning success (Chaudron 1988).

Gardner (1990:9) concludes that there is little evidence convincing him of the importance of personality factors in language learning. He attributes this to the "generally poor results" in existing studies and the lack of a clear theoretical model for linking personality and language learning. After the Interagency Language Roundtable Symposium on Language Learning Aptitude, however, he volunteered that he planned to revise the section of his paper in which he minimizes the role of personality factors before it is published (personal communication 1988); much of this revised opinion was based on the information provided during this conference (see Ehrman 1990 and Oxford 1990b).

Interaction of cognition and affect. It is conventional to separate cognition (abstract reasoning and similar processes) and affect (mental processes that involve feelings). Considerable work has been done in cognitive psychology to examine their interaction, however, e.g. Clark and Fiske (1982). Work in clinical psychology has also shown a close link between cognition and affect: one particularly interesting example is the work of John Gittinger (n.d.), in which evidence from the Wechsler Adult Intelligence Scale is used to build a complete personality model that encompasses both normal and pathological functioning. The second language acquisition literature also addresses the subject of the interface between cognition and affect in a number of ways. Some representative works from general psychology and second language acquisition include the following.

Gallwey's *The Inner Game of Tennis* (1974), a general work, distinguishes between the performing self and observing-judging self. This distinction relates directly to work in cognition and information processing theory: it is necessary to differentiate between behaviors that benefit from conscious mediation—often helpful when a behavior is being acquired—and those for which such conscious attention can be destructive once automatic acquisition has taken place (Lefebvre-Pinard 1983). The matter of critical, conscious self vs. automatic, performing self relates directly to the matter of performance anxiety, its deleterious effects, and some ways to cope with such anxiety. In fact, *The Inner Game of Tennis* has been useful to some FSI learners who were particularly affected by performance anxiety.

The impact on language learning success of interactions of learning style, learning strategies, and other variables of setting and personality are becoming increasingly clear (a fairly exhaustive list of these variables is to be found in Swan 1987). Certainly instructional methodology has a major effect. For example, there appears to be a correlation between general intelligence and performance in formal, classroom-based instruction (Swain and Cummins 1986), but "more informal programmes which stress interpersonal skills and language do not show the same stratified performance patterns" (Somerville-Ryan 1987).

Studies of the interaction of motivation and learning strategies represent an intersection of affect and cognition. Oxford and Nyikos (1989) report motivational level to have the most powerful effect on reported use of four out of five categories of language learning strategies. Development of motivation by interest in the task was the only one of a large number of strategies listed by 14 good language learners to be mentioned highly by all (Pickett 1978). McGroarty (1987) found that learners of Spanish whose motivation was presumed to be low tended to avoid authentic practice opportunities despite their availability. More indirectly, Politzer and McGroarty (1985) indicate that strategies may differ depending on the purpose for which the language is being learned. Similarly, the work of Ehrman and Oxford (1989), Oxford and Ehrman (1988), and Oxford (1986b) reports more frequent use of authentic language use strategies among adult learners learning languages for career reasons, from which we could infer that the learners are (instrumentally) motivated to practice.

Acquisition can be blocked by anxiety or other negative affect, a phenomenon referred to by Krashen (1982) as the 'affective filter'. Performance can also be enhanced by positive experience: Isen et al. (1982) describe the way that artificially induced positive mood can enhance creativity (but may reduce willingness to engage in tasks that require focused attention, unless they are deemed very important). Such findings may affect language learning in differential responses to such tasks as grammar study (which usually requires focused attention) or free conversation (which can engage creativity).

The study. The remainder of the present paper addresses some of these issues of learning strategy, learning style, motivation, and anxiety, using one of the dimensions of the Myers-Briggs Type Indicator (MBTI) model of personality structure as an organizer of general learning style. Just as personality provides order and predictability in the life-span story of an individual through the choices and decisions the person makes among the many alternatives available (Datan et al. 1987; Wheelis 1973), so learning style variables serve as a way to organize choices among the wide range of affective responses and learning strategies available to an individual. The MBTI thinking-feeling dimension is here used as that learning style organizer.

Subsequent sections describe the sample and procedures used and the results of the interview material. The results are followed by a general discussion, a short treatment of the relationship of the findings to learning success, and concluding observations.

Sample and procedures. The data reported on below are taken from a series of interviews of 21 members of the foreign affairs community, language learners at the Foreign Service Institute: one was a student of Thai, two of Korean, two of Japanese, and the remainder of Turkish. They were enrolled at FSI between 1986 and 1990, for periods ranging from 24 to 44 weeks of full-time intensive study. All 21 were satisfactory students, though some were relatively weak and some were exceptionally strong. Their age range was 25-50 years old; 13 were male; 8 were female. FSI language training is aimed at enabling students to undertake work overseas in foreign-affairs-related settings; it is therefore language for special purposes that is aimed at an advanced level of proficiency. Much of the instruction is communicative, though all of the programs in which these students participated had grammar-based textbooks and considerable emphasis on accurate as well as fluent communication. Students also received training in reading, especially unfamiliar reading material.

All students took the Myers-Briggs Type Indicator; this instrument is scored on four scales: extraversion/introversion (refers to focus of attention and energy); sensing/intuition (refers to ways of taking in information); thinking/feeling (refers to ways of making decisions and coming to conclusions); judging/perceiving (refers to need for closure and structure in daily life). (The MBTI is described in detail in Ehrman 1989; Ehrman 1990; Myers and McCaulley 1985; and Myers with Myers 1980.)

The present discussion focuses on the thinking/feeling scale. When I undertook the study of which the present report is a part (Ehrman 1989), I had anticipated that the sensing/intuition scale would be primary, because it addresses how people learn. Although it was indeed very important, the results of my analysis of the interviews showed that the thinking/feeling scale was at least as important. The thinking/feeling scale reflects how people make decisions; it also reflects a great deal about their interpersonal interactions. A person who prefers thinking judgment likes to decide on impersonal grounds, values objectivity, and will put truth over tact. (This is the 'owl' of the title of this paper.) A feeling type, or 'dove', uses subjective, value-based criteria for decision making, puts interpersonal harmony above all else, and may put tact over truth.

Interviews were usually part of the normal progress-reporting and end-of-training process; a few were specially arranged. I took notes during the interviews, and analyzed my notes for approaches to learning indicated by each of the learners. Some of these approaches were formal strategies of the sort described by Oxford (1986b) and others. Others were more general affective statements of likes, dislikes, fears, and enthusiasms. The student behaviors and attitudes were further analyzed according to the four MBTI dimensions and by a three-way grouping of 'behaviors characterizing or enhancing learning', 'liabilities', and 'behaviors characteristic of people of opposite preference'. Clear regularities appeared for all four MBTI scales.

Language learning success was evaluated through teacher ratings. A good student was one for whom rapid learning was achieved with relatively little effort or discomfort to both student and teachers. Conversely, a weak student was one for whom the process of language learning was costly for both sides.

Results. Results are reported for students preferring thinking judgment and for students preferring feeling judgment. In addition, the influence of the sensing/intuition scale on thinking and feeling is addressed, because the two poles of this scale colored the way thinking and feeling were realized (sensing refers to a practical, matter-of-fact, sequential approach to learning; intuition is a term used to refer to a more theoretical, imaginative, nonsequential and inferential approach).

Thinking. Fourteen, or two-thirds, of this subsample preferred thinking. All reported a pervasive tendency to analyze, which was applied to self, to language, to learning patterns, to readings, to grammar, and so on. They exhibited an analytical detachment from the social environment and impersonality in their assessment of their program and teachers. Thinkers also indicated a strong need for self-control, as well as control of content.

Thinker liabilities were for the most part the negative side of the detachment and control needs that were mentioned as assets. Detachment could become carelessness of the feelings and needs of others, and control needs frequently led to destructive performance anxiety, especially for the thinkers who also preferred intuitive perception (learning). Thinkers also reported speech production difficulties.

Thinkers indicated sporadic access to feeling characteristics in the form of valuing interpersonal relationships, forming alliances with classmates, working to maintain interpersonal harmony, and acceptance of their own and others' feelings. These were at best secondary, however.

Thinkers commented extensively about their teachers, and mostly with an objective, analytical tone. They tended to be most positively impressed by dedication, ability to maintain control without becoming authoritarian, concern for individualization and variety, availability, amount of preparation for classes, patience with students, sticking to what they thought right despite student pressure, teamwork, and complementary mix of talents.

Feeling. The seven feeling learners, one-third of the subsample, reported being highly influenced by their relationships with those around them. Good relationships with teachers were especially helpful, as was a nonthreatening, cooperative atmosphere. Few specific cognitive strategies were mentioned.

Feeling types rejected use of analysis, indicated overdependence on external harmony, and disliked "boring" materials.

Thinking characteristics sometimes accessed by feelers included a willingness to tolerate pressure by teachers and acknowledgement of the ability to analyze, even if it was not often applied.

Feelers' impressions of teachers exhibited greater subjectivity and interpersonal involvement than did those of their thinking classmates. They liked their teachers' motivation, conscientiousness, interest in individual student learning, imagination, variety, and going out of the way to be agreeable, liveliness, and variety of interests. The teachers were described as considerate of different student needs and pace of learning, having interest in individual students and their progress, showing pleasure in student progress, pleasure in their own profession, flexibility, and sensitivity to student state of fatigue or mood.

Combinations of preferences. People who make regular use of psychological type find that the individual scales or dimensions are even more valuable when they are treated in combination with each other. Any of the scales can usefully be combined with any other and can be used to account for various aspects of behavior. The whole of any given combination tends to be more than the sum of the parts. However, several scale combinations are more often used than others; among these are the combinations of sensing and intuition with thinking and feeling.

Characteristics of members of this sample who fell into these four combination categories (sensing-thinking, sensing-feeling, intuition-thinking, intuition-feeling) are sketched here. These sketches are consistent with common descriptions of these combinations (see Hirsh and Kummerow 1987).

The six learners who preferred sensing and thinking were largely matter-of-fact, systematic learners. They all made regular use of step-by-step hard work. They tended to need a clearly outlined curriculum and interim, specific goals and objectives. For the most part, they were facilitated by routine. Imagination and search for meanings did not play much of a role in their approach to the language learning task.

The three sensing feelers were facilitated by harmonious relations with their teachers, but they did not talk about it directly, perhaps because they could take such relations for granted: many of their teachers were sensing feelers, too. On the other hand, they did address the importance to their learning of their relations with their classmates. Perhaps this was because, unlike their relations with their teachers, they could not take harmony with their classmates as much for granted, because of the diversity of types among the students and an element of competition. Sensing feelers were generally solid, businesslike learners who took study seriously but who were not much oriented to experimentation and exploration of multiple possibilities.

The five intuitive feeling learners cited the fewest actual language learning strategies or techniques. Most of the elements occurring in their descriptions of their learning could be categorized as a generalized affiliative orientation rather than as specific social strategies for learning. They frequently mentioned the importance of bonding with teachers and peers (reflecting feeling sociability combined with intuitive global, nonanalytical grasp of language). As the only two-scale combination group in this sample to have all top-rated students, they demonstrated the natural communication skills by which intuitive feelers are typically characterized (see e.g. Myers and McCaulley 1985). As a group, they tended to reject analysis as a spontaneous strategy but profited from external reminders to make use of it.

In contrast to the intuitive feelers, the eight intuitive thinkers were extremely analytical. In fact, one described herself as "analyzing everything." Their desire to understand the 'why' as well as the 'what' of the language led to intense curiosity, much of which they satisfied by their own investigations and researches. They were consistent users of formal model building strategies, using thinking analysis to find out how the language works and intuition to see the relations among the parts and levels. They had very high achievement needs, which were often two-edged swords: on the one hand, these needs caused the intuitive thinkers to work hard and explore intently; on the other hand, these needs sometimes led to overcomplexity and performance anxiety.[2]

Discussion. Female thinkers had more in common with the male thinkers than they did with female feelers, and vice versa. Thus the thinking/feeling dimension of the MBTI provided more information about language learning than did sex differences in this qualitative study. These findings contradicted the data from the quantitative study reported in Ehrman and Oxford (1989); this difference may stem from the fact that there was far more variation in occupation and interests in the quantitative (larger sample) study. Personality type (as expressed by occupational self-selection, e.g. into the Foreign Service) may thus be a more powerful variable in language learning than sex of the student.

Thinking. Statistical findings relating MBTI type and language learning strategies on the Strategy Inventory for Language Learning (SILL, Oxford 1986a) indicated that thinkers used no learning strategy factor more often than did feeling types (Ehrman and Oxford 1989). The interview data yielded contrasting results, in which thinkers reported many more specific behaviors and strategies than did feelers. The interviews provided other information about the instrumental approach of the thinkers, which appeared especially clearly in what thinking types appreciated in their teachers and the program: professionalism, effort, performance, and competence of their teachers. This doubtless also reflected many of the characteristics that the thinkers liked best about themselves.

Unquestionably, the most salient thinker strategy found in the interviews was analysis. Every one of the thinking students mentioned doing analysis in

---

[2] Intuitive thinkers were able to combine intuitive insight and inferencing skills with thinking analysis; however, they hindered themselves affectively. Their instructional metho-dology conflicts were minimal. The intuitive feelers in this subsample were all excellent learners; their primary consistent liability was a distaste for analysis, for which they com-pensated by a more global acquisitional approach. However, other intuitive feelers, not in this subsample, have had difficulty in the program and have even failed. Their primary defects appeared to be memory retention and a really underdeveloped ability to use cognitive skills that was not characteristic of any of the students in this subsample.

some form, whether of the language, of his or her own learning patterns, or of content. Thinkers also expressed a strong need for control, including both self-control and control of knowledge. These two aspects of control merged in thinkers' general 'competence hunger', which tended to focus on reaching for knowledge and conceptual mastery. A visible sign of competence is one's profession, hence the thinkers' professional identity was of great importance to them (especially to the intuitive thinkers, who defined themselves by their intellectual competence). Control strategies were adaptive for the most part, but they became maladaptive when they led thinkers to require perfection of themselves, thus sometimes producing disabling anxiety.

Also both adaptive and maladaptive was the detachment of the thinkers. Detachment helped some thinkers get out of the anxious, perfectionistic mode; sensing thinkers seemed to use detachment in this way more readily than intuitive thinkers. Sensing thinkers were able to take in stride a great deal that happened in language training, did not ordinarily take difficulties personally, and could often evaluate their own progress in a balanced way. On the other hand, the negative side of detachment was insensitivity and occasionally strained relations with others. It was not feelers but thinkers (though only three of them) who were at all characterized by strained relations with teachers and classmates. Some thinking types—not necessarily those who had friction with others—expressed concern about maintaining relations with others, suggesting that they knew that interpersonal relations came less naturally to them, and they had to work harder to maintain such relations.

Thinker interpersonal anxiety may be significant as an explanation for the competence hunger of most of the thinkers in the subsample. Feeling is a relatively undeveloped function for thinkers, and so they may not have as much confidence in their relations with others as do feeling types for whom the interpersonal is usually a strength. I speculate that many thinkers in the subsample may have experienced anxiety about their personal acceptability. They are likely to have displaced this anxiety onto achievement needs. Intuition may have exacerbated the anxiety, because where sensing is grounded and often matter-of-fact and realistic, intuition is imaginative about negative possibilities as well as positive ones. That is, intuition, which is usually optimistic when well developed, can be distorted by anxiety that the less socially oriented thinkers may feel in a socially stressful situation.

Only thinkers reported difficulty with self-esteem issues, including loss of professional identity, loss of control, and high self-expectations. Almost all of those who had such difficulties were intuitive thinkers. Although such a small sample of thinkers—only 14—is far too small a basis for making sweeping generalizations, this observation about the propensity of intuitive thinkers to vulnerable self-esteem compared to sensing thinkers is consistent with my informal experience with a great many other students.

This thinker anxiety, especially evident in intuitive thinkers, contrasts with the self-acceptance exhibited by the feelers in the subsample. It is tempting to wonder which came first, a sense of acceptability leading to development of the feeling function, or a propensity toward feeling leading to higher self-esteem and reinforcing acceptability because the feeler is oriented to pleasing others.

A characteristic for which the thinker is well known in psychological type theory is the tendency to respond to stimuli with criticism rather than with appreciation. This trait of describing their glass as half empty rather than half full was quite characteristic of all the thinking types in their interviews. They sometimes had to be asked what they appreciated in the course. When asked, they were quick to cite many virtues of teachers and course; it was not that they did not appreciate the good qualities of the training, but they sometimes needed overt reminding to mention the positive side. It seems likely that thinkers see what is good, but because they think it is self-evident, and they do not like to proclaim the obvious, they tend to focus on what seems less obvious: how to make the adequate even better. (To be sure, they may not always even grant adequacy.) Unfortunately, the thinkers' critical tendency sometimes compounds their other social liabilities.

Thinkers can function without interpersonal harmony, considering external strife irrelevant and often tuning it out. This may seem contradictory to the interpersonal anxieties thinkers experience that were described above as a possible source of their competence hunger. In fact, there need be no contradiction. At one level, some thinking types may lack confidence in their interpersonal acceptability, but they may cope with what seems to be a weakness by reducing social harmony needs to a less important place in their day-to-day lives. Despite their ability to detach, however, thinkers in fact do even better without external emotional upheavals.

Aspects of a training program that is likely to help thinkers do their best include a businesslike but not demeaning and regimented atmosphere, task-oriented camaraderie, and a curriculum that permits the student to feel in control of the material. The nature of an optimal curriculum is likely to differ somewhat for sensing thinkers and intuitive thinkers. Although both will appreciate a sense of order and organization in the syllabus, sensing thinkers will depend on it more than intuitive thinkers and may well be handicapped and slowed down without such order. Intuitive thinkers will be critical if it is not present, but they will usually be able to function effectively (if complainingly) in its absence. Topics like literature and domestic life which are not directly task-related will probably be accepted best if their relationship to the task is made clear. Intuitive thinkers who are confident of their language learning ability will be frustrated by lack of opportunity to find their own structure, both in the study plan and in the language itself, so opportunities for autonomous functioning should be elements in programs for thinkers, especially intuitive thinkers. Self-confident intuitive thinkers can be highly innovative and creative language learners if given the freedom to follow their inclinations.

Feeling. In the interviews, feeling students reported far more concern for social, interpersonal issues than for any other aspect of their language learning. Although feelers reported relatively high use of all strategies on the SILL and particularly of general study strategies in the quantitative investigation (Ehrman and Oxford 1989), their interviews reported few specific strategies, especially relative to thinkers. Interview data suggested that the high use of general study strategies reported on the SILL might be because doing assignments was the least that was required for pleasing teachers, and pleasing others is very important for feelers.

In contrast with thinkers, feelers were spontaneous and liberal with praise for their teachers and general appreciation for the program. Their relatively few critical comments focused on subject matter (too relentlessly work-related) or on their own comparatively low interest in activities calling for analysis. This relative lack of criticism could come from the tendency of feelers to appreciate rather than criticize, or it could result from the fact that their primary needs for harmony and acknowledgement of their individuality were being met (or some of both).

The feelers appreciated interpersonal qualities of the teachers. Specifically, they cited teacher interest in individual students and the teaching team's consistent and harmonious teamwork. Where thinkers evaluated teachers on their ability to perform the teaching task, feelers appreciated them for their personal and interpersonal contributions. Feelers reported that their learning was greatly facilitated by bonding with their teachers and by teacher interest in them as individuals and in their progress. Teacher interest in individual students came up repeatedly in feeler comments. It is remarkable that this factor was not mentioned by any of the thinkers. What the feelers admired and appreciated might have reflected their own ideals and the behavior in themselves with which they identify: caring about the personal and the interpersonal.

None of the feelers experienced friction with others. It was more important for them to suppress their irritation with disruptive classmates in the interest of interpersonal harmony than to exert the control that mattered to their thinking colleagues. Several feelers commented that congenial classes lowered tension for them; others remarked that they accepted others without asking 'why'; and several liked the MBTI because it made students more sensitive to each other.

Feelers were not ordinarily troubled by doubts of personal acceptability. This freed them to put energy into learning rather than protection of self-image. Some of the perfectionistic anxiety that was so deleterious to thinkers seemed to stem from lack of assurance about the degree to which they were accepted and acceptable; the feelers in the subsample did not describe experiencing this phenomenon.

Feelers reported themselves as interested in topics and materials that were not directly related to their overseas jobs. They specifically mentioned the way in which such topics might contribute to better understanding of

Turkish people. These observations can be interpreted as the thematic feeler interest in people, rather than in impersonal tasks.

The only specific learning strategy that was consistently mentioned in interviews by the feelers was analysis—usually to reject it. Feeling students sometimes would admit to an ability to use analytic skills, but almost all said that they disliked the process or that they had to force themselves. Perhaps the lack of interest in analytic work came from the fact that feeling students did not find that they needed it, that other skills served in its place. It could also be a matter of differentiation of themselves from the thinkers, who were almost completely identified with analysis. The remark made by one of the feelers about his perception of thinking as distant, aloof, and self-centered, and the comments by several about not being 'hung up' on competence suggest that these feeling students were keenly aware of the differences between them and their thinking classmates. It is also evidence of the fact that feelers can be critical, but they do not express criticism reflexively, as the thinkers seem to do.

The detrimental side of the personal orientation of the feelers in the subsample was their interpersonal vulnerability, expressed in a dependence on continuous evidence of bonding and harmony. It was only the feelers, for example, who described discouragement when teacher attention was diverted to the students who were ending their training and who normally received intense 'care and feeding' at this time. It was only feelers who described discouragement when they did not receive enough positive feedback from teachers. Feelers described themselves as context-sensitive and affected by interpersonal atmosphere; thinkers did not.

An ideal classroom for a feeler would be one in which relationships were harmonious at all times. Teachers would be accessible for the bonding and identification that aid feelers and would take overt and consistent interest in the students, not only as learners but as people. Cooperative learning would be a frequently used technique. Feelers are likely to appreciate a tool like the MBTI to help them build fellowship with their classmates and as a norm of acknowledging each others' needs. The optimal curriculum for feelers is orderly and sufficiently structured that it does not draw attention and energy to itself and to its own deficiencies. Content is wide-ranging, with material that is work-relevant but not exclusively so. Attention to culture and values is pervasive.

Learning success. The unexpected salience of the thinking/feeling scale confirms the importance of the affective side of language learning and puts to rest any lingering thought that learning in general and language learning in particular is a chiefly cognitive process. The prominence of the thinking/feeling scale, which reflects in part an individual's degree of sensitivity to others, is also indicative of the significance of social factors in language learning. This finding is consistent with research which has emphasized that adult intelligence increasingly involves the ability to adapt to and cope with the intrapersonal and interpersonal problems of daily living as well as abstract problem solving: such social intelligence is an aspect of post-formal-operations thinking (Rybash et al. 1986).

The social nature of communicative language learning almost certainly made a difference to relative success in this sample. Among these students, although there were excellent students of all psychological type preferences, a greater proportion of feeling types were rated by their teachers as good students and a smaller proportion as problematic. Their advantage may be a result of motivational factors (interest in the people and culture reflecting integrative motivation) and their ability to access affective strategies to maintain self-esteem and social affiliation approaches to enlist help. The thinkers as a group were more hindered by their anxiety and were much less likely to be able to make regular use of interpersonal skills in this intensely social situation.

It is important to keep in mind that no individual is monolithically characterized by thinking or feeling characteristics only (or any of the other MBTI poles). A mature person can show, for instance, both thinking and feeling skills, though psychological type theory would say that they would not have equal facility. Such a person would be able to operate using thinking and feeling (or sensing and intuition) for any given task, if not simultaneously, at least in rapid succession. It appears that in type terms, effective language learning depends on the ability both to mobilize consistently the strengths associated with one's native preferences, as expressed by the four letters in the MBTI type, and to access skills associated with less preferred functions and attitudes as needed.

A good example of such a learner appears in Stevick's recent book (1989) based on interviews of seven gifted language learners. I know that one of these seven learners, "Gwen," is an intuitive thinking type on the MBTI; she has a very strong preference for thinking judgment. She reports herself as heavily affected by interpersonal factors and as making extensive use of analytic strategies. "Gwen" is a good example of a person who relies successfully on strategies associated with both preferences.

Some learners access the less preferred skills by conscious self-discipline and hard work. Others achieve such access as a result of normal maturation—this is definitely one of the advantages an older learner may have over a younger one. And some are simply fortunate in having access to cross-type skills as a result of such environmental accidents as upbringing or schooling: for example, most educated feelers can access thinking skills because education in Western culture offers constant training in analytical skills. The converse is not true, however, which puts thinkers at a disadvantage in situations where feeling skills are needed.

Students who used metacognition to self-regulate seemed to have an edge. They were aware of themselves as learners, observed themselves and the effects of their behavior, often introspected about why and how, and evaluated their success. When the self-evaluation was done in a self-accepting way (with affective strategies like self-reinforcement or positive self-talk as a conscious or unconscious cushion), students could adapt effectively to the learning demands and could take steps to meet their needs. When the self-evaluation was done in a self-flagellating way (without a positive affective balance), the metacognition was distorted and an impediment to effective learning. In general, the feelers in this subsample could better access the constructive kind of metacognition supported by positive affect; of the thinkers, the matter-of-fact sensing thinkers were less vulnerable as a group to neurotic, destructive metacognition than were the intuitive thinkers.

Concluding observations. The study of which this report is a part (Ehrman 1989; Ehrman and Oxford 1989) is one of several that show the great variation among successful language learners. Stevick's (1989) seven gifted language learners are all quite different from each other and rely on dramatically different strategies. Schneiderman and Desmarais (1988) review some of the neurological elements that have been investigated for second language talent; in the same volume, Novoa, Fein, and Obler (1988) refer to these findings to describe a specific case of an individual of normal intelligence, whose approach is clearly different from that of any of the 21 individuals in my sample (two of whom are profiled briefly in the Appendix) or the seven in Stevick's. This subject differs from the others both in the fact that he is of only normal (rather than superior) general intelligence and in his choice of specific learning strategies and cognitive style, e.g. informal contacts with native speakers, use of the media, and unusually rapid verbal memory. However, it is interesting that he shares with many of them a high motivation, a somewhat nonconformist self-concept, and a willingness to take linguistic risks.

I have attempted here to find regularities in the many different approaches to successful learning that these different cases document by using relatively broad-gauge personality factors. The findings for thinking/feeling alone are seen to have implications for prediction of preferred approaches to the learning task (strategies and attitudes), the probable nature of motivation for learning (instrumental vs. integrative), the kinds of factors that are likely to interfere with learning, and the kinds of classroom intervention that are most likely to reach these different learner types.

Language learning for communicative proficiency is a social, interpersonal matter for a social, interpersonal purpose. Trust and the ability to reduce interpersonal boundaries are helpful; these seem to come more easily to feeling types in a situation that is not characterized by interpersonal disharmony. Hostile competition is likely to be disruptive to both personality types, for different reasons: thinkers may be vulnerable to self-focus and reduced self-esteem, with concomitant reduction of cognitive efficiency because failure and success are organizing principles of their self-structure; feelers may find themselves dysfunctional when they cannot count on the mutual acceptance of those around them, since their self-structure is dependent on their sense that they are in harmony with their social environment. For different reasons for thinkers and feelers, the findings in this paper support classrooms which promote cooperative learning and reduce hostile competition.

Appendix: Two successful students

The following brief descriptions show how two top-rated students achieved exceptional results in their training. On all four MBTI scales they are opposites, showing that ultimately any learner can maximize his or her assets and the learning strategies associated with his or her personality.

Melissa, an extraverted intuitive feeling judger (ENFJ), was an A+ student. As a result of an accident of timing, she received most of her training in an individual class. Naturally, this arrangement had great advantages for her, because it permitted her to learn in a style entirely compatible with her needs and at her own rate. On the other hand, it was not as satisfying to her affiliation needs as a group class would have been. She was able, however, to mobilize her strongest function, extraverted feeling, to build close relationships with her teachers, who then provided her the companionship that motivated her. Her interview notes contain almost no information about specific cognitive techniques used. This absence of information about cognitive strategies might suggest the degree to which successful language learning is influenced by affective, motivational, relational matters; or it might imply that as an intuitive feeler, Melissa was most likely to focus on these affective issues, rather than the strictly cognitive. Melissa was clearly a risk-taker. Meeting the affiliation needs of her dominant function appears to have enabled her to take and profit from these risks.

Dennis, an introverted sensing thinking perceiver (ISTP), was described as one of the best students ever to go through the difficult and demanding Japanese program. His performance was rated A+ by his teachers. Much of Dennis's success came from his ability to actualize his sensing skills through systematic application more characteristic of judging than the perceiving he really preferred. On the other hand, he also had the relaxed approach and adaptability to a new environment typical of perceiving. Dennis's strongest function, by theory, is introverted thinking. It seems likely that his analysis of the situation and development of a plan were examples of constructive use of his thinking, as was his ability to detach himself from destructive self-talk that affected many of his classmates. Dennis used a visual but concretizing metaphor, in which he compared Japanese grammar to an engine to be assembled. He was self-sufficient but relaxed in his relations with his teachers and fellow-students. Although he reported himself as disadvantaged by such communicative teaching techniques as round-robin story telling, he found ways to compensate for them; this was typical of his entire matter-of-fact approach to the learning process.

References

Alpert, R., and R. Haber. 1960. Anxiety in academic achievement situations. Journal of Abnormal and Social Psychology 61:207-15.

Anderson, J.R. 1982. Acquisition of cognitive skill. Psychological Review 89:369-406.

Bailey, K.M. 1983. Competitiveness and anxiety in adult second language learning: Looking at and through the diary studies. In: H.W. Seliger and M.H. Long, eds. Classroom oriented research in second language acquisition. Rowley, Mass.: Newbury House.

Bailey, K.M., M.H. Long, and S. Peck. 1983. Second language acquisition studies. Rowley, Mass.: Newbury House.

Bates, E. 1972. Language and context. New York: Academic Press.

Beebe, L.M. 1983. Risk taking and the language learner. In: H.W. Seliger and M.H. Long, eds. Classroom oriented research in second language acquisition. Rowley, Mass.: Newbury House.

Beeman, P., R. Martin, and J. Meyers. 1972. Interventions in relation to anxiety in school. In: C. Spielberger, ed. Anxiety: Current trends in theory and research. New York: Academic Press.

Berman, R.A. 1987. Cognitive components of language development. In: C.W. Pfaff, ed. First and second language acquisition processes. New York: Newbury House.

Bialystok, E. 1981. A theoretical model of second language learning. Language Learning 28. 69-83.

Bialystok, E., and M. Frohlich. 1978. Variables of classroom achievement in second language learning. Modern Language Journal 62:327-66.

Brown, H., and H.D. Brown. 1987. Principles of language learning and teaching. 2d ed. Englewood Cliffs, N.J.: Prentice-Hall.

Busch, D. 1982. Introversion-extraversion and the EFL proficiency of Japanese language students. Language Learning 32:109-32.

Bush, M.D. 1989. The personality and attitudinal dimensions of language aptitude. Paper presented at the Interagency Language Roundtable Invitational Language Aptitude Testing Symposium, 1988. In: T. Parry and C.W. Stansfield, eds. Language aptitude: Past, present, and future research. Englewood Cliffs, N.J.: Prentice-Hall.

Campione, J.C., and A.L. Brown. 1984. Learning ability and transfer propensity as sources of individual differences in intelligence. In: P.H. Brooks, R.D. Sperber, and C. McCauley, eds. Learning and cognition in the mentally retarded. Baltimore: University Park Press. 265-94.

Carrell, P. 1984. Evidence of a formal schema in second language comprehension. Language Learning 34.2:87-112(b).

Carroll, J.B. 1963. Research on teaching foreign languages. In: N.L. Gage, ed. Handbook of research on teaching. Chicago: Rand McNally.

Carroll, J.B., and S.M. Sapon. 1958. Modern language aptitude test. New York: Psychological Corporation.

Carroll, J.B. 1990. Cognitive abilities and foreign language aptitude: Then and now. Paper presented at the Interagency Language Roundtable Invitational Language Aptitude Testing Symposium, 1988. In: T. Parry and C.W. Stansfield, eds. Language aptitude: Past, present, and future research. Englewood Cliffs, N.J.: Prentice-Hall.

Chamot, A.U., and J.M. O'Malley. 1987. The cognitive academic language learning approach: A bridge to the mainstream. TESOL Quarterly 21:227-49.

Chastain, K. 1975. Affective and ability factors in second language acquisition. Language Learning 25:153-61.

Chaudron, C. 1988. Second language classrooms: Research on teaching and learning. New York: Cambridge University Press.

Clark, M.S., and S.T. Fiske. 1982. Affect and cognition: The seventeenth annual Carnegie symposium on cognition. Hillsdale, N.J.: Erlbaum.

Clement, R., P.C. Smythe, and R.C. Gardner. 1978. Persistence in second language study: Motivational considerations. Canadian Modern Language Review 34:688-94.

Curral, S.C., and R.E. Kirk. 1986. Predicting success in intensive foreign language courses. Modern Language Journal 70.2:107-13.

Curran, C.A. 1972. Counseling-learning: A whole-person model for education. New York: Grune and Stratton.

Darke, S. 1988. Effects of anxiety on inferential reasoning task performance. Journal of Personality and Social Psychology 55:499-505.

Datan, N., D. Rodeheaver, and F. Hughes. 1987. Adult development and aging. Annual Review of Psychology 38:153-80.

Day, R.R. 1984. Student participation in the ESL classroom or some imperfections in practice. Language Learning 34:69-102.

Day, R.R. 1985. The use of the target language in context and second-language proficiency. In: S.M. Gass and C.G. Madden, eds. Input and second language acquisition. Rowley, Mass.: Newbury House.

Ehrman, M.E. 1989. Ants and grasshoppers, badgers and butterflies: Qualitative and quantitative investigation of adult language learning styles and strategies. Ann Arbor,Mich.: University Microfilms International.

Ehrman, M.E. 1990. The role of personality type in adult language learning: An ongoing investigation. Paper presented at the Interagency Language Roundtable Invitational Language Aptitude Testing Symposium, 1988. In: T. Parry and C.W. Stansfield, eds. Language aptitude: Past, present, and future research. Englewood Cliffs, N.J.: Prentice-Hall.

Ehrman, M.E., and R.L. Oxford. 1989. Effects of sex differences, career choice, and psychological type on adult language learning strategies. Modern Language Journal 73:1-13.

Ehrman, M.E., and R.L. Oxford. 1990. The Interaction of Adult Language Learning Styles and Strategies. Modern Language Journal, in press.

Eysenck, M.W. 1979. Anxiety, learning, and memory: A reconceptualisation. Journal of Research in Personality 13:363-85. Cited in Darke (1988).

Eysenck, M.W. 1982. Attention and arousal (cognition and performance). Berlin, West Germany: Springer-Verlag. Cited in Darke (1988).

Fischer, K.W., and L. Silvern. 1985. Stages and individual differences in cognitive development. Annual Review of Psychology 36:613-48.

Flavell, J.H., P.I. Botkin, C.C. Fry, W. Wright, and P.G. Jarvis. 1968. The development of role-taking and communicative skills in children. New York: Wiley.

Foss, K.A., and A.C. Reitzel. 1988. A relational model for managing second language anxiety. TESOL Quarterly 22:437-52.

Frawley, W., and J.P. Lantolf. 1985. Second language discourse: A Vygotskyan perspective. Applied Linguistics 6.1:21-43.

Frawley, W., and J.P. Lantolf. 1984. Speaking and self order: A critique of orthodox L2 research. Studies in Second Language Acquisition 6.2:143-59.

Frederiksen, N. 1984. Implications of cognitive theory for instruction in problem solving. Review of Educational Research 54.3:363-407.

Gallwey, W.T. 1974. The inner game of tennis. New York: Random House.

Gardner, R.C. 1978. Social psychological aspects of second language acquisition. In: H. Giles and R.N. St. Clair, eds., Language and social psychology. Baltimore: University Park Press.

Gardner, R.C. 1990. Attitude, motivation, and personality as predictors of success in foreign language learning. Paper presented at the Interagency Language Roundtable Invitational Language Aptitude Testing Symposium, 1988. In: T. Parry and C.W. Stansfield, eds. Language aptitude: Past, present, and future research. Englewood Cliffs, N.J.: Prentice-Hall.

Gardner, R.C., and W.E. Lambert. 1972. Attitudes and motivation in second language learning. Rowley, Mass.: Newbury House.

Gittinger, J.W. n.d. Origins of the personality assessment system. PAS Journal. 13-28.

Graham, C.R. 1984. Beyond integrative motivation: The development and influence of assimilative motivation. Paper presented at the International Convention of Teachers of English to Speakers of Other Languages, Houston, Texas, March.

Gregg, K.R. 1984. Krashen's monitor and Occam's razor. Applied Linguistics 5:79-100.

Guiora, A.Z., W.R. Acton, R. Everard, and F.W. Strickland. 1980. The effects of benzodiazepine (valium) on permeability of ego boundaries. Language Learning 30:351-63.

Guiora, A.Z., B. Beit-Hallami, R.C. Brannon, C.Y. Dull, and T. Scovel. 1972. The effects of experimentally induced changes in ego states on pronunciation ability in second language: An exploratory study. Comprehensive Psychiatry 13.

Guiora, A.Z., R.C. Brannon, and C.Y. Dull. 1972. Empathy and second language learning.Language Learning 22:111-30.

Hall, R.H., T.R. Rocklin, D.F. Dansereau, L.P. Skaggs, A.M. O'Donnell, J.G. Lambiotte, and M.D. Young. 1988. The role of individual differences in the cooperative learning of technical material. Journal of Educational Psychology 80.2:172-78.

Hirsh, S.K., and J.M. Kummerow. 1987. Introduction to type in organizational settings. Palo Alto, Calif.: Consulting Psychologists.

Horwitz, E.K. 1987. Linguistic and communicative competence: Reassessing foreign language aptitude. In: B. Van Patten, T.R. Dvorak, and J.F. Lee, eds. Foreign language learning: A research perspective. New York: Newbury House.

Horwitz, E.K., M.B. Horwitz, and J. Cope. 1986. Foreign language classroom anxiety. Modern Language Journal 70:125-32.

Isen, A.M., B. Means, R. Patrick, and G. Nowicki. 1982. Some factors influencing decision-making strategy and risk-taking. In: M.S. Clark and S.T. Fiske, eds. Affect and cognition: The seventeenth annual Carnegie symposium on cognition. Hillsdale, N.J.: Erlbaum.

Jacobus, F. 1990. The relationship between cognitive development and foreign language proficiency. Paper presented at the Interagency Language Roundtable Invitational Language Aptitude Testing Symposium, 1988. In: T. Parry and C.W. Stansfield, eds. Language aptitude: Past, present, and future research. Englewood Cliffs, N.J.: Prentice-Hall.

Knowles, M.S. 1978. The adult learner: A neglected species. 2d ed. Houston: Gulf.

Krashen, S.D. 1978. Individual variation in the use of the monitor. In: W.C. Ritchie, ed. Second language acquisition research: Issues and implications. New York: Academic Press.

Krashen, S.D. 1982. Principles and practice in second language acquisition. San Francisco: Pergamon.

Krashen, S.D., and T. Terrell. 1983. The natural approach: Language acquisition in the classroom. Oxford: Pergamon.

Labouvie-Vief, G. 1985. Intelligence and cognition. In: J.E. Birren and K.W. Schaie, eds. Handbook of the psychology of aging. 2d ed. New York: Van Nostrand Rheinhold.

Lalonde, R.N., and R.C. Gardner. 1984. Investigating a causal model of second language acquisition: Where does personality fit? Canadian Journal of Behavioural Science 16:224-37.

Lefebvre-Pinard, M. 1983. Understanding and auto-control of cognitive functions: Implications for the relationship between cognition and behavior. International Journal of Behavioral Development 6:15-35.

Lett, J., and F.E. O'Mara. 1990. Predictors of success in an intensive language learning context: An explanatory model of classroom language learning at the Defense Language Institute. Paper presented at the Interagency Language Roundtable Invitational Language Aptitude Testing Symposium, 1988. In: T. Parry and C.W. Stansfield, eds. Language aptitude: Past, present, and future research. Englewood Cliffs, N.J.: Prentice-Hall.

Linville, P.W. 1982. Affective consequences of complexity regarding the self and others. In: M.S. Clark and S.T. Fiske, eds. Affect and cognition: The seventeenth annual Carnegie symposium on cognition. Hillsdale, N.J.: Erlbaum.

Lozanov, G. 1979. Suggestology and outlines of suggestopedy. New York: Gordon and Beach.

McDonough, S.H. 1981. Psychology in foreign language teaching. London: George Allen and Unwin.

McGroarty, M. 1987. Patterns of persistent second language learners: Elementary Spanish. Paper presented at the annual meeting of Teachers of English to Speakers of Other Languages, Miami.

McGroarty, M. 1988. The 'good learner' of English in two settings. Research report to the Center for Language Education and Research, UCLA.

Myers, I.B., and M.H. McCaulley. 1985. Manual: A guide to the development and use of the Myers-Briggs Type Indicator. Palo Alto: Consulting Psychologists Press.

Myers, I.B., with P. Myers. 1980. Gifts differing. Palo Alto: Consulting Psychologists Press.

Naiman, N., M. Frohlich, H.H. Stern, and A. Todesco. 1978. The good language learner. Research in Education Series No. 7. Toronto: Ontario Institute for Studies in Education.

Naiman, N., M. Frohlich, and A. Todesco. 1975. The good second language learner. TESOL Talk 5.1:58-75.

Novoa, L., D. Fein, and L.K. Obler. 1988. Talent in foreign languages: A case study. In: L.K. Obler, and D. Fein, eds. The exceptional brain: Neuropsychology of talent and special abilities. New York: Guilford.

O'Malley, J.M., R.P. Russo, A.U. Chamot, G. Stewner-Manzanares, and L. Kupper. 1985. Learning strategy applications with students of English as a second language. TESOL Quarterly 19.3:557-84.

Oxford, R. 1985. A new taxonomy of second language learning strategies. Washington, D.C.: ERIC Clearinghouse on Languages and Linguistics.

Oxford, R. 1986a. Development and psychometric testing of the Strategy Inventory for Language Learning (ARI Technical Report). Alexandria, Va.: U.S. Army Research Institute for the Behavioral and Social Sciences.

Oxford, R. 1986b. Second language learning strategies: Current research and implications for practice. Los Angeles: Center for Language Education and Research, University of California at Los Angeles.

Oxford, R. 1990a. Language learning strategies: What every teacher should know. New York: Newbury House/Harper and Row.

Oxford, R. 1990b. Styles, strategies, and aptitude: Important connections for language learners. Paper presented at the Interagency Language Roundtable Invitational Language Aptitude Testing Symposium, 1988. In: T. Parry and C.W. Stansfield, eds. Language aptitude: Past, present, and future research. Englewood Cliffs, N.J.: Prentice-Hall.

Oxford, R., and M.E. Ehrman. 1988. Psychological type and adult language learning strategies: A pilot study. Journal of Psychological Type 16.

Oxford, R., and M. Nyikos. 1989. Variables affecting choice of language learning strategies by university students. Modern Language Journal 73:291-300.

Parsons, A.H. 1983. Self-esteem and the acquisition of French. In: K.M. Bailey, M.H. Long, and S. Peck, Second language acquisition studies. Rowley, Mass.: Newbury House.

Pask, G. 1988. Learning strategies, teaching strategies, and conceptual or learning style. In: R.R. Schmeck, ed. Learning strategies and learning styles. New York: Plenum.

Pickett, G.D. 1978. The foreign language learning process. London: The British Council.

Politzer, R.L., and M. McGroarty. 1985. An exploratory study of learning behaviors and their relationship to gains in linguistic and communicative competence. TESOL Quarterly 19.1:103-24.

Pritchard, D.F.L. 1952. An investigation into the relationship of personality traits and ability in modern languages. British Journal of Educational Psychology 22:147-48.

Reiss, M.A. 1985. The good language learner: Another look. Canadian Modern Language Review 41:511-23.

Richards, F.A., and M.L. Commons. 1984. Systematic, metasystematic, and cross-paradigmatic reasoning: A case for stages of reasoning beyond formal operations. In: M.L. Commons, F.A. Richards, and C. Armon, eds. Beyond formal operations: Late adolescent and adult cognitive development. New York: Praeger.

Rubin, J. 1975. What the 'good language learner' can teach us. TESOL Quarterly 9.1:41-45.

Rybash, J.M., W.J. Hoyer, and P.A. Roodin. 1986. Adult cognition and aging: Developmental changes in processing, knowing, and thinking. New York: Pergamon.

Schneiderman, E.I., and C. Desmarais. 1988. A neuropsychological substrate for talent in second-language acquisition. In: L.K. Obler and D. Fein, eds. The exceptional brain: Neuropsychology of talent and special abilities. New York: Guilford.

Schumann, J. 1975. Affective variables and the problem of age in second language acquisition. Language Learning 25:209-35.

Schumann, J. 1976. Second language acquisition research: Getting a more global look at the learner. Papers in Second Language Acquisition. Proceedings of the Sixth Annual Conference on Applied Linguistics, 1975. Language Learning, Special Issue No. 4:15-28.

Scovel, T. 1978. The effect of affect on foreign language learning: A review of the anxiety research. Language Learning 28:129-42.

Seliger, H.W. 1983. Learner interaction in the classroom and its effects on language acquisition. In: H.W. Seliger and M.H. Long, eds. 1983. Classroom oriented research in second language acquisition. Rowley, Mass.: Newbury House.

Showers, C., and N. Cantor. 1985. Social cognition: A look at motivated strategies. Annual Review of Psychology 36:275-305.

Slobin, D.I. 1971. Developmental psycholinguistics. In: W.O. Dingwall, ed. A survey of linguistic science. College Park, Md.: University of Maryland Linguistic Program.

Smart, J.C., C.F. Elton, and C.W. Burnett. 1970. Underachievers and overachievers in intermediate French. Modern Language Journal 54:415-22.

Somerville-Ryan, R.B. 1987. Taking slow learners to task. In: C.N. Candlin and D. Murphy, eds. Language learning tasks. Lancaster Practical Papers in English Language Education, vol. 7. Englewood Cliffs, N.J.: Prentice-Hall International.

Spielberger, C., Gorusch, and Lushene. 1970. State-trait anxiety inventory. Palo Alto: Consulting Psychologists.

Steitz, J.A. 1985. Issues of adult development within the academic environment. Lifelong Learning 8:15-17.

Stevick, E.W. 1980. Teaching languages: A way and ways. New York: Newbury House Publishers.

Stevick, E.W. 1989. Success with foreign languages: Seven who achieved it and what worked for them. Englewood Cliffs, N.J.: Prentice-Hall.

Strong, M. 1984. Integrative motivation: Cause or result of successful language acquisition? Language Learning 34(3):1-13.

Swain, M., and J. Cummins. 1986. Bilingualism and education. London: Longman.

Swan, M. 1987. Non-systematic variability: A self-inflicted conundrum? In: R. Ellis, ed. Second language acquisition in context. Englewood Cliffs, N.J.: Prentice-Hall International.

Van Dijk, T.A., and W. Kintsch. 1983. Strategies of discourse comprehension. New York: Academic Press.

Verma, P., and H. Nijhavan. 1976. The effect of anxiety, reinforcement and intelligence on the learning of a difficult task. Journal of Experimental Child Psychology 22:302-8.

Vygotsky, L.S. 1934/1962. Thought and language. Trans. by E. Hanfmann and G. Vakar. Cambridge, Mass.: MIT Press.

Weinstein, C.E. 1988. Assessment and training of student learning strategies. In: R.R. Schmeck, ed. Learning strategies and learning styles. New York: Plenum.

Weinstein, C.E., A.C. Schulte, and E.C. Cascallar. 1984. The Learning and Study Strategy Inventory (LASSI): Initial design and development. Alexandria, Va.: U.S. Army Research Institute for the Behavioral and Social Sciences.

Wheelis, A. 1973. How people change. New York: Harper and Row.

Missing link: Evidence from research on language learning styles and strategies

Rebecca L. Oxford
University of Alabama

The theme of the 1990 Georgetown University Round Table on Languages and Linguistics lends itself to discussion of language learning styles and strategies, the focus of this paper. At no other moment in recent history have we seen such a strong and interactive combination of theory, practice, and research taking hold in the sister fields of language learning and second language acquisition; and I am pleased that language learning styles and strategies are a major part of this exciting ferment.

This year, three major books on language learning strategies are being published (Cohen 1990; O'Malley and Chamot 1990; Oxford 1990b), following Wenden and Rubin's (1987) important book of three years ago. A recent landmark dissertation (Ehrman 1989) has explored the interrelationship of styles and strategies for language learning. Interest in language learning styles and strategies is continuing to rise as teachers, students, and researchers have begun to see the central role of the learner, not just the teacher, in the language learning process. Discussion of language learning styles and strategies is "shifting the instructional focus to the learner," as stated in the well-chosen title of this year's *Northeast Conference Reports* (Magnan 1990), a book which all of us should read carefully.

Because language learning styles and strategies, more than many other aspects of language skill development, focus on the learner in highly specific and classroom-relevant ways, they can be seen as a 'missing link' in our understanding of the language learning process. We can expect the current trends in theory, research, and practice to strengthen and solidify the link that is now being forged.

My purpose here is to provide a general overview of existing research on language learning styles and strategies. Rather than trying to summarize all the relevant research (an impossible task for this short paper), I will highlight some of the most interesting and most important research, including ongoing strategy investigations that have not yet been discussed in print elsewhere. I will underscore the key themes, with the intent of portraying the area of language learning styles and strategies as accurately as possible within a brief space. (For more in-depth coverage of previous research, see Oxford and Crookall 1989; Oxford 1989, 1990a, 1990c; Skehan 1989; Ehrman 1989; Wenden and Rubin 1987; O'Malley and Chamot 1990.) In the current paper I am also going to take some calculated risks by speculating and extrapolating from existing research. I will thus state new conceptual linkages and implications that have never before been expressed, as far as I know, at least in the theoretical framework of language learning styles and strategies.

Definitions and relationships. Language experts sometimes make a strong distinction between formal, classroom-based 'learning' and informal, out-of-class 'acquisition' of nonnative language skills. However, the terms 'language learning style' and 'language learning strategies' are applied with great frequency in discussions of second language acquisition (note the intriguing title of O'Malley and Chamot's 1990 book, *Learning Strategies in Second Language Acquisition*), as well as in discussions of foreign language learning. To keep things simple, I dispense with the awkward, double terminology of styles and strategies for 'language learning and/or acquisition'. I adopt common convention by using the simpler terms, 'language learning style' and 'language learning strategy', in a rather broad way to refer to an individual's characteristics in developing target language skills in either a formal or informal setting.

Because styles are usually at the root of an individual's natural strategy preferences, it is logical to start with styles and then move to strategies. Throughout this chapter, the term 'language learning style' is used to encompass four aspects of the learner: (1) cognitive style, i.e. preferred or habitual patterns of mental functioning; (2) patterns of attitudes and interests that affect what an individual will pay most attention to in a learning situation; (3) a tendency to seek situations compatible with one's own learning patterns; and (4) a tendency to use certain learning strategies and avoid others (Lawrence 1984). Learning style is pervasive (Willing 1988) and is a mixture of cognitive, affective, and behavioral elements (Oxford and Ehrman 1988). At least 20 dimensions of learning style have been identified (Parry 1984; Shipman and Shipman 1985; Oxford 1990a, 1990c).

'Language learning strategies', in contrast to styles, are much more specific. They are the often-conscious steps or behaviors used by language learners to enhance the acquisition, storage, retention, recall, and use of new information (Rigney 1978; Oxford 1990b). Strategies are malleable and teachable (Brown, Campione, and Day 1981; Oxford 1990a; Chamot and Kupper 1989; O'Malley and Chamot 1990). However, when left to their own devices and if not overly pressured by their environment to use a certain set of strategies, students typically use learning strategies that reflect their basic learning style (Ehrman and Oxford 1988, 1989; Ehrman 1989, 1990).

Let us see how the style-strategy relationship works in some specific cases. Gary has a global, feeling-oriented learning style, so he generally chooses 'globalizing' strategies such as guessing, searching for the main idea, engaging in social conversation without having to know all the words, and being sensitive to the social-emotional content of a given interaction. In contrast, Anne's analytic, heavily thinking-focused style pushes her to prefer strategies that involve dissecting words and sentences into their component parts and analyzing the structure of the new language in detail. She does not readily concern herself with social and emotional subtleties.

As an intuitive-style learner, Irene tries to build a mental model of the target language; she deals best with the 'big picture' in a nonlinear, random-access mode. Susan, whose style is sensing instead of intuitive, prefers language learning materials and techniques (such as flashcards and Total Physical Response) that involve combinations of movement, sound, sight, and touch and that can be applied in a sequential, linear manner.

Claudia has a closure-oriented style, and so she plans her language study sessions and does all her lessons on time or early. To avoid the ambiguity that she hates, she sometimes jumps to hasty conclusions about language rules, conversational intent, or cultural norms. Oliver, whose style is more open than closure-seeking, approaches the new language as though it were an entertaining game to play. He has a high tolerance for ambiguity, doesn't worry about comprehending everything, and does not feel the need to come to rapid conclusions about the way the language works. Finishing assignments on time is not a natural priority for him.

We have just met global Gary, analytic Anne, intuitive Irene, sensing Susan, closure-seeking Claudia, and open Oliver. Notice how some of their characteristics overlap from one person to another. For instance, Gary and Irene both display a love of breadth, but Gary applies it directly in social functioning while Irene uses it to create a grand mental design of the new language. All these characters illustrate the multiplicity of stylistic dimensions (and corresponding strategies) present in all of us, to one degree or another.

Styles. The subject of the upcoming discussion is the set of three style dimensions that I personally consider to be the most significant for language learning at this stage of my research on the subject, though further research may lead to slightly different conclusions. The first of these dimensions, analytic vs. global processing, appears to be uniquely important and seems to underlie, or at least relate strongly to, a number of other dimensions: field independence vs. field dependence, left-brain vs. right-brain hemisphericity, sharpening vs. leveling of detail in memory, reflection vs. impulsivity, thinking vs. feeling, and sensing vs. intuition. The second potentially salient style dimension for language learning is tolerance vs. intolerance of ambiguity, which may be the foundation of other dimensions, such as judging vs. perceiving and flexible vs. constricted thinking. Sensory preference (visual, auditory, tactile, kinesthetic, or a combination of one or more of these) comprises the third crucial style dimension.

Analytic vs. global processing and its likely correlates. The distinction between analytic and global processing may be the most important of all style differences in language learning. Schmeck (1988) suggests that focused/detailed vs. global/holistic processing—which I simplify by using the common dichotomy of analytic vs. global—is a fundamental, perhaps *the* fundamental, dimension of learning style in any subject area, as discussed later in this paper. However, analytic vs. global processing is not as thoroughly researched as other style aspects, such as field independence vs. field dependence, which I will discuss shortly. Little foreign or second language research has been conducted directly on analytic vs. global processing, but some indirect hints exist about the probable salience of this dimension. One study providing such hints showed that in terms of grammatical competence, foreign graduate students enrolled in American engineering and science programs, who would be expected to have an analytical style due to their choice of academic major, outperformed their less analytical peers, who were enrolled in other programs (Politzer 1983).

Field independence vs. field dependence has received a vast amount of research attention in the language learning area and elsewhere, much more than the underlying analytic vs. global processing dimension which it probably represents. Many researchers view field independence vs. field dependence as "the perceptual aspect of a more pervasive analytic-global cognitive style" (Kogan 1971), with field independence being associated with the analytic pole and field dependence with the global pole.

It is important to realize that the main instruments related to the field independence vs. dependence dimension actually measure only field independence, with field dependence inferred and operationally defined by the lack of field independence (Brown 1987; Ehrman 1989)—a negative definition which may reveal a bias in researchers' value systems. That is, scientists who conduct research are most often analytically oriented; therefore field independence, which is basically analytic, is their focus with field dependence, the global opposite, defined only by the absence of the favored trait. Therefore, to be totally accurate, field dependent should really read 'nonfield independent'.

Field independent learners on tests involving embedded figures easily separate key details from a complex or confusing background, while their field dependent peers have difficulty doing this but are more adept than field independent learners in social, globally oriented situations. Field independent learners show significant advantages over field dependent learners in certain tasks in their own native language, such as speech perception (DeFazio 1973), sentence disambiguation, and grammatical transformation (Witkin and Goodenough 1977).

However, results have been mixed regarding an advantage for field independent individuals in foreign language learning. For instance, a number of important studies found no differences between field independent and field dependent learners in foreign language skills like reading and listening (e.g.

Tucker, Hamayan, and Genesee 1976; Bialystok and Frohlich 1978), though a different study (Naiman, Frohlich, Stern, and Todesco 1978) discovered that field independent learners surpassed field dependent learners in listening. Despite their mixed findings regarding performance on specific skills, some of these very studies, along with research by Parry (1984), found a rather consistent advantage for field independent learners in overall foreign language achievement and proficiency in traditional classrooms. Hansen and Stansfield (1981) uncovered a strong linkage of field independence with grammatical competence but not with communicative competence.

The picture is thus very confusing, with no clear answer about whether field independent learners have an advantage in language learning. One particularly important area that surprisingly has been left unstudied is whether the superior social skills that have been documented for field dependent people give them an edge over field independent individuals in a social or conversational setting.

The field independence vs. field dependence dimension has been marked by a significant sex difference, with males tending toward independence and females toward dependence (Shipman and Shipman 1975). This sex difference may be culture-bound (Witkin and Berry 1975).

The analytic vs. global processing dimension is also tapped, if only indirectly, in studies of 'brain hemisphericity'. The left hemisphere of the brain deals with language through analysis and abstraction, while the right hemisphere recognizes language as more global patterns, either auditory or visual (Willing 1988). Leaver (1986) suggests that right-brain learners—those who prefer the global processing conducted by the right hemisphere—are more adept at learning intonation and rhythms of the target language, while left-brain learners deal more easily with analytic elements like grammatical structure and contrastive analysis. Right-brain learners may be better at lower proficiency levels and left-brain learners at higher levels that demand greater analysis and control, according to Leaver. She also suggests that hemispherically balanced (integrated) people perform well as learners of foreign languages. Hemisphericity research is at a very early stage, and we should not yet rely on it completely. However, it holds great interest as related to analytic vs. global processing in language learning.

Sharpening of detail in memory—a stylistic trait that seems very analytic to me—was found by Parry (1984) to be related to language learning success in conventional language classrooms; its opposite, leveling or blurring of detail in memory, was not helpful. This aspect of what appears to be analytic vs. global functioning involves long-term memory processes rather than instantaneous or short-term memory. Since most of language learning is related to ability to store material in and retrieve material from long-term memory, sharpening vs. leveling of detail in memory is probably very relevant to certain aspects of language learning, and Parry's statistically significant findings highlight this possibility. Therefore, it is unfortunate that so far the sharpening vs. leveling dimension has not yet been widely studied in the language learning field.

Another dimension which I believe to be related to analytic vs. global processing is reflection vs. impulsivity. Reflection, which involves systematic, often analytic, mental investigation of hypotheses, is often contrasted with impulsivity, the quick and uncritical acceptance of initially selected hypotheses. In some foreign language research, reflective subjects perform much more effectively than impulsive subjects because of the latter's premature, inaccurate responses (Parry 1984). However, reflective tendencies may be helpful in some kinds of language programs but not in others. One might imagine that reflection would be helpful in a setting in which accuracy rather than fluency was the main goal, as is the case in many traditional language classrooms.

However, in a communicative setting, strong analysis and reflection might not be as useful as in more traditional classrooms. In a set of ongoing investigations involving the Myers-Briggs Type Indicator (MBTI; Myers and McCaulley 1985) in a long-term, communicative, intensive foreign language program (Ehrman and Oxford 1988, 1989; Ehrman 1989), Madeline Ehrman and I have found that thinking-type students who showed characteristics that seem to resemble reflectivity—analyzing not just the language but also their own language performance in great detail—were not necessarily the best language learners after all. Feeling-type people, who tended to be more socially attuned than their analytically oriented colleagues, often performed more proficiently in the program. In fact, some of the analytic, thinking types were very self-critical, upset about not reaching perfection, and overly anxious. Language performance was actually harmed by their overreliance on analytical reflection. In discussions with my co-researcher, I invented the term 'perverted metacognition' for this type of reflection because of its harsh, self-chastising tone and its negative implications for performance. What might be called 'positive metacognition', a tendency toward positive, nonself-flagellating behaviors involving evaluating, planning, and organizing, is often viewed as one of the cornerstones of successful learning, as discussed later in this paper. Only when the analytic reflection involved in metacognition is negatively twisted into self-condemnation does it become harmful to the learner. During this process, analytic reflection may become a tool for globally negative self-talk that lowers motivation and self-esteem, thus illustrating in a negative way the inextricable bonding among cognitive, metacognitive, and affective aspects of language learning.

In the Ehrman-Oxford studies, the dimension of sensing vs. intuition (as measured by the MBTI) also appears to be related to elements of analytical vs. global processing. Sensing-type people who were learning languages intensively showed great practical interest in facts and details, which might be viewed as analytical components of the whole language; and they chose to learn sequentially, following a clearly definable series of steps in a serial-processing mode. On the other hand, intuitives were much more global, searching for general patterns and broad meanings rather than attending to small details. Instead of learning sequentially, they preferred a random-access mode that allowed them to move in and out freely in their globalizing way, as though they owned the entire 'language territory' from the start and did not have to inch their way along. Intuitives also favored a parallel-processing mode, in which several strands of learning were dealt with at the same time. Both random-access and parallel-processing modes contrasted with the serial-processing mode noted in the sensing learners.

Tolerance of ambiguity. I have just discussed some of the fascinating offshoots of the analytic vs. global processing dimension, which seems likely to be central to language learning. Now I turn to tolerance of ambiguity, which also logically appears to be a potentially important dimension of language learning style. Learning a language and its corresponding culture is a difficult endeavor, often fraught with ambiguity and uncertainty on many levels: emotional, sociocultural, and linguistic. Therefore, it is not surprising that research indicates better language learning performance by students who can more readily tolerate ambiguity (Chapelle 1983; Chapelle and Roberts 1986; Naiman, Frohlich, and Todesco 1975).

The Ehrman-Oxford studies of adults in an intensive foreign language learning situation suggest that the perceiving vs. judging dimension on the MBTI is very important and that it might be related to tolerance vs. intolerance of ambiguity. Learners who did not feel the need to reach closure quickly (the so-called perceivers), and who were therefore assumed to be more tolerant of ambiguity, performed more proficiently than learners who needed rapid closure, known as the judging types (Ehrman and Oxford 1988, 1989; Ehrman 1989, 1990b). Research on the influence of tolerance vs. intolerance of ambiguity on language learning success is neither extensive nor ironclad, but the existing results may lend some credibility to the presumed importance of this dimension.

Parry (1984) found that flexible thinking, as opposed to constricted thinking, was a significant predictor of language learning success in traditional high school language classrooms. Flexibly thinking students performed better in language learning than did constricted thinkers. I speculate that flexible thinking is important because of an underlying relation to tolerance of ambiguity; conversely, constricted thinking may be related to intolerance of ambiguity.

Sensory preferences. Little research has been done on language students' sensory preferences—visual, auditory, tactile, kinesthetic, or a combination of senses—although these preferences represent a style dimension that is probably very important in learning a new language. Reid (1987) studied sensory preferences of ESL learners and found that those preferences were strongly influenced by national origin. Koreans were the most visual in their preferences. Japanese were the least auditory and the least kinesthetic of all nationalities. Students of most other nationalities were strongly kinesthetic and tactile in their preferences. ESL students' choice of academic and career specialization was related to their sensory preferences. In a different discussion, Semple (1982) suggests that children might progress from the kinesthetic sense to the visual, with auditory preference constituting a possible later development.

Certainly, the appropriate development of materials, textbooks, and methods for language instruction depends crucially on the developer's understanding of sensory preferences of learners. The publishing industry is beginning to address the notion that language learners have different learning styles based on sensory preferences. Therefore, publishers are now developing multimedia packages: texts full of beautiful, authentic materials and photos of the target country and people; full-color overhead transparencies keyed to textbook lessons; video and interactive videodisc; increasingly sophisticated audiotapes; printed and illustrated flashcards; and in some instances, even prepackaged Total Physical Response realia such as miniature houses and cars. I applaud the astute efforts of publishers, and at the same time I urge researchers to provide more data on what students actually need based on a comprehensive, realistic, scientific assessment of their sensory preferences.

Further discussion and speculation about style. I cannot draw completely firm conclusions about language learning styles, because style-related research, while seemingly plentiful, is thinly scattered over large numbers of dimensions. However, without being overly simplistic, I think it is possible to speculate that analytic vs. global processing is the most important style dimension for language learning, since it seems to underlie or relate strongly to field independence vs. field dependence, left-brain vs. right-brain hemisphericity, sharpening vs. leveling, reflection vs. impulsivity, thinking vs. feeling, and sensing vs. intuition, and since it has proven so significant in studies in other subject areas outside of language learning.

My own ideas about the centrality of analytic vs. global processing are supported by Schmeck's highly important work (1988), which synthesizes the research on learning styles. Schmeck describes a general learning style continuum (without particular reference to second or foreign language learning). At one pole of the continuum, according to Schmeck and others in that volume, are analytic (focused/detailed) processing, field independence, reflection, narrow categorization, serial-processing, and left-brain dominance; and at the other pole are global processing, field dependence, impulsivity, broad categorization, parallel processing, and right-brain dominance. As is obvious, Schmeck's conceptualization is remarkably similar to the one that I have independently posited, based on research on style research in the language learning area.

Other potentially important style dimensions for developing skills in a second or foreign language are tolerance vs. intolerance of ambiguity and sensory preferences such as visual and auditory, as suggested in the foregoing discussion. Though research on language learning styles is somewhat sparse concerning these two dimensions, nevertheless existing research findings suggest that these dimensions are likely to be very important.

Different styles for different settings and purposes. I can speculate with some degree of certainty that one particular style may be more functional in one setting than in another. For instance, Martha Nyikos and I (Oxford and Nyikos 1989; Nyikos and Oxford, forthcoming) found that analytically prone students were more prevalent, and therefore probably more comfortable, in a higher education setting where memorizing and grammatical analysis were the norm; and the Ehrman-Oxford studies (Ehrman and Oxford 1988, 1989; Ehrman 1989, 1990; Oxford and Ehrman 1988) discovered greater progress among socially oriented, feeling-type adult learners than among analytical learners in an intensive language instruction program that was highly communicative. As an aside, it is possible that the proficiency guidelines designed by the American Council on the Teaching of Foreign Languages may seem difficult to many learners whose school experiences have been almost always in the analytic rather than the global mode.

Common sense, combined with research findings, suggests that nonclosure seekers—who can cope with ambiguity and do not need to feel completely in control—may be more likely than closure seekers to adapt well to total immersion programs and learning the new language 'in country'. Similar comments might be made about intuitives, who, unlike sensing learners, may not require a step-by-step, linear progression in learning but are comfortable with the more haphazard progression that characterizes immersion programs, living in the country of the target language, or any other communicative experience.

Certainly, much more research needs to be conducted on which learning styles operate most effectively in different settings and for different language learning purposes. Additional research is essential to determine just how much individual learners can adapt their styles to fit the materials, methods, and intensity of a given instructional program, and to what degree the program (which generally reflects the policies and priorities of its sponsoring institution) should try to adapt to the stylistic preferences of individual learners.

Teaching and learning style conflicts. The importance of teaching style has been highlighted by recent research and theory. Teaching styles have been classified as directive, authoritative/friendly, cooperative/tolerant, repressive, businesslike, uncertain/drudging, aggressive/uncertain, tolerant/uncertain, and friendly/tolerant by a Dutch research team (Wubbels, Brekelmans, Creton, and Hooymayers 1988); and as command, practice, reciprocal, self-check, inclusion, guided discovery, convergent discovery, divergent, learner-designed individualized, learner-initiated, and self-teaching, according to two researchers in the United States (Mosston and Ashworth 1990). Teaching styles can also be described in the same terms I have used for learning styles: analytic vs. global; tolerant vs. intolerant of ambiguity; and visual, auditory, tactile, kinesthetic, or some combination.

Teachers tend to mirror their learning preferences in their teaching style. The teacher who has a global learning style may favor such activities as open-ended, oral role-plays or jigsaw listening; frown on the use of the blackboard; and enjoy a classroom characterized by 'organized chaos'. In contrast, the analytical instructor may enjoy the systematic presentation of difficult points and patterns, follow a detailed plan for classroom practice involving incremental steps, and use analytic error correction (Lavine, personal communication, March 1990).

There is no problem as long as students share their teacher's style preference; they feel comfortable with the learning environment and corresponding classroom techniques and materials. However, problems arise when the teacher's style differs radically from an individual student's style, or from the overall stylistic tendency of a group of students. Learners who exhibit a style preference different from the teacher's may be plagued by constant anxiety and unconsciously—or consciously—react negatively to the teacher, the environment, and the subject matter. Academic success in a particular course is also likely to be linked to the style match or mismatch: students whose learning style matches the teacher's style are more likely to achieve good grades than those whose styles are in opposition to the instructor. What can be done when such a mismatch occurs between teaching style and learning style? Should the teacher try to adapt his or her own teaching style? Should the teacher go so far as to individualize the instruction, in order to provide the kind of learning most favorable to every student? Should the student(s) adapt, being taught new stylistic modes so as to cope with the situation and obviate the style conflict? Should learners and teachers be matched on the basis of style similarities, so that style conflicts will not arise in the first place (Dunn and Dunn 1972)?

Handling different styles in a single group and a single class period. Mosston and Ashworth (1990) suggest that lessons can be organized as a series of episodes, each of which has a different objective, a different or same subject matter, and a different style, with the teaching style (or, more accurately, the teaching-learning style) chosen that best matches the objective, e.g. for a memory-related objective, command and practice styles might be highly relevant. They also clearly state that learners can be taught to relate to and use different styles associated with diverse objectives; in other words, students are not stuck in one style but can instead become adept at tapping multiple styles.

In general terms, I agree with these conclusions but want to add that the teacher should do more than to orient teaching styles to the demands of particular tasks; the teacher should also pay attention to students' own existing style preferences. This does not imply total individualization of instruction according to students' learning styles. In most instances, complete individualization is not practical or feasible, nor is it necessary or even desirable, but attention should be paid to a limited number of major learning style dimensions present in the class. If my speculations are correct about the three major dimensions named above—analytic vs. global processing, tolerance vs. intolerance of ambiguity, and sensory preferences—being the most important for language learning, it is immediately possible to narrow down the range of individual stylistic differences about which teachers need to be concerned. If future research tells us that there are just two key dimensions, such as analytic vs. global processing and sensory preferences, then the situation is simplified even more. What this means in practice is that teachers need to assess students' styles (on whatever style dimensions appear to be the most important according to formal research or teachers' own observations) and then gear their instruction to the needs of students in different style categories, such as visual/analytic, visual/global, kinesthetic/analytic, kinesthetic/global, and so on.

The 4MAT curriculum design model (McCarthy 1980), based on Kolb's four-quadrant learning style model, suggests that teachers should orient instruction to all the different categories of learning style present in the classroom, which the Kolb model says are four. Though I find Kolb's style categories somewhat abstract, nevertheless the idea of providing instructional options for a limited number of major style groups is highly appealing—as long as those style categories are identified as the ones most important and relevant to language learning. In this way, though the individual learner's needs are viewed as central, the teacher does not have to prepare 15 or 20 or 30 different 'prescriptions' or 'lessons' for that many individual students; the teacher has to provide materials, methods, and activities that relate to the main stylistic dimensions. This should not be too difficult, as long as multiple media are available to cater to various sensory preferences, and a variety of analytic and global-communicative tasks are used, some of which require more immediate closure than others.

Grouping students according to style. A frequently raised stylistic issue is whether students should be grouped according to their learning style, with all the students who prefer analysis grouped together and all of the globals in another group, or with visual, auditory, and tactile learners separated. Dansereau's research (1983, 1985) indicates that in small-group activities or pairwork, it often helps to place students together who have the same basic learning style; and this is true even if one student in a given style group is more advanced in language learning than another. However, Ehrman (personal communication, March 1990a) suggests that learners thus segregated into style groups may miss out on an opportunity to 'stretch' themselves by learning new style possibilities from their peers, who are often the best teachers. Probably a compromise position, which allows students to work with their stylemates a large portion of the time but also permits cooperative learning with students who have a different style preference, is the most useful means of dealing with this issue. Students should be allowed and encouraged to form their own groups occasionally (Lavine, personal communication, February 1990), but some guidance from the teacher in doing so might be useful. Future research can and should tell us more about the merits or demerits of grouping students by style.

Strategies. I have explored the area of language learning styles in some depth, pointing out the limitations of current research results and speculating on classroom implications and further research that is needed. The discussion of styles is a good stepping stone to talking about language learning strategies, that is, the actual behaviors learners use to control and improve their own learning.

Research by Ehrman and Oxford (1988, 1989) has tried to probe the existing relationships between styles and strategies and has found them to be very strong. We have found that learners can—and indeed in some instances should—be taught to apply strategies that are useful yet do not coincide fully with their basic learning styles. That is, learners can learn to use strategies outside of what I call their 'stylistic comfort zone'. For instance, a highly analytic learner can learn, perhaps with some effort, to make global inferences when necessary; and a global learner can be taught to use contrastive analysis if that strategy is seen as potentially useful. A visually oriented student can continue to use memory strategies that involve purely visual associations but can also be trained to tap memory strategies that combine motion and touch with visual imagery.

Though style-strategy combinations and strategic movement beyond one's comfort zone are tantalizing areas for research, they have not yet been the focus of research on language learning strategies. In general, researchers have looked at strategies in isolation from styles, except for a few investigations that have been mentioned above. The primary concern of most strategy researchers has been on strategies, divorced from the underlying style dimensions that might elucidate strategy choices that students make. Researchers have, on the other hand, spent a great deal of time considering the strategies of what have been called 'good language learners', and a lesser amount of time examining the strategies of unsuccessful or just average learners. Research on these topics has used a variety of techniques, such as diaries, think-aloud procedures during a language learning task, teacher or researcher observations, and student surveys (see Oxford and Crookall 1989 and Cohen 1987 for methodological details).

Strategies of successful learners. Research both outside the language field (e.g. Brown, Bransford, Ferrara, and Campione 1983) and investigations with language learners (see reviews by Ehrman 1989; Oxford 1989; Skehan 1989; Oxford and Crookall 1989) frequently show that the most successful learners tend to use a variety of learning strategies that are appropriate to the learning material, the task, and to their own needs, goals, and stage of learning. Many types of strategies are used by successful learners. One very important type is metacognitive strategies (strategies that engage cognition in order to consider one's own learning, in other words thinking about one's own learning). These involve organizing, focusing, and evaluating learning and seeking the necessary opportunities to put new knowledge into practice. Use of these metacognitive behaviors—along with cognitive strategies such as analyzing, reasoning, taking notes, and summarizing—might be considered part of any operational definition of truly effective learning. Metacognitive strategies might also be viewed as part of a generally reflective approach or style, which was mentioned earlier.

Successful learners often employ 'memory strategies', such as grouping, labeling, making associations, and visual imagery, and what I call 'compensation strategies' such as guessing and using synonyms and gestures. (Memory strategies and compensation strategies are often classed as subsets of cognitive strategies but in fact have very specialized functions: for the former, entering new information into memory by assimilating it to existing schemata or accommodating those schemata to the new information; and for the latter, compensating for the lack of not yet acquired subject knowledge.) Competent learners may also use 'social strategies', such as asking questions or cooperating with others (Kagan 1986), and 'affective strategies', such as positive self-talk, self-reward, and anxiety reduction (Oxford 1990b), although social and affective strategies are not encouraged by most branches of our educational system and therefore do not necessarily show up as strong predictors or correlates of effective language learning in typical studies.

In an early study of successful language learners, Rubin (1975) suggested that such learners are willing and accurate guessers; have a strong, persevering drive to communicate; are often uninhibited and willing to make mistakes in order to learn or communicate; focus on form by looking for patterns; take advantage of all practice opportunities; monitor their own speech and that of others; and pay attention to meaning. Similar but not identical strategies and characteristics of good language learners were cited by Naiman, Frohlich, and Todesco (1975).

The adult language learners in an intensive, long-term language program (Ehrman and Oxford 1988, 1989; Oxford and Ehrman 1988) were considered successful in that they all reached the proficiency goals that were set for them, although some learners experienced much more strain than others in doing so. These learners were highly motivated to learn the new language for career purposes, and their motivation (along with a rather communicative instructional methodology) seemed to influence their frequent choice of strategies aimed at searching for and communicating meaning. (For more on motivation, see Gardner 1978, 1990; Gardner and Lambert 1972; and the discussion below of influences on strategy choice.)

Strategies of average and unsuccessful learners. Nyikos (1987) found that the average, typical language learners she studied, most of whom were studying a language to meet a university foreign language requirement, used only a narrow range of strategies and were generally unaware of the strategies they used. In contrast, Chamot, O'Malley, Kupper, and Impink-Hernandez (1987) discovered that even ineffective language learners were aware of and used a number of strategies, with the only difference between effective and ineffective learners being that the effective ones reported greater frequency and greater range of strategy use. Vann and Abraham (1989) found yet a different situation, discovering that unsuccessful language learners actively use strategies and can often describe those strategies, but that the strategies they apply are often inappropriate to the situation.

In an ongoing diary study in which I am involved (Lavine and Oxford forthcoming), even average language learners spontaneously and rather precisely describe using a significant number of language learning strategies for listening comprehension and vocabulary learning (though they had fewer strategies for learning grammar and therefore felt at a loss in that area). The most common strategies included organizing one's learning, trying out new strategies, writing/listing as an aid to memorization, and employing a sequential approach to studying (first do this, then do that). In terms of general strategy categories, students used mainly cognitive, memory-related, and limited metacognitive behaviors, all of which were finite, familiar, and did not involve much risk-taking, guessing, or self-direction.

In the Lavine and Oxford study, in order to capture the strategies mentioned by average and ineffective learners along with those cited by their more successful classmates, we were forced to expand a typology containing 62 strategies to a list of 139 strategies; and the worse learners averaged almost as many strategies as the better learners. Thus the quantity of strategies does not necessarily appear to be the determiner in language learning success. We found, just as did Vann and Abraham in their study, that unsuccessful learners used strategies in a less targeted, less appropriate way than did successful learners. We found that the best learners combined strategies in an especially 'strategic' way that reflected strong metacognitive planning, organizing, and evaluating the use of the strategies themselves. In our diary study, the average and unsuccessful language learners were somewhat deficient in these powerful metacognitive tools.

Without linking the degree of language learning success with the use of various kinds of strategies, some studies have simply assessed the average frequency of use of various kinds of strategies in 'typical' groups of high school, university, and adult students. For instance, Chamot and O'Malley's studies (e.g. Chamot, O'Malley, Kupper, and Impink-Hernandez 1987; O'Malley, Chamot, Stewner-Manzanares, Kupper, and Russo 1985; O'Malley, Chamot, Stewner-Manzanares, Russo, and Kupper 1985) have found that across many different foreign and second language groups students used rather simple, basic cognitive strategies, such as note-taking and repetition, more often than metacognitive strategies; that the most commonly employed metacognitive strategies involved planning with little use of self-monitoring of errors or self-evaluation; and that social-affective strategies were infrequently reported.

Martha Nyikos and I (Oxford and Nyikos 1989; Nyikos and Oxford, forthcoming) found that typical university students of five different foreign languages made heavy use of analytic, formal practice strategies, probably because of the institution's use of analytic, discrete-point testing. These university students relied heavily on the teacher and/or the text for direction, were motivated mainly by grades, and shunned authentic language practice. Nyikos (1990) and McGroarty (1987) in other university studies found that foreign language learners stuck to traditional, analytic, noncommunicative strategies and did not take the risk to seek out communication opportunities—even when such opportunities were abundant, as in the McGroarty situation. Young (forthcoming) found that similar university students were very anxious about language learning in general, had low situational self-esteem in the language classroom, and were very unrealistic in their expectations, believing that two years should be enough to develop language fluency. High motivation was unlikely to thrive in such a situation. (On the topics of beliefs and anxiety, see also Horwitz, Horwitz, and Cope 1986; Horwitz and Young 1991.) My own observations say that Young's portrayal of ordinary foreign language students at the university level is accurate. If this is indeed a true picture, it is not surprising that—given university students' language learning anxiety, self-esteem problems, unrealistic ideas, and low motivation—they tend to use strategies unconducive to the development of communicative competence.

However, ordinary, unexceptional learners in an intensive, university-run ESL program (Oxford, Talbott, and Halleck 1990) demonstrated far more frequent use of many kinds of learning strategies, including numerous communicatively oriented strategies, than did typical university students learning foreign languages in the studies mentioned above. A rather wide range of strategies was found for ordinary students learning ESL in six additional samples from around the United States (Oxford, Nyikos, Rossi-Le, Eyring, and Lezhnev forthcoming). The probable difference is that the second language learners, in contrast to the foreign language learners, had an immediate need to communicate in the language and therefore felt an urgency to use whatever strategies they could think of to help them communicate.

Some influences on strategy choice. Elsewhere I have reviewed research on factors which appear to influence the learner's decision to use particular strategies and ignore others (see Oxford 1989, 1990a). Martha Nyikos and I (Oxford and Nyikos 1989; Nyikos and Oxford forthcoming) have carefully examined the variables affecting strategy choice among 1,200 foreign language learners at a large university and have found motivation to be the single most powerful influence on the choice of strategies, with the most motivated learners using more strategies and more different kinds of strategies. I mentioned the important role of motivation earlier when speaking of the adult language learners in the Ehrman-Oxford studies. In many studies, females have reported using a variety of strategies more frequently than males (Oxford, Nyikos, and Ehrman 1988). In the Oxford-Nyikos report, more experienced learners and learners majoring in nontechnical fields used strategies that involved greater functional, communicative practice.

A number of other studies, taken together (see Oxford 1989, for details), suggest that other variables in addition to sex, motivation, years of experience in language learning, and academic major might influence choice of strategies. Ethnicity/nationality, language learning purpose, the nature of the task, institutional expectations, and classroom reward systems are also highly influential in terms of the behaviors that a learner decides to use. I have mentioned before the possibility of teacher-student style conflicts in the classroom; such conflicts are likely to play a strong role, as yet not completely defined, in learners' choice of language learning strategies, and no doubt affect learners' attitudes toward the course, the teacher, the language, and the culture.

Other predictors or correlates of language learning strategy choice are beginning to be examined in some studies in which I am now participating. For instance, with Victoria Talbott and Gene Halleck I am looking at the relationship between strategy choice on the one hand, and on the other hand, self-image as measured by a projective instrument (the Twenty Sentences Test), nationality, sex, career orientation, and other factors. We are examining the relationship of all these factors to proficiency in learning the language. To my knowledge, this is the first time strategies have been correlated with self-image. My colleagues and I will share our results as soon as we have completed further analyses.

Strategy training studies. Although Jack Richards (1990) has championed the use of the terms 'education' and 'development' to replace the word 'training' in the language learning field, nevertheless 'training' has commonly been the term chosen by almost all specialists in the area of learning strategies. Therefore, I will use that word in discussing strategy training—that is, efforts designed to teach students to use more appropriate learning strategies.

Several strategy training studies outside of the language field have produced useful findings concerning ways to teach strategies to students (e.g. Brown, Bransford, Ferrara, and Campione 1983; Brown, Campione, and Day 1981; Brown and Palinscar 1982). 'Blind training', in which the tasks or materials cause the student to use particular strategies, does not provide explicit information to the student about the nature or importance of the strategies and not surprisingly is not particularly useful. 'Informed training', which tells the learner what a particular strategy does and why it is useful, results in improved performance on the task, maintenance of the strategy over time, and some degree of transfer of the strategy to other tasks. However, 'strategy-plus-control training' (or what I call 'completely informed training') informs the learner about the nature and use of the technique, as well as how to transfer, monitor, and evaluate its use. This is the most successful of the three strategy training modes, according to research.

Despite the limited range of strategies taught in formal strategy training studies, along with significant methodological problems (e.g. too short a time span for strategy training, lack of follow-up on permanence of strategy maintenance, difficulty of the language task, inadequate integration of strategy training into ordinary classroom language work, lack of adequate comparison groups in some instances), it is clear that strategy training has positive effects in many language skill areas. Certainly, more research needs to be done to determine which strategies are most important to teach, how they should be clustered for optimal use, and the precise timing and presentation of strategy training as part of regular language learning events. As this research occurs, it would be wonderful if researchers could start building in an affective strategy component (for details, see Oxford 1990b), so that learners could begin to control the powerful feelings and attitudes surrounding language learning as well as the cognitive and metacognitive skills necessary to develop language proficiency. Examples of affective strategies woven into informal, nonresearch-oriented strategy training as part of ordinary classwork are found in Oxford, Crookall, Cohen, Lavine, Nyikos, and Sutter (1990).

Conclusions. I have discussed the important role played by learning styles and strategies in the development of skills in a new language. Styles and strategies are directly relevant to the language classroom. Greater understanding of the styles learners naturally use would help teachers adapt instruction to the needs of individuals, whether in like-style or mixed-style classroom groupings. The analytic vs. global dichotomy seems to be a very important style dimension for teachers to consider, along with two other dimensions: first, tolerance vs. intolerance of ambiguity; and second, sensory preferences (visual, auditory, tactile, and kinesthetic). Many other style dimensions that may be relevant to language learning are probably correlated with or subsumed by these three dimensions. I am not saying these three are the only important style aspects, but current research suggests to me that they should be close to the top of the list in our future investigations. Current tests of language aptitude could be supplemented by measures that assess these or other salient dimensions of students' learning style, so that decisions about placement, tracking, and instructional design can be made in the most well-informed manner possible (Oxford 1990c).

Language learning strategies, because of their specific and behavioral nature, are teachable. When we realize that the use of appropriate strategies is often directly related to successful language performance, and that strategy use can indeed be improved through strategy training, the topic of language learning strategies becomes very compelling to researchers, teachers, and students alike. Language learning strategies are frequently a reflection of the person's underlying learning style, but if properly motivated and aided through strategy training, learners can start tapping important strategies that may not necessarily be in the strategic repertoire formed by their natural style preferences.

At the beginning of this paper, I said that now is a time of great ferment. It is a time when theories (especially cognitive schema theories, humanistic psychology theories, clinical psychotherapy theories, second language acquisition theories, and various other concepts involving cognition and affect) are percolating everywhere in a highly inderdisciplinary manner. It is a time when research is intense and high-profile. It is a time when teachers and administrators are actually communicating with researchers and theorists—and vice versa. It is a time when the terms 'action research' and 'teacher research' finally have the opportunity to become more than just hoped-for ideals. Most importantly of all, it is a time when students are starting to take their rightful place at the center of our attention (although we still remember the roles of the teacher, the institution, or the society at large). Concern for learning styles and strategies is crucially involved in these important trends. Learning styles and strategies are becoming an increasingly strong link in our understanding of language learning processes.

References

Bialystok, E., and M. Frohlich. 1978. Variables of classroom achievement in second language learning. Modern Language Journal 62:327-66.

Brown, A.L., J.D. Bransford, R.A. Ferrara, and J.C. Campione. 1983. Learning, remembering, and understanding. In: J.H. Flavell and E.M. Markham, eds. Carmichael's manual of child psychology, vol. 1. New York: Wiley.

Brown, A.L., J.C. Campione, and J.D. Day. 1981. Learning to learn: On enabling students to learn from texts. Educational Researcher 10:14-21.

Brown, A.L., and A.S. Palinscar. 1982. Inducing strategic learning from texts by means of informed, self-control training. Topics in Learning and Learning Disabilities 2:1-17.

Brown, H.D. 1987. Principles of language learning and teaching. (2d ed.) Englewood Cliffs, N.J.: Prentice-Hall.

Chamot, A.U., and L. Kupper. 1989. Learning strategies in foreign language instruction. Foreign Language Annals 22:13-24.

Chamot, A.U., and J.M. O'Malley. 1987. The cognitive academic language learning approach: A bridge to the mainstream. TESOL Quarterly 21:227-49.

Chamot, A.U., J.M. O'Malley, L. Kupper, and M.V. Impink-Hernandez. 1987. A study of learning strategies in foreign language instruction: First year report. Rosslyn, Va.: InterAmerica Research Associates.

Chapelle, C.A. 1983. The relationship between ambiguity tolerance and success in acquiring English as a second language in adult learners. Unpublished doctoral dissertation, University of Illinois.

Chapelle, C.A., and C. Roberts. 1986. Ambiguity tolerance and field independence as predictors in English as a second language. Language Learning 36:27-45.

Cohen, A.D. 1987. Studying learner strategies: How we get the information. In: A.L. Wenden and J. Rubin, eds. Learner strategies in language learning. Englewood Cliffs, N.J.: Prentice-Hall. 31-42.

Cohen, A.D. 1990. Second language learning: Insights for learners, teachers, and researchers. New York: Newbury House/Harper and Row.

Dansereau, D.F. 1983. Cooperative learning: Impact on acquisition of knowledge and skills. Technical Report 586. Alexandria, Va.: Army Research Institute for the Behavioral and Social Sciences.

Dansereau, D.F. 1985. Learning strategy research. In: J.W. Segal, S.F. Chipman, and R. Glaser, eds. Thinking and learning skills: Relating learning to basic research. Hillsdale, N.J.: Erlbaum. 209-40

DeFazio, V.J. 1973. Field articulation differences in language abilities. Journal of Personality and Social Psychology 25:351-56.

Dunn, R.S., and K.J. Dunn. 1972. Learning styles/teaching styles: Should they . . . can they . . . be matched? Educational Leadership 36:238-44.

Ehrman, M.E. 1989. Ants and grasshoppers, badgers and butterflies: Qualitative and quantitative investigation of adult language learning styles and strategies. Ann Arbor, Mich.: University Microfilms International.

Ehrman, M.E. 1990, March. Personal communication.

Ehrman, M.E. 1990. The role of personality type in adult language learning: An ongoing investigation. Paper presented at the Interagency Language Roundtable Invitational Language Aptitude Testing Symposium, 1988. In: T. Parry and C.W. Stansfield, eds. Language aptitude: Past, present, and future research. Englewood Cliffs, N.J.: Prentice-Hall.

Ehrman, M.E., and R.L. Oxford. 1988. Ants and grasshoppers, badgers and butterflies: Qualitative and quantitative investigation of adult language learning styles and strategies. Paper presented at the Symposium on Research Perspectives in Adult Language Learning and Acquisition, The Ohio State University, Columbus, Ohio.

Ehrman, M.E., and R.L. Oxford. 1989. Effects of sex differences, career choice, and psychological type on adult language learning strategies. Modern Language Journal 73:1-13.

Ehrman, M.E., and R.L. Oxford. 1990. The interaction of adult language learning styles and strategies. Submitted for publication.

Gardner, R.C. 1978. Social psychological aspects of second language acquisition. In: H. Giles and R.N. St. Clair, eds. Language and social psychology. Baltimore: University Park Press.

Gardner, R.C. 1990. Attitude, motivation, and personality as predictors of success in foreign language learning. Paper presented at the Interagency Language Roundtable Invitational Language Aptitude Testing Symposium, 1988. In: T. Parry and C.W. Stansfield, eds. Language aptitude: Past, present, and future research. Englewood Cliffs, N.J.: Prentice-Hall.

Gardner, R.C., and W.E. Lambert. 1972. Attitudes and motivation in second language learning. Rowley, Mass.: Newbury House.

Hansen, J., and C.W. Stansfield. 1981. The relationship of field dependent-independent cognitive styles to foreign language achievement. Language Learning 31:349-67.

Horwitz, E.K. 1988. The beliefs about language learning of beginning university foreign language students. Modern Language Journal 72:283-94.

Horwitz, E.K., M.B. Horwitz, and J. Cope. 1986. Foreign language classroom anxiety. Modern Language Journal 70:125-32.

Horwitz, E.K., and D.J. Young. 1991. Language learning anxiety. New York: Newbury House/Harper and Row.

Kagan, S. 1986. Cooperative learning and sociocultural factors in schooling. In: Beyond language: Social and cultural factors in schooling language minority students. Sacramento: California State Department of Education, Bilingual Education Office. 231-32.

Kogan, N. 1971. Educational implications of cognitive styles. In: G.S. Lesser, ed. Psychology and educational practice. Glenview, Ill.: Scott Foresman. 242-92.

Lavine, R.Z. 1990, March. Personal communication.

Lavine, R.Z., and R.L. Oxford. Forthcoming. Language learning diaries: Let the learners tell us. Submitted for publication.

Lawrence, G. 1984. A synthesis of learning style research involving the MBTI. Journal of Psychological Type 8:2-15.

Leaver, B.L. 1986. Hemisphericity of the brain and foreign language teaching. Folia Slavica 8:76-90.

McCarthy, B. 1980. The 4MAT system. Oakbrook, Ill.: Excel, Inc.

McGroarty, M. 1987. Patterns of persistent second language learners: Elementary Spanish. Paper presented at the annual meeting of Teachers of English to Speakers of Other Languages, Miami.

Magnan, S.S., ed. 1990. Shifting the instructional focus to the learner. Middlebury, Vt.: Northeast Conference on the Teaching of Foreign Languages.

Mosston, M., and S. Ashworth. The spectrum of teaching styles. New York: Longman.

Myers, I.B., and M.H. McCaulley. 1985. Manual: A guide to the development and use of the Myers-Briggs Type Indicator. Palo Alto: Consulting Psychologists Press.

Naiman, N., M. Frohlich, H.H. Stern, and A. Todesco. 1978. The good language learner. Research in Education Series No. 7. Toronto: Ontario Institute for Studies in Education.

Naiman, N., M. Frohlich, and A. Todesco. 1975. The good second language learner. TESOL Talk 5:58-75.

Nyikos, M. 1987. The effect of color and imagery as mnemonic strategies on learning and retention of lexical items in German. Unpublished dissertation, Purdue University, West Lafayette, Ind.

Nyikos, M. 1990. Seven studies of language learning strategies. Paper presented at the annual meeting of the American Educational Research Association, San Francisco.

Nyikos, M., and R. Oxford. Forthcoming. A large-scale, factor-analytic study of language learning strategy use in a university setting: Interpretations from information-processing theory and social psychology. Submitted for publication.

O'Malley, J.M., and A.U. Chamot. 1990. Learning strategies in second language acquisition. Cambridge: Cambridge University Press.

O'Malley, J.M., A.U. Chamot, G. Stewner-Manzanares, L. Kupper, and R.P. Russo. 1985. Learning strategies used by beginning and intermediate ESL students. Language Learning 35:21-46.

O'Malley, J.M., A.U. Chamot, G. Stewner-Manzanares, R.P. Russo, and L. Kupper. 1985. Learning strategy applications with students of English as a second language. TESOL Quarterly 19.3:557-84.

Oxford, R. 1989. Use of language learning strategies: A synthesis of studies with implications for strategy training. System 17:235-47.

Oxford, R. 1990a. Language learning strategies and beyond: A look at strategies in the context of styles. In: S. Magnan, ed. Shifting the instructional focus to the learner. Middlebury, Vt.: Northeast Conference on the Teaching of Foreign Languages.

Oxford, R. 1990b. Language learning strategies: What every teacher should know. New York: Newbury House/Harper and Row.

Oxford, R. 1990c. Styles, strategies, and aptitude: Important connections for language learners. Paper presented at the Interagency Language Roundtable Invitational Language Aptitude Testing Symposium, 1988. In: T. Parry and C.W. Stansfield, eds. Language aptitude: Past, present, and future research. Englewood Cliffs, N.J.: Prentice-Hall.

Oxford, R., and D. Crookall. 1989. Language learning strategies: Methods, findings, and instructional implications. Modern Language Journal 73:404-19.

Oxford, R., D. Crookall, A. Cohen, R. Lavine, M. Nyikos, and W. Sutter. 1990. Strategy training for language learners: Six situational case studies and a training model. Foreign Language Annals 22:197-216.

Oxford, R., and M.E. Ehrman. 1988. Psychological type and adult language lerning strategies: A pilot study. Journal of Psychological Type 16:22-32.

Oxford, R., and M. Nyikos. 1989. Variables affecting choice of language learning strategies by university students. Modern Language Journal 73:291-300.

Oxford, R., M. Nyikos, and M. Ehrman. 1988. Vive la différence? Reflections on sex differences in use of language learning strategies. Foreign Language Annals 21:321-29.

Oxford, R., M. Nyikos, L. Rossi-Le, J. Eyring, and V. Lezhnev. Forthcoming. Analysis of language learning strategy data from multiple groups of adult ESL learners. Submitted for publication.

Oxford, R., V. Talbott, and G. Halleck. 1990. Language learning strategies, attitudes, motivation, and self-image of students in a university intensive ESL program. Paper presented at the annual meeting of Teachers of English to Speakers of Other Languages, San Francisco.

Parry, T.S. 1984. The relationship of selected dimensions of learner cognitive style, aptitude, and general intelligence factors to selected foreign language proficiency tasks of second-year students of Spanish at the secondary level. Unpublished dissertation, The Ohio State University, Columbus.

Politzer, R.L. 1983. An exploratory study of self-reported language learning behaviors and their relation to achievement. Studies in Second Language Acquisition 6:54-68.

Politzer, R.L., and M. McGroarty. 1985. An exploratory study of learning behaviors and their relationship to gains in linguistic and communicative competence. TESOL Quarterly 19:103-24.

Reid, J.M. 1987. The learning style preferences of ESL students. TESOL Quarterly 21:87-111.

Richards, J.C. 1990. Integrating theory and practice in second language teacher education. Paper presented at the annual Georgetown University Round Table on Languages and Linguistics, Washington, D.C. (in this volume).

Rigney, J.W. 1978. Learning strategies: A theoretical perspective. In: H.F. O'Neil, Jr., ed. Learning strategies. New York: Academic Press.

Rubin, J. 1975. What the 'good language learner' can teach us. TESOL Quarterly 9:41-45.

Schmeck, R., ed. 1988. Learning strategies and learning styles. New York: Plenum.

Semple, E. 1982. Learning style: A review of the literature. (ERIC Document Reproduction Service No. ED 222 477).

Shipman, S., and V.C. Shipman. 1985. Cognitive styles: Some conceptual, methodological, and applied issues. In: E. Gordon, ed. Review of Research in Education 12:229-91. Washington, D.C.: American Educational Research Association.

Skehan, P. 1989. Individual differences in second-language learning. London: Edward Arnold.

Tucker, G.R., E. Hamayan, and F. Genesee. 1976. Affective, cognitive, and social factors in second-language acquisition. Canadian Modern Language Review 23:214-26.

Vann, R., and R. Abraham. 1989. Strategies of unsuccessful language learners. Paper presented at the annual meeting of Teachers of English to Speakers of Other Languages, San Francisco.

Wenden, A., and J. Rubin. 1987. Learner strategies in language learning. Englewood Cliffs, N.J.: Prentice-Hall.

Willing, K. 1988. Learning styles in adult migrant education. Adelaide, South Australia: National Curriculum Research Council.

Witkin, H.A., and J.W. Berry. 1975. Psychological differentiation in cross-cultural perspective. Journal of Cross-Cultural Psychology 6:4-87.

Witkin, H.A., and D.R. Goodenough. 1977. Field dependence and interpersonal behavior. Psychological Bulletin 84:661-89.

Wubbels, T., M. Brekelmans, H. Creton, and H. Hooymayers. 1988. Teacher behavior style and learning environment. Paper presented at the annual meeting of the American Educational Research Association, New Orleans.

Young, D.J. Forthcoming. Understanding and coping with language anxiety: A summary of theory and practice. Submitted for publication.

Language learning in a study abroad context: The effects of interactive and noninteractive out-of-class contact on grammatical achievement and oral proficiency

Barbara F. Freed*
Carnegie-Mellon University

Introduction. Study abroad programs are becoming increasingly common on American campuses. With the recent emphasis on global education and internationalizing the curriculum, growing numbers of institutions are taking steps to expand opportunities for study abroad. While the overall benefits of study abroad are widely acclaimed, little is actually known about the effects of a study abroad experience on the participants in such programs. In fact, although it has recently been noted (Goodwin and Nacht 1988:16) that "mastery of a modern language has traditionally been perceived as the most direct educational benefit of study abroad," there have been few studies of the impact these experiences have on the linguistic skills of those who spend time in these programs. Indeed, there has been scant attention to the linguistic experiences students have while they are abroad.[1]

Nonetheless, it has been popularly assumed by students and teachers alike that those students who spend time in study abroad programs are the most likely to "pick up the language," become fluent, and achieve the greatest proficiency in their use of the language. Indeed, the oft quoted study by Carroll (1967) supports the belief that students who spend time in study abroad situations are more proficient than those who do not. A more recent study by Cox and Freed (1989) comes to a similar conclusion. A related assumption, also supported by professional discussion (Bialystok 1978; Rubin 1975; Seliger 1977; Stern 1983) is that students who seek to use the target language the most, both in and out of the classroom, will be the ones who ultimately make the most progress.

---

* Appreciation is expressed to Henry Gleitman for his assistance in matters of experimental design, statistical analysis and comments on previous versions of this article. Appreciation is also extended to Lila Gleitman for suggestions regarding the design of the study, to Cynthia Fisher for invaluable help with the statistical analysis, to Virginia Young for assistance with the coding of the data, to Kathryn McMahon for logistical support in France, to Shearer Weigert, Barbara Klaw and Stacy Gayman, my research assistants, to Nina Spada for comments on a previous version of this paper, and to the Consortium for Language Teaching and Learning which supported the study.

[1] For a recent study on the linguistic experiences of students in a study abroad context, see Kaplan 1989.

There has been, however, conflicting evidence which suggests that informal, out-of-class contact, which presumably provides more linguistic input and obligates use of communicative strategies, does not necessarily enhance (Day 1985; DeKeyser 1986; Krashen and Seliger 1976; Krashen, Seliger, and Harnett 1974; Spada 1984, 1985) and may even impede foreign language proficiency (Higgs & Clifford 1982). Of the formal studies of the effects of out-of-class contact, only one (Martin 1980) has found that informal contact leads to increased proficiency, while a second one suggests, but does not demonstrate, that increased contact "probably results in more second language acquisition" (Parr 1988:12).

This study was therefore motivated by the desire to assess the impact of informal out-of-class contact on the linguistic skills of American foreign language students. In this respect the study differs from most previous studies in which the subjects were, or had been, students of English as a Second Language.

The purpose of this study was to investigate the effects of out-of-class contact on American students of a foreign language who were living and attending classes in a study abroad context. The underlying question which this study sought to answer was the following:

> Do those students who pursue the most informal contacts out of the classroom make the greatest gains in achievement and proficiency during a six-week summer study abroad program?

This is not, of course, a simple question. It seemed to us that it was at least possible that many interviewing variables would confound the results. For example, it is reasonable to hypothesize that more highly motivated students would be more likely to seek contacts in the target culture. Or, for instance, that students who are less concerned about speaking "correctly" would be more likely to pursue contacts outside the language classroom. One might further hypothesize that students with a greater aptitude for foreign language learning might feel more confident and would be likely to look for more opportunities to use the language outside of class. We also considered a possible effect of instructional levels. It did not seem unreasonable to assume that higher level students would be more likely to interact with native speakers than would beginners. Nor was it unlikely that students at different instructional levels would benefit in different ways from the interactions they had. We also considered the possibility that different types of contact within the target culture might have differing effects on ultimate achievement and proficiency. We therefore addressed a series of related questions which include the following:

1. What, if any, difference exists between students at various levels of study and the likelihood of their pursuing out-of-class contact?
2. What relationship exists between motivation and student attitudes toward correctness in speech and the likelihood of pursuing out-of-class contact?

3. What is the relationship between aptitude and the likelihood of pursuing out-of-class contact?
4. What, if any, difference exists between students at various levels (beginning, intermediate, advanced), the likelihood of their pursuing out-of-class contact and the effects these out-of-class contacts have on their achievement and proficiency?
5. Are different effects observed between qualitatively different types of out-of-class contacts? That is, are there differences between interactive and noninteractive types of contact?

This paper addresses the basic question which motivated the study as well as questions 1-5. It is organized in the following way: (1) there is a description of the design of the study, which includes the subjects, the questionnaires and tests used to collect information on student motivation and aptitude; (2) a description of the instruments used to measure achievement and proficiency; (3) a description of the measures used to gather information on the students' out-of-class contacts; (4) a description of the method of observation, data collection and analysis, and, finally, a discussion of the results of the study.

Design.

Subjects. The original subjects in this study were 40 undergraduate students who, during the summer of 1988, participated in a six-week study abroad program, sponsored by the University of Pennsylvania. Two students were eventually eliminated from the study: one because he was found to have learning disabilities which seriously affected his performance; the second because his proficiency in English was slightly limited. The program was held in Tours, France. The students ranged in age from 18-25, the majority being between 18-22. Of the students, 14 were male and 24 were female. Thirty students were native speakers of English; the other eight were native speakers of Chinese, Spanish, Tamil, Ukrainian, or Taiwanese. All of these students possessed near native proficiency in English. On arrival in France the students' knowledge of French varied considerably. Some had had no previous study of French while others had completed between one and three years of college French or the equivalent. This distribution was equally true for the native and nonnative speakers of English who participated in the study.

All students were enrolled in two French courses: language, literature, civilization or a combination of the two. Those at the lower levels of study took two related language courses (e.g. Elementary French 1 and 2). Those at more advanced levels combined either two language courses (advanced grammar and composition), one language and one literature or civilization course, or two literature courses. There were no control groups per se. The only control existed by virtue of students studying at various instructional levels and therefore receiving different types of instruction. For purposes of analysis, students were divided into four groups based on their previous study of French: beginners (6 students), intermediate (9 students), high intermediate (15 students), and advanced (8 students). (The terminology used here is general and is not intended to correspond in any way to the ILR ACTFL ranges.) These groups also corresponded to the students' levels of study while in Tours.

During their stay in France, students lived either with French families or in the university residence. Thirty-two students lived with families; six lived in the dormitory. While it might be assumed that those who lived with families had greater opportunity for informal contacts, this was not necessarily the case. Some families lodged as many as 12 foreign students, so the opportunities for personal interaction with native speakers were not necessarily greater for a student in a family situation than for one who lived in the university residence. Adjustments for different living situations were made in the analysis of out-of-class contact.

Motivation questionnaires and aptitude tests. To assess student attitudes and motivation toward studying French, all students were given a modified version of the motivation questionnaire developed by Glicksman, Gardner, and Smythe (1982).[2] Students were also asked to complete a questionnaire which measured their attitudes toward correctness in speech (based on questionnaires used by Ely 1983; Abraham 1983; and DeKeyser 1986).[3] They were also given the Modern Language Aptitude Test (MLAT).

Achievement and proficiency tests. As a measure of grammar and reading comprehension, the College Entrance Examination Board Language Achievement Test (CEEB) was used, both as a pre- and posttest. This is a traditional discrete point multiple choice test. In order to assess functional oral language proficiency, the ILR-ACTFL Oral Proficiency Interview (OPI) was administered, also as a pre- and posttest. This test provides one global score for various aspects of interactive language use. The OPI was administered by trained, but not always certified OPI testers. The ratings, however, were given by two highly experienced and certified OPI testers. The interrater reliability was 100%.

Measures of out-of-class contact. A variety of observation and self-report instruments was utilized to assess students' informal out-of-class contacts.

---

[2] Modifications include removing certain items from the original questionnaires and substituting French for French Canadian.

[3] The questionnaire combined elements from the Ely (1983) and Abraham (1983) questionnaires as used in DeKeyser (1986).

Language contact profile.[4] The primary measure of informal contact outside the classroom was a questionnaire designed to measure out-of-class contact. The Language Contact Profile (LCP) originally used by Seliger (1977) and later adapted by Bialystok (1978), Spada (1984), and Day (1985), was used as the basis of this self-report questionnaire on informal contact with native speakers outside of the classroom.

The questionnaire includes a wide range of questions which elicit information on the students' background and language learning history, as well as a series of questions related to their out-of-class contacts while in France. These questions were divided into two general categories. The first measures interactive contacts, those involving direct social contact with native speakers of French, either family members or friends. Points were allocated according to living situations (with families or in the university residence; with small families who spoke only French or in larger family situations where English and other languages were spoken) and the number of hours per day they spent speaking French with family members and friends. Many of the questions had subparts which elicited more information about the kind of activities students engaged in while speaking with their friends. The second set of questions measures noninteractive contacts: those which were media related. These questions measured time spent listening to the radio, watching television, reading French books and newspapers, going to the movies, etc. Noninteractive activities were those weighted toward the literate end on an oral-literate continuum. The LCP, therefore, provided information on the total amount of time students were engaged in out-of-class contact, as well as data regarding qualitative differences in the type of contact. (The LCP is included in the Appendix to this paper.)

Diaries. In an effort to overcome the self-report limitations of the LCP, we asked students to keep a bi-weekly diary. Students were requested to record their experiences, interactions and, to the extent they were willing to do so, their feelings about these events. Their diary entries were collected twice a week.

Interviews. In a further effort to substantiate the data recorded in the LCPs, all students were interviewed by one of three research assistants at the end of the program. These interviews were based on the data recorded in the students' LCPs and their general out-of-class contact during their six-week stay in France. During the interview, students were asked to reflect on the nature of their progress and their language learning experience.

---

[4] The LCP as used by Day (1985) was the basis for the LCP in this study. However, it was revised to fit a study abroad situation and expanded, as suggested by Spada, to provide for qualitative as well as quantitative differences in types of out-of-class language contacts.

Observations. In addition to data provided by the students themselves, a sample of 21 students (roughly divided among the four levels) was observed by the research assistants. These observations were informal and ethnographic in nature. The research assistants attempted to observe students' interactions with native speakers outside of the classroom. This was done to further enhance the self-report data and to gain some insight into the nature of the native speaker, nonnative speaker interaction. These observations included informal observation of students in typical target language encounter situations, as well as in class.

Method. Just before or immediately after arriving in France, all students were pretested on the CEEB and the OPI. At the beginning of the six-week program, all students completed the questionnaires on motivation and attitude toward correctness. They were also given the MLAT. With the exception of the MLAT, each of these measures was administered a second time during the program. The two questionnaires were given again during the fifth week of the program and the CEEB and OPI were used as posttests at the conclusion of the program.

Students were also asked to complete the LCP on two separate occasions: at the end of the third week of class and again during the last week of the program. There were two reasons for giving the LCP twice. The first was that their LCP scores might have changed as a result of increasing interactions with native speakers in the community, as their skills increased during the course of the program. The second reason was to reduce the suspicious effect of self-report data. We believed that if the scores on the two LCPs were found to be highly correlated, then test-retest reliability would be a measure of validity. As mentioned earlier, diaries were collected from all students twice a week and student interviews were conducted during the last week of class.

During the six-week program students pursued their regular course of study with no involvement from the investigator. There was no manipulation of course materials, instructional approach, or requirements. Course instructors were essentially unaware of the research project.

Analysis. Analysis of the data falls into several categories:

1. The relationship between student level of study and the likelihood of their pursuing out-of-class contact.
2. The relationship between attitudes toward correctness, motivation, and the Language Contact Profile (LCP).
3. The relationship between the MLAT and the LCP.
4. The relationship between the LCP (both interactive and noninteractive aspects of out-of-class contact) and the results on the pre- and posttests of grammar, reading comprehension (CEEB), and the oral proficiency interview (OPI).

Beyond these general categories for the group as a whole, analysis focuses on differences between groups of students enrolled at various levels of study. We attempted to determine whether or not beginning, intermediate, high intermediate, or advanced students were more or less likely to pursue out-of-class contacts in a study abroad environment and to what extent these contacts affected their achievement and proficiency as measured by the two tests.

The various aspects of out-of-class contact, as measured by the LCP, were standardized by converting them to z scores which were then averaged. The relationship of this average to other variables, as listed in 1, 2, 3, and 4 above, was then assessed by appropriate regression analyses.

Preliminary inspection of the student diaries, related student interviews, and out-of-class observation by the research assistants suggested that these were flawed measures. As a result they were not included in this analysis.[5]

Results. As described here, the basic question which motivated this study was whether or not students who maintained the greatest amount of out-of-class contact would be those who made the greatest gains in achievement and proficiency during a six-week study abroad program. Since other variables were suspected as possible confounding factors, we also addressed several related questions. The results will be reported in response to these individual questions.

What, if any, difference exists between students at various levels of study and the likelihood of their pursuing out-of-class contact of either the interactive or noninteractive variety?

While it might reasonably be expected that more advanced students would be more likely to engage in informal out-of-class contacts, we began our study by measuring the mean score of out-of-class contact as measured by the LCP with student level of study. (Remember that students were divided into four general levels: beginner, intermediate, high intermediate, and advanced.)

As seen in Table 1, the more advanced students, those in the high intermediate and advanced levels, were far more likely to pursue informal contact in the French-speaking community than were students at the beginning and intermediate levels. This is not particularly surprising. This finding was true for the total amount of out-of-class contact as well as for the different types of contact. That is, the more advanced students tended to seek both

[5] In reading the student diaries, we found enormous variation in their descriptions and learned that the students misconstrued or misunderstood the diary task. Furthermore, some students resented having to write or submit diary entries and others regarded this as homework; other enjoyed keeping the diaries. This made it almost impossible to analyze the diary data. For similar reasons the data from the student interviews were not analyzed and presented in this report. Lack of sufficient consistency on the part of the research assistants yielded highly variable reports on both the student interviews and informal observations.

more interactive contact (time spent speaking with French friends and family) and noninteractive contact (time spent reading books, watching TV, etc.).

Table 1. Mean and standard deviations of total out-of-class contact (occ), interactive out-of-class contact and noninteractive out-of-class contact scores by level of study.

		Level of Study			
		Beg. *(n=6)	Int. (n=9)	High Int. (n=14)	Adv. (n=6)
Total OCC (z-scores)	Mean	-0.49	-0.84	0.38	0.66
	SD	3.75	2.25	2.20	3.26
Interactive OCC	Mean	-0.04	-0.62	0.35	0.43
	SD	3.68	2.16	2.34	3.29
Noninteractive OCC	Mean	1.78	1.88	3.50	4.09
	SD	1.75	1.22	1.79	2.53

* The number of subjects may vary from table to table or column to columns because a few subjects had either a missing test score or missing values that prevented the calculation of complete out-of-class contact scores. Missing observations are left out.

Moreover, as seen in Table 1, students at all levels were, not surprisingly, more likely to seek opportunities for less threatening types of noninteractive contact than were they to pursue interpersonal interactive contacts.

To what extent does motivation and/or student attitudes toward correctness in speech relate to the likelihood of pursuing out-of-class contact?

To test the relationship between motivation and the likelihood of pursuing out-of-class contact as measured by the LCP, as well as the relationship between student attitudes toward correctness and out-of-class contact (again as measured by the LCP), we performed a regression analysis to see if motivation and/or attitudes toward correctness predict scores on the LCP. There was no evidence of such a relationship; the regression did not begin to approach significance ($F = 1.46$, ns). We concluded that neither a high mean score on two questionnaires measuring motivation, nor a low mean score on questionnaires measuring attitudes toward correctness, predicts the likelihood of pursuing out-of-class contact.

This result struck us as somewhat surprising so we decided to separate the out-of-class contact scores as measured by the LCP into its two component parts, interactive and noninteractive. Again we found that even by separating these two distinct components, out-of-class contact cannot be predicted by motivation or attitudes toward correctness. The relevant F-ratios were 1.32 and 2.53, respectively, neither of which is significant.

In a further attempt to understand this finding, we decided to look at motivation and attitude toward correctness across all four levels of study: beginner, intermediate, high intermediate, advanced. This was based on the assumption that beginners, even if highly motivated, might be less likely to pursue out-of-class contact than more advanced students who had greater communicative skills. We therefore added level of language study to the regression analysis of motivation and attitude toward correctness as they affect various aspects of the LCP, both interactive and noninteractive. We again found no effect. (The relevant F-ratios were 1.00 and 2.35, respectively, both nonsignificant.)

Since motivation and attitude toward correctness in speech are not correlated, there was no reason to suspect that they would interfere with each other in a regression analysis. Nonetheless, to be certain that there was no confounding of results by looking at scores on the motivation questionnaire and those on the correctness questionnaire, we separated these and looked at simple correlations to see if the result was any stronger. Once again, we confirmed that neither motivation nor attitudes toward correctness in speech affect the likelihood of pursuing out-of-class contact. This finding was true for students at all levels of study. (The respective r's were 0.26 and -0.08, both nonsignificant.)

The one exception to this finding was a positive relationship between motivation and the likelihood of pursuing out-of-class contact of the noninteractive variety ($r = 0.36$, $p < 0.03$). That is, those students who were more motivated to learn French were somewhat more likely to pursue noninteractive opportunities to use the French language outside the classroom; they reported spending more time attending French movies, reading French newspapers, and the like. Other than this, there is basically nothing to suggest that motivation or attitudes toward correctness affect the tendency to pursue out-of-class contact.

Given these findings, these variables (motivation and attitudes toward correctness) were left out of all subsequent analyses.

What is the relationship between aptitude and the likelihood of pursuing out-of-class contact?

We had hypothesized that students who possessed greater aptitude for language learning might also have a greater tendency to look for opportunities to interact in the target culture. We therefore looked at the relationship between aptitude as measured by the MLAT scores and the LCP, which measured out-of-class contact. Using a regression analysis, we once again found no correlation between student scores on the aptitude test and the likelihood of their pursuing out-of-class contact (F = 1, ns). These findings were maintained for the group as a whole, with no effect of level. This variable also was left out of future analyses.

Having found that motivation, attitude to correctness, and aptitude for language learning exert no effect on the likelihood of students pursuing informal contacts in the French-speaking community, we turn to the principal question of the study.

Do those students who pursue the most out-of-class contact as measured by the LCP make the greatest progress in achievement and proficiency during a six-week study abroad program?

The primary data to answer this question derived from the LCP and the difference scores on the pre- and posttests, which measured grammar (CEEB) and oral proficiency (OPI). As described previously, students completed the LCP questionnaire twice during the program: at the midpoint and again at the end of the program. The scores on the two LCPs were found to be highly correlated with correlation coefficients of 0.78 (p 0.0001) for noninteractive scores and 0.72 (p. 0001) for interactive scores. This finding enhanced our confidence in the self-report data. We interpreted this high correlation as encouraging evidence that the students were responding more or less truthfully to the questions on the LCP. Therefore, for all future comparisons, we used the mean score of the two LCPs.

Having bolstered our confidence in the LCP itself, we turned to analyses of the effects of informal out-of-class contact on growth in achievement and proficiency. We looked first at the relationship between out-of-class contact and oral proficiency (as measured by the OPI), and then at the relationship between out-of-class contact and achievement (measured by the CEEB).

With respect to growth in oral proficiency, there is no evidence of the effect of out-of-class contact on OPI scores (F = 1.68, ns). It is important to point out, however, that there is relatively little change over the six weeks, in the OPI pre- and posttest scores, for students at any level. (In fact, only for the six students at the beginning level, is there a significant difference in pre- and post-OPI test scores.)

To assess the effect of out-of-class contact and change in grammatical achievement, we calculated the difference between the students' CEEB pre- and posttest scores, as seen in Table 3.

We next performed a multiple regression analysis of CEEB change as a function of overall LCP scores as well as level of study. Table 4 shows CEEB changes as a function of level of study. In this analysis we collapsed beginners and intermediate level students into one group (labeled Level 1) and high intermediate and advanced level students into another (labeled Level 2). We also established low vs. high groups for overall out-of-class contact (where low and high are defined by scores below and above the overall LCP mean). We found an overall significant regression ($F = 7.70$, $p < 0.0005$, $R^2 = 0.43$), but upon further analysis, the primary contributor to this effect was found to be the students' level of study. That is, as shown in Table 4, the lower the students' level of study, the greater their improvement from the CEEB pre- to the posttest. By contrast, the more advanced students, those in Level 2, not only showed no growth on the CEEB as an effect of overall out-of-class contact, but the findings were in fact reversed. So, while the level effect is strong at the beginning level, there is little evidence of an independent effect of overall out-of-class contact score on CEEB change.

Table 2. Mean and standard deviations of OPI pre- and posttest scores by student level of study.

		LEVEL OF STUDY			
		Beg. *(n=6)	Int. (n=9)	High Int. (n=15)	Adv. (n=8)
OPI Pre-	Mean	1.83	3.22	4.20	4.75
	SD	0.75	0.44	0.68	1.04
OPI Post-	Mean	3.33	4.56	4.87	5.62
	SD	0.82	1.01	0.64	1.41

* The number of subjects may vary from table to table or column to columns because a few subjects had either a missing test score or missing values that prevented the calculation of complete out-of-class contact scores. Missing observations are left out.

On the face of it, out-of-class contact seems to have little or no effect on CEEB improvement. To determine whether this is really so, we decided to look more closely at the type of out-of-class contact the students had in the target community. We therefore analyzed the interactive (direct oral/social, involvement with friends, family, etc.) and noninteractive (media-related activities: French movies, TV, radio, newspapers, books, etc.) components of the LCP and their potential relationship to changes in achievement and/or proficiency.

To this end, we performed a multiple regression analysis of CEEB change as a function of interactive and noninteractive aspects of the LCP, as well as level of study. Table 5 shows mean CEEB change as a function of level of study and degree of interactive out-of-class contact. Table 6 presents corresponding results for noninteractive out-of-class contact.

Table 3. Mean and standard deviations of CEEB pre- and posttest scores by student level of study.

		LEVEL OF STUDY			
		Beg. *(n=6)	Int. (n=9)	High Int. (n=15)	Adv. (n=8)
CEEB Pre-	Mean	370	471	582	649
	SD	63	71	84	98
CEEB Post-	Mean	511	588	645	681
	SD	100	64	67	103

* The number of subjects may vary from table to table or column to columns because a few subjects had either a missing test score or missing values that prevented the calculation of complete out-of-class contact scores. Missing observations are left out.

Table 4. CEEB improvement as a function of overall out-of-class contact and student level of study.*

	OUT-OF-CLASS CONTACT	
	Low	High
LEVEL 1	124.29	128.75
LEVEL 2	60.00	45.00
MEAN	92.14	86.88

* Level 1 = Beginners and intermediates.
Level 2 = High intermediate and advanced.

Low and high overall scores are defined as below and above the relevant mean scores of the LCP for the group as a whole.

As Tables 5 and 6 show, when out-of-class contact is analyzed in this manner, it does indeed have an effect on CEEB change, but this effect goes in an opposite direction for the two components.

Table 5. CEEB improvement as a function of interactive out-of-class and student level of study.*

	INTERACTIVE OUT-OF-CLASS CONTACT	
	Low	High
LEVEL 1	118.33	132.22
LEVEL 2	55.83	48.18
MEAN	87.08	90.20

* Level 1 = Beginners and intermediates.
Level 2 = High intermediate and advanced.

Low and high overall scores are defined as below and above the relevant mean scores of the LCP for the group as a whole.

Table 6. CEEB improvement as a function of noninteractive out-of-class contact and student level of study.*

	NONINTERACTIVE OUT-OF-CLASS CONTACT	
	Low	High
LEVEL 1	136.92	60.00
LEVEL 2	45.56	56.43
MEAN	91.24	58.22

* Level 1 = Beginners and intermediates.
Level 2 = High intermediate and advanced.

Low and high overall scores are defined as below and above the relevant mean scores of the LCP for the group as a whole.

As Table 5 shows, the more interactive contact students have, the greater their CEEB improvement. However, this effect is present only for the lower levels of study; it was either absent or reversed for the more advanced students. These findings are statistically upheld by the multiple regression analysis, which showed a t-value of 2.62 ($p < 0.02$) for the effect of interactive out-of-class contact, and a significant interaction between this variable andlevel ($t = 2.84$, $p < 0.01$).

Table 6 shows that the effect of noninteractive out-of-class contact went in the opposite direction: the greater the degree of noninteractive out-of-class contact, the less CEEB change was observed at the lower level. But again, this effect was reversed for more advanced students where more noninteractive contact had an effect on CEEB change. These findings are again upheld by the multiple regression analysis, which showed a t-value of 2.97 ($p < 0.01$) for the effect of noninteractive out-of-class contact, and a significant interaction between this variable and level ($t = 2.75$, $p < 0.01$).

With respect to oral proficiency, separating interactive and noninteractive types of out-of-class contact once again had no effect on OPI scores. Given the little variation in OPI scores there was no significant effect at any level.

Discussion. This study was undertaken in an attempt to learn more about the effects of informal contact on learners' acquisition of a foreign language. In particular, we were anxious to gain further insight into the effects of out-of-class contact on the achievement and proficiency of foreign language students studying in the native speaking environment.

We began by looking at the potential interaction between motivation, attitudes toward correctness in speech, aptitude, and the likelihood of pursuing out-of-class contact. With little exception, we found essentially no relationship between any of these variables and student tendency to pursue informal contact.

In attempting to explain these findings, we suggest the possibility that this self-selected group of students, who chose to study abroad, might fall into the upper range of a motivation continuum. That is, these students may have been more motivated generally than the average student population.

We considered a similar explanation for the lack of correlation between high aptitude and the likelihood of pursuing out-of-class contact. However, it cannot be said that the aptitude of this group of students was necessarily any higher than for any other group of students. In fact, at the beginning and intermediate levels (where students had not yet satisfied the university's foreign language requirement) there may even have been some students with a low aptitude for foreign language learning. There is also the added possibility that the validity of the MLAT is in question. At least one recent study (Goodman, Freed, and McMannus 1990) has found no strong correlation between MLAT scores and the tendency to do well or poorly in communicatively oriented language classes.

With respect to the major purpose of this study, we have found, consistent with most previous studies, that the amount of out-of-class contact in general does not seem to influence measurable class progress.

At face value, it even looks as if our intuitions were all wrong. We might be led to question the long-held belief in the linguistic benefits of study abroad and the value of contact with native speakers in authentic encounter situations. However, such a counterintuitive and improbable finding obliged us to look further. By refining our analyses, we found some exceptions to the general lack of effect.

Further analysis did reveal an interaction between the likelihood of pursuing out-of-class contact and progress made on traditional tests of grammar and reading comprehension. This effect was particularly true for students at the beginning and intermediate levels, but was totally absent (in fact, it was slightly reversed) for higher level students. Level of study, therefore, seems to be an important variable in predicting change in performance as measured by an achievement test.

More specifically though, it is not the amount but rather the type of contact which interacts with level to predict a change on achievement test scores. That is, spending time with family and friends in a variety of social contexts appears to be more meaningful in predicting this change (at the lower levels of study) than is time spent interacting with different types of media: books, newspapers, movies, TV, etc. In fact, those lower level students who spent more time in literate-oriented activities actually demonstrated less growth on the CEEB.

It is important to remember that informal interactive contact with native French speakers did not predict change for students at the high intermediate and advanced levels. One possible explanation for this finding is that higher level students demonstrate less change on a standardized test of grammar. (The CEEB has a known ceiling and the higher level students are closer to the upper level of these scores. They have, in effect, less room to demonstrate growth.) It is the lower level students who predictably make the greatest progress on such tests. It is equally true that higher level students who have more or less mastered the language of daily activities profit less in a general way from oral/social interaction. For those students, interaction with language materials weighted toward the literate on an oral-literate continuum (reading books and newspapers in French, watching TV, and going to the movies) seems to make an important difference. This explanation corresponds with the conclusions drawn by Parr (1988). In an analysis of students' perceptions of the benefits of various types of language-related experiences in a study abroad situation, Parr reported that "beginners sensed that the social interaction was of more benefit to them than the media" (Parr 1988), while advanced level students "perceived (greater) importance for media activities" (Parr 1988). In this respect, we must consider the very real possibility that different types of activities interact in different ways with the process of language learning at different stages in the acquisition process. Such a hypothesis might explain the puzzling finding that lower level students who spent more time in noninteractive activities profited less from this type of involvement.

The interaction of level with out-of-class contact of the interactive type needs to be considered in light of Spada's (1984, 1985, 1986) study of the effects of out-of-class contact on intermediate level students. Her results showed an interaction between instructional variation and out-of-class contact. These findings may very well be related to our own finding of the effects of instructional level. Spada found that out-of-class contact accounted for differences in learners' progress on tests of grammar when the instruction represented a combination of form-based and meaning-based teaching, rather than instruction which represented an exclusive focus on communication (1986:196-97, and personal communication). Interestingly enough, it is precisely at the beginning and intermediate levels in our study, that instruction tends to be more form-focused. While classes at the beginning and intermediate levels in our study had a 'communicative approach' to language learning, there was at the same time a clear focus on form. Such a focus was less apparent in the high intermediate level and advanced level language classes, and essentially absent in the advanced level literature and civilization courses.

Spada also found a negative relationship between amount of out-of-class contact and progress on tests of reading and discourse activity for intermediate level students (1986:194-95). Her interpretation was that "high contact" learners spend more time in interactive contact situations, while "low contact" learners spend more time in noninteractive (reading and listening) situations. In our study, it was the more advanced learners (as opposed to the intermediate level students in Spada's study and the beginning and intermediate level students in our own study) who sought more noninteractive contact.

By contrast and perhaps surprisingly, informal contact out of the classroom, appeared to have no measurable effect on functional oral proficiency as measured by the OPI. While unlike Spada's results, which found a positive correlation between interactive contact and students' oral abilities, our finding supports other studies which found no relationship between tests of oral skills and amount of out-of-class contact (Day 1985).

Conclusion. This study has provided a new look at the effects of informal language contact on the achievement and proficiency of the second/foreign language learner. In particular, it has focused on the foreign language student in a study abroad context. It has gone beyond previous studies of the effects of informal out-of-class contact by providing data on students engaged in study at various levels. In addition, the study has built upon Spada's initiative in attempting to refine the distinction between amount and type of out-of-class contact. While new measures of out-of-class contact were added to this study (diaries, student interview, and informal observation), these instruments were not sufficiently developed to be useful in this study. They provided, however, a first step in designing measures to complement a self-report language contact profile and to provide insight into various types of interaction.

Before suggesting possible implications for classroom practice based on these findings, it is important to underscore the limitations of this study. These include the number of subjects (38 students), the length of the study (six weeks), and most importantly, the testing instruments which provided gross measures of achievement and proficiency.

As has been previously noted, the OPI which utilizes one global holistic score for various aspects of language use is not sufficiently refined to capture growth in oral skills, particularly in a six-week period. Except for students at the very beginning level, there was little variation in OPI scores. We therefore found it difficult with this type of analysis to demonstrate any effect of out-of-class contact. In order to demonstrate change, future studies will have to utilize more finely tuned analyses; those which will reveal, with specificity, development in students' lexical breadth, syntactic complexity, stylistic sensitivity, sociolinguistic and pragmatic competence, and cohesion and coherence in language use.

Beyond tests of oral abilities, there remains the very real concern that the achievement tests used in this and other studies are not sensitive enough to capture the overall linguistic progress of our students. The use of the CEEB itself is now called into question for use in a study of this type. As mentioned earlier, advanced level students are close to the upper levels of what this test can measure. It remains counterintuitive to believe that out-of-class contact has little, if any, effect on measurable performance. We may not be defining 'progress' properly, we may not be looking at the right constellation of skills, and we may not be using the appropriate measurement devices.

In addition, the possibility remains that the effects of out-of-class contact are not immediately obvious and/or that they are not sufficiently strong in a short-term program. The effects of informal contact may be evident in a retest situation, both in terms of overall student retention and in students' ability to make future progress. Once again, the hypothesis that serious consideration must be given to different types of linguistic involvement interacts in different ways with the process of language learning at different stages in the acquisition process. For this and other reasons, future studies will also have to include students at various levels of study.

Finally, it may be that there are other variables that have not been measured. For example, as demonstrated by DeKeyser (1986), individual differences in personality may account for differences in the likelihood of pursuing out-of-class contact and the impact these activities make on the language learner.

Given the preliminary nature of this study, it is premature to draw firm conclusions regarding practice. Nonetheless, we might tentatively suggest some general implications for the classroom and for study abroad programs that seem to emerge from this study.

First among these is the suggestion that prestudy abroad proficiency will determine to some extent both the amount and type of out-of-class activities students will be able to pursue and from which they will be able to benefit.

Second is the strong possibility that form-focused classroom instruction interacts in positive ways with informal out-of-class contact. Finally, activities and interaction of a social/oral nature seem to benefit students at the lower level, while students at upper levels appear to profit from involvement with a variety of media which provide for interaction with extended discourse in reading and listening.

In conclusion, it is to be anticipated that future studies of this type will help elucidate the relationship between formal instruction, informal language contact, and the acquisition process itself. In a related fashion, such studies will also provide important information that will permit us to organize study abroad programs to maximize their potential for language growth.

References

Abraham, Roberta. 1983. Relationships between the use of the strategy of monitoring and the cognitive style. SSLA 1983:17-32.

Bialystok, Ellen. 1978. Language skills and the learners: The classroom perspective. In: C. Blatchford and J. Schachter, eds. On TESOL '78. Washington, D.C.: TESOL.

Carroll, John B. 1967. Foreign language proficiency levels attained by language majors near graduation from college. Foreign Language Annals 1:131-51.

Cox, Ronald, and Barbara F. Freed. 1989. The effects of study abroad on form and function: A comparison of differences in the language of students who have studied abroad and those who have not. MS.

Day, Richard. 1985. The use of the target language in context and second language proficiency. In: Susan Gass and Carolyn Madden, eds. Input in second language acquisition. Rowley, Mass.: Newbury House.

DeKeyser, Robert. 1986. From learning to acquisition? Foreign language development in a U.S. classroom and during a semester abroad. Unpublished Ph.D. dissertation, Stanford University.

Ely, Christopher. 1983. A causal analysis of the affective, behavioral and aptitudinal antecedents of foreign language proficiency. Unpublished Ph.D. dissertation, Stanford University.

Glicksman R., Robert Gardner, and P. Smyth. 1982. The role of integrative motive on students' participation in the French classroom. Canadian Modern Language Journal 38:625-47.

Goodman, Joan, Barbara F. Freed, and William McMannus. 1990. Determining exemptions from foreign language requirements: Use of the modern language aptitude test. Contemporary Psychology.

Goodwin, C., and M. Nacht. 1988. Abroad and beyond: Patterns in American overseas education. Cambridge: Cambridge University Press.

Higgs, Theodore, and Ray Clifford. 1982. The push toward communication. In: Theodore Higgs, ed. Curriculum, competence and the foreign language teacher. Skokie, Ill.: National Textbook Co.

Kaplan, Marsha. 1989. French in the community: A survey of language use abroad. French Review 63.2:290-99.

Krashen, Stephen, and Herbert Seliger. 1976. The role of formal and informal environments in second language learning: A pilot study. International Journal of Psycholinguistics 3:15-20.

Krashen, Stephen, Herbert Seliger, and D. Harnett. 1974. Two studies in adult second language learning. Kritikon Literarum 2:220-28.

Martin, G. 1980. English language acquisition: The effects of living with an American family. TESOL Quarterly 14:388-90.

Parr, Patricia. 1988. Second language acquisition and study abroad: The immersion experience. Unpublished Ph.D. dissertation, University of Southern California.

Rubin, Joan. 1975. What the 'good language learner' can teach us. TESOL Quarterly 9:41-51.

Spada, Nina. 1984. The interaction between type of instruction, informal contact, learner opinions and second language proficiency. Unpublished doctoral dissertation, University of Toronto.

Spada, Nina. 1985. Effects of informal contact on classroom learners' proficiency: A review of five studies. TESL Canada Journal 2:51-62.

Spada, Nina. 1986. The interaction between types of contact and types on instruction: Some effects on the second language proficiency of adult learners. SSLA 1986:181-99.

Seliger, Herbert. 1977. Does practice make perfect: A study of interaction patterns and L2 competence. Language Learning 27:263-78.

Stern, H. H. 1983. Fundamental concepts of language teaching. London: Oxford University Press.

The cognitive basis for second language instruction

J. Michael O'Malley
Georgetown University

Efforts to explain the basic principles underlying second language acquisition have tended to focus on linguistic and social features of language rather than the cognitive mechanisms involved in memory storage and retrieval. Analyses of the linguistic and social characteristics of second language acquisition are essential to comprehend the substantive and interactive aspects of language. A complementary analysis of the learning processes themselves is useful to support a better understanding of how second language phenomena are stored in memory and are acquired. To the extent that the learning processes underlying second language acquisition are similar to those underlying all learning, this analysis will also aid in inspecting the connection between second language acquisition and processes involved in learning other information including academic content. Furthermore, an analysis of the processes involved in learning will assist in examining the instructional procedures that contribute to second language acquisition and in viewing the obstacles to effective learning.

This paper will describe the basic principles of cognitive theory that underlie learning processes and extend these principles to research and theory in second language acquisition and instruction. The first part of the paper will provide a brief overview of cognitive theory and highlight the evidence for asserting that learning a second language has parallels with the active, strategic processes that occur with all learning. The second part of the paper will describe special learning processes referred to as learning strategies or mental processes that assist in the comprehension, learning, and recall of new information. In a third section, the paper will examine selected constructs in second language acquisition to determine how they can be explained using cognitive theory. The fourth and final part of the paper will provide recommendations drawn from cognitive theory for instructional design in second language acquisition.

Cognitive theory. Recent psychological theories of learning have proposed that the way in which information is acquired cannot be understood without an analysis of the cognitive processes involved in the selection, interpretation, and construction of knowledge (e.g. Anderson 1980, 1983, 1985; Brown, Bransford, Ferrara, and Campione 1983; Shuell 1986). Cognitive theories in particular have been concerned with the mental processes underlying how information is stored in memory and how information is learned. In examining these two major phenomena, a number of other topics have emerged, such as attention, encoding of language-based information, and language production. The original conception of memory processes in cognitive theory differentiated memory into short-term memory, in which a limited amount of new knowledge was retained for only short periods, and long-term memory, in which there were fewer limitations on the amount or duration over which information could be retained. What enables long-term memory to accomplish the end purpose of collecting, retaining, and providing for the retrieval of large amounts of information is the organization of memory into schemata or interconnected frameworks of concepts. These views have not gone unnoticed in the second language field (e.g. Carrell, Devine, and Eskey 1988; Rivers 1983).

Since the advent of information processing theory, this conceptualization of memory and learning has been greatly enhanced by a new understanding of how information is stored in long-term memory and through an expanded view of the process of learning. One of the elements that has been added is the differentiation of short-term memory into a component that stores information and a 'working memory' that manipulates the information contained in short-term memory (Anderson 1985). The following discussion will highlight other newer views, focusing in particular on how information is maintained in long-term memory and on the stages of skill acquisition. The aspects of cognitive theory that are emphasized here provide for the representation of complex cognitive skills in memory as production systems (Anderson 1980, 1983, 1985), a view that has continued to be expanded and revised (e.g. Anderson 1987; Singley and Anderson 1989).

Representation in memory. Information is said to be stored in long-term memory as either declarative or procedural knowledge (Anderson 1983, 1985). The distinction between these two types of memory lies not only in how each is stored, but in how each is learned. 'Declarative knowledge' consists of the facts that we know, i.e. the information that we can declare or describe. This type of information is typically acquired through a mental encoding process that distills the essence of the ideas represented or the language used to represent them. The original language sequences used to convey the information are abstracted so that only a meaning-based representation of the ideas is retained as a proposition (Kintsch 1974). Propositions can be organized, linked, and represented as 'schemata', or configurations of interrelated concepts that define a larger or more inclusive concept. Concepts are said to be linked or connected through their strength of association. When a concept is evoked, other related concepts along linked pathways are also evoked through 'spreading activation'. Declarative knowledge can be learned readily through establishing associations with existing knowledge, but retrieval and application of declarative knowledge can be slowed by the time required for spreading activation. The principal value of schemata is that they facilitate making inferences about concepts and assimilating new information to existing memory structures. Although declarative knowledge can be learned rapidly, it also can be easily forgotten, as can be discovered from attempts to recall information learned in high school content areas.

'Procedural knowledge' refers to the ability to perform various skills, including complex cognitive skills, such as the ability to solve problems, apply strategic modes of thought to learning, and the ability to use language. Procedural knowledge is represented in memory through production systems, a series of condition-action sequences, or IF-THEN connections, that determine the direction and flow of thought or behavior. The following example represents a production system for pluralization (Anderson 1980):

IF the goal is to generate a plural of a noun,
and the noun ends in a hard consonant,
THEN generate the noun + /s/.

The conditions and actions may be either internal thought processes or external behavior. One of the principal values of production systems is their self-modifiability, or change resulting from experience, in ways that capture the elements of learning and development (Klahr, Langley, and Neches 1987). This is illustrated in the following example, where the production system acts like an hypothesis-testing mechanism for a Piagetian balance beam task (adapted from Langley 1987):

IF you have a balance beam with sides A and B,
and the weights are equal,
THEN predict the sides will balance.

IF you have a balance beam with sides A and B,
and side A has the greater weight,
THEN predict that side A will go down.

IF you have a balance beam with sides A and B,
and the weights are equal,
and side B has the greater distance,
THEN predict that side B will go down.

A young learner's experience with balances and weights will lead to the accumulation of world knowledge and to the modification of inaccurate predictions. This important principle is the basis for learning and for the self-modifiability of production systems. Another feature of production systems is that they can act on and modify declarative knowledge. This principle is illustrated in the following simple example:

IF I want to know the branches of government,
and I think there are two branches,
and my latest analysis shows there are three branches,
THEN modify my knowledge to contain three branches.

Many production systems are far more complicated than those illustrated here and require multiple steps, condition-action statements, and sequences with options and subgoals for new directions depending on the conditions met in previous steps. Because of this complexity, the procedural knowledge represented in complex cognitive skills like problem solving and language is difficult to learn and may require extensive opportunities for practice. Nevertheless, once learned, procedural knowledge operates efficiently and rapidly and is retained over long periods. Production systems have been used to represent such diverse actions as reading (Thibadeau, Just, and Carpenter 1982), mathematical computations (Brown and Burton 1978), solving algebra word problems (Bobrow 1968), playing chess (Newell and Simon 1972), using grammatical rules (MacWhinney and Anderson 1986), and using communicative competence in language (O'Malley and Chamot 1990).

Stages of skill acquisition. The cognitive theory of skills acquisition indicates that complex cognitive skills are acquired through a three-stage process in which the skills gradually become proceduralized or automatic (Anderson 1983, 1985). In the first, or 'cognitive stage', learners are provided with rules or condition-action sequences for task performance. This stage entails conscious analysis of the task requirements and the activities that are likely to lead to the desired performance or task solution. Knowledge of the task and task requirements is largely declarative at this stage and can be described by the learner. Task performance at this stage has been referred to as controlled processing, or as processing that requires the attention of the learner and places demands on short-term memory (Shiffrin and Schneider 1977). In the 'associative', or second stage, two main changes occur in task performance. First, errors in the original declarative representation are detected and eliminated, and second, the connections between components of the complex skill are strengthened. This strengthening leads to efficiency in task performance and reduction in the time required to perform the task. In a third, or 'autonomous stage', the performance becomes increasingly fine-tuned. Execution of the skill is nearly automatic and the skill can be performed effortlessly. The skill is said to have been proceduralized through the construction of a propositional representation of action or thought sequences that is converted into production systems. Task performance at this stage of acquisition is referred to as automatic processing (Shiffrin and

Schneider 1977) to signal that little attention on the part of the learner is required and that there are few demands on short-term memory.

The transition of a condition-action rule from declarative knowledge to procedural knowledge occurs through 'knowledge compilation', which has two components: proceduralization and composition. In proceduralization, declarative knowledge of condition-action sequences is stored in long-term memory as propositional representations and ultimately as production systems. In composition, individual productions are combined into larger productions. Anderson indicates that knowledge compilation in learning problem-solving skills is more efficient when analogies or sample problems with opportunities for practice are incorporated into new learning (Singley and Anderson 1989). However, knowledge compilation is insensitive to the accuracy of the underlying declarative knowledge used as input, so that repetition of erroneous compiled productions can lead to what is known in second language acquisition as fossilization (see Schumann elsewhere in this volume and Selinker 1972).

Extensions of cognitive theory. There are three basic ways in which this expression of the theory can be expanded. The first concerns the role of rules in the proceduralization of a skill. The theory (Anderson 1980; Singley and Anderson 1989) indicates that the shift from the cognitive to the autonomous stage occurs through knowledge compilation, which begins with a rule-based performance and ends with automatic execution of a skill. Most of the tasks to which the theory has been applied have well-defined rules that are conveyed as part of instruction, as in mathematical problem solving and computer programming. Learner-generated rules have been of interest theoretically mainly for clarifying differences between novices and experts (Gagné 1985). In second language acquisition, rules evident in the cognitive stage would be synonymous with the grammar-based rules learned in classrooms.

This analysis needs to be extended in second language acquisition since the rules for language use are difficult to identify and may be the self-generated rules evident in interlanguage (Selinker 1972) as easily as the formal rules of language structure. Furthermore, the rules may be used for varied aspects of language performance, including what Canale and Swain (1980) refer to as communicative competence (sociolinguistic knowledge, discourse knowledge, and strategic knowledge, as well as grammatical knowledge). The learner-derived rules for second language acquisition are often functional because they produce desired social consequences and therefore have more importance than the inaccurate rules found in most comparisons of experts and novices. The rules may enable individuals to function effectively with oral or written texts and lead to correct interactive solutions. Many of these rules may be gained through experience as much as through formal exposure to classroom instruction.

A second way in which the theory can be extended is to incorporate social modeling into the proceduralization of cognitive skills. Modeling is intended here to mean a demonstration of a complex skill or its components by an expert or near-expert performer that is observed by the learner. Two key ingredients in the acquisition of a second language, according to Faerch and Kasper (1985), are modeling and hypothesis testing. The exclusion of modeling from a theory based on artificial intelligence and computer analysis is not surprising, despite the potential of modeling to influence learning. The role of modeling in the proceduralization of a highly complex skill nevertheless is limited by the constraints of short-term memory to hold a full representation of the skilled performance. This points to the importance of knowledge compilation of smaller chunks of proceduralized skills that combine to produce a reasonably close approximation to the modeled skill (Gagné 1985). In order to advance beyond the cognitive stage, and to refine the skills in the associative stage, individuals test hypotheses based on prior declarative knowledge. In second language acquisition, the declarative knowledge is synonymous with the rules for all four aspects of communicative competence and is derived from personal or formal knowledge of either the native language or the second language. Learners test and revise hypotheses by analyzing second language input, assessing the feedback received from language production, consulting native speakers or texts, or making intentional errors to elicit repair from a native speaker (Faerch and Kasper 1985). In no small measure, second language acquisition resembles the psycholinguistic guessing game that Goodman (1971) described in the process of reading. However, it is an informed guessing game based firmly on declarative knowledge, procedural skills, knowledge of modeled performance, and intelligently devised hypotheses.

Another possible extension of the theory concerns its implications for instruction of complex cognitive skills. Individuals may resist instruction that is exclusively rule-based due to the excessive demands on short-term memory. Presumably, an individual would be required to retrieve the rules for executing the next steps in an action sequence from long-term memory, check to ensure that the rules apply as predicted, apply the rules to the execution of the skill, check the outcomes, and immediately thereafter retrieve new rules to guide subsequent steps in the action sequences. Delays in performance due to the limited capacity of short-term memory and the slow pace of spreading activation make this an untenable approach to learning and instruction. A preferred method for teaching may be to provide ample opportunities to practice complex skills with feedback (Gagné 1985). Effective instruction of complex cognitive skills could involve modeling the desired performance and providing cues at critical points where the complete skill has been forgotten. The components of complex skills requiring composition would be rehearsed until they are automatic before being integrated into a complete performance.

Some of these extensions of cognitive theory have emerged from a need to expand the content to which the theory of memory and learning processes applies. As Black and Lehnert (1984) note, the theory provides the general mechanism for learning and cognition but does not specify the particular kind of knowledge to which these mechanisms apply. In second language acquisition, the kind of knowledge to which the theory applies is best understood through analysis of the interaction between linguistics and cognitive psychology.

Learning strategies as cognitive skills. All individuals are viewed in cognitive theory as learning most effectively through active, dynamic mental processes. Learning strategies are intentional mental processes that individuals use to select, organize, acquire, or integrate new knowledge or to change their motivational or affective state to enhance learning (Weinstein and Mayer 1986). Strategies may be used with simple learning tasks, such as vocabulary development, or with complex tasks such as mathematical problem solving, reading narrative and expository texts, listening, and written and oral language production. Learning strategies have become a key ingredient to a number of instructional systems (e.g. Chamot and O'Malley 1987; Jones, Palincsar, Ogle, and Carr 1987; Weinstein 1978, 1982) and therefore are given considerable attention here to illustrate their role in second language instruction.

Strategy types. Three types of learning strategies have been described based on the level and type of processing involved (O'Malley, Chamot, Stewner-Manzanares, Kupper, and Russo 1985a): metacognitive strategies, cognitive strategies, and social-affective strategies. The general term 'metacognition' can entail either analysis and awareness of task demands, or use of metacognitive strategies in learning, two separate but interacting processes (Brown et al. 1983). 'Metacognitive strategies' are higher order executive skills that may entail planning for, monitoring, or evaluating the success of a learning activity (Brown et al. 1983). Metacognitive strategies may be more generalizable across tasks than are cognitive strategies. Specific examples of metacognitive strategies with examples drawn from second language acquisition are as follows:

- **Planning.** Specifying the conditions for a learning task, the organization of the task, or the elements of the task required for successful performance.

- **Selective Attention.** Paying attention to specific aspects of a task, as in planning to listen for key words or phrases.

- **Monitoring.** Reviewing attention to an ongoing task, monitoring comprehension for information that should be remembered, or monitoring production while it is occurring.

- **Evaluating.** Reviewing comprehension after completion of a receptive language task, or evaluating language production after it has taken place.

'Cognitive strategies' operate directly on new information, manipulating it in ways that enhance learning. Cognitive strategies may be more limited to specific learning tasks than are metacognitive strategies. Three broad groupings of cognitive learning strategies are rehearsal, organization, and elaboration (Weinstein and Mayer 1986). 'Rehearsal' consists of repetition or review of task information, and 'organization' is the restructuring or reclassification of items to be learned. 'Elaboration' involves linking new information to concepts in long-term memory or linking related parts of a new text. Elaboration is a key strategy affecting the learning of declarative information, and subsumes a variety of other strategies that rely at least in part on information already contained in long-term memory, such as

- **Inferencing.** Guessing at the meaning of words or phrases, predicting the next items or information in sequence, or predicting conclusions.

- **Summarizing.** Synthesizing information or identifying the main ideas and associated details.

- **Deduction.** Applying or analyzing rules to understand or produce language.

- **Imagery.** Using visual images (either generated or actual) to understand or remember new information.

The third type of learning strategy is 'social/affective strategies', or strategies that influence the individual's motivational state, conceptualization of learning, or use of social interaction to enhance learning. Specific examples of social/affective strategies are asking questions for clarification, cooperative learning, and self-talk, or assuring one's self about the potential effectiveness of one's learning approaches or outcomes. Social/affective strategies are potentially applicable with a variety of learning tasks, as are metacognitive strategies.

Representation of strategies in memory. Strategies are represented in memory as procedural knowledge once they have become automatic. Procedural knowledge is also the fundamental mechanism for cognitive control (Anderson 1980). The condition-action sequences represented in production systems provide for an internal testing mechanism by which the applicability of any strategy or strategy combination to a specific task can be determined. These action sequences also provide for a device by which the learner can plan future courses of action and exert control over the learning process.

Planning is a key metacognitive strategy involved in both language reception and production.

The basis for grounding learning strategies in production systems is that strategies can be described in terms of a conditional (IF) clause and one or more action (THEN) clauses, just like production systems. The following examples illustrate the way in which production systems parallel learning strategies (strategies are italicized):

IF the goal is to comprehend a concept in a written text,
and I know the concept is not at the beginning,
THEN I will *scan* through the text to locate the concept.

IF the goal is to comprehend an oral or written text,
and I am unable to identify a word's meaning,
THEN I will try to *infer* the meaning from context.

IF the goal is to comprehend and remember an oral passage,
and I have heard a complete passage or thought expressed,
THEN I will *summarize* the passage to ensure I understand.

Cognitive theory contains a number of ways of representing strategies such as elaboration, inferencing, and organization. Elaboration is based on the existence of schemata representing declarative knowledge in long-term memory. Individuals faced with new information in short-term memory bring forth complementary schema-based concepts from long-term memory and manipulate them in working memory to find commonalities or differences in the concepts or the way they are organized. Elaboration occurs through spreading activation by directing activation toward pathways or linkages that are related to the new information, directing activation away from unrelated pathways, and enabling the reconstruction of the original meaning of a text based on inferences drawn from schemata. Organization is a basic mental process that is used in comprehension to segment oral or written input based on meaning or other features that contribute to an understanding of meaning. Organization and classification are useful in building the precursors to schemata when the learner has only a scant understanding or knowledge of the new information.

Descriptive research. There has been an increasing number of studies of learning strategies in cognitive psychology and no small number in second language acquisition. While some of the second language acquisition studies were concerned with definition and classification of strategies (e.g. Naiman, Frohlich, Stern and Todesco 1978; Oxford 1985; Rubin 1975), other work has been concerned with strategy descriptions with different types of students, contexts, and tasks (O'Malley et al. 1985a; Oxford and Ehrman 1987; Oxford, Nyikos and Crookall 1987; Rubin 1981; Wenden 1987). The methodology used to collect strategy information from students in these studies has included analysis of oral or written protocols, questionnaires (requesting information on strategies used with specific language tasks), group and individual retrospective interviews (asking questions about language tasks performed in the past), and concurrent interviews or 'think aloud' tasks (interrupting students while they are performing a task and asking them to describe what they are thinking).

Results from a number of descriptive studies in second language acquisition suggest the following conclusions (O'Malley and Chamot 1990):

- Learning strategies in second language acquisition do not appear to be any different from learning strategies involved in performing first language receptive and productive tasks;
- Students use strategies with classroom language tasks and with language tasks that occur outside the classroom, such as functional language tasks;
- Students designated by teachers as effective language learners use strategies more frequently than students designated as less effective language learners, use a greater variety of strategies, and alternate between a top-down and bottom-up approach depending on the task characteristics and difficulty;
- The principal strategies that differentiate more effective from less effective learners on listening comprehension tasks are monitoring, elaboration, and inferencing;
- Students use metacognitive and cognitive learning strategies with all four language skills (listening, speaking, reading, and writing);
- The specific strategies students select for a task often depend on the nature of the task demands, as when students select deduction and translation for classroom grammar tasks; and
- Certain strategies tend to occur together, such as using previously acquired knowledge to comprehend new information, which cooccurs with inferencing and imagery.

These conclusions support some of the theoretical assumptions about strategy use and provide the basis for concluding that mentally active, strategic approaches to learning a second language are part of the regular experience of successful learners. The question that remains to be addressed is whether or not strategies can be incorporated into instruction, as will be discussed in the following section.

Strategy instruction and transfer. A number of writers have commented on the difficulty of strategy instruction and the problem of strategy transfer (e.g. Derry and Murphy 1986; Nisbet and Shucksmith 1986). Students seem to have difficulty in adopting and applying new strategies for learning across a variety of tasks that differ from those used in the original learning. They also have difficulty in retaining use of the strategies over time, unless the strategies have been used extensively with learning tasks. These difficulties are consistent with the cognitive view that learning strategies are procedural knowledge as represented in production systems. Production systems are acquired slowly and may require a complex series of steps to perform a strategy with additional steps required to effect successful transfer.

Strategy transfer is largely based on a pattern-matching condition in which individuals look for common stimulus features or patterns between new tasks and contexts and those included in the original learning or instruction (Singley and Anderson 1989). Prior associational patterns can conflict with the pattern match, however, leading to use of a previous or inefficient strategy that is counter to the intent of strategy instruction. Because production systems are goal oriented, however, the specific goal of a production can take salience over prior habit formation and result in the use of the new strategy. This goal-oriented, pattern-matching approach is likely to be more efficient than simple repetition of a strategy with new materials and is referred to by Perkins (1989) as the 'high road' to transfer. Learner intentionality and awareness of the purposes of strategy training are therefore important components of strategy instruction. One possibility for increasing student awareness of the conditions required for transfer is to encourage students to assess their own strategy uses, thereby gaining metacognitive awareness of the conditions for learning and characteristics of different tasks.

Although this discussion of transfer applies specifically to instruction of learning strategies, it also applies more generally to instruction designed to counter ineffective or inaccurate language patterns, such as fossilization. A high road to countering fossilization might consist of modeling accurate uses of the language, pattern matching to the accurate language model, and self-assessment to encourage metacognitive awareness. Learning strategies and language use should follow the same learning patterns because they are both represented in memory as production systems. If learners profit from metacognitive awareness, strategy instruction should be more effective when learners are informed about potential strategy applications.

Strategy instruction can be either direct, in which students trained to use strategies are informed of the purpose and anticipated benefit of the strategies, or embedded, where students apply strategies but are uninformed concerning the intent or purpose of the strategies (Derry and Murphy 1986). More recent studies of strategy instruction have successfully included an informed or direct strategy training component that has resulted in strategy use, transfer, and retention over time (Palincsar and Brown 1984; Weinstein and Mayer 1986).

From the small number of studies that have been conducted of learning strategies in second language acquisition, the following conclusions can be reached (O'Malley and Chamot 1990; O'Malley, Chamot, Stewner-Manzanares, Russo, and Kupper 1985b):

- Students can learn to use strategies with both integrative and discrete language skills when the teacher provides direct training on strategy use;

- Second language performance of students taught to use strategies is significantly better than the performance of students who received no strategy instruction, but the effects depend on the task, task difficulty, and the level of support for strategy use and transfer; and

- Strategy transfer requires extensive cued support for strategy use even with highly similar tasks presented in the same classroom where initial instruction occurred.

There is a need for additional research on strategy instruction in second language acquisition. While there has been extensive research on child development and strategy use in the native language (e.g. Flavell 1985), few developmental studies have been done with second language tasks. Another important area of inquiry is to conduct further controlled experimental research with strategy interventions. However, much of the research on strategy instruction in classrooms has been initiated and presented by researchers rather than teachers. One of the needs evident in this field is for more information on staff development to support teachers in adopting instructional models that include a learning strategy component. One of the few studies of this type reported that foreign language teachers will adopt strategies and instruct their students on how to use them in natural classroom environments for teaching Spanish at the high school level and Russian at the college level (Chamot, Kupper, and Impink-Hernandez 1988).

Cognitive analysis of second language constructs. One way to apply cognitive theory to second language acquisition is to use it in analyzing some of the language constructs that have been introduced in the second language literature. This section contains a brief analysis of second language constructs based on knowledge of declarative and procedural knowledge in cognitive theory. Other constructs analyzed from a cognitive perspective are discussed elsewhere (O'Malley and Chamot 1990).

Declarative knowledge. One of the principal questions concerning second language acquisition that can be addressed through cognitive theory is the way in which meaning in two languages is represented in memory. Individuals may have separate stores of information in long-term memory, one for each language, or a single information store accompanied by selection mechanisms for using the first (L1) or the second language (L2) (McLaughlin 1984). In cognitive theory, information stored in memory has a meaning-based representation that is independent of the specific language sequences that led to the proposition or abstraction of meaning. Schemata contain connections and pathways that may be linked initially to an individual language but may transfer as a unit given a recognized pattern match and the availability of sufficient proficiency in L2. It is possible that the memory systems are discrete to the extent that they are distinctly language related, as in poetry, and contain common elements when they are not, as in knowledge of academic content (Hakuta 1986). Cummins' (1984) proposed "common underlying proficiency" is consistent with the notion that the concepts and propositions in schemata are transferred as a unit with sufficient knowledge of L2. In fact, evidence from second language research indicates that individuals actively search memory pathways for information in L1 that can be linked to new information experienced through L2 (O'Malley et al. 1985a).

Procedural knowledge. Two examples of the use of production systems in second language acquisition are discussed in this section. The first is based on a further analysis of common underlying proficiency, and the second illustrates the use of production systems in the analysis of communicative competence. An analysis of the acquisition of grammar using a cognitive model can be found elsewhere (MacWhinney and Anderson 1986).

Initial evidence supporting the notion of common underlying proficiency was based on correlations between scores on reading tests in L1 and L2 (Cummins 1984). Because the correlations were of sufficient magnitude, Cummins assumed that the memory store (declarative knowledge, presumably) had common elements. However, this picture is confounded by the fact that individuals tend to apply strategies used for reading in L1 to new reading tasks in L2, and that more effective readers will have a greater repertoire of strategies to apply than less effective readers. Thus, at least part of the strength of association between reading scores in L1 and L2 can be attributed to transfer of reading strategies such as predicting, inferencing, elaboration, and summarizing. As McLeod and McLaughlin (1986) indicate, however, even advanced ESL students may not transfer to English strategies from L1 such as the use of top-down processing, in which they use contextual clues to extract meaning from text. The general principles for supporting strategy transfer that were discussed above should be applied in strategy instruction to enable such students to capitalize on strategies that are effective in L1.

Another familiar construct in second language acquisition is communicative competence. The use of production systems to describe processes underlying communicative competence is based on the differentiations Canale and Swain (1980) make among sociolinguistic competence, discourse competence, strategic competence, and grammatical competence. Applying procedural knowledge to analyze communicative competence as procedural knowledge will illustrate one of the characteristics of production systems, namely, that goals of a production can subsume subgoals and that each subgoal has its own condition-action statements. An imagined conversation between a native speaker of English and a nonnative speaker at about the intermediate level of English proficiency might proceed along the following lines (adapted from O'Malley and Chamot 1990):

1. IF the goal is to engage in conversation with Sally,
   and Sally is monolingual in English,
   THEN the subgoal is to use my second language.

2. IF the goal is to use my second language,
   THEN the subgoal is to initiate a conversation.
   (sociolinguistic competence)

3. IF the goal is to initiate a conversation,
   THEN the subgoal is to say a memorized greeting formula.
   (discourse competence)

4. IF the goal is to say a memorized greeting formula,
   and the context is an informal one,
   THEN choose the appropriate language style.
   (sociolinguistic competence)

5. IF the goal is to choose an appropriate language style,
   THEN the subgoal is to say, 'Hi, how's it going, Sally?'
   (sociolinguistic competence)

6. IF the goal is to say, 'Hi, how's it going, Sally?'
   THEN the subgoal is to pay attention to pronouncing the
   sentence as much like a native speaker as possible.
   (grammatical competence for pronunciation)

   etc.

This illustration shows that the rules of grammar are only a part of the complex rules that govern language use in natural settings. The illustration also shows the goal-directed nature of communicative interactions and the adaptability of goals as the conversation proceeds. Although one set of goals is portrayed, the speaker may change goals and move the conversation in different directions at any time. A more general model of conversation would contain multiple branching and exit opportunities in addition to a greater variety of subgoals that establish the direction of the conversation. Individuals engaging in conversations such as the one portrayed here do so efficiently despite the large number of options for the different components of communicative competence because many of the decisions have become proceduralized and place little burden on short-term memory. In other cases, the individual may need to pause, reflect on a rule in one of the areas of communicative competence, and deliberate over which direction to follow in the conversation. Productions may be represented by declarative or procedural knowledge depending on the individual's prior exposure to rule systems, the transfer of similar rules from L1, and prior opportunities for communication in comparable settings.

Implications for instruction. There is a considerable amount of new information available about how students learn a second language. Rivers' (1983) appeal for teachers to know as much as possible about the way students learn and the way they learn a language is particularly relevant given this analysis. In the following discussion, the implications of cognitive theory for second language instruction will be indicated. Implications for instruction in learning strategies are identified separately due to their significance in instruction. The recommendations for instruction are based in part on recommendations made previously in the literature on second language acquisition, as will be noted.

1. Determine students' mental structures and existing knowledge through asking questions or encouraging discussion that enables them to elaborate on their prior knowledge.

2. Enable learners without existing schemata to use organization and classification to create the components on which later schemata will be established.

3. Minimize load on short-term memory whenever possible and support meaning-based connections to long-term memory. Avoid drill and practice as in grammar drills due to the limitations of short-term memory, since students may not encode the underlying principles. Instead, provide opportunities for students to establish connections in long-term memory with meaningful text (Rivers 1983).

4. Encourage students to construct meaning from text in a variety of ways including elaborating, predicting, inferencing, and summarizing.

5. Provide repeated opportunities for observation of modeled performance, practice with feedback, and composition of the elements of a complex skill in order to support proceduralization. Introduce new procedures that are part of a complex skill only when the component procedures show evidence of proceduralization and automaticity so as not to overload short-term memory.

6. Provide students with varied opportunities to engage in hypothesis testing with language in natural interactive settings (Faerch and Kasper 1985; Rivers 1983). Cooperative learning is one mechanism that can support the use of hypothesis testing in interactive settings.

7. Provide at least one activity following presentation of a rule so that students have opportunities for applications (Rivers 1983).

Learning strategies

8. Enable learners to set goals and establish control over their own learning, including evaluating their own performance, with repeated opportunities for practice. Encourage student awareness of their own strategies by discussing which strategies to use with classroom tasks.

9. Use embedded and informed training of learning strategies in order to maximize opportunities for practice with authentic materials accompanied by metacognitive awareness. Make certain that students are aware of the importance of using strategies with their learning. Model strategy use for students and verbalize the strategy while doing so.

10. Provide ample support for strategy transfer including pattern matching (i.e. identifying similarities) to similar tasks with cues for continued strategy use. Continue this support for as long as is warranted until transfer is evident and strategies are used automatically with the new materials.

11. Enable students to select learning strategies from a list of strategies that are appropriate to the task. This will encourage their metacognitive awareness of the conditions for learning the task.

12. Assess and encourage self-assessment of the students' use of strategies with all four language skills and provide students with feedback concerning their strategy applications. This also supports metacognitive awareness of tasks and strategies.

Conclusions. An analysis of recent advances in cognitive psychology has provided a number of directions for second language instruction. What these advances suggest is that naturally active, directed learning processes students use can be an asset for instruction if teachers are able to recognize and support effective learning procedures, analyze language learning tasks to identify declarative and procedural requirements, and build a model of instruction in which students are supported directly in an informed way to apply strategic procedures in their learning. This calls for the teacher to be aware of the procedures students use in learning and to integrate strategic processes into their instruction so that they become a natural part of instruction both for the teacher and the student.

References

Anderson, J.R. 1980. Cognitive psychology and its implications. San Francisco, Calif.: W.H. Freeman.

Anderson, J.R. 1983. The architecture of cognition. Cambridge, Mass.: Harvard University Press.

Anderson, J.R. 1985. Cognitive psychology and its implications. 2nd ed. New York: W.H. Freeman.

Anderson, J.R. 1987. Production systems, learning, and tutoring. In: D. Klahr, P. Langley, and R. Neches, eds. Production system models of learning and development. 437-58. Cambridge, Mass.: MIT Press.

Black, J.B., and W.G. Lehnert. 1984. Review of: The architecture of the mind. Contemporary Psychology 29:853-54.

Brown, A.L., J.D. Bransford, R.A. Ferrara, and J.C. Campione. 1983. Learning, remembering, and understanding. In: J.H. Flavell and M. Markman, eds. Carmichael's manual of child psychology, vol. 3. 77-166. New York: John Wiley.

Brown, J.S., and R. Burton. 1978. Diagnostic models for procedural bugs in basic mathematical skills. Cognitive Science 2:155-92.

Canale, M., and M. Swain. 1980. Theoretical bases of communicative approaches to second language teaching and testing. Applied Linguistics 1:1-47.

Chamot, A.U., L. Kupper, and M.V. Impink-Hernandez. 1988. A study of learning strategies in foreign language instruction: Third year and final report. Submitted to the U.S. Department of Education. McLean, Va.: Interstate Research Associates.

Cummins, J. 1984. Bilingualism and special education: Issues in assessment and pedagogy. Clevedon, England: Multilingual Matters.

Derry, S.J., and D.A. Murphy. 1986. Designing systems that train learning ability: From theory to practice. Review of Educational Research 56:1-39.

Faerch, C., and G. Kasper. 1985. Procedural knowledge as a component of foreign language learners' communicative competence. In: H. Boete and W. Herrlitz, eds. Kommunikation im (Sprach-) Unterricht. 169-99. Utrecht: University of Utrecht.

Flavell, J.R. 1985. Cognitive development. Englewood Cliffs, N.J.: Prentice-Hall.

Gagné, E.D. 1985. The cognitive psychology of school learning. Boston, Mass.: Little, Brown and Company.

Goodman, K.S. 1971. Psycholinguistic universals in the reading process. In: P. Pimsleur and T. Quinn, eds. The psychology of second language learning. 135-42. Cambridge: Cambridge University Press.

Hakuta, K. 1986. Mirror of language. New York: Basic Books.

Jones, B.F., A.S. Palincsar, D.S. Ogle, and E.G. Carr. 1987. Strategic teaching and learning: Cognitive instruction in the content areas. Alexandria, Va.: Association for Supervision and Curriculum Development.

Kintsch, W. 1974. The representation of meaning in memory. Hillsdale, N.J.: Lawrence Erlbaum.

Klahr, D., P. Langley, and R. Neches, eds. 1987. Production system models of learning and development. Cambridge, Mass.: MIT Press.

Langley, P. 1987. A general theory of discrimination learning. In: D. Klahr, P. Langley, and R. Neches, eds. Production system models of learning and development. 99-161. Cambridge, Mass.: MIT Press.

MacWhinney, B., and J.R. Anderson. 1986. The acquisition of grammar. In: I. Gopnik and M. Gopnik, eds. From models to modules. 3-25. Norwood, N.J.: Ablex.

McLaughlin, B. 1984. Second-language acquisition in childhood: Volume 1, Preschool children. Hillsdale, N.J.: Lawrence Erlbaum.

McLeod, B., and B. McLaughlin. 1986. Restructuring or automatization? Reading in a second language. Language Learning 36:109-26.

Naiman, N., M. Frolich, H.H. Stern, and A. Todesco. 1978. The good language learner. Toronto: Ontario Institute for Studies in Education.

Nisbet, J., and J. Shucksmith. 1986. Learning strategies. Boston: Routledge and Kegan Paul.

O'Malley, J.M., and A.U. Chamot. 1990. Learning strategies in second language acquisition. Cambridge: Cambridge University Press.

O'Malley, J.M., A.U. Chamot, G. Stewner-Manzanares, L. Kupper, and R. Russo. 1985a. Learning strategies used by beginning and intermediate ESL students. Language Learning 35:21-46.

O'Malley, J.M., A.U. Chamot, G. Stewner-Manzanares, R. Russo, and L. Kupper. 1985b. Learning strategy applications with students of English as a second language. TESOL Quarterly 19:285-96.

Oxford, R.L. 1985. A new taxonomy for second language learning strategies. Washington, D.C.: ERIC Clearinghouse on Languages and Linguistics.

Oxford, R.C., and M. Ehrman. 1987. Effects of sex differences, career choice, and psychological type on adults' language learning strategies. Manuscript. Washington, D.C.: Center for Applied Linguistics.

Oxford, R.L., M. Nyikos, and D. Crookall. April, 1987. Learning strategies of university foreign language students: A large-scale, factor analytic study. Paper presented at the annual meetings of the Teachers of English to Speakers of Other Languages, Miami.

Palincsar, A.S., and A.L. Brown. 1984. Reciprocal teaching of comprehension-fostering and comprehension-monitoring activities. Cognition and Instruction 1:117-75.

Perkins, D.N. 1989. Teaching metacognitive strategies. Paper presented at the annual meetings of the Amereican Educational Research Association, San Francisco.

Rivers, W. 1983. Communicating naturally in a second language: Theory and practice in language teaching. Cambridge: Cambridge University Press.

Rubin, J. 1975. What the 'good language learner' can teach us. TESOL Quarterly 9:41-51.

Rubin, J. 1981. Study of cognitive processes in second language learning. Applied Linguistics 11:117-31.

Selinker, L. 1972. Interlanguage. International Review of Applied Linguistics 10:209-31.

Shiffrin, R.M., and W. Schneider. 1977. Controlled and automatic human information processing, II: Perceptual learning, automatic attending, and a general theory. Psychological Review 84:127-90.

Shuell, T.J. 1986. Cognitive conceptions of learning. Review of Educational Research 56:411-36.

Singley, M.K., and J.R. Anderson. 1989. The transfer of cognitive skill. Cambridge, Mass.: Harvard University Press.

Thibadeau, R., M.A. Just, and P. Carpenter. 1982. A model of the time course and content of reading. Cognitive Science 6:167-203.

Weinstein, C.E. 1978. Elaboration skills as a learning strategy. In: H.F. O'Neill, Jr., ed. Learning strategies. 31-55. New York: Academic Press.

Weinstein, C.E. 1982. Learning strategies: The metacurriculum in community college teaching. Journal of Development and Remedial Education 5(2):6-7, 10.

Weinstein, C.E., and R.E. Mayer. 1986. The teaching of learning strategies. In: M.C. Wittrock, ed. Handbook of research on teaching. 315-27. 3rd ed. New York: Macmillan.

Wenden, A. 1987. Metacognition: An expanded view on the cognitive abilities of L2 learners. Language Learning 37:573-97.

Cognitive instruction in the second language classroom: The role of learning strategies

Anna Uhl Chamot
Georgetown University

Introduction. Cognitive instruction is based on an understanding of the mental processes that take place in students' minds as they seek to understand, store, remember, and produce information or perform skills. By understanding how students learn, teachers can design more effective instruction. Interest in the role of cognition in second language acquisition is not new. In fact, the developing links between cognitive psychology and linguistics have been chronicled, analyzed, and applied to language teaching by Wilga Rivers for more than twenty-five years (see, for example, Rivers 1964, 1976, 1983, 1990). In the last ten years, a number of second language researchers have turned their attention to cognitive theories of learning (Bialystok 1981, Ellis 1984, Faerch and Kasper 1987, McLaughlin 1987, Spolsky 1985).

In current cognitive theory, information is said to be stored in memory either as declarative or as procedural knowledge (Anderson, 1985, Gagné 1985). This distinction has important implications for instruction because the two types of knowledge are learned in quite different ways. Declarative knowledge, or the concepts, events, and facts we know about, is best learned by associating new information with prior knowledge and building on existing schemata (Gagné 1985). On the other hand, procedural knowledge, or the skills and processes that we know how to perform, is best learned through observation of an expert model and extensive practice accompanied by feedback (Gagné 1985). In cognitive instruction, the teacher first identifies the type of knowledge required by a learning task, and then designs appropriate instructional activities. The teacher's focus is on how the learner learns, rather than on how the teacher teaches. Because some learners are far more effective than others in mastering both declarative and procedural knowledge, interest in identifying the strategies of effective learners has emerged in recent years and has led to a considerable amount of research in first language contexts and initial research in second language contexts.

Current interest in learning strategies evolves from the premise that less effective students can be taught to use strategies that will enable them to learn more effectively. Considerable success in teaching students to apply learning strategies has been reported for first language reading comprehension, memory training, and problem solving (Derry and Murphy 1986). Research on learning strategy instruction in second languages is less extensive, but shows promise of contributing to the improvement of language instruction.

Learning strategy identification studies have uncovered a rich variety of strategies that learners of second and foreign languages employ as they seek to understand, remember, and use the new language (O'Malley and Chamot 1990, O'Malley, Chamot, and Küpper 1989, Oxford 1990, Politzer and McGroarty 1985, Rubin 1981). Some of these strategies, such as note-taking or outlining, are the observable study skills that are a familiar feature of the academic classroom. Other learning strategies, however, are not observable. For example, a student reading a difficult text might be thinking, 'Do I understand this? Does it make sense?', and, by using this type of comprehension monitoring, may be able to identify areas of difficulty. Another student reading the same text might be thinking, 'What do I already know about this topic? How does this new information fit in with what I already know?', and by actively elaborating on prior knowledge, may build a deeper understanding of the text. This type of nonobservable strategy has been identified through interviews with students, questionnaires, and 'think-aloud' interviews in which students are asked to describe their thoughts as they work on a language task (Chamot, Küpper, and Impink-Hernandez 1988, Chamot and Küpper 1990, O'Malley et al. 1989). These mental learning strategies are perhaps even more important in assisting students to learn more effectively than are the more traditional observable strategies.

Learning strategies for second and foreign languages can be classified into three major categories (Chamot et al. 1988, O'Malley and Chamot 1990, O'Malley, Chamot, Stewner-Manzanares, Küpper, and Russo 1985, Rubin 1987):

(1) Metacognitive strategies. Self-regulatory strategies in which learners think about their own thinking, and plan, monitor, and evaluate their own learning endeavors.

(2) Cognitive strategies. Task-appropriate strategies in which learners actively manipulate the information or skills to be learned.

(3) Social and affective strategies. Strategies involving interaction with others for the purpose of learning, or control over one's own affective state. Table 1 defines specific strategies within this classification.

This paper provides an overview of the issues and implications of cognitive theory for instruction in second language learning strategies, discusses some recent research on strategy instruction in both first and second language

Table 1. Learning strategies taught in the cognitive academic language learning approach (CALLA) (From O'Malley and Chamot 1990).

Metacognitive strategies:

Advance organization. Previewing the main ideas and concepts of the material to be learned, often by skimming the text for the organizing principle.

Advance preparation. Rehearsing the language needed for an oral or written task.

Organizational planning. Planning the parts, sequence, and main ideas to be expressed orally or in writing.

Selective attention. Attending to or scanning key words, phrases, linguistic markers, sentences, or types of information.

Self-monitoring. Checking one's comprehension during listening or reading, or checking one's oral or written production while it is taking place.

Self-evaluation. Judging how well one has accomplished a learning task.

Self-management. Seeking or arranging the conditions that help one learn, such as finding opportunities for additional language or content input and practice.

Cognitive strategies:

Resourcing. Using reference materials such as dictionaries, encyclopedias, or textbooks.

Grouping. Classifying words, terminology, numbers, or concepts according to their attributes.

Note taking. Writing down key words and concepts in abbreviated verbal, graphic, or numerical form.

Summarizing. Making a mental, oral, or written summary of information gained through listening or reading.

Deduction. Applying rules to understand or produce language or solve problems.

Imagery. Using visual images (either mental or actual) to understand and remember new information or to make a mental representation of a problem.

Auditory representation. Playing back in one's mind the sound of a word, phrase, or fact in order to assist comprehension and recall.

Elaboration. Relating new information to prior knowledge, relating different parts of new information to each other, or making meaningful personal associations to the new information.

Transfer. Using what is already known about language to assist comprehension or production.

Inferencing. Using information in the text to guess meaning of new items, predict outcomes, or complete missing parts.

Social and affective strategies:

Questioning for clarification. Eliciting from a teacher or peer additional explanation, rephrasing, examples, or verification.

Cooperation. Working together with peers to solve a problem, pool information, check a learning task. or get feedback on oral or written performance.

Self-talk. Reducing anxiety by using mental techniques that make one feel competent to do the learning task.

classrooms, and describes instructional models for learning strategy instruction in the ESL and foreign language classroom.

Instructional issues. A number of issues related to learning strategy instruction need to be considered. Some of these have to do with curriculum, methodology, materials, teacher preparation, and student characteristics.

Curriculum. An unresolved issue in designing a learning strategy curriculum is whether the instruction should be provided as a separate 'learning to learn' course or should be integrated with regular classroom instruction. A number of researchers in first language contexts recommend separate strategy training programs because students (especially low-achieving students) can focus all of their attention on the strategies themselves, rather than having to attend simultaneously to both the strategy and the content to be learned (Derry and Murphy 1986, Jones, Palincsar, Ogle, and Carr 1987).

However, other researchers strongly recommend integrated strategy instruction, pointing out that learning in context is more effective than a separate skills approach (Wenden 1987), and that practicing strategies on real school tasks facilitates transfer to similar tasks (Campione and Armbruster 1985, Chamot and O'Malley 1987). An additional argument for providing students with challenging tasks on which to practice learning strategies is that students may be more likely to perceive the utility of the new strategies for a difficult task than for an easier task that they can accomplish successfully using familiar strategies that they have already automatized.

Methodology. A methodological issue in strategy instruction appears closer to resolution. This issue concerns the advisability of embedded or direct strategy instruction. In embedded instruction (sometimes referred to as blind or uninformed strategy instruction), the teacher has students apply the strategies through a variety of activities but does not inform the students of the intent or purpose of the strategies. In direct or self-control strategy instruction, on the other hand, students are informed of the purpose and anticipated benefit of the strategies and are given explicit instruction on how to apply the strategies (Garner 1987). Research indicates that embedded strategy instruction does not lead to transfer, but that direct instruction is linked to the maintenance of strategies over time and their transfer to new tasks (Brown, Armbruster, and Baker 1986, Garner 1987, Palincsar and Brown 1984, Wenden 1987, Weinstein and Mayer 1986, Winograd and Hare 1988).

Materials. A third issue important to instruction is the selection or development of materials to use with students during learning strategy instruction. The instructional materials now available for language strategy instruction are quite varied in their approach. For example, some address the student directly by providing suggestions and exercises for becoming more effective learners (see Brown 1989, Rubin and Thompson 1982), while others provide teachers with extensive information about different strategies and suggestions for activities to promote their use (see Oxford 1990). Some provide explicit lesson plans and student materials for explaining and practicing the strategies (see Chamot, Küpper, Barrueta, Toth, and Thompson, forthcoming; and Ellis and Sinclair 1989). Others focus on applying strategies to the learning of academic content as well as language (see Chamot 1987, Chamot and O'Malley 1988, and Chamot, O'Malley, and Küpper, in press).

Teacher preparation. A fourth important issue is the preparation of teachers to provide learning strategy instruction in their second or foreign language classrooms. Little information is to be gleaned on teacher training from research on strategy instruction in first language contexts (Derry and Murphy 1986). In second language contexts, learning strategy instruction has most frequently been carried out by the research team, with teachers as observers or assistants (e.g. Cohen and Aphek 1980, Hosenfeld, Arnold, Kirchofer, Laciura, and Wilson 1981, O'Malley, Chamot, Stewner-Manzanares, Russo, and Küpper 1985). For learning strategy instruction to become widely used in the language classroom, teachers need to have the information and skills to provide the instruction. This implies additions to the teacher preparation course sequence and/or in-service staff development. Our own experience indicates that teachers tend to need time to understand the difference between teaching and learning strategies and to implement direct learning strategy instruction in their classrooms (Chamot and Küpper 1990; O'Malley and Chamot 1990).

Student characteristics. A fifth issue to be considered in strategy instruction is student characteristics. What the student brings to the task of learning and applying strategies to the second language will have a profound effect on the course of strategy instruction. Motivation, aptitude, learning style, age, cultural background, and language proficiency need to be considered in planning for strategy instruction.

Motivation obviously plays a dominant role in students' ability to profit from learning strategy instruction. Since motivation is closely allied to self-regulation, it has been considered a component of metacognition (Jones et al. 1987). Researchers in first language contexts have recommended that motivational training be added to learning strategy instruction, suggesting a number of classroom activities that integrate cognitive and motivational instruction, such as modeling, scaffolding, and cooperative learning (Jones et al. 1987, Paris 1988).

The concept of aptitude is, in our view, more of a strategic ability that can be learned than an innate trait (O'Malley and Chamot 1990). In other words, the student lacking in language learning aptitude is merely a student who has not yet learned effective learning strategies.

A student's individual learning style may lead to a predisposition for one type of learning strategy over another. This indicates that students need to experience a variety of strategies so that they can select the ones that are most effective for them. However, it is also important for students to learn strategies that are particularly valuable in language learning (such as focusing attention, monitoring comprehension, elaborating prior knowledge, using deduction and induction, and questioning), even if they are not a perfect match with their individual learning styles (O'Malley and Chamot 1990).

Additional research is needed concerning the effects of age and cultural background on learning strategies in second language acquisition. Strategies have been identified with bilingual elementary school students (Chesterfield and Chesterfield 1985; Padron and Waxman 1988), but studies of instructional interventions with young students have so far been restricted to first language contexts (e.g., Carpenter, Fennema, Peterson, Chiang, and Loef 1988, Gagné 1985, Pressley, Levin, and Ghatala 1984). Cultural background or prior educational experiences may predispose students to adopt one strategy while rejecting another. This appeared to be the case in one ESL study (O'Malley et al. 1985), but additional work in this area is obviously necessary.

The level of students' language proficiency needs to be considered for learning strategy instruction in the second or foreign language classroom. The options are to delay instruction until students have developed sufficient proficiency in the language to understand and talk about strategies, present the instruction through the native language, or teach beginning students the language they need to discuss learning strategies. The last two options appear preferable because they enable the teacher to provide learning strategy instruction at the beginning as well as at more advanced levels of language study. On the other hand, it has been suggested that learner training can be effectively initiated at the lower intermediate level of language proficiency because students can engage in activities in the second language and can also reflect on their early language learning experiences (Ellis and Sinclair 1989).

In considering these and other issues, research and practice point to a number of generalizations that can be made about learning strategy instruction in the language classroom:

(1) Strategy instruction should be integrated with the language curriculum so that it becomes a part of the second or foreign language class.
(2) Learning strategy instruction should be direct so that students are made aware of its purposes and anticipated effects. This means that teachers should name the strategies, explain them, and show students how to apply the strategies by modeling them.
(3) Materials selected for learning strategy instruction should be appropriate for the content of the course and for the teacher's greater or lesser need for specific direction.
(4) Teachers may need assistance in implementing learning strategy instruction. Methods of strategy instruction could be provided at either the preservice or in-service level.

(5) Motivational training should accompany learning strategy instruction. Recommendations include modeling by the teacher, scaffolding instruction so that students gradually assume more and more control of their own learning, and cooperative learning in which all students achieve success.
(6) Ineffective language learners should have top priority for strategy training, and they should be encouraged to believe that their difficulties are due to lack of strategies rather than to lack of aptitude.
(7) Students should be offered a menu of learning strategy options so that they can select those that work best for them.
(8) Teachers should be aware of the effect that age and cultural background may have on learning strategy use, and be able to make adaptations when either of these factors appears to impede strategy use.
(9) Students should be taught the language needed to understand and talk about strategies from the beginning level of language instruction, or the learning strategy instruction at this level should be provided through the native language.

Research on learning strategy instruction. In the last fifteen years, extensive research on learning strategy instruction in first language contexts has been conducted, while the number of studies with second language students has been rather modest. However, many of the findings of first language strategy instruction research appear to have considerable potential for second and foreign language classrooms.

In first language strategy instruction, the area of reading comprehension strategies at both elementary and secondary levels has been the object of extensive research. A variety of strategies have been taught, including differing combinations of metacognitive, cognitive, and social/affective strategies (for comprehensive reviews of reading comprehension strategy instruction, see Derry and Murphy 1986 and Garner 1987).

In metacognitive strategy instruction, students engage in activities to promote 'awareness' of their own cognitive processes, to 'monitor' their comprehension while reading, and to 'regulate' their reading comprehension with repair strategies as needed (Haller, Child, and Walberg 1988).

Several studies have sought to improve reading comprehension through instruction in the use of the cognitive strategy of 'elaboration', or meaningful association of new information with prior knowledge. Effective readers use elaboration to construct meaning by making explicit connections between the text and their individual schemata, which can consist of knowledge frameworks about the world in general or specific knowledge about discourse structure such as story grammars (O'Malley and Chamot 1990). Expert use of elaboration leads to top-down or meaning-driven reading, and is also used for other language skills by effective learners (Chamot, Küpper, and Impink-Hernandez 1988; O'Malley, Chamot, and Walker 1987). In first language contexts, students have been successfully taught to recognize, generate, and evaluate elaboration strategies with texts they wanted to remember (Gagné 1985, Weinstein 1978).

A number of studies have taught a cluster of learning strategies for reading comprehension, rather than individual strategies. Two examples of multiple strategy programs which have increased reading comprehension are Informed Strategies for Learning (ISL) (Paris, Cross, DeBritto, Jacobs, Oka, and Saarnio 1984), and Reciprocal Teaching (Palincsar and Brown 1984). In the ISL program teachers provided direct instruction in the strategies by naming the strategies, showing students how to use them, providing guided practice, and relating the strategies to reading in other content areas (Garner 1987). In Reciprocal Teaching, students work cooperatively to develop comprehension of a written text by taking turns to 'teach the text'. This consists of using the cognitive strategies of 'summarizing' and 'predicting', the social strategy of 'questioning', and the metacognitive strategy of 'selective attention' to areas of difficulty (O'Malley and Chamot 1990).

Evidence for the effectiveness of strategy instruction on reading comprehension in first language contexts continues to accumulate. A recent meta-analysis of the effect of instruction of metacognitive strategies on reading comprehension indicates that the answer to the question, 'Can comprehension be taught?' is a resounding 'Yes' (Haller et al. 1988). Extending this research to second language comprehension instruction, including both listening and reading, appears quite promising.

In second language learning strategy instruction, early research efforts focused on memory strategies for learning vocabulary, while more recent studies have sought to teach strategies for integrative language tasks.

Various mnemonic techniques have been used to facilitate vocabulary learning (Thompson 1987). Probably the most extensively researched of the mnemonic strategies is the 'key word method' in which students learn sets of vocabulary words by associating each word with an auditory and imagery association (Atkinson and Raugh 1975; Pressley, Levin, and Delaney 1982). This strategy has been effective in promoting recall of foreign language vocabulary, appears to work best with concrete rather than abstract vocabulary, and is most facilitative when learners generate their own key words (Thompson 1987).

Simple paired associations have also been successful in helping students recall vocabulary, especially when students made their own associations for the words (Cohen and Aphek 1980).

We have trained ESL students to learn vocabulary by first 'grouping' words in a personally meaningful way, and then making a mental 'image' of a context in which the words in each group appeared (O'Malley et al. 1985). This two-step process was used successfully by experimental group Hispanic students, whereas control group Asian students using rote-repetiton strategies outperformed the experimental Asian group who had been trained on the new strategies. This led us to conclude that students who have already developed effective strategies for a particular type of language task may quite reasonably object to being asked to replace it with a new strategy, especially when study time is limited (O'Malley and Chamot 1990).

A number of second language strategy instruction studies have focused on integrative language skill areas rather than on separate components of skills, such as vocabulary. In one study, reading strategies were taught to high school French students following a model of direct training in which students were informed of the nature and value of strategies and provided with activities to identify and evaluate their own reading strategies (Hosenfeld et al. 1981).

In the ESL study mentioned above, we provided strategy instruction on listening comprehension and language production, as well as on vocabulary (O'Malley et al. 1985; O'Malley, Russo, Chamot, and Stewner-Manzanares 1988). In the listening comprehension instruction, experimental group students learned how to pay 'selective attention' to main ideas by using linguistic markers, how to 'take notes' on a T-List, and how to improve their comprehension through 'cooperation' with classmates. We had mixed results on the listening comprehension tests accompanying the instruction. On the less demanding and more interesting human interest texts, students in the experimental groups performed significantly better than those in the control group. However, the same effects were not found for the more demanding academic texts in which, in addition, the cues to use the strategies were deliberately faded. Our conclusions were that students needed additional practice with the strategies, that listening texts need to be of sufficient interest to motivate students to use the strategies, and that difficulty level and fading of cues need to be adjusted more gradually. The language production task, on the other hand, revealed significant differences favoring the experimental groups. In this task students were given a choice of topics and had to prepare and present a one-minute talk. The strategies taught were functional 'planning', in which students had to organize their ideas into an introduction, main body, and conclusion, and 'cooperation', in which students worked in small groups to practice and revise their presentations.

In the ESL study described above, instruction in learning strategies was provided by the research team. In an extension of this work, we have more recently conducted learning strategy instruction research in which the regular classroom instructors provided the instruction to foreign language students (Chamot and Küpper 1989, 1990; Chamot, Küpper, and Impink-Hernandez 1988; O'Malley and Chamot 1990).

In the first of these foreign language learning strategy instruction studies, we worked with Spanish and Russian instructors to develop a series of learning strategy lessons for high school Spanish students and college Russian students, then observed the strategy instruction. Our major purposes were to find out if foreign language instructors would be able and willing to teach learning strategies in their classes, to capitalize on the instructors' expertise to select appropriate strategies to teach, and to document the actual implementation process.

We were able to gain the participation of four of the seven instructors whose students had previously been involved in two strategy identification studies (for a description of these studies, see Chamot and Küpper 1989, and O'Malley and Chamot 1990). This led to the realization that not all teachers have the time or inclination to add yet another component to a crowded curriculum.

Participating instructors decided to teach strategies for listening comprehension, reading comprehension, and speaking. Table 2 describes the strategies taught for each skill and how they were used by each instructor.

Table 2. Foreign language course development study: Major learning strategies taught for different tasks (From: O'Malley and Chamot 1990).

Task	Description	Strategies	How used
Listening comprehension	Students listened to tape of authentic dialogues between shoppers and salesperson, then completed comprehension exercise.	Selective attention	Focus on specific items while listening.
		Elaboration	Use what you know.
		Inferencing	Make logical guesses.
		Transfer	Recognize cognates.
Reading comprehension	Students identified reading strategies in L1, then aplied same strategies to L2 paragraph with new words underlined	Inferencing	Use immediate and extended context to guess words.
		Deduction	Use grammar rules to identify word forms
		Elaboration	Use prior knowledge.
		Transfer	Recognize, use cognates.
Speaking	Students worked in groups to prepare sections of difficult reading to retell to class so that all would understand it	Substitution	Use synonyms, paraphrases and gestures to communicate meaning.
		Cooperation	Work in pairs or groups to plan and evaluate task.
		Self-evaluation	Check own ability to communicate.

As could be expected, each instructor implemented strategy instruction in a slightly different way. All provided direct instruction by informing students of the purpose and value of the strategies. Most of the instructors also named the strategies. Strategy instruction and discussion took place in English, as the students were still limited in their second language proficiency. Although only one of the instructors asked students to identify strategies they used on similar tasks in their native language as a first step toward transferring those strategies to the foreign language, this procedure seemed so successful and so congruent with the critical role that cognitive theory assigns to prior knowledge, that we decided to incorporate this step into our subsequent strategy instruction study.

Our current learning strategy instruction study builds on what we have discovered through our own previous research and that of others, and is designed to make language learning strategy instruction easily accessible to all foreign language classroom teachers. This two-year study is developing and field testing a Resource Guide for learning strategy instruction in French, Russian, and Spanish (Chamot and Küpper 1990; Chamot, Küpper, Barrueta, Toth, and Thompson, forthcoming). In the first year of the study, foreign language instructors designed and implemented lessons to teach their students how to use language learning strategies in one skill area (writing, listening, or reading), the actual instruction was implemented and observed, students were interviewed to ascertain their reactions to the instruction, and pre- and post-strategy instruction think-aloud interviews with students were conducted. Results of the first-year student interviews on reactions to strategy instruction indicate that students found that too many strategies were introduced at once, that the division of writing strategies into three phases (planning, composing, revising) did not accurately reflect the actual writing process, and that knowing the name of a strategy helped them focus. Some students felt that the strategies were repetitious of what they had learned in native language instruction in earlier years or else conflicted with what they were currently learning in their English classes. In the pre- and postinstruction think-alouds, less effective students who learned to use strategies improved their comprehension and performance. Originally effective students showed little change in their think-alouds, whereas the average and less effective language learners were able to profit from the instruction. Our conclusions were that learning strategy instruction is probably most useful for students who are not encountering success in their language learning, and that the instruction needs to be modified so that students are not overwhelmed by the sheer number of strategies. Evidence from think-alouds indicates that while students may be aware of strategies on a 'declarative' level, for most the strategic approach has not yet been 'proceduralized', even after a semester of instruction. We concluded from these results that strategy instruction is most useful for students who are encountering difficulties in their foreign language learning, and that additional opportunities to practice the strategies are necessary for many students.

In the second year of the current study, the learning strategy lessons have been revised as a result of both teacher and student evaluations, and are being field-tested by foreign language teachers in a different school district. Revisions based on the field testing are being made, instruction for learning strategies for speaking is being developed, and students are being interviewed to find out about their perceptions of the utility of strategy instruction. Preliminary results of this study indicate that teachers are able to use the Resource Guide with their students and are generally willing to provide learning strategy instruction. It is also apparent that strategy instruction is exceedingly complex and needs to take into account both teacher ability and interest and student perceptions of the value of learning strategies.

Instructional models for second language learning strategies. Instructional models should include a theoretical framework, a curricular scope and sequence, methodological direction, guidelines for or examples of specific lessons, and suggestions for evaluation of student achievement. Most of these components are represented in the various models that have been proposed for learning strategy instruction in first or second/foreign language contexts. Table 3 illustrates two sample scope and sequence frameworks that have been implemented for learning strategy instruction in first and second language contexts.

Common elements in these frameworks are: activation of students' prior knowledge about strategies (through assessment or discussion/self-report of current strategy use in L1 and/or L2); explanation and demonstration of strategies (through rationale, description, naming, modeling, and discussion); active practice of strategies (through think-alouds, cooperative learning, discussion, role-playing, peer tutoring); evaluation of strategy use (through identification of successful strategies, analysis of strategy use, think-alouds, relating strategy use to successful performance); transfer of strategies to new tasks (through discussion of metacognitive and/or motivational aspects of strategy use, practice in using strategies on similar tasks, feedback on strategy use for different tasks).

The framework proposed by Jones and her colleagues (1987) is a component of the Strategic Teaching Model, which is based on cognitive learning theory and its applications to instruction for English-speaking students in all content areas. In this model, learning strategy instruction plays a key role, with teachers modeling the strategies by thinking aloud to their students. The Strategic Teaching model identifies three instructional phases: preparation, presentation, and application/integration. The preparation phase serves to activate students' prior knowledge of the lesson's topic and to set goals. In the presentation phase, students interact with the new information presented through active practice. For example, students may organize the information graphically, or they may increase their understanding of a text through Reciprocal Teaching. In the third phase of the lesson, students evaluate their own learning by referring back to the goals identified in the preparation phase and then restructuring their prior knowledge to include the new information.

Table 3. Scope and sequence frameworks for learning strategy instruction (Adapted from O'Malley and Chamot 1990).

First Language Context	Second Language Contexts
Jones et al. 1987 All subjects	O'Malley and Chamot 1988 Content-based ESL
1. Assess strategy use with: - think aloud - interviews - questionnaires.	1. Preparation: Develop student awareness of different strategies through: - small group retrospective interviews about school tasks - modeling think-aloud, then having students think aloud in small groups - discussion of interviews and think-alouds.
2. Explain strategy use by: - naming it - telling how to use it, step by step.	2. Presentation: Develop student knowledge about strategies by: - providing rationale for strategy use - describing and naming strategy - modeling strategy.
3. Model strategy by: - demonstrating it - verbalizing own thought processes while doing task.	3. Practice: Develop student skills in using strategies for academic learning through: - cooperative learning tasks - think-alouds while problem solving - peer tutoring in academic tasks - group discussions.
4. Scaffold instruction by: - providing support while students practice - adjusting support to student needs - phasing out support to encourage autonomous strategy use.	4. Evaluation: Develop student ability to evaluate own strategy use through: - writing strategies used immediately after task - discussing strategy use in class - keeping dialogue journals (with teacher) on strategy use.
5. Develop motivation by: - providing successful experiences - relating strategy use to improved performance.	5. Expansion: Develop transfer of strategies to new tasks by: - discussions on metacognitive and motivational aspects of strategy use - additional practice on similar academic tasks - assignments to use learning strategies on tasks related to cultural backgrounds of students.

The Strategic Teaching Model has been applied to different content areas of the curriculum, focusing mainly on the declarative knowledge required in social studies, science, and literature. Procedural knowledge is addressed in mathematics, analysis of literary texts, and reading comprehension in general. Since the model is intended for use in first language contexts, language skill development is not addressed directly except for explicit strategies for gaining meaning from text.

In second language instruction we have developed a model for content-based ESL that is grounded in cognitive theory and our own research with second language learning strategies (Chamot and O'Malley 1986, 1987, in press). The Cognitive Academic Language Learning Approach (CALLA) is designed to develop the academic knowledge, language skills, and learning strategies of limited English proficient students in upper elementary and secondary schools. The model integrates instruction in cognitively appropriate content topics from the mainstream curriculum, development of the language skills needed for learning in school, and direct instruction and practice in using learning strategies to acquire both procedural and declarative knowledge.

The CALLA lesson plan model states objectives for content, language, and learning strategies. Lessons are divided into five phases. In the preparation phase, both teacher and students find out what is already known about the lesson's topic through brainstorming or a concrete experience, and the strategy of 'elaboration' of prior knowledge is directly taught and discussed. In the presentation phase of the lesson, new information is presented and explained to students with different types of contextual reinforcement, such as demonstrations, visuals, and graphic organizers. Some of the strategies that can be taught for this phase are 'selective attention' to key ideas, 'monitoring' of comprehension, 'inferencing', 'note-taking', and 'questioning'. In the practice phase of the CALLA lesson, students have the opportunity to practice the new information actively, usually in cooperative learning activities.

In addition to 'cooperation', the learning strategies practiced will depend on the task undertaken. For example, if the task is to gain information from reading, students might be asked to develop oral or written 'summaries', or to find the meanings of new words through 'inferencing' and/or 'resourcing'. If the task is to develop a product, students might use strategies such as 'organizational planning', or 'grouping' and 'imagery' to make a graphic organizer such as an illustrated classification chart. After practicing, students move into the evaluation phase of the lesson. The major purpose of this phase is to develop in students the strategy of 'self-evaluation' through activities such as using checklists to evaluate their own work or writing self-evaluation journals or learning logs in which they reflect on their own learning processes. Finally, in the expansion phase of CALLA lessons, students engage in a number of activities designed to foster higher order thinking and integration of new concepts into existing schemata. Transfer of learning strategies to new contexts is featured during the expansion phase.

The CALLA model is being implemented in a number of school districts in both bilingual and ESL programs. In conducting staff development workshops, we have discovered that teachers of many different kinds of students find the model can be applied to their own situations. For example, ESL teachers have been able to incorporate learning strategy instruction with beginning level students. Mainstream teachers find that CALLA teaching provides greater support to educationally disadvantaged English-speaking students, and indicate that CALLA can be used to implement a whole-language or language-across-the-curriculum approach to instruction. Special education teachers, who generally are already teaching learning strategies, find that CALLA's integration of language and content is beneficial to their students. We believe that CALLA also has potential application in the foreign language classroom. Although our current classroom research is focusing on direct instruction of learning strategies for language skills, addition of academic content, particularly at more advanced levels of language study, could be an effective way to develop a broader range of proficiency.

In our view, CALLA can be applied to different instructional settings because of its theoretical framework, which is grounded in cognitive learning theory (O'Malley and Chamot 1990).

Conclusions. This paper has provided an overview of some basic issues that are important in considering the implementation of learning strategy instruction in the second or foreign language classroom. These issues—which include curriculum design, methodology, materials selection, teacher preparation, and attention to student characteristics—need to be considered prior to establishing a language learning strategy instructional program.

The discussion of research on learning strategy instruction in first and second language contexts, and its impact on teachers and students, indicates that direct learning strategy instruction can have a positive effect on students' achievement in both content and language areas. The research also indicates that these effects will most likely benefit students who are experiencing limited success in their language learning endeavors.

Finally, I have suggested some criteria for evaluating instructional models, and have described representative models from both first and second language contexts which meet these criteria.

In conclusion, the evidence from first and second language research and practice indicates that direct teaching of learning strategies can make a very positive contribution to cognitive instruction in second language classrooms.

References

Anderson, J.R. 1985. Cognitive psychology and its implications. 2d ed. New York: W.H. Freeman.

Atkinson, R.C., and M.R. Raugh. 1975. An application of the mnemonic keyword method to the acquisition of Russian vocabulary. Journal of Experimental Psychology 104:126-33.

Bialystok, E. 1981. The role of conscious strategies in second language proficiency. Modern Language Journal 65:24-35.

Brown, A.L., B.B. Armbruster, and L. Baker. 1986. The role of metacognition in reading and studying. In: J. Orasanu, ed. Reading comprehension: From research to practice. 49-75. Hillsdale, N.J.: Lawrence Erlbaum.

Brown, H.D. 1989. A practical guide to language learning. New York: McGraw-Hill.

Campione, J.C., and B.B. Armbruster. 1985. Acquiring information from texts: An analysis of four approaches. In: S.F. Chipman, J.W. Segal, and R. Glaser, eds. Thinking and learning skills. vol. 1:297-317. Hillsdale, N.J.: Erlbaum.

Carpenter, T.P., E. Fennema, P.L. Peterson, C.-P. Chiang, and M. Loef. 1988. Using knowledge of children's mathematics thinking in classroom teaching: An experimental study. Paper presented at the annual meeting of the American Educational Research Association, New Orleans, April.

Chamot, A.U. 1987. Language development through content: America: The early years and America: After independence. Reading, Mass.: Addison-Wesley.

Chamot, A.U., and J.M. O'Malley. 1986. A cognitive academic language learning approach: An ESL content-based curriculum. Washington, D.C.: National Clearinghouse for Bilingual Education.

Chamot, A.U., and J.M. O'Malley. 1987. The cognitive academic language learning approach: A bridge to the mainstream. TESOL Quarterly 21.3:227-249.

Chamot, A.U., L. Küpper, and M.V. Impink-Hernandez. 1988. A study of learning strategies in foreign language instruction: The third year and final report. McLean, Va.: Interstate Research Associates.

Chamot, A.U., L. Küpper, M. Barrueta, S. Toth, and I. Thompson. Forthcoming. Learning strategy instruction in the foreign language classroom: A teacher's resource guide. McLean, Va.: Interstate Research Associates.

Chamot, A.U., and L. Küpper. 1989. Learning strategies in foreign language instruction. Foreign Language Annals 22.1:13-24.

Chamot, A.U., and L. Küpper. 1990. A study of learning strategy instruction in the foreign language classroom: First year report. McLean, Va.: Interstate Research Associates.

Chamot, A.U., and J.M. O'Malley. 1988. Language development through content: Mathematics Book A. Reading, Mass.: Addison-Wesley.

Chamot, A.U., and J.M. O'Malley. In press. The cognitive academic language learning approach: A resource guide for teachers. Reading, Mass.: Addison-Wesley.

Chamot, A.U., J.M. O'Malley, and L. Küpper. In press. Content plus: Content and learning strategies for ESL students. Boston, Mass.: Heinle and Heinle.

Chesterfield, R., and K.B. Chesterfield. 1985. Natural order in children's use of second language learning strategies. Applied Linguistics 6.1:45-59.

Cohen, A.D., and E. Aphek. 1980. Retention of second language vocabulary over time: Investigating the role of mnemonic associations. System 8:221-35.

Derry, S.J., and D.A. Murphy. 1986. Designing systems that train learning ability: From theory to practice. Review of Educational Research 56:1-39.

Ellis, R. 1984. Classroom second language development. Oxford: Pergamon.

Ellis, G., and B. Sinclair. 1989. Learning to learn English. Cambridge: Cambridge University Press.

Faerch, C., and G. Kasper. 1987. From product to process: Introspective methods in second language research. In: C. Faerch and G. Kasper, eds. Introspection in second language research. 5-23. Philadelphia, Pa.: Multilingual Matters.

Gagné, E.D. 1985. The cognitive psychology of school learning. Boston, Mass.: Little, Brown and Company.

Garner, R. 1987. Metacognition and reading comprehension. Norwood, N.J.: Ablex.

Haller, E.P., D.A. Child, and H.J. Walberg. 1988. Can comprehension be taught? A quantitative syntheses of 'metacognitive' studies. Educational Researcher December 5-8.

Hosenfeld, C., V. Arnold, J. Kirchofer, J. Laciura, and L. Wilson. 1981. Second language reading: A curricular sequence for teaching reading strategies. Foreign Language Annals 14.5:415-22.

Jones, B.F., A.S. Palincsar, D.S. Ogle, and E.G. Carr. 1987. Strategic teaching and learning: Cognitive instruction in the content areas. Alexandria, Va.: Association for Supervision and Curriculum Development.

McLaughlin, B. 1987. Theories of second-language learning. London: Edward Arnold.

O'Malley, J.M. 1988. The cognitive academic language learning approach. (California/Louisiana). Journal of Multilingual and Multicultural Development 9.1 and 2:43-60.

O'Malley, J.M., and A.U. Chamot. 1988. How to teach learning strategies. In: A.U. Chamot, J.M. O'Malley, and L. Küpper. The cognitive academic language learning approach (California/Louisiana). Training Manual 121-22. Arlington, Va.: Second Language Learning.

O'Malley, J.M., and A.U. Chamot. 1990. Learning strategies in second language acquisition. Cambridge: Cambridge University Press.

O'Malley, J.M., A.U. Chamot, G. Stewner-Manzanares, R. Russo, and L. Küpper. 1985. Learning strategy applications with students of English as a second language. TESOL Quarterly 19:285-296.

O'Malley, J.M., A.U. Chamot, and C. Walker. 1987. Some applications of cognitive theory to second language acquisition. Studies in Second Language Acquisition 9:287-306.

O'Malley, J.M., A.U. Chamot, and L. Küpper. 1989. Listening comprehension strategies in second language acquisition. Applied Linguistics 10:4.

O'Malley, J.M., R.P. Russo, A.U. Chamot, and G. Stewner-Manzanares. 1988. In: C.E. Weinstein, E.T. Goetz, and P.A. Alexander, eds. Learning and study strategies: Issues in assessment, instruction, and evaluation. 215-31. San Diego, Calif.: Academic Press.

Oxford, R.L. 1990. Language learning strategies: What every teacher should know. New York: Newbury House.

Padron, Y.N., and H.C. Waxman. 1988. The effects of ESL students' perceptions of their cognitive strategies on reading achievement. TESOL Quarterly 22:146-50.

Palincsar, A.S., and A.L. Brown. 1984. Reciprocal teaching of comprehension-fostering and comprehension-monitoring activities. Cognition and Instruction 1:117-75.

Paris, S.G. 1988. Fusing skill and will: The integration of cognitive and motivational psychology. Paper presented at the annual meeting of the American Educational Research Association, New Orleans, April.

Paris, S., D. Cross, A.M. DeBritto, J. Jacobs, E. Oka, and D. Saarnio. 1984. Improving children's metacognition and reading comprehension with classroom instruction. Paper presented at the annual meeting of the American Educational Research Association, New Orleans, April.

Politzer, R.L. and M. McGroarty. 1985. An exploratory study of learning behaviors and their relationship to gains in linguistic and communicative competence. TESOL Quarterly 19:103-23.

Pressley, M., J.R. Levin, and J.D. Delaney. 1982. The mnemonic keyword method. Review of Educational Research 52:61-91.

Pressley, M., J.R. Levin, and E.S. Ghatala. 1984. Memory strategy monitoring in adults and children. Journal of Verbal Learning and Verbal Behavior 23:270-88.

Rivers, W.M. 1964. The psychologist and the foreign language teacher. Chicago, Ill.: University of Chicago Press.

Rivers, W.M. 1976. The second-language teacher and cognitive psychology. In: W.M. Rivers, Speaking in many tongues. Rowley, Mass.: Newbury House.

Rivers, W.M. 1983. Communicating naturally in a second language: Theory and practice in language teaching. Cambridge: Cambridge University Press.

Rivers, W.M. 1990. Connections, schemas, scripts, and all that: Cognitive psychology revisited. Plenary paper at annual convention of Teachers of English to Speakers of Other Languages, San Francisco March, 1990.

Rubin, J. 1981. Study of cognitive processes in second language learning. Applied Linguistics 11:117-31.

Rubin, J. 1987. Learner strategies: Theoretical assumptions, research history and typology. In: A. Wenden and J. Rubin, eds. Learner strategies in language learning. 15-30. Englewood Cliffs, N.J.: Prentice-Hall International.

Rubin, J., and I. Thompson. 1982. How to be a more successful language learner. Boston: Heinle and Heinle.

Spolsky, B. 1985. Formulating a theory of second language learning. Studies in Second Language Acquisition 7:269-88.

Thompson, I. 1987. Memory in language learning. In: A. Wenden and J. Rubin, eds. Learner strategies in language learning. 43-56. Englewood Cliffs, N.J.: Prentice-Hall International.

Weinstein, C.E. 1978. Elaboration skills as a learning strategy. In: H.F. O'Neill, Jr., ed. Learning strategies. New York: Academic Press.

Weinstein, C.E., and R.E. Mayer. 1986. The teaching of learning strategies. In: M.C. Wittrock, ed. Handbook of research on teaching. 315-27. 3d ed. New York: Macmillan.

Wenden, A. 1987. Incorporating learner training in the classroom. In: A. Wenden and J. Rubin, eds. Learner strategies in language learning. 159-68. Englewood Cliffs, N.J.: Prentice-Hall International.

Winograd, P., and V.C. Hare. 1988. Direct instruction of reading comprehension strategies: The nature of teacher explanation. In: C.E. Weinstein, E.T. Goetz, and P.A. Alexander, eds. Learning and study strategies. 121-39. New York: Academic Press.

Yes, but . . . What kind of theory? What kind of practice? What kind of research?

Nina Garrett
Carnegie Mellon University

The interdependence of theory, practice, and research is a notion which most Georgetown University Round Table speakers are likely to accept as desirable, but are equally likely to see as a goal not yet achieved. Theoretical linguistics is developed with virtually no reference to language teaching; much language teaching practice is independent of (or even hostile to) linguistic theory, and foreign language teaching has so far been only marginally affected by language acquisition research; research on language acquisition takes place under a number of different rubrics, only some of which are related either to theoretical linguistics or language teaching. Charles Ferguson (1989) speaks eloquently of the need to build principled connections between these endeavors, and especially to develop the value of language learning data to linguistic theory, so that the flow of wisdom is not automatically thought of as unidirectional. We must also admit, though, that there is a whole range of problems in the classroom to which linguistic theory is quite irrelevant—not all of language teaching practice needs to be rooted in linguistic theory, and classroom language learner data contribute nothing to most work in linguistics.

We cannot, therefore, simply take the stance that interdependence is a general desideratum. And even where the 'lack' of interdependence is problematic, that is only one side of the coin. The other side, 'inappropriate' interdependence, may be even more serious. Much language teaching practice is based on inappropriate theory, quasi-theory, or ideology masquerading as theory. Studies that are cast as SLA research are often inappropriately based on pedagogical manipulations motivated by ideological rather than theoretical considerations, so that what is in fact 'methods' research is used to support or refute theoretical hypotheses of SLA. And theoretically motivated research on SLA in children or outside the classroom context is routinely used to support claims about how language learning by adults should be guided, i.e., to make pedagogical prescriptions.

The real point of the Round Table's theme this year, therefore, is not just the suggestion that current work in each of these three areas should take closer cognizance of related work in the others, but rather the much more complex issue of how—or even whether—we can conceptualize a discipline in which their interdependence can be seen to be intellectually coherent. What changes in our perspective on and in our practice of each of the three endeavors are required to make the concept of interdependence meaningful? *What kind of linguistic theory—what kind of language teaching practice—what kind of language acquisition research* fit together?

I argue here for an approach in which a psycholinguistic understanding of second language acquisition (SLA) provides the basic conception for a discipline which establishes principled relationships between theory, practice and research. At this admittedly early stage of its development, SLA is still too often used as a trendy label for the research that goes along with ESL, or for second or foreign education generally, or for applied linguistics—a label which itself has no widely agreed-upon meaning. If SLA is to achieve disciplinary status, an understanding of its theory has to be primary. So—what kind of theory?

The role of theoretical linguistics in SLA, or the extent to which current linguistic theory should dominate model-building in SLA, continues to be a topic of debate. Flynn's work (this volume) demonstrates that significant work in SLA is being undertaken from within the work on theoretical linguistics which uses a parameter-setting model. But theories of linguistic 'competence' or knowledge that focus on the abstract constraints imposed by Universal Grammar on the development of syntax cannot of themselves directly account for or predict the phenomena of most immediate interest to language learners and teachers in understanding the way language operates in actual communication. Concern for the role played by sociolinguistic, pragmatic, and discourse factors has led language teachers, among others, to insist on seeing 'linguistic competence' in the context of 'communicative competence'. But in working out the implications of that axiom for SLA, we have lost sight of the fact that, like linguistic competence, the notion of communicative competence derives from a theory of 'language knowledge'. Communicative competence originally meant the combination of all these extended kinds of knowledge—the knowledge of what is sociolinguistically and pragmatically appropriate in discourse, added on to the knowledge of what is grammatical.

But even extending linguistic competence to include knowledge of other systematicities than syntax does not solve the question of its role in SLA. Language teachers insist that their concern is not so much to arrive at a description of learners' 'knowledge' as to understand what they can *do* with it—in other words, not so much with 'competence' as with 'performance'. As Widdowson reminds us (this volume), 'performance' in the Chomskyan sense functions mostly as a wastebasket to which are consigned all the data that would confuse an understanding of the idealized knowledge of language. It is true that, in trying to account for language acquisition and language processing, linguists do address performance issues, but they do so from a perspective which still distances the theory from the kind of performance which concerns language teachers, because of a subtle ambiguity in the way the key questions are put.

When theoretical linguists ask 'How do people process language?' or 'How do people acquire language?' they are looking for abstract principles which explain how it is formally to be accounted for that language can be processed or can be acquired, the formal constraints on universal grammar and on particular language systems which result in the particular kind of language knowledge which is assumed to 'underlie' performance. But when SLA researchers or language teachers ask 'How do people process or acquire language?' they do not want to account for the formal or abstract potential but to understand how processing and acquisition actually happen—the process by which real people in real time express and comprehend contextualized meaning in culturally authentic discourse, and how they learn to do this in a second language.[1] That kind of performance question falls under the rubric of psycholinguistics rather than theoretical linguistics. (We need not address here the question of whether linguistics and psycholinguistics are two sides of the same coin or whether one subsumes the other: theories of language knowledge and of language performance must complement each other.) Nonetheless, given contemporary emphasis in foreign language education on communicative language proficiency rather than abstract knowledge of language, it will be clearly more useful in the effort to develop a coherent discipline with interdependent theory, practice, and research not to demand of theories of competence that they explain or predict performance but rather to consider how a theory of performance could more directly support SLA research and teaching practice. (To keep the references clear, I shall refer to theories of performance as 'psycholinguistic', and use the term 'linguistic' for theories of competence.)

A focus on performance subdivides into two areas of inquiry: processing and acquisition. Processing refers generally to all the mental activities of recognizing, interpreting, organizing, storing, accessing, selecting, and mustering language knowledge that go on in actual comprehension and production. For the purposes of SLA theory and research, and for the purposes of language teaching, *the crux of processing is the mapping of meaning or function onto language form.* To 'speak French' is to map meaning onto the forms (lexical and grammatical) of the French language in much the same way as do the native speakers of some variety of French. Some of that meaning could be considered generic human meaning, but for the most part

---

[1] I am indebted to Elizabeth Platt for discussion of this point.

the meanings conveyed in a language are as culturally shaped as the forms used to map them. And to 'learn French' is to develop that mapping ability over time—which involves learning not only the French forms but also the French meanings.

A theory of mapping is therefore logically prior to a theory of acquisition: if what is acquired is mapping ability, we have to know what that ability is before we can study how it is acquired, how it changes over time. A performance theory of language acquisition thus hinges on a theory of mapping, and both are crucial to SLA research and teaching practice.

One of the major barriers to language teachers' recognition of the potential importance of this psycholinguistic understanding of SLA as a paradigm for our research is a widespread misperception that 'psycholinguistics' refers particularly to the learning of grammar and is therefore in conflict with a communicative, sociolinguistically sensitive, and culturally contextualized approach to language learning. Nothing could be further from the truth: psycholinguistics is concerned with the way *all kinds of meaning* are communicated in language. Every adult utterance expresses or implies semantic, sociolinguistic, pragmatic, and discourse meaning; all of these kinds of meaning are rooted in the cultural context of language, and all of them are realized in communicative language use through complex and interrelated choices of vocabulary and grammar. How those choices are systematized by individuals in their own production and comprehension is the subject of language mapping, and it is precisely this mapping which communicative language teaching tries to help learners understand and acquire.

But before we can develop the implications for research and practice of this psycholinguistic version of SLA, we must arrive at a coherent sense of the relationships between the several different kinds of theories that play a role in this complex discipline. Lyons (this volume) articulates one widely accepted distinction when he refers to autonomous syntax as constituting one part of a binary pair and sociolinguistics, semantics, psycholinguistics, pragmatics, and discourse analysis as the other. (He uses the terms 'microlinguistics' and 'macrolinguistics' to label the distinction.) In contrast, I argue that we should not include the psycholinguistic in either of these categories, but should instead see it as functioning in a different plane entirely.

Autonomous syntax has been the main province of theoretical linguists whose goal is to describe knowledge of language. But theories of semantics, sociolinguistics, pragmatics, and discourse *are likewise theories of language knowledge*. They describe knowledge not only of what is grammatical but also of what is appropriate. They are not of themselves theories of language 'use' or language 'ability'. That is why sociolinguists, semanticists, etc., so often refuse to label themselves 'applied linguists'; they are just as much theoretical linguists as are syntacticians. In sharp contrast, that part of psycholinguistic theory which addresses 'language processing' postulates the constraints on, and the mechanisms of, the ability to organize, store, access, and use all these kinds of knowledge of language, both micro- and macrolinguistic knowledge, in actual language performance, in comprehension and production. Another part of psycholinguistic theory addresses 'acquisition', the development over time of learners' ability to perform, to organize, store, access, and use language knowledge more or less as do native speakers of the language being acquired. Second language acquisition theory is thus a subdivision of psycholinguistic theory, and classroom SLA theory in turn a subdivision of that. Seeing SLA as belonging under psycholinguistics therefore does not in any way conflict with an individual researcher's desire to focus on the particularly sociolinguistic aspects of learners' form-meaning connections, or on pragmatic aspects, or on cultural or psychological constraints on acquisition, or on the particular qualities of classroom discourse.

What kind of research does this kind of theory suggest and support? The development of a research agenda within this paradigm poses for us some serious challenges. In the first place, it suggests that it may be premature to study how pedagogical manipulation and experimentation can affect acquisition until we know much more about how acquisition happens when pedagogical factors are held constant; evaluating pedagogical method is not the point of SLA research. Research on classroom-based learning cannot be pedagogy-independent, but it can and should be pedagogy-neutral if it is to have validity as *basic* research in SLA. Current communicatively oriented methods provide a good array of well-founded techniques for making the classroom an affectively encouraging, dynamic, interactive environment for communication. If teachers are trained and materials designed to promote communicative activities, we can explore in depth how individual learners map meaning onto form in a new language in such an environment without confusing the issue with pedagogical experimentation. (That is not to say that pedagogical experimentation is never good research; obviously it can be. But it should not be confused with psycholinguistic research.)

Unfortunately, much of the research carried out under the rubric of SLA in the foreign language context is not based on psycholinguistic theory or any theoretical paradigm consonant with it. Some so-called SLA research is really pedagogical research, manipulating instructional variables in attempts to find evidence supporting one or the other side of the ideologically motivated debate on whether we should teach grammar. Most SLA research has been carried out in other research contexts than the foreign language classroom, and while no challenge is here implied as to the appropriateness of its implications for its own domains, we must be extremely cautious about extrapolating to ours, for a number of reasons.

First, cross-linguistic studies in first and second language acquisition carried out by researchers in psychology and developmental psycholinguistics (such as Slobin 1985, MacWhinney 1989, among others) demonstrate that the dominant mapping constraints in English are highly unusual. MacWhinney notes that the fact that most of the work on language processing has been done on 'an exotic language' should give us serious pause.[2] The same is true, perhaps to an even greater extent, in second language acquisition.

Second, a good deal of SLA research has been based on hypotheses and research models derived from work on 'child' first language acquisition--but a sizable corpus of studies by MacWhinney and his collaborators shows that children often start out with mapping strategies for their native language which are quite different from those of adult native speakers. When we are dealing with adult learners we cannot assume that their mapping strategies in a second language will or should be those of children learning that language as their first.

Third, almost all SLA research takes as the object of its study learners' language 'product', not the processing by which they arrive at that product. If we want SLA research to contribute to a theory of performance, we should not focus on learner utterances as evidence of their interlanguage as 'idiosyncratic linguistic system' and subject that system to linguistic analysis—i.e. study how learner knowledge deviates from native speaker knowledge—because that approach gives us by definition insights into 'idiosyncratic competence' of learners, which is not enough for our purposes, either theoretical or pedagogical. A linguistic description of learner errors does not of itself tell us why the individual learner made that particular error in that utterance in that communicative context. The appearance of a certain structure or word order in learner language—whether it is correct or incorrect—cannot be taken as evidence that the learner is using that structure to map the same meaning or function as would be conveyed if a native speaker used it. If we assume, as we often do, that a learner's error indicates inadequate learning of a 'form' or its use in a paradigm, when in fact it represents an inadequate understanding of the 'function' that is supposed to be mapped by it, or of the relationship between the learner's intended meaning and the second language context for that meaning, then we can (and we often do) come to unwarranted conclusions about the nature of SLA.

A psycholinguistically motivated SLA research agenda must thus be based on the axiom that the primary object of study is the idiosyncratic processing by which learners map meaning onto the forms of the second language. The study of how this mapping changes over time so as to approximate more closely that of the native speaker is logically subordinate, although it may well be the principal focus of any given study; we cannot understand how mapping changes over time unless we can understand how it operates at one point in time, so acquisition research in this paradigm must consist of two or more mapping studies. Roughly speaking, the variables of interest in such research will be of three kinds—cognitive and psychological variables of the individual

---

[2] "We have also found that the English pattern ... represents an extreme that is unmatched in any other Indo-European or non-Indo-European language that we have studied to date. Think of the implications: 98% of the sentence processing studies in the literature to date have been carried out in an exotic language!" (MacWhinney and Bates 1989, Preface, xiv.)

learner, characteristics of the relevant language forms in the learners' native and goal languages of (perhaps in other languages as well), and characteristics of the meanings or functions being mapped onto the forms (again in the several languages); but in psycholinguistic terms none of these can be explored entirely in isolation from the others. Into the first category fall psychological characteristics of individual learners': cognitive style, age, language learning background, intelligence, motivation, anxiety, memory, etc., and how these influence idiosyncratic connections between meaning and form. The second includes linguistic and psycholinguistic features of both the first and the second language. What are the formal features involved in a particular form-function mapping? How unambiguously do they convey the function in question? How difficult are they to process—for example, are they salient or unstressed? How transparent is the similarity or difference between the use of this form in the second language and its real or apparent analogues in the first?

The particular kinds of meaning or function involved in the mapping include concepts of all kinds—sociolinguistic, semantic, pragmatic, etc.— which can only be understood in the context of the cultural presuppositions that define the communicative environment. In SLA research we must constantly allow for the interaction of two sets of cultural presuppositions that constrain mapping at all levels in the first language and the second. (In other words, we must understand mapping problems in terms of a contrastive analysis of meaning as well as of form.)

The hypotheses and research methodologies of SLA, therefore, can and should borrow not only (not even primarily) from microlinguistics and the already recognized domains of macrolinguistics, but from cognitive psychology, psycholinguistics (particularly cross-linguistic studies of language processing) and cultural studies. The latter field—really a set of fields—should be of particular interest to us because of the intellectual and the politico-academic importance of building connections between our research and other bodies of theory whose relevance to SLA is usually only vaguely acknowledged. Anthropology, communications, history, literary criticism, philosophy, political science, semantics, semiotics, stylistics—all these disciplines deal with the ways human beings in specific cultures construct their understanding of reality and their experience, and how they communicate that understanding in language form. We work with adults whose native language already encompasses some level of all these kinds of meaning, and we must concern ourselves with how they now learn to map them in a second language. The study of language mapping and language acquisition is thus quintessentially interdisciplinary.

And if we understand our discipline in this framework, we can abolish second-class citizenship for language teachers. SLA research and publications motivated by any of these relevant bodies of theory can lay claim to recognition for intellectual significance and cannot be dismissed as 'merely pedagogical'. This perspective also opens up a wide range of opportunities for individual faculty members to use their own interests and training in theoretically respectable SLA research. Language teachers whose research interests lie in literary scholarship or criticism can explore how literary language conveys meaning different from that of nonliterary discourse, how learners come to understand what makes a text literary both in their first language and in a second. Language teachers who focus on linguistics can investigate, for example, how learners develop the appropriate L2 concepts of discourse that underlie choices of syntactic structure, or the problems encountered by speakers of a morphologically complex language in mapping case relations or aspect in an uninflected language. (Selinker, this volume, argues convincingly that we should reconsider some of the work in contrastive linguistics that was abandoned when that approach to SLA was devalued, because our understanding of what might be productively contrasted has become much more sophisticated.) Those who concern themselves most with sociolinguistic features of language use can explore the influence of social setting, deference relationships, classroom discourse, etc., on SLA. Interest in individual learner characteristics suggests a research focus on the influence of particular psychological variables. Contemporary work in cultural studies is developing theoretical frameworks for understanding a variety of semiotic systems, for studying the texts of culturally disenfranchised groups, and for exploring the cultural significance of 'texts' in the form of film, television, and music, and that work could be just as significant to language teachers as it is to scholars in those other fields.

What kind of language teaching practice does this paradigm support? When SLA research is understood to be rooted in and contributing to a theory of 'performance', principled connections can be made between theory and practice at every point, because communicative language teaching is after all dedicated to the proposition that the point of language learning is performance, rather than only language knowledge—even the knowledge commonly referred to as communicative competence. This perspective does not change the goals to which language teaching is currently committed; it provides a better theoretical foundation for them. (How nice to have ideology independently supported by theory—and vice versa!)

Perhaps the most important contribution of this perspective is that it does away with the counter productive debate over the teaching of grammar, in which so many discussions of language teaching have bogged down. If communicative language performance is the ability to make, and make communicative use of, connections between meaning and form, it can hardly be learned without understanding both meaning and form simultaneously and in terms of each other; it is pointless to contrast 'a focus on form' with 'a focus on meaning' (cf. Garrett 1990). A psycholinguistic approach has strong implications for the reworking of standard foreign language textbook presentations of language form, which conventionally 'explain' structures almost entirely in terms of surface collocations or in terms of their relationship to supposedly equivalent structures in English. Form should instead be presented and explained in terms of its representation of different kinds of meaning; psycholinguistic theory (as well as common sense) suggests that students will both remember it better and be better able to make use of it in their own communication attempts. (However, neither theory nor common sense has to be accepted on faith; research must be designed to confirm this prediction, although a major prerequisite for such pedagogical research will be developing appropriate materials and training teachers to conceive of language teaching this way.)

This perspective also reinforces growing concern about the unconsidered use of 'authentic data' in language teaching—texts, video, and audio materials that are created not for purposes of language pedagogy but for communication between native speakers of the foreign language. Both Nostrand (1989) and Kramsch (1989) argue that students should not be allowed to take authentic documents in whatever medium at face value, because 'authentic data' (either linguistic or cultural) of the second language are all too likely to be interpreted by students in the context of the linguistic and cultural presuppositions (many of them unconscious) students bring from their native language and culture unless teachers are sophisticated enough to mediate the experience and help students to reflect critically on both. The broad psycholinguistic version of SLA set forth here provides a framework for the genuine integration of the teaching and learning of 'culture' with the teaching and learning of 'language'. In a way, this is simply a restatement of the claim of the preceding paragraph: meaning and form must be understood in terms of each other.

To sum up, then, I have suggested that if we really want to aim for a principled, coherent interdependence of theory, research, and practice, we need first of all to establish a coherent metatheoretical framework for SLA. Theoretical linguistics is a valid and important enterprise, and language teachers should understand the SLA research which is done within that paradigm. But an understanding of SLA as it takes place in real people in real time in real contexts requires a theory of psycholinguistic performance which is consonant with, but not the same thing as, a theory of linguistic knowledge. If SLA research is understood as the study of the variables that influence the kinds of meaning conveyed by language, how language form conveys meaning, and how learners come to make both correct and appropriate use of the connections between these, it will contribute significantly both to such a theory and to language teaching practice. The components of the answer to the question of what kind of theory, practice, and research can be postulated as truly interdependent are already available to us. They add up to a new paradigm of SLA as a discipline in its own right, with its own theory, research, and practice.

References

Ferguson, C.A. 1989. Language teaching and theories of language. In: Georgetown University Round Table on Languages and Linguistics 1989. Washington, D.C.: Georgetown University Press. 81-88.

Garrett, N. 1990. Theoretical and pedagogical problems of separating 'grammar' from 'communication'. In: B.F. Freed, ed., Foreign language acquisition research and the classroom. Lexington, Mass.: D.C. Heath.

Kramsch, C. 1989. Media materials in the language class. Contemporary French Civilization xiii, 2.

MacWhinney, B., and E. Bates, eds. 1989. The crosslinguistic study of sentence processing. Cambridge: Cambridge University Press.

Nostrand, H.L. 1989. Authentic texts—cultural authenticity: An editorial. Modern Language Journal 73:1.

Slobin, D.I., ed. 1985. The crosslinguistic study of language acquisition. Hillsdale, N.J.: Lawrence Erlbaum Associates.

www.ingramcontent.com/pod-product-compliance
Lightning Source LLC
LaVergne TN
LVHW090757070826
844660LV00022B/1008